KT-447-334

TRAVELLERS

U.S.A. & CANADA

SURVIVAL KIT

by
SUSAN GRIFFITH
& SIMON CALDER

Published by Vacation Work, 9 Park End Street, Oxford

First published February 1985
Second Edition January 1989

TRAVELLERS SURVIVAL KIT — USA & CANADA
by Susan Griffith & Simon Calder

ISBN 1 85458 008 X (softback)
ISBN 1 85458 009 4 (hardback)

Cover Design

Mel Calman

Miller Craig & Cocking Design Partnership

Maps and illustrations by William Swan

Printed by **Gibbons Barford Print,** Wolverhampton, England

Contents

CANADA

Regional Chapters

MAPS

Acknowledgments

We are grateful to the following people for their contributions to this revised edition:

New York	Melody Daniels, Chester Krone and Cathy Packe
Boston and New England	Sarah Ellison Caldwell and Roger Brown
Chicago and the Midwest	Janet Renard and Luke Olivieri
Miami and Florida	Christopher Caldwell, Diane Krone and Steve Annett
New Orleans and the South	Julie Hunnisett, Winston Krone and Heather Maclean
Texas	Chester Krone
Denver and the Rockies	Sarah Ellison Caldwell
Los Angeles and the Southwest	Jon Wilson, Nicholas Cowan and Chester Krone
San Francisco and the Northwest	Diane Krone and Peter Wise
Hawaii	Frank Partridge and Liz Mardall
Toronto and Ontario	Katherine Peel and Douglas Hutchinson
Montreal and Quebec	Sylvie Strobel and Louise Collins
Atlantic Provinces	Chris McKinnon
Vancouver and British Columbia	Ambrose Marsh and Nicholas Kenrick

Many other individuals and organizations have assisted with comments and criticisms, especially Ian Barlow, Ian Curtin, Cath Dobbie, Mary Griffith, Ben Howard, Ciaran Lynch, Sally Mitchell, Jeremy Olsen, Scarlett O'Sullivan, Garry Richardson, Sarah Rosen-Webb, Steve Rout and William Teesdale.

Preface

The mechanics of daily life for visitors to the world's richest continent can be complex and baffling. The *Travellers Survival Kit USA & Canada* sets out to guide the traveller through the North American maze, from automated public transport systems to automatic fast food restaurants, from telephones to time zones, state taxes to city taxis.

North America specializes in extremes of climate, achievement and personality. One of the surprisingly tricky features of preparing this book was sorting out the rivals for the tallest building, busiest airport, largest Chinatown and most dangerous city. But not everything is vying to be the biggest and best. The America you find will not always be the brash and superficial place you might expect from films and television.

During the writing of this book the number of dollars you could buy with £1 sterling has fluctuated alarmingly between $1 and $2. It is now more important than ever to know where to find the bargains. If you do, you'll be pleasantly surprised at how affordable North America can be. This book tells you how to get to and around the USA and Canada safely, cheaply and enjoyably, and how to find the best value in food, drink, accommodation and entertainment.

Susan Griffith & Simon Calder
January 1989

BEFORE YOU GO
USA and Canada

RED TAPE

Passports. A full ten-year passport is required for travel to both the USA and Canada. Application forms are available from post offices and should be sent with the appropriate fee, photographs and supporting documents to your regional passport office. Allow at least one month for processing by mail. If you're in a tearing hurry or realize your existing passport is soon to expire, you can usually obtain one in person if you're prepared to queue all day at a passport office.

For visits to the USA, your passport must have a minimum of six months to run. This rule is not rigidly enforced but nonetheless could be used as a reason to deny you entry. If your passport is lost or stolen while travelling, contact first the police then your nearest Consulate. Obtaining replacement travel documents is easier if you have a record of the passport number and its date and place of issue.

Visas. At present, British visitors to the USA who meet certain conditions do not require a visa for a leisure or business trip of up to 90 days. Note that this scheme is only experimental and may be withdrawn at any time (particularly if the authorities feel the system is being abused). Check the latest position by ringing 01-499 7010. You must hold full British citizenship and have a ticket refundable only in the country of origin. You must be travelling on a carrier which has agreed to take part in the scheme: this includes the major transatlantic airlines, but not all charter carriers. When you check in for your flight you will be required to sign a declaration to the effect that you are of sound mind and body and have neither suspect political affiliations nor criminal convictions. Upon arrival in the USA you must expect to spend longer at immigration than travellers with visas. Another drawback for those without visas is that side-trips to Canada or Mexico are possible only if you travel across the border with a carrier participating in the scheme.

If you do not meet these conditions, get a visa. You can apply by post, using an application form which is free from most travel agents or the US Embassy Visa Branch, 5 Upper Grosvenor Street, London W1A 2JB. You must supply two passport photographs, evidence of financial resources, and a good reason for leaving after a temporary stay. "Financial resources" can take the form of a receipt for travellers cheques, a photocopy of credit cards or a statement from a US citizen assuming responsibility for you. "A good reason to leave" might be a commitment to a job, a family or a pet. A statement to this effect signed by yourself or, preferably, a letter from your employer, college or social security office outlining the commitment should be regarded as sufficient proof of your intention to return.

The form also asks if you intend to work or study in the United States. Whatever your intentions, the correct answer is "no", which is also the appropriate answer when you are asked if you have a contagious disease, a serious mental illness or a criminal conviction, and whether you have been a member of a Communist organization or participated in atrocities perpetrated by Nazi Germany.

These documents, plus your passport, should be posted to the Visa Branch at the above address; allow three weeks for processing. If there are any irregularities in your application (such as omitting to sign or date it) you'll need at least another fortnight to sort it out. Some travel agents and visa specialists can obtain a visa within 24 hours. Assuming you get one, it will be valid either indefinitely or for a specified time; and entitle you to either one or multiple applications for entry, with a maximum stay of six months for each visit. The norm is to issue a multiple one. If your old passport contains an indefinite multiple entry visa, be sure to hang on to it, even after your passport expires. If you carry both passports when you travel to the States you'll have no need to re-apply for a visa.

It is important to note that an American visa is no more than a permit to apply for entry to the USA. It does not guarantee that you will have no problems when you reach American soil — see *Red Tape: Immigration,* page 27.

British visitors to Canada do not need visas for stays of up to three months. For information about working visas see *Work,* page 340.

INSURANCE

Everyone has heard horror stories of visitors to North America becoming destitute after having to pay enormous medical bills because they had insufficient insurance. Although all North Americans enjoy free emergency treatment in Britain courtesy of the National Health Service, there is no reciprocal agreement for the benefit of travellers to North America. Health care in the USA and Canada is extremely expensive. All but the poorest natives belong to health insurance schemes, and it is imperative that you be covered.

Policies valid in the USA and Canada usually cost more than those for the rest of the world, since the high cost of health care means the level of medical cover is around twice that deemed necessary elsewhere. Select a policy which offers at least £250,000 of cover. Any less might cause your premature departure from hospital in the event of a serious accident or illness. The cover provided by most policies is fairly standard: delay and cancellation insurance of up to £2,500; around £250,000 for medical expenses and emergency repatriation; £500,000 for personal liability; £20,000 for permanent disablement cover; lost or stolen baggage up to £1,000 (sometimes valuable single items are excluded); and cash to a maximum of £250. Every airline, tour operator and travel agent is delighted to sell you insurance because of the high commission (sometimes over 40%) it yields. Shopping around can save you money or get better cover for the same premium. In particular, Endsleigh Insurance (Cheltenham Spa, Glos GL50 3NR) offers good rates for its worldwide ISIS scheme. In 1988, for example, one month of cover from most travel agents cost around £50, but Endsleigh charged only £35 for a similar policy.

If you stay longer than expected, you can buy a new policy from any insurance broker in the USA or Canada, but note that these policies do not cover the cost of repatriation to your home country. You can also insure yourself as required for risky activities such as skiing or scuba diving, for which a more expensive policy covering dangerous sports is required.

Protection against claims for negligence could prove to be as valuable as health insurance. For instance, if you cross a road without looking and cause a driver to swerve, the owners of the dog that the driver subsequently hits may sue you. They will no doubt claim that you have caused inestimable grief and a court might award huge damages against you. Fortunately, most travel policies cover third party liability of this kind. Note, however, that negligence while driving is not covered (see *Driving: Insurance*).

Three groups of travellers are automatically insured. Clients of some travel agents receive several weeks' insurance with full-price air tickets, effectively giving a discount on the air fare. Holders of Diners Club cards (annual subscription £20) who use the card to pay for travel or accommodation expenses receive full cover; note that this is substantially better than the travel accident insurance provided by most credit card companies which merely gives compensation for accidents while in transit. Members of the British Airways Executive Club receive travel insurance as a free benefit of membership; there is no requirement to travel on BA. The annual subscription of £70 compares well with the cost of two months' cover, and provides insurance for an unlimited number of trips.

If you are unfortunate enough to have to claim on your insurance, the golden rule is to amass as much documentation as possible to support your application. In particular, compensation is unlikely to be paid for lost baggage or cash unless your claim is accompanied by a police report of the loss.

MONEY

Travellers Cheques. Dollar travellers cheques ("travelers checks") are readily accepted at face value by virtually every enterprise in North America. They are treated as cash, and real dollars and cents are given in change. With a sufficient supply of travellers cheques, it is possible to avoid banks completely. Travellers cheques are much more useful than sterling cash, since many small banks may lack facilities for changing sterling on the spot. The normal charge for travellers cheques is face value plus 1%, in addition to the currency exchange commission for changing sterling to dollars. Buy them in Canadian or US dollars as appropriate. Travellers cheques in sterling or other currencies can be changed only at *bureaux de change* and major banks.

The most easily negotiable travellers cheques are American Express, Thomas Cook and Visa. Possessing just one $10 American Express travellers cheque entitles you to use their customer mail service (addresses for mail collection given in regional chapters). They are sold by Lloyd's Bank and the Royal Bank of Scotland in Britain. Visa cheques are issued by Barclay's, the Co-op, Yorkshire and the Trustee Savings Bank, and Thomas Cook cheques by Midland Bank and Thomas Cook offices. If you buy a less well-known variety you should be prepared to change cheques for face value in cash at any American bank rather than spending the cheques direct.

Carry your passport as ID when paying for goods or services with travellers cheques. Low denomination cheques (ideally $10) are more welcome than high ones, especially if you are buying an inexpensive item. Don't be put off by the signs in shops, gas stations and restaurants saying "No Checks". this usually refers only to personal cheques.

Keep a separate record of the cheques you have, and where and when the last was cashed. Note the toll-free phone number provided with the cheques so that you can claim a refund quickly and easily. This usually involves a trip to the nearest branch of the issuing bank or travel agent; some also have emergency arrangements with hotels and car rental outlets to give you $200 to tide you over until the next working day. American Express normally issues replacement travellers cheques as soon as you have completed a detailed form at one of its offices. But if you don't have the numbers of the cheques (or you have a less well-known brand), the process can take several days. There is no charge for replacing lost or stolen travellers cheques.

Cheques. A British cheque book will be virtually useless. Unless you have a charge card (American Express, Diners Club or AirPlus) which allows you to cash cheques against it, leave your cheque book safely at home. Details of how to open a bank account in North America are given under *Money* in the USA and Canada sections.

Credit and Charge Cards. A reasonably civilized life in North America is impossible without a credit or charge card. You can use one to pay for goods or services almost anywhere whether a campground in Colorado or a phone call in Phoenix. More importantly, a card is the accepted guarantee of your financial reliability when hiring cars, booking rooms or clearing immigration. Credit cards are free and allow you to pay off the debt over a long period of time at a high rate of interest, whereas charge card companies impose a joining fee (about £25) plus an annual subscription of around £20 and then let you spend up to a discretionary limit which is not pre-set, as long as you pay off in full each month. Consider asking the card issuer to increase your credit limit before you leave for North America. Even if you think you can keep your spending under control, hotels and car rental companies often "block out" hundreds of dollars of your account temporarily, in case you fail to pay your bill or steal the car. Thus you might believe (correctly) that your spending is well inside the limit, but find that your card is rejected next time you try to use it.

It is therefore worth carrying at least two credit/charge cards, which also helps on the odd occasion when one is not accepted. When buying petrol, be prepared to pay with cash or travellers cheques. Oil companies issue their own credit cards (which are difficult for temporary visitors to obtain) and most gas stations do not accept other cards.

When you use a card, don't be alarmed if you have to wait while the number is checked with the issuing company; checks for stolen or abused cards are more frequent than in Britain You may well be asked for supporting ID and for your address and telephone number. You might also be given the carbons from the credit card voucher, since a favourite scam among American villains is to use them to make counterfeit cards bearing your name and number. Keep all sales vouchers until you return home, since it is not unknown for unscrupulous traders to add an extra digit or two to their copies. Also, keep a separate record of the numbers of your cards and of the emergency telephone line to call in case of loss or theft. Report any loss to the local police and immediately call the card company toll-free or collect.

Access and Visa credit cards can be used anywhere displaying the MasterCard or Visa signs respectively. Visa seems to be the more widely accepted, perhaps because its design is the same on either side of the Atlantic. Visa cards are issued in Britain by Barclay's, the Co-op Bank, TSB and a few others: pick up an application form at any branch. You do not need to have an account with the bank concerned. Access cards are unique to the UK, and so you may have problems in out-of-the-way places. If you encounter difficulties, point out the minature version of the MasterCard symbol on the front of the card. Access cards are issued by Lloyds, Midland, NatWest and Clydesdale Banks, and by the Royal Bank of Scotland group. You can use British credit cards to draw cash at most cash machines, banks or *bureaux de change* displaying the appropriate Visa or MasterCard symbol.

The major charge cards are American Express and Diner's Club. Each company constantly tries to outdo the other with free fringe benefits when you charge tickets, car hire or hotels to the card before you travel. Both offer free life insurance during the journey. Furthermore, if your journey is delayed by more than four hours, you immediately qualify for around $100 of expenses (hotel rooms, meals, drinks, etc). You charge these items to the card and send in the receipts along with supporting evidence. If your baggage arrives late — or not at all — you can claim extra spending on a scale which increases with the time that your luggage is delayed. Where Diner's Club really scores is by providing free health insurance, which will save you the cost of the annual subscription on just one trip. Normally you cannot use American Express or Diner's Club cards to withdraw cash as you can with Visa or Access. However, members can write personal cheques for cash and travellers cheques at American Express offices (addresses in the major cities are listed in the geographical chapters) or, with a personal identification number, at airport dispensers. Diner's Club members can cash cheques at branches of Citibank.

Emergency Cash. Running out of cash, travellers cheques and available credit need not spell disaster. British Consulates can cash a personal cheque for up to £50 in an emergency, though they do so reluctantly. You can do this only once. If you can survive for a week or two, persuade a relative or friend to send you an International Money Order (IMO) in sterling or dollars, which costs around £5. Your friend then sends the IMO through the post. If you have funds in your own bank account, you can cable the bank to telegraph cash to a specified North American bank. Choosing a bank associated with your own in Britain will save time but even so you must allow 48 hours in major cities and longer in the depths of North Dakota or Nova Scotia. If weekends or public holidays intrude, you may have to wait a week. If you have a refundable airline ticket, you could cash it in to sustain yourself until help arrives, and then buy another.

If you are near a branch of Thomas Cook (principal addresses in regional chapters you can arrange for a telegraphic transfer from a Thomas Cook branch office in Britain via New York or Toronto. This takes 24-48 hours and costs approximately £15. If there is no real urgency, Thomas Cook can send a banker's draft in American or Canadian currency. This goes by ordinary airmail post (about seven days), costs around £5 and must be paid into a bank account in the USA or Canada.

Provided you have an interesting story to tell, you might approach the local (small town) newspaper. If they print it, they might slant it in the form of a request for assistance. Soft-hearted North Americans will respond with cash and invitations.

The information under *Work* could suggest a solution to a cash flow crisis. But, as a last resort, your government will get you home. Once their efforts to find someone to pay your fare have failed, then they will reluctantly put you on a plane. Your passport will be removed upon your arrival, and will not be returned until you have paid the authorities for the flight plus handling charge.

PLANNING AHEAD

This book should give you some good ideas about where to go, how to travel and so on. But you can supplement this with information on specific interests — from American football to zoology — by contacting US or Canadian tourist offices before you go. Their London addresses are:

US Travel & Tourism Administration
22 Sackville St
London W1X 2EA
01-439 7433

Canada House
Trafalgar Square
London SW1Y 5BJ
01-629 9492

They can also help with comprehensive lists of accommodation, details of available tours, etc., allowing you to plan some or all of your itinerary. You might also want to contact state or province tourism authorities; addresses for the USA are shown on page 118, for Canada on page 354. In addition, members of motoring organisations should ask for free information on driving and services provided by affiliated organizations in North America.

Some of the best unlimited travel deals by air and bus are available only to people who book and pay for them abroad. Look under *Getting Around* for each country to see the offers available and details of how to book.

Phoning Ahead. You can find most numbers in the USA and Canada from Britain by dialling international directory enquiries on 153. To call a number in North America from Britain, dial 0101 followed by the area code (for New York 212, for Toronto 416, etc.) and then the number. So to call the British Embassy in Washington (code 202) you should dial 0101-202-462-1340. If you wish to make a collect (reverse-charge) call to the USA you can dial straight through from the UK to the American operator on 0800-890011, a call which (for you) is free.

Before ringing relations to announce your arrival, or calling a hotel to make a booking, estimate what the time is at your destination; see *Time,* below. Also bear in mind that your conversation will cost a minimum of 70p per minute (8pm-8am) and a maximum of 95p per minute (3pm-5pm).

Travellers' Clubs. If you lack friends and relations in America, you might consider joining an organisation which arranges hospitality exchanges. For example members of the Globetrotters Club (BCM/Roving, London WC1 3XX) can request a list of members in the USA, Canada and other countries who have expressed a willingness to provide hospitality to other globetrotters. Membership costs £7 and the list of members costs £1.

Servas International is an organization begun by an American Quaker which runs a worldwide programme of free hospitality exchanges for travellers, to help the cause of peace and international understanding. To become a Servas traveller, it is necessary to be vetted by a member (to weed out freeloaders) and to pay a joining fee of about £10/$15. If you are interested, contact Servas at PO Box 885, London W13 9TH (tel: 01-352 0303) or, in the USA, at Room 406, 11 John St, New York, NY 10038.

A new non-profit organisation called Students International Lodging Exchange (STILE) is worth investigating. A membership fee of $29 entitles you to have an entry in two directories (published in May and November) of student members willing to swop accommodation. You then contact your fellow members in the places you wish to visit (and in turn are contacted by them). STILE may be contacted in Europe at 9 rue Charcot, 92200 Neuilly-sur-Seine, Paris, France (tel: 1-47 47 28 82) or in the USA at 210 Fifth Avenue, New York, NY 10010.

Handicapped Travellers. Before your flight to North America you may wish to consult *Care in the Air,* a free booklet published by the Civil Aviation Authority, 129 Kingsway, London WC2B 6NN; and a guide to London and Scottish airports obtainable free from the British Airports Authority, 130 Wilton Road, London SW1V 1LQ (tel: 01-834 9449). Every airline gives free assistance to handicapped travellers, and will provide a wheelchair at 24 hours notice. Some airlines, including British Airways, Pan Am and TWA, require a medical certificate of fitness to travel.

The Royal Society for Disability and Rehabilitation have a holidays officer who can provide specialist advice. Write to RADAR at 25 Mortimer Street, London, W1N 8AB, or call 01-637 5400. Mobility International exists to promote international travel for the disabled; their UK office is at 62 Union St, London SE1 1TD (tel: 01-403 5688). See *Help and Information* in the introduction to the USA or Canada for details of similar organizations at your destination.

WHAT TO TAKE

Maps. Free maps issued by the US Travel and Tourism Administration and Canada House are sufficient to locate most towns and establish the distance between them. Good state maps can be requested from Exxon Touring Service (1251 Avenue of the Americas, New York, NY 10020) or from the state tourism offices (addresses in *Help and Information*). If you plan to drive, see the section on Routes and Maps in the *Driving* chapter. For a larger selection of specific city and regional maps, visit Edward Stanford Ltd, 12-14 Long Acre, London WC2E 9LP (tel: 01 836 1321).

Electrical Items. If you're taking an electric razor, hair dryer or anything else electrical you'll need a plug adaptor and possibly a voltage transformer. The standard North American mains plug has two pins (live and neutral) plus an optional third (earth). Buy a suitable adaptor before leaving, since convertors which accept British three-pin plugs are difficult to find in North America. If the appliance does not have a voltage selector, you'll also need a transformer to step up the American 110 volts supply to operate 240 volt equipment.

Medications. Any prescribed drugs (except contraceptives) which you intend to take with you should be accompanied by a doctor's letter explaining why you need them. Take a good supply: drug prescriptions are expensive in North America, and many insurance policies will not meet the cost of medication for pre-existing conditions. Do not take any non-prescribed drugs stronger than aspirin or Alka-Seltzer, and then only in the original packs. Customs officers are highly sensitive about drugs of all kinds. Some which can be bought over the counter in Britain (such as certain cough mixtures, any headache remedy containing codeine, and kaolin and morphine) are available only on prescription in the USA and Canada.

Other Necessities. If you want to keep in touch with the goings-on in the rest of the world, take a short-wave radio. The BBC World Service broadcasts on various frequencies to North America, predominantly in the 49 metre band.

Literary travellers should take plenty of reading matter with them. Although there are thousands of bookshops selling millions of books, it is sometimes hard to find any English novel older than a year or two. So whether your tastes are for Iris Murdoch or Georgette Heyer, don't expect to find their complete works wherever you go.

What Not to Take. Leave your jewels and flashy clothes at home; they will only attract unwelcome attention from street criminals.

GETTING THERE . . . AND BACK

Air. A score of scheduled airlines operate non-stop flights from Britain to at least 30 North American cities. Dozens of wide-bodied jets — plus a couple of Concordes — fly between Britain and North America every day. Fares range from £200 for a low season return flight to the East Coast, to £4,000 for a supersonic trip to Dallas and back.

Finding the most appropriate and economical flight requires some research or the services of a reliable discount travel agent. Fares and conditions change constantly; for example, a Virgin Atlantic promotion in 1989 offered London-New York flights for £89, with the return flight just $99. Before parting with your cash, check with travel agents, airlines and *Business Traveller* magazine for the best deal. It is always worth looking for special offers particularly in the off-season. Outside the peak season (usually June to September plus the Christmas period), most aircraft fly with empty seats and the airlines periodically compete to fill these seats at almost any price. At certain times the major airlines offer low-cost standby fares to all the American cities served by flights from Britain. Or by ringing around the bucket shops which advertise in the *Times, Independent, Guardian* and *Time Out* you can fly from Heathrow to New York on a lesser known scheduled airline (Air India, Kuwait Airlines, etc) for considerably less than the official fare. If you intend to fly around North America using an airpass (see page 48 for the USA, page 343 for Canada), bear in mind that some airlines specify the carriers you must use to cross the Atlantic.

Every travel agent in Britain has plenty of brochures for APEX (advance purchase on scheduled flights) and charter air fares. Cheap return fares are almost always subject to advance booking requirements of 14 or 21 days. If you fail to travel on your booked flight, you lose your money, and changes to your itinerary are either impossible or very expensive. Most operators allow open-jaw returns, where you fly out to one city and return from another. These are generally permitted only within the USA or within Canada: you can't fly out to San Francisco and back from Vancouver on a cheap ticket.

The following agencies specialize in cheap return flights to North America: American Airplan (PO Box 267, Walton-on-Thames, Surrey KT1 4SA; 09322-46166), Poundstretcher (Airlink House, Hazelwick Avenue, Crawley, West Sussex RH10 1YS; 0293-519233) and Slade Travel (15 Vivian Avenue, London NW4 3UT; 01-202 0111). Most tour operators have special deals such as car hire for a nominal $1 per week. Take this into account when choosing the best bargain. If you intend to travel to the West Coast and Hawaii, a round-the-world ticket might suit you better; prices start at around £700 from the discount travel agencies which advertise in *Time Out*.

Airport Tax. Departure taxes from Britain and Canada are included in the fare you pay. Tickets to the United States are subject to a $10 Federal Inspection Fee; and upon leaving the USA, an International Passenger tax of $3 is payable in addition to the fare. Some individual airports levy extra taxes on departing travellers.

Baggage. All transatlantic airlines allow two pieces of baggage to be checked in free, as long as the dimensions of the larger (length plus breadth plus width) do not exceed 65 inches, and those of the smaller, 55 inches. It is quite feasible to take your own bicycle to and around the USA. Airlines will accept bikes as checked baggage providing they are boxed (with pedals removed and handlebars placed at right-angles) and the tyres deflated to avoid mid-air explosions.

Schedules. Transatlantic flights from Britain depart between 10 am and 7 pm and arrive in North America in the afternoon or evening (apart from Concorde, when you arrive an hour or two before you set off). If you are taking an onward flight, clearly the earlier you arrive the better, to avoid expensive overnight stays en route.

Air Courier Flights. If you are prepared to put up with some restrictions, the cheapest way across the Atlantic is as a casual air courier. You role is to fill the aircraft seat while "time-sensitive documents" travel in the hold as your baggage. The disadvantages include being limited to one piece of hand luggage only, having to get to the airport several hours before the flight leaves, and being restricted to a set number of weeks for return flights. Nevertheless the savings on normal fares are considerable. Sadly flights on Concorde are no longer an option except for those with contacts in the business, and acting as a casual air courier is now so popular that you need to book well in advance.

Several companies recruit casual couriers for flights from London Heathrow. Call DHL on 01-890 9393 then ask for "CPJ Travel" (the part of the organization which deals with casuals). Your call is put through to an answering machine which gives details of flights and conditions, and quotes a fare of £150 for one week in Miami, New York or Toronto (November-April only). You leave your name and address and are sent an application form and if your application is successful you will be contacted within eight weeks of departure. The extension number for further enquiries is 3407. TNT (01-561 2345) also uses an answering machine, on which you can request a flight to New York; fares vary. IML (01-890 8888) has flights to New York for £90-£199 return and to Chicago for £90-£150. Bookings are taken up to three months in advance. Inflight (0932 857455-6) acts as an agency for other courier companies, and quotes fares of New York (one or two weeks) for £175, and Los Angeles (two weeks) for £250.

Sea. If economy is not essential, you might consider a sea voyage to North America. Cunard's *Queen Elizabeth II* still plies between Southampton and New York about a dozen times a year taking five days. Standby fares for young people under 26 are sometimes available for around £400. You are entitled to take a great deal of luggage free of charge on board, which can be a major advantage for emigrants. It is also possible to book a berth on a freighter, though these are usually not much cheaper than luxury liners. For further information, you might refer to *Freighter Travel News* (1745 Scotch Avenue SE, Salem, OR 97309) or *Ford's Freighter Travel Guide* (22151 Clarendon Street, Woodland Hills, CA 91365).

Getting Back. Classified advertisements in local newspapers in the USA and Canada often quote "bargain" flights from North America to Britain. Unfortunately most of these are heavily restricted, or available for round-trip travel only. The most reliable and efficient discount travel agents seem to be those operated primarily for students, but which also offer good deals to normal people. In the USA, contact a branch of Council Travel (or its sister company Council Charter) or the Student Travel Network - STN. Within Canada, Travel CUTS has offices in most major cities.

TIME

Travelling by land or air across the North American continent can be chronologically confusing. The continent straddles eight and a half time zones, which means that at 7.30 pm in Newfoundland, it is only noon in the Aleutian Islands of Alaska. However, the bulk of the North American continent is divided into five zones, while Hawaii, Alaska and Newfoundland account for the others. The maps on pages 46 and 334 show where the boundaries lie.

Time zone changes, whether at state/provincial borders or otherwise, are rarely signposted. If you really need to be exact about the time in order to catch a flight or because your visa expires at midnight, check locally if you suspect you might have travelled into another zone. Another complication arises from Daylight Saving Time which begins on the first Sunday in April (later than in the UK) until the last Sunday in October. To confuse things further, Arizona, Hawaii, parts of Indiana and most of Saskatchewan do not observe Daylight Saving.

Atlantic Standard Time is four hours behind Greenwich Mean Time, Eastern Standard Time is five hours behind, Central Standard Time six, Mountain Standard Time seven and Pacific Standard Time eight. Thus noon in London corresponds to 8 am in Halifax, 7 am in New York and Toronto, 6 am in Chicago and Winnipeg, 5 am in Denver and Calgary, and 4 am in Los Angeles and Vancouver. Bear this in mind when telephoning, not just from Europe but also within North America; a 9 am call from New York would disturb the slumbers of most Californians. If you watch any coast-to-coast news programmes, you'll notice that the studio clock has no hour hand.

If you travel west across North America, you "gain" time; suppose you took three days to drive from east coast to west, then each day would appear to have 25 hours. In the reverse direction, the day last only 23 hours. Flights across the continent work in the same way as transatlantic flights: the day is "stretched" flying west and "squeezed" going east. To compound this effect, west-east flights are faster in real time due to the wind assistance of the jet stream.

The USA has stubbornly rejected the 24-hour clock used by the rest of the world. In timetables, many times are given in local time using the 12 hour clock. The convention is that times printed in light type are before noon, those in **bold** after noon.

The usual way to ask the time is to enquire "what time do you have?" The answer is not "well, my doctor's given me six months to live". North Americans use *before* and *after* where Britons say *to* and *past*. Thus 1.10 is "ten after one" and 1.5 is "ten" before two". An alternative to the latter is to say "ten to two".

U.S.A.

THE PEOPLE

Africans	derogatory term applied to black people
buppie	black urban professional (see yuppie)
Canuck	Canadian
GLC	Gay and Lesbian Community
GOP	Republican Party (Grand Old Party)
hick	country bumpkin
honky	black term for a white man
hop	a dance
horsebag	derogatory term, usually (but not always) applied to women
jap	Jewish American princess; any rich spoiled girl
klutz	a physically or socially inept person
limey	Englishman (comparable in tone to Yank)
Mister Charlie	black term for a white man
Native American	American Indian
ofay	black term for a white man
Okie	poor farmer (originally referred to Oklahomas who fled the dust bowl during the Depression
preppy	lifestyle and dress associated with socially elite prepatory schools, e.g. button down shirts and penny loafers
redneck	ignorant yokel, often violently right wing, prevalent in the South
school	university or college as well as school
WASP	White Anglo Saxon Protestant
Yankee	usually a New Englander, but to Southerners, all Northerners
yuppie	young urban professional, who frequents single bars and psychoanalysts

At the last official count there were 245,110,000 Americans. You will be relieved to discover that not all American gentlemen dress in loud checks nor do they all have blue-rinsed wives who nag them to hurry and take a photo or who gush over the antiquity of 1920s architecture. On their home territory they can be most open, generous, uncomplaining and relaxed people you could ever hope to meet, not to mention well-dressed and polite.

Like every nationality, they have their egocentricities. You can't fail to notice the pride they take in living in the richest major country in the world with its much vaunted belief in freedom, democracy and justice. This sometimes blinds them to the abject poverty in which some of their fellow citizens live, and also to the dark side of American foreign policy. Of course there are many informed, well-balanced Americans with a keen interest in all things foreign, including you. But there is also a general air of narrow-mindedness which can be irritating and amusing by turns. As was demonstrated in a recent survey by the National Geographic Society, many

Americans have a very dodgy grasp of European geography; don't be unduly surprised to be asked what is the capital of London. Some young people really do seem to exist on a diet of soft drinks and fast foods while shuttling between divorced parents who bicker over who will pay the orthodontist's bill (you will see many sets of metal braces called "railroad tracks" in place of teeth). Young thrusting professionals exude self-confidence by day and consult psychoanalysts by night. The middle aged and elderly are kept busy by regular visits to their plastic surgeons. Everybody seems to judge you (and each other) in terms of material wealth.

But despite a higher degree of conformity among Americans (partly because of the power of the media and advertising) there are plenty of folks who don't conform to these or any other norms. If you are expecting everyone in the States to act like the archetypal New Yorker or wheeler-dealer in *Dallas* you are in for a great surprise. There are areas in the States just as remote as places in northern Scotland; where small villages have only a post office and gas station; where farmers are like farmers everywhere and where people work and go home to their family and friends; where crime is virtually unknown or treated with horror and shock.

ETHNIC BACKGROUND

The USA is the most cosmopolitan country in the world. Every shade of skin, each of the earth's 160 nationalities and scores of the world's languages are represented. But the nation is not quite the melting pot it might seem; although most citizens take pride in being American — they will describe themselves as Irish-American, Polish-American, Korean-American — there is not much large-scale intermixing between racial groups. The neighbourhoods of every city are often delineated along ethnic lines, more so than in Britain. Despite official denials, there is a clear racial hierarchy in terms of material wealth: the White Anglo-Saxon Protestants (WASPs) are at the top, followed by the descendants of other immigrants from Europe, then Asians and finally blacks and Hispanics (Spanish-speaking Americans) competing for last place. The number of Hispanics (including large numbers of naturalized Americans from Mexico known as Chicanos) has risen steadily to 18 million, and the Population Reference Bureau estimates that by the year 2000 they could surpass blacks (currently numbering 27 million), and become the largest minority.

Sadly, there is considerable racial sensitivity which frequently surfaces. It may be a casual racist comment made by someone of your own race. Or you may witness interracial attacks (either verbal or physical) on the streets. Even among people who appear to be tolerant, you need to tread warily to avoid inflaming concealed prejudices.

American Jews play a significant role in the ethnic composition of America, particularly in and around New York. Numbering around six million (twice as many as in Israel), they exert a political, business, intellectual and artistic influence disproportionate to their numbers. Despite their valuable contribution to American culture, there is still a strong streak of anti-Semitism running right through American society, as evidenced by the blunder made by the liberal candidate for the leadership of the Democratic Party, the Reverend Jesse Jackson, who used the term of abuse "hymies" for Jews while campaigning.

Indians. The only true native people of the USA are thought to have crossed over what is now the Bering Strait from Asia many thousands of years before Europeans reached America, and wandered down settling the continent. Some tribes, such as the Sioux, settled in tepees on the plains of the Midwest. The Navajo, Ute and others chose to dwell in the caves of the Rockies and the west. As soon as the white man arrived, the native peoples were successively invaded, murdered, killed off by epidemics and sequestered. At the end of the nineteenth century, the comparatively few survivors were dispossessed of their remaining land and shunted off to reservations designated by the federal government in desert and mountain regions. Although over half the states of the Union have Indian names (MiciZibi = "great river", Iowa = "one who puts to sleep"), Indians were not made US citizens until 1924.

Gradually the condition of the modern Indian is improving. Having Indian blood is now a matter of considerable pride. The term "Native American" has been adopted to replace the 500-year-old misnomer. In recent years, they have been politically active in securing land, money and official encouragement in their struggle to maintain their culture. Their traditional handicrafts are held in great esteem and marketed more fairly than they once were. The rest of America has become aware of the plight as the profile has increased.

Inevitably, traditional ways have been altered by contact with the twentieth century. Modern Indians travel in pick-up trucks rather than on horseback, and live in houses or tarpaper shacks not wigwams. Any wigwams you see are likely to be plastic tourist attractions. All the same, Indian reservations can provide a fascinating insight into the lives of an aboriginal people. Three quarters of a million Indians still live on reservations. Although reservations are subject to federal law, they are intended to be autonomous communities. When a public highway enters a reservation, there are often signs saying something like "You are now entering the exclusive Navajo nation, and your entrance constitutes consent to the laws of the Navajo people and the jurisdiction of their court". There is still one tribe in Florida (the Miccosukee) who have not formally made peace with the United States.

If possible get into the heart of a reservation — although entrance to certain villages is forbidden — and avoid the tourist-orientated periphery. Take care to respect the practices of the Indians. Do not take photographs or make tape recordings without the permission of the subjects. Some who have absorbed enough of the market ethic will insist on payment for pictures; others will be offended. Behave circumspectly and be especially deferential to the elders. Many Indians feel resentment towards white people, and have no intention of compromising their beliefs and rituals for the sake of curious visitors.

MAKING FRIENDS

It is very easy to make friends with Americans. They are not suspicious when foreigners address them, and they love to talk to strangers on trains, buses and in restaurants. Furthermore, they are not an overly critical or subtle people and will accept overtures of friendship at face value. Especially if their own ancestry is British, they will be delighted to befriend you, perhaps because they regret the lack of history in their own culture.

So even if you don't start your trip with a list of friends, acquaintances and distant relations to visit, you'll soon meet the natives in the usual places — youth hostels, bars, national parks, etc. Sooner or later you will be invited into an American home. Try to be punctual, polite and full of praise for the United States. Although many Americans have a hearty sense of humour, they seldom direct it at themselves or their country.

Don't be surprised if you are continually addressed as "sir" or "ma'am", since Americans use these titles indiscriminately. After just one meeting, they may greet you with an intimacy which seems to you inappropriate. Relax and enjoy these social differences. Be as outgoing and yet respectful as you can, and they will respond with generosity second to none.

Sex. The media give the impression that Americans worship sex almost as much as money. Although some observers might place motor cars or food above both, it is not a great exaggeration to say that a "meaningful relationship" and, more starkly, sex is of overwelming importance to many Americans. To others the topic is anathema. Religious fundamentalists devote more energy to attacking pre-marital sex, contraception and homosexuality than any other subjects. Displays of affection between gay people which go unnoticed in New York and San Francisco could get the practitioners shot by Southern rednecks.

If the opportunity for casual sex presents itself, you should be aware of some of the possible consequences. The whole spectrum of venereal diseases, most of which are curable if irritating, flourish amid such sexual freedom. However, genital herpes is an unpleasant, incurable complaint with an ever-growing number of sufferers; there are now dating agencies specifically for people with the complaint. But for several years the threat of the disease AIDS — the acquired immune deficiency syndrome — has been a much more serious matter. On average someone in the USA is diagnosed as having AIDS every ten minutes, and at least one million Americans are believed to be infected by the AIDS virus HIV. One result has been a decrease in casual sex among male gays, although there are still plenty of homosexual bars which specialize in the easy pick-up. Sado-masochism can be found in cities with a large gay community, but is strictly out-of-bounds elsewhere. Lesbian bars are rare; female homosexuals meet primarily through discussion and action groups devoted to lesbian rights and problems.

There are other hazards facing the prospective sexual athlete, notably legal difficulties. The age of consent for both males and females is 18 in some states. Intercourse with someone below the age of consent is known as "statutory rape", and is not legally distinguished from forcible rape: 80% of men in American prisons for rape are there for statutory rape. There are also laws against transporting minors over state borders so be cautious of picking up adolescent hitch-hikers. Homosexual activity among both men and women is illegal in most states, but rarely prosecuted when conducted discreetly. Even heterosexual sex between people not married to each other is classified as "unlawful intercourse", although convictions are virtually unknown. Unmarried couples should encounter no problem checking into a motel or hotel.

Paid sex exists as it does everywhere. the cheapest variety is provided by sleazy massage parlours and the poorly-paid waitresses and dancers in topless bars. Hookers in the $25-$50 range work dingy hotels, motels and bars in every large city. In the event of a police crackdown (usually preceding a local election), the women suffer rather than their clientele. The customer risks disease and a possible mugging. One notable exception is the state of Nevada: Reno and Carson City have licensed brothels and regular staff medical examinations.

Language. Americans have certainly done interesting things to the English language. Pedants will have to steel themselves. "Tonite" is flashed up everywhere, accommodation has inexplicably become a plural, and so on. The energy associated with the American lifestyle seems to be reflected in their love of dynamic verbs ("grab forty winks", "fire off an application") and of inventing verbs ("to gift", "to emote"). The best example of this is the New Yorker who elevatored up to his penthouse, to wash and tuxedo before going theatering.

American slang can be a delight. Be sure to commiserate with someone who tells you he has just "struck out" (a baseball term meaning failed, often in the context of attracting a partner), and don't disagree when someone says of another person that he or she is "out-to-lunch" (i.e. weird, inattentive). "Chill out" now means calm down and "to spin your wheels" is to make no progress. The coining of the term "yuppies" to refer to young urban professionals has led to many variations: Buppies (black urban professionals), Guppies (gay), Puppies (pregnant). Wall Street jargon has entered the American language and is creeping across the Atlantic: "user-friendly", "interface" and "on-line".

This book uses British words and spellings except for proper names such as the World Trade *Center*. To help you overcome some linguistic difficulties, each chapter in the first part of this book begins with a glossary. For a full treatment of this facinating subject, consult the *British/American Dictionary* by Norman Moss (Hutchinson, £3.95).

In England, one's speech often identifies one's education and social class, but in America those distinctions are not nearly as obvious. Someone with a PhD in geology from the University of Washington in Seattle will sound very much like a blue-collar worker for the local Boeing aircraft factory. And don't panic when you are not understood right away. Speak slowly and distinctly; the natives are not used to your English either. Perhaps suprisingly, English is the official language in only 16 states. And as the Hispanic population increases, Spanish is becoming more widespread: in New York City, Texas and the Southwest USA, you can expect to see many bilingual signs. Those who have learned Castilian Spanish in Europe should note that Spanish-speaking Americans have been just as disrespectful to their tongue as have English-speakers.

Listen also for the colourful slang employed by blacks, much of which is impenetrable. There are pockets of interesting dialects across the country such as the Cajun *patois* heard in Louisiana, and Gulla, a dialect spoken by blacks living on a coastal strip in South Carolina and Georgia which contains many West African words. There is also a theory that the American accent is closer to the way Elizabethan was spoken than is the present BBC accent, though of course this is difficult to prove. There is some American vocabulary which was in common or dialect usage in England several centuries ago, but is now archaic. For example Americans talk about "shucking" peas (i.e. shelling) which is a 17th century English word. Or they talk of a "whole slew of boats", meaning large numbers, from the Irish "sluagh". Cookie was originally a Scottish word for plain bun. Going on a drinking "jag" (prolonged spree) was an English dialect word.

Religion. Church attendance is much higher in the USA than it is in Britain, and many Americans practise their religion with fervour a uncommon in Europe. One of the first things you may notice is that every hotel and motel room is equipped with a bible, placed there by the Gideon Society, an association of Christian commercial travellers. The "Moral

Majority" (a subspecies of Christian fundamentalists) use their literal interpretation of the Bible to denounce many liberal causes from racial integration to toleration of homosexuality. There are entire television networks funded by private donations which broadcast the message of salvation 24 hours a day. Try to tune in to a televised faith healing or revival meeting. A source of considerable amusement to liberal Americans is the susceptibility of TV evangelists to sex and fraud scandals. Nevertheless viewers continue to send millions of dollars to preachers who use tactics such as the threat of their imminent demise to appeal for funds. A popular satirical postcard reads "Honey — if God had meant us to be rich, He would have made us TV evangelists".

Of course their are many other influential religions. The Roman Catholic Church claims a membership of over 50 million. Much smaller in number but also influential (especially in Utah) is the Jesus Christ of Latter Day Saints, better known as the Mormons, who derive their teachings from one Joseph Smith who had visions of the Angel Moroni in New York early in the nineteenth century. The closest approximation of the Church of England is the Episcopal Church which has around three million members.

Cult religions have suprisingly large and enthusiastic followings, from offbeat meditating sects in California to the Unification Church (Moonies). Since many of these groups have energetic recruitment policies, be wary of offers of meals and accommodation or a chance of having a personality test (this latter is a popular tactic of the Church of Scientology). Whereas it is usually not difficult to brush off religious pitches in Britain, American zealots are not so easily deterred and you can soon become embroiled in an unpleasant contest of wills. On the other hand, Hare Krishna have free vegetarian restaurants and take-away temples in most large cities, where you can find delicious food in exchange for enduring half-hearted attempts to convert you.

If you do wish to attend church services, enquire at the local tourist office or consult the Yellow Pages. To make a change from sitting in a pew, you can attend full religious services in the comfort of your own (or hired) car. Drive-in services are conducted at drive-in cinemas and cater for the physically or socially handicapped. You park next to speaker posts which are used to transmit the sermon and music, and prayer books are handed around by pedestrian "greeters".

Politics. The political system of the American democratic republic is highly complex and quite unlike Britain's constitutional monarchy or Canada's parliamentary democracy. Federal, state and local officials from US President to district Sanitation chiefs are all democratically elected. The federal legislature of the United States of America is Congress, and is composed of the Senate with 100 Senators (two elected per state) and the House of Representatives with 435 elected members.

Every leap year there is a Presidential election, preceded by an interminably long campaign. The first stage is a series of primary elections during which party supporters vote for their favourite presidential candidate. The choice is sealed at the two party conventions in summer, which are huge, colourful and expensive media events. Finally, after nearly a year of campaigning, the President is elected in November and formally inaugurated in January. Instead of electing the President and Vice President directly, the voters of the USA vote 535 non-office-holding people to make up the Electoral College which in turn elects the President and Vice President. A great deal of razzamatazz surrounds the election of politicians and politics seems increasingly to be just a branch of showbusiness.

The two main parties — the Republicans (officially called the Grand Old Party or GOP) and the Democratic Party — have dominated American politics for many decades. Although there are a few other political organisations, they very seldom have representation at a national level. As you might expect from the party that has produced Ronald Reagan and George Bush the Republican Party is fairly right wing. In contrast Michael Dukakis is a typically liberal Democrat. Travellers should take care when discussing politics. Any viewpoint which might be constructed as anti-American is best kept to yourself unless you really want a heated argument. Radical politics do exist, but tend to be issue-based: the peace movement is growing and the environmentalist lobby has commanded respect for years. But so has the Ku Klux Klan.

IMMIGRATION

If you arrive by public transport — air, sea, bus or train — you should be given an Arrival/Departure record card and Customs Declaration form to fill in before you arrive. If you drive or walk across an international border, you'll be asked to fill them in at the frontier. Try not to make any mistakes on the forms, and complete them only in blue or black ink: otherwise the officials will make you rewrite them. If you don't have a definite address in the USA, you can always choose a hotel from this book rather than leaving the section blank. The US authorities have instituted a system of "pre-clearance" when travelling from some foreign airports: visitors arriving direct from points in Canada, and Shannon in Ireland, proceed through immigration before take off.

The queue for immigration at most American airports is very long and very slow, so be prepared for an ordeal. The shortest queues are at little-used airports such as Anchorage Alaska or Charlotte North Carolina, rather than busy gateways like Los Angeles or the New York airports. Hand the officer your forms plus your valid passport, plus an old passport if it contains an unexpired American visa. Have ready any documents which you think may prove your status as a desirable alien, and be as polite as possible. It may be that they simply ask you: "What is your job, Sir/Madam?" "Brain surgeon". "Do you enjoy it?" "Yes". Stamp. However, if they suspect you of trying to work illegally or to undermine the American Way of Life, or they simply don't like your face, the questioning will be more aggressive. Your chances of getting through easily are improved if you happen to be white, English-speaking and smartly-dressed.

It makes sense to have as much in your favour as possible. In descending order of effectiveness, this means having:
— an onward or return air ticket. (If this is a refundable ticket, you can usually claim a refund as soon as you are safely through immigration).
— an official-looking letter from someone in your home country explaining why you will have to return home after a designated period
— travellers cheques. A wad of low denomination cheques looks more impressive than a few of higher value. Immigration officers will be looking for at least $100 for every week of the requested stay. It helps to flash a few credit cards. If necessary, you can buy travellers cheques up to your credit limit on a credit card and then send the money home to pay off the loan as soon as you're through
— an invitation from an American citizen accepting full responsibility for your keep. Again, this should look as official as possible. (If he has reason to doubt you, the officer won't hesitate to telephone this person at any time of the day or night)
— a large amount of American dollars or foreign currency (pounds not pesos)
Assuming they agree to admit you, one copy of the Arrival/Departure card will be stapled to your passport. The passport itself will be stamped, and the date to which you are allowed to remain in the USA written in. If you've done well, you will get six months; if the officer has admitted you grudgingly, you may get much less. This is entirely at the discretion of the immigration officer.

Overstaying. The chances of arrest for overstaying a week or two are very remote, but your non-compliance will probably be noticed when you leave, and be noted on your file should you ever wish to return.

An altogether less risky procedure is to request a visa extension before your allotted time expires, which you may do at any office of the US Immigration and Naturalization Service. Look in the telephone directory to find the nearest, and phone first to check opening hours. Take along all the evidence you can amass to justify your claim. They will probably assume that you are working illegally, so adequate proof of your means of support is essential. Taking along a US citizen who will vouch for you is recommended. Get an "Application for Issuance or Extension of Permit to Re-enter the USA". It may be sufficient to say simply you want to continue your travels. Or it might be safer to invent a plausible excuse such as your parents are joining you so you wish to extend your stay. If you apply more than once, use a different regional office. Some people have remained legally in the country for as long as a year.

Departure. There are no passport controls upon leaving the USA. If you are flying out, the check-in clerk will remove the Departure card from your passport. Travellers who cross by land into Canada should surrender the card to the Canadian border officials; leaving for Mexico, hand it in at the US side of the frontier.

CUSTOMS

After surviving immigration and collecting your luggage, hand in your completed Customs Declaration form to the inspector and hope that he will be content with this. There is no need to declare gifts whose total value does not exceed $400. The inspectors are naturally more concerned with rich returning Americans that with modest-looking British travellers. In addition to questions about the value of what you are bringing in, you will be asked whether you have any fresh foods (if you say yes, they'll probably confiscate them) and whether your footwear have been on a farm in the previous month (ditto). Do not be over-scrupulous in answering such questions.

Some airports have a "red" and "green" channel system, as in Europe. If you have goods to declare, go through the red channel and discuss terms with the officer; payment may be made in cash, travellers cheques or by any major credit card. Even if feel that you have no goods to declare you will still be stopped and your Customs Declaration inspected. At all other customs posts, it is highly probable that your baggage will be given a thorough going over.

Alcohol and Tobacco. Travellers who have been out of the USA for over 48 hours and have not imported goods duty free in the previous 30 days can bring in 200 cigarettes and 50 cigars (not Cuban). These may, however, be subject to a few cents state tax on each pack. Visitors over 21 may import one litre (34 fl oz, slightly more than a US quart) of any alcoholic drink, unless this is prohibited by the state you arrive in.

Prohibited Goods. The Commissioner of the US Customs Service makes its purpose icily clear:

> The US Customs Service is proud to serve you. Our intention is to protect the American way of life. Together we can end the devastating impact of illicit drugs, maintain the integrity of our economy by protecting US products, trademarks and immigration laws, support a healthy economy by depositing in the national treasury duties levied on foreign goods, and guard our agricultural well-being from contaminated products.

The importation of even a small amount of cannabis will get you in a lot of trouble if you are caught. As well as drugs and anything vaguely agricultural, the following are prohibited: liqueur-filled chocolates, obscene publications, video tapes, pirate tapes or books, "seditious and treasonable material", lottery tickets and anything made by forced labour.

Restricted Goods. The booklet *Know Before You Go* is free from the US Customs Service (PO Box 7407, Washington, DC 20044) and contains details of items which require a permit, for example guns, goods made in Cuba, North Korea, Vietnam, etc.

Other Goods. If you are seen to have over $400 worth of gifts, you may have to pay duty at 10%-12%, however there are discounts depending on the country of origin of your gifts. Under the Generalized System of Preferences, intended to aid the economies of developing countries, you can bring in duty free, for example, music boxes from any of the 140 countries on the list except Taiwan.

Currency. There are no restrictions on the amount of money you may take to or from Britain. If you take more than $10,000 into or out of the USA, you are supposed to declare the fact on a form which is supplied by customs officers at the border.

Returning to Britain. Apart from the culture shock induced by returning from southern California to a wet Monday morning at Gatwick, your biggest problem is likely to be bringing in exotic and expensive purchases. You are allowed only £32 worth of purchases duty free; beyond that you'll pay duty of around 15%. Custom officers in the UK have lists of the serial numbers of valuable items such as cameras with which they can trace the country of sale, so don't be too daring. If you pay duty on expensive purchases, retain the receipt for future use.

The duty free alcohol limit is one litre of spirits or sparkling wine, plus two litres of still wine. The standard size for spirits sold in North American duty free shops is 40 fl oz (1.4 litres). This is technically more than you are allowed, although you are unlikely to encounter problems. Similarly, bringing in three standard bottles (750 ml) of wine will take you marginally over the limit, but most customs officers turn a blind eye. You may also bring back 200 cigarettes or 50 cigars or 250 g (9 oz) of tobacco.

A large number of visitors to the USA are not satisfied with a fortnight or a month's holiday. They find the American way of life so addictive that they look for ways of earning money in order to extend their stays and to get to know one place well. Furthermore they find their transatlantic accents a definite bonus in their job search. A car is equally valuable but more expensive to acquire. But the visa situation is discouraging.

Working Visas. The US government authorizes a limited number of Exchange Visitor Programmes or EVP's. Participants who qualify for these programmes are then given a J-1 visa which authorizes them to take paid summer employment in the USA, and to apply for a social security number. The two main EVP's are sponsored by the British Universities North America Club (232 Vauxhall Bridge Road, London SW1V 1AU; 01-630-0344) and Camp America (Dept TK, 37A Queens Gate, London SW7 5HR; 01-589-3223). Most J-1 visas are issued to students; however, non-students are eligible for certain jobs in American summer camps. Contact these organizations as early as possible for details, and to set the slow-moving procedures in motion.

A few Australian and New Zealand students are now permitted to work in the USA under the auspices of the Council of International Educational Exchange in New York (205 E 42nd St, New York, NY 10017). Antipodean participants must be full-time students with a minimum fund of $1,500 and a return ticket to Los Angeles on one of the group flights departing Australia in November or December. The worst restriction is that work can be accepted only between 1st November and 19th March, though the organizers in Australia (Student Services Australia, P O Box 399, Carlton South, Victoria 3053) are trying to extend the dates so that the period extended until Easter to at least cover the entire ski season. The cost of registration is $180.

The lucky few who have influential contacts or specialized skills which they can market in the USA may be eligible for other working visas. For the H-2 "Temporary Worker" visa you must leave all the paperwork to your American employer. The processing of his or her application will take between four and six months while the authorities decide whether it is true that no eligible American citizen could do the job. The H-3 "Industrial Trainee" visa is possible for people in certain lies of work and study. For a list of official programmes request a copy of *Summer Programs in the USA* from the Educational Advisory Service, 6 Porter St, London W1M 2HR.

Casual Work. You may want to consider the possibility of picking up casual work without having a working visa. A new immigration bill came into effect in 1987 / 8 which for the first time made it unlawful for employers knowingly to hire illegal aliens; the penalty for ignoring the new law is a fine of up to $10,000. Social Security cards and/or green cards are meant to be produced when applying for jobs. Exceptions are bound to occur, but on the whole it has become more difficult to pick up casual work in fast food restaurants, fruit orchards, fishing boats, landscape gardening firms, etc. There are rumours that anyone caught working illegally may be banned permanently from obtaining a US visa, though this scaremongering prophecy has yet to be fulfilled. Good bluffers continue to find cash-in-hand jobs on the strength of invented social security numbers. In such a situation, it is better to rely on newspaper adverts and direct personal contact. Building sites are reputed to be among the best bets, especially in New York and California. Wages are often $8-$10 an hour.

Harvests. As in Europe, fruit and vegetable harvests across the United States rely on itinerant pickers from the citrus harvests of Florida (October to May especially in Desoto County) to the wheat harvest in the Great Plains (mid May to August). In the southern and eastern states, soft fruits (strawberries, peaches) are harvested in May and June, followed by tobacco in July and August. Apple-picking in September in the north-eastern USA can be lucrative. And any of the leading wine-producing states (California, Washington, Idaho, New York) have opportunities for grape-pickers: the further north the location, the later the harvest. Always enquire locally about possible openings.

Summer Camps. Many American parents send their kids to camp for part of the summer. Thousands of young people are needed to teach them sports and other activities, feed them and prevent them from running riot. There are two major organizations in Britain which recruit camp staff on a large scale, both of which are geared largely but not exclusively to students. Camp America accepts applicants who are 18 years or older as camp counsellors, kitchen/maintenance staff or family companions. BUNAC recruits anyone aged between 19 and 35 who is able to satisfy the counsellor requirements. They have a subsidiary programme, called "KAMP" (which is primarily open to students) for people who prefer to do domestic work in summer camps rather than look after kids. None of these programmes pays high wages, but after your registration fee of about £50 has been accepted, your return air fare to the States will be paid for you, plus you receive $250-$400 pocket money at the end of the nine week work period. It is an excellent way of making friends with young Americans who often invite their fellow camp counsellors to their homes after camp is finished. Three smaller summer camp recruitment programmes are Camp Counselors USA (CCUSA), 26 3rd Street, San Francisco, CA 94103, the International Counselor Exchange Program (ICEP), 38 W 88th St, New York, NY 10024, and the YMCA's International Camp Counsellors Program (ICCP), c/o YMCA Centre, Fairthorne Manor, Curdridge, Southampton SO3 2GA.

Tourism. Although some might consider the proliferation of fast food establishments a blight on the land, they are often useful places in which to pick up some extra cash. There is a high turnover of staff, and a methodical series of enquiries along a strip of hamburger and pizza restaurants — especially in resort town like Myrtle Beach South Carolina, Ocean Beach Maryland, Ann Arbor Michigan, along Cape Cod, or the beaches of Southern California or Florida — should eventually be rewarded. The main disadvantages with this sort of job are erratic or insufficient hours, lack of accommodation and low wages. It is not uncommon to be paid a fraction of the minimum hourly wage ($3.35 at the time of going to print) since employers exploit the fact that serving staff receive generous tips.

Ski resorts are also worth investigation over the winter season which lasts from November to April in the high Rockies. Large ski resorts include Vail and Aspen in Colorado, Big Sky Montana, Sun Valley Idaho and Stow Vermont. Try to show up at least a few weeks before the first customers and ask in all the shops, bars, day care centres and hotels.

A number of foreign nationals have found employment through recruitment agencies in Florida with cruise ships which ply the Caribbean. Hours are long, wages (but not tips) are minimal, but most enjoy the experience. Try contacting Stella Cruise Services in Miami (305-358-4433) which employs for about 20 ships, Windjammer Cruises (P O Box 120, Miami Beach) or Premier Cruise Lines (101 George King Boulevard, Cape Canaveral, Florida 32920).

Fishing. Without some mechanical skills, plenty of physical stamina and a little experience at sea, it will be very difficult to get a place on one of the West Coast shrimp, salmon or tuna boats. Earnings can be very high — over $1000 a month — so you may decide it's worth the trouble of visiting the docks (and visiting them often) at Kodiak, Chignik, Petersburg, Ketchikan or Wrangell in Alaska, or Newport and Astoria in Oregon. You can also try at fishing ports along the Gulf of Mexico, though these are not so good a bet. You have a better chance of finding work in the fish processing plants in any of these towns. Alaska offers the best prospects because of the size of its fishing industry and the relatively low population. Although much of the recruitment is done through Seattle, there are still many last-minute on-the-spot opportunities. Ask at the seafood packing factories well before the seasons begin. Most fishing seasons peak in July and August, though shrimping begins in Kodiak in April when it is easier to land a job.

Parks. Although there are a great many seasonal jobs in national parks, the hiring is done months in advance by a government agency which taken on Americans almost exclusively. Logging and forestry jobs are also very hard to get because of high wages and strong unions. You might, however, be able to get a job planting trees between February and April (try Alabama and Mississippi).

Chances are much better in theme and amusement parks, which are so popular with American. A number of these, as well as many other jobs, are listed in the annual Summer Employment Directory of the United States (distributed in the UK by Vacation Work, 9 Park End St, Oxford). Jobs at commercial attractions throughout the USA range from selling hotdogs at massive amusement parks to dismantling rides for small travelling carnivals. The earlier in the year you can present yourself to the Personnel Director or carnival owner the better, but it is always worth asking about any last-minute openings. Get a list of the local attractions from the tourist information office.

Doing something constructive for the environment might hold out more appeal. Volunteers are recruited in numbers by the American Hiking Society (P O Box 86, No. Scituate, Massachusetts 02060) to build and maintain trails, etc. from the Daniel Boone National Forest of Kentucky to Volcanoes National Park in Hawaii. Camping accommodation is arranged and in most cases food and partial travel expenses are provided. There is a registration fee of $25. Other organizations worth contacting for similar programmes are AMS, Box 298, Gorham, New Hampshire 03581, and the Sierra Club Service Trips, 730 Polk St, San Francisco, CA 94109.

Selling. The "Sales" section of the classified advertisement columns of most big city newspapers is usually larger than any other employment category, and if you are determined and outgoing you should be able to come up with something. Many people find that selling products over the telephone is less intimidating, but it is not potentially as high paying. Most selling jobs will pay on a commission basis so earnings will be unreliable and seldom turn out to be as high as the adverts imply. But your foreign charm may make you a more successful salesperson than you expected. Jobs on ice cream vans are advertised nearly as often as encyclopaedia-selling jobs, and should not be too difficult to obtain in large cities, assuming you can drive.

To pick up a little emergency cash ($8-$12), some hospitals pay for blood donations.

Domestic. Au Pair in America (37 Queen's Gate, London SW7; 01-584-2274) and Experiment in International Living (West Malvern Rd, Upper Wyche, Malvern, Worcs. WR14 4EN) offer J-1 visas to young women and a few men with some childcare experience, willing to work one year with an American family. Many British women who are not eligible for these programmes continue to take up nannying jobs (provided they get past the inevitable inquisition at immigration) and earn up to $400 a week.

auto-teller	cash dispenser
change purse	purse
check	cheque *or* bill in a restaurant or bar
checking account	current account
dime	ten cent coin
greenback	dollar (slang)
make change	give change
nickel	five cent coin
penny	cent
purse	handbag
quarter	twenty-five cent coin
savings account	deposit account
sawbuck	ten dollar bill (slang)
smackers	dollars (slang)
two bits	twenty-five cents (slang)

In recent years, the number of dollars that you can buy for one pound has varied between $1 and $2. Inflation is currently about 5%.

Coins. 1c (penny), 5c (nickel), 10c (dime), 25c (quarter), 50c (half dollar), $1. The term penny, nickel, dime, and quarter are not slang words but official names — rather like farthing, florin and crown. However, "buck" or "greenback" are pure slang for dollar.

All but the penny — which is bronze — are silver in colour. Half-dollar coins are rare. $1 coins (called "silver dollars") are found almost exclusively in gambling cities. The nickel and quarter are very similar in size, but the quarter has a serrated edge. Quarters are easily the most useful coins — for telephones, launderettes, coin-operated newspaper vending machines, luggage lockers and exact-change buses — so keep a supply.

Notes. $1, $2, $5, $10, $20, $50, $100, $1,000 and $10,000. Each denomination of note is the same size, is exactly the same shade of green and has a broadly similar design. You should check notes very carefully, and keep denominations as low as possible to avoid the risk of errors. Notes above $20 may be treated with suspicion, as counterfeiting of high-value notes is commonplace.

BANKS

Hours. Banks are normally open 9am-3pm, Monday to Friday. Many large banks in urban areas stay open later especially on Fridays, and operate for a few hours on Saturdays. At other times, you can change foreign currency only at a few hotels of the *bureaux de change* in major international airports. Be warned that the exchange rates offered at these places are often grossly unfavourable.

Cash Machines. Money machines ("auto-tellers") can be found in shopping malls, at airports and in the lobby of almost every bank. When the rest of the bank is closed, you may have to insert your card into a slot at the door to the lobby in order to gain entry. As elsewhere in the world cash machines are linked together by computer into several networks, allowing customers of other banks to draw funds; this includes holders of Access and Visa cards who can get cash by keying in their Personal Identification Number (PIN). Note that the system is not yet functioning perfectly, so after successfully drawing cash from a Cirrus network machine in one city, your card may be rejected by a similar machine elsewhere. In addition, if your card is damaged or accidentally placed in a magnetic field, it will be unceremoniously rejected by all machines. Therefore you should not rely upon this method alone for getting cash.

Drive-In Banks. Various systems are employed to serve those unwilling or unable to leave their vehicles. Sometimes an auto-teller is placed at car window height outside a bank. Or there may be a Heath Robinson network of pneumatic tubes to transfer cheques and cash, with negotiations carried on through microphones and loudspeakers. The most human version involves driving up to a window and conducting transactions face-to-face. Drive-in banks can also be used by cyclists, motorcyclists and even pedestrians.

Opening a Bank Account. The American banking system is highly disparate and relatively primitive. Most banks have only a few local branches, and there are no nationwide banks of the size and influence of British clearing banks; the nearest contender is the Bank of America. So choosing a bank for your account will probably depend on the enticements offered; interest on current accounts, for example, or free giveaways to new customers.

Opening an account in the USA is quick an easy. You need only pay in a few dollars, show some identification and provide a mailing address. You may be asked for a reference, although many banks will waive this requirement in ceaseless search for new clients. If you have opened a current account (called "checking account"), you will soon receive a cheque ("check") book and an auto-teller card. Deposit accounts are called "savings accounts".

Statements are sent out monthly. You are not allowed to go overdrawn without prior negotiation with the bank; in the USA this is taken more seriously than in Britain, and bouncing cheques should be avoided.

If you have sufficient capital (a minimum of $500), you can open a US dollar bank account in Britain. The Bell Savings Bank of Philadelphia (9 South 69th St, Upper Darby PA 19082) offers interest-bearing accounts for overseas clients. The system functions remarkably efficiently: you get monthly statements, a cheque book and an auto-teller card linked to the Plus system. Running the account costs nothing since correspondence is pre-paid and there is even a toll-free number from the UK (0800 89 1024). Within Pennsylvania you can call 1-800-222-2781 for customer service, from elsewhere in the USA 1-800-523-4175. If you can't afford the initial $500 alone, you can team up with a (trustworthy) friend to open a joint account.

Once you have a cheque book, you might be tempted to use it. Be warned that for any store, gas station or hotel to take a cheque, you must be able to produce two pieces of identification: a major credit card, plus something with your photograph on (a passport will do if you don't have an Amercan driving licence). You will be expected to give your home and local addresses, telephone number and even your social security number, and the assistant may circle one letter in the acronym COINS; this stands for Caucasian-Oriental-Indian-Negro-Spanish, and is designed to help the police to identify and trace frauders. Not surprisingly, most people prefer to use credit cards.

TIPPING

There is a strong tradition of tipping for service in North America, especially in restaurants and bars. Servers of food and drinks are notoriously uderpaid (often below the statutory minimum wage), and it is common knowledge that most rely on tips for their livelihood. So, as a general rule, be as generous a you can, but don't go to the extremes of some Americans who even tip air stewardesses.

Most guide books recommend a tip of 15% or even 20% in all situations: tax drivers, waiters, bartenders and so on. You will have to use your discretion, as Americans do, when deciding whether this is excessive. Taxi drivers are usually content with 10% (although they loath to admit it) and some passengers simply round up the fare to the nearest dollar. Restaurant customers who leave more than 15% are susally on expenses. If you pay by credit card, often the "total" box will be left ominously blank. The idea is that you add on the amount you wish to leave as a tip. Most restaurant staff prefer you to leave a cash tip (for tax purposes) so you should fill in the total amount as it appears above.

In bars you need to tread more carefully. Often the waiter will present you with the bill ("check") as each round is delivered. You can guarantee that if you don't tip, or at least round up to a convenient amount, you will receive lousy service all evening. (If you have the audacity to ask for change for a ten dollar note on a bill for $9.50, you are certainly in for a dreary evenings). Should you merely be having a couple of beers and standing at the bar, no bartender should take offence if you choose not to tip. If you intend to make a night of it, however, placing a $5 or $10 bill on the bar at the start of the session should ensure good service. To avoid both unnecessary social embarassment and spending more than necessary, try to keep an eye on how the other customers are tipping. Many of the establishments we recommend are used to budget travellers, and so are not unaccustomed to people who cannot afford to tip.

area code	dialing code
automated attendants	computer-generated telephone operators
busy signal	engaged tone
cable	telegram
call collect	reverse the charges
Fedex	common abbreviation for Federal Express, an overnight delivery company
general delivery	poste restante
letter carrier	postman or woman
long distance	trunk call
night letter	overnight telegram
special delivery	express post
telephone booth	phone/call box
toll-free number	numbers (beginning 1-800) which are free
unlisted number	ex-directory
wire (vb)	to send a telegram
zip code	postal code

TELEPHONES

The American telephone system is a pleasure to use. Although owned and operated by numerous independent companies it is extremely efficient. And despite slight regional variations in price, it is also cheap. This is either the reason for or the result of the fact that Americans are the greatest telephone-users in the world making between two and three calls a day (compared to less than one in Britain).

Everything is slick and computerized, from the solid-state push button dialling system to the electronic voice that admonishes you for calling the wrong number and tells you how to do it right. If you ring directory enquiries ("information") you will not hear the riffling of pages, but rather a gentle keyboard tapping which can find the number — and repeat it to you in synthesized voice — almost before you've finished spelling the name. When you call a business, the reply is quite likely to be from an answering machine which plays canned music to keep you entertained until a human being comes on the line saying "Hi, this is Betty Lou, how can I help you?"

Tones. The dial tone is a constant buzz or low frequency continuous note. You should hear this as soon as you pick up the receiver, unless it is the type of payphone which requires money before dialling (see below). The ringing tone is long with long pauses. The engaged tone (or "busy signal") is a repeated short beep, with short pauses in between. The unobtainable tone — a piercing continuous note — is rare; you are more likely to get an electronic operator who offers an alternative number.

Interactive Telephones. The "touch-tone" system — whereby each key emits a different tone when pressed — is almost universal within North America. Push button phones have buttons bearing the symbol # and ★ in addition to the normal ten digits. Used in the right combinations, these enable your telephone to perform a variety of amazing tasks, such as calling back an engaged number automatically, or diverting incoming calls to another number. A telephone is no longer a telephone; it's a computer terminal.

You may find that are often called upon (by an electronic voice) to perform a task before achieving the desired aim. For example, calling Amtrak for train information (on 1-800-USA-RAIL), you should press 1 for arrival times and 2 for other information. Interacting with a telephone is no more difficult than operating a cash dispenser. One feature which may confuse the British is that you may be called upon to press the "pound" key; in fact, this is the # key. The simplest function (and possibly the most useful for foreign visitors) involves pressing # after dialling an international number. This indicates to the exchange that you have finished dialling and helps to speed your call through.

Numbers. All American telephone numbers take the form (111) 222-3333, where 111 is the area code and 222 is the exchange. These numbers are often replaced by the letters: for instance, the British Airways number is (800) AIR-WAYS; or a cinema might be 231-FILM. This presents no problem, since dials and push buttons are marked with both letters and numbers. Don't mistake the zero button which calls the Operator for the letter 'O' which coincides with the number 6, nor the numeral 1 for I. Note that it is not accepted practice to say "double-three double-seven". Americans expect to hear three-three-seven-seven.

Local calls are made by dialling the last seven digits. Call to numbers within the same area code are not necessarily local: for a definition of "local", consult the directory or call the operator. Any calls outside this local district are long distance ("toll calls"). To call a long distance number with the same area code, dial 1 plus the last seven digits, e.g. 1-222-3333. For long distance calls to a different area, dial 1 plus the area code plus the seven digit number, e.g. 1-111-222-3333.

The international prefix is 011. This should be followed by the country code (44 for Britain), then the STD code minus the first zero, then the number. So to call Vacation Work you should dial 011-44-865-241978. For further information on international calls, dial 1-800-874-4000; this call costs nothing.

Directories. As in Britain, the introductory pages of the phone book contain a wealth of useful information. Directories are made up of the "white pages" (the regular alphabetical listing), the "yellow pages" (the trade directory) and the "blue pages" (a very thin section listing government organizations). In large cities, the yellow pages usually constitute a separate volume and may be divided into two sections: Consumer & Household, which contains all the listings an individual might need, and Business & Industrial for commercial enterprises.

The almost universal number for local directory enquiries is 411, but check first in your directory or the notice next to payphones. To find a non-local number within your area, dial 1-555-1212. For numbers in another area, add the area code, e.g. 1-111-555-1212. If you don't know the area code, just dial 411. Directory enquiries are free from payphones, but often charged for from private phones.

Operator Services. The universal number for the operator is 0. This can also be used to contact emergency services if you can't get your hands on the correct emergency number (normally 911). If you are trying to make an urgent call, but repeatedly get the engaged signal, the operator will interrupt the conversation for a charge of 70c.

Dial direct whenever possible: unless you can prove the direct-dial mechanism is faulty, going through the operator increases the cost of a call by a minimum of $1.75. If you get a wrong number, ring 211 immediately and explain the fault. They should credit your bill or allow a further call from a payphone.

Dial-a-Service. Every large city has an astonishing range of numbers to call for "useful" services. The phone book will list the most helpful, but not necessarily the most exotic. For the price of a local call, you can find respectable information such as weather reports or transport timetables. But you can also dial-a-soap opera (one episode each day, sponsored by advertising), dial-a-prayer, dial-a-joke or even dial-a-heavy breather. Or try the "Tipster's Confidential" number, a hot line to the FBI which enables you to grass on your mates in complete secrecy.

Public Telephones. Because such a high proportion of Americans have their own telephones, public telephone booths in the US are not as numerous as in Britain, and virtually non-existent on residential streets. But you should be able to locate them on downtown street corners, in laundromats, gas stations, bars, restaurants and shopping malls. Airports and bus stations have banks of them. Do not make the mistake of going to a post office to make a call as you would in Europe, since the post office and the various independent telephone companies are absolutely separate. Unfortunately there are not public telephone offices in the US and long-distance calls must be made from an ordinary phone booth. Although most booths have doors (the kind of phone booth used by Superman), others are fixed to a post, and enclosed in a clear plastic shell which affords little protection against noise and the elements.

Because of regional variations in the way payphones work, always read the instructions. Normally you insert the minimum fee (usually 25c) in nickels, dimes or quarters. This gets you the dial tone and allows you a local call which may or may not be of limited duration. If you don't get a reply, replace the receiver to get your money back. If you are calling the operator, directory enquiries, a "toll-free" number or an emergency service, the machine will return your money as soon as the call connects. However, a growing number of payphones require you to pay only when the connection goes through. Among other benefits this enables people without the right change to call an ambulance.

Long distance numbers can be dialled direct: but you may have to select the telephone company you wish to use. Some payphones have half-a-dozen different possibilities. In general, AT&T is expensive, Sprint is cheap. Before the number is connected a voice (either human or computer-generated) will cut in to tell you the cost for the first three minutes. You should have a large pile of nickels, dimes and quarters handy; the pile will be enormous if you are making an international call. The call will finally be put through after all your money has dropped through. If no one answers, replacing the receiver will initiate a flood of loose change. Should you get a reply, then after three minutes the same voice will cut in to advise you of the cost for extra minutes. Alternatively, you may just hear a "beep" after three minutes. If you continue to speak, the operator will wait until your conversation is finished before ringing you back immediately to ask for more money. If you don't pay, then the cost will be charged to the number you have called.

There is an increasing number of payphones which accept credit cards, including your humble Access or Visa. You lift the reciever, wipe your card through the electronic reader, and dial. Apart from saving you the bother of amassing coins, you can pay for as little time as one minute (rather than the minimum of three minutes for coin-operated phones). When your credit card statement appears it will show not just the call charge but also the number dialled; bear this in mind if you're calling someone you shouldn't be, or using someone else's card.

There are payphones aboard some Amtrak trains which accept all major credit cards and allow direct dialling almost anywhere in the world: a one minute call to the UK cost $7.50. Air travellers can take advantage of the *Airfone* system used by many airlines. This allows you to make calls to anywhere within the USA from an aircraft in flight. Telephones are built into armrests and the wall of the cabin. To release the handset, you insert a major credit card (e.g. Access or Visa). You dial in the normal manner for long distance calls. When you replace the receiver at the end of your call the credit card is automatically debited with the charge ($7.50 for the first three minutes, $1.25 for each minute thereafter) before being released Directory enquiries are free.

Private Telephones. If you're staying in one place for a month or more, it may be worth getting a phone installed, since this process is much simpler, quicker and cheaper than it is in the UK. You may even be assigned a telephone number on the spot when you ask for one to be installed. The cost of installation is around $25. Monthly charges, which are much lower than in Britain, usually entitle you to a certain number of free local calls, and sometimes an unlimited amount.

Having a phone of your own also helps when making calls from payphones. Subscribers can obtain a telephone "calling card". This looks just like a credit card, and bears a number which you key into virtually any payphone. The charges appear on your monthly bill. Calling cards issued by foreign telephone companies (including British Telecom) are not acceptable.

Charges. The cost of using the telephone is low by international standards, particularly if you take advantage of cheap-rate periods and toll-free numbers. Local calls from private telephones are either free or very cheap (around 10c). Most householders, restauranteurs or barkeepers will let you use their phone to call local numbers without a second thought. And if you need to make a long distance call from a friend's phone, you can be sure that the call will be individually itemized on their next monthly bill and reimbursement can be exact. Do not be tempted to use hotel telephones for long distance calls, for there are often steep surcharges.

Try to make long distance calls when the cheap rates apply. There is an evening rate (35% discount) from 5pm-11pm Sunday to Friday. The night and weekend rate (50% off) is 11pm-8am daily, all day Saturday and 8am-5pm on Sundays. for example a three minute call from New York to Los Angeles during the cheapest period costs around 60c, depending upon the network used. The daytime rate is about three times as much. Calls to Alaska, Hawaii, Canada and Mexico cost slightly more, though off-peak calls can be made at substantial savings. No off-peak discounts apply to operator-assisted calls; direct-dial calls from payphones benefit from discounts, but cost more than the private rates.

For calls made from a private telephone on the East Coast to the UK and Ireland, the standard rate is applied daily from 7am to 1pm, local time. The discount rate (25% off) is 1pm to 6pm, and the "economy" rate (40% off) from 6pm to 7am. A one minute call dialled direct to Britain from a private phone during the cheapest period costs 99c, with additional minutes at 60c each; this is a great deal cheaper than using a payphone, when the minimum three minute call would cost $5.75.

Numbers with area code 900 belong to commercial enterprises who provide information such as share prices or ski conditions. Charges are set by the companies and are generally expensive, e.g. $1 for the first minute.

Toll-Free Calls. The American version of the Freefone system is very easy to use, and you should take maximum advantage of it to smooth your travel planning. A "toll-free" number has the prefix 800 in place of the area code, and should be dialled as a long distance number, e.g. 1-800-USA-RAIL for Amtrak. It is accepted practice to call businesses and government agencies toll-free. Many organizations advertise their toll-free numbers widely, and they are usually listed in telephone directories alongside the ordinary number. A free call to the 800 directory assistance number (1-800-555-1212) will get you any publicly available toll-free number. A toll-free number may change from area to area in order to minimize the cost to the business. For example, the toll-free number for the Nebraska Tourist Division differs depending on whether you're calling from inside or outside the state.

Because of the expense involved, organizations try to discourage callers from using toll-free numbers within the city in which they are based. A company based in San Francisco for example, might advertise its numbers as "765-4321 within San Francisco, (800) 123-4567 elsewhere". However, if you want to save the cost of a local call, you can always try the toll-free number or call the company collect.

About the only disadvantage of toll-free numbers is that they cannot be dialled from outside North America, even if you're prepared to pay for the call.

POST

The US Postal Service does not match the efficiency of the telephone system. There is usually only one daily delivery, and (in rural areas) sometimes none at all. A small — but nevertheless alarming — proportion of letters arrives in tatters, accompanied by an apologetic note from the government monopoly which runs the postal system.

A letter should take from two to four days within the States, and about a week to get to Europe. There are anomalies such as a letter from New York might arrive in LA before one posted at the same time arrives in a small Massachusetts town. Not surprisingly, private companies have begun to compete by offering guaranteed overnight delivery. The leading firm is Federal Express (often abbreviated to Fedex) which has offices in most large towns. In retaliation, the US Mail provides an Express Mail Service at post offices: for $8.75 you can send a package weighing up to 8 oz with guaranteed next-day delivery to many parts of the USA.

Post Offices. Since there are no sub-post offices of the kind found in Britain, post offices are thin on the ground and a little harder to find. They are identified by a blue sign bearing an eagle and the words US MAIL. Post offices are usually open 9am-5pm Monday to Friday, 9am-noon Saturday. Central post offices in most large cities offer a 24 hour lobby service where you will find change and stamp machines, mail boxes large enough to accept parcels, scales and tables of postal rates.

Larger post offices have a daunting array of counters which offer a bewildering variety of services. Read the signs listing the services offered by each window carefully, in order to avoid queuing at the income tax counter when you only want to buy a stamp.

Mail Collection. Mail boxes are blue and look rather like rubbish bins. They are found on many downtown street corners, often positioned to allow drivers to post letters without leaving their cars. However, mail boxes are rare in the suburbs. Instead, each house has a delivery/collection box fixed to a post at the end of the drive: the postman picks up mail as well as delivering it. There is a flag attached to the box which is raised to indicate that mail is waiting to be collected even if there is nothing to deliver.

There is usually only one collection each day. Collections in city centres are more frequent, but the last is at around 6pm, earlier at weekends.

General Delivery. This is the American equivalent of *Poste Restante.* Letters should be addressed c/o General Delivery, City, State (plus zip code if known). They will arrive at the main post office, from where they can be collected upon production of ID. The service is free, but advance notification should be given, and mail will be held for a maximum of 30 days before being returned to sender.

Post Office Box Numbers. Many Americans rent boxes for incoming mail at post offices. This is not necessarily because they are transients, or because they want to keep their address a secret: in some country areas or small towns there are no door-to-door postal deliveries, and rural folk just pick up their mail from town along with their groceries. Boxes are cheap to rent. You are given a key which you can use whenever the post office is open.

Zip Codes. The Americans invented post codes. The zip code is supposed to speed mail to its destination, and is universally used. It is a five-digit number identifying a small town or area of a city, and runs from 00001 (in northeastern New England) to 99999 (in Alaska). Mail without a zip code will get through eventually, but may take a day or two longer.

A statewide list of zip codes is included in the back of local telephone directories, but it does not always break down the cities that have more than one zip code. That type of street-by-street information is included in the official zip code directory which is available for reference at any post office.

Stamps. Sold at post offices, from machines at airports and bus stations, (where $1 buys you 95c worth of stamps) and at many shops which sell postcards (where the mark-up may be in excess of 100% so that four quarters might buy you three 15c stamps). Some air mail stamps do not bear values, but instead use a code letter. You don't need to know what the codes mean: just ask for a stamp for an airmail letter to Britain, or whatever.

The first class letter rate is 25c for an ounce. This ensures that your mail is sent by air where this is beneficial, but does not necessarily mean next day delivery. Air mail letters to Europe cost 45c for half an ounce; aerogrammes are 39c; postcards sent by air mail cost 36c. It is customary for the sender to add his or her name and address to every piece of mail. If you post a letter with insufficient stamps, you can expect to find it returned to you with a demand for extra postage.

Parcels. All parcels must be securely wrapped and clearly addressed. The counter clerk at the post office will not hesitate to send you away to re-wrap a parcel if he considers it not to meet US Mail regulations. Charges increase according to distance: parcels to neighbouring states cost far less than those being sent across the country. All parcels are sent overland unless you pay a lot more for air mail. When sending parcels abroad you'll need to complete a customs declaration form, which is free from post offices.

TELEGRAMS

Telegrams (cables) cannot be sent from Post Offices. Western Union handles all telegrams, and has branches in all but the smallest American towns. Call 1-800-325-6000 to send a domestic cable, 1-800-435-7984 for international. Within the USA, cables cost around 25c per word with a minimum of twelve words ($3). Abroad, a cable of the same length costs about $10. Each word of the address must be counted, apart from the name of the country.

Fax. The US Mail has taken even more of a hammering recently due to the proliferation of facsimile machines, yet another disincentive for people to use the postal service. You can even send a fax from a payphone-type machine: the Pay Fax company has installed credit card operated machines in hundreds of public places.

Americans benefit from the most sophisticated and expensive health care in the world: 11% of the national income of the USA is spent on health, compared to 6% in Britain. The whole medical industry has a decidedly unhealthy preoccupation with wealth that makes the British health service seem a paragon of selfless care and efficiency. But if you are adequately insured, an encounter with American medicine should not alarm you. If you arrive without adequate health insurance, ring any office of the ubiquitious Blue Cross for information about visitors' cover.

If you take precautions against the extremes of temperature, the USA is a healthy place to be. You need no vaccinations. Drinking water is safe everywhere, food is usually hygienically prepared and there are few contagious diseases to worry about. As long as you don't run foul of the more threatening varieties of flora and fauna (humans included), there is little to worry about unless you're unlucky enough to get caught in an avalanche, tornado or earthquake.

Emergency Procedure. Dial the emergency number — usually 911 — for an ambulance. (This also alerts the police). The paramedics will take you to the nearest hospital. This is fine so long as you can produce evidence that you are insured, but if your insurance has expired, you face the choice between astronomical hospital bills or finding a free ("public") hospital. Most large cities — but no small towns — have such a hospital, usually run by charity and with highly stretched resources. They will treat you until you are able to leave under your own steam.

Doctors. In Britain, GPs are valued and respected members of the community although not terribly well-paid. In the USA, physicians are right at the top of the professional tree in terms of prestige and wealth. American doctors don't just sit at desks prescribing cough remedies or referring patients to specialists. Their surgeries are miniature hospitals, where X-rays are taken, blood samples tested and full medical screenings take place. For these services they are extremely well-paid by the insurance companies of wealthy patients and the public *Medicaid* and *Medicare* schemes for the poor and the aged respectively.

If you need to see a doctor, you'll have to rely upon a personal recommendation or ploughing through the Yellow Pages until you find a willing practitioner. If you happen to be in a city which has a British Consulate, ring them for a list of recommended doctors. Night calls and weekend work are usually out of the question, and even during working hours it can be difficult to get an appointment if the doctor has a full workload or is playing golf. The minimum fee will be about $50.

Hospitals. In view of the above, and the fact that most travellers will be seeking instant treatment rather than long-term screening, it is usually best to go for treatment at a hospital. Anyone will direct you to the nearest general hospital. Except in a real emergency, do not go to the accident unit (sometimes called "Emergency", comparable to Casualty in the UK). Admission charges are very high to discourage use by non-urgent cases. Instead, ask at the reception desk to see the duty physician. The policy for charging varies from one hospital to another. At some you may have to pay for minor treatment and prescribed drugs and subsequently reclaim the cost from your insurance company. At others, sight of your policy is sufficient. For major surgery, no hospital will insist on cash in advance.

Be cautious when seeking treatment. For example if you go to a hospital complaining about abdominal pain, you may find your appendix has been removed almost as fast as you can produce your insurance certificate. This is not entirely due to the greed of surgeons working on a piece-rate system; it is also because of past litigation against doctors who have failed to diagnose appendicitis correctly and whose patients have subsequently died of peritonitis.

Pharmacies. Most over-the-counter drugs are cheaper than in Britain. If you are prescribed medication in a hospital, it will normally be supplied by the in-house pharmacy. Otherwise you need to take the prescription to a drug store. Late-night pharmacies are listed in each regional chapter under *Help and Information*. Prescription medicines are charged for at the full market rate, which can be frighteningly high. Save all receipts for prescription drugs so you can claim the cost from your insurance company.

Dentistry. Your friendly neighbourhood dentist ("orthodontist") has more in common with NASA Mission Control than a simple drilling-and-filling operation. Vast amounts of expensive technology are employed in dental surgeries. Together with the inflated salary of the dentist and his assistants, this means that even a simple filling costs at least $50. Crowns and other complications can increase the price tenfold. Don't be tempted to go beyond the bounds of your insurance policy, which probably covers only emergency treatment. An achingly-infected tooth constitutes an emergency. If it is driving you wild with pain, oil of cloves is an effective local anaesthetic to tide you over. Failing that, swish a mouthful of whisky around the offending tooth. Don't be tempted to dissolve an asprin on it, since this will only make your gums ache.

HEALTH HAZARDS

Sunburn. If you travel anywhere in the continental USA in summer, you must be careful to avoid sunburn. The most effective protection is to stay out of the sun, particularly between 10am and 3pm. The next best precaution is to encourage gentle tanning. Start with less than an hour of sun a day to get your pallid skin used to the idea. Use a lotion with a high protection factor to screen the burning rays, but remember that most of it will wash away if you bathe. Seawater, perfume and after-shave will increase the rate of burning. Aspirin delays but does not reduce the reddening process and thus may increase your suffering. The best way to avoid sunstroke or heat exhaustion is to remain in the shade as much as possible, and wear a wide-brimmed hat. Wear loose cotton clothing for maximum comfort.

If you are like most sun-starved travellers and ignore this advice, treat the resulting burns with cold, damp towels or take a long cold bath. Apply after-sun cream or yoghurt to the affected areas and drink gallons of fluids.

Cold Weather. Americans cope with the cold by eating well, sleeping well, overheating their homes and wrapping up well before venturing outside. Temperatures already below freezing can be reduced dramatically by the wind chill factor. If you're out in the cold, it is essential to stay dry to avoid frostbite or exposure.

Creatures to Avoid. Humans apart, the USA has several lethal species wandering around. Grizzly bears, rattlesnakes and alligators are perhaps the best known. While it is not necessarily pleasant to meet them, they will usually be at least as frightened as you. The simple expedient of walking, swimming or running away normally works and they will probably do the same. A lot of nonsense is also talked about sharks. The closest you'll ever come to one is likely to be at Sea World in Orlando or the clockwork Jaws at Universal Studios in Hollywood. Even if a shark swims up to you while you bathe, a sharp tap on the nose should send him on his way. Many species of snake thrive in the US, especially in the swampy areas of southern states. Ask local park rangers or well-informed locals to describe the dangerous versus the harmless, ones and find out if there is a first aid hut before venturing into the wilds.

Smaller animals can be a bigger nuisance. Dingy hotel and motel rooms in the southern states are infested with cockroaches. Although they are harmless, they can be upsetting. You might be tempted to invest in a cockroach trap known as the Roach Motel — "they check in, but they don't check out". Ignore any lizards you may see edging up the wall: they keep the insect population down and are to be encouraged. Mosquitoes are a summer hazard in Alaska and the northernmost states of the continental USA. Use a heavy-duty insect repellant; take local advice on the most effective brand. The chigoe fly is fond of sand dunes and beaches. It is an unpleasant creature which burrows into the sole of your foot to lay eggs. The only way to remove it is to conduct a little excavation with the aid of sterilized needle. Scorpions and black widow spiders are a serious nuisance in southern areas; remember to shake out your shoes since they will bite only if you annoy them.

Plants to Avoid. Poison ivy, which is unknown in Britain, is very widespread in North America. An encounter with it is much worse and longer-lasting than a brush with stinging nettles. It is especially a nuisance for children who find it impossible to prevent themselves from scratching the irritated skin and thereby spreading it. Unfortunately the plant looks like an unassuming ivy, though you should make an effort to learn to recognise the three pointed leaf.

Whereas there are many delicious wild berries unfamiliar to Europeans (boysenberries, huckleberries, wortleberries, etc.) there are also many poisonous varieties. Ask the locals before munching. As in Europe there are dangerous toadstools and mushrooms. There is also an abundance of hallucinogenic mushrooms, especially in mountain areas.

Smog. The chief constituents of smog are ozone, sulphur dioxide and other petrol-engine emissions. Smog is at its worst during climatic inversions. When these occur in Los Angeles or Denver (the worst culprits), a sickly yellow pall hangs over the city. Healthy young people find their eyes watering and their throats burning. Young children, the elderly and infirm suffer greatly. If you suffer from a nasal or chest complaint, you may be wise to avoid the worst cities and to keep a check on smog forecasts in other areas. Weather reports in Los Angeles include the "eye irritation level" along with routine data on temperature and humidity.

Acts of God. The United States suffers from most forms of natural disaster: earthquakes and volcanic eruptions on the West Coast, avalanches and flash floods in the Rockies, tornadoes in the Midwest, hurricanes in the South and fierce electric storms in most parts of the country. While travelling in danger areas, pay attention to advance warnings of eruptions or tornadoes and don't hesitate to evacuate. If you are caught out in the open during a thunder storm, stay out of water and well away from tall objects which act as potential lighting conductors. Cars are relatively safe places to be because of the insulating effects of rubber tyres. You may also get caught in a sandstorm if you are travelling in desert areas; sit it out in a car if possible.

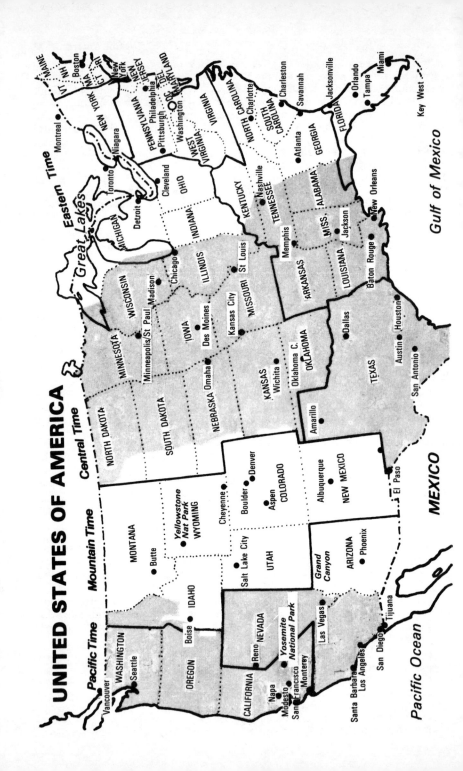

Getting Around

boardwalk	raised wooden promenade by seaside
box car	goods wagon on a train
brakeman	guard on a train
caboose	last wagon on a goods train
coach class	economy class as opposed to first, club or custom
el	elevated railway running above a city street
freight car	goods wagon
first floor	ground floor (and hence the second floor is the same as the British first floor, etc.)
hack stand	taxi rank
one way ticket	single
pavement	road surface
ramp	slip road
redcap	railway or airport porter
round trip	return ticket
sidewalk	pavement
smoky bears	policeman
streetcar	tram
subway	underground railway
tramway	cable car
truck	lorry
yard bull	railway yard patrolman

You should never underestimate the size of the USA when planning your itinerary and choosing your modes of travel. It is over 3,000 miles by road from Miami to San Francisco or from Boston to Seattle. While part of the great American experience is to travel overland from coast to coast, do not undertake this lightly: whether driving, motorcycling or travelling by bus or train, you are not going to enjoy a trip telescoped into a few days. (If you try hitch-hiking, predicting if — and in what condition — you will arrive is arguably a more appropriate problem than "when"). Flying is no way to get a sense of the vast expanses between urban America. But air travel is the fastest and most efficient way to visit cities far apart, and using one of the bargain airpasses on sale it need not be too expensive. The best value unlimited travel tickets are undoubtedly Amtrak's rail passes, but the limited network restricts your choice of destination. Greyhound bus passes allow you to reach far more places. Or you may choose to visit just one region of the USA, in which case you might prefer to travel on ad-hoc basis. The following pages outline the options available.

AIR

Every day more than a million Americans catch a domestic flight. Often they give no more thought to catching a plane than to catching a bus, and for many air journeys the fare will be similar. Airlines in the USA fly to more places more often than in any other country. For example between New York and Washington there are over 100 flights each way every day on a dozen different airlines. To find your way around the maze of services, consult the monthly *Official Airline Guide* at any library or travel agency, which will also give you some idea of the fares.

For visitors to the USA, air travel is a sensible way to cover the vast distances between interesting places. On heavily-travelled routes with competing airlines, fares are very low with extremely frequent flights. If you know your itinerary in advance, you can buy an airpass, some of which offer remarkably good value. Even if you plan to take only one or two flights, buy your domestic tickets before leaving Europe to qualify for the 30% Visit USA discount. Or if you want to fly free of charge you can try for a trip as an air courier. All of these ways of saving money are described below.

Fares. Air fares in the USA are crazy. It can cost over a hundred dollars to fly 30 miles between two towns in Maryland, but only $99 for a promotional New York-Miami fare. As a general rule, the more airlines that compete on a particular route, the cheaper the fares. The most heavily discounted routes are along the Eastern Seaboard (as far south as Miami) and along the West Coast, within Texas, and on coast to coast flights. Also, you can save around 30% by travelling off-peak (early morning, late evening, all day on Saturdays and Sundays before the evening rush) or "night coach". If you are able to book and pay seven days in advance, you can benefit from various APEX deals. Or you might find a "twofer" promotion, where two can travel for the price of one. When bargain-hunting, pay particular attention to smaller airlines such as Midway, New York Air and America West, who fly from little-used but not necessarily inconvenient airports.

There are many seemingly illogical bargains to be had. Sometimes it is cheaper to buy a return ticket and leave half unused than it is to buy the normal one-way ticket. Or if your flight continues beyond the city at which you want to disembark, it may cost less to buy a ticket to the aircraft's eventual destination and hop off when it touches down where you want to be (assuming you are carrying only hand luggage.) Fares change literally daily and airlines which file low promotional fares boast loudly about them in the press. So keep your eyes open, try to find a sharp-witted travel agent or call the airlines for free.

It is also worth checking the classified ads for unwanted tickets being sold by private individuals. As long as your gender corresponds to the one stated on the ticket you'll have no problem.

Visit USA (VUSA). Most airlines offer reductions of about 30% on flights within the USA to visitors who buy tickets abroad at least a week before travelling to North America. You must provide proof of residence abroad and show your transatlantic ticket. Sample fares are New York-Los Angeles $300, Los Angeles-San Francisco $40 and San Francisco-Chicago $250. Note, however, that unrestricted flights on these routes may often be found at lower fares once you've arrived. VUSA tickets are most valuable on routes with little or no competition, which are unlikely to be discounted.

Airpasses. If you plan to travel extensively in the USA, an airpass can be invaluable. Most airlines sell you a pass for a specified number of flights, usually a minimum of four costing $399. This in itself is excellent value since you could, for example, fly New York - Miami - Los Angeles - Seattle -New York. Additional flight coupons usually cost only $25-$45 each, which makes a longer itinerary a bargain. Bear in mind that there are usually strings attached, such as specifying that you must buy the pass before you leave for the USA at least one week before you use it, and that you sometimes have to fly the Atlantic on a particular airline. In addition, no carrier has a truly comprehensive network within the USA.

Some advertised airpasses will strike you as incredibly good value, such as America West's two-sector airpass for $89 (tel: 01-839 9381). The catch is that all flights are routed through Phoenix or Las Vegas where a compulsory plane change uses up a sector.

Two of the larger airlines, Northwest and Delta, have unlimited travel passes valid for 30 days for $399. These involve travelling standby, but if you choose your flight times carefully to avoid peak periods you should rarely be disappointed. And several carriers have excellent deals priced in sterling, e.g. under £200 for three flights anywhere on the TWA network. Look out also for airpasses offered by small regional airlines: for example, Hawaiian Air will take you around eight Hawaiian islands for $177.

Fares and conditions change frequently, so call the airlines at their UK offices:

American	0800-010151	Northwest	01-629 4090
Continental	01-679-5531	Pan Am	01-409-0688
Delta	01-668 0935	TWA	01-636 4090
Hawaiian Air	01-631-3199	United	01-997 0179
Jet America	01-839 9384	US Air	0800-777333

Reservations. You should reserve a seat in advance for all domestic flights except the walk-on shuttle flights linking Boston and Washington with New York. You do not need to pay for the ticket at the time of reserving a seat, and can pay later at any travel agency, at the airport or in some cases on board the aircraft. So if there is an outside chance you may wish to travel on a particular flight, phone the airline toll-free and reserve a seat as early as possible.

MAJOR DOMESTIC AIRLINES IN THE USA

Call the following toll-free numbers for fares and reservations of flights within the USA:

American Airlines	1-800-433-7300	Delta	1-800-221-1212	Pan Am	1-800-221-1111
America West	1-800-247-5692	Eastern	1-800-Eastern	TWA	1-800-221-2000
Braniff	1-800-Braniff	Midway	1-800-621-5700	United	1-800-241-6522
Continental	1-800-525-0280	Northwest	1-800-225-2525	US Air	1-800-428-4322

Reservations can also be made through the airline's office in Britain or through your transatlantic carrier. There is no penalty for failing to turn up. If you do not have a reservation, arrive at the airport well before departure time and ask to be put on the waiting list. On average, 15% of passengers booked on a domestic flight don't show up.

Overbooking. Because of their liberal reservations policies, airlines routinely overbook flights by 15%. If every passenger with a reservation shows up, some have to be turned away and put on a later flight. But all airlines give "denied boarding compensation" (DBC) to victims. This may be equivalent to the price of your ticket or a more exotic prize such as a return ticket to any destination on the airline's domestic network. If the airline staff ask for volunteers to be "bumped", don't hesitate to step forward. If, however, you fail to show up by the time specified for check in, you forfeit your rights to a seat or DBC.

Smoking. The days of the smoking passenger are numbered. Smoking is prohibited on all flights scheduled to take two hours or less. Some airlines, notably Northwest, have banned smoking on all flights within North America. Pipes and cigars are prohibited on all airlines.

Coping with Airports. American airports can be very large with separate terminals miles apart. Phone your airline ahead of time to find you which terminal they use. Once you have successfully located the right terminal and checked in, don't sit about waiting for your flight to be announced; you're normally expected to turn up at the correct gate as shown on the numerous information screens. The absence of passport control on domestic flights means that friends, relations or belligerent Moonies can escort you all the way to the departure gate, where security checks take place. Don't be tempted to make jokes of the "careful how you open that —there's a bomb inside" variety. Any such levity will be taken seriously and the FBI may be called in to question you while your plane takes off. Smokers may be dismayed to learn that smoking is either allowed only in specified areas, or banned entirely within the terminal building.

Baggage. The usual allowance is the same as on transatlantic flights, i.e. two reasonably-sized suitcases (or, indeed, a rucksack plus a bicycle box) with no weight restriction. Cabin baggage rules are usually strictly enforced, so don't bank on taking on more than one small bag. The maximum compensation for lost baggage is $750 per passenger.

Frequent Flyer Schemes. Most American airlines operate a system whereby loyal customers are rewarded for the amount of flying they do. If you fly 30,000 miles on Pan Am, for example, you qualify for a free ticket anywhere in the USA. If you are travelling on an airpass it is suprising how quickly the miles mount up. Membership of all these schemes is free, and you can join at the check-in counter before you fly.

There is a booming business in selling tickets which airlines give away to frequent fliers. Most cities have a "coupon broker" who acts as a middleman between buyers and sellers and uses the classified sections of newspapers to advertise his wares. Note, however, that many airlines now insist upon ID for travellers using free tickets.

Free Flights. Even if you don't fly enough to earn a free ticket, it is possible to get around as a freelance air courier. Check the Yellow Pages under *Air Couriers* and offer your services to any of the companies listed such as DHL and TNT. The personal delivery of documents is a booming business and often the courier companies need extra staff for one-off journeys. The more flexible you are over dates and destinations, the better your chances. Some companies might even offer you a free flight to London after you have proved to them your trustworthiness.

If you prefer the idea of flying free in a private aircraft, see *Hitch-hiking*.

BUS

Bus travel is the accepted alternative to flying in the USA. The network of long distance routes is dense, services are frequent, and journey times are as fast as the speed limits allow. It is also very easy to travel by bus: terminals are invariably in city centres, tickets may be bought at any time and reservations are not needed since relief buses are usually laid on when necessary. The vehicles — always called buses not coaches — have reclining seats, air conditioning and a "rest room". So long distance bus travel need not be an ordeal. There are also frequent rest stops where you can stretch your legs and your horizons. Smoking on buses is severely restricted. Federal law prohibits the use of pipes and cigars. Cigarette smoking is allowed only in the rear three rows of seats, which tend to fill up quickly (with both people and smoke.) In some states, notably California, smoking is banned completely.

By far the largest operator is Greyhound, which recently took over Trailways. Its London address (for buying unlimited travel passes or other tickets in advance) is 14-16 Cockspur Street, London SW1Y 5BL (01-839 5591). There are hundreds of other smaller bus companies serving individual areas, and your ticket or pass on Greyhound may be valid on their services. There seem to be no rules governing this, so it is always necessary to check locally.

Bus Passes. Greyhound offers a range of Ameripasses valid on all its services plus those of some other bus companies. To get the best deal, buy your bus pass before you fly to the States from a travel agent or direct from the Greyhound office in London. Seven days unlimited travel costs £65, 15 days £95 and 30 days £140. You can buy extra days for £10 in the UK or $15 in the USA; at the current rate of exchange it is cheapest to extend your pass in North America. You can do this at any major Greyhound terminal.

Fares. Journeys covering routes of similar length can have radically different fares, and so it is not possible to give a mileage cost. For example the 400 mile trip from New York to Buffalo costs about the same ($75) as the 650 mile journey from St Louis to Dallas.

Handicapped Travellers. Buses are not the most accessible form of transport for the disabled. However the Greyhound "Helping Hand" fare allows a handicapped passenger and attendant to travel for one fare.

Alternative Operators. In addition to conventional bus companies, there are a few more enterprising operators using imaginatively converted vehicles. *Green Tortoise* and *Grey Rabbit* buy up obsolete Greyhound buses, rip out the seats and install mattresses and bunk beds for 25 passengers. Most of the driving takes place at night. The days are spent swimming, whitewater rafting or exploring canyons. As a result, progress is not rapid: the Boston-San Francisco route (via New York and Los Angeles) takes 11 days. Fares and frequencies vary wildly, but as a rough guide there are two transcontinental journeys per month in summer, with additional runs to the South in winter and up the West Coast as far as Alaska in summer. The coast-to-coast fare is about $250 one-way, plus an optional $50 for communal food. The free benefits such as side trips to hot springs, swimming holes and Caesar's Palace make for a fascinating journey through the USA.

Up-to-date fares and schedules are displayed at YMCAs and colleges, or contact the operators direct:

Green Tortoise,
Box 24459,
San Francisco, CA 94124
(415) 821 0803 within California
1-800-227-4766 from other states

Grey Rabbit,
2000 Center St,
Berkeley, CA 94704
(503) 224-RIDE within Oregon
1-800 RABBITS from other states.

TRAIN

The American railroad system which encouraged the development and exploitation of an entire continent, is sadly not what it once was. By the 1960s it was run down, bankrupt and in danger of total collapse. It was saved by a massive injection of federal funds and the creation in 1970 of the National Railroad Passenger Corporation — *Amtrak*. This nationalized concern operates a network that is thinly spread and little used by most Americans. Those who do travel by train tend to be more out-of-the-ordinary than most business travellers or holidaymakers. This is not suprising since rail fares for long trips are often no cheaper than flying and take several days longer. The tracks upon which the modern carriages run are still owned by the old freight companies who show little enthusiasm for investing in new track. So journeys tend to be rather bumpy.

However, trains score over planes in the fast, dense networks of the Chicago area and the Northeastern corridor. The Boston-New York-Washington line features 120mph *Metroliners* and city centre to city centre journeys are often faster than by air. Trains are also a very good way to view the country particularly from the double-decker *Superliners* used on long journeys. Instead of the endless freeways which comprise the view of most car drivers and bus passengers, railroads cut through dramatic scenery and America's backyards.

Reservations. Book before you leave for North America if you can plan ahead that far, especially for long distance trains in summer and around public holidays. The Amtrak office in London is at 16 Bedford Square, WC1B 3JA (01-637-7961). Although this office gives advice and information, it does not sell tickets or make reservations. Instead contact a travel agent or Amtrak's General Sales Agents in the UK:

Compass Travel
9 Grosvenor Gardens,
London SW1W 0BH
01-828 4111

Thistle Air
22 Bank St
Kilmarnock KA1 1QJ
(0563) 31121.

Within the USA, reservations can be made free at any time by calling (toll-free) 1-800-USA-RAIL or by personal application at travel agents, stations or city tickets offices. When you reserve a seat or sleeper, you'll be given a reservation number and a time limit by which you must pay for your ticket. If you don't have a reservation but seats are still available, you'll be assigned a seat and sold a ticket at the departure station. If you get on a train without a ticket, you must pay the one-way fare plus a $5 charge. However, if the ticket office was closed at the time, you don't pay the charge and may buy a round-trip or discounted ticket. The Amtrak timetable (free from US travel agents or the Amtrak Distribution Center, Box 7717, Itasca, IL 60143) advises passengers to be at the station 30 minutes before departure. Arriving that early is only necessary if you don't have a set reservation or if you have large amounts of luggage to check in.

Fares. Regular one-way rail fares are slightly higher than on buses. Short journeys cost around 15c per mile. The rate decreases to 10c per mile over long distances. If you are able to travel outside peak periods, then return excursion fares offer a 35% reduction. For short journeys, the times to avoid are 1 pm-7 pm on Fridays and Sundays. On longer trips, peak times are usually at weekends and holidays.

Your ticket entitles you to an unlimited numnber of free stopovers, and it is much cheaper to buy a through ticket to your eventual destination rather than paying fares between the intermediate points. Even so, $300 for the 2242 rail miles from Chicago to Los Angeles is an expensive way of travelling between the two cities. It is cheaper by air. Moreover, the basic price buys only a second class ("coach") reclining seat on the train. Pillows and blankets are provided free on overnight trains. For a proper sleeping berth, you must pay a supplement of between 25% and 100% of the regular fare. A similar premium is charged for custom class (first) or use of the club car. The high-speed Metroliners cost about 20% more than the corresponding coach fares. Advance reservations are essential for any of these special facilities.

You're also going to need refreshment. A federal law requires that food and drink be provided on any rail journey of over two hours, but does not specify that prices should be moderate. Most low-budget travellers take their own supplies. Alcohol is available on most trains, but its sale is subject to the licensing laws of the state through which the train is travelling.

If a husband and wife are travelling together, one pays full fare while the spouse pays half fare. Any children aged 12-21 also pay half fare, those aged 2-11 quarter fare. Foreign visitors who buy tickets in advance can benefit from "International Gateway" fares, e.g. $50 from New York to Niagara or $30 for the round trip between Los Angeles and San Diego.

Rail Passes. USA rail passes represent extremely good value for money. Each is valid for 45 days. They are available only from travel agents outside North America, and must be used within 90 days of the date of sale. The national pass costs $299, i.e. less than $7 per day. There are also four regional passes. The Eastern pass (valid on all Amtrak services east of Chicago and New Orleans) is $159. For everything west of Chicago and New Orleans, the Western pass costs $239, while a pass covering only the Far Western region (the west coast, plus lines inland as far as Denver and El Paso) is $159. Finally, 45 days travel around the (admittedly limited) Florida rail network costs only a dollar a day. These prices include only basic coach class travel; however, you can upgrade to custom class or Metroliner services upon payment of the appropriate supplement. Note that seat reservations (see above) are advisable and can be made at any time after purchase of the rail pass.

Baggage. Each fare-paying passenger can take three pieces of luggage, one of which may be a bicycle. Baggage is checked in airline-style and conveyed in a separate car, so make sure you have everything you need for the journey before you check in. The maximum liability for lost luggage is $500. Amtrak accepts bicycles as checked baggage when boxed; suitable boxes are sold at many stations for $5. You need not tip the station redcaps who help with your luggage, but they won't turn down a dollar or two.

Handicapped Travellers. Amtrak makes special provision for those with a travel-related handicap. Deaf people with access to a teletypewriter should call (toll-free) 1-800-523-6590 for information and reservations. Specially designed sleeping accommodation for overnight trains and assistance with wheelchairs are available upon request at the station or by calling 1-800-USA-RAIL.

GETTING AROUND CITIES

The public transport systems are described in detail under each *City* section. However, there are a few guidelines on finding your way around which are true for all American cities. American cities are not like their European namesakes. With a few notable exceptions (San Francisco, Boston) they consist of a central business district, where offices and condominiums tower over wasteground parking lots, an inner-city ring of menacing squalor punctuated by freeways and sprawling, identical suburbs. In all but the oldest or most hilly cities, streets are laid out in a strict grid pattern. They intersect at right angles and form squares or "blocks". Distances within cities are given in blocks; there are usually between ten and twenty blocks to a mile. The use of the grid system enables "grid references" to identify easily a specific location. For instance, the Empire State Building is on the corner of 34th St and 5th Avenue in New York. For reasons of conciseness, Americans omit unnecessary words like "street" or "avenue". Thus the above example will be abbreviated to "34th and 5th".

Just because the street number in an American address is extremely high, e.g. 7765, it does not mean that the roads must be very long. Buildings in the first block of a street will be numbered from 1 to 99, but with random gaps in between: thus 99 Park Avenue could be next door to 80 Park Avenue. The second block is numbered from 100 to 199, the third 200-299 and so on. Occasionally the system breaks down: if a new building is erected between numbers 112 and 113, it will be numbered 112½. Short streets follow the numbering system of the longer parallel road. So the numbers in a street could begin at 600 and run to 799. In most cities there is a mathematical formula to pinpoint street numbers to within a block: ask the locals.

Taxis. One popular image of American taxi drivers — as monosyllabic bruisers whose sole conversation consists of telling you they can't change a bill over $10 — is misplaced. Taxi driving is a common way for students to finance themselves through college, so your driver may be on the verge of qualifying for a PhD in Philosophy or Business Administration. Professional drivers, having "seen life", are often fascinating characters and will take pride in pointing out places of interest in their city. They also rise to the occasion if you tell them you're in a hurry. Their motivation is not always financial: taxi drivers have been known to turn down tips and even in New York City, taxis have stopped and offered a free trip to people who look as though they need a ride.

Fares. Expect to pay around $1.50 for the first half mile and $2 a mile thereafter. Extras are charged for additional passengers, baggage, nights, Sundays and public holidays. Leaving the city limits will increase the meter charge by 50-100%. This makes airport journeys particularly expensive; at some airports an official taxi-sharing scheme cuts the cost, and at others you can simply pair up with fellow travellers.

Finding a Cab. Taxis are large saloons, with the driver protected from passengers by a bullet proof screen and are usually either bright yellow or black and white checks. Taxis may be hailed in the street; their signs are illuminated when free, although you'll often find drivers who are not prepared to take you to an unfavourable location. "Hack stands" (taxi ranks) are few and far between. This is relatively easy in affluent downtown areas, impossible in suburban and dangerous in inner city ghettos. Avoid unlicensed cabs at all costs. They are particularly prevalent at airports. At best, you'll be wildly overcharged; at worst, driven to an isolated patch of wasteground and robbed. The genuine article can usually be identified by the medallion on the bonnet. Taxis will respond to radio calls for no extra charge. Consult *Taxis* in the Yellow pages.

City Cycling. Many city cyclists wear smog-masks, and American drivers' ideas on how to share the roads with cyclists are not well-developed. Bicycle couriers have won a fearsome reputation for ignoring red lights, running into pedestrians and generally behaving abysmally. In cities some drivers seem to regard any cyclists as fair game. Even so, bicycles provide the visitor with a cheap and effective means of enjoying cities and the surrounding countryside.

Using a crash helmet in cities is not taking precautions too far; the majority of American cyclists wear them. Visitors unused to city traffic will find that a one- or three-speed bicycle with upright handlebars is safer than a ten-speed racer. Bad surfaces leave a lot to be desired; beware of potholes and streetcar tracks. It is essential to make yourself as visible as possibly to American motorists. Fluorescent gear is particularly necessary at dawn or dusk. Although lights are not obligatory everywhere for night cycling, anyone who rides without them must have suicidal tendencies. Many Americans use lights strapped to an arm or leg, but the fixed variety are safer. Riding more than two abreast (or single file in cities) is foolhardy and illegal. Bicycles are not permitted to use freeways, and on strategic bridges must use the separate track provided. More and more cities are designating bicycle routes. American cyclists stick their left arm out to signal a left-hand turn, the same arm bent up at the elbow to indicate right and bent down to indicate an imminent stop.

DRIVING

beltway	ring road
divided highway	dual carriageway
expressway	motorway
fenders	wings
freeway	motorway
grade crossing	railway level crossing
gridlock	traffic jam in all directions
hood	bonnet
muffler	exhaust
no passing	no overtaking
no standing	no parking
parkway	yet another variation on the theme of motorway, landscaped with trees and grass
pavement	road surface
pull-off	lay by (on a motorway)
rotary	roundabout (very rare)
RV	recreational vehicle (camper van)
sedan	saloon car
sidewalk	pavement
smoky bear	highway patrolman (CB slang)
speed zone	a zone in which the speed limit is lower than 65 mph
station wagon	estate car
stop lights	traffic lights
stick shift	gear shift, or more broadly any car without automatic transmission
superhighway	motorway
tags	licence plates (slang)
thruway	motorway
trailer	caravan
trunk	boot
turnpike	toll motorway
U-Haul	small trailer, rather like a horse box, for moving goods
Winnebago	camper van (trade name that has become a generic term)

In America the car is king. Successive oil crises have encouraged the fashion for compacts at the expense of the gas-guzzling monsters of the 50s and 60s, but the cult of the automobile continues. A driving licence is regarded almost as a birthright and you will see high school parking lots jammed with the cars of 16-year-old commuters. Motorists guard their vehicles jealously, whether brand-new Cadillacs or dented pick-ups. One benefit of such fervour for the open road is the best highway network in the world, though coupled with one of the lowest speed limits: 65mph. Despite this economy measure, the USA still manages to consume almost one-third of the world's petrol.

Licences. A full British licence is sufficient for up to a year. However, the police, and anyone else who asks for your licence as identification, are frequently suprised at the absence of a photograph, and astounded at an expiry date well into the 21st century. An International Driving Permit (obtainable from the AA or RAC) bears a photo and will avoid problems and enable you to go out without your passport. Remember to carry your licence with you whenever driving; unlike in Britain, you are not given five days grace.

If you stay for a year or more you will need a licence issued by the state authorities, whereupon they may confiscate your British licence. To qualify, you must take a written examination based on state motoring law, have an eyesight test and undergo a road test. Apply for a test at the local office of the State Highway Department; it can be arranged within a few days, although some states require you to hold a learner's licence for a month before the test. The examination is usually pathetically easy, since driving is regarded as an essential skill. If you pass you pay between $5 and $25 for a licence valid for two, three or four years. Renewals are automatic upon payment of a further fee. Unlike in Britain, you are permitted to drive vehicles with manual transmission ("stick shift") even if you take the test in an automatic. Your licence will state whether or not you wear glasses. In big cities, there are agents who can issue an ID card to non-drivers. These official-looking documents cost $6 and may smooth the way for you in bars, etc.

The minimum age for holding a full licence is 15 in Mississippi, 21 in Colorado and Georgia, and 16, 17 or 18 in all other states. Under various schemes, learners as young as 14 are allowed on the road and people below the minimum state age can often drive as long as they have their parents' written permission.

Petrol. Fuel is sold in litres or US gallons (3.8 litres) which are 20% smaller than Imperial gallons (4.7 litres). There are wide variations in cost. Expect to pay $1-$1.40 per US gallon (26c-40c per litre). Prices are lowest among competing suburban gas stations, and highest on the freeways and in small towns where no competition exists. The most solid advice is to avoid places which do not boldly display their prices: they usually have something to hide. In a string of gas stations along a suburban highways, the first and last tend to be more expensive. Prices fluctuate continuously, so keep your eyes open for exceptionally good deals.

It is not always obvious whether a station is self-service or not. If you are served by an attendant, you might have to pay a little extra, but you'll get your windscreen cleaned and oil checked. Most late-night and 24 hour gas stations require you to pay the cashier before filling commences. Oil can be bought most cheaply at large discount stores, e.g. Bradley's.

By law, recent cars must run on lead-free petrol ("unleaded gas"). This has a very low octane rating, but engines are fitted with a catalytic convertor which enables them to run without knocking. Leaded petrol ("regular") is still available at most gas stations, and is usually cheaper than the unleaded variety. To avoid the possibility of filling up with leaded fuel, the tanks of unleaded vehicles will not physically accept the hoses for leaded fuel.

ROAD SYSTEM

American roads vary in size from New Jersey Turnpike (with up to eight lanes — in each direction!) to the Ranch-to-Market roads in rural Texas. In quality, they range from the freeways of California (where the only imperfections are the lane studs designed to prevent drivers drifting sideways) to the dirt-tracks of the Rockies and the mud-tracks of the Mississippi Delta.

Just as the Eskimo language is said to have 17 words for the word snow, so do Americans seem to have a large vocabulary for the word motorway. Roads are classified as freeways (which include Interstates, Turnpikes and some Federal Highways) or other roads. There are thruways, parkways, expressways, superhighways and beltways (i.e. ring roads). Like British motorways, freeways are dual-carriageways with "grade-separated" junctions, i.e. entrance and exit is by slip road (ramp) leading above or below the freeway. On other roads, there are the usual impediments such as traffic lights, bicycles and pedestrians, but almost no roundabouts (called "rotaries") as found in Britain.

American methods of numbering roads are not always logical. There are often optional variations to a particular route, identified by a variety of suffixes. Some will bear the suffix N,S,E or W (for north, south...). Or they may not give any geographical clue, and just be appended "Alt" (alternative) or A,B,C, etc. Other sophistications include the alternatives "Business" and "Thru". The sensible long-distance traveller will always choose the latter; business routes simply divert highways through industrial and commercial areas for the benefit of local traders. A good road map is essential for navigating through the myriad of choices.

Interstates. The Interstate and Defense Highway System (so called because the original funding came from the Defense Department) provides a comprehensive network of inter-urban roads of motorway standard i.e. with two lanes plus a hard shoulder in each direction. Some charge tolls, in which case they are know as Turnpikes. Each Interstate bears the prefix I - and is marked on maps and roads signs with a red, white and blue shield. Those which run predominantly east-west are even-numbered, those running north-south are odd-numbered. The lowest numbers are in the south and west, the highest in the north and east. For example, I-5 runs up the West Coast and I-95 up the East Coast; I-10 crosses the country along its southern edge, I-90 along the northern border. Most Interstate numbers have one or two digits; three-digit Interstates are short urban spur motorways. The first digit is the prefix (eg I-610, a spur from I-10 around New Orleans) and theoretically denotes whether the spur goes around the city (even numbered prefixes) or into the city (odd-numbered prefixes, eg I-395 into Washington DC). Three-digit interstates are not exclusively numbered; for example, I-295 recurs several times during the course of I-95.

Some interstates bear the names as well as numbers, such as the "Golden

State Freeway" or "Dan Ryan Expressway". Since these names are prone to change or vanish altogether after a few miles, they should be ignored in favour of numbers whenever possible. Names may, however, be unavoidable if they are part of local parlance. When giving directions, a native might say "take the New England Thruway as far as Boston Post Road" and expect you to know he means "1-95 as far as US 1". A good map or road atlas will help with the translation.

No Interstates (unless they are Turnpikes) have service areas of the kind that brighten the lives of European motorists. Instead, fuel and refreshments are obtainable at gas stations and restaurants located adjacent to junctions. The generic term for these is "truck-stops". They are easy to spot (look for a cluster of huge neon signs) and occur at reasonable intervals even in remote areas. Picnic sites and rest areas are becoming more common as part of a campaign to persuade drivers to rest more frequently.

Except in urban and strategic bridges and tunnels, emergency telephones are never provided. In the event of a breakdown you are supposed to wait (with hazard lights flashing) for a passing patrol car.

Turnpikes. Turnpikes are toll motorways; some are part of the Interstate system, others not. They are found mostly in the north-east, although the states of Florida, Kansas and Oklahoma also have them. They are known by name for example the Will Rodgers Turnpike (Oklahoma) and the Garden State Parkway (New Jersey). Tolls are payable upon entry to or exit from the turnpike, and sometimes during the journey. The longest continuous stretch of turnpike, the 900 miles from New York to Chicago via Philadelphia and Pittsburgh, costs about $30. You will usually be given a card upon entrance to the turnpike and pay at tollbooths for the distance travelled.

Tolls on shorter turnpikes are often collected by throwing quarters into a basket, but usually need more than one: the New Hampshire Turnpike costs 75c for example. You may see the occasional driver go straight through without paying, but don't be tempted to follow suit. Some gates have concealed barriers which rise if the toll is not paid, and others operate police checks on non-payers; they note your licence plates and radio ahead to a waiting patrol car. Fines are heavy.

Federal Highways. These roads bear the prefix US, and are marked on maps and signs by a white shield with black lettering. They are equivalent to British 'A' roads, duplicating Interstates on some routes and providing links between them. They range in quality from fast dual carriageways, largely indistinguishable from Interstates (e.g. US 101 between Los Angeles and San Francisco) to little more than suburban streets; US 1, which runs down the east coast from Maine to Florida, is colloquially known as "everybody's Main Street". Adhering rigidly to the course of a Federal Highway is not recommended if you are in a hurry. Like Interstates, north-south Federal Highways are odd-numbered, east-west even numbered.

State Highways. These show an even greater variation in quality than Federal Highways. Some are almost of freeway standard, others simply gravel tracks. Road numbers on maps are marked in ovals, squares or circles or even inside a printed outline of the state. Since the numbering system is at the discretion of state authorities, numbers on through-routes often change at state borders.

Maps and Routes. To obtain maps in advance, you must write to the main tourist information office in each state (addresses on page 118). In addition, the more tourist-conscious states give away Official State Highway maps to personal callers at tourist offices, including the "Welcome Centers" located on main routes just inside the state line. Many visitors find it easier to invest $6.95 in a Rand McNally road atlas; these are cheaper when combined with advertising material and sold by banks, insurance companies, etc. Most gas stations have a stock of good oil company maps, but these are not usually free. Cheaper maps are sold in supermarkets with their branch locations superimposed. Free maps can be picked up from car hire desks at airports: just ask.

Route advice can be obtained locally at tourist offices or simply by asking at gas stations. For those who prefer to plan in advance the AA and RAC will supply their members with a package containing a map of the USA, a catalogue of travel publications and a form for requesting route information. This information is supplied by their counterpart American Automobile Association (AAA, known as "Triple A" in America). If you ask for advice about a specific journey , you'll be a sent a strip map showing the recommended route. Do not write direct to the AAA: all requests must go through an affiliated motoring organization in your own country, so letters to the AAA will go unanswered.

Road Signs. Signs giving instructions or warnings are usually spelt out explicitly: "No U-Turns", "Do Not Stop On The Tracks" for example. Some pictorial signs are being introduced, but there should be few problems for motorists familiar with European pictorial signs. One of the ones you may not be familiar with is a black X in a yellow circle with RR; this indicates a railway crossing which may or may not have an automatic gate.

Direction signposts are a diferent matter. Although main routes are well signposted for much of their courses, approach to cities leave a lot to be desired. For instance, driving to New York City is no problem until you get within ten or twenty miles of the city. Then the signs for New York disappear to be replaced by options like "George Washington Bridge", "Midtown Tunnel" and so on. Plan your approach to large cities in advance with the aid of a good road map.

RULES OF THE ROAD

Drive on the right. Try not to get too annoyed when for the umpteenth time you hit the windscreen wipers instead of the indicator.

Freeways. Interstates, turnpikes and freeway-standard stretches of federal highways have the same rules. These include no stopping except in an emergency, no U-turns and a wide range of prohibited traffic: pedestrians, bicycles, animals, etc. Although technically you are not allowed to go slower than 40-50 mph, this is rarely enforced.

In urban areas there are no "fast" or "slow' lanes. Note that slip roads sometimes join and leave the outside lane. When driving on a multi-lane freeway it is usually best to avoid the extreme nearside and outside lanes, since these have the unnerving habit of becoming exit lanes. On some stretches of urban freeways, one lane is reserved for buses and "pool" cars during rush hours. A pool car is defined as any vehicle carrying the minimum number of passengers shown on the attendant road signs, usually two or four, driver included.

Although freeways outside cities technically have a through (slow) lane and a passing (fast) lane, many drivers choose a lane at random and stick to it. Others switch from one to another at will. Overtaking on the right is legal everywhere except in Connecticut, Maryland and Nebraska.

Other Roads. A single or double solid line along the centre of the road should not be crossed. U-turns are prohibited in city centres ("business districts") and elsewhere as posted.

The traffic light sequence is red-green-amber-red, or sometimes just red-green-red. At less busy times, there may simply be a flashing amber light which means "proceed with caution". In most places you are allowed to turn right against a red light, as long as you first come to a complete stop and give way to other cars, pedestrians, etc. Sometimes a sign may restrict this privilege to certain hours, or prohibit it entirely. You may be allowed to turn left from the extreme left lane of a one-way street into another one-way street. Before trying either of these manoeuvres, observe the practice of local drivers.

The octagonal STOP sign — or flashing red light — instructs drivers to come to a complete standstill before proceeding. Especially in cars with automatic transmission, it is very tempting not to bother. But the widely-practised "rolling stop" is a favourite target for traffic police keen to boost their takings. A common arrangement at crossroads is the "four-way stop", where each road is controlled by a stop sign or flashing red light. The accepted convention is that the first vehicle to arrive and stop at the cross roads has priority. When you approach a road obstruction at the same time as another vehicle coming in the opposite direction, the first one to flash their headlights takes the right-of-way. Do not interpret flashing headlights as meaning "go ahead, mister" as it sometimes does in Europe!

School buses have absolute priority. They are bright yellow ("National School Bus Chrome" is the official colour) and are fitted with lights that flash when taking up or discharging passengers. When this happens, all traffic — whether travelling in the same or opposite direction — must stop and wait. This law is taken very seriously. The only exception to it is that vehicles travelling in the opposite direction on a divided highway do not have to stop. Other vehicles which will assert priority include streetcars (trams) and the cable cars of San Francisco.

Many railroad crossings are unguarded. Some have flashing lights and/or a bell to warn of approaching trains, but others rely upon the good sense of the motorist. If you stall on a crossing, your battery should have sufficient power to allow you to crawl out of danger using the starter motor.

Speed Limits. The usual 65 mph maximum on good roads in rural areas is not universally respected. Driving at around 70mph seems to be the norm; many drivers of cars with cruise controls (which keep the speed constant until the accelerator or brake is operated) set them at about 72 mph, known as "truckers speed".

Of course, lower limits are often posted. Typically these are 55 mph on urban freeways, 50 mph for two lane highways in rural areas; 25-30 mph in residential districts; 15-25 mph in business districts; and 15 mph near schools when the kids are around. Watch for 30 mph and 35 mph zones just after you leave a freeway. Sometimes these speeds are enforced very strictly. Such zeal is usually attributed to traffic cops in small towns, especially in the southeastern USA, which reputedly depend upon speeding fines for a substantial part of their municipal revenue.

Detection techniques vary from state to state. They include the use of "Vascar" speed guns (where a policeman points the device at your car and takes an instant reading), unmarked police cars, helicopters, aircraft and radar. Signs warning of these traps are usually posted. Many states permit the use of in-car radar detectors, which sound an alarm when radar is in use; devices which jam the radar system are illegal. Some states are less than enthusiastic about the 65 mph limit: in Idaho the maximum fine for driving on freeways at over 65 mph but no more than 70 mph is a paltry $10 plus nominal $5 court costs.

If you must drive faster than the legal limit, travel with a group of vehicles doing roughly the same speed; the police are unlikely to book an entire convoy. The speed of trucks and cars equipped with CB radio should be closely observed, since their drivers are in contact with others who can warn of impending speed traps. These vehicles can be spotted by their distinctive antennae.

Penalties. If you are stopped for exceeding the limit, or for another "minor violation" (such as an illegal turn, or failing to halt at a stop sign), be obsequious and show your British passport: you might get away with a warning. Pleading unfamiliarity with American motoring practice may help. As with British traffic wardens, the most crucial point is to persuade police not to start writing. But don't despair if the officer starts scribbling: he may only be filling out an official caution, described as a "Friendly Warning" in some states.

If you do get a ticket, you have a choice of various courses of action. Some states allow spot fines, others have to take you to court although the penalty is often fixed at the time of the offence. In the spot-fine states, you can elect to go to court if you wish. However, the spot fine — around $50 for up to ten miles over the limit, plus an additional $10 fine for each mile per hour — will usually be less than that per hour imposed by the court. In the court states, you can waive your right to a hearing by sending the amount of the fine to the court in advance.

Some travellers, particularly those about to leave the USA with no immediate plans to return, may be tempted to opt for a court appearance and then skip the hearing. An immediate impediment to this is that some states require a deposit to assure your appearance which is often more than the fine you face. A longer-term drawback is that disobeying the summons (the ticket issued at the time of the offence) is a much more serious crime in law than the one you were originally stopped for. Your non-appearance will forever remain on your record in some police computer, ready to haunt you next time you're in the country.

You might find your vehicle "tagged", i.e. seen performing a traffic violation but not stopped, and later summonsed for the offence. If you are driving a rented car, the rental company will receive the summons and may well debit your credit card account to cover the fine.

Parking. Most cities are divided into zones for the purposes of controlling parking. Generally, suburban areas are unrestricted, except for the main thoroughfares that pass through them. Downtown, on-street parking is either metered or prohibited. Meters accept quarters; 25c buys up to half an hour with a maximum of two hours. Meter feeding is prohibited: the officers chalk the time they checked your car on the pavement, and therefore can tell if you have returned to insert some more coins. Erasing or amending the chalk mark will also incur a fine. Although you'll see plenty of cars parked illegally, it is not a good idea to join them unless you know the territory well.

There are certain places where you should never park. Avoid any stretch of kerb painted red, which means no parking at any time. You'll often see a tempting 20-foot gap between cars in an otherwise crowded street. The reason is probably the presence of a fire hydrant. Parking is prohibited within ten feet of hydrants, and this law is enforced strictly by towing offending vehicles away. Fire stations, ambulances and schools have a zone clearly marked on the roadway in front of them, which is similarly out-of-bounds. In addition temporary parking restrictions are often imposed in winter to allow snow ploughs to clear the streets.

Parking controls are enforced by city police together with private firms. The latter are paid on a piece-rate basis and hence are particularly zealous. Several techniques are employed. The most extreme is towing away; beware of signs showing a red axe embedded in a car. If your car is removed, the local police precinct station will tell you how to recover it and how much you will have to pay (at least $50).

Wheel clamps which immobilise cars are widely employed. Their colloquial name is the Denver Shoe, after the city in which they were first introduced. Details of where to go to pay the charge (about $30) for releasing your vehicle will be attached to the screen. You can expect to wait at least an hour or more at busy times for release.

Downtown parking lots cost upwards of $10 a day. Wasteground lots are cheapest, but not necessarily secure after dark. Be warned that car parks which cater primarily for commuter traffic often lock their gates overnight. If using an automated car park, be sure to follow the instructions; if you try to leave by the wrong exit, spikes may be activated and do serious damage to your tyres.

Supermarkets, banks and other establishments often have free parking for customers' use only. They enforce the system by issuing a token with which you leave the car park at the conclusion of your business. Those who are not customers must pay a great deal to get out.

Parking a large American car can be tricky. Some drivers deliberately bump adjacent vehicles, relying on the law which requires that bumpers (fenders) be designed to withstand a 5 mph collision without damage.

Alcohol. Drunken driving is taken much more seriously than it is in Britain. Every state has an "implied consent" law, whereby the act of driving implies a willingness to undergo a chemical test for drink. Some states set up road blocks to check every car and pick out drunk drivers. Otherwise, police must have some reason to stop you: if you drive with a blown headlight bulb, expect to be stopped and asked if you've been drinking. The officer will ostentatiously sniff the air around you, and may decide to administer a test. This may take the form of a breath test, or an analysis of blood, urine or saliva. The penalties for non-compliance are as serious as those for failing the test.

The blood-alcohol level above which you are deemed to be driving while intoxicated ("DWI" in highway patrol parlance) is 0.08% in most states. If your count is below the DWI level but above 0.05%, then you may still be charged with "driving under impairment". This is usually brought only as a secondary charge following an accident or a blatant case of reckless driving. However, DWI will earn you a heavy fine and withdrawal of your licence at the very least, possibly combined with some community service or treatment for alcoholism. Some states have mandatory 48-hour prison sentences for first offenders. If you hit someone while intoxicated, the penalties become much more severe. There is an extremely strong lobby against drunk drivers in the USA, comprised mainly of mothers who have lost children in road accidents where the offender was drunk.

Alcohol affects everyone differently according to their weight, metabollism and tolerance. As a very rough guide we include a chart from the *Wyoming Drivers Manual* in which a drink is defined as a can of beer, a glass of wine or a shot of spirits.

WEIGHT	DRINKS (ONE HOUR PERIOD)											
100	1	2	3	4	5	6	7	8	9	10	11	12
120	1	2	3	4	5	6	7	8	9	10	11	12
140	1	2	3	4	5	6	7	8	9	10	11	12
160	1	2	3	4	5	6	7	8	9	10	11	12
180	1	2	3	4	5	6	7	8	9	10	11	12
200	1	2	3	4	5	6	7	8	9	10	11	12
220	1	2	3	4	5	6	7	8	9	10	11	12
240	1	2	3	4	5	6	7	8	9	10	11	12

PRUDENT UP TO 0.05	DO NOT DRIVE 0.05 - 0.09	DO NOT DRIVE 0.10 AND UP

Carrying alcohol within the passenger compartment of a vehicle is a serious offence in most states. Alcohol must be transported in sealed containers which are locked in the boot ("trunk"). Some drivers attempt to circumvent the law by using the "brown bag" technique, which involves taking surreptitious gulps from a bottle of liquor concealed in a brown paper bag. It is sometimes an offence to carry alcohol — even if locked beyond reach of the occupants — across state lines (particularly in the southern states) or city limits. However, this is one transgression which is unlikely to be detected.

Driving under the influence of illicit drugs, although difficult to detect, incurs penalties similar to those for drunk driving.

HIGHWAY HAZARDS

Breakdowns. Drivers of rented cars should follow the procedure described by the company concerned on the rental agreement; if necessary, call the agency collect to negotiate repairs or a replacement vehicle. Those who have bought or borrowed vehicles should either join the AAA or be members of an affiliated motoring organization. On production of a valid AA or RAC certificate members will receive the same privileges as full members of the AAA. These benefits include a limited breakdown service, activated by calling (toll-free) 1-800-336-HELP. Members are entitled to 30 minutes of mechanical help at the scene of the breakdown or towing to a garage up to two miles away. Additional charges for towing, labour and parts come out of the motorist's pocket.

Summer Driving. Although some drivers regard it as essential, air conditioning increases petrol consumption dramatically, as does the practice of driving with all the windows open or the roof down. For air conditioning to function properly, you must keep all the windows closed. Don't be alarmed at the drips of condensation when you stop.

Should your vehicle start to overheat, check the radiator level and turn the heater full on. Use the highest possible gear to keep your speed up but the revs down; this maximizes the cooling effects of the air. Always carry plenty of water to keep the radiator topped up — and to drink while you're waiting for help to arrive. If you do break down on a desert, stay in your vehicle until another car comes along.

Petrol expands with heat, so the energy value of a gallon bought at midday is less than that of a gallon bought early in the morning when temperature are lower. Fill up early.

Winter Driving. Many of the same areas which suffer from excessive heat in summer are afflicted by severe snow and ice in winter. The most dangerous time to travel in snowy conditions is while the snow is actually falling. As soon as it stops, the ploughs (plows) come out in force. Don't park on main roads if there's a chance of snow, or your car may get ploughed away. The Interstate system is promptly cleared, although the passing lane may be slushy and a lower speed limit imposed. If you intend to drive on roads which may be cut off by snow, take sustenance, blankets, candles and a shovel.

Driving on ice is an altogether more frightening prospect. A warning that sometimes appears on signs is "Bridges Freeze First": an apparently clear road can turn into an ice rink as you cross a bridge. The worst driving of all is in freezing rain (black ice). Traction is almost nil; you should brake, turn or accelerate only with the utmost care. The conditions for freezing rain — warm air at cloud level enclosing a patch of sub-freezing air at ground level — make it rare and usually short-lived. It eventually turns to snow, sleet or rain, depending on whether the warm air cools down or the cold air warms up.

Mountainous Areas. At high altitudes, engines function less efficiently and produce far more carbon monoxide due to the lower density of oxygen. Also, because there is less oxygen, people are more susceptible to the effects of carbon monoxide (which makes you first drowsy, then unconscious, then dead). If driving at altitude, keep a window partially open even in winter. Do not run your engine while stationary.

If two vehicles meet face-to-face on a single track mountain road, the convention is that the driver heading downhill must reverse back up the slope until a suitable passing place is reached.

Other Drivers. Many American motorists are on a short fuse, and on the road as elsewhere racial tensions exist; the car or truck is often used as an equalizer. So pay attention to other traffic at all times, and try to blend in with it. Never stare at another driver, nor protest when a motoring discourtesy is committed against you that does not cause actual damage.

INSURANCE

Many visitors to the USA assume that American motor insurance policies include unlimited third party cover, as European policies do. They are wrong. There are very serious risks to British drivers without sufficient cover: you could be maimed yet unable to claim against an uninsured motorist, or — if you cause an accident — be crippled financially for life.

Vehicle insurance requirements vary greatly from state to state. In 12 states, insurance is not obligatory at all, subject to proof of financial resources sufficient to meet a moderate claim (say $20,000). In others, third party insurance is compulsory but with a similarly low level of cover. The lowest is $20,000 (Florida), the highest $50,000. So you must ensure that you and your passengers have sufficient medical insurance (see *Before You*

Go). This will provide some compensation for being hit by an uninsured or hit-and-run driver. Wise American drivers buy "uninsured motorist" insurance to protect themselves in such cases, but this is not easily available to foreigners.

You should have at least half a million dollars' worth of third party cover in case you cause an accident in which someone is injured. Law suits against negligent drivers can quite easily reach this level. A basic policy covering fire, theft, accident damage and third party claims up to the state minimum will cost about $100 for three months. The cost of increasing the third party cover to a more substantial amount is not expensive, costing around $20 for three months.

Before renting a car, find out the amount of third party cover. If it is below half a million dollars ask if you can extend it: some agencies increase the cover on payment of a dollar or two per day on top of the normal hire charge. If they do not, go elsewhere. The standard cover from Avis and Hertz is around $1 million. Insurance policies of the cheapest car rental firms restrict the use of a hire car to one or several states. This is especially common for cars hired in Florida. Some policies are actually nullified if an offence is committed by the policyholder at the time of the accident. Since most accidents result from some transgression of the law, this is tantamount to driving without insurance. So read the small print. If someone offers to lend you a car, check their policy to make sure it extends to you and provides adequate cover; if in doubt, decline politely.

Some states have a "no-fault" insurance law for accidental damage to vehicles. Each driver's insurers pay for his own damage, even if one party has absolutely no responsibility for the accident. This system does not encourage careful driving.

CAR HIRE

Every American city has a swarm of vehicle rental agencies. They range from small local outfits with a few beaten-up cars to the multinational chains of Avis, Budget and Hertz. Competition is intense. The cheapest regular rates for compacts are around $20 a day plus 10c per mile, or $30 unlimited. "Standard" or "full size" cars are most costly. Rates vary considerably from one state to another: New York is most expensive, Florida and California the cheapest. For example a one week rental from National Car Rental costs $159 USA-wide, $129 for just California/Nevada and $99 in Florida, with unlimited mileage. To these rates should be added around $5 per day for collision damage waiver (CDW) cover, plus local taxes. You must also check the level of insurance cover offered by the rental company. If it meets only the minimum requirements you should buy extra cover (including uninsured motorists insurance if possible).

Most hire cars have automatic transmission, which makes driving easy but increases petrol consumption. "Stick-shift" (manual) rental cars are rare, but will save a few dollars if you find one. Air conditioning is an expensive extra, but may be worthwhile in summer. If you rent from a chain of agencies, it is possible to drop off the car at a different location but this can be expensive.

Conditions of Booking. You will normally be asked to produce a major credit card, though sometimes it is possible to leave a hefty cash deposit instead. You must be at least 18 years of age for some companies, 21 for others. (Sometimes the insurance premiums are higher for younger drivers). A full British driving licence is sufficient, though you may be asked to show the photograph in your passport as well.

Don't try to avoid paying for any parking or speeding tickets; the hire company will simply charge the fine to your credit card. If you are going to be late returning the vehicle, you should let the hire company know. Most rental agreements specify a return time, allowing one hour's grace. If you are late, you will be driving without insurance cover and may even be presumed to have stolen the car. Remember the possible gain or loss of an hour if you change time zones. Be sure to return the car with a full petrol tank (assuming you have taken the car on an "out full, back full" basis) since rental agencies always charge dearly for fuel.

Cheap Deals. For a real bargain, book ahead. Many fly-drive holidays sell flights and a week's car rental for little more than the cost of an APEX ticket. Off-season, a second week's rental may be thrown in free (but you still have to pay extra for adequate insurance and local taxes). Every package tour operator to the USA offers low cost car rental. Independent travellers can also benefit by booking ahead: in 1988 Avis were offering a week's unlimited mileage in Florida for $79. Call them in London (01-848 8733) for their latest deal. You may be tempted by discounts offered to you because you have flown with a particular airline, belong to a certain club, etc. by the major car hire chains. The 10% discount usually applies only to the most expensive tariff, and local deals will be cheaper.

Once you are in the States, you can find the best deal by ringing around a few firms in the Yellow Pages. Most rental companies offer special weekend rates. You can also try for a cheap one-way deal: in a few locations (such as Florida) incoming one way rentals drastically exceed those going the other way. It may be possible to hire a car for a nominal sum as long as you deliver it to, say, New York. Ring around the big companies and ask if they have any "returns". U-Haul (who rent out vans) are also worth a try. They may even pay for fuel.

Rent-a-Wreck and Ugly Duckling are nationwide chains specializing in old, noisy and scruffy but mechanically sound cars at about half the rates charged by the other big companies. Call 1-800-228-5958 toll-free for Rent-a-Wreck reservations, 1-800-854-3380 for Ugly Duckling. One drawback is that the cars tend to be large "gas-guzzlers" so what you save on rental you may squander on fuel. Another is the three-day minimum hire that some outlets impose. Local companies copying the idea, with names like "Fender Benders" or "Rent-a-Heap-Cheap," are usually cheapest of all.

Recreational Vehicles (RVs). To solve all your accommodation problems at a stroke, hire one of these camper vans. Rental charges will seem astronomical — at least $500 per week — but the freedom and flexibility they provide could offset this. Because of the limited availability of RVs, it is worth booking well in advance. The US Travel and Tourism Administration in London (address on page 116) will provide you with a list of agents who can arrange bookings. If you own a camper van at home, you can swap vehicles temporarily with a American family: contact Change Wheels at CW House, 84 Fallowcourt Avenue, London W12 OBG.

DRIVEAWAYS

An attractive alternative to an expensive one-way car rental is provided by the "driveaway" system, a perennial feature of American motoring. Americans often want to be able to use their cars in different parts of the country without the bore of driving there themselves. Therefore, they are prepared to pay upwards of $250 to companies which organize deliveries. Look up "Auto Delivery" in the Yellow Pages; All American Auto Transport, Nationwide Car Transport and Dependable are three of the largest agencies. These companies arrange insurance and wait for people like you to phone and offer to drive. Apparently foreign visitors are considered more reliable than local drivers. The most common routes are coast to coast (in either direction), from the northeast to Georgia/Florida around Christmas, and back again in the spring, and from many places in the Midwest to Texas.

You contract to deliver the car within a certain number of days and miles, both of which are negotiated before you start. For example, delivering a car from New York to San Francisco may entitle you to 3,200 miles and seven days. (When this trip was first made by automobile in 1903 it took over two months). The amount of latitude depends upon how desperate driveway companies are to secure your services. In summer, when countless travellers are trying the same trick, you may not get a car at all; if you do succeed you will probably be allowed less generous deadlines and mileage limits. At other times of the year, you should face less competition and have more scope for negotiation. If companies are sufficiently anxious to meet their delivery commitments, they may even offer to pay for fuel. Some owners have been known to add a cash incentive in order to jump the queue.

You need to be over 21 (although some agencies reduce this to 18 or 19 years) and hold a full driving licence. All potential drivers and passengers must register at the start, and you may not pick up hitch-hikers. But there is nothing to stop you teaming up with fellow travellers in advance and splitting petrol costs and driving. Your passport and licence will be photocopied, you will have thumb prints taken and pay a deposit of up to $200. This is refunded by the recipient of the car at its destination.

Driveaways fall under the auspicies of the Interstate Commerce Commission, whose enforcement agency is the FBI. If you fail to deliver the car on time, they will start looking for you after a day to two.

When you pick up the car, it should have a full tank of petrol and be in good working order. Check the bodywork and agree the condition with the consignee, to avoid the risk of paying for existing damage. Should the car break down en route, pay any repair bills up to $50 yourself and reclaim this from the recipient. For larger amounts, call the owner collect and ask them to cable the cash to the garage. Also request an extension of your permitted time to take account of the delay involved. If you have an accident, you will have to negotiate according to circumstances and the state of the car.

If all goes well, driveaways provide a cheap and effective way to cross the continent. With careful route planning you can take in many places of interest. The vehicles on offer will predominantly be large, modern and expensive in fuel (e.g. 15-20 mpg) but this is offset by the opportunity to sleep in the car to save on accommodation costs.

BUYING A CAR

A good way to see America is to buy a car and sell it at the end of your trip. Prices for decent secondhand cars start at about $500 and are generally much lower than in the UK.

Choosing a Car. A cheap, old model will minimize losses if resale should prove difficult. One of the better bets is a Volkswagen Beetle. They are economical to run, and reasonably reliable; if you do hit problems, then almost every mechanic will have some idea how to fix it. The air-cooled engine behaves very well in hot weather. There is a thriving trade in secondhand VWs which makes buying and reselling relatively straight-forward. A 15-year-old Beetle will cost $300 - $500, depending on condition, a VW Camper about twice that amount. Japanese cars are also good value.

Old American cars offer greater space and comfort, but use more fuel and are prone to breakdowns. Lesser-known vehicles such as the Austin America (known in Britain as the 1100) are so unfamiliar to American mechanics that any problems may be terminal. Unless you are an expert on a particular car, choose a popular model. Try to buy in an area of the USA not subject to snow. So much salt is used to clear it that rust is a major problem.

The easiest way to get a car is to buy from one of the used car salesmen whose premises line the main highways out of every city. Unless a dealer is recommended to you by someone whose judgment you trust, you will have to gauge the dealer's honesty yourself. Although it is impossible to trust the salesman's patter, at least you are offered an immediate choice and can expect the paperwork to be completed with despatch. Transactions will normally be in cash, though in some cases a credit card will be accepted.

Cars sold privately are usually cheaper. Check advertisements in local newspapers and on college noticeboards. It is important to satisfy yourself that the seller actually owns the vehicle by checking the Certificate of Title against his driver's licence. You will probably never see the vendor again, so give the car a thorough going-over before parting with any money. The price of a vehicle is likely to come down rapidly if you can produce a bundle of ready cash. Some states impose a tax on the private sale of vehicles, and it is the purchaser's responsibility to pay this.

Legal Requirements. Every vehicle has a Certificate of Title, the American equivalent of the British "log book" or Registration Certificate. The seller must endorse this across to you. You then send it to the Division or Registrar of Motor Vehicles for the state, who will issue you with a new certificate. There may be a small fee for this, and for the transfer of licence plates to your name. (Some states require only a rear number plate.) However, the number plates may be retained by the vendor, particularly if they are the personalized variety (as found, for example, in California). You must then apply for new plates. This will cost you more, so take it into account when agreeing on the price of the vehicle.

Resale. Although it's probably better to buy a cheap heap and drive it into the ground, you may want to try to resell. If you are selling the car in the state (geographical, not mechanical) in which you bought it, there will be few problems. If you have sufficient time to sell privately, then wait for someone to answer your advertisement. Should you fail to find a buyer in time, your only choice is to hawk the vehicle around a few local dealers and accept the least derisory offer.

Many visitors who buy a car and drive across the continent will not want to return to the state of purchase just to sell their car. To sell legally in another state, you will normally have to re-register the vehicle in the state in which you wish to sell. This takes time and money, not least for buying new number plates. Once it is re-registered, proceed as above. The alternative is to sell to an individual or dealer who is prepared — for a suitable reduction in price — to accept the legal complications of buying an out-of-state car.

MOTORCYCLING

The Hell's Angels of the USA rejoice in the title of the "one-per-centers", which arose from a claim that while 99% of American motorcyclists are law-abiding citizens, one per cent are troublemakers. Unfortunately for the remainder, they have earned all bikers an undeservedly poor reputation. Prejudice can manifest itself at truck stops, gas stations and — more worryingly — on the open road. Motorists probably won't acually try to run you down, but may well fail to give you due consideration. Even so, many visitors are prepared to put up with such ill-feeling in return for the freedom and economy that a motorcycle allows.

Buying a Motorcycle. When exchange rates are favourable, it is quite possible to buy a brand-new bike in the States, use it throughout your visit, then ship it back and pay import duty for less than the price of the same machine in Britain. If you intend to sell before returning, then buy secondhand to avoid the inevitable depreciation on a new motorcycle. Most dealers sell both new and used bikes. They charge state tax on sales. Buying privately may avoid tax and secure a better bargain. The legal requirements for buying and selling are the same as for *Buying a Car,* above. When you buy a bike, get a very strong lock at the same time.

Hiring a Motorcycle. Contact the Harley Owners Group (3700 W Juneau, PO Box 453, Milwaukee, Wisconsin 53201; 414-935-4522) for details of their Fly & Ride programme. If you join the club, you will be eligible to rent a Harley Davidson bike in Florida (Orlando or Miami), California, the Rockies or Hawaii for about $300 a week.

The minimim age for riding a moped ranges from 12 in New Mexico to 16 in most other states. For motorcycles above 50 cc, the lower limit in between 14 and 18 years. Licences are required by motorcyclist in every state except Mississippi. A British motorcycle licence will suffice. In some states, helmets are obligatory and must be reflective. Elsewhere, helmets must be worn only by riders under 18 or 19. In Delaware, every biker must carry a helmet but only those under 19 need actually wear them.

Any bike whose engine is larger than 50 cc is allowed on freeways. If you intend to ride a motorcycle, you are strongly advised to take out insurance well beyond the minimum level required by law.

HITCH-HIKING

Hitch-hiking in the USA is not what it is in Europe. It is harder to get lifts, the distances to be covered can be immense, police hassles are endless and a high proportion of drivers who give lifts can best be described as weird. Many lift-givers are drunk, or insist on smoking dope while driving, or are just plain crazy. It is questionable whether hitching in its traditional form is a worthwhile form of transport for anyone save inveterate hitchers and those down to their last few cents. As a result, an American definition of hitch-hiking now encompasses far more than thumbing lifts. It covers freight-hopping on the railways, getting rides on private yachts and aircraft, and the growing practice of ride-sharing.

Hitching out of Cities. Most American cities are criss-crossed by a maze of limited-access freeways, which are a nightmare for the hitcher. It is essential to have a good map to identify the road you want and to plan how to reach a suitable junction. Some hitchers specialize in asking drivers at downtown gas stations to recommend a suitable spot, and sometimes even get a free ride out to the driver's choice.

Signs are essential for leaving large cities, and advisable elsewhere. A two-letter code is usually sufficient: NY, LA, SF etc. Add "Please" if you're feeling polite and desperate. "Home to Mom" has also been known to work. Brandishing a Union Jack usually helps even though many drivers may mistake it for the Canadian flag.

Cities are best avoided altogether by hopping from one truck stop to another. There is usually through traffic to guarantee a ride past big cities en route. Occasionally you may be seized by an urge to get out and visit a city; when you come to leave, directions to hitching spots are given under *Arrival and Departure* in each regional chapter.

Hitching on Freeways. It is universally illegal to hitch from the main carriageway of limited-access highways, and yet everyone does it until told to move on. The ramps are disputed territory; a sign saying "No Hitch-hiking" at the start of a ramp is ignored at your peril. Turnpikes invariably have toll booths at junctions. If the toll collector is in a good mood, he will let you stand where the traffic is travelling slowly and may even solicit a ride on your behalf. More likely, though, he will warn you off his territory and not hesitate to call the police if you argue, so it's best to stay a few hundred yards up or downstream.

Drivers. A fair amount of academic research into hitch-hikers has been carried out in the USA. Much of it is concerned with the kinds of drivers that hitchers attract, and the conclusion reached is that motorists generally pick up people like themselves. Experienced hitchers recommend three disguises; the casual-but-clean approach; wearing a suit an tie and carrying a suitcase rather than a backpack; or making the most of your European connections by wearing full Tyrolean mountain gear or a kilt and sporran, though this could well attract the weirdos. You then have some chance of being picked up by normal human beings. This can be a definite advantage in view of the many strange characters currently driving around America, many of whom are religious cranks, drink or drug abusers or perverts of various kinds. If you do get a lift with a dubious character, you might try to gain your freedom by feigning sickness or slamming the gear lever into a low gear and leaping out. Beware of the central locking systems fitted to many American cars. The best policy is to avoid problems by turning down any drivers whose sobriety or motivation you suspect. Sometimes the motorist will be pleasant company but a dangerous driver; just ask to be set down if you're anxious.

Some drivers will demand payment for a ride before you get in. Whether or not you agree to this depends upon how desperate you are for a lift. If you do decide to pay, make sure you agree a figure in advance. Claim poverty and settle on a figure as low as possible in order to emphasize that you're not worth robbing. And don't hand over all the cash until you reach your agreed destination. It is not unknown for drivers to extract payment from hitchers, eject them after a few miles, then drive on to pick up the next unsuspecting victim. You should also be wary of a driver who asks you to step out to see if his tail lights are working. Many a hitcher has been left helpless on the road after the vehicle pulls away with his luggage.

The Law. Despite former FBI director J. Edgar Hoover's warning that "the beckoning thumb of the hitch-hiker can be a lure to disaster in disguise", there is no federal law prohibiting hitching. Instead, there is a mass of piecemeal state and municipal legalisation. Some states ban the soliciting of rides entirely, although this is easily circumvented by the accepted local custom of *smiling* at the oncoming traffic. Other states permit thumbing except if you are standing on the road surface. In fact the laws are often vague, and many police officers use their powers of stop-and-search at their discretion to check for drugs and weapons, and often invoke local vagrancy laws to arrest hitchers carrying less than the statutory $10 or so. Penalties for contravening anti-hitching laws range from a $10 spot fine to 30 days in the local jail. If you are concerned, ring the local police station and ask them what the local laws are.

Fortunately, foreign visitors — especially clean, tidy and polite foreign visitors — are frequently immune from the worst penalties of the law. Rather than fining or arresting you, the police will tend to warn you off a freeway ramp or order you to hitch outside the city limits. Some may decide to give you a ride, and you are not expected to decline this offer. This will usually be to the county or state line. In fact standing close to the state borders is a good idea since there is a real "no man's land" on interstates between the last exit in one state and the first in the next.

CB Radio. The use of citizen's band radio in the USA is more than a passing fad. Almost all trucks, and many private cars, are fitted with CB. Unfortunately truck drivers are far less prone to pick up hitchers due to strict company regulations. But if you are lucky, you'll get a ride in a truck and be able to listen to your driver talk about delays ahead, summon help to accidents, and warn of impending presence of "smoky bears" (highway patrolman) looking for speeding vehicles. (However, the combination of CB jargon, radio interference and a southern drawl will render many conversations entirely incomprehensible). They also chat to one another to while away the endless hours of tedium on transcontinental freeways. In the course of such conversations, there is a chance that a driver who has picked you up will ask other drivers to take you further along your route, and arrange an exchange at a convenient truck-stop.

Boat Hopping. For a free ride on a private yacht, find a yacht marina and offer your services as a crew member. Any maritime experience will be valuable but not essential if you can offer another skill such as handyman, cook or cleaner. The best chances are at San Diego, San Francisco, the Chicago lakeside, Boston, Long Island Sound near New York, New Orleans and Miami. The last two are particularly promising for voyages around the Caribbean.

Hitching on Aircraft. There is a great deal of private aviation in the USA, made up of amateur pilots and corporations who fly key executives around in private planes. Over 750,000 Americans have private pilots' licences. They operate mainly from the hundreds of small airfields dotted around the States. Many people have successfully hitched rides by the simple expedient of asking. The duty officer at an airfield should be able to tell you who is flying where, and it's up to you to use your powers of persuasion with the pilots concerned. Maximize your chances by travelling light and being slim: in small aircraft every pound in weight is significant. Pilots use the same criteria as drivers when choosing hitch-hikers, so be clean, tidy and a great conversationalist.

Ride Sharing. Most cities operate a car-pooling service for commuters, but since this is probably of little interest to long-distance traveller don't get excited when you hear about a municipal "Ride Board". More useful are the ad hoc systems which can be found in large cities. Community radio stations and college noticeboards are full of requests for passengers and drivers to share expenses on long journeys. Many cities have ride referral agencies (look for this heading in the local Yellow Pages) which charge a fee for matching drivers with passengers. Their advantage is that they have plenty of people on their books and so if you're not tied to an exact departure date, you'll probably find a suitable ride. There is one nationwide agency which deals in rides throughout the USA and Canada: Travel-Mate, which has offices in New York (1-800-243-8588) and Virginia (1-800-368-3137) One-off membership costs $20. They also deal in ride-sharing on private aircraft. Other agencies provide services whereby several riders deliver a driveaway car or club together to buy a cheap car, drive to their destination, then sell the car and split the proceeds.

However you fix up your ride, the customary arrangement is to divide the cost of oil and gas equally, and to share the driving; check that the owner's insurance covers you adequately before taking the wheel. If you register jointly for a driveaway, there is no problem about insurance.

Freighthopping. The art of riding illicitly on freight trains has enjoyed something of a renaissance recently, perhaps as a reaction to the increasing dangers of hitch-hiking. Although it is against federal law, many railway employees are not averse to your hopping a lift. The idea is to find a railroad freight yard and identify a train to take you someway towards your destination. You do this by asking friendly-looking switchmen (the people who operate the points) or experienced hoboes. Your adversary is the yard bull, the security officer whose job consists of preventing theft and vandalism, but also of catching freighthoppers. Once you find a train, you must look for a safe place to hide, which with increasing containerization is becoming trickier. The ends of bulk grain loaders are reputed to be secure if uncomfortable. When you arrive at the next yard, you repeat the procedure until you finally reach your destination. For further information and an explanation of the jargon (e.g. "hotshot" for express freight train and "pussy" for hostile security guard) consult *The Freighthopper's Manual for North America* by Daniel Leen, available from the author at Box 191, Seattle, WA 98111 ($7.95).

Accommodation

apartment	flat
bathroom	often a euphemism for toilet
coeducational/coed	mixed (male and female)
condominium/condo	flat which can be bought outright
dormitory	student hall of residence, usually with single rooms
duplex	an apartment occupying two floors
efficiency unit	self-catering apartment, sometimes in motels
elevator	lift
faucet	tap
half-bath	a room with a toilet and sink but no bath

outhouse	outdoor toilet
roomer	lodger
roommate	flat or house sharer, who does not necessarily share the same room
rooming house	a house in which rooms are let
RV	recreational vehicle (camper van or mobile home)
washroom	toilet/bathroom

One of the most regrettable facts for the traveller in North America is that there is nothing comparable to the family-run pensions and cheap and cheerful hotels which can be found throughout Europe. The cheap hotel you find near the Greyhound bus depot will not be in the same league as the cheap hotel you'll find near French or Italian railway stations. Not only will it be more expensive, but it is likely to be run-down and inhabited by low life. Most travelling Americans stay either in modern expensive chain hotels or in motels. Fortunately the network of low-budget hostels is expanding, and those who enjoy a little more luxury can buy vouchers in advance which give substantial discounts at motel and hotel chains. The most comprehensive guide to budget-priced lodgings is Frommer's *Where to Stay USA,* published in association with the Council on International Educational Exchange; the 1989 price is $10.95.

HOTELS

Chains such as Holiday Inn, Hilton, Sheraton and Ramada specialize in providing predictable clean rooms the world over. The rates, too, are uniformly expensive starting at around $50 per double room per night. But foreign travellers can make substantial savings by purchasing accommodation vouchers in advance when buying transatlantic air tickets. All North American tour operators offer discount vouchers for hotel chains including Days Inn, Howard Johnson and Holiday Inn. Typically a voucher costs £30 and allows up to four people to occupy a room. You may, however, have to pay substantial surcharges to stay in more upmarket places.

Whereas there is an endless choice of lavish upmarket establishments, the number of older, dingy but respectable hotels varies from city to city, but is usually disappointingly small. The few there are get booked up early, so reserve in advance if you possibly can.

Hotel rates in America are quoted per room not per person. Singles — where they exist — are only slightly less than doubles, so it is much more economical to travel with a friend. If you are planning to stay for a week or more, it is always worth asking at the outset for a discount. You can get excellent weekend deals in big city hotels, as most places slash their rates to attract custom when business people are thin on the ground. They may still cost more than many of the budget places recommended in this book, but should be substantially more luxurious. If you are not on a particularly tight budget and are looking for inns and hotels with character look for the series of accommodation guides called *Country Inns, Lodges and Historic Hotels* to various regions of North America.

MOTELS

Apart from youth hostels (see below) the cheapest and most comfortable accommodation can often be found in motels. Motels dot the approach roads of every American city, advertising their facilities: swimming pool, colour TV, air-conditioning and free ice are common. The price of a room will seldom drop below $20; motels without neon signs are usually the cheapest. They are not called motels (motor-hotels) for nothing. Most are awkward to reach by public transport, but if you are driving around the US, they are a sensible (if somewhat predictable) option. The Big 6 chain of motels is about the cheapest, and they make it easy to book a room in your next motel for the price of the call. Also watch for Regal 8 (1-800-851-8888), Super 8 (1-800-843-1991), Days Inn, Red Roof Inns (1-800-THE-ROOF) and Susse Chalet. Howard Johnson's offer more upmarket accommodation for more upmarket prices ranging from $33 for a double in Montgomery Alabama to $100 in New York City. Best Western Motels are middle-of-the-road in price and facilities.

BED & BREAKFAST

American tourists who have for years been smitten with the British institution of bed and breakfast have finally succeeded in importing the idea into their homeland. Most regions of tourist interest and many large cities now have bed and breakfast associations. Unfortunately rates are not at the familiar £10 level, but more like $50 for a double. Although this competes favourably with hotel prices it is by no means the cheapest accommodation available. In many cases, though, it might be the most interesting. Once you've seen one motel you've seen them all, but bed and breakfast homes vary greatly according to the personality and taste of the owner, and they can provide a unique glimpse of middle class American life. You may even get along with the host so well that you are asked to stay longer without paying, or invited back in the future free of charge

The addresses for B & B registers are given in the regional *Accommodation* sections whenever possible. Look out for the *Bed and Breakfast Guide to the U.S. and Canada* by Bob and Ellen Christopher ($4.95), *Bed and Breakfast USA* available for $5.95 from the Tourist House Association of America, PO Box 335-A Greentown, Pennsylvania 18426, or *Bed and Breakfast American Style* from Berkshire Traveller Press, Stockbridge, Massachusetts for $10.95. In the UK, you can contact Home Base Holidays, 7 Park Avenue, London N13 5PG (01-886-8752)

BUDGET ACCOMMODATION

Student travel offices in North America and abroad sell a useful booklet called *Sleep Cheap: North America*; the UK price is £2.

Youth Hostels. Buying a youth hostels membership for £7 ($17 in the US) might turn out to be the wisest investment you can make in preparation for your American travels. And since 20% of the clientele is British, you'll meet like-minded travellers. Youth hostels are the cheapest places to stay, ranging from $5 for the simplest shelter to $12 for a superior hostel. There is usually a 25% surcharge during the winter (October 15 - April 15) to offset heating costs. Hostellers can expect to have to perform a small chore before leaving each day. Some larger hostels even offer the option of doing several hours work in exchange for your board, allowing you to stay for free. There are nearly 300 hostels, but unfortunately they are not distributed evenly over the country. Whereas areas like the Colorado Rockies, the San Francisco Bay area and the Great Lakes are amply provided with hostels, there are many states (Alabama, Arkansas, Oklahoma, etc.) which do not have a single hostel. Some hostels are located inside national parks where they often have a monopoly on accommodation.

In addition to the regular hostels operated by American Youth Hostels, supplementary accommodation is sometimes made available to hostellers in YMCAs, church halls, university residences, etc. Beds are normally available to non-YHA members also, but for a higher fee. Another variation on the usual kind of purpose-built hostel is the home hostel, which is simply a private residence open to youth hostellers for the same price as a hostel. Many hostels permit camping on their property for a small fee. All of this specified in the *American Youth Hostels Handbook* available from YHA in Britain (14 Southampton St, London WC2) for £7.50 including postage or $5 from any hostel office in the USA excluding postage. The national headquarters is at PO Box 37613, Washington DC 20013-7613; tel: (202) 783-6161. To complement the network of AYH hostels, some cities have low-cost hostels without the restrictions on timekeeping, alcohol, etc., that many travellers find tedious. Details are given under the *Accommodation* heading where applicable.

YMCAs. There are over 50 centres where you can spend the night, and most Y's now accept both men and women. Prices vary from $10 single in small towns to about $40 double in big cities. The average seems to be about $20 single and $30 double (though doubles are not always available).

Despite the wholesome reputation of YMCAs — most are complete with swimming pools and fitness rooms — they do seem to attract a number of down-at-heel locals. Partly for this reason, it is important to book ahead, especially for Boston, New York or San Francisco and other centres in heavy demand. Book through the central office in New York (356 W 34th St., New York, NY 10001; 212-760-5856) at least two months in advance; otherwise the booking fee is $3. Full payment must be made in advance to reserve the room.

Camping. Almost 60 million Americans go camping every year, and that can mean anything from backpacking with a pup tent to living in comfort in a plush RV. There are almost 18,000 campgrounds serving these campers, some private, many in national or state parks and forests. Campers and campsite managers are often funds of information on events and eating places in their area.

Whereas government-run campsites are normally inside designated parks or recreation areas, private sites may be within automobile access of cities and other tourist attractions. The best known network of 700 commercial campsites is called KOA ("Kampgrounds of America") which are not intended for the back-to-nature camper (although tenters are welcome). The cost of a night's accommodation (including TV and games facilities, possibly a swimming pool, etc.) is around $10-$15, so they are not much cheaper than motels. In high summer, they are frequently full. You can obtain their clearly laid out directory either at one of their sites, or in advance from their headquarters, Billings, Montana 59114, by sending $1 to cover surface postage.

LONGER TERM ACCOMMODATION

College Dorms. If you plan to be in a college or university town for a week or more during the summer months, it is worth writing to the University Housing Office to see whether they let travellers stay in student rooms. Some college residences are allocated to summer schools and conferences, but others are open to itinerants. Bookings should be made early. Travelling students may be given preference if rooms are scarce.

Rented Accommodation. If you are staying for a week or more, you might be able to find space in a rooming house, where rents might be as low as $60 a week. Check in the "Furnished Rooms" column of the newspaper classifieds. You could also try to arrange to sublet a room or a flat during the summer by checking in the personal columns of the campus newspaper. Most ads appear March/April/May. You can also find self-catering apartments often known as "efficiency units"; enquire at the local tourist office.

House Exchange. If you want to live in an American home and have it all to yourself, you might want to participate in a house exchange. The two main requirements are that you are willing to spend two or three weeks in one place and that you have a house in a desirable location (London, the Cotswolds) which you are willing to trust to strangers. There are several agencies which charge a fee of (around £30) for publishing your house specifications in a register which is then distributed to all members. For some reason this has not yet become a big business, and many of the agencies are run by individuals from their homes. Try Home Base, 7 Park Avenue, London N13 5PG (01-886 8752) or Intervac, 6, Siddals Lane, Allestree, Derby DE3 2DY (0332 558931).

Eating and Drinking

à la mode	with ice cream
au jus	with gravy
automat	a restaurant where food and drink are taken from coin-operated machines
bittersweet	plain (as in chocolate)
broiled	grilled
brown-bag (vb)	to eat or take a packed lunch
brownie	a heavy chocolate cake, almost like fudge
brunch	late morning meal, often a social occasion
busboy	general restaurant dogsbody, table wiper and water pourer
Canadian bacon	thin gammon steak
candy	sweets
candy bar	chocolate bar (occasionally still called "Hershey bar")
car hop	waiter/waitress at a drive-in restaurant
carry out	take away
check	bill
chiffon	frothy eggwhite dessert, often used as a filling for pies
chips	potato crisps
cookie	sweet biscuit
cracker	savoury biscuit
diner	basic restaurant which serves unpretentious American food
doggie bag	bag provided by a restaurant for taking away left-overs
easy over/over easy	fried eggs, turned
eggplant	aubergine
English muffin	muffin (toasted, flat crumpet)
entree	main course
frank	frankfurter (hot dog)
french fries or fries	chips
greasy spoon	basic diner
grits/hominy grits	rural Southern dish of coarsely ground grains
gumbo	okra stew or any stew, characteristic of Louisiana

hash browns	chopped potatoes fried in bacon fat and shaped into flat cakes
hush puppy	small deep fried cornmeal cake (Southern)
jello	jelly
jelly	jam
lox	smoked salmon
maitre d'	head waiter
muffin	leavened cake in the shape of a cupcake, often made of bran or with blueberries
munchies	peckishness often arising after indulging in controlled substances
pastrami	smoked beef with seasoning
popsicle	ice lolly
potato chips	crisps
quick and dirty	a cheap caff
sack lunch	packed lunch
scrod	young Atlantic cod or haddock
seafood	any fish (including freshwater)
sherbet	sorbet
shrimp	prawns
succotash	mixture of corn and beans (Iroquois Indian word)
sunny side up	fried eggs which have not been turned
surf n' turf	seafood and steak
take-out	take-away
tenderloin	fillet steak
truck stop	transport cafe
zucchini	courgette

Over five million people are employed in the catering industry to minister to the avid eating-out habits of Americans. Although the kitchen of the average American is equipped with all manner of time-saving gadgets, the owner can regularly be found dining elsewhere. Consequently there is a huge range of eating establishments from basic diners to trendy vegetarian cafes, from authentic Ethiopian restaurants to the ubiquitous steak and seafood places serving "surf 'n' turf".

There are some ethnic cuisines which seem to have flourished in America even more than in their own countries or origin: pizzas can be tastier in Chicago than in Calabria, Dim Sum more appealing in San Francisco than in Shanghai, and the tacos spicier in Texas than in Tijuana. Chefs in the USA have nurtured the French concept of *nouveau cuisine* and serve it in much larger portions, a style becoming known as *nouvelle Americain*. There is also a great deal of over-priced, mass produced, artifical garbage masquerading as food. A brief account of the kind of eating establishments to be found in most urban centres, followed by a run-down of the most common ethnic cuisines, should help the discerning traveller to find well prepared food at a reasonable price.

RESTAURANTS

It is impossible to make many useful generalizations about American restaurants, since the range of style and ethnic style and ethnic cuisine is enormous. Many do tend to be gimmicky. There will be no understatement on the menu, the decor will be unusual in some way and the staff may be dressed up as if on safari or as characters from a cartoon strip. It seems that the publicity manager and interior decorator are paid more than the chef. One advantage of this corny mentality is that many restaurants will bake a cake for a special occasion if given prior warning and the waiters may even sing happy birthday to your embarrased companion. Often there are dress requirements for customers. Men may be refused admittance, even from fairly modest establishments, for wearing jeans or failing to wear a jacket and tie. Enquire when booking, or turn up prepared. If you book in advance you may be asked for your credit card number. If you don't show up for the reservation your account will be charged to an amount representing the average cost of a meal.

Restaurant service is attentive to the point of being obtrusive. "Hi, I'm Ron and I'll be looking after you this evening. I hope y'all enjoy your meal." It is very tempting to think that this ritual is intended to lead to a generous tip.

Many travellers are bemused by the number of staff clamouring to serve them. You may be seated by the hostess or maitre d' (pronounced may-tradee), waited on by Ron and the bar waiter and cleaned up afterwards by the busboy. Ron is the only one you should consider tipping, though there is usually a system by which tips are pooled and shared.

Check the menus to see whether the price of the entree includes a starter, bread, salad and dessert. Some restaurants offer small helpings called "petite dinners". This may well be sufficient since the portions served in most restaurants verge on the obscenely large. If you can't finish your meal and want to save the leftovers for breakfast, ask for a doggy bag. Lunch in smart resturants is usually cheaper than dinner, even though the menu may be the same. Other restaurants charge less for meals consumed at an unfashionable time of day: many offer "early-bird specials" for people prepared to eat dinner before 6pm.

Restaurant proprietors are keenly aware of the new fad for healthy living and almost every menu has some appetizing vegetarian choices. Vegetarians will not have to make do with undressed green salads and cheese omelettes. The *Organic Traveller* can be obtained from Small Press Distributors, 1636 Ocean View, Kensington, California 94707. It describes and rates vegetarian resturants throughout North America.

Fast Food. McDonalds, Kentucky Fried Chicken and Taco Bell are the culmination of the American desire for familiar, palatable food served instantly. Since the first McDonalds opened in the mid 1950s the company has sold 65 million burgers. It has also employed, at sometime or other, one in five of the American workforce. And the company claims that in any year 95% of Americans eat at McDonalds. Most fast food outlets are national chains, so the burger you eat in Los Angeles is exactly the same —down to the last gram of monosodium glutamate — as the burger you ate in Boston. With a few exceptions, the antiseptic decor is identical from state to state, the prices and muzak will be the same, and the staff will be wearing the same uniforms and same forced smiles. Americans adore standardization, and these places were flourishing even before Colonel Sanders experimented with his first unfortunate chicken. Most connoisseurs maintain that Wendy's and Burger King are preferable to McDonald's, and the International House of Pancakes better than Taco Bell or Pizza Hut.

Although this kind of dining experience is not likely to be memorable, it is a cheap and efficient way to eat. A quarter-pounder with all the trimmings, plus large fries and a soft drink won't set you back more than $3. Fast food can also be nutritious: you can order a McSalad rather than a Big Mac. Many fast food outlets have drive-in service. You park your car beside an intercom, relay your order to the staff inside, and wait for a waitress (who may or may not be wearing rollerskates) to bring out a tray, laden with burgers and root beers, and clip it to your car window. Alternatively, you drive round to another window where you pay, pick up your meal and drive away.

Diners. The first diners were gleaming steel caravans made in New Jersey, driven to suitable roadside locations throughout America and mostly owned by immigrants from Southern Europe. Now the term is loosely used to describe any unpretentious truckstop or city cafe with a long menu and low prices. There is a counter with stools where you can watch your meal being prepared, or chairs and tables where you are waited upon by the blue rinsed wife of the proprietor. The European influence on proletarian American food lives on only in the names: "bologna", "hamburger", "frankfurter" and "wienie" (from Vienna hot dog).

Roadside diners are becoming an endangered species due to the growth of "family restaurants" or "roadhouses", which are national chains dealing in standardized, portion-controlled meals. But away from the Interstates, on the edges of small towns, you can still find genuine diners. Although they used to pride themselves on their hearty home-cooking (stews, casseroles, etc.) they now have conformed to the tyranny of the hamburger. But the star turn is breakfast. John Steinbeck once said "I've never had a really good American dinner, but I've never had a really bad American breakfast". Competition is keen and for as little as 99c you can enjoy some of the following, and, for a little more, all of them: cereal, eggs, bacon, toast, jelly, hash browns, pancakes, syrup and unlimited coffee. Don't be surprised if everything (except the coffee) arrives on the same plate. After unsuccessfully trying to keep the syrup from the eggs and the jelly from the bacon you'll give up and eat them all together as Americans do. Brunch, eaten between 11am and 2pm, especially on Sundays, is like breakfast only more so. If you're ordering eggs the waiter will ask you how you want them done. If you want them fried, you'll have to specify if you want them "sunny side up" (unturned), "over" (turned) or "easy over/over easy" (turned but runny).

The lunch special may be stew, bread and coke and very cheap. You may see signs saying "no substitutions". This means you cannot have, say, french fries instead of a baked potato for the same price. To avoid embarrassment and extra expense, stick to the fixed menu.

Coffee shops are upmarket versions of diners with slightly fancy decor. They serve a range of egg dishes, fry ups, toasted sandwiches and pancakes. Many city hotels have a coffee shop on the ground floor which stays open late even all night. Drug stores often have a counter which serves cheap breakfasts and other snacks.

Mealtimes. Americans tend to dine much earlier than Europeans. Lunch is usually eaten at noon and dinner (usually called "supper") between 5.30 amd 6.30. But in cities you can eat at any hour of the day or night. Some diners and coffee shops advertise breakfast 24 hours a day. You can usually find an all-night drug store food counter, bus station cafeteria or hotel coffee shop. Diners and coffee shops which do not stay open all night generally open at 5 or 6 am and serve breakfast until 11 am.

In small towns, dinner may not be served after 7.30 pm. But there will doubtless be a local fast food joint open later or a 24-hour truckstop on a nearby highway. Fancy restaurants in big cities serve throughout the evening as they do in Europe.

Payment. In fast food joints you always pay at the time you get the food. At other places, you get either a computerized print-out or a scrawled bill ("check") to which tax, but not service has been added. You might also find, therefore, a note from your waiter saying "It's been a pleasure to serve you — Ron". At upmarket restaurants you pay at your table. At diners, take the check to the cash desk on the way out. You may find that each member of your party gets an individual bill, which is the management's way of avoiding fraud. There is no problem paying with a recognized travellers cheque (see *Money*) or cash. Most restaurants also accept credit cards, but make sure of this before ordering if you have no other means of payment.

Delicatessens. The "deli" is a mainstay for American consumers, especially busy office workers. Delis usually serve bagels with cream cheese or lox (salmon) and sandwiches prepared from several varieties of bread and a score of fillings. Order as snappily as you can. The two great deli sandwiches are pastrami (smoked beef) and corned beef, served on rye bread with mustard only. These cost about $3.

Street Snacks. The hot dog was allegedly invented at the 1904 St Louis World's Fair. Over 80 years later it is still going strong. Street vendors positioned at busy corners do a roaring trade in tasty hot dogs at a dollar each, with the American apology for mustard included in the price. They also do side orders of french fries and soft drinks. You can buy a slice of pizza for $1 from street stands. Pretzel vendors are unfamiliar to most northern Europeans. Pretzels are glazed salty curls of pastry and seem to be very popular.

Cheap Deals. Fixed price buffets, normally called "smorgasbords" in America, are very popular especially at Sunday lunchtimes, but also on week nights. You can help yourself to whatever you like as often as you wish. A variation found in many restaurants is a serve-yourself salad bar. You are given a bowl and possibly only a single run at the salads on offer. The art is to begin with the densest salad (coleslaw, meats, potato salad) and build up your pile with progressively less dense ingredients. Finish up with lettuce and perhaps a tomato or two to anchor down the construction. To avoid undue spillage, apply dressing to each layer rather than all at once at the end. Many restaurants, particularly pasta joints, have "all you can eat" specials. For about $7 you are entitled to endless helpings of the day's special dish, usually spaghetti bolognese.

FOREIGN CUISINES

You are probably familiar with American favourites such as steak, fried chicken and fruit pies (blueberry, pumpkin, pecan, banana cream are all delicious) and some of the most familiar ethnic cuisines such as French, Italian and Indian. Although there are a few surprises (e.g. when French cuisine collides with southern influences in Louisiana), most travellers will be able to cope. But there are a number of ethnic cuisines which are rarely found in Britain, yet which are ubiquitous throughout the States: principally Mexican and various Far Eastern cuisines (Chinese, Japanese, Korean and Vietnamese). You might also try a soul food restaurant which will probably feature ribs and cornbread, or an American Indian place serving Native American specialities such as sopapillas (deep-fried puff bread).

Tex-Mex. This term refers to the Americanization of Mexican food. Despite its name, it is not confined to Texas and can even be found in Alaska. Although often disparaged by gourmets for not being as fiery or as authentic as the original, it has the advantage of superior quality beef and pork, and has contributed some dishes of its own such as chilli con carne.

The basic menu of Tex-Mex is tortilla (made of maize), rice, refried beans (beans which have been boiled, mashed and fried with chillis) and various kinds of sauce made from chilli peppers. A tortilla is not a Spanish omelette but a round, flat unleavened bread, a little like a papadum, which takes many forms. Wrapped around meat or cheese, and oven baked, it becomes an *enchilada*. Fried, folded and filled with meat, cheese or salad, it becomes a *taco*. Toasted and broken up into squares or triangles, it becomes *tostados*, which are served either with a hot chilli sauce or with guacamole (mashed avocado, lemon and a hot green chilli sauce called *salsa verde*). This is enjoyed either as an hors d'oeuvre or as a snack to accompany beer or margaritas (see below). Nobody drinks wine with Tex-Mex food.

To this basic menu has been added stuffed sweet and hot peppers known as *chilli rellenos; fajitas,* steak skirts marinated and charcoal grilled; *carne asada fajitas* covered with a sauce of tomatoes, chillis, onions, chopped avocado and cilantro (coriander) leaves, all eaten within a tortilla.

Finally there is the *nacho;* the supreme Tex-Mex snack, which may be purchased at rodeos, baseball games, and other events. In essence, it's a *tostados,* topped with refried beans and cheese, popped into the oven until the cheese melts, and then crowned with a coin-shaped slice of chilli called a *jalapeno.*

If your budget allows it, start your Tex-Mex meal with a margarita, a delicious and potent cocktail made with two parts tequila (a Mexican liquor made of fermented cactus juice), one part fresh lime juice, a dash of triple sec or Cointreau, shaken over crushed ice, and served in a glass whose dampened rim has been impregnated with salt. Again, if your budget allows it, wash down Tex-Mex with Mexican beer.

Tex-Mex food with a more Mex than Tex flavour is good value and can be found at cafes and restaurants with a predominantly Mexican American clientele. There are many fast food chains offering Tex-Mex food, the most popular of which is called Taco Bell, though the quality of the food can't compete with small family-run Mexican restaurants.

Chinese. In Britain almost all Chinese restaurants are Cantonese. America is also dominated by Cantonese cuisine, but it is also easy to find Szechuan (Setch-*wahn*), Mandarin and even Hunan restaurants too. In Szechuan cuisine there is less reliance on glutinous sauces and more use of hot spices. Mandarin cooking (whether the Beijing or Shanghai varieties) uses a great deal of oil. You can tell an authentic Chinese restarant by the number of Chinese people eating there, the absence of an English menu and the appearance of the soup at any time apart from the beginning of the meal.

Many Chinese restaurants offer *Dim Sum,* a luncheon tradition in which trolleys of small pastry parcels are wheeled to your table and you choose as many as you like. These contain various exotic combinations of meat, vegetables and noodles. Your bill is calculated according to the number of empty dishes at your table. Dim Sum is usually served from 11 am to 3 pm, and is especially popular on Sundays.

Chop suey may sound oriental, but was in fact invented in New York in September 1896. Most oriental restaurants distribute chopsticks but will provide a knife and fork if specially requested. At the end of the meal each diner gets a "fortune cookie", an edible hollow biscuit containing a slip of paper claiming to tell your fortune but more often contains a piece of solid American philosophy such as "He who works hard prospers greatly."

Japanese. There is a strong Japanese influence even in the most American restaurants. Steak or chicken teriyaki have entered the reper- toire of American dishes. Whereas originally this meant that the meat had been marinated in soy sauce and rice wine prior to grilling, ususally it will merely have been basted with a sweet and sour barbecue sauce.

Eating out in an authentic Japanese restaurant is possibly the most foreign experience you will enjoy in the USA. The meal is served in a long series of courses in no apparent order: it seems to be simply the order in which the cook finishes each item. You will need to allow a full three hours, much of which will be spent drinking *sake* (hot rice wine) while you wait for the next plate of goodies to arrive.

The fish will arrive raw. Although this may sound disgusting, it is in fact rich, tender and tasty. You may also have a bowl of raw egg in which to dip *sukiyaki:* stir-fried beef, bamboo shoots, noodles and bean curd. *Tempura* are pieces of fish or vegetables deep fried briefly in batter. Do not expect pudding as the final course. You will get a bowl of boiled rice.

If a full-blown Japanese meal seems too much for you, try a snack of *sushi.* These are small rice-and-seaweed packages covered with fish, eggs or vegetables.

Korean. In culinary terms as well as geographically, Korea is halfway between China and Japan. There is one major difference in the restaurants; you have to go prepared to cook your own meal. Although dishes of elaborately sculpted vegetables and spicy sauces are ready made, the marinated meat arrives raw along with a small stove. Using chopsticks, you scatter the meat onto the stove and cook it to your satisfaction. If you plead ignorance, a waiter will come to your rescue.

Vietnamese. The food is a spicy approximation to Cantonese cooking, but with some French sophistication.

SUPERMARKETS

If your stomach is confused by such an array of cuisines, and your budget is stretched, one alternative is to buy your snacks from a supermarket. With so many good raw ingredients to choose from, it is easy to put together a cheap nutritious picnic. A visit to a supermarket could reward you with three large avocadoes for a dollar. Or, for $3 a pound, you can blend your own "Trail-Mix" from bins containing dried bananas, coconut, almonds and yoghurt-covered raisins. Make sure you are carrying a decent tin and bottle opener.

Because of the constant threat of legal action by dissatisfied customers and stringent enforcement by the United States Department of Agriculture (USDA), food is usually safe and of good quality. By British standards it is also cheap. Beef and chicken, fruit, salad vegetables and milk are particularly good value. Items usually sold only in health food shops in Britain can be found on supermarket shelves at lower prices. The cost of food depends on the size of the store (large supermarkets, especially those in suburban malls, are cheapest, corner shops most expensive) and on the origin of the produce. California is cheapest for fruit and vegetable, the Midwest cheapest for meat, everything is cheap in Texas and everything except salmon is expensive in Alaska.

Beware of beautiful-looking fruit which is tasteless. All supermarket fruit is of a uniform size and shape; like so much in North America, it won't be marketed if it doesn't conform. The Californians are busy developing the square tomato because it will pack better, and most people who have tried them say they taste nothing like the real thing. Even worse is the aim of poultry breeders. As one New England farmer boasting on the radio explained, "When they asked for more breast meat, we bred turkeys with meatier breasts, until they couldn't support the weight and began to fall on their faces. Then we bred them with bigger feet."

To find the best bargains, read the full page advertisements in local newspapers proclaiming the latest loss leaders (a term unknown in the USA). If you find that a store, whether grocery or otherwise, has sold out of a particular special offer, ask for a "rain check". This is a voucher which entitles you to buy at the offer price when new stocks arrive.

Another idea is to join a food co-op, especially popular on the West Coast. By volunteering your labour for a few hours, you can become a member of a co-operative, which sells produce very cheaply from a large number of outlets.

A growing trend is towards "generic" packaging. This means that packets and tins are unbranded, bearing only the name of the product plus the bar code and statutory information on additives, etc. Generic products are almost always cheapest, but don't let the low price put you off. Food and drink in generic packs often comes from the same factory as branded goods; savings made on packaging and advertising are passed on to the consumer. But branded food can be cheaper if you cut out the coupons from newspaper advertisements, offering 15c off a tin of beans or a bar of soap. Some stores operate "double coupon value" promotions, where your 15c coupon is worth 30c and so some products cost next to nothing.

Low-budget travellers in search of a hot meal should look out for supermarkets equipped with a microwave oven. If you buy a prepacked "TV dinner" or similar culinary atrocity, they will heat it up for you free of charge. As in Britain, takeaway food in some states is free of tax when cold, but taxed when above room temperature.

Free Deals. The bakery and/or delicatessen counters at most supermarkets offer various free morsels designed to tempt you into buying. You will, however, have to tour a great number of deli counters to find enough to constitute a square meal. A better bet is to buy one drink at a happy hour (see *Drinking*) and then munch your way through the free hors d'oeuvres.

Some food factories which offer free tours and samples are listed under each city. Elsewhere, ask at the local tourist information office whether there are any others nearby. If you happen to be in Hershey, Pennsylvaina, be sure to join a tour of Hershey's chocolate factory.

DRINKING

barkeep	bartender
blitzed	drunk
brown bagging	drinking illictly from a can or bottle concealed in a brown paper bag
BYO	bring your own (bottle)
chaser	long drink (usually beer) to follow a spirit; sometimes vice versa
cold duck	mixture of red and sparkling white wine (also a brand name for a wine made in Ontario)
excise laws	licensing laws
fifth	a bottle of spirits (i.e. a fifth of a US gallon)
float	ice cream drink

happy hour	half price drinking period, usually late afternoon and early evening
highball	whisky and soda or ginger ale
hooch	spirits
iced tea	cold tea with sugar and lemon
jag	prolonged drinking binge
loaded	drunk
malted (milk)	drink like a milkshake
Margarita	popular tequila cocktail (see eating: Tex-Mex)
Martini	**the** American drink: 3 parts gin, 1 part vermouth, served with an olive
Mint Julep	bourbon and mint cocktail associated with Southern planters
Old Fashioned	bourbon, bitters, sugar and fruit
regular coffee	white coffee (sometimes with sugar)
regular tea	tea without milk (often called clear or black tea)
root beer	soft drink
sarsaparilla	soft frink flavoured with the American plant of the same name
set-up	soda or soft drink for mixing with spirits
shot	measure of spirits (not standard but usually about equal to a UK double)
soda (pop)	carbonated soft drink
speakeasy	illegal drinking establishment, originally from Prohibition
straight/straight up	neat, no ice
suds	workingmen's slang for beer
tea	could mean "iced tea", especially in the South
to drink one's face off	to go on a drinking binge
to tie on a bag	„ „ „ „ „
Tom Collins	gin, lemon juice, soda and sugar
water cooler	drinking fountain found in most public buildings
white lightning	crude, powerful homemade whisky

Social drinking in the USA does not revolve around neighbourhood pubs as it does in Britain. In fact there *are* no neighbourhood pubs, since suburbia is almost entirely devoid of bars. Although in some small towns you can still find a bar which serves as the focus for the local community, this concept barely exists in cities. People tend to go to bars not for a quiet chat with friends, but for an expensive night out on the town when conversation is usually rendered impossible by the noisy crowds and the loud music (often live). The closest equivalent to a place for a quiet drink is the cocktail lounge, where business people and office workers stop for a drink on their way home.

Attitudes towards drunkenness also differ. Displaying the effects of drink is a social misdemeanour, and jolliness or rowdiness after a night on the town is regarded with disdain. Leaning heavily on the counter is sometimes enough to earn a reprimand from the bartender. If you don't sit up straight, he'll refuse to serve you, and the bouncer who checked your ID at the door won't hesitate to eject you. Once outside, if you stagger around drawing attention to yourself you'll be a prime target for both police and muggers. But despite all the problems, going drinking is still a good way to see a slice of life or to make friends.

Licensing Laws. The multifarious collection of legislation governing the sale and consumption of alcohol in America, called excise laws, makes Britain's licensing laws seem positively progressive. In some small towns in the Bible Belt, Prohibition has never ended. Getting a drink in Utah requires advance planning and military precision. State drinking laws can be modified by municipal legislation, and frequently are. Alcohol is often banned completely from Indian reservations. The result is a maze of anomalies prescribing what strength of liquor may be sold to whom between which times. The only way to find out is to enquire locally.

As a general rule, bars open at some time between 9 am and noon and close between midnight and 3 am. Sunday opening, if permitted, is for shorter hours. The drinking age is 21 virtually everywhere in the USA, as a result of pressure from the lobby against drunk driving. Age limits are very strictly enforced by both the management and the police. Always carry your passport or other ID showing your date of birth; even if you are obviously over 21, you will probably be required to prove your age. There is a considerable trade in unofficial identification cards. You can buy ID over-the-counter at print shops, and the assistant will print whatever you require: a false age, an address in the USA, a false social security number, etc. Note, however, that young people who use these to buy alcohol are guilty of fraud as well as under-age drinking.

Container Laws. These cover the heinous crime of drinking in a public place, an offence almost everywhere in the USA. The laws are not taken terribly seriously. Most Americans — including picknicking families as well as alcoholics — circumvent the law by drinking from a bottle or can concealed in a brown paper bag.

Off-Licences. Every state — except New Hampshire — imposes duty on alcohol in addition to sales tax. The rate varies roughly in proportion to the historical influence of the local temperance movement, and is heavier on spirits than beer or wine. Mormon-dominated Utah has the highest prices, but even these are low by British standards.

It is much cheaper to buy liquor from shops than to drink in a bar or restaurant. Beer comes in two standard sizes: 12 fl oz and 16 fl oz. Bottles and cans are sold individually or in packs of six. If you are able to shop around, you should find six-packs for $2-$3.

Many states have "bottle laws" offering a 5c or 10c deposit on returned beer or soft drink bottles or cans (but not usually wine, spirit or fruit juice bottles). The deposit will be added at the check-out in addition to the advertised price. You may get a few pennies for returning aluminium cans, and indeed many down-and-outs scrape a living by collecting them.

The standard size for wines and spirits is 750ml (1⅓ pints), known in common parlance as a "fifth", i.e. a fifth of a US gallon. Cheap foreign wine costs upwards of $2.50 per bottle; Californian and other American wine is more expensive. Bourbon starts at around $7 per bottle.

In a few states, you can buy any kind of alcohol at any time of the day or night. In others, beer and wine can be sold at any time while the sale of spirits is restricted to certain stores at certain times. Many states have a monopoly on the sale of liquor: it can only be bought from official State Liquor Stores within restricted opening hours and at standard prices. It is therefore pointless to shop around. There are some counties (particularly in Texas and Utah) where the sale of alcohol is totally prohibited. In West Virginia, drinks are sold only to members in private clubs; however temporary membership is exceedingly easy to obtain.

The minimum drinking age applies to purchases of alcohol. If there's any doubt about your age, shops are supposed to ask for your ID. In practice, supermarkets rarely bother. But if a supermarket check-out girl is under age, she will ask an elder colleague (or you) to ring up the price of, say, a six-pack of beer. Otherwise she would technically be in breach of the law by selling you alcohol. (If you consider this to be yet another bizarre American custom you should know that the same practice has been known to happen in Tesco).

Bars. The stereotype of an American bar is not hard to find; look for a plastic-upholstered shell deserted except for a solitary drunk, a pair of desultory pool players and an adulterous couple conspiring in a darkened corner. It will probably have pictures of nude women and baseball stars as decoration. Single women will feel distinctly uncomfortable in such a place. The wild west saloon, with sawdust on the floor and only bourbon behind the bar, has died out more or less completely. The cocktail lounge has established itself as the primary venue for self-respecting drinkers, especially in big cities. Cocktail lounges approximate to British wine bars in style and clientele, but with a little more sophistication: for instance you may find your drink chilled with frozen grapes rather than ice cubes. You are waited upon at your table, and pay after each round or upon leaving. Either way, you'll be expected to leave some change in the waiter's saucer. Singles bars are a special case of cocktail bars. Customers willingly pay high prices for the privilege of eyeing up one another in the hope of finding the perfect partner. Even if you have no intention of doing likewise, the behaviour in singles bars provides an excellent spectator sport.

Many bars double as places to hear music or dance or both. Depending on the quality of the music, an admission fee or cover charge will be levied. Alternatively the price of drinks will be weighted.

Happy Hours. To drink on a low budget, choose a happy hour every time. The first thing to realize is that happy hours are rarely as short as 60 minutes. Most stretch for two hours or more in the late afternoon and early evening. If you see a sign saying "Happy Hour Forever", it probably refers to cheap drinks all night rather than in perpetuity.

The simplest form of happy hour is where all drinks are half price. Other variations include "All Drinks 99c", "Half Price Draft Beer During Football Game" or "Two Highballs for the price of one." There is nothing to prevent you piling up a supply of drinks at happy hour prices as long as you pay upon serving to avoid disputes when settling up.

An added bonus of many happy hours is the range of free food on offer. The more up-market establishments (where you might never be able to afford drinks outside happy hours) often provide free hors d'oeuvres such as guacamole dip or cheese and biscuits. With a little determination and a thick skin it is possible to wolf down a complete meal while you linger over a solitary cocktail.

Free Drinks. Some clubs and bars offer free drinks all evening to single females. They are not necessarily the sorts of places that your mother would like you to visit. Others with music have ladies' nights when women are excused the cover charge but still pay for their drinks. Otherwise, tours of breweries, wineries and distilleries are invariably followed by free tastings. The South is best for distilleries; the Midwest for breweries; and Northern California for wineries. Addresses are given under the regional sections.

Beer. Almost all beer sold in the USA is pasteurized, pressurized lager brewed from maize or even rice, rather than from barley; it is invariably served ice cold. America, like other countries, has beer snobs. The best-regarded beers are Canadian (Molson), Mexican (XX, pronounced Dos Equis) and Filipino (San Miguel), rather than the standard American varieties like Budweiser, the best seller, and Michelob. Naturally the foreign brews are more expensive.

Canned and bottled British beers are available at the more up-market establishments, but cost the earth. Drinking Guinness is considered chic.

There is a relatively new trend for "boutique breweries" to start up brewing beers with some character; usually these are not marketed outside their immediate area. Try, for example New Amsterdam Bitter in Manhattan, Cartwright beer in Oregon and New Albion ale in California. In bars and restaurants, beer is sold by the glass, can or bottle in measures of 12 fl oz, costing $1.50 or more. Many establishments also sell pitchers. These are jugs filled with a quart or half-gallon (32 or 64 fl oz) of draught beer. They provide considerable savings on buying by the glass, with prices starting as low as $4 for a half-gallon jug. Whereas the cost of drinking in a pub in Britain is not much more than buying beer at an off licence, the difference is much greater in the US. As a result, a great deal more beer drinking goes on in private homes in America than in Britain.

It is not considered normal to add lime or lemonade to beer in America. However, some people attempt to pep up Budweiser by adding tomato juice: ask for a "Bud and blood", which is not nearly so disgusting as it sounds. A variation on beer is malt liquor, which is simply canned beer without the hops. As a result it tastes sweet and insipid. The leading brands are Colt 45 and Schlitz. Another variation, brought about by the quaint licensing legislation in some states, is "three-two beer" of 3.2% alcohol, about the same as Watneys special bitter but weaker than most other American beers.

Wine. House wine in restaurants and cocktail bars is usually Italian plonk. A half litre carafe in a typical restaurant might cost $3. Californian wine is highly regarded in the USA and can be extremely good. But it usually isn't as cheap as one might have expected. Decent Italian and Chilean table wines are often cheaper. Look for wine as cheap as $3 a bottle in off-licences. Californian rose or "blush" wines are popular and reliable, and the cabernets (red) and rieslings (white) are occasionally outstanding. Cheap blended Californian wines known as jug wines are a real bargain, for example $5 for a magnum of Gallo red wine. Christian Brothers, Inglenook and Paul Masson (familiar to all Sainsbury's shoppers) are most reliable brands. Some wine is produced in other parts of the US, notably the Finger Lakes regions of upstate New York and the excellent soil of Idaho and Washington State. There is an increasing number of cottage wineries producing more varied vintages.

At cocktail bars, a favourite tipple among the diet-conscious is white wine and Perrier. An undiluted glass of wine in a cocktail bar costs at least $2 outside happy hours. Sangria, a mixture of cheap red wine and fruit juices, has been somewhat superseded by "coolers", blends of rough white wine, juices and sugar. Beware of the effect of coolers (particularly if you plan to drive) and note that the sugar and flavourings added to the poor quality of the wine can lead to an almighty hangover.

Spirits. A fair shot of neat spirit (approximating to a double English measure) costs at least $2. The most popular is bourbon, a whisky distilled from maize, which originated in Bourbon County, Kentucky. Jim Beam and Jack Daniels are the superior brands. Rye whisky, such as Canadian Club and Seagrams 7, tastes rather like a dubious blend of Scotch. Try mixing it with Seven-up; ask for a "7 and 7". The genuine article, like Johnny Walker Black Label, can be twice as expensive. Vodka is gaining popularity; American-made Smirnoff is cheaper but weaker than the imported Polish and Russian varieties. Spirits are rarely drunk neat ("straight up"). Usually they are served "on the rocks" or they form the basis for mixed drinks. The term "cocktail" originated in Louisiana as a corruption of *coquetier,* meaning egg-cup and is now used as a term for any drink containing a spirit and mixer.

The first cocktail was probably the mint julep, made from bourbon, fresh mint and sugar. Mixing drinks became necessary during Prohibition to diguise the disgusting taste of illegal hooch. The term "highball" is used to describe simple drinks such as whisky and soda, gin and tonic or rum and coke. Short stiff drinks include Martinis (vermouth — not necessarily Martini — swamped by gin), Manhattans (vermouth and bourbon) and Black Russians (vodka and Tia Maria). The Tequila Sunrise uses orange juice and grenadine to make a longer, less potent drink; beware of the salt which is applied liberally to the rim of the glass. The ever-popular Margarita also relies on tequila. The Daiquiri is simply white rum and lime, but often comes with crushed banana or strawberries as well. Every cocktail comes with lashings of ice unless you specify otherwise, plus assorted miniature umbrellas, cherries and so on. Before you order make sure that your drink will be freshly made. Some bars sell only pre-mixed cocktails straight from the can. On average a cocktail will cost $3.

However you take your poison, you should remember that American spirits are generally stronger than in Britain: 80° or 90° proof rather than 70°. And since they are poured by hand, you could seriously underestimate the rate at which you are drinking. You might want to adopt the practice favoured by many serious drinkers in the USA of drinking a chaser (a long drink, usually beer) after each shot.

Soft Drinks. There is no stigma attached to abstaining from alcohol and drivers are socially and legally encouraged to drink in moderation or not at all. There are plenty of non-alcoholic drinks to choose from. Still or sparkling mineral water (usually imported) is sold for about the same price as beer. Bear in mind that in a blind tasting of mineral water, New York tap water was the outright winner among still waters; in the sparkling category, ordinary soda water easily beat some of the top name European mineral waters.

Seven-Up, Sprite, Coke, Pepsi and root beer (a vaguely medicinal-tasting fizzy drink devoid of alcohol) and many other varieties are collectively known as "soda pop" or "soda". They cost about 50c for a 12 fl oz can from vending machines located at every garage, bus station and motel. Soda is the strongest drink you can hope to find at most diners and fast food outlets. It is served in regular (large) or large (enormous) paper cups, along with a small glacier's worth of ice. As a reaction to the health fad of low calorie, low caffeine soft drinks, the trendiest cola at present is Jolt, which advertises itself as having "all the sugar, twice the caffeine". If you are at all concerned about your health, choose instead a freshly-squeezed fruit juice or a non-alcoholic cocktail.

You should try to pay at least one visit to a soda fountain, a veritable soft drinks emporium. For a dollar or two you can sample a fizzy chocolate and ice cream milk shake (malt). At least it contains real milk: most of the synthetic slush sold as shakes by fast food chains has never been near a cow.

Coffee. American coffee is almost always filtered or percolated from fresh beans and is generally excellent. The "bottomless cup" — where you can get endless free refills — is standard practice. Coffee is either "with" or "without cream"; the term "white" is not used. Coffee is also either "regular" or "Sanka", a brand-name for decaffeinated coffee. The price of a bottomless cup starts at 50c.

Tea. In *The Tea Lover's Treasury,* James Norwood Pratt suggests that the Boston Tea Party episode has given the American people "a prenatal disinclination for tea." The American idea of what constitutes a cup of tea is usually insipid and fairly disgusting. You are given a cup of hot water and a tea bag and left to get on with it. Milk or lemon may be supplied if you're lucky. Tea costs 50c upwards, but you only get one cup.

If you ask for tea in the southern states, you'll get iced tea unless you specify the hot version. Iced tea can be a deliciously cooling brew of double strength tea poured over ice cubes, lemon and sugar. Unfortunately, it is sometimes made from powder or served straight from the can, when it bears little relation to the genuine article.

barracker	sports fan
bunco game	crooked card game
cotton candy	candy floss
couch potato	television addict
craps	popular gambling game with dice
creamed	soundly beaten
exacta	racing forecast
Ferris wheel	big wheel at a fun fair
field hockey	hockey; by "hockey" Americans mean ice hockey
first balcony	upper circle in a theatre
hands-on (display/ museum)	participatory, practical involvement, "user-friendly"
high roller	big spending gambler
hootenany	jamboree, rave-up, often implying a square dance
jock	keen athlete
loge	front of the dress circle at the theatre
mezzanine	dress circle in a theatre or cinema
movie theater	cinema
place (vb)	to come second in a horse race
orchestra	front stalls in a theater
road team	away team
scalper	ticket tout
show (vb)	to come third in a horse race
stock company	repertory theatre company
summer stock	repertory company which works in resort areas during the summer
taxi dancer	a girl who dances with customers at a dance hall, for a price
theme parks	American-style amusement parks
Tony Awards	Broadway theatre awards named after Antoinette Perry
twofers	two-for-the-price-of-one theatre tickets

With so much disposable income, Americans spend a lot of time going out and in the process support a massive entertainment industry. Whether your tastes are for Baroque chamber music or naked female mud wrestling, there is much to take in. Of course the big cities have most to offer, but smaller communities also have ways of satisfying Americans' deeply felt need for a good time.

Tickets. You can buy a ticket for almost any musical, theatrical or sporting event anywhere in the country from any branch of Ticketron. This is a national chain of ticket agencies linked by computer, often located in Sears stores. Because the promoters get so much business through Ticketron you are unlikely to have to pay a surcharge as is normally the case with British ticket agencies. Ticketron are also worth trying for cut-price tickets for local events on the day of performance. Most large cities now have booths selling half-price theatre tickets on the day; details are given in each regional chapter, but in general the booth is located in the theatre district.

The terminology for the location of seats in auditoria may be confusing: the "orchestra" equates to the front stalls in a British theatre, while Americans describe the dress circle as the mezzanine.

MUSIC

Serious Music. When rich Americans hear the word "culture" they reach for their wallets. It is not over-cynical to suggest that the reason why serious music, ballet and opera are so well patronized is because of the desire to impress. For instance Cleveland (not generally noted for its sophistication and class) boasts an orchestra of world-renown. This pattern is repeated in cities throughout the USA, and in all the arts. Whatever the motives for such bulk-purchase of culture and prestige, serious music lovers should take advantage of prices subsidized by local wealth and patronage. Tickets are by no means cheap — up to $30 for a concert, $50 for an opera or ballet — but represent a bargain in view of the costs of staging these extravaganzas.

Most of the top orchestras—such as the Boston Symphony, the Chicago Symphony, the Los Angeles Philharmonic, the New York Philharmonic and the Philadelphia Orchestra—have a winter season at their main downtown concert hall and a summer season in a more informal setting such as a park or pavilion.

Popular Music. Whatever your taste in pop music, you will find something to object to in America. The birthplace of jazz, the blues and rock and roll also produced the Muzak Company, purveyor of anonymous background music to be played in lifts, restaurants and supermarkets. There are more radio stations than in any other country and yet most of them limit themselves to repeating identical playlists of the top forty 24 hours a day.

Although there has always been a strong overlap between the British and American charts, the last fifteen years have revealed a major difference in national tastes. The mainstream of American music has been dominated by AOR — "Adult Oriented Rock" — smooth, clean and highly produced. The best selling albums over the last ten years have been produced by mature musicians such as Dire Straits and Michael Jackson, who perform very professional, uncontroversial music. In defence of this music, it does sound rather more acceptable when played loud in an open convertible driving down the freeway on a sunny morning than it does when heard in a bedsitter on a rainy afternoon in Barnsley. The most lively American music at present seems to be "new Country", with musicians such as Dwight Yoakam, K. D. Lang and Nanci Griffith putting a sharper edge on a style which has been widely ridiculed for many years.

British trends such as punk rock were hardly noticed in America outside certain trendy Anglophile quarters. Only "safe" bands such as the Police, who were introduced in Britain as part of the "new wave" bandwagon, made much impression on the US charts. But, in recent years, British music has begun once again to influence American music. This new trend is largely due to the advent of MTV, the 24-hour cable channel showing undiluted rock videos, which found that the quality of the professional videos produced by young British artists was far superior to those produced by native performers.

Outside the world of the top forty the American musical world is far more healthy. Those with a particular taste in, say, country and western or jazz-rock should be able to find radio stations, record shops and clubs to cater for their needs; America's vast population means that "minority interest" groups form a viable market. The regional chapters of this book advise you on local musical specialities: even more detail can be found in *"Honky Tonkin'* — *A Travel Guide to American Music"* (Travelaid Publications).

Nostalgia buffs stand a better chance of seeing vintage bands such as the Grateful Dead or Crosby and Nash, or Crosby, Stills and Nash, or even (in a good year) Crosby, Stills, Nash and Young in America than back home. There are even some British bands such as Jethro Tull and the Kinks who are now more popular in America than in their native land, and correspondingly spend more time touring there. Keep your eyes open, and you will find something to your taste.

Opera. The leading opera companies perform in San Francisco, New York (both the Met and the City Opera), Seattle, Chicago, Boston and (unexpectedly) Santa Fe. There are sometimes substantial reductions for students or for people willing to accept standing room.

Dance. As in many things, New York leads the US in dance with several excellent companies including the renowned New York City Ballet. The National Ballet performs in Washington DC, and there are also very good companies in Pittsburg, Philadelphia and San Franciso. The two most important touring companies are the American Ballet Theatre and the Martha Graham Dance Company.

THEATRE

Mainstream drama is confined to the 37 theatres of Manhattan's Broadway (the "Great White Way") plus conventional theatres in most large cities. The latter often survive on a diet of touring companies from Broadway, or provide a testing ground for new plays before they move to New York. Many Broadway plays originate in Britain: at the time of going to press, five shows were playing simultaneously in both London and New York.

If you are interested in more experimental theatre, you might prefer to visit an "Equity-waiver theatre". These are theatres with 99 seats or less, so-called because they do not need to pay union rates. Therefore they can afford to stage experimental material. The best examples are the "off-Broadway" or "off-off-Broadway" theatres in New York. Because of their small size, "Equity-waiver" theatres are chronically short of money. Even after buying your ticket you'll be asked for extra donations before, after and even during the show.

Theatrical life outside the big cities and university campuses includes Shakespearean festivals in unlikely and out-of-the-way small towns (several of which are called Stratford). These can be most entertaining, if only for the specactacle of a Hamlet with a rich English accent playing against minor characters with southern drawls. Many stock companies play in repertory theatres located in summer resort areas. Although they tend to confine themselves to lightweight farces, the quality of the productions can be high.

Tickets for Broadway-standard shows are expensive; $50 for a reasonable seat is not unusual. They can be booked through Ticketron or by phoning the theatre box office direct and paying by credit card, or even by going along in person. For less popular productions, just go along to the local half-price tickets booth where unsold seats are sold off on the day of performance.

CINEMA

Watching television has not quite replaced going to the movies and box office receipts are graudally increasing after three decades of decline. Cinemas fall into three categories: "first-run", found mostly in New York and Los Angeles, which premiere films; "second-run", which approximate to local cinemas in Britain and show films on general release; and "re-run" cinemas, which specialize in showing old classics. Advance booking is necessary only for first-run cinemas, which charge $6-$10 a seat. These tickets can be bought through Ticketron agencies. Second-run cinemas cost between $3 and $5. You shouldn't pay more than $3 at a re-run cinema, except for all-night sessions, and some cinemas charge only 99c.

Drive-ins. Ever since they were invented in Camden New Jersey in 1932, the huge screens of drive-in cinemas have towered above small town America. You simply pay at the gate, drive into a parking place, clip a tinny loudspeaker to your car window and watch the movie. They rarely show new releases, nor seldom old classics. It seems that adolescent culture in some small towns has not progressed at all since the 1950s. Sadly, videos have undermined the popularity of drive-ins, and many now stand abandoned as reminders of the lost innocence of youth.

TELEVISION

All the stories you have heard about American television are true. There are countless stations, programmes (even live sport shows) are interrupted every few minutes for a batch of commercials, and most children spend longer in front of the box than at school. The average adult watches 28 hours a week. Wherever you are and whatever the time you can be certain of a choice of viewing. Even the crummiest hotel or motel will boast a TV in every room, albeit with numerous dead flies attached to the screen. Airports and bus stations have coin operated televisions built into arms of the chairs.

Having seen a few programmes you may find it hard to comprehend the addiction. British television takes only the "best" American entertainment, what remains is even more excessive than *Dallas, Dynasty* or the *Dukes of Hazzard.* Quiz shows are inordinately popular, often with prizes of up to $100,000. Most of the questions concern other television programmes. Although news broadcasts and documentaries have occasional flashes of brilliance, serious political analysis is usually sacrificed to the cause of sensationalism. Pictures of violent death are shown in gory detail, then re-run forwards, backwards and in slow motion. Michael Caine once said he could find out more of actual importance in ten minutes of listening to the BBC World Service than from watching three and a half hours of local TV in California.

Reception. Programmes are mostly so ghastly that the poor reception experienced in many ares can be something of a blessing. Snowy pictures and fuzzy sound are the rule rather than the exception. Even when reception conditions are perfect — close to transmitters or where cables are wired in — the image is far from perfect. The USA has had colour television since 1952 and uses a relatively primitive transmission system. There are only 525 lines on the screen, as opposed to the more usual 625.

Operation. There are no televisions with simple push-button selectors as found in Britain. Older sets have rotary dials, often showing numbers which bear no relation to numbers of each channel: Channel 3 might appear at "42" on the dial. More modern TVs have remote control handsets with which you can select a channel with repeated button-pushing. The station you have selected is displayed in red digits next to the screen. But again, there is not necessarily any correlation between the number shown and the channel of the station as quoted in newspapers or in the *TV Guide* (a combined *Radio Times/TV Times*). If you seriously want to watch a particular programme, accost a friendly local to help tune in.

Networks. Most of the stations which transmit programmes belong to one of the three national networks: ABC, CBS and NBC. The competition between them is intense. Programme ratings are compiled overnight and series terminated abruptly the next morning should they make a poor showing. Heavy self-censorship is practised to avoid outraging vocal minorities: even the mildest swearwords are wiped from the soundtrack of late night movies, and anything resembling a sex scene is cut before transmission. The contents of films are listed in graphic detail in newspapers: *The Postman Always Rings Twice* is described as containing "Adult Language —Adult Situations — Brief Nudity — Violence."

This search for mass audiences drags programmes quality down to the lowest common denominator. The result is a diet of dehumanizing game shows and soap operas so dire as to make *Neighbours* seem intellectual. Should you become addicted to one of these gripping sagas, don't despair if you miss an episode. Several "dial-a-storyline" numbers will give you an instant 60-second update on the latest goings on. And if you want to see a game show being recorded, head for Hollywood where they give out free tickets in the streets.

Public Broadcasting. An antidote to the overwhelmingly tasteless networks is provided by the many regional stations that make up the Public Broadcasting Service (PBS). They show documentaries, discussion pro-grammes and high quality foreign drama. Instead of interrupting the programmes with advertising, PBS stations spend a great deal of air time appealing for donations and displaying messages of gratitude to their commercial sponsors.

Cable. In all but the most rural areas, cable TV offers a supplementary repertoire of 24-hour TV programming. In the large cities, it is not uncommon to find 50 or more channels in addition to the regular network and PBS stations.

To receive these additional channels, viewers pay a monthly subscription fee to the local cable company. These fees reduce the need for advertising, which is part of the attraction of cable TV. Some channels, particularly the movie channels, require an additional monthly charge from the viewer.

There are few restrictions on what may be shown on cable TV. You may watch evangelism or pornography; local council meetings or heavy rock. The range of channels available will depend upon the local cable company and the nature of the franchise agreement it has with the municipality. Many of the channels are transmitted by satellite and are available across the country. They include the movie channels Cinemax, Home Box Office (HBO) and Home Theatre Network (HTN); a Disney channel and a Playboy channel; MTV (rock videos); Country Music Television and the Nashville Network; Cable News Network (CNN); and the sports channel, ESPN. which sometimes shows British soccer matches.

Satellite TV. The USA and Canada are served by about 20 TV satellites, each with a capacity to transmit up to 24 channels. Most transmissions from the satellite are for the exclusive use of local cable TV companies, which act as the middlemen, passing the satellite signal, through a cable network, to individual subscribers. The contracts between the satellite owners, programmers and local cable TV companies are exclusive, so direct reception of the satellite signals is illegal. Nevertheless a growing number of Americans are tuning in with their own back yard "dish" antennae realizing that ownership of a dish is legal and that it is virtually impossible to enforce a law that attempts to control the way you convert the satellite signal after it has entered your home. Since the direct satellite TV viewing audience includes many electronics buffs, the satellite owners' expensive attempts to scramble their signals have invariably failed, since the plans for descramblers are soon in circulation.

RADIO

Many travellers find American radio a better source of entertainment and information than television. There are 50,000 radio stations in the USA, so you should find something to your liking. As long as you don't anticipate serious programmes of the kind found on BBC Radio 4, you won't be disappointed. If you have access to a short wave radio, you might want to tune into the BBC World Service on the 49 metre band; alternatively, over 300 stations carry BBC World Service news. In big cities you can find any kind of music at the turn of the dial: MOR (middle of the road), AOR (adult oriented rock — mostly album music), Urban Contemporary (black music); top forty hits, golden oldies, country and western, jazz, gospel, reggae and classical music. The speech content is equally diverse, from the latest West Indies cricket score or Dow Jones Index to ferocious fundamentalist sermons.

The choice of station thins out considerably as you move away from large cities. In vast tracts of Texas and the Midwest you'll find only two or three stations, whose entire output seems devoted to country and western music plus the odd farming programme. Technically, stations range from hi-tech automated affairs (where everthing is on tape and the engineer monitors the output on a transistor radio at the local bar) to shoestring stations run by a man, dog and a pile of records. If you want to look around a station, just phone up and ask. Most stations will be delighted by your interest and may even put you on the air.

Radio stations are classified as AM or FM depending upon the mode of propagation. These correspond to medium wave and VHF respectively. Some stations broadcast simultaneously on both wavebands, but most use only one. Frequencies are quoted in kHz (AM) or MHz (FM). With a few exceptions, each radio station is identified by a four letter code; for stations east of Mississippi, the first letter is W; in the west, it is K.

FM. Most FM broadcasts are high-quality stereo. Historically, the lower end of the FM dial (below 92 FM) was reserved for non-profit stations, mostly student stations, offering classical music and intellectual discussions. Although this is no longer strictly true it is still a fairly accurate guide. The speech content on these stations is largely community information; meetings, lost cats, ride-sharing etc.

AM. Sound quality is worse on AM, but the signals travel much further. Although there are no real national radio networks in the USA, several stations cover the eastern half of the country on AM. You are most likely to find news and top forty stations on AM: the phrase "AM Rock" is widely used to describe modern commercial pop music.

NEWSPAPERS

Once again the USA has earned another superlative, with more daily newspapers (1600) than any other country. The biggest seller is *USA Today* which is put together in Virginia and transmitted by satellite to printing plants all over the USA. It tends to be bland — some Americans refer to it as *McPaper*, the journalistic equivalent of junk food — but nonetheless it sells 5.3 million copies daily. The only other truly national newspapers are the *Wall Street Journal* and the *Christian Science Monitor.* Other newspapers are either regional (e.g. the *Los Angeles Times*, serving the Southwest) or local (e.g. the *Santa Barbara News-Press*, serving a small patch of the Pacific coast). Although it is possible to buy the *New York Times* in Los Angeles or vice-versa, most Americans stick to their local regional paper. Most rely heavily on syndicated features, so you can read the same article in Washington then a week later in Chicago.

Most newspapers are broadsheets — the same size as the *Independent* or *Guardian* — and approximate in style, if not in breadth of coverage, to British "quality" papers. Tabloids are confined to large cities and place more emphasis on sport and sensationalism than serious news.

Papers cost 25c-50c. Sunday editions cost twice or three times as much but are truly enormous, containing a dozen or more sections. They are often on sale on Saturdays. There are no newsagents as are familiar in Britain; the few Americans who don't get a daily paper delivered buy them from vending machines at downtown street corners and shopping malls. You put in coins to the required amount, whereupon the door opens. You are trusted to take only one copy and to close the door firmly afterwards.

Being highly localized, most newspapers are good at information about what's on. Many cities also have weekly listings magazines which are more detailed: these are described in each *Entertainment* section.

Foreign newspapers can be found at specialist news kiosks in city centres. They are usually expensive and out of date: if you have an insatiable craving for the *Times*, expect to pay $3 for a two-day-old copy. The cheapest and most up-to-date British newspaper is the *Financial Times*, printed locally and costing $1. For a free read, try larger libraries or the reading room of the British Consulate, though these will be even more outdated.

MUSEUMS AND GALLERIES

The enormous budgets of many American art galleries guarantees a wealth of visual art. Whereas it is not so suprising to find collections at the National Gallery in Washington or the Metropolitan Museum of Art in New York which are equal to the National Gallery in London or the Hermitage in Leningrad, you would not expect to find art galleries in Buffalo or Malibu. Again it is a case of abundant financial resources compensating for an arguable absence of cultivation and refinement in the average citizen. Because of their large endowments, many museums are free; others post a suggested donation which you are at liberty to ignore if you have the nerve.

In addition to museums of art and sculpture, there are many eccentric collections, often located in out-of-the-way places, for example the Museum of Fire Engines in New York City or the Balzekas Museum of Lithuanian Culture in Chicago.

America specializes in museums of science and technology. Whereas Europeans excel at preserving and restoring their past. Americans are more future-oriented. Even people with no scientific background or interest find these displays fascinating. Many of them are "hands-on" museums which invite visitor participation.

RECREATION

At times you will be tempted to think that America is a nation of joggers. Track suit and running shoe manufacturers have made a killing (not to mention osteopaths and physiotherapists). On the whole Americans are sporty: they ski, sail, waterski and canoe as a matter of course. Most children are exposed to outdoor recreations at summer camp or at their family's holiday home (called a "cottage"). Although there are many spectacular hiking trails, usually in mountainous areas or parklands, there is no tradition as there is in Britain of simply going for a weekend walk in the country, partly because of the supremacy of the motorcar, and partly because there are very few pedestrian rights of way in rural areas.

There are also many less energetic recreations favoured by Americans. Mini-golf courses and bowling alleys proliferate and are a good place to see American families at play. Golf is a more proletarian sport in American than in Britain, and there are many public golf courses where it is possible to hire clubs and play a round of golf for a modest fee. In prosperous America, it is not surprising to find a high density of swimming pools, skating rinks and tennis courts, which are either free or nearly free. Pool halls provide a less wholesome alternative; take care not to "foul on the eight-ball" (ask the locals for an explanation).

Every affluent American seems to have a hot tub (large pool which holds up to half a dozen bathers) or a jacuzzi with the additional feature of swirling water. if you don't happen to be invited to share a private one, you can rent one for a few dollars at the more legitimate massage parlours or at a jacuzzi joint in city centres.

SPORT

Perhaps the most popular way to be idle in the US is to watch sports either on television or live. Try to see a big league game if at all possible. Even if you don't understand all the rules and strategies, the antics of both players and fans provide ample entertainment. Furthermore, despite the frenzy generated by cheerleaders, music and instant video replays, there is virtually none of the hooliganism (except on the field) that taints some spectator sports in Britain.

Ball Games. The major American spectator sports have few practitioners elsewhere. This is historically because America has had no empire to adopt its pastimes (as Britain has introduced cricket and rugby to its former colonies). To gain a thorough understanding of each sport would require a degree course in the subject, but a brief sketch of each game may help.

Baseball is like rounders, only the ball is harder (so players wear large gloves). After three fair throws by the pitcher a batter is out. But if he hits the ball, he runs to the first of four bases, and further if he feels he can getaway with it without being run out. The equivalent of hitting a six at cricket is a home run. Each of the nine innings ends when a team has three "outs" (i.e. loses three wickets in cricketing terms). If there is a tie, they go into extra innings. The major leagues are the American and the National, each divided into East and West divisions. The baseball season starts slowly in April and climaxes with the World Series in October.

American football is understandably called "football"; to refer to it as American is as strange as talking of "British cricket". The aim is to cross the opponents' base line with the ball, a slow process achieved by a series of plays in ten yard stages. Like rugby, the players use hands, feet and shoulders to move the oval ball — and the other team — around. College football culminating in such famous New Year events as the Rose Bowl in Pasadena and the Orange Bowl in Miami, is followed almost as avidly as professional football, whose season can last from August to December. Ice hockey can also be a vicious game, but the Canadians are the best exponents: see *Canada—Sport.*

Basketball is played from September to March. Although the aims and rules of the game are fairly straightforward, the degree of skill displayed by players is phenomenal. Try to see a major league game.

Many Americans consider soccer to be an inferior import, although this attitude may change as the USA is to host the 1994 World Cup. The Americans have done appalling things to the game in the name of entertainment — instant large screen replays, emasculating the offside rule, etc — and purists should certainly avoid the bastardized indoor game. The American Soccer League has Northern and Southern divisions, with five teams in each, and the season runs from November to May. Most league players are foreign, particularly British and Cuban.

Motorsport. As you might expect from a nation where the car is king, motor and motorcycle racing are taken to the ultimate in the USA. Major events are held from spring to autumn. At Easter, half the motorcyclists in America congregate in Florida for the Daytona Beach speedway events, a long weekend of beer and bike racing. Non-enthusiasts might prefer to be elsewhere, since the reputation of the spectators is considerably worse than that of English football fans.

Little trouble surrounds the Indianapolis 500, which is held at the end of May each year, and provides a great spectacle. The 300,000 people who attend make this the biggest single spectator event in the world and pay $10 million at the turnstiles. The race itself lasts three hours, with the winner averaging nearly 170 mph.

The Indy 500 is but one in the 12 or 13 race Indy Series for big-engined single seater cars. About half the races, which are held around the country, are on tailor-made tracks and the remainder are on street circuits. For times and locations of the big events, consult the racing calendars published in the New York editions of *Motor Sport* magazine. The Detroit Grand Prix for Formula One cars was due to move to a new circuit from 1989, replacing the former race around bumpy city streets, but at the time of writing this world championship event had been cancelled and future races seemed uncertain. Be warned that accommodation becomes very scarce during race meetings in cities like Indianapolis which are quiet industrial backwaters for much of the year. You need to book up early (and pay four times the going rate), or be prepared to sleep rough along with many other less wealthy racegoers.

For spectacle, the highly professional M.A.S.C.A.R. series for stock cars should not be missed. In America, "stock car" means a highly developed but production line based vehicle — not an old banger — and America's top drivers participate in the series. Demolition Derby and drag racing events are less well patronized. Events are advertised on fly posters and in the local press, and for a few dollars you can see screaming hulks of metal reach 60 mph in the blink of an eye, or knock bits off each other.

Horse Racing. The sport of kings is largely restricted to the flat in the USA, though there is some jumping. Off-track betting is legal in only three states — Connecticut, New York and Nevada. Like high class greyhound tracks, the courses are normally surrounded with glass-enclosed grandstands. Racing takes place on most days of the week, usually from noon to 6 pm. On race days local newspapers often carry advertisements attracting customers with the lure of a free drink or snack. For a complete list of events and a guide to form, try the *Racing Form,* the American equivalent to *The Sporting Life,* or contact the Thoroughbred Racing Association (3000 Marcus Avenue, Lake Success, New York 10040).

Admission is cheap: around $5 entitles you to a seat if one is available, and an extra couple of dollars will reserve you a seat. If you get a seat and wish to move around, the accepted custom is to place a sheet of newspaper on the seat to reserve it. If you book a meal you automatically get a seat facing the track, and can place bets and receive winnings without moving. Those without seating are consigned to the "standees' enclosure". Unfortunately there are no bookies to add colour to this area.

To follow the fortunes of your chosen steed, you can hire binoculars for about $2. All betting is based on the totaliser ("tote") system, in which the total money staked — less the operator's cut — is shared among the winners. There are various booths accepting stakes from $1 to $1,000 or more. Some of the terminology is the same as in Britain, though if you plan to make a study of it, consult the locals. A forecast (first and second in a race) is known as an "exacta". To "place" means to come second, to "show" means to come third. An "each-way" bet is a bet on a horse to win, place or show. The types of bet will be explained in the official programme, as will the history of horses and riders.

In the three states where off-track betting (OTB) is legal, totalisator bets can be placed at OTB offices. These are identical in appearance, decor and clientele to British betting shops.

The richest event in the racing calendar is the $3 million Breeder's Cup Classic, held at Hollywood Park California in early November. Next most valuable is the Arlington Million, held at the end of August at Arlington Park in Chicago. Other big races are the Florida Derby (Gulfstream Park near Miami, early April), the San Juan Capistrano Handicap (Santa Anita near Los Angeles, mid-April), the Kentucky Derby (Louisville, the first Saturday in May) and the Belmont Stakes (New York, early June). If you like horses, visit the Kentucky bluegrass country. The world centre of the thoroughbred is Lexington, which has a Horse Park complete with farm, racetrack and museum. Several stud farms in the area welcome visitors.

While the best thoroughbreds are groomed in Kentucky, the top races are held in neighbouring West Virginia. Betting on greyhounds operates in the same way as for horse racing. Harness racing (trotting) is popular in the small towns of the Midwest and elsewhere, and attracts surprisingly large interest. The biggest annual event is the $1.5 million Woodrow Wilson Classic at Meadowlands in late July.

AMUSEMENT PARKS

Whether internationally famous like the Walt Disney creations, or known only to afficionados of the roller coaster and Ferris wheel, the billion-dollar industry of amusement parks is for many people the number one reason to visit the USA. A few high-minded entrepreneurs have tried to shift the emphasis towards education-through-entertainment, however, the biggest queues at Walt Disney World in Florida are not for the multicultural EPCOT Center but for Space Mountain, arguably the ultimate fairground ride.

The usual practice is to buy an unlimited-ride ticket for $10-$20 per day. The only restriction on the number of rides is the time taken up by queuing. At peak periods (weekends and public holidays) you can waste half the morning standing in line for the star attraction, though the management takes pain to keep queues informed of the likely waiting time.

Darien Lake near Buffalo boasts a roller coaster named the Thunderball Express, which turns passeners upside down five times in a couple of minutes. But the title of the biggest roller coaster in the world has been snatched by Magic Harbor at Myrtle Beach, South Carolina. Brought to you by the people who run the Blackpool Pleasure Beach, the attractions include imported Thwaites Lancashire Ales.

The Midwest seems to have more than its fair share of amusement parks but for the best selection you have to go to Southern California. Disneyland near Los Angeles attracts the biggest crowds to its imaginative rides and quasi-educational exhibits. More sedentary visitors may prefer nearby Knott's Berry Farm, a genteel collection of rides, sideshows and shops. Patrons of Magic Mountain just north of LA are unashamed thrill-seekers. For a complete rundown of these and other attractions — such as the Grizzly River Rampage in Nashville or the Loch Ness Monster coaster in Virginia — consult *Amusement Parks of America* by Jeff Ulmer, published by Doubleday.

Rodeos. Most rodeos remain loyal to their cowboy roots, with modern-day cowboys competing in bronco-busting, steer wrestling and calf-roping events. Others offer less traditional but equally exciting contests such as barrel racing. Try to see a rodeo in a small Midwestern or Southwestern town rather than at the grander, more commercialized venues such as Buffalo Bill's Wild West show in North Platte, Nebraska or Dodge City Days in the "Cowboy Capital of the World", Dodge City, Kansas. For a calendar of upcoming events, contact the International Rodeo Association, American Fidelity Building, Box 615, Paul's Valley, Oklahoma 73075 (405-238-6488).

Other Attractions. Fairs, festivals, jamborees and parades are times when

Americans are at their most colourful and gregarious. State Fairs provide a chance to see log splitting and pie baking contests and plenty of other esoteric activities. There are Kite Festivals, Garlic Festivals, Apple Blossom Festivals, Blue Grass Music Festivals, Tobacco Spitting Contests (recently won by a native of Mississippi with a spit measuring just short of 27ft) and countless others. Some are very local; some attract participants from all over the country to compete in raw egg swallowing, fiddling or snow sculpting. There are also corn roasts, clam bakes and chilli cook-outs. In addition there is a wealth of ethnic celebrations from Czech to Celtic. Ask at the state tourist office for details of local festivals.

GAMBLING

Casinos. Most forms of casino gambling are banned throughout North America. The exceptions are in the State of Nevada and Atlantic City, New Jersey. Both were almost destitute until they introduced gambling, and now the sole raison d'etre of these two areas is to permit Americans to dispose of surplus cash in the forlorn hope of accruing even more. The gambling industry is so highly developed that there are two ways for visitors to try to make money: the first to gamble; the second (and much more certain) is to take advantage of the extraordinary deals designed to extract as much as possible from gamblers by tempting them with free offers.

The casinos realize that the more punters who can be tempted to the city, the more money will flow into the coffers of the casino operators. Some people will go to any lengths to gamble, but most need an incentive. To tempt the marginal gambler, gambling "resorts" offer low-cost meals and accommodation.

For richer travellers who wish to play the tables seriously, a couple of ground rules follow. Firstly, the casino almost always wins. The odds are only very slightly in its favour, but over a period of time the resources of the richest punter are drained. Secondly, the free cocktails that magically appear by your side are strictly an investment on the part of the casino; by dulling your rational senses, they hope to persuade you to part with much more cash than you intended.

Numbers. Americans indulge in many forms of illicit gambling, the most prevalent of which is the "numbers game". This is particularly popular in northern industrial areas, where factories employing many blue-collar workers are ideal territory for the operators of this racket. If you are spending some time in the States, you might be asked to take part. One version works like this: each participant picks a number from 1 to 999 and stakes a dollar. The winning number is the last three digits of a publicly-quoted index, such as the closing price of pork belly futures. If the number comes up, then he wins $500. With a payout of only half the amount staked, this is clearly a mug's game.

Blue Laws	legislation restricting opening on Sundays
cigar store	tobacconist
cut-outs	discontinued records
drug store	chemist dispensing medicines as well as many other items, comparable to Boots; often with a snack counter
five and dime	downmarket chain store (e.g. Woolworths) which used to sell items for 5c and 10c
jumper	pinafore dress
layaway	putting a deposit on an article to be paid for and collected at a later date
make change	give change
notions	haberdashery
pants	trousers
pantyhose	tights
pocket book	wallet/purse
purse	handbag
raincheck	promise of the same article at the same price at a later time
rummage sale/ garage sale	jumble sale
schlock	cheap, crummy merchandise (slang)
sneakers	plimsolls
sweater	jumper
thread	cotton
twofers	items sold at two-for-the-price-of-one
underwear	pants
vest	waistcoat

America is the ultimate consumer society. Americans are spoilt for choice, and it is easy to get caught up in their seemingly endless shopping spree. You can begin at stores bearing familiar names like Woolworth and Safeway before moving on to smart, expensive department stores such as Bloomingdale's and Neiman-Marcus, where high quality products can cost a fortune. For example, Neiman-Marcus sells an exercise bicycle built into a video cubicle showing scenic rides, for slightly less than the cost of a new car. But for those with less exotic tastes, there are thousands of less pretentious stores with vast amounts of good quality merchandise. J.C. Penney has been compared to Marks & Spencer, but with changing rooms. In fact Marks & Spencer now owns Brooks Brothers, a chain of men's clothing stores with a reputation for quality.

To meet more basic human needs there are mammoth supermarkets, cut-price stores and plenty of 24-hour shops. American factories often have a retail outlet on the premises from which they sell seconds at such good bargains that people drive hundreds of miles to shop at them. Beware that Americans can be remarkably straightlaced. Stores and truck stops often bear signs saying "No shirt? No shoes? No service!"

The prices of virtually everything are lowest at suburban shopping malls. A typical mall (pronounced, roughly, "moll") is a sprawling, covered air-conditioned centrally-heated shopping centre. At one end there might be a large discount department store such as K-Mart; at the other, a super-market. In between are all manner of shops most of them chain stores, interspersed with banks, laundromats and fast food restaurants. Most are situated on main roads in middle class suburbs, a few miles from the city centre, and surrounded by acres of parking lots plus a gas station or two. Teenagers favour them as hang-outs. They are usually only accessible by car. But in recent years there has been a tendency away from new suburban developments, and towards the refurbishment of obsolete shopping areas in city centres, which is good news for those without transport.

Suprisingly, some European goods are actually cheaper in the USA than in their country of manufacture. Even if you don't understand the economics, you may want to take advantage of the fact that Shetland sweaters can be cheaper in Dallas than Dundee, and books published in Oxford cheaper than in Oxford bookshops.

Sales Tax. Each state levies a tax on the sale of everything except basic foodstuffs. The rate varies from nil (in five states) to 7.5% in Connecticut; all are in the table below. Taxable and tax-exempt items vary from state to state; some states exempt shoes and books others don't. In addition, individual cities can add their own percentage to these figures. For example, sales tax in New York State is 4%, but more than twice that in New York City. Quoted prices almost never include sales tax. So if you're down to your last $5, don't try to buy something advertised at $4.99. On expensive purchases, sales tax becomes a significant extra, so try to buy in a low-tax state. If you are intending to have a purchase shipped directly out of the state or the country, it is always worth asking if you can be exempted from the sales tax. Regulations vary according to the state and the item. It is not worth doing this merely to save the tax, since shipping charges would probably cancel out any saving, but it might be useful to reduce the amount of luggage you have to carry. Some states are now introducing legislation allowing foreign visitors to avoid sales tax on items which they themselves will take out of the country; again, ask around.

STATE SALES TAXES (%)							
Alaska	nil	Illinois	4	Montana	nil	Rhode Island	6
Alabama	4	Indiana	5	Nebraska	3.5	S. Carolina	4
Arizona	4	Iowa	4	Nevada	5.75	S. Dakota	4
Arkansas	3	Kansas	3	New Hampshire	nil	Tennessee	4.5
California	4.75	Kentucky	5	New Jersey	6	Texas	4
Colorado	2.5	Louisiana	3	New Mexica	3.5	Utah	4
Connecticut	7.5	Maine	5	New York	4	Vermont	4
Delaware	nil	Maryland	5	N. Carolina	3	Virginia	3
DC	6	Massachusetts	5	N. Dakota	3	Washington	6.5
Florida	5	Michigan	4	Ohio	5	W. Virginia	5
Georgia	3	Minnesota	6	Oklahoma	2	Wisconsin	5
Hawaii	4	Mississippi	5	Oregon	nil	Wyoming	3
Idaho	4	Missouri	4.1	Pennsylvania	6		

Hours. While there are individual variations, most downtown shops open from 9.30 am to 5, 5.30 or 6pm, Monday to Saturday. There is usually at least one late-night shopping evening per week, when stores remain open until 9 pm. Suburban shopping malls stay open until 9 pm every week night. Sunday opening is subject to state and/or local laws, which often allow small corner shops to stay open, but prohibit the large department stores.

In addition, most towns have all-night supermarkets selling food and drugs. Outside large cities, they are often adjacent to 24-hour gas stations. Look for the ubiquitous 7-11 chain (so called because they originally opened from 7 am-11pm) which stay open all night in some locations.

Complaints. Despite — or perhaps because of — being the world's number one capitalist country, the USA has a very high degree of consumer protection legislation on its statutes. Paranoia about the expensive consequences of law suits means that a politely-worded complaint with just a hint about future legal action will usually be successful in getting a replacement or refund on faulty goods. Consumer consciousness has also led to a very liberal returns policy, and few questions are asked if you return an item which looks unused. For expensive purchases (over $150), buy with a credit card: you should then be able to claim against the credit card company if the company goes out of business and you are stuck with faulty goods.

Tobacco. Never underestimate the sensitivity of Americans to smoking. State and federal laws make it an offence to light up in virtually any enclosed public place, and there are tight rules on smoking in offices, shops and even some parks. The smoker is rapidly becoming a social leper, and even offering a cigarette to an American may cause offence. The health warnings carried on every pack of cigarettes do not mince words. One example: "Smoking by pregnant women may result in foetal injury, premature birth and low birth weight". See *Getting Around* for details of smoking restrictions on aircraft, trains and buses, and read the regional chapters for details of local restrictions such as the New York City law which forbids smoking within 20 feet of a hotel reception desk.

The smoker will already be familiar with many American brands, such as Marlboro (the world's biggest-selling cigarette), Camel and Winston. Less well known abroad are the ultra low tar brands, whose advertising makes you wonder whether they are more satisfying than inhaling fresh air. Try True ("less than 0.1 mg tar) if you think you'd like to give up. British or European cigarettes can be found only in specialist tobacco shops: the popular Benson and Hedges brand taste nothing like its British namesake. Menthol cigarettes are very popular: the top selling brand is Kool.

A pack of 20 cigarettes costs less than a dollar in the tobacco-producing state of North Carolina. other states impose much higher rates of duty, with correspondingly higher prices; about $1.50 for 20 is the norm. Smokers from neighbouring states make day trips to North Carolina to stock up. Imported brands cost around twice as much, so try to acquire a taste for the local cigarettes.

The cheapest way to buy cigarettes is in cartons of 200 at supermarkets. For single packs, try gas stations or drug stores: there are few tobacconists as such. Look out for special promotions along the lines of "two packs for the price of one". Choosing your cigarettes can be a daunting prospect; you have to decide between "Regular" and "Lite" (high or low tar), between "Regular" (king-size) and "100" (even longer), between "flip top" and "soft pack", and between untipped and filtered. Whichever you finally choose, you'll probably get a free book of matches thrown in. Most Amercan smokers buy from the cigarette machines found in bars, bus station and hotel foyers.

American and European cigars are widely available, but the import of Cuban cigars is a federal offence. Pipe smoking has not been promoted in the USA as a less dangerous alternative to cigarettes, and is something of a dying art. But with perseverance you can find decent tobacco and well made pipes.

Few Americans roll their own cigarettes from tobacco. As a result, Europeans who smoke roll-ups in the USA are frequently presumed to be smoking marijuana. If you wish to avoid embarrassing situations (such as being thrown out of a restaurant) or the attention of the police, stick to tailor-mades. Furthermore, although papers are sold in every shape, size and colour, good tobacco is hard to find. Some rolling tobacco ("natural tobacco") is soaked in bourbon and tastes disgusting.

Clothing. The best bargains can be found in factory outlets. Inexpensive new clothes may also be found at "off-price" stores. Located in unfashionable suburban areas, they pile clothes high and sell them cheap. Branches of J.C. Penney are much easier to find. Try to buy clothes at sale times: shortly after Christmas, in mid—February (around Washington's birthday) and at the height of summer.

Secondhand clothes, clean and in reasonable condition, can be bought cheaply at Salvation Army and Goodwill charity shops. These are usually located in dilapidated areas of many cities. At the other end of the market is the "preppy" wardrobe: corduroy trousers, Oxford cloth shirts, collared T shirts, Shetland sweaters, etc. Jeans are always a good buy, and Levi 501s can cost as little as $16.99.

Men's clothing sizes are the same in Britain and the USA, except shoes (see below). Women's dress sizes involve subtracting two from the British size: British size 10 is US size 8, British size 12 is US size 10 and so on. Slightly built women should check the "Boys" or "Teens" department for jeans. Short men should investigate the "Undergraduate" department for all kinds of clothes. For both men's and women's shoes, sizes vary as follows:

British	3	4	5	6	7	8	9	10	11
American	4½	5½	6½	7½	8½	9½	10½	11½	12½

Jogging shoes are particularly good value at around £10 in discount department stores.

Books and Records. American bookshops are packed with thousands of cheap paperbacks. The selection in small towns is more pulpy than in their British counterparts. Records (analogue and Compact Disc) and audio cassettes are one third cheaper than in Britain. Check out the remaindered sections of both book and record shops. Most record shops sell cut-price albums; look for the holes punched through the record sleeve which gives rise to the term "cut-outs".

Photography. Top-name film costs around $3.50 for a 24-exposure 135 or 110 cartridge. The one-week processing services offered through supermarkets charge about $10 for 24 prints, and you may get a free film or a second set of prints thrown in. Some specialist shops offer same-day or even on-the-spot processing at surprisingly competitive prices. Cameras bought in the USA can be considerably cheaper than in Britain, but do not always carry worldwide guarantees. Unless your future travel plans will allow you to return the camera should something go awry, the absence of after-sales service may discourage you. Remember that the extreme heat that you will encounter in the Southern states can have an adverse effect on your colour film.

Spectacles. Even after paying an optometrist for a sight test, a pair of glasses or contact lenses costs much less than in Britain. Travellers who plan to stock up on cut-price eye wear can get a free NHS sight test in Britain and take the prescription to the US for making up. The cheapest place is likely to be a department store.

Electrical goods. The American electrical supply is 110 volts at 60 cycles per second. Britain uses 240 volts at 50 cycles per second. This is more than enough to burn out most American electrical appliances. Most Japanese audio equipment has voltage and frequency selectors on the back allowing them to be used anywhere. Most American-made equipment does not. You can buy a transformer to reduce the voltage, but the difference in frequency means that cassette recorders and record players will run at the wrong speed.

Do not buy a home computer, television or video cassette recorder made for the American market: the 525-line system used makes them incompatible with British television equipment. Similarly, pre-recorded video cassettes will not work on machines designed for use in Britain.

New York and Miami are about the best places for shopping for electrical and photographic equipment. Prices average 60% less than their British equivalents.

The leading chain of stores for all things electrical is Radio Shack (which trades as Tandy in the UK), but prices are often lowest in the electrical department of discount department stores.

Garage Sales. Although Americans may donate clothes to Salvation Army or Goodwill Stores, they are likely to dispose of their other superfluous possessions at a garage sale and keep the money themselves. Garage sales are a phenomenon usually confined to summer weekends, The vendor simply displays his chattels in his garage (or, more likely, on the front lawn) and waits for the eager buyers who learn of the sale through local papers, fly posters, leafleting or word of mouth. All prices are fully negotiable: anything still around towards the end of the sale is likely to be knocked down cheaply. Even if you don't pick up the bargain of a lifetime, a garage sale is great fun and gives an insight into how American communities operate.

Gifts. America has great scope for gifts with which to astonish your friends and relations. The most obvious examples include Disney toys, stetsons, baseball caps and T-shirts saying "my folks went to Pittsburgh and all I got was this lousy T-shirt". T-shirts with arty, imaginative or outrageous designs are sold everywhere. Trendy boutiques specialize in "preppy" clothes (a combination of Sloane Ranger/King's Road chic and American college casualness) and designer jeans. Regular jeans are cheaper and tougher. A current fad is for safari-style wear sold by the Banana Republic chain, whose shops are always entertaining.

Indian handicrafts are one of the few remnants of native American culture. Be cautious when shopping on or near reservations unless you are sure you can distinguish tourist trash from the real thing. Shops set up in large cities by the various Indian nations which pride themselves on marketing the authentic products of Indian artisans are probably more reliable. For specific recommendations on handicraft centres and other unusual ideas for gifts, see the regional chapters.

When buying presents, remember that any purchases above the duty free limit of £32 will attract duty of around 15% upon import to Britain.

The Great Outdoors

biking/bike	cycling/pedal cycle
diamondback	domestic American rattlesnake
dude ranch	ranch style holiday resort
flashlight	torch
garter snake	harmless snake with three lengthwise stripes
parka	anorak (both are Eskimo words)
poison ivy	shrub which gives a painful skin rash on contact
pup tent	low one-man tent
RV	recreational vehicle (camper van)
skinny dipping	swimming in the nude
smudge	smoky fire to drive away insects
trailer	caravan
white-out	drifting snow which reduces visibility to zero

Visitors from a crowded island such as Britain sometimes have difficulty coming to terms with the sheer vastness and emptiness of the USA. Much of the terrain is not merely uninhabited, it is uninhabitable. The stark beauty of the wilderness is in complete contrast to the brash commercialization of the cities. The two extremes frequently collide, when a billboard or diner blots out the landscape, or a neon city like Las Vegas rises out of the desert.

Americans have abused their environment shamelessly, not only in pursuit of wealth but also of personal freedom. Recently an eccentric millionaire who owned an island off the Florida coast had his island entirely coated in purple plastic as a work of art.

Despite the efforts of American entrepreneurs to despoil the landscape, there are still many beautiful places where the traveller can find quietness and solitude on coastal cliffs, in the mountains or on the lakes and waterways. Large areas are protected from exploitation, being designated National or State Parks. The most famous of these (Grand Canyon, Yosemite, Yellowstone) can be appallingly crowded, but many are so large that a day's hike will remedy this. Most have excellent facilities for camping and "nature interpretation". They make the best of the Great Outdoors easily accessible and should not be missed.

Many indigenous species of wildlife can be seen while travelling in the wilds of America, from the endearing little chipmunk (an Algonquin word for the North American squirrel) to the grizzly bear. There are many unique small mammals and marsupials such as raccoons, possums, skunks and gophers as well as larger ones like elk and moose. The groundhog (or woodchuck) gives its name to February 2; if the groundhog sees his shadow on Groundhog Day (a fairly safe bet), he returns to his burrow and winter continues six weeks longer. The decline of the population of bald eagles (the symbol of the United States) seems to have been reversed in the past few years. For a description of dangerous species and ways to remain safe in the bush, see *Health: Creatures to Avoid* (page 44) and *Canada: The Great Outdoors* (page 351).

National Parks. The National Park system includes national monuments, historic sites and national seashores, but the prime attractions are the 37

National Parks. They range in size from the 3,472 square miles of Yellowstone in Wyoming to the single volcanic crater of Haleakala in Hawaii. In all, the National Park Service controls 77,000,000 acres of land. Common to all of these parks is a set of regulations to preserve the environment, such as no smoking in some areas (to prevent forest fires), all garbage to be disposed of, and of course no hunting. But the parks encourage all kinds of outdoor activity and there are excellent networks of trails.

One feature which may take you by surprise the first time is that you have to pay an entrance fee to at least half the parks. The charge for a vehicle and its occupants is around $5. If you intend to visit several parks, you can obtain a yearly Golden Eagle Passport for $25 from the National Park Service, Interior Building, Washington DC 20240. This entitles you, your vehicle and other occupants to free admission. There is also a free Golden Age Passport for those over 62 and a free Golden Access Passport for the disabled, giving both categories free entry anywhere in the system and 50% off the regular camping and user fees. Hitch-hikers of course will get in free in any case; cyclists and hikers may have to pay a nominal admission of $1.

Another idea which takes some getting used to for people accustomed to wandering freely around the wilderness elsewhere in the world is that some regions off the beaten track are accessible only if you have a permit for "backcountry" use. The person to approach, by mail or directly, is the Superintendent of the park. As well as issuing permits for hiking or camping, he or his staff can tell you everything you could possibly wish to know about the geology, ecology and history of the park.

There is normally a choice of accommodation. The larger parks have simple wooden shelters for the free use of hikers, and ample camping facilities. For a little luxury there are log cabins or (if you don't mind not blending in with the surroundings) ordinary motel rooms. That said, you should plan ahead if you decide to visit the parks. There are crowds at most of them during the summer, and many shut down entirely or offer only limited services in the winter. Walled facilities are generally in short supply, and bookings have to be made as much as six months in advance. Camping facilities outdoors are usually on a first come, first served basis, so it makes sense to arrive early if you want the better campsites.

Many of the National Parks are mentioned in the regional chapters. For further details ask the USTTA for their free brochure *The Great Outdoors of the USA,* or buy the *Backpackers Sourcebook* by Loelle Liebrenz. American Youth Hostels, PO Box 37613, Washington DC 20013-7613 produces a useful brochure called Discount Storeroom which lists many more specialized books.

If you are interested in donating some of your time and labour to maintaining footpaths in national parks, you can become a volunteer with the American Hiking Society. You should have some experience as a camper and hiker and be prepared to work hard for ten days in rugged terrain. Food may or may not be provided free of charge depending on the project's finances. For further details, contact Kay Beebe, AHS Volunteer Vacations, PO Box 86, North Sciutate, Massachusetts 02060; (617) 545-4819.

For information on camping in the national parks, send for the *Guide and Map: National Parks of the United States* from the National Park Service, Public Inquiries Office, 18th and C Sts, NW, Washington, DC 20240; for a complete list of national forests, request the free brochure FS13, *Field Offices of the Forest Services* from the US Forest Service, Office of

Information, PO Box 2417, Washington, DC 20013. The National Park Service also encourages campers to use lesser-known national parks in its brochure *Lesser Known Areas of the National Park System,* usually available free from local offices of the Park Service.

State Parks and National Forests. Although not quite on the grand scale of some national parks, don't overlook these reserves. With planning, you can cross the USA staying in a different one each night if you're travelling by car. Rates vary from park to park, as does the quality of accommodation, but in general you should pay no more than $7 a night. 'Campground Full' signs are a rare sight.

National forests, inasmuch as they often border or surround national parks, are well worth exploring, though, by and large, camping in them tends to be primitive. The advantage over national parks is that they are usually free. You'll need detailed maps, and a sense of adventure.

Organizations. For people (particularly first-time visitors) who might feel more relaxed with an experienced guide or other campers, there are six major organizations to contact:

Yosemite Institute, PO Box 487, Yosemite, CA 95389 (209-372-4441)
American Wilderness Alliance, 4260, E Evans Ave, Suite 3, Denver, CO 80222 (303-758-5018)
American Forestry Association, 1319 18th St, NW, Washington DC 20036 (202-467-5810)
Sierra Club, 530 Bush St, San Francisco, CA 94108 (415-981-8634)
Nature Expeditions International, PO Box 11496, Eugene OR 97440 (503-484-6529 or 800-634-0634)
Appalachian Mountain Club, 5 Joy St, Boston, MA 02108 (617-523-0636)

The Sierra Club has local branches all over the USA. Their organized outings could be unkindly compared to boy scout hikes — you have to take a turn with the camp chores — but many travellers find the trails a good way to explore lesser known areas and to meet people. Apart from one or two week "Highlight Trips" around the western states, they organize plenty of one-day outings which are advertised in local newspapers.

More regimented and rigorous are the"wilderness skills" courses offered by Outward Bound in various mountainous loctions in the northern states. They are expensive — $750 for a week — but if you are interested, contact Outward Bound, 384 Field Point Rd, Greenwich CT 06830 (1-800-243-8520).

Connoisseurs of flora and fauna are in for a treat, since there are many species unique to North America. Buy a field guide such as *Audubon Society Beginner Guides* to birds or reptiles and amphibians or wildflowers for about $4 each. Or join a naturalist tour such as the one operated by Questers, 257 Park Avenue South, New York 10010 (212-673-3120). The National Wildlife Federation has programmes of field trips and classes. Contact them at 1412 16th St NW, Washington DC 20036 (703-790-4371).

WATER SPORTS

Waterskiing. Waterskiing was invented on a Minnesota lake in 1922. Although it has been somewhat upstaged by windsurfing, waterskiing is still popular on lakes and in calm coastal areas throughout the US. Many resorts make it easy for the beginner to participate in this realatively simple activity. Renting the skis and someone to tow you in a motor boat is not prohibitively expensive.

Canoeing. Canoeing, kayaking and rafting are various ways of experiencing the inland waterways of the US. Canoes for several paddlers (known in Britain as "Canadian canoes") are the most popular way of exploring the calm lakes and backwaters of the Ozarks, the northern Midwest and so on. You don't need any experience for this. However if you want to tackle the rivers in a kayak, which in North America refers to a one-man enclosed boat versatile enough to be taken on turbulent waters, you'll need some previous training and practice. There are many canoe rental outlets (about $20-$25 a day) and complete outfitters who supply camping equipment and all the food you will need for a leisurely week canoeing. For a free list of outfitters, write to Grumman Boats, Marathon, NY 13803.

Those who lack canoeing experience can still experience the thrills of the fast rivers of New England, the Rockies and even the Grand Canyon by joining a white water rafting expedition. The inflatable rafts are virtually unsinkable. Many rafting organizations arrange for you to be returned to your point of departure after the trip which lasts a half day, one day or sometimes longer.

The latest watersport craze is "tubing" which means floating down rivers in an inner tube. You can either rent these for $3-$6 a day (which usually includes transport back to your starting point) or you can buy your own at any truckstop for $10.

Swimming. America has produced more Olympic swimming champions than any other country. Like other forms or exercise, it is taken seriously and most children take formal lessons at their local suburban swimming pool. The majority of hotels have pools, which in the summer offer a much needed respite from the heat. University campuses have Olympic-sized pools which may be open to the public for a minimal fee. Municipal pools, though often smaller and more crowded, are often cheaper. But most Americans will share their backyard swimming pool as readily as their phone.

Disused quarries, gravel pits and ponds are also popular swimming holes. Lakes and rivers will be colder and potentially more dangerous if there are rapids and whirlpools. Subterranean activity in many parts of the country produces free natural jacuzzis. Since most of these are sulphur springs, you will have to take a shower soon afterwards to rid yourself of the smell. "Skinny dipping" (nude bathing) is popular though on crowded resort beaches it is unlawful to change let alone disrobe entirely.

Windsurfing and Surfing. Windsurfing was popularized about 20 years ago in California by attaching a mast and sail to a surf board. After a few hours of professional tuition (around $10 an hour in small groups) you should be able to start, turn, tack and sail along at a good few knots. Every coastal and inland lake resort will offer windsurfing instruction and hire facilities.

One of the principal entertainments in Southern California and Hawaii is watching and admiring the top surfers. If you're a beginner, be very cautious of the pounding breakers. The Atlantic coast and the Gulf of Mexico provide a gentler introduction to the sport.

For an interesting variation, try landyachting. By putting a set of wheels on a sailboard, you can travel along hard-packed beaches at up to 50mph. The sport is relatively undeveloped, but enthusiasts can be found on Floridan and Californian beaches.

HUNTING AND FISHING

Hunting and freshwater fishing require permits issued by the state authorities. Hunting licences for non-residents are much more expensive than for residents, ranging from $4 to hunt waterfowl in Oklahoma to $400 to hunt bighorn sheep in Wyoming. Fishing licences are generally cheaper, seldom above $5 for three days. Contact the state government department of Natural Resources (Fish & Wildlife Division) for further information about seasons and where to purchase a licence.

The traveller who has adapted to the bitter winters of the Midwest or New England might wish to try ice-fishing from a "fish-house". These are wooden huts erected on frozen lakes around a small circular hole which permits fishing inside the hut. The catch can then be barbecued on the spot. Some temporary ice communities even have their own bars and cinemas. Some states require all fish-houses to be cleared by the last day of February to avoid mishaps on melting ice.

CYCLING

Cycling is enjoying a renaissance in the States because of its economy and health-giving properties. The film *Breaking Away* set in the small Midwestern university town of Bloomington illustrates the joys of cycling and how seriously many Americans take it.

In the summer of 1976 the TransAmerican Trail for cyclists was opened. It wends its way along 4,250 miles between Oregon and Viginia through national parks, prairies, deserts, farmlands and country towns. Strip maps of the route are available from American Youth Hostels, PO Box 37613, Washington DC 20013-7613. Almost every state has marked bikeways, which state tourist offices will be able to tell you about. If you want to plan your own bicycle route, stick to back roads, canal towpaths, abandoned railway lines and beaches with hard-packed sand.

Buying or Renting a Bicycle. Cycle shops offer a selection ranging from one-speed runabouts to ten-speed racers. The best, and most expensive models are French and Japanese imports. Prices are perhaps slightly lower than in Europe: the cheapest ten-speed costs around $150 new, $100 in good secondhand condition. You might want to consider a mountain bike with wide tyres suitable not only for off-road riding but for pot-holed city streets. Some cycle shops hire out bicycles for around $20 per day. A returnable deposit or major credit card is required.

There is often a roaring trade in used bicycles, especially on and around college campuses. Because of the high level of theft, anyone with a decent bike removes the front wheel and uses a Citadel or Kryptonite lock to fasten it plus the rest of the bike to an immovable object. Few bicycles are fitted with mudguards since Americans simply don't cycle in inclement weather.

Further Information. There is a wealth of cycle touring information published in the USA, including strip maps of bicycle trails and maps for negotiating city centres. For an overall impression try *The American Biking Atlas and Touring Guide* by Sue Browder, published by Workman, 231 E 51st St, New York 10022. Details of other publications can be obtained from the Cyclists' Touring Club, 69 Meadrow, Godalming, Surrey.

SKIING

There are a few states in the Deep South where skiing is not feasible, but virtually every other state in the Union provides facilities for skiing, even if they have to make the snow artificially. But it is generally accepted that the best skiing is confined to the Western Sierras, the Rockies, Vermont and New York State. There are few package tours to be had, so it is normally a matter of turning up at a highly developed resort and finding your own accommodation, hire shop, instructor and cable car ("tramway"). This can become very expensive; most skiers do not expect much change from $100 a day. People in the Rockies in the spring should look around for late-season ski deals, e.g. $12 lift tickets and "Women Ski Free".

To make sure the investment is worth your while, there are several numbers to call for ski conditions: New Hampshire (900) 976-3700; New Mexico (505) 984-0606; Utah (801) 521-8102; Colorado (505) 984-0606; Vermont (900) 976-3740.

One of the advantages of learning to ski or improving your technique in North America is that the instruction will be in English. Most resorts teach the Graduated Length Method (GLM) — the American equivalent of "Ski Evolutif" — which starts complete beginners on very short skis and allows them to progress to longer skis as their proficiency increases. Experienced skiers may find American resorts a little too regimented (piste stewards equipped with walkie-talkies enforce "slow skiing" zones where runs converge), but the USA is certainly a good place for beginners.

In addition to basic downhill skiing, the cross country variety is very popular. Write to the National Park Service (Department of the Interior, Washington DC 20240) for literature about parks which have cross-country trails, or to the Ski Touring Council (West Hill Rd, Troy, Vermont 05868) for cross country routes throughout the country.

To find untracked snow in higher mountains, a group of experienced skiers can club together to hire a helicopter and take up the increasingly popular sport of heli-skiing. An interesting variation is offered at some resorts where you can balloon up to the top of a mountain and then ski down. Other attractions include renting a Sony Walkman for music while you ski, or an outdoor hot tub for relaxation afterwards.

Even out of season, ski resorts are often very good bases for outdoor activities. You can often find golf, tenis, rafting, fishing and horse riding facilities at a single mountain centre, and acccommodation is cheaper than during the ski-season. For an annotated list of ski resorts, consult *The Morrow Book of American Resorts* edited by Thomas Tracey.

RANCHES

City slickers get a taste of the great American outdoors on dude ranches, which are popular from Montana to Texas. If the cowboy life appeals to you, you will have to be prepared to pay for it, since dude ranches are usually more like posh resorts than working farms (usually over $500 a week per person). Ask the Dude Ranchers' Association (PO Box 471, La Porte, California 80535) for their *Vacation Directory.*

Fifth Amendment	the right to remain silent when arrested
jay walking	crossing a street not at an intersection
Mann Act	Congressional Act that prohibits men from taking women across state borders for "immoral purposes"
mugger money	a cache of about $50 which will satisfy a potential mugger and prevent him from searching for more
patrolman	ordinary policeman

Despite the statistic that the United States has the highest rate of serious crime in the world, the dangers of violent attack on travellers are greatly exaggerated. It is true than many ordinary citizens own guns, availing themselves of the second amendment to the Constitution which protects the right to keep and bear arms, and also that there are more murders in Chicago and Miami than in Britain. But the huge majority are internecine killings. According to a recent survey, London is the seventh most dangerous city in the world just below Los Angeles but above New York. Murder of travellers is mostly confined to victims of psychotics and addicts, or more often, those who fail to behave in the accepted manner while being mugged. And mugging is not nearly as widespread as popular reports would have us believe. If you take care in choosing where to go and in comporting yourself correctly, it is highly improbable that you will be mugged. You are more likely to fall victim to a pickpocket, hotel thief or someone out to pick a barroom fight.

The most crime-ridden cities are not necessarily the ones you would expect. According to recent FBI statistics, the top ten cities on the crime index were: Atlantic City (New Jersey), Odessa (Texas), Miami (Florida), Gainesville (Florida), Lubbock (Texas), Bakersfield (California), Savannah (Georgia), New York City, Sacramento (California) and Stockton (California). Miami, Houston and Odessa have the highest murder rates in the country. The most violent state seems to be New York with nearly one violent crime per 100 population, and the safest is Nebraska with only 61 violent crimes per 10,000 population. The prevalence of violent crime is much higher in the southern states than in the north, which is arguably attributable to the warm climate.

How to avoid a Mugging. Despite the display of ostentatious American wealth all around you, never let it be known that you are worth robbing (unlike the New York bank robber who was mugged on his way to the getaway car). If you count your holiday cash in a crowded bar, don't be surprised if you're attacked on the way home. Leave your expensive watch or jewellery at home, and give some thought to where you'll carry your documents and money. The important rule is not to have all your valuables in one place, so that even if you are robbed or mugged you will have an emergency fund intact.

Find out which areas of a city a native would hesitate to visit. After dark, wherever you are, stick to well-lit main thoroughfares. Always walk purposefully. Don't stop every few yards to peer at a map; work out your route beforehand. Never appear drunk even if you are. And if you are shaking with terror, try to disguise your fear. Stride across the street to avoid the attentions of the gang of malevolent youths who are following you.

How to be Mugged. If you find yourself being mugged, there are several sensible precautions you should have taken to minimize personal danger and loss. Ideally, you should carry $50-$100 in cash. Any less than this, and the villain will become belligerent and search for hidden wealth to make his attack worthwhile.

Most muggers are young males who operate alone. You can expect to be grabbed from behind and threatened by a gun or, more likely, a knife. After your initial spasm, stay completely still and don't try to resist. Muggers can be extremely wound up and will not hesitate to use this weapon if things go wrong; they are highly susceptible to sudden or unexpected movement so do exactly as you are told. Direct your attacker's hand to the wallet or purse. When the mugger has your cash, he may also remove your watch or jewellery and promptly run away into the shadows. You are now at your most vulnerable; trembling with shock and fear, and without the "mugger money" to pay off subsequent attackers. Stay still and silent until you are sure he has gone. Flag down a cab if you can find one, explain your predicament and ask to go to the nearest police precinct station. It is a rare taxi driver who will refuse you. At the station, your story won't arouse much interest. Collect the number of the police report to facilitate your insurance claim, and ask for a lift home.

The above pattern is the ideal. If, instead, you are set upon by a gang intent upon mindless violence as much as theft, there is little you can do except to protect your head and play dead.

Pickpockets and Bagsnatchers. Theft by stealth rather than violence is a growth industry in the USA. Some pickpockets allegedly learn their craft in Bogota Colombia, the theft capital of the western hemisphere. Pickpocketing and bagsnatching are most prevalent at airports, in subways and bus stations, where tired travellers are plunged into a frenetic and confusing enviroment. Money belts and pouches worn next to the skin will foil most pickpockets; avoid moving in crowds and treat unusual events with suspicion. Tricks like dropping a handful of change or spilling coffee on someone are employed by pickpockets to distract attention.

Make sure your luggage is in your sight, if not necessarily in your hands, to deter bagsnatchers. And beware of well-dressed strangers who ask you to watch their case while they visit the toilet. When it comes to your turn to go, don't feel morally obliged to ask the stranger to do the same for you. Travellers who entrust their belongings in this way often find no sign of luggage or stranger upon their return.

Hotel Theft. Burglary is extremely popular in America. Nothing appeals to the burglar more than the prospect of rich pickings in hotel and motel rooms. If you have to relinquish your key when going out for the day, make sure you hand it to the reception clerk rather than leave it lying on the desk. But despite precautions, access to unattended rooms presents few problems to the professional thief. It makes sense to keep all your valuables in the hotel safe while you're out and about. Even when you're asleep in your room, the odd burglar may still try to make off with your belongings. Most are so stealthy that you won't wake up; if you do, pretend to be asleep to avoid unpleasant consequences.

Be wary of opening your door to callers who claim to be the hotel staff. Some villains simply knock on a door and, when it opens, threaten the occupant with a gun or a knife. You are usually forced to stand in the bath while he goes through your possessions. Fortunately, most rooms are equipped with spy holes through which you can size up the caller. Phone the reception desk to check his credentials if you're suspicious. If your room has no telephone, ask him to let himself in. Most genuine employees (and unfortunately some thieves) have a master key.

Violence. There is a great deal of tension in American society. Although the more overt demonstrations of racism such as those practised by the Ku Klux Klan have largely subsided, there can be considerable conflict between different ethnic groups. When the short fuse of underlying racial tension is inflamed by drink, drugs or unbearably hot weather, the consequences are often frightful. It is not safe for blacks to venture into poor white or Hispanic ghettos, nor for whites or Asians to wander through black neighbourhoods. The racial character of an area can change dramatically within a block or two. If you are in any doubt, stick to main throughfares which are generally safe territory. Even when driving, you should keep all doors locked and windows closed and not hesitate to follow the custom of ignoring red lights if you feel threatened.

You may notice an undercurrent of paranoia in some settings which manifests itself in aggressive behaviour. Barroom brawls are frequent occurences, so avoid heated arguments when out drinking. Bars which have lots of souped-up cars and motorcyles parked outside, and large burly men with platinum blondes inside are best avoided.

Confidence Tricksters. It is not always easy to distinguish between con-artists, religious fanatics and people who are genuinely trying to help. As a rule, the unsavoury characters who hang around bus stations and hotel bars do not fall into the latter category. Any stranger who engages you in a conversation which eventually turns into a suggestion that you should part with some money — to place on a "fixed" horse race, as a partner in some fabulous financial deal or for a prostitute who subsequently fails to deliver — is almost certainly a con-artist. Smile, explain that you're penniless and waiting for cash to be sent from Europe in a week or so, and walk away.

Never become involved in any illicit street card games such as "Spot The Lady" or with pool sharks who might let you win the first time to build up your confidence (and the amount you're willing to bet on the game) but will clobber you in the end.

THE LAW

The lawmakers in Congress are supplemented by the legislatures of 50 states and of thousands of counties and cities. The result is a vast amount of piecemeal legislation which makes it difficult for travellers to keep track of the law. For example, few visitors can be expected to know that it is illegal to draw faces on window blinds in Garfield Montana, or that riding on a bus in the Indiana town of Gary is unlawful if you've eaten garlic within the previous two hours. Even without these eccentric ordinances the reams of statutes and civil case law result in thousands of trials, retrials and appeals which keep the highly litigious legal profession in business. A million "peace officers", equipped with all sorts of menacing hardwear and supplemented with equally many armed security guards, attempt to keep some sort of order. Yet there are still areas where police fear to tread.

Police. In addition to the police force, there are a large number of armed security guards technically without the rights of publicly-employed police, but you are not advised to test this out. When dealing with police, remember that you are in a nation where guns are almost as common as tennis rackets. Any sudden movement, or even slouching with your hands in your pockets, could be misconstrued. Don't consider offering a financial inducement to get out of trouble. The vast majority of policemen would be outraged at an attempt to bribe them and would add the offence to your charge sheet.

Enforcers of the law fall into four broad categories: city police, state police (who operate the highway patrol), the National Guard and the FBI. Each state has a National Guard, civilian reservists who are called up to deal with civil unrest. The Federal Bureau of Investigation concerns itself with major offences and crime across state borders. You are unlikely to become involved with them unless you are an international drug dealer or fail to deliver a driveaway car.

A fifth category is the US Secret Service, whose chief function is to protect present and past Presidents. They are easily identified by their ill-fitting gabardine suits with bulges under the shoulder and a hearing aid (actually a radio device) in one ear. Finally, the men with white hats, gloves and holsters are Military Police concerned only with deserting soldiers and drunken sailors.

Arrest and Summons. Offences are categorized as misdemeanours (dropping litter, smoking marijuana in liberal states) or felonies (robbery, carrying marijuana in conservative states). You are certain to be arrested for a felony and likely to be summonsed for a misdemeanour. In an arrest you are frisked for concealed weapons (just like on TV), possibly handcuffed and "helped" into the back of a police car. You will have the Fifth Amendment — the right to remain silent — quoted at you (just like on TV). At the station you are charged before being put in a cell. This is the time to phone the British Consulate, an attorney or the local Legal Aid office and anyone who might stand bail for you. It is preferable to be summonsed. Legally this is equivalent to arrest and is answerable in court, but it allows you to avoid the cells.

Drugs. Among middle-class Americans, smoking marijuana at a private gathering is considered as natural as drinking beer, and joints are offered round as casually as cigarettes. But the laws on drugs are complicated and often extremely harsh. Each state fixes its own penalties. The possession of a small amount of cannabis for home consumption is legal only in Alaska. It has been decriminalized in 11 states which means that you will only get a fine if caught with less than an ounce. In all but two of the other states, it is a misdemeanour, but in Arizona and Nevada it is a felony which means that it is punishable by lengthy prison sentences. The most common penalty is up to a year in prison and a fine of $1,000. Penalties for possessing harder drugs, including cocaine and the very popular "crack" are severe as are those for dealing of any kind and carrying marijuana in a vehicle. Parents form a very strong lobby and maintain pressure for exemplary punishment of anyone who could conceivably be corrupting their kids.

Of course theory and practice are two different things. In many cities, people smoke grass openly (especially in under-policed neighbourhoods) and dealers hang about ostentatiously on street corners with no apparent fear of the law. In the course of a short visit it is unlikely you'll be able to ascertain where it's safe.

Other Laws. Laws affecting the motorist or hitch-hiker are mentioned in the relevant sections of *Getting Around.* If you are a pedestrian, beware the dreaded jay-walking law. You must cross downtown streets at intersections and never diagonally. If a policeman sees you scooting across mid-block or crossing against a red light, he may well slap you with a hefty fine.

There are also strict laws affecting minors in many states. If you drive an under-aged person over a state border, you may be committing a federal offence. These laws are designed to prevent kidnapping. In some localities, there may even be a curfew for minors.

Help and Information *i*

TOURIST INFORMATION

The American government tourist office is called the United States Travel and Tourism Administration (USTTA). Its British office is at 22 Sackville St, London W1X 2EA (01-439 7433); its US headquarters is at 14th and Constitution Avenues NW, Washington, DC 20230 (202-377-2000). Call in or write with an outline of your plans. Within the USA you can use the toll-free USTTA Hotline, 1-800-255-3050.

The national tourist office holds only a small proportion of the available travel literature. Most travel promotion is done at state level, so if you know in advance which states you'll be concentrating on, write to the travel offices (all addresses and phone numbers below) or to the city tourist offices given under *Help and Information* for each region.

When you call or write to a state tourist office, mention any special interests such as theatre, cycling or ornithology, since many offices have leaflets on all sorts of subjects. But don't expect a personal reply to your enquiry. And don't expect a detached or discriminating tone in the bumph; be prepared for the hard sell. It is still a worthwhile exercise for the road map and the list of forthcoming events.

Emergencies. If you need emergency medical assistance see the chapter *Health.* For dealing with a financial crisis see *Money.* In the *Help and Information* section of the regional chapters are listed the addresses of the post office, American Express, Thomas Cook and telephone numbers for emergency medical treatment.

Travelers' Aid. This voluntary organization began life in the 19th century. In the predominantly male West it was popular to advertise for brides in British provincial newspapers. A Chicago lawyer, alarmed at the plight of women who travelled to the USA but took fright upon meeting their potential husbands, established Travelers' Aid to help them escape. This role has decreased significantly. Nowadays the Travelers' Aid bureaux at airports and bus stations cater for any foreign visitors in need of succour. If all your money and documents have been stolen, they will contact the Consulate and a relative at home to help you out. If you arrive at nightfall in an unfamiliar city, they will help to arrange (paid) accommodation and advise you of areas to avoid.

The resources of Travelers' Aid are stretched. It should be emphasized that they should only be used in an emergency. And if you need medical help, go direct to a hospital: Travelers' Aid are not equipped to deal with health problems.

Consulates. There are eight British Consulates-General in the US in addition to the Embassy in Washington. These are located in New York, Atlanta, Boston, Cleveland, Houston, Los Angeles, San Francisco and Chicago. In addition there are British Consulates in Anchorage, Dallas, Kansas City, Miami, New Orleans, Norfolk, Philadelphia, Portland, Seattle and St Louis. Unless you lose your passport, are destitute and want to be repatriated or there is a revival of the American Civil War, you won't need to consult the addresses which are provided in the regional chapters. (If you lose your money, try to have them cash a cheque for up to £50 as mentioned under *Money*). If your passport is lost or stolen, notify the police immediately, and go to the nearest consulate where you will be issued with travel documents which will allow you to complete your stay and take a one-way trip back to Britain. It is also worth notifying the local Immigration & Naturalization Service of the loss, to avoid suspicion of overstaying.

Handicapped Travellers. The American travel industry is highly aware of the problems facing handicapped travellers and makes careful provision for ease of access. Hertz and Avis rent cars adapted with hand controls at normal rates subject to ten days notice. Greyhound Bus Lines and most American airlines allow an escort to travel free with a handicapped passenger. Amtrak provide specially-designed compartments on all long-distance trains. Potomac Tours, 1919 Pennsylvania Avenue NW, Washington DC 20006 (1-800-424-2969) operate escorted rail tours for handicapped groups to various areas of the northeastern USA.

Accommodation presents few problems as long as you book well in advance. Every hotel in the Holiday Inn chain has one or two rooms for handicapped guests. Other hotels specialize in catering for the disabled. For example, the Vista International in New York has 18 rooms equipped with hydraulic lifts for baths and showers, plus a large fitness centre complete with physiotherapists.

PUBLIC HOLIDAYS

Although all holidays are legislated by the state rather than the federal government, in practice most states observe the holidays legislated for federal employees as below. Banks, most businesses and some restaurants are closed on the following days:

January 1:	New Year's Day
January 16:	Martin Luther King's Birthday
February (3rd Monday):	Presidents' Day
May (last Monday):	Memorial Day (except Alaska, Louisiana, Mississippi, South Carolina)
July 4:	Independence Day
September (1st Monday):	Labor Day
October (2nd Monday):	Columbus Day (32 states only)
November 11:	Veterans' Day
November (4th Thursday):	Thanksgiving
December 25:	Christmas

In addition, there are many other holidays celebrated, such as Lincoln's birthday which is widely observed in the north and neglected in the south.

Details are given in the *Calendar of Events* at the end of each regional chapter.

STATE TOURIST OFFICES

Where a telephone number beginning 1-800 is listed, you may call toll-free from within the USA.

Alabama Bureau of Tourism and Travel: 532 S Perry St, Montgomery, AL 36104. Tel: (205) 832-5510; 1-800-392 8096 within Alabama; 1-800-252 2262 from outside the State.

Alaska Division of Tourism: Pouch E, Juneau, AK 99811. Tel: (907) 465-2010.

Arizona Office of Tourism: 3507 N. Central Avenue, Suite 506, Phoenix, AZ 85012. Tel: (602) 255-3618.

Arkansas Department of Parks & Tourism: 1 Capitol Mall, Little Rock, AR 72201. Tel: (501) 371-7777; 1-800-482 8999 within Arkansas; 1-800 643-8383 from outside the State.

California Office of Tourism: 1030 13th St, Suite 200, Sacramento, CA 95814. Tel: (916) 322-1396; 1-800-TO CALIF.

Colorado Tourism Board: 225 West Colfax, Denver, CO 80202. Tel: (303) 892-1112; 1-800-433 2656.

Connecticut Department of Economic Development: 210 Washington St, Hartford, CT 06106. Tel: (203) 566-3948; 1-800-842-7492 from northeastern states only.

Delaware State Travel Service: 99 Kings Highway, PO Box 1401, Dover, DE 19903. Tel: (302) 736-4271; 1-800-282 8667 within Delaware; 1-800-441-8846 from outside the State.

Washington DC Convention & Visitors Association: 1575 I St NW, Suite 250, Washington, DC 20005. Tel: (202) 789-7000.

Florida Division of Tourism: 126 Van Buren St., Tallahassee, FL 32301. Tel: (904) 488-8230.

Georgia Department of Industry & Trade: PO Box 1776, Atlanta, GA 30301. Tel: (404) 656-3590.

Hawaii Visitors Bureau: 2270 Kalakaua Avenue, Room 801, Honolulu, HI 96815. Tel: (808) 923-1811.

Idaho Travel Council: State Capitol Building, Room 108, Boise, ID 83720. Tel: (208) 334-2470; 1-800-635-7820.

Illinois Department of Commerce & Community Affairs: 310 S. Michigan Avenue, Suite 108, Chicago, IL 60604. Tel: (312) 793-2094.

Indiana Department of Commerce, Tourism Development Division: 1 N Capitol, Suite 700, Indianapolis, IN 46204. Tel: (307) 232-8860; 1-800-2 WANDER.

Iowa Tourism and Film Office: 600, E Court Avenue, Capitol Center, Suite A, Des Moines, IA 50309. Tel: (515) 281-3100; 1-800-345 IOWA

Kansas Travel and Tourism Department: 503 Kansas Avenue, 6th Floor, Topeka, KS 66603. Tel: (913) 296-2009.

Kentucky Travel Development Department: Capital Plaza Tower, Frankfort, KY 40601. Tel: (502) 564-4930; 1-800-225 TRIP.

Louisiana Office of Tourism: Box 44291, Baton Rouge, LA 70804. Tel: (504) 925-3860.

Maine State Tourism Office: 189 State St, Augusta, ME 04333. Tel: (207) 289-2423.

Maryland Office of Tourist Development: 45 Calvert St, Annapolis, MD 21401. Tel: (301) 269-3517; 1-800-331-1750.

Massachusetts Division of Tourism: 100 Cambridge St, Boston, MA 02202. Tel: (617) 727-3201.

Michigan Department of Commerce, Travel Bureau: Box 30226, Lansing, MI 48909. Tel: (517) 373-0670; 1-800-5432 YES.

Minnesota Travel Information Center: 240 Bremer Building, 419 N Robert St St Paul, MN 55101. Tel: (612) 296-5029; 1-800-642 9747 within Minnesota; 1-800-328-1461 from outside the State.

Mississippi Division of Tourism: Box 22825, Jackson, MS 39205. 1-800-962-2346.

Missouri Division of Tourism: Truman State Office Building, Box 1055, Jefferson City, MO 65102. Tel: (314) 751-4133.

Montana Travel Promotion Bureau: 1424 Ninth Avenue, Helena, MT 59620. Tel: (406) 449-2654; 1-800-548-3390.

Nebraska Tourism Division: Box 94666, Lincoln, NE 68509. Tel: (402) 471-3796; 1-800-742-7595 within Nebraska; 1-800-228-4307 from outside the State.

Nevada Commission on Tourism: Capitol Complex, Carson City, NV 89710. Tel: (702) 885-4322.

New Hampshire Office of Vacation Travel: Box 856, Concord, NH 03301. Tel: (603) 271-2343.

New Jersey Division of Travel & Tourism: CM 826, Trenton, NJ 08625. Tel: (609) 292-2470.

New Mexico Tourism & Travel Division: Bataan Memorial Building, Santa Fe, NM 87503. Tel: (505) 827-6230; 1-800-545-2040.

New York Division of Tourism: 1 Commercial Plaza, Albany, NY 12245. Tel: (518) 474-4116; 1-800-CALL NYS (from north-eastern states only)

North Carolina Travel & Tourism Division: 430 N. Salisbury St., Box 25249, Raleigh, NC 27611. Tel: (919) 733-4171; 1-800- VISIT NC.

North Dakota Tourism Promotion Division: Capitol Grounds, Bismarck, ND 58505. Tel: (701) 224-2525; 1-800-472-2100 within North Dakota; 1-800-228-4307 from outside the State.

Ohio Office of Travel & Tourism: Box 1001, Columbus, OH 43216. Tel: (614) 466-8844; 1-800-BUCK EYE.

Oklahoma Tourism & Recreation Department: 500 Will Rogers Building, Oklahoma City, OK 73105. Tel: (405) 521-2409; 1-800-652-6552 from nearby states only.

Oregon Division of Tourism: 595, Cottage St, NE, Salem, OR 97310. Tel: (503) 373-1200; 1-800-223-3306 within Oregon; 1-800-547-7842 from outside the State.

Pennysylvania Bureau of Travel Development: 416 Forum Building, Harrisburg, PA 17120. Tel: (717) 787-5453; 1-800-VISIT PA

Rhode Island Department of Economic Development, Tourist Promotion; 7 Jackson Walkway, Providence, RI 02903. Tel: (401) 277-2601; 1-800-556-2484 (from northeastern states only).

South Carolina Division of Tourism: Edgar A. Brown Building, 1205 Pendleton St, Suite 110, Columbia, SC 29201. Tel: (803) 758-8735.

South Dakota Division of Tourism: 221 S. Central, Pierre, SD 57501. Tel: (605) 773-3301; 1-800-952-2217 within South Dakota; 1-800-843-1930 from outside the State.

Tennessee Department of Tourist Development: 601, Broadway, Box 23170, Nashville, TN 37202. Tel: (615) 741-2158.

Texas Travel & Information Division: Box 5064, Austin, TX 78763. Tel: (512) 475-5956.

Utah Travel Council, Council Hall, Salt Lake City, UT 84114. Tel: (801) 533-5681.

Vermont Travel Division: 134 State St, Montpelier, VT 05602. Tel: (802) 828-3236.

Virginia State Travel Service: 202, N Ninth St, Suite 500, Richmond, VA 23219. Tel: (804) 786-4484.

Washington State Tourism Development Division: 101 General Administration Building, Olympia, WA 98504. Tel: (206) 753-5600; 1-800-544-1800.

West Virginia Travel Development: Building 6, Room B-564, Charleston, WV 25305. Tel: (304) 348-2286; 1-800-CALL WVA.

Wisconsin Division of Tourism: Box 7606, Madison, WI 53707. Tel: (608) 266-2161.

Wyoming Travel Commission: Frank Norris Jr Travel Center, Cheyenne, WY 82002. Tel: (307) 777-7777; 1-800-CALL WYO.

New York
City and State

New York may not have London's grandeur, Paris's romance nor Venice's beauty, but what it does have is vitality. To a New Yorker those other cities with their various claims to greatness don't matter a fig. New York is a place of extremes: it has the best and the worst in every category. It pulsates with energy. It is no more possible to tire of New York than it is of life. When you're on a high, New York will back you up and open its doors to pleasure. When you're down, it won't care. New York is no place for the weary, nor for the poor. You need energy and vitality to match the city's, and enough money to enjoy its opportunities.

New York is known as the "Big Apple", an expression which originated among the blacks who migrated from the South, to describe anything very, very big. Although the city may not always be equal to the task of feeding, clothing, educating, informing, entertaining, heating, cooling, policing and protecting its seven million people, it tackles the job with great gusto. Somehow, it has enough left over to cope with over 17 million visitors as well.

One hundred hospitals and five medical centres cater to New Yorkers' health needs. Seven thousand underground cars carry 1½ billion riders annually. Two thousand and fifty schools and 91 colleges, universities and technical schools educate the city's young and old. Fourteen thousand sanitary engineers (dustbin men) take away four million tons of refuse annually and keep 7,500 miles of streets clean and free of snow. Fifteen TV stations, not counting cable TV channels and over 30 radio stations provide

New Yorkers with news, music, sports and comedy. Theatres, ballets, concert halls, 125 museums, five zoos, a planetarium and an aquarium entertain New Yorkers. Two baseball teams, two football teams, one soccer team, two ice hockey teams and three racetracks make the Big Apple a sportsviewer's (and punter's) paradise. Those into active sports have 538 municipal tennis courts, 13 golf courses, 37 outdoor and 11 municipal indoor swimming pools, and facilities for boating, biking, riding and jogging.

No one knows how much energy the energetic city consumes, but it's a lot. Energy is required to heat, cool and light the city's huge area and to propel New Yorkers up and down hundreds of storeys in lifts. Some 1.2 billion gallons of water must be brought in daily, so that New Yorkers can drink, cook, bathe and launder their clothes. One could go on with mind-boggling statistics for pages. They give an impression of how awesomely huge and splendidly organised the city is.

Metropolitan New York is divided into five boroughs which together cover an area of 300 square miles. The island of Manhattan (almost always called "New York" by natives and visitors alike) lies in the mouth of the Hudson River and is the place in which the visitor will spend most of his or her time. The other boroughs are Brooklyn, Queens, the Bronx and Staten Island. Their residents are described derisively by Manhattan people as the "B & T" (bridge and tunnel) crowd. The Bronx is the only borough which is on the mainland and is mainly known for its slums, which the City has recently tried to disguise by erecting cheery vinyl facades to cover up shattered tenements and burned out buildings. Brooklyn and Queens are part of Long Island, which stretches 350 miles out into the Atlantic, and Staten Island occupies its own island which is connected to the mainland by one of the longest suspension bridges in the world.

Almost every New Yorker and many non-New Yorkers believe (with some justification) that New York is where everything important happens. If you can make it in New York, you've made it: there is no higher achievement. You haven't reached the heights until your talent has been recognized in the Big Apple. As a former Governor of New York, Al Smith, once observed about New York versus the rest of the country, "When you're west of the Hudson River, you're camping out."

New Yorkers are quirky, proud and arrogant. They are the products of a defiantly artificial megalopolis whose towering architecture, success/money ethos, and extreme urban style of life can overwhelm all but the most resilient. Against the odds, the true New York not only survives but flourishes. In the heat of battle with their environment, New Yorkers ignore the past and future and concentrate on the present, in which they stretch their capacities for work and play to the limit.

THE NATIVES

Few New Yorkers want to know about their city's history: its discovery by the Dutch in 1524, its acquisition by the British in 1775, the building of Central Park in the 1860's, the construction of famous skyscrapers during the 1930s following the Wall Street crash and so on. As the visit soon discovers, many natives believe the history of the city started with their (or their parents' or grandparents') arrival. "The story of New York" wrote Anthony Burgess, "is a story of immigrant battling with immigrant", and perhaps it is this continuous battling that makes the New Yorkers so hard.

What is not open to question is the fact that successive waves of immigration have produced a city with the greatest ethnic diversity of any in the world. Indeed, in New York, the minorities seem to be the majority: over three million blacks and Hispanics make up almost half the population, American-Italians constitute just under 10%, and American-Irish about 7%. Almost 250,000 Asians (mainly Chinese, but now including Vietnamese and Koreans) and some 300,000 German-Americans, Austrian-Americans and Swiss-Americans are also there. On top of that, there are large communities of Hungarians, Greeks, Filipinos and Indians. To complicate matters further, there are 700,000 people who are racially unclassifiable. There are at the very least 56 different ethnic origins represented in the Big Apple, because that's how many different foreign language newspapers are published in the city. Visit the Museum of Immigration in the pedestal of the Statue of Liberty, which illustrates the contributions which immigrants have made to the USA, or the museum on nearby Ellis Island where all prospective immigrants were processed between 1892 and 1924, and which came to be known as the "Island of Tears".

The wide ethnic diversity is reflected in the city's numerous religious and folk festivals: you can celebrate Chinese New Year, march in the St Patrick's Day or Pulaski Parades, sing along to the guitars and bongo drums of the Puerto Rican block parties on San Juan Bautista's Day, follow the procession carrying Our Lady of Carmel through the streets of downtown "Little Italy" or quietly observe in the company of American-Japanese the solemn rites of the Feast of Obon held on Riverside Drive above the Hudson River.

An ethnic self-consciousness accompanies the ethnic diversity, and this cosmopolitanism contributes in large measure to the Big Apple's fascination. When blacks and Jews and Poles and Chinese don green caps and wave little green flags, singing "When Irish Eyes are Smiling" on St.Patrick's Day, you may think you understand the intention or the hope of the melting pot theory. But predominant in the consciousness of New Yorkers is the firm belief of not being melted in that pot, of retaining a separate identity.

Class, as well as race, divides New Yorkers. Millionaires, the middle classes, yuppies, 15,000 vagrants sleeping rough (1,000 of which die unidentified and unclaimed each year) and over one million welfare recipients crowd together in the city, though the gap between rich and poor is very seldom bridged. Panhandlers (beggars) are numerous and persistent, but you should quickly cultivate resistance to their approaches. Some shops sell T-shirts reading "NO spare change". What unites New Yorkers of all classes and races is simply that New York, for better or worse, is their city, that living within its 300 square miles bestows a unique privilege, burden, opportunity and right to voice an opinion on how it ought to be run. Every New Yorker is an authority on New York; every New Yorker will insist that he or she alone knows the best place to eat, shop, sleep or visit. Ask directions on a street, and two New Yorkers will argue about the best way for you to get there, and often give two completely contradictory answers. Moreover, each will give you the directions with utter certainty that he or she is right, the other wrong.

On the other hand there are unexpected demonstration of fellowship among New Yorkers. Recently a man arrived at his parked car just as the meter expired and at the moment a traffic warden was about to summon the towing squad. When the warden persisted despite the man's protests, 15 passers-by climbed onto the car to prevent it from being towed away.

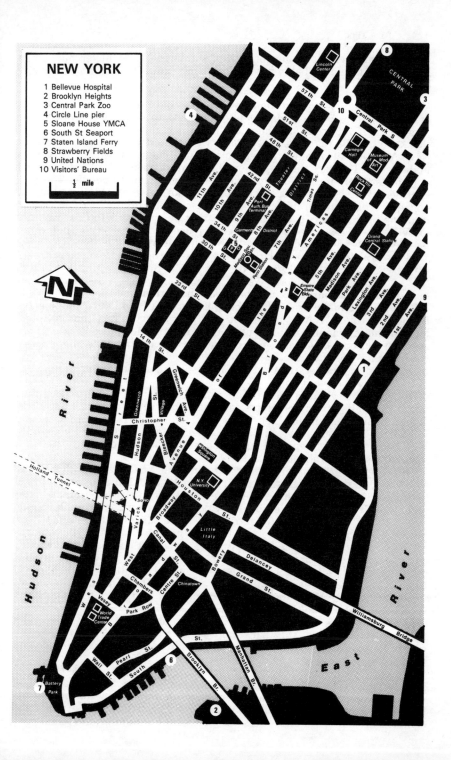

The spontaneous expression of citizen solidarity could never happen in Britain, and would probably not take so flamboyant a form in any other city in the world.

Making Friends. The reputation New Yorkers have earned for pugnacity is understandable. Being cocksure is often hard to distinguish from being aggressive. If you tread on someone's toes, you can expect to be abused, but this shouldn't be taken very seriously. Everyone does it to everyone else. New Yorkers also have a reputation for coldness which is simply undeserved. They are the most open of all American city dwellers, open not only to fads, art forms, life-styles and ideologies, but to people. Too self-confident for shyness and to curious for caution, they think nothing of engaging complete strangers in intimate conversations. To their way of thinking, if someone's in a public place, that person wants to talk. This ties in with their exaggerated image-consciousness. Those who find other people's confessions and self-revelations unwelcome had better avoid New Yorkers. Exploring new relationships and tasting new experiences are active goals of most denizens of the Big Apple. Surprisingly, it has one of the nation's lowest divorce rates among big cities, possibly because "meaningful associates" and "cohabitees" have replaced spouses.

If you can't make friends in the Big Apple, it's unlikely you'll make friends anywhere. New Yorkers not only lack reserve, they tend to spend an inordinate amount of time out of their homes and flats. Weekends are spent at museums, concerts, poetry readings, or in the city's many parks. Evenings are spent on the town. Following cocktails and dinner, there can be opera, disco, ballet, theatre, a concert, nightclub, jazz joint, film, party or bar — anywhere but home.

Discos of every variety are excellent places to meet people, though it's not cheap to hop from one club to another when there may be a $10 cover charge (which does include a drink or two). Many have a short lifetime and fads change. A quick glance at the *Village Voice, Soho News, After Dark* or *New York Magazine* should give you an idea of which place is currently "in", but it's still wise to call ahead.

The singles bars play an even greater role in NYC than in other cities. You will find the average singles bars along 1st and 2nd Avenues between 60th and 85th Streets. Often they live cheek by jowl with ordinary pubs and clubs. Inside, you can enjoy every decor and crowd imaginable. Some, like Friday's, Maxwell's Plum and Elaine's are said to attract celebrities, but instead act as a magnet for gawking out-of-towners. The restless search for partners dominates the atmosphere of many of these bars, though stiff competition means that there are just as many losers as winners. If your main ambition is to see celebrities, you could try lurking outside the Dakota Apartments, Central Park West and 72nd St where many stars have lived, including John Lennon: Strawberry Fields, dedicated to his memory, is just across the street in Central Park.

If your object is not so much sex as a stimulating conversation, there is the regular New York City bar. Many visitors and New Yorkers feel you have a better chance to meet people here than in the noise, riot, crush and light show atmosphere of a popular disco.

Except for San Francisco, there is probably no other city in the USA with such a visible gay population, both male and female, and bars play and important part in the social interaction. The Oscar Wilde Memorial Bookstart is a good place to investigate the gay scene, for it is here that you can pick up journals, newspapers and postings of both male and female gay events. Here, too, you can find copies of the *Gayellow Pages,* a listing of goods and services for the gay community. You can also call National Gay Task Force (741-5800) or the Lesbian or Gay Switchboards for additional information. The gay scene in New York has come a long way from Victorian drawing rooms with men standing about wearing green carnations and making *bon mots.* The spectre of AIDS, though, has cast its shadow over the gay community. 'Safe sex' is the byword now, but it by no means eliminates all risk.

Among the best places to meet people are the campus and bars, cafes, bookstores and restaurants of the neighbourhoods surrounding the campuses. New York University (NYU) is downtown beside Washington Square; check in the Loeb Student Center for university events open to the public. Columbia University is uptown not far from Harlem. To get the flavour of the area around Columbia, drop into Marvin Gardens Restaurant, West End Cafe or Green Tree Hungarian Restaurant, all within a five minute stroll of Columbia University. Remember, too, that because of the vast number of Americans who go back to university to start second careers or to undertake post-university work or adult education, one is just as likely to strike up conversation with men or women in their 30s and 40s as with people in their 20s.

Those looking to make friends among college people might also appreciate the folks they are likely to meet at museums, gallery openings and in the queues waiting to get into concerts, films or plays where common interests are an easy opening to conversation. Or loiter around the Citicorp Center (53rd St at Lexington Avenue; 559-4259) where you and others like you will be entertained by the chamber music or jazz. The free summer concerts of the New York Philharmonic in Central Park (see *Music)* are especially friendly occasions with a mood of celebration.

You'll notice in most parks baseball and softball games materialize whenever enough enthusiasts gather for a few informal innings of play. You'll also see rugby, soccer, frisbee and maybe even cricket played impromptu in the Upper East Side area of Central Park facing 5th Avenue. It is easy to meet people with similar interests this way, both New Yorkers and expatriates.

CLIMATE

In general, early spring is windy and rainy; May and June are ideal; July and August are oppressively hot, often going above 90°F/33°C and stiflingly humid; autumn is generally delightful with a surprising range of colour in the foliage; and from December through February, there are snowstorms, icy conditions and slush underfoot which makes walking treacherous. Call 976-1212 for weather information.

When deciding on your travelling wardrobe, remember that the city buildings are over-cooled in summer and over-heated in winter by fanned central heating.

Getting Around

ARRIVAL AND DEPARTURE

Air. New York's airports are not the best introduction to the city or the country. Even before you land, your flight is likely to be delayed because of crowded airspace. Once you touchdown, you can face a wait of two hours or more to clear immigration and customs. In addition, the problems of changing flights or travelling into Manhattan are considerable. For details of airport links, call 1-800-AIR-RIDE toll-free.

Kennedy International Airport (JFK). Most international flights arrive at JFK, about 15 miles east of Manhattan. In 1988, readers of *Business Traveller* magazine voted it worst in the world for both immigration and customs clearance. The fastest way into the city is by helicopter ($70). A taxi will cost at least $40. To avoid being taken on a circuitous route, ask the driver to use either the Manhattan Bridge (for the south of Manhattan) or the Queensboro (59th St) Bridge; this will give the impression that you know your way around, so a scenic diversion via the Bronx is less likely. Next quickest (at least in theory) is the Carey Transportation bus ($8) running to Manhattan's Grand Central Station and the Rockefeller Center, although services are unreliable. During the morning rush hour the JFK Express is the best bet: for $6.50 you take a shuttle bus to Howard Beach subway station, with a connecting express train to Brooklyn and midtown Manhattan. The cheapest way into town ($2) is to take bus Q10 from the inner ring road to a regular subway station: Lefferts Boulevard for the A line (fastest to south Manhattan) or Union Turnpike/Kew gardens for the E line (quickest to midtown).

When changing aircraft, note that JFK has five terminals linked by a slow and irregular shuttle bus which arrives at and departs from the ground level of each terminal and travels anticlockwise; for a faster ride, cross to the inner ring road and catch the clockwise yellow shuttle bus, intended for staff. A direct bus service runs to La Guardia ($7, about 30 minutes), while to reach Newark you need to take a bus or subway to Manhattan then travel out.

Newark International Airport (EWR). Continental, Virgin Atlantic and several other carriers fly into Newark, ten miles southwest of Manhattan. Confusingly all international arrivals are at Terminal C, while Virgin Atlantic departures leave from Terminal A. A taxi to New York City involves paying a $10 surcharge plus the toll and is likely to cost $40-$50. More cheaply, you can take the New Jersey Transit bus to Manhattan's Port Authority Bus Terminal, or the Olympia bus to the World Trade Center and Penn Station. There are departures every 20-30 minutes, and the one-way fare is $6, The journey time can be anything from 20 to 120 minutes. To cut the journey cost to $2, take the local bus to downtown Newark then a PATH train to Manhattan. This will not be a pleasant experience at night.

La Guardia (LGA) This airport is much closer to Manhattan than the other two airports. It handles domestic and Canadian flights, including the Trump Air and Pan Am shuttles to Boston and Washington DC. Note that the Pan Am shuttles use the Marine Terminal, a mile from the rest of the airport. You can reach this splendid art deco, former seaplane terminal in 30 minutes by launch from Wall St or E34th St in Manhattan for $18; call 1-800-54 FERRY for details. To get to the Marine terminal by public transport, take the subway to Jackson Heights and connect to bus Q47. For the other terminals, use the same subway stop but take bus Q33. Carey Transportation buses run to all La Guardia terminals from the Rockefeller Center and Grand Central Station for $7. A taxi costs $15 or so.

New York is the best place in the USA to buy cheap international air tickets. Students should try Council Travel, 205 E 42nd St (661-0311) for the best deals; in summer 1988 you could fly to London on Pan Am for $199. Its sister organization, Council Charter (same address, 661-0311 or 1-

800-223-7402) sells cut-price tickets to non-students on both scheduled and charter flights. For other agencies, check the advertisements in Saturday's *New York Times.*

Bus. You arrive by bus at the Port Authority Bus Terminal, 8th Avenue and 41st St (564-8484); the Greyhound number is (635-0800). It is widely held view that the best pickpockets in the city operate at the Bus Terminal. If you want to escape from Manhattan, the Catskill Mountains are less than 100 miles away; the two hour bus journey to Monticello on the Short Line Bus System (736-4700) costs about $30.

Train. The two Amtrak terminals are Grand Central Station (42nd St and Park Avenue) and Penn Station (34th St between 7th and 8th Avenues). A shuttle bus operates between the two stations. Grand Central is the terminal for services to Canada and some suburban trains, but most fast trains serve only Penn. The Long Island Railroad (739-4200) can take you from Penn Station to Montauk at the tip of Long Island for $15 one way, a three hour journey. The route along the east side of the Hudson River from Grand Central is also a scenic outing (532-4900).

Driving. Think carefully before attempting to bring a car into Manhattan. Road signs on the outskirts seem designed to confuse; instead of signs to, for example, "Downtown", you are offered options of various crossings to Manhattan, or obscure freeway names which are of no use to drivers unfamiliar with the city. On most crossings to Manhattan (but not Brooklyn or Manhattan Bridges) a $2 toll is levied; if you plan to cross frequently, you can buy a pack of 20 tokens for $34. The authorities are at present looking for ways to keep cars out of Manhattan, and proposals include a $10 per day tax on visiting motorists. If you are still not deterred, see page xxx for the problems of parking in the city.

Hitch-hiking. Around Manhattan the overwhelming majority of traffic is local, so it is well worth investing a few dollars on public transport to get away from the city. The closest reasonable proposition for I-80 west and I-95 north is the Manhattan approach to George Washington Bridge; take the subway to 181 St station and stand somewhere on the tangle of approaches to the bridge, holding a sign and smiling wanly. For I-95 southwest, take a train from Penn station to Metropark New Jersey, close to the suburb of Iselin and with relatively easy access to the Interstate.

Driveaways. Among the many auto driveaway companies listed in the Yellow Pages, one welcomes foreign drivers (you are invited to call in advance) and has a minimum age limit of 19 rather than the usual 21: Dependable Car Travel Services, in Suite 301 at 1501 Broadway (840-6262). Although competition for cars from New York is intense in summer, with patience and persistence you should find one.

CITY TRANSPORT

City Layout. It is not as easy as you might think to find your way around Manhattan. Avenues run north-south, streets run east west. Broadway traces a crooked diagonal from the south to the northwest. It is relatively easy to navigate in central Manhattan, but you should bear in mind that 3rd and 5th Avenues are separated by three others (Lexington, Park and Madison), and that 8th Avenue becomes Central Park West north of 59th St. Avenue of the Americas is usually known as 6th Avenue. In the south of

Manhattan the grid system collapses into disarray, exacerbated by the underpasses and flyovers leading to bridges and tunnels.

Fifth Avenue runs through the centre of the city and is the dividing line between East and West in street addresses. You will also hear people talking about downtown, midtown and uptown divisions of the city. Downtown or lower Manhattan is the southern tip of the island including Wall Street, Chinatown and Greenwich Village; Midtown extends from roughly 14th St to 59th St and uptown is north of 59th St,which forms the southern boundary of Central Park, all the way north to the Bronx, including Harlem.

Walking. New York is a pavement town and you are likely to do a lot of walking in it, so bring comfortable shoes or buy jogging shoes with hard rubber studs which are especially designed to save wear and tear on feet in cities. Even the city's yuppies wear running shoes to work.

The pavements of New York are a constant source of entertainment. On Easter Sunday join in the traditional see-and-be-seen promenade along 5th Avenue (near the Museum of Modern Art). Many areas such as Wall Street, Greenwich Village, SoHo, 5th Avenue and Central Park are best appreciated on foot. You can walk to Brooklyn Heights across the architecturally striking Brooklyn Bridge which offers a vantage point from which to view the harbour and skyline of Manhattan. This is especially stunning at sunrise when you can watch the play of lights on the glass and steel facades of the buildings.

Walking tours are listed in the *New York Magazine.* Adventures on a Shoestring (300 West 53rd St, 265-2663) arranges more off-beat walking tours. If you want to walk on your own, investigate *Flashmaps* at $4.95 each, a well-organised series of individual neighbourhoods.

Bus. The Metropolitan Transit Authority runs buses on all north/south avenues and major east/west crosstown streets. Buses have no conductors and drivers won't give change. Board at the front of the bus and deposit $1 in coins or an MTA token (which can be bought at booths in subway stations) in the box beside the driver. If you don't have change, fellow passengers will help. Ask for a free transfer if your trip requires changing buses.

The Culture Bus Loops I and II are special tours created by the New York Transit Authority to help visitors see the Big Apple. They take you virtually to the front doors of many of New York City's major museums, tourist attractions and places of historical interest. The loop which includes Lower Manhattan takes you to the World Trade Center, Greenwich Village and across the East River to Brooklyn Heights. The other loop includes midtown and uptown attractions such as the Rockefeller Center and Central Park. The Culture Bus Loops operate on Saturdays, Sundays and some holidays. Buses ply the route every 30 minutes in the winter, 20 minutes in the summer, and make 22 stops. You can get off at any or all of the stops, take in the sights then catch a later bus. A free 44-page guidebook crammed with information about 124 points of interest along the loop will act as your guide. A ticket costs $3 in exact change or tokens, and is valid all day. Phone 1-718-330-1234 for further information.

Subway. The New York subway is one of the fastest and most extensive (240 miles of track) underground railways in the world. It can also be the most frightening, confusing and unpleasant. Be sure to pick up a detailed map of the system given away at stations and tourist offices, since you cannot rely on finding a map once you have entered the system. Unfortunately the subway map is horribly confusing and even a simple journey requires considerable study and planning. It is also very difficult to ask for directions since ticket sellers are shielded behind layers of bullet proof (and sound proof) glass.

The subway map explains some of the peculiarities of the system, whereby express trains miss out certain stations at certain times of the day. Find out if your destination is a "local" or an "express" stop. If you are still in doubt, ring Transit Information on 1-718-330-1234 and explain where you are and where you want to be.

Originally run by three competing companies, IND, IRT and BMT — names which are still used by many New Yorkers — the system is now run by the New York City Transit Authority. It provides round-the-clock service and a $1 token will, if you wish, take you around the entire sytem. You can buy a "Tenpak" at ticket booths, but this saves only queuing rather than cash. To enter the system, simply drop a token into the turnstile slot and walk through.

Weighed against the advantages of speed and economy is the fact that the subway is filthy, noisy, and especially at night, a semi-degenerate world of its own, unpredictable, potentially dangerous. There is an independent 3,000-strong special police force called the Transit Police. In addition, there is a group of volunteers called "Guardian Angels", male and female vigilantes in red berets who ride unarmed, relying on their karate skills and teamwork rather than weapons. For details about how to maximise your safety on the subway, see the section *Crime and Safety.*

Suburban Trains The subway extends into the outlying boroughs, but to get across to New Jersey or to the northern and eastern suburbs you need to use the suburban train networks. New Jersey is served by the Port Authority Trans-Hudson (PATH) railway, with the main Manhattan terminus at the World Trade Center. Long Island can be reached on the Long Island Rail Road (LIRR), and the northern suburbs on Metro North; trains on both these systems leave from Grand Central.

Car. Don't bother with motoring in the city: the traffic is frantic; streets are so potholed that axles are always being broken; there is very little legal street parking and midtown garages cost at least $15 per hour (municipal garages are cheapest). Parking law in the city is so complex that an entire book is devoted to the subject. Glen Bolovski's *New York City Alternate Side of the Street Parking Calendar* details all the rules and highlights the 30 days each year when normal restrictions are lifted. The book is available from the author (who no longer drives) at PO Box 2499, Grand Central, New York 10163. If the police take your car to the "docks", it's going to cost a minimum of $60 to retrieve it, plus a $35 ticket and an unpleasant visit to the pound which is surrounded by armed guards. There is a service called Auto Baby Sitters at 827 Sterling Place, Brooklyn (1-718-493-9800), which is simply a secure long term car park.

You may decide to rent a car for a weekend drive out-of-town. But car rentals in NYC are often twice as expensive as they are in Florida or California. The best deals are booked up early, especially over a holiday period, so make reservations well in advance.

Taxis. There are exactly 11,787 licensed taxis in the city, a number unchanged since the Depression. New Yorkers are inveterate taxi users, so you may find competition stiff, especially in foul weather. Avoid cabs which are not yellow, since these are probably unlicensed, and look for the identity card with a photo of the driver displayed inside. Unlicensed drivers prey upon tourists in locations such as Grand Central Station and the Port Authority bus terminal; some purport to have been sent by your hotel. You might be asked to pay $20 after a trip of only a few blocks, and you won't get your luggage back until you pay up. Be especially cautious if you are taking a taxi from JFK. There are many stories in circulation of drivers who will take you to Manhattan via New Jersey, charging upwards of $200. If you are ripped off or have a complaint, phone 747-0930 giving the driver's name and number

The initial charge is $1.15, plus 15c for each additional eighth of a mile, plus a 50c surcharge from 6pm-6am. You will have to pay any bridge or tunnel tolls in addition to the mileage charge. Don't hesitate to ask any taxi driver about New York; many of them are fountains of quirky information. But don't be tempted to smoke in the back of a cab, since this carries a fine of $50.

Cycling. The bicycle courier fraternity takes pride in the fact that one of its number won an Olympic gold medal for speed cycling. Despite the antagonism generated by the couriers' antics, cycling is growing in popularity as a means of getting around the city and there are some demarcated cycle routes. But there are major problems: potholes, inclement weather, theft, and motorists who just don't seem able to spot cyclists in their rear view mirrors, nor remember to check before opening car doors. Still if the prospect doesn't frighten you, it is a quick and cheap way to get around the Big Apple.

Cycing is also a popular Sunday recreation for New Yorkers. Bicycles can be rented for about $5 per hour or $20 per day, with a deposit of $50 or credit card. Sunday, with its limited traffic, is an excellent day for exploring lower and midtown Manhattan. Traffic is prohibited from Central Park on the weekends, so this is a good time to rent a bicycle and watch New Yorkers at rest and play. Try Metro Bicycles which has six branches including one at 1311 Lexington Avenue at 88th St which is handy for Central Park (427-4450); Loeb Boathouse in Central Park at about 72nd St (360-8111); or Sixth Avenue Bicycle, 546 6th Avenue at 15th St (255-5100), well situated for bicycle forays into Greenwich Village and SoHo.

Ferries. If you would like to get an idea of Manhattan from the water that surrounds it, then take a Circle Line tour leaving from Pier 83, West 43rd St (563-3200), price $15; the boat tour lasts about three hours, leaving every 45 minutes. It runs between mid-March and late November.

New York's favourite boat ride is the Staten Island Ferry. At 25c, it must be one of the cheapest water voyages per mile in the world. You get good views of the Statue of Liberty and the skyline of Manhattan. There's not much point in getting off on Staten Island so you might as well stay on board and save a quarter. The service runs every half an hour day and night from Battery Park at the southern tip of Manhattan, which is a good place for a pre-ferry picnic.

Accommodation

Hotels. Manhattan is by no means a cheap place for accommodation and you won't want to stay in any other borough. As prices for property have skyrocketed, small inexpensive hotels and low-priced rooming houses have all disappeared. In Manhattan, a one-room flat with a bathroom and kitchenette in a good, safe neighbourhood fetches over $1000 a month. Competition is fierce for any reasonably priced hotel rooms which are still around. It may well be worth making a transatlantic call to one of the hotels listed below. Otherwise you could trudge the streets of Manhattan for hours or else pay a very high price. Remember to add 8¼% sales tax to the price of a room plus $1.50 occupancy tax. Bed and breakfast accommodation is exempt. A little-enforced law prohibits smoking within 20 feet of a hotel reception desk.

Head for the New York Convention and Visitors Bureau, 2 Columbus Circle (397-8222) and pick up two free pamphlets: *Hotels* with addresses, phone numbers and rates and *I Love New York at Night Packages.* Check the Travel Section of the *New York Times* for hotel adverts offering weekend package deals: two for the price of one, sometimes with breakfast or theatre tickets thrown in. The following hotels often participate in the scheme: Bedford, 118 E 40th St (697-4800), Beverly, 125 E 50th St (753-2700) and Carter Hotel, 250 W 43rd St (944-6000).

Below are a few suggestions of reasonably priced hotels, but phone ahead for reservations:

Chelsea Hotel, 222 W 23rd St (243-3700). A bohemian landmark in whose lift Leonard Cohen met Janis Joplin, and where Bob Dylan wrote "Sad Eyed Lady of Lowlands"; $85 double.

Clinton Herald Square Hotel, 19 W 31st St, between 5th and 6th Avenues (279-4017), $50 double.

Franklin Hotel, 164 E 87th St (289-5958) $50 double.

Hotel 17, E 17 St. Squalid but only $30 double.

Rio Hotel, 132 W 47th St (382-0600), $60 double.

Hostels. The new International Youth Hostel on Amsterdam Avenue between 103rd and 104th Streets (431-7105) is to open in the summer of 1989 . Housed in the former Associated Residence for Respectable Aged Indigent Females, it costs $19 per night. There is a 25 bed hostel at 515 W 42nd St just a few blocks from the Port Authority Bus Terminal called the Travel Inn Motor Hotel. Ring 695-7171 to reserve. Prices range from $15 to $35 depending on whether you have a room to yourself or share with up to three others. The Chelsea Centre Hostel (511 W 20th St) is well situated and clean; expect to pay $15-$20 per person including breakfast. Book in advance on 243-4922.

YMCA. Ys which accept both men and women charge approximately $27-$30 per person in a double. Try the massive William Sloane House, 356 West 34th St (695-0291); the YMCA Vanderbilt (244 E 47th St, 755-2410) handy to Grand Central Station and with sauna, pool, laundry and library; and the YMCA West Side (5 W 63rd St, 787-4400) near the Lincoln Center, where the fee for a double is about $40.

You might also want to check out a three night package deal on one of the Ys mentioned (others are not coeducational), plus three breakfasts, two dinners, sightseeing tour and dinner in Chinatown, plus Circle Line cruise around the Manhattan (itself costing $15), all for around $100: contact The Ys Way, 356 W 34th St, New York, NY 10001 (760-5856).

Bed and Breakfast. Because of the high cost of other accommodation in New York, bed and breakfast can be particularly good value. In Manhattan contact New Yorkers at Home, 301 E 60th St, New York, NY 10022 (838-7015) or Urban Ventures, PO Box 426, New York 10024 (594-5650), which has 850 listings starting at $35 but more often $60-$80. You can book in advance through the UK office at 139 Round Hey, Liverpool L28 1RG (051-220 5848).

Student Residences. The International Student Center, 500 Riverside Drive (678-5036), for foreign visitors only, offers singles at $20 for the first night, $15 thereafter. International Student Centers are located at 38 W 88th St (787-7706) or Broadway at W 55th St, where a dormitory bed is around $10 for students. New York University sometimes has rooms for students costing $15 single; contact the Undergraduate Housing Secretary, NYU, 54 Washington Square S (598-2083). Finally the Fashion Institute of Technology, 230 W 27th St (760-7885) charges $90 per week during June and July only.

Longer Term Accommodation. Check the sublet columns in the *New York Times* and the *Village Voice*. New Yorkers are prepared to let out rooms for as short a time as one or two weeks if it will make them a few extra dollars.

Eating and Drinking

Where to eat follows money and precedes sex as a New Yorker's favourite topic of conversation. Recommending places to eat in the Big Apple is both fraught with difficulties and perhaps unnecessary, since there are so many good places and publications galore on dining in New York. Coffee shops abound on every corner, and are excellent and colourful places to eat breakfast, pastries or a Mediterranean speciality. Also watch for the diners with signs: "Two eggs, any style $1.49". Don't feel you have to sit down to eat. Street food like sausages, souvlaki and tempura is delicious and cheap. Take it to a park bench if you're tired. From more than 25,000 eating places, here are some suggestions which have reputations for good food at reasonable prices served with no frills. Not all accept credit cards and, unlike pricier restaurants won't expect men to wear jackets and ties. The eating places are listed geographically, moving from downtown to uptown.

Sloppy Louie's 92 South Street near South Street Seaport (952-9657) has long been one on the cities most colourful eating spots in which you sit at long tables in the company of dock workers, stockbrokers and tourists and eat the best fish and shellfish in town.

Hong Fat 63 Mott St in Chinatown (962-9588) open 24 hours, unspoilt by success and rude waiters. Try shrimp and black bean sauce at 4am, a dish considered by many New Yorkers to diminish the next morning's hangover. There are good restaurants all along Mott St, e.g. at numbers 13, 21, 81 and 113.

Say Eng Look 5 East Broadway (732-0796) in Chinatown. Popular for lunch, specializing in Peking cuisine (try Moo Shu Pork).

Umberto's Clam House, 129 Mulberry St (431-7545) in Little Italy bordering Chinatown. Serves Italian style seafood, outdoor seating in summer, open late, frequented by the local "Godfather" types. Sit at the counter and watch the squid, conch and shrimps cooking.

Luna 112 Mulberry St (226-8657). Superb family-run Italian restaurant.

Ratners 138 Delancy St (677-5588) in Lower East Side. Strictly kosher dairy and convenient for Sunday brunch when you're bargain hunting at the nearby street market on Orchard St. Try blintzes (stuffed crepes) or matzo-bri (egg pancakes with matzos soaked in milk)

Ray's Pizza, 465 6th Avenue (at 11th St) plus several other locations. Excellent pizzas.

Nathan's Famous (several locations throughout Manhattan). Famous for its hot dogs, french fries, and meat and seafood delicatessen. Good value fast food.

Horn & Hardart Automat, 200 E 42nd St. Cafeteria, coin-operated selections, bliss for those who would like to avoid the human touch; great place to crash as you can sit as long as you like (7.30am-11pm). Excellent value.

Carnegie Delicatessen 854 7th Avenue (near West 55th St) renowned for its unsurpassed pastrami on rye bread, sour pickles and cole slaw, not to mention its corned beef hash. Open 6.30am to 4am. Sandwiches are not cheap, e.g. $6.95 for corned beef but since they give you 12 ounces of cold cuts on a sandwich, it's understandable.

V&T Pizzeria, 1024 Amsterdam Avenue (663-1708) on the Upper West Side. A favourite with students from Columbia University.

Moving up a notch, it is well worth spending a little more to enjoy some truly excellent food. The following restaurants are, at the time of writing, providing excellent food at reasonable prices:

Eat, 11 St Mark's Place between 2nd and 3rd Avenues (477-5155). A small (and hard to find) bistro/cafe with consistently good food; vegetarians are well catered for.

Cherry Restaurant, 335 Columbus Avenue between 75th and 76th Streets (874-3630). From the outside it looks like a typical old coffee shop, but you go through to a comfortable eating area with a menu combining New York favourites with Japanese influence. Try Long Island Duck ($10).

Nick's Coffee and Pizza Shop, 736 11th Avenue (757-2432). Open all hours except 5am-6am, there is a seemingly infinite variety of pizzas plus excellent home-made yoghourt and baklava.

The best (or at least the most prestigious) restaurant in Manhattan is the *Russian Tea Rooms* on W 57th St between 6th and 7th Avenues. If you're not famous, the waiters will point out people who are. Expect to pay at least $40 per head.

You need to add about a quarter to all menu prices to estimate the final total: 8¼% tax is added to the bill, and it has become an accepted convention to give twice this amount as a tip (it is also relatively easy to calculate by doubling the tax figure). Some restaurants even add 16½% to the bill as a "suggested" service charge.

As well as the obvious areas such as Chinatown and Little Italy, New York has numerous concentrations of other ethnic restaurants. For seafood, go to 2nd Avenue at E 77th St and 3rd Avenue at E 79th St. There is a huddle of Indian, Pakistani and Bangladeshi restaurants on Lexington Avenue between 27th and 28th Streets. W 14th St is the place for Hispanic restaurants, while for soul food try Lenox Avenue around 126th St. South of E 9th St along 2nd Avenue you will find many Ukranian and Polish places; the best Russian food is at Brighton Beach and Coney Island in the borough of Brooklyn. Still in Brooklyn (but much closer to Manhattan), Lebanese restaurants can be found along Court St and Atlantic Avenue.

Picnics. As in other great gastronomic cities, the picnic lunch is both economical and delicious, and fixings can be bought at any corner store.

For a gourmet picnic or just to drool, visit one of the Big Apple's famous food emporiums. For example, Balducci's (422 6th Avenue in Greenwich Village) has exotic varieties of fresh fruit, cheese (try Monterey Jack from California, a tasty American speciality), sliced Virginia ham, smoked turkey and pastries, which, though not cheap, are fresh and fantastic. Take your picnic a few blocks east to Washington Square Park where there is folk singing, comics trying out their routines (including some talented young comics a bit too raw for TV) and assorted instrumentalists. Then there is Zabar's, 2245 Broadway (uptown near 80th St and the Museum of Natural History) which is famed for its chopped chicken liver on pumpernickel bread and its coffee cake topped with pecans and peach ice cream. For a choice of eight varieties of smoked salmon (among other things) visit the long-established Murrays deli on Broadway.

The recent proliferation of Korean greengrocery stores is good news for budget picnickers. Most of these stores have a salad bar on the premises, where you can choose your own salad and pay according to weight: $2.50 to $4 per pound is the usual price range.

Pizza, which sells for between $1 and $1.50 per piece, is good value and is enough for lunch. At the better places, the pizzas are made of good quality cheese, tomatoes, olive oil, spices and other ingredients. Other tasty snacks can be had from the Edible Pickle Works (Delancy and Essex Streets) which offers a delicious range of pickles for 50c; or Lock, Stock and Bagel (opposite Madison Square Garden) which sells 30 types of bagel.

DRINKING

New York has all manner of bars: cocktail, ethnic, artistic bars, neighbourhood affairs, hard drinking bars. They may stay open until 4am every night except Saturday when they must close at 3am (on the theory that if you drink up an hour earlier, you will be in better shape to spend Sunday morning at church or with the family). Bartenders would like to think that tipping is standard, but most New Yorkers don't bother unless they're drinking something other than beer and they have had more than a couple of cocktails or glasses of wine, or they have occupied a stool at the bar.

One bar definitely deserves a visit. McSorley's Old Alehouse (15 East 7th St) has been called "more a state of mind than a place." It is an Irish workingman's bar in a run down Ukrainian neighbourhood which serves only beer, dark and light, and cheese. Its slogan "good ale, raw onions and no ladies" has had to be adapted slightly to the age of feminism, and both sexes are now welcome. Queues form most evenings and every weekend.

Here is a random selection of other bars and a brief summary of their character:

Puffy's, 81 Hudson St at West Broadway. Unchic.

Raoul's, 180 Prince St. Punk hangout.

Cedar Tavern, 82 University Place. An artists' bar.

Kettle of Fish, 114 MacDougal St. New York University student hangout.

West End Cafe, Columbus Avenue, near W 112th St. Cheap food and jazz as well as 70 kinds of beer.

Riviera Cafe, Sheridan Square, junction of 7th Avenue South and W 4th St Greenwich Village. Best street cafe/bar.

Village Corner Tavern, Bleecker St at La Guardia Place. Free jazz on Sunday afternoons.

Chumley's, 86 Bedford at Barrow. Former speakeasy and literary bar.

P J Clarke's, 915 3rd Avenue at 55th St. Semi-chic old pub with a good atmosphere and tasty salads (but avoid the burgers.)

Blue Bar, at the Algonquin Hotel, 59 West 44th St. Established literary chic bar.

Kellers, 384 West St. Grandfather of gay bars.

Andre's, 8th Avenue at 125th St. Biggest and best known gay bar in Harlem.

Tennessee Mountain, 143 Spring St. Monday night "barbecue and brew"; for $15 you get ribs or beef plus all you can drink.

New Amsterdam Brewery, 26th St and 10th Avenue. Barn-like pub-brewery, always crowded and noisy, with several interesting beers and good snacks. Call 255-4100 if you want to join a tour of the brewery.

White Horse, Hudson and Bleecker Streets, Greenwich Village. Dylan Thomas reputedly drank his last drink here, and a bar has been named after him. The tavern sells draught beer by the Imperial pint ($3) and serves excellent fish and chips.

Entertainment

From the dazzling view at the top of the World Trade Center to the frenetic activity of the New York Stock Exchange. New York is endlessly entertaining. Make use of the excellent tourist advice centres which have current schedules of city events. From June through August, leading theatre groups perform Shakespeare, jazz, dance, opera, puppet shows, pop and folk music — much of it free — in the parks and plazas of buildings. Phone 755-4100 for daily schedules. For the summer entertainment in Central Park arrive early with a picnic basket and plenty of beer or wine.

The monumental complex for the performing arts is the Lincoln Center at 65th St and Columbus Avenue (877-1800). It houses the Met (Metropolitan Opera Company), New York Philharmonic Orchestra, New York City Ballet, the New York State Theater and the Julliard School of Music whose students sometimes perform free concerts. During the day the central plaza is enlivened by buskers, assorted street characters and outdoor cafes. Tours, including some behind-the-scene glimpses of the Opera, are available daily from 10 am to 5 pm (877-1800, ext 512.) The Center is most impressive at night when the buildings and fountains are brilliantly lit.

In addition to some of the best theatre, music and art in the world, there is plenty of spontaneous street entertainment and free performances in parks and city squares. For example, visit the Citicorp Center at 53rd St and Lexington Avenue. This trend-setting skyscraper, 59 storeys high, with a metallic finish reflecting the clouds, blue skies and sunsets, built on stilts delicately straddling a bright courtyard with shops (including a gourmet coffee shop called "Slotnick's daughter"), restaurants and even a church, is a classic Big Apple blend of monotheism and monetarism. In a deal with the city, Citicorp agreed that ground space would be set aside for people to sit, relax, shop, picnic or dine and be delighted by entertainment provided daily — chamber music, jazz, trios, etc.

The five block dockland area of the South Street Seaport has rejuvenated lower Manhattan by making it a place to stroll, sit and enjoy concerts, buskers and puppet shows. A restored printer's shop offers maps and maritime souvenirs and there are several early vessels including a square rigger docked at the piers, which may be toured for $5. On your way to this area located at Fulton and South Streets, notice the giant mural paintings which cover the side of a brick building in an amusing *trompe l'oeil* of a bridge tower which appears to be part of the real Brooklyn Bridge visible above the building.

New York Magazine published on Monday and the *New Yorker* on Wednesday carry comprehensive entertainment listings and witty critiques. The *Village Voice* is an excellent source of what's on in the city.

The information in this chapter should sustain you for a short stay in New York, but for longer visits you might wish to invest in a specific guide book. The Michelin *New York City* guide provides comprehensive details on virtually every place of interest, while for the lowdown on nightlife try *The Rough Guide to New York* (RKP, 1987 edition £4.95.)

Buildings of Interest. Le Corbusier called the architecture of New York City a catastrophe, but "a magnificent catastrophe". The Empire State Building, immortalized by a love-sick gorilla, is located at 5th Avenue and 34th St (736-3100). Despite its loss of the title "World's Tallest Building" which it held for 40 years, it is still worth going up to the open observatory on the 86th floor or the glass-enclosed one on the 102nd floor, especially on a clear night (it's open till midnight).

The Rockefeller Center lies between 5th and 6th Avenues, and between 48th and 52nd Streets. It has an observation roof which affords a panoramic view of Manhattan unsurpassed even by taller downtown buildings. Check on the tours available by calling at the Information Desk in the lobby or ringing 246-4600. The Center's most famous landmark is the golden statue of Prometheus, floating above a sunken plaza that is used as an outdoor cafe in summer and ice rink in winter when a giant Christmas tree is put in place. A tour allows you to take a leisurely stroll through the pedestrian walkways or glimpse the luxurious atrium-styled interiors of shops and restaurants. The architectural centrepiece of the Center is the 19-storey RCA Building at 30 Rockefeller Plaza. Completed during the Depression, the socio-realist murals reflect the preoccupation with the shortage of work by exalting it.

Located downtown at Liberty St, the twin towers which make up the major part of the World Trade Center stand 110 storeys high. Two months after completion in 1974, the WTC was replaced by the Sears Building in Chicago as the tallest building in the world. On a clear day, visibility extends for 100 miles. The observation deck on the 110th floor of WTC 2 is open except in bad weather. The tower is open 9.30 am to 9.30 pm daily; the cost is $2.95 (call 466-4710). The Windows on the World restaurant at the top of WTC 1 is another option: a weekend buffet brunch costs $25, and the view is free.

The United Nations headquarters are spread over several acres on the East River. The entrance lies at 1st Avenue at 46th St (963-7113). Free tickets to sessions of the General Assembly and Security Council are obtainable from the Information Desk before debates begin at 10.30 am and 3 pm on a first-come, first -served basis. Guided tours take place daily from 9.15am to 4.45pm and cost $4.50 ($2.50 for students).

The Statue of Liberty in New York Harbour was the creation of sculptor Barthold and engineer Eiffel, and was given to the city by France in 1884. A lift takes visitors halfway up and then a stairway gives access to the observation platform in the crown. The price (including the hourly ferry ride from Battery Park) is $4.

Apart from these well-documented landmarks, there are thousands of less celebrated buildings: in particular, the world's largest cathedral — St John the Divine on 110th St — is a breathtaking construction as well as a lively centre for performing arts. It stages a Bach Festival, a silent film festival, free theatre and dance, and hosts Sunday afternoon concerts.

Museums and Galleries. Manhattan has more museums per square mile than any city in the world. It is advisable to phone ahead for information on special exhibitions. Many of the city's museums are closed on Mondays; some offer free admission on Tuesday evenings and most give student discounts. A number of museums are not allowed to charge admission because of their charter. Instead, they have a "suggested contribution" of about $5. If you really can't afford to pay bear in mind that New Yorkers have free entry to most British museums. If you happen to be in New York in mid-June, there is a stretch of 5th Avenue known as the "Museum Mile" which is closed to traffic while promenaders are allowed to visit the museums within that area free of charge. It's a festive occasion with clowns, street musicians, etc.

More art and antiquities are amassed in the Metropolitan Museum of Art than anywhere in the world. With 248 galleries, still only a quarter of the collection is on display at any one time. In addition to the many Old Masters, the American wing is of special interest for its extraordinary collection of furniture and decorative arts from early colonial times (1630) to the nineteenth century. The museum is on 5th Avenue at 82nd St, on the edge of Central Park (535-7710). It opens daily except Mondays from 9.30am to 5.15pm, with late opening on Tuesdays to 8.45pm.

If you would like to get away from the hustle and bustle of Manhattan, you can visit the Cloisters and have a picnic in Fort Tryon Park, accessible by bus number 4 which runs along Madison Avenue, or by a special bus from the Metropolitan Museum ($4 return). Overlooking the Hudson River and George Washington Bridge, this unusual attraction houses bits and pieces from four mediaeval French monasteries, purchased and reassembled on behalf of the billionaire Rockefellers. The park itself has varied terrain with footpaths and a small botanical garden.

The Museum of Modern Art at 11 West 53rd St (956-7070) has an astonishing collection of masterpieces from 1880 to the present from Monet's water lillies (stunningly displayed in a room of their own) to household objects of superior design. Other museums are the Frick Collection (1 East 70th St near 5th Avenue, 288-0700) housed in an elegantly furnished nineteenth century mansion, and the Guggenheim (5th Avenue at 89th St, 860-1313) in a building designed by Frank Lloyd Wright.

The Museum of the City of New York located on 5th Avenue and 103rd St (534-1672) is as varied as the city it celebrates. It contains dolls' houses, model ships, period rooms, toy collections and multi media shows. The Cooper-Hewitt Museum (2 East 91st St and 5th Avenue, 860-6868) is a working museum of design, including an extensive collection of fabrics. The American Museum of Natural History (79th St and Central Park West, 769-5100) has the best collection of dinosaurs in the world, the golfball-sized "Star of India" diamond and literally millions of other items. The Hayden Planetarium is nearby, with its 2½ ton Zeiss Projector. Call 724-8700 for times and programmes.

The Brooklyn Museum is out of the way but worthwhile (Eastern Parkway and Washington Avenue, 638-5000). It contains primitive art from Africa, a highly acclaimed Egyptian collection and early American paintings. For a large collection of Americana, visit the Museum of

American Folk Art tucked away at 55 West 53rd St (581-2475). You will find patchwork quilts, samplers, weathervanes, whirligig toys and carvings in the folk tradition. For more contemporary objects, go to the American Craft Museum at 40 W 53rd St (696-0710). If you are interested in native American culture, visit the Museum of the American Indian (Broadway at 155th St, 283-2420).

Two hi-tech "museums" are recommended for excellent hands-on exhibits: the New York Hall of Science out at Flushing Meadows in Queens (718-699-0675), and the AT & T InfoQuest Center (Madison Avenue and 56th St, 605-5555). Finally, the latest jewel in New York's crown is the American Museum of the Moving Image in Astoria, Queens (35th Avenue and 36th St, 718-784-0077). Located in a redevelopment movie studio, if offers the chance electronically to try on Scarlett O'Hara's dress and to dub sound effects on a TV commercial. Admission costs $4, and a free transfer bus links the museum with 3rd Avenue and 56th St in Manhattan.

Music. According to one school of thought, New York City has left London far behind as the musical capital of the world, and there is no doubt that the Big Apple ranks high on the list of musical cities. Apart from the New York Philharmonic which is among the best orchestras in the world (phone 874-2424 at the Lincoln Center for details), Brooklyn boasts two symphony orchestra, the Bronx has one, and there are others in Queens and Manhattan. Performing at the Carnegie Hall represents the highest dream of many musicians (247-7549). Chamber music ensembles are beyond counting. Among the famous ones are the Guarneri and the Juliard Quartets. For concerts of chamber music go to the peaceful courtyard garden of the Frick Museum on Sundays. A music lover will also find Chinese opera, Jewish choirs, balalaika orchestras, choral groups and neighbourhood musicians brought together by a love of music-making.

One of the highlights of the summer are the free concerts given by the New York Philharmonic in Central Park two or three times a month. As many as 100,000 people gather on blankets to eat picnics (from peanut butter sandwiches to caviar) and enjoy the music. More modest free concerts are held at the World Trade Center at lunchtime in summer and at the IBM Atrium (56th St and Madison Avenue). Branches of the Manhattan Savings Bank employ pianists to entertain the lunchtime queues of customers, and you're welcome to sit and listen even if you have no business to transact.

Jazz of all kinds is alive and well in the Big Apple. You can hear it in clubs, on fifth floor "lofts" and in college concert halls. Try Bradley's (cool), Eddie Condon's (Dixie), Mikell's (informal), Jimmy Ryan's (Dixie), Michael's Pub (cool — where Woody Allen occasionally plays clarinet on a Monday), Village Gate (bop), and the Village Vanguard (mainly cool). Sweet Basil, Lush Life and Fat Tuesdays are also interesting and reliable. Most jazz joints charge about $7 at the door; if entrance is free, drinks will be expensive and there may be a minimum. (This minimum may be waived if you stay at the bar instead of a table, but the bar is usually noisy). Most clubs have three sets, the first at 10pm, the second at midnight and the final one at 3am. Call the Jazzline (463-0200) for a daily recorded announcement of what's on, or pick up a jazz news sheet at the information Center in Times Square.

Here is a selection of venues for other kinds of music.

Bottom Line, 15 West 4th St (228-7880). Full range of pop/rock/folk/ country.

Max's Kansas City, 213 Park Avenue, near 17th St (777-7871). Everything including one of the weirder crowds in town.

The Mudd Club, 27 White St near Broadway (227-7777). New wave/house, and very crowded.

Dan Lynch, 221 2nd Avenue (677-0901). Blues. No cover.

Tramps, 125 East 15th St near Irving Place (777-577). Blues.

Lone Star Cafe. 5th Avenue and 13th St (242-1664). Country 'n Western.

O'Lunney's, 915 2nd Avenue near 38th St (751-5470). Country 'n Western

The Bitter End, 147 Bleecker St (637-7030). Folk, and first date for Joni Mitchell and Bob Dylan.

For rock music consult the *Village Voice* listings. Major concerts are staged at the Radio City Music Hall in the Rockefeller Center (541-9436) and in Madison Square Gardens (563-8300).

Theatre. The Broadway theatre district around the Times Square area has the greatest concentration of theatres in the world. When looking for Times Square, remember that it is not really a square at all, but merely a widening of Broadway above 42nd St. Hit shows are usually sold out months in advance, particularly if they are musicials. Tickets can be ordered by credit card (usually with a surcharge) though Tele-Charge on 239-6200, Teletron on 246-0102 or Hit-Tix on 564-8038. Call the New York City on Stage information line on 587-1111 for current productions.

Both more fun and adventurous is Off-Broadway, a term used to describe smaller theatres beyond the trade union authority and trade union wages. Many a play has started Off-Broadway and made it to Broadway. Tickets cost between $10 and $20. Productions at the Circle Repertory Theater (99 7th Avenue S), the Public Theater (425 Lafayette St) and Manhattan Theater Club (321 E 73rd St) are all worth investigating.

Fringe theatre or Off-Off-Broadway theatre may be held in a drab room in a slum district, in a church meeting room or an old loft with crumbling board benches. Very avant-garde. See the *Village Voice* for details.

Tickets for Broadway shows are very expensive, seldom available for less than $20, and more often $45 for plays, $60 for musicals. Try the TKTS booths (at the World Trade Center, with short queues, and in Bryant Park, on 42nd and Sixth) for half price tickets on the day of performance. There are normally queues formed well in advance of the 3pm opening. You will also find tickets touts outside theatres charging exorbitant prices, despite the bye-law which makes it illegal to sell tickets marked up by more than $2.

Since New Yorkers are theatrical their everyday lives, check out some theatre in in the wider sense of the word. There is the New York Stock Exchange at 20 Broad St in the Wall St area, which welcomes visitors to watch the frantic activites from the free public gallery overlooking the trading floor. It is open to spectators from 9.20am to 4pm, Monday-Friday; call 656-5168. Or you might like to sit in on a court case at the Criminal Court, 100 Centre St. Trials in the US are highly publicized, even televised, and you might be able to attend one which you have been reading about in the papers. For especially bizarre cases that might have come out of the Mad Hatter's Tea Party, drop into the nearby Small Claims Court and see what people will sue for.

Nightlife. Every taste is catered for, from the most glittering and expensive floor shows to the sleaziest topless bars, from chic discos to old-fashioned ballrooms. And New Yorkers pride themselves on the exotic parties they give in their own apartments or homes.

For a night of dancing try "Heartbreak" (Varig and Vandem Streets) which is a cafeteria by day and a 60s/80s rock and roll club by night; admission is $15. For something different, try the clubs which serve as training grounds for young comics who may go on to become the next Lenny Bruce or Woody Allen. Among the best of these are Catch a Rising Star (1487 First Avenue), Improvisation (358 W 44th St) and Comedy Cellar (117 MacDougal St). The humour may be slightly obscure for non-New Yorkers. The cost might be $15 plus a minimum of two drinks.

There is no legalized gambling in New York City unless you include the racetracks and the State Lottery. If you're into the higher forms of wagering — roulette, black jack, craps — head for nearby Atlantic City.

Cinema. Films are taken very seriously in New York. The New York film Festival, at the Lincoln Center in mid-September to early October, is so serious that in order not to be vulgar and commercial like the Cannes Film Festival, no prizes are awarded. You can see previews of soon-to-be-released Hollywood blockbusters as well as experimental art films. Ring 362-1911 for Festival details.

The Museum of Modern Art has a fine film library and shows films daily, usually Hollywood classics.

Check local papers and magazines for prices and times of new releases. Admission charges start at $7 for a seat during the evenings; matinees are cheaper. As befits a serious cinema-going audience, New Yorkers are especially keen on foreign art films. There are more subtitles in Manhattan than in the rest of the country put together. In addition to the art cinemas like Cinema Studio (Broadway and 66th St, 877-4040) or Film Forum (57 Watts St, 431-1590), there are many cinemas which specialize in revivals. Programmes change frequently. Among the best known are the Cinema Village (8th St Playhouse) and the forerunner of them all, the Thalia (95th St and Broadway).

Special Events. In addition to jazz, film and dance festivals, there are many ethnic celebrations in which to participate. Depending on the lunar calendar, Chinese New Year (known as Tet) is celebrated with week long festivities, fireworks and parades in Chinatown. Phone the Chinese Community Center, Mott Street, for the exact dates in late January/February (226-6280). If you are a fan of fireworks, try to be in New York on the 4th of July, when spectacular fireworks are set off from barges in the Hudson River. Riverside Drive on Manhattan's West Side provides the best vantage point.

Most businesses along 5th Avenue close on March 17th when the annual St Patrick's Day Parade takes place. Regardless of race or religion, everyone becomes honorary Irish and joins the parade past St Patrick's Cathedral and along the edge of Central Park to 86th St. Many marchers head for the ethnic Irish bars on the Upper East Side for green coloured beer and stronger stuff. Bar-room celebrations can quickly flare up, so avoid political or religious discussions. Beware also of adolescent revellers who often choose this particular day to exceed their capacity.

Other parades include the Hallowe'en Parade through Greenwich Village on October 31, a bizarre affair which starts at dusk just west of Washington Square Park. On the last Thursday in November, Macy's Department Store sponsors the Thanksgiving Day Parade on Broadway from 77th St and Central Park West to their store. Starting at 8.30am, you can see building-tall helium-filled balloons of Kermit, Snoopy, Bullwinkle and other cartoon characters. Call 397-8222 for further information. The tree lighting ceremony at the Rockefeller Center is held a couple of weeks before Christmas, followed by an (oddly secularized) Christmas carol sing-along. A few weeks later you can join the New Year's Eve revellers in Times Square.

SPORT

Baseball. Half the home games of both New York City teams are played at night under spectacular floodlights. Except during the last few weeks, when teams may be in contention to win division titles and get into the World Series, you should be able to pick up tickets at the box office on the day of the game. New York City's two teams are the Mets (National League) who play in Shea Stadium in Flushing, Queens (507-8499) which can be reached by subway line 7 to Willets Point/Shea Stadium Station, and the Yankees (American League) who play in Yankee Stadium in the Bronx (293-6000) which can be reached by subway lines CC, D and 4 to 161st Street Station. You should stick with the crowd when leaving the stadium on your way home by subway since the neighbourhood is decidedly unsafe.

Football. Tickets to the games of both New York City teams are hard to come by because of the many season ticket holders. The Jets play in Giant's Stadium at the Meadowland Sports Complex in East Rutherland, NJ, about six miles from midtown; if you're lucky enough to get a ticket, dress warmly as Meadowland is notoriously cold and windy in the autumn and winter. Meadowland is easily reached by bus from the Port Authority Bus Terminal.

Basketball. Tickets are usually available on the night at prices ranging from $10 to $20, unless it's near the end of the season and there's a close race. New York's team is the Knickerbockers (Knicks for short) who play at Madison Square Garden, 7th Avenue and 33rd St. If you visit Harlem, you will notice a high density of basketball hoops and young lads dribbling and shooting baskets. Because green parks are so rare, the locals have adapted their sports preferences to the concrete jungle.

Ice Hockey. The season lasts from October to April, with availability of tickets fluctuating according to the whims of the fickle fans. New York's two teams are the Rangers who play at Madison Square Garden (564-4400), tickets $10 and $20; and the Islanders whose games on ice held at Nassau Coliseum on Long Island (516-794-9100).

Tennis. The best time of year for tennis is early September, when the US Open Tennis Championships are held at the National Tennis Centre, Flushing Meadows, Queens (592-9300). Last minute tickets will be available only from ticket touts at outrageous prices. There is professional tennis at Forest Hills (268-2300) also in Queens.

Horse Racing. Turf fans will be delighted to hear there is year round flat racing. From October to April you can place your bets at Aqueduct (the "Big A") Racetrack in Queens (subway lines A and CC), and then from April to October at Belmont on Long Island (Long Island Railroad); call 739-4200 for special fare and admission deals to Belmont. There is off-track betting (known as OTB) as well as racetrack betting in the state of New York. Dial 976-2212 for results. Trotting, called "harness racing", takes place as Roosevelt Raceway on Long Island (718-895-1246); take the Long Island Railroad from Penn Station.

Participation. Get a free copy of the *Green Pages*, a guide to New York City Parks and a source of information on activities ranging from archery to tennis. The *Green Pages* is available from information booths in all main parks. Jogging is undoubtedly the favourite. The most popular venues are Central Park, along the East River Promenade, and, for a vista of the Hudson River and New Jersey beyond (with its gorgeous sunsets thanks to pollution), the West Side Highway below 42nd St.

In October, crisp days and golden foliage make an ideal setting for the New York City Marathon, which starts at the Staten Island side of the Verrazano Bridge and ends 26 miles and 365 yards later (after touching all five boroughs) at the Tavern on the Green in Central Park. The race is run on the third or fourth Sunday of October. A circus atmosphere prevails. Entry is by mail, and only 16,000 applicants are chosen. Write for an application form to the Road Runner Club, PO Box 881, FDR Station, New York, NY 10150, or their headquarters, 9 East 89th Street, New York, NY 10028 (860-4455).

Bicycling enthusiasts have their own annual event, the 50-kilometre Bicycle Challenge held in the second week in July.

During the winter, every snowfall brings out the skiers and tobogganers in Central Park, Prospect Park in Brooklyn and Van Cortland Park in the Bronx. Skis can be rented and instruction obtained at the latter two parks (965-6511 and 543-4595 respectively). You'll be amazed to find how hilly some areas of New York are.

For indoor ice skating year round, try The Sky Rink, 450 West 33rd Street (695-6555) or watch the disco skating Friday and Saturday nights. There's outdoor skating (subject to weather) from October to April at the Rockefeller Center Rink, and the Wollman Skating Rink in Central Park at 59th Street (397-3158).

You can rent roller skates at several locations near Central Park from mobile vans set up along Columbus Avenue between 70th and 80th Streets, from the Skate Connection, 349 West 14th St (243-6353). There are also indoor rinks: Village Skating, 15 Waverley Place (677-9690) which is ideal for beginners; and the Roxy, 515 West 18th St (691-3113) for serious disco skaters.

Several beaches where you can sunbathe and swim in the ocean can be reached by subway: Coney Island in Brooklyn (with its famous amusement park); Orchard Beach in the Bronx; and Rockaway and Jacob Riis in Queens (the west end of the beach is a favoured meeting place for gay men; it can be reached by subway line 3 to Flatbush, then bus Q35). The finest public beach is Jones Beach on Long Island, an hour by bus from the Port Authority Bus Terminal. Unfortunately, most of New York's beaches were closed down during the summer of 1988 due to pollution ranging from medical waste to decomposing rats. For further information on how to reach the beaches and the condition they are in, phone the Parks Department on 360-8111.

Parks. Central Park is Manhattan's saving grace, an oasis of calm in the midsts of chaos. It covers 840 acres in the middle of the island, stretching from 59th St to 110th St and bounded by 5th and 8th Avenues. Despite the large number of New Yorkers in serious need of rest and relaxation, it is so big that overcrowding is rarely a problem. One of the most pleasant parts is Strawberry Fields, a gently rolling grassy area dedicated to the memory of John Lennon. It is on the west side of the park, close to the Dakota apartment building where Lennon lived and died. Central Park also offers one of the best views of the awesome scale of Manhattan. Although the top of Belvedere Castle is only 100 feet high, the panorama allows you to marvel at the sheer hugeness of the city.

The *Green Pages* gives details of nearly forty other large parks in New York City, including Fort Tryon Park at the far north of Manhattan (with delightful views of the Hudson and disturbing views of urban decay) and Prospect Park in Brooklyn (which contains Brooklyn Botanic Garden).

Zoos. The zoo in Central Park recently reopened after several years of reburbishment, and is a small but well-organised and illuminating place. It is divided into a "Tropical Zone", "Temperate Territory", "Polar Circle" and "Edge of the Icepack", ranged around a sea lion pool. A noble effort has been made to recreate natural environments but this does not deter hardened New York kids from taunting the animals. With the exception of the sea lions, most of the residents seem to spend their lives hidden or asleep, and so if you visit especially to see a Japanese snow monkey you may be disappointed. Admission is $2 for adults, $1 for children and senior citizens. Central Park Zoo is on the east side of the park at 64th St. It opens daily at 10am; closing time varies according to season, so call 220-5111. There is a small Children's Zoo adjacent, for which admission is just 10c.

One good reason to venture out to the Bronx is to visit some of the 4,000 residents who dwell in imaginative settings — caves, an island in a lake, hollow trees and meadows — in the 265 acre Bronx Zoo (367-1010). Carefully arranged habitats and camouflaged moats seperate the animals from the onlookers; you can also observe the wildlife from the tramway over the 'African Veldt' or take the 'Bengali Express', a monorail to view the Asian Animals. Charges vary according to season, so phone 220-5100. Admission is free Tuesday to Thursday. The zoo is open daily from 10am to 5pm; many outdoor exhibits are closed during the winter. You get to the zoo's entrance at 185th St and Southern Boulevard by subway to Pelham Parkway.

Adjacent to the zoo is the New York Botanical Garden which offers free admission. In the spring, the azaleas and rhododendrons brighten the hemlock woods and the Bronx River rushes through the steep narrow gorge that bisects the garden. A series of Victorian glasshouses, recently restored, contain tropical flora and desert plants. The garden is open from 10am to one hour before sunset. It's not Kew, but it's not far off.

SHOPPING

New York City abounds in speciality shops, such as the Erotic Bakery at 246 E 51st St which sells rudely sculptured cakes and confectionery from $2.50 or the Last Wound-Up (E 19th St and Broadway) which deals in amazing wind-up toys. There is a shop which sells nothing but seashells, another that sells only kites and a bookshop which carries only mystery novels. But unless you have precise requirements and plenty of time and stamina, stick to the department stores. Start with the top two stores; Macy's (Herald Square, between 7th Avenue and Broadway, 695-4400) and Bloomingdale's (59th St between Lexington and 3rd Avenues, 355-5900). Both stay open late on Thursday evenings and Macy's is also open Monday to Friday evenings and on Sunday afternoons.

At the other end of the price spectrum, there are two chain stores which specialize in leftover merchandise (including some quality stuff) from big-name or bankrupt shops Weber's (2064 Broadway, 505 5th Avenue and 390

6th Avenue) and Odd-Lot (33 W 34th St and 585 8th Avenue) have everything from cosmetics and clothing to furniture and food at low prices.

Remember that 8¼% sales tax will be added at the cash till except on necessities such as medicines, groceries and infants' clothing.

Flea markets are held between April and November and sell jewellery, antiques, clothes and all manner of junk; visit Sixth Avenue at W 26th St on Sunday, or 8 Greene St in SoHo on weekends.

Clothing. Madison Avenue from about 42nd St north has a wealth of men's and women's speciality shops from the classics at Brooks Brothers on 44th St (now part of Marks & Sparks), to the striking designer fashions of Saint Laurent Rive Gauche on 70th St. The clothes are expensive, partly because of the shops' high rents. Also try the famous Fifth Avenue department stores such as Saks, B Altman and Lord & Taylor.

The following two stores cater for both men and women. The Gap (145 E 42nd St near 3rd Avenue) which has the most complete selection of jeans in the Big Apple, and the Unique Clothing Wearhouse in Greenwich Village (718 Broadway near Washington Place) which has trendy, inexpensive clothing, as well as surplus and workmen's clothes. The cheapest jeans in town are sold at the huge Canal St Jeans, which has Levi 501s for $16.99. One of New York's most colourful sights is the racks of new clothes being wheeled out of the Garment District (7th Avenue between 23rd and 40th Streets) to stores throughout Manhattan.

Charity shops regularly receive donations of fashionable clothing from department stores as well as from individuals. Two within a short walk of each other are Repeat Performance on 3rd Avenue at 84th St and Trishop on 3rd Avenue at 92nd St.

The Lower East Side, a predominantly Jewish area, is at its liveliest on Sundays (closed on Saturday, the Jewish Sabbath). You'll find Orchard St south to Canal St jammed with shoppers bargaining ("hondling") with stall keepers. Open front stores are bursting with merchandise. You may hear of designer clothes and shoes being snapped up from pushcarts for a song, but *caveat emptor;* many of the goods are seconds or shop-worn, though undeniably cheap. Stores here and elsewhere in New York close for Passover in late March, Rosh Hashanah in early September, Yom Kippur later in the same month and Hanukkah in early December.

Americana. For American folk art, such as patchwork quilts, try Spirit of America (269 E 4th St in Greenwich Village) or America Hurrah (316 E 70th St on the Upper East Side). The best place to find American Indian Jewellery is at the American Indian Community House, 849 Broadway; this is shortly to move to new premises. Among their wares may be found Zuni "squash blossom" necklaces and silver "concha" belts. For well made artifacts from around the world, visit the UN shop, which also sells UN stamps. You can buy anything from Albanian post cards to Zambian jewellery and since the UN occupies "international territory" no tax is levied. A great collection of New York post cards can be found at a shop called "Untitled" (159 Prince St).

Jewellery. On 5th Avenue at 57th Street, Tiffany's (755-8000) vies with its great competitor Cartier's, 5th Avenue and 52nd Street (753-0111) and other posh jewellery stores for the most stunning eye-catching window displays and opulent interiors. All have some small items at modest cost that recipients back home would be impressed by, such as Tiffany's silver 'snowflake' charm at around $30. Downtown in SoHo and Greenwich

Village, shops and galleries sell hand-crafted silver and gold pieces, as well as a large selection of unusual rugs.

THE MEDIA

Leaving aside the numerous New Jersey, Westchester County and Long Island stations, there are 45 AM and FM radio stations operating in New York City. Try WCBS (880 AM) which broadcasts only news, and its sister station WCBS (101.1 FM) for "solid gold music". The Brooklyn-based WKRB (90.0 FM) has probably the best new music. WLIB (1190 AM) is the all black news and information station which broadcasts cricket scores five times daily from 7.15 to 5.30pm, once or twice daily at weekends.

One tour available from the Information Desk in the lobby of the Rockefeller Center takes you behind the scenes of NBC TV studios, another backstage at Radio City Music Hall, home of the precision dance troupe, the Rockettes. You can get tickets to locally produced TV shows from the Visitors Bureau at 2 Columbus Circle. There is an interesting Museum of Broadcasting at 1 E 53rd St (752-7684) which allows the public access to famous old television and radio programmes. There are tapes of the McCarthy hearings and videos of the Apollo moonshots, which you can watch or listen to at playback consoles. Apparently the most popular request is the Beatles on the Ed Sullivan Show in 1964. Note that the museum will be moving to 23 W 52nd St (between 5th and 6th Avenues) in 1990/91.

The *New York Times* (known locally as the *Times*) is arguably America's best newspaper. The tabloid *Daily News* has been called America's worst, although it boasts a circulation of 1,300,000. *New York Newsday* at first sight seems to be another dismal tabloid, but it's not at all bad. The *Village Voice* ($1 weekly) is an excellent left-of-centre paper whose value to the visitor for recommending entertainment, accommodation, etc. cannot be over-emphasized. New York has a flourishing alternative press, e.g. the bimonthly feminist newspaper *Womanews* and the gay guide *NY Native*. The free *New York Press* can be picked up at bars and restaurants; its reviews and listings are surprisingly good for a free newspaper.

There are many misapprehensions in Europe about street crime in New York City. Surprisingly, it rates only ninth in the crime statistics for American cities; and has the strictest gun control laws in the USA. The theoretical odds are 32,000 to 1 that you will be the victim of one of the 225 daily muggings, and much longer that you will one of the four people murdered on the average day; and if you avoid endangering yourself by walking around drunk and disorderly in neighbourhoods you should avoid, the odds rise dramatically.

Certain sensible precautions such as those described in the introductory section *Crime and Safety* should stave off most dangers. The great majority of residents live in New York without incident, and do not dress in bullet proof fabrics (though there are shops in the city which sell them). On the other hand, there was one fellow who was mugged twice in the same evening. The first time he was reeling home under the influence of too much drink; the second under the influence of too many knocks on the head. If he hadn't been drunk in the first place, there probably would have been no first or second assult. Keep enough money after a pub crawl for a taxi home.

Still, there is no denying that New York is a dangerous town. There are sections of it you simply should not visit. If you want to see the burned out shells of Harlems buildings, go through it in a bus. (Harlem is north of Central Park and between 125th and 156th Streets.) You need only walk a few blocks and you may be in a completely different and possibly risky neighbourhood, even if it doesn't look particularly slummy. It is easier to avoid tough, dangerous, hostile slum neighbourhoods which are known by everyone. There is a depth of ill-feeling you cannot conceive of unless you have been getting the short end of the stick for generations on account of your nationality or colour, so don't go into them. In particular avoid the South Bronx, south of Fordham Road, the Bedford-Stuyvesant area and the Lower East Side (east of First Avenue and south of 12th St.) Also do not go into Central Park after dark. You should exercise caution in Chinatown, the Bowery and the area west of Broadway to the waterfront. Never be rude to a policeman unless you want to be given a hard time.

The subways are notoriously dangerous. Here are some precautions: when waiting at a relatively deserted station, stand in the clearly marked and brightly lit "off-hours" waiting area which has an intercom to the Transit Police. Travel in the central cars where the guard travels. Avoid isolated cars and deserted exits; stick with the crowds wherever possible. Don't display jewellery or wallets and don't sit next to the doors where pickpockets often operate. Try to memorize your route ahead of time so that you don't betray your unfamiliarity with the system by consulting a map en route.

Drugs. New York is a druggy town. Around the Cooper Union building in the Bowery downtown, you will see pedlars hawking openly with pitches of considerable invention: "I've got the herb that's superb, the smoke that's no joke. Don't pass until you've tried my grass". Further on a block at St Mark's Place, you'll pass a dozen or so people bombed out on something or other they've just purchased. At parties you could be offered cocaine. And, if for some inexplicable reason you're in a slum, heroin is available. The possession of cannabis has been all but decriminalized. Using cocaine could mean prosecution, but it's a middle and upper class activity due to the price; the police seldom make a fuss and rarely raid parties in high rent apartments. It is still illegal, and in view of the prison conditions at prisons such as Utica, you will want to do your best to avoid arrest.

Sin. It is no surprise that sin is for sale in New York. The boys and girls operating on the streets in the Times Square area are so tough, say the cognoscenti, that their spit bounces. Prostitutes encountered in bars in mid-Manhattan have been known to lead prospective clients back to a mugging ambush. Abstinence is advised, especially in view of the prevalence of AIDS and other diseases.

Creatures. Not all of the threats to your safety in New York take the form of muggings. It is reputed that dozens of crocodiles inhabit the sewers of the city as a result of pet owners who have flushed their reptiles down the toilet once they become too big for their aquariums. You are unlikely to escape Manhattan without confrontation with a cockroach; these harmless insects infest even expensive hotels and apartment buildings, and are said to be more numerous than humans. And if you are worried about rodents, be consoled that according to one Police Commissioner, three times as many people in New York are bitten by other people as are bitten by rats.

Help and Information *i*

The area code for Manhattan and the Bronx is 212, and 718 for the other boroughs.

Information: The New York Convention & Visitors Bureau, 2 Columbus Circle, New York, NY 119 (397-8222 / 8200). Tourist Information Desks may also be found in the Rockefeller Center and in Times Square. If you write in advance stating your specific interest, they will try to put you in touch with relevant organizations.

British Consulate - General: 845 3rd Avenue (752-84).

American Express: 15 East 42nd St (687-37) and nine other offices in Manhattan.

Thomas Cook: 2 Penn Plaza (967-5800).

Post Office: 8th Avenue and 33rd St (967-8585).

Western Union Telegrams: 962-7111.

Medical Emergencies: Bellevue Hospital, 1st Avenue at East 27th St (561-4141).

Dental Emergency Service: 679-3966.

24 hour drugstore: Kaufman Pharmacy, 557 Lexington Avenue (755-3300).

Emergencies: 911.

Fire: 682-2900.

Crime Victim Hotline: 577-7777.

Legal Aid Society: 8 Lafayette St. (577-3300).

Travelers' Aid: 42nd St between Broadway and 7th Avenue (944-13). Also in the International Arrivals building at JFK Airport (718-656-4870).

New York Transit Authority: 33-1234.

Lost and Found: 374-4925.

Handicapped travellers may obtain useful information for their visit to New York City at The Easter Seal Society, 194 Washington Avenue, Albany, NY 12210 (518-434-4103); and at The Junior League of New York, 13 East 80th Street, New York, NY10021, who publish a booklet *Access to New Work City* that contains information on transport, museums, stores and hotels.

New Yorkers believe in the telephone. Not only can you dial Dr Joyce Brothers, the psychologist, for advice on mental problems, you can contact a representative of the Almighty through Dial-a-Prayer (246-4200) or get a laugh on Dial-a-Joke (976-3838).

Don't neglect calling the New York Public Library (340-0849) if you have a serious or not-so-serious question about New York or any other subject. Their reference section is more than likely to come up with a brief answer to any question you have remarkably quickly. For years, bets have been settled by a call to the Library.

Further Afield

Just as some Londoners refer to The North as everything beyond Watford, so native New Yorkers refer to everything above Manhattan as Upstate New York. It matters little to them that this region is only a fraction smaller than the whole of England. It is seen merely as a quaint backwater, a place to visit on the weekend. The locals upstate complain bitterly about the invasion of weekend New Yorkers, who have caused land and house prices to sour and who swagger around the small country stores with their fashionable clothes and their loud voices. But there are still plenty of undiscovered places. The ideal guide book for independent travellers who prefer not to rent a car is Theodore Scull's *Carefree Getaway Guide for New Yorkers* (Harvard Common Press 1988, $9.95). It describes excursions from Manhattan using public transport alone.

The Hudson Valley. Cutting a north/south swathe between the Taconic Mountains to the east and the Catskills to the west, the Hudson River is crossable by seven bridges. If the Big Apple has turned sour on you, drive up the tree-lined Taconic State Parkway to Albany, the not-very-interesting state capital, and on to Montreal if you are so inclined on the Northway (I-87). You may stop in at any of the towns along the river, such as Poughkeepsie, Hyde Park (site of F D Roosevelt's home and the Vanderbilt Mansion) and Rhinebeck which retains some of its Dutch influence. The oldest wine district in the country is in the Valley; Benmarl Vineyards near the town of Marlboro is particularly picturesque and is open to visitors. It is also possible to take a Hudson River Day Line cruise; the nine hour round trip cruise costs about $25.

Saratoga Springs. Forty-five minutes north off the Northway, is Saratoga Springs. This once elegant spa town has recently had its downtown and beautiful old hotels and inns restored. In the summer the Philadelphia Orchestra, New York City Ballet Company and other top classical and popular performers put on two months of stunning entertainment at the Performing Arts Complex. The famous harness and flat race tracks are located "just around the corner" from the concert area. The flat races take place in August and are attended by the rich and famous. This is your chance to wear your top hat and tails or carry a parasol. There are many fine restaurants in and around Saratoga Springs, but rooms are very hard to find in the summer.

Finger Lakes. In addition to the beautiful scenery, you will find the Finger Lakes area dotted with wineries. After you have been around one or two of them, you may come to share the local enthusiasm for wines produced in the area.

Niagara Falls. Continuing west past the lakes you will come to the large industrial city of Buffalo (where there is an excellent art gallery called the Albright-Knox), and nearby Niagara Falls, which form a boundary between the US and Canada. The view is best from the Canadian side. Many visitors are disappointed by the extent of the tourism industry surrounding the falls, but for all the cliched postcard pictures, seeing 200,000 cubic feet of water spill over a crest 3,172 feet wide every second is worth a detour. Most accommodation around the falls is devoted to honeymooning couples, although the Youth Hostel on the US side accepts non-members for $12 per night.

Catskill Mountains. Visitors to this modest mountain range occupying the area in the southern part of the state between the Hudson River and the Pennyslvania border, find a host of diversions, from vineyard-visiting to hang gliding. The ski slopes at Hunter Mountain and Plattekill Bowl get very crowded at weekends. The Ice Caves Mountains are a fantastic remnant from the age of the glacier. There is also a renowned Game Farm where 2000 animals and birds roam freely.

The Catskills are sometimes called the Borscht Belt, since this has been a traditional resort area for the East Coast Jewish population: nowadays it is frequented by everyone regardless of religion or money. Big name entertainers and famous show people have made their start at the clubs here.

The Adirondacks. There are fewer than 43 peaks over 4,000 feet high in this six million acre state park. This mountainous and forested region takes up the whole of northern New York State. The landscape is not unlike that of Scotland, although the weather in summer is much more predictable. If you get off the principal route, through this genuine wilderness, be sure you have enough petrol and a place to stay when the chilly nights fall.

Whiteface Mountain Memorial Highway leads visitors to one of the most spectacular views in the Adirondacks. But it is better, if you have time, to abandon your car and take to some of the thousands of miles of hiking trails. You will see Park Ranger stations all along the way, where you can seek advice about routes and camping facilities. For information on ski tours to upstate New York contact Sportiva Sporthaus, 145 East 47th St (421-7466). The principal ski resorts are Adirondack, Lake Placid and Whiteface Mountain.

Calendar of Events

early February	Overland Ski Marathon, Panama to Westfield
March 17	St Patrick's Day Parade, NYC
mid May	9th Avenue International Festival, NYC
mid June-mid July	International Festival of the Arts, NYC
(even-numbered years)	
early August	Harlem Week, NYC
August	Lincoln Center Out-of-Doors Festival, NYC
early September	US Open Tennis Championships, Flushing Meadow, NYC
mid September	Buffalo—Niagara Falls Marathon
October 31	Hallowe'en Parade, Greenwich Village,
early November	NYC Marathon
late November	Macy's Thanksgiving Day Parade, NYC
early December	Tree Lighting, Rockefeller Center, NYC

Boston and New England

Boston Common

**Connecticut   Maine   Massachusetts   New Hampshire
Rhode Island   Vermont**

Known locally as "Beantown" and "The Hub", Boston is the home of John Adams, Paul Revere, the Kennedys, a famous strangler (later electrocuted) and perhaps even Mother Goose. The city is also the scene of the famous Tea Party, and is one of several eastern cities that lay claim to the title, "Birthplace of the Revolution". It is now the second largest financial centre in the nation with a greater metropolitan population of nearly three million and it has what New Yorkers refer to as "quality of life" in abundance.

Boston's hinterland consists of Massachusetts — home state of Michael Dukakis —and the five other states of New England. The three southern states of Connecticut, Rhode Island and Massachusetts are dominated by urbanization and big industry, but the cities are more provincial than New York or Washington and the residents friendly. There is a high concentration of Ivy League colleges in peaceful campus settings. (The Ivy League comprises eight north-eastern universities, including Harvard and Yale, with high academic and social status.) The three northern states represent another contrast, despite weekending New Yorkers. In the far northern woods and mountains of Maine, New Hampshire and Vermont, time is meaningless, and bear and moose are more populous than people.

The austere Atlantic coasts, starting in Rhode Island and running up through Maine — which has more coastline than California — are neither terribly cosmopolitan nor backward. The string of charming seaside towns that dot the coast from Newport beach to Bar Harbor are the most appealing places, outside of Boston, to visit in New England.

THE NATIVES

Like most American cities, Boston is a racial and social melting pot, with large contingents of Irish, Hispanics, Chinese, Italians, French Canadians and blacks. Races have segregated themselves geographically. South Boston (known as Southie), for instance, is predominantly Irish. Roxbury has traditionally been black (and poor) but is now being settled by yuppies. Chinatown and the Italian North End are close to the centre of the city.

Including the separate municipality of Cambridge across the Charles River, Boston boasts America's highest concentration of colleges and universities, dominated by Harvard and the Massachusetts Institute of Technology (MIT). There is a vast student population of 100,000 in the Boston area, making it a young and energetic place with a vigorous intellectual and artistic life.

Making Friends. Boston has its share of bars, singles and otherwise, that might prove suitable meeting places, but it also offers interesting prospects for meeting people. Picking the right spot to eat your meal in Quincy Market, for instance, or spreading out your blanket on the Boston Common or the Charles River Embankment on a hot summer weekend, could bring you within talking distance of the man or woman of your dreams. Investing $10 or $20 on a whale watching trip or deep sea fishing cruise could also bring you into contact with people of similar interests. Look for ads in the local papers or tourist literature, or check through the "Boats — Excursions" and "Boats — Rental and Charter" headings in the Yellow Pages.

The colleges and universities are the focal points of most social and cultural activities. You can meet people in the bars and coffee houses around the various campuses or at events open to the public. If all else fails, you can always resort to the personal ads in the *Phoenix*. All tastes are catered for, and most of the ads are graphically explicit.

CLIMATE

New Englanders take pride in the region's abruptly changing, unpredictable weather. Surprise blizzards occur as late as May and the most promising sunny afternoon can degenerate into heavy showers in an hour. Summer officially lasts from Memorial Day (end of May) to Labor Day (early September), during which you can rely on hot weather most of the time. The city gets stiflingly muggy, on average heating up to 35°C/95°F. Fortunately, it is easy to escape to a nearby beach for refreshing sea breezes; evenings on the beach can be cool, so have a sweater handy. Remember, too, when you plan your beach trips, that New England is not touched by the Gulf Stream, so the Atlantic is cold even when the weather is extremely hot.

From September, expect rapidly decreasing temperatures, often falling below freezing for weeks on end, especially in Northern New England near the Canadian border, and occasionally dropping below —18°C/0°F between December and February. Expect a lot of snow and ice in these months, too. Winters are excellent for skiers particularly in the mountainous sections of Vermont and New Hampshire. For Boston weather information, dial 567-4670

Getting Around

ARRIVAL AND DEPARTURE

Air. Boston's airport is Logan, located on reclaimed marshland just three miles northeast of the city. As you touch down, you will have the impression of landing in the water, since the runway is very close to the bay. Information about flights and facilities is available on 482-2936.

All international flights arrive at the International Arrivals Terminal. Waits can be long at immigration since most aircraft from Europe arrive during the afternoon. Domestic flights arrive at terminals A,B,C or D depending on the airline.

The airport is only ten minutes from downtown Boston in light traffic, but the journey can take an hour or more in busy periods. Going north, the airport exits directly on Route 1A, which leads to I-95 for Maine and New Hampshire. The fastest and most reliable journey into town is on the Airport Water Shuttle, a launch which runs from Logan Dock (a short bus ride away from the airport terminals) to Rowes Wharf on Atlantic Avenue. The service operates every 15 minutes Monday-Friday between 6 am and 8 pm, and half-hourly at weekends from noon to 8pm. A cheaper method is to take the Massport International Shuttle Bus number 22 or 33 (free) to the Airport subway station, from whence the journey costs 60c. Two airport buses are operated by Airways Transportation (267-2981) and Hudson Bus Lines (395-8080) to the downtown hotels; the cost is $3.25 and $4 respectively. Hudson Bus Lines will also take you straight from Logan to other towns in Massachusetts and New Hampshire.

Taxis will be waiting for you at designated taxi stands and can be useful if you have a lot of luggage or are going to a destination not served by the boat, bus or subway. There is also a Share-a-Cab system which you can find out about at a desk inside the terminal. Dial 1-800-23 LOGAN for more details of ground transportation arrangements.

Bus. The Greyhound Terminal is 10 St James Avenue (432-5810); the nearest subway stop is Arlington.

Train. There are two main Amtrak stations in Boston (North and South), both adjoining subway stops. Call 482-3660 for information, or toll-free 1-800-USA-RAIL. Trains leave South Station (a beautifully restored Beaux Arts building) every two hours to New York, and there are less frequent services west to Springfield and beyond. The New York service offers 35% discounts on round trip fares if you travel on ordinary trains (rather than Metroliners) and avoid peak periods.

Commuter rail services run from South and North Stations. For information call 227-5070. The Massachusetts Turnpike (I-90) is the watershed between the two areas of service.

Driving. There are long lists of car hire firms in the Yellow Pages from which to choose. Of those at the airport, the best are Budget, American International, Econo-Car and Thrifty. Better deals may be found just a five minute shuttle bus ride away, e.g. at Ajax, among the suburban rental offices listed in the Yellow Pages, and of course at the discount places like Rent-a-Wreck.

Driveaways. You should have little trouble finding a car to Chicago, Denver or the west coast, except at the ends of term. Around November, the biggest demand will be for people to drive cars to Florida.

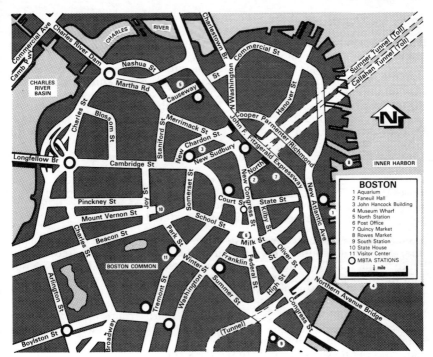

Ride-Sharing. Check under "Rides" in the *Phoenix* classifieds, or on college bulletin boards.

Hitch-hiking. Because of the complexity of the road system in and around Boston, a sign always helps to get a lift, even though it may seem obvious where you are heading. The high student population has made hitch-hiking a common, if unpredictable, form of transport even within and between Boston and Cambridge. When heading out of town, natives will probably advise you to pick any suitable downtown ramp on to the urban highway network, but this can be both dangerous and frustrating.

Instead, try the following: going south on Route 3 (to Cape Cod), Route 24 (to Fall River) or I-95 (to Providence), take the train from South Station to Route 128 Station, at the Route 128/I-95 intersection. Stand on either I-95 south, or, for Route 3 or 24, on Route 128 south. The westbound I-90 (Massachusetts Turnpike) to Springfield, New York City and all points west and south is the only road that is hitchable from a downtown location, namely the Massachusetts Avenue ramp (subway to Auditorium). If you are going north on I-95 (to coastal New Hampshire and Maine), take the subway to Airport and hitch up Route 1A; this leads to Route 1, which joins I-95 at Danvers. Heading north on I-93 (to most places in New Hampshire and Vermont), take the subway to Wellington then bus 100 to the West Fellsway ramp on to I-93. This is the best route to take if you wish to make a pilgrimage to Lowell, home town of Jack Kerouac. There is a memorial to the author of *On The Road,* bearing passages of his writing.

CITY TRANSPORT

The Massachusetts Bay Transportation authority (MBTA) runs buses, a subway network and, under contract to other companies, a commuter rail service. The entire system, especially the subway, is known simply as the "T". The sign for stations and bus stops is a black T in a white circle.

For route and service information, call 722-3200 on weekdays and 722-5000 other times. Route maps cost 75c from the Boston Visitor Center at the Prudential Center and on Boston Common, the MBTA information desk in Park Street Station, the MBTA Customer Service office on the fourth floor at 50 High St, or Waldenbooks bookshops. Bus drivers carry free timetables of their individual routes. Services run from about 5.30 am to 1 am.

Buses. Buses (50c flat fare) take exact change or 60c subway tokens. You place the money or token in a machine as you board the bus, under the watchful eye of the driver. There are no transfers.

Double Deckers. Mainly for tourists, a small fleet of surplus London buses operates at ten minute intervals from 10 am to 4 pm daily on a cross-town route from the Prudential Center to Faneuil Hall, passing the major downtown shopping areas and tourist attractions. The flat fare is 50c.

Double deckers also ply a sightseeing route in a loop to the north and east of Boston Common, tying together all the sights of the so-called "Freedom Trail", the one and a half mile tourist route around the city centre marked by a red line along the pavements. A flat fare of 50c gives you the equivalent of an all-day pass: you can get off and on as often as you like, thus taking your own time to see the sights.

A similar (single decker) sightseeing shuttle is run by Hub Bus Lines (776-0630) on the same route, but only between May 15th and October 15th.

Subways. If you don't have a subway map, plan your route carefully from the poster maps on station platforms On the trains themselves, you will see single line maps only of the route you are on. If you need to change, remember which station you want before you board the train. The subway system consists of four colour-coded lines (red, green, blue and orange) which intersect at the four downtown stations (State, Washington, Park Street and Government Center). Other passengers are an excellent source of advice. The subway system is small enough that many Bostonians have the route map committed to memory.

To enter the subway system, you need a token, costing 60c at the desk at the entrance. You ride without a ticket and have unlimited travel until you resurface. Extra fares are charged for travel on the green line west of Reservoir and to the southern extremes of the red line.

Cheap Deals. Children and senior citizens travel at half fare. A number of monthly passes are available, depending on how much of the system you want to use — just buses, just subway, both, just one subway line, etc. They are available at banks during the last week of the preceding month. For example, the all subway monthly pass costs $22 (excluding travel to the distant suburbs of Riverside and Quincy). For information about passes, call 722-5218.

Car. Boston drivers are reputed to be among the worst in the world, and the road system is particularly difficult to navigate, with an elaborate one-way system. There are two one-way tunnels leading in and out of the city (Sumner and Callahan respectively), both of which charge a 30c toll.

Parking is so bad in the centre of town that the best advice is to pick a suburban subway station and leave your car there. In central Boston, on-street parking is either metered or restricted in some way, so your best bet is to park in a multi-storey lot for around $12 a day. The most central are on Dalton, Charles and Sudbury Streets.

Taxis. Taxis can be found cruising or at many taxi stands. There are several companies to choose from but fares are standardized. A taxi ride between North End and the Prudential Center for example will cost about $6.00 plus a tip in light traffic; in heavy traffic the fare can be astronomical. For information or complaints, contact the Cab Association of Boston, 253 Sumner St (462-8316). So bad was the reputation of Boston taxi drivers for rudeness and poor navigation that they are being put through a "Customer Care" course.

Cycling. You can rent bikes by the hour, the day or the week, from the Herson Cycling Company, 1250 Cambridge St, Cambridge (876-4000); or Community Bike Shops, 490 Tremont St, Boston (542-8623). Boston is good undulating cycling terrain, but get yourself a good lock and chain, and learn from the natives who always lock both wheels as well as the frame to an immoveable object. Write to the Massachusetts Department of Environmental Management, Division of Forests and Parks, 100 Cambridge St, Boston, MA 02202 for a free series of maps covering ten one-day rides in the greater Boston area, or just pedal along the 18-mile bike path that runs through Boston and Cambridge along the Charles River.

Ferries. You can choose from a half-hour lunchtime cruise around Boston Harbour for $2, indulge in a few hours' island-hopping in the Harbour, or take a longer trip to Cape Cod for example. Bay State Cruises (723-7800) runs express ferries from Boston to Martha's Vineyard via the Cape Cod Canal. The three-hour trip costs $30 one-way, $50 for a day return. There are also ferries to Provincetown in Cape Cod from the Commonwealth Pier in South Boston (subway to Aquarium, then the shuttle ferry from Long Wharf). These services operate only in summer.

Accommodation

Hotels/Motels. Expect to pay at least $30 for a single room, $20 per person for a double in a motel on the freeway or in the distant suburbs. Susse Chalet is a good franchise to try (287-9100). In town, barely decent rooms start at about $75.

Hostels. The International Youth Hostel is excellently located a few blocks west of the Prudential Center near the Back Bay Fens Park. The address is 12 Hemenway at Haviland (536-9455 or 731-5430). The cost of $6.25 in winter is raised to $7.50 in summer when reservations are particularly important. The rest of Massachusetts is well provided with youth hostels.

Ys. The YWCA at 40 Berkeley St (482-8850) is Boston's most central Y for both men and women. A dormitory bed costs $22. Otherwise call 536-7940 for information on other YWCA dormitories in the area; or 536-7800 for YMCAs.

Guest Houses. Guest houses are cheaper than hotels, but for the best prices you have to go out of the centre of Boston. There is a string of them on

Beacon St in Brookline. Try Anthony's Townhouse (566-3972), Beacon Inn (566-0088); Beacon Street Guest House (232-0292) or Beacon Plaza (232-6550).

Bed & Breakfast. Since advance reservations are advisable in summer, selected addresses and phone numbers are given below. These agencies act as clearing houses for tourists wishing to stay in a family setting. Prices are comparable to hotel room prices. Try: Bed and Breakfast Area Wide, 73 Kirkland St, Cambridge 02138 (576-1492); Bed and Breakfast Associates, PO Box 166, Babson Park, Boston 02157 (872-6990); Bed and Breakfast Brookline/Boston, PO Box 732, Brookline 02146 (277-2292); City Cousins, PO Box 194, Concord 01742 (369-8416); Greater Boston Hospitality, PO Box 1132, Brookline 02146 (734-0807); New England Bed and Breakfast, 1753 Massachusetts Avenue, Cambridge 02138 (489-9819); and Host Homes of Boston, PO Box 117, Newton 02168.

Residences. Try the Northeast Hall Residence at 24 Bay State Road (MBTA to Kenmore). In the summer, a double room starts at $25.

Longer Term. If you are staying more than a night or two, you might find weekly boarding or renting arrangements, starting as low as $50 a week in the off-season, in the "Furnished Rooms" section of the *Boston Globe* classifieds, but don't expect a royal suite. You may also strike lucky in the "Sublets" ads in the *Phoenix* classifieds. For longer term stays (several months), look under "Housemates" in the Phoenix. Places tend to come open at the ends of term in December, May and August.

The Boston University Department of Rental Property Management has a few surplus apartments available during the summer, with monthly rents starting at about $500. Advance booking is required, and you will have to put up a security deposit equal to one month's rent. Call 353-4101 for more information.

Camping. Nothing in the immediate Boston area, but there are campgrounds on Cape Cod and the North Shore (Gloucester, Salem area), both at least one hour's drive from Boston. The *Massachusetts Campground Directory* is free from the Division of Tourism, 1 Cambridge St, Boston 02202 (727-3201).

Eating and Drinking

Boston is renowned not only for its baked beans, but for its seafood which is excellent throughout New England. For traditional New England fare, try clam chowder (made with milk not tomatoes as in the counterfeit Manhattan variety) with a piping hot blueberry muffin. Legal Seafoods in Boston and Cambridge serves outstanding fresh fish a la carte. If you're feeling wealthy head out on Northern Avenue and splurge on a seafood dinner at Jimmy's Harborside, 243 Northern Avenue (423-1000). Menus also feature clams, mussels, lobsters and other shellfish. Try a "Steamer", a huge bowl of steamed soft-shell clams. Fresh fish available includes bluefish, swordfish, scrod (young cod) and shark. One of the best known seafood restaurants (because it is the oldest in Boston) is the informal and bustling Union Oyster House at 41 Union Street (227-2750) near the old city centre. Not only does it serve the best clam chowder in town, it's historic — a French prince lived there once.

If seafood does not appeal, try any of the small lively Italian restaurants in the North End, especially along Hanover Street. The European is a capacious pasta and pizza place — a North End institution. For more sophisticated Italian cuisine go down Richmond Street to Felicia's —Felicia is the chef-owner. Chicken verdicchio is her speciality and always superb. Jacob Wirth's, on Stuart Street near the theatre district, is one of Boston's oldest restaurants and yet undiscovered by tourists. It's a German pub featuring excellent sausages of various types, saurbraten and, of course, beer. Boston has the nation's third largest Chinatown — after San Francisco and New York — but you have to walk through a seedy pornography and prostitution district they call the "Combat Zone" to get there. Go for dim sum at the Imperial Tea House on Beach Street. Along "Mass Ave" in Cambridge there are dozens of good little ethnic restaurants — Greek, Ethopian, Middle Eastern, Japanese — which tend to be inexpensive since their primary clientele are impoverished academicians. Bostonians eat more ice cream per capita than anyone, and there are ice cream parlours everwhere. Herrell's and Steve's are the fiercest rivals, both chains started by the same man — Steve Herrell. Emack and Bolio's leads the pack in interesting flavours.

At Quincy Market (the middle building at Faneuil Hall Market Place —Boston's version of Covent Garden) you can invent your own menu by buying food from different vendors, and eat it in a common seating area on a terrace or under a glass roof. Durgin-Park Restaurant is one of the most famous restaurants in the Faneuil Market, where a dinner of Yankee roast beef or oyster stew will cost over $20. Sailors have been eating there for over a century.

Go for drinks — not the overpriced, mediocre food — at the Top of the Hub, the restaurant with a view, located on the top floor of the otherwise unattractive Prudential Center, which, until recently, was Boston's tallest building. (That honour now goes to the nearby John Hancock Building, built in a fit of pique to outdo the rival insurance company's attempt to impress).

DRINKING

Drinking establishments as well as restaurants advertise widely in the *Boston Globe* and *Phoenix*. Those with live entertainment receive a short critique in the *Phoenix's* very thorough listings column of the "Boston After Dark" section. Bars are open until 1 am. All states observe "Blue Laws' which forbid the sale of package liquor on Sundays. Wine and beer is usually sold in food stores as well as in liquor stores in Massachusetts; New hampshire's state government has a monopoly on liquor sales, but the prices are so low that people drive in from all over New England to stock up.

The Black Rose on State Street in Boston and the Plough and Stars in Cambridge are good basic pubs with the addition of nightly music. Clarke's in the financial district has outdoor seating in fair weather. The Boston Brewery offers an impressive selection of its own lagers, ales and stout. Elsewhere, seek out locally-brewed Harpoon, Samuel Adams and Moosehead. For Guinness and an Irish ambience, visit the pubs along Dorchester Avenue.

The inspiration for the television series *Cheers* was the Bull and Finch at 84 Beacon Street, although it bears little resemblance to the Hollywood studio set version. For British pub atmosphere, try the Sevens at 77 Beacon Hill, which has a young unpretentious clientele. Prices are reasonable and there is a good range of beers.

Entertainment

The standard route for determined sightseers is the Freedom Trail which links 16 sites and buildings of historic interest. It is marked by a thick red line on the ground and crosses some of the bleakest parts of town as well as some of the most picturesque. Pick up the map from the Park Street Visitor Information Center (subway to Park Street) and set off from there. Free maps of the city, showing public toilets among other things, are available from the National Historic Park Service, in State St. Maps and brief guides are available for $1 from the Visitor Center on Boston Common.

Excellent views of the city and environs, sometimes stretching as far as the mountains of New Hampshire, may be obtained from the observation floors of the Prudential Center or the John Hancock Building. The engineers seem to have solved the problem which afflicted the latter when it was first built, and huge sheets of glass are no longer liable to fall out on a windy day. The old Trinity Church nestling at the base of the skyscraper provides a remarkable contrast of old and new, and makes a lovely photograph.

All current entertainment is listed in the "Boston After Dark" section of the *Phoenix* and in the weekly calendar included with Thursday's *Boston Globe*. Tickets for most theatrical and musical events can be bought from Concert Charge (426-8181) or try the Bostix kiosk at Faneuil Hall (subway to Government Center; 723-5181 for recorded information), which offers half-price tickets on the day of the performance. The kiosk's hours are 11 am to 6 pm Monday to Saturday; noon to 6 pm on Sunday.

Museums. Boston has some of the best museums of art and science in the country. Visit the Museum of Fine Arts (465 Huntington Avenue, 267-9377) or the nearby charming Gardner Museum (280 The Fenway, 734-1359) for a comprehensive collection of the visual arts. For modern art, visit the Institute of Contemporary Art (955 Boylston, 266-5151).

Boston has its share of viewer-participation or "hands-on" museums such as the Museum of Science and Charles Haden Planetarium (Science Park, 742-6088). If you want to re-visit the scene of the Boston Tea Party, when the early colonists demonstrated their dislike of British taxes on traded commodities by dumping 342 chests of tea into Boston Harbour in 1773, go to Museum Wharf at 300 Congress St (338-1773). You can tour a full size replica of one of the three ships and even heave a chest of tea overboard (which is subsequently winched up for the next tourist). Close by, the new Children's Museum (adjoining the giant milk bottle on Museum Wharf) takes hands-on exhibits to extremes. You can make computerised rock music or clamber around a replica sewer system. No child on a visit to Boston should be deprived of a day at the Children's Museum.

On the grounds of Harvard University lie a half dozen internationally acclaimed museums. The Fogg and Sackler museums hold the bulk of Harvard's massive art collection. The Busch-Reisinger is dedicated to Germanic art. The Peabody Museum houses artifacts from ancient civilisations and at the adjacent Botanical Museum the celebrated Blaschka glass flowers are displayed. Ring the Harvard operator (495-5000) and ask to be connected with the particular museum to find out opening hours.

The New England Aquarium (742-8870) is a short stroll from Faneuil Hall and well worth it to see the comical penguins and seals, as well as the 1,999 other species of sea-life exhibited there.

Music. Boston attracts major musical performances of every type. For rock groups, either Boston or Hartford, Connecticut is the usual New England stop on a national tour. In the summer, Boston Common is the location for a series of outdoor concerts. Check the *Phoenix* listings for upcoming concerts. Tickets for rock concerts can be bought at Strawberries record shops (there are 15 of them in Greater Boston) or at Ticketron (720-3450)

For local new music in a bar setting try the Rathskellar — known as "the Rat" near Boston University in Kenmore Square or Nine Landsdowne Street (the address is epinymical). Jazz lovers will want to spend at least one evening at Montana's (160 Commonwealth Avenue). Boston is also strong on folk music, and in 1987 you could have seen Tracy Chapman for free at clubs around the universities.

For classical music, Boston has opera and ballet companies, a symphony orchestra, many chamber orchestras and the Boston Pops Orchestra, which gives free concerts at the Hatch Shell Auditorium on the Charles River Embankment in July. At the Hatch Shell you can also see free Boston Ballet performances in August.

Film. With movies, too, Boston usually gets the pick, but the first run cinemas are the priciest ($4-$6). Queues form early so be sure to telephone the theatre to find out when ticket sales start.

Nightlife. Many bars offer live musical or comic entertainment, with some of the best jazz in town being played at corner dives around Faneuil Hall and at Inman Square, Cambridge. The universities are naturally the focal points of most nightlife. In particular, try Harvard and Kenmore squares.

Theatre. The theatre is alive and well in Boston, and many productions which open here move on to Broadway. Downtown, the Wilbur (423-4008), the Schubert (426-4520) and the Colonial (426-9366), and in Cambridge the American Repertory Theatre (597-8300) are the most prominent playhouses in the area.

SPORT

Ticketron (542-5491) handles all the city's sports events. Most visitors will see Boston in the baseball season (April to September). The team is the Red Sox and they play at Fenway Park (MBTA to Kenmore; 267-8661). At other times of the year, spectators go to the Sullivan Stadium in Foxboro to watch the New England Patriots play football (1-800-543-1776), and to the Boston Garden (North Station) to see the Boston Celtics play basketball (523-3030) or the Boston Bruins play ice hockey (227-3200). For the homesick, the *Boston Sunday Globe* prints English, Scottish and Irish soccer results.

Horse racing fans can go to Suffolk Downs (567-3900) in East Boston. Dog racing is held at Wonderland Park (284-1300) in Revere. Betting at the track only in both cases.

The Boston Marathon takes place each year on Patriot's Day, the nearest Monday to April 19.

SHOPPING

There is a sales tax of 6% on everything except clothes and food (but restaurant and take-out meals are taxed). Regular shopping hours are 9.30 am to 5 pm but many downtown department stores stay open until 9pm on Mondays and Thursdays. Shopping malls also stay open until 9pm every night, and some corner stores and supermarkets (such as Purity Supreme or Heartland) stay open 24 hours.

Boston offers many different kinds of shopping experience, from the Dickensian (Beacon Hill) to the ultra-modern (Prudential Center) and renovated-trendy (Faneuil Hall). The main downtown department stores are located on Washington Street. Cambridge's main shopping area is around Harvard Square.

New England generally is renowned for its handicrafts from patchwork quilts to scrimshaw, an unusual folk art of carved or engraved whale teeth, bones or shells.

An interesting exercise in American capitalism takes place every Monday morning at Filene's Department Store Basement on Washington Street. After two weeks on sale at full price, the cost of an item drops by 25%; after three weeks, by 50%; after four weeks 75%; and after five weeks without a buyer, the item is given away to charity.

For good deals on books, records and cameras, check the Harvard Coop stores (rhymes with hoop) at Harvard Square or on the MIT campus on Massachusetts Avenue in Cambridge, or at 1 Federal Street, Boston. If you want to call first, they have toll-free numbers: 1-800-343-5570 from within Massachusetts, 1-800-792-5170 from elsewhere.

Harvard Square is the best place in the United States to shop for books. On Brattle Street, Wordsworth and the Paperback Booksmith carry an impressive array of titles at slightly discounted prices. The Harvard Bookstore on Mass Avenue has a positively mouth watering selection of new, used and out-of-print books. Schoenhoff's, on Mt. Auburn Street carries a wide selection of foreign language books.

A trip to Haymarket — two blocks north of Faneuil Hall — makes for a pleasant expedition on a Saturday or Sunday morning when local farmers and fishermen set up stands in a bustling open air market.

THE MEDIA

Newspapers. The *Boston Globe* is the leading newspaper, but in the last few years, Rupert Murdoch's *Herald* has been capturing an increasingly larger market share. Incidentally, the *Herald* publishes the crossword puzzle from the London *Sunday Times* each week. The weekly *Phoenix* started out as an underground paper and has retained that image despite being taken over by big business. It comes out on Tuesdays and excess copies are distributed free at college campuses a day or two later. For a full range of European newspapers, try Out of Town Newspapers Inc., on Harvard Square in Cambridge (354-7777)

Radio. The USA's foremost classical music station is WCRB, broadcasting to Bostonians on 102.5 FM. It shares programmes with BBC Radio 3, and transmits concerts from Tanglewood (*see Further Afield*). For good 24 hours stereo rock, try WBCN (104.1 FM) or WFNX (101.7 FM). For top 40, the best known station is WXKS (107.9 FM) which advertises itself as "Kiss-108".

At the lower end of the FM dial are grouped a number of student and other non-profit stations, most noteworthy of which is WGBH (89.7 FM) which has a varied menu of classical music and current events programmes. Another good non-profit station is WBUR (90.9 FM) with programming from Boston University. MIT's station is WMBR (88.1 FM)

On the AM dial, there is very little worth listening to. Of historical significance, though, is WBZ (1030 AM), owned by Westinghouse, which in 1921 became the nation's first licensed broadcast station. (KDKA in Pittsburgh, also a Westinghouse station, had put out programmes the previous year, but without a licence.) Unfortunately WBZ now offers 24 hours of mediocre music and generally dull chat shows that can be heard across 38 states and the southeast and south-central portions of Canada. For news listen to WEEI (590 AM) or WRKO (700 AM).

Boston has its share of street crime but is not in the same league as New York or Detroit. Boston Common should be avoided by single women at night, and anyone is likely to meet with trouble in the red light district, also known as the "Combat Zone" around Park Square between Chinatown and the Greyhound Station.

Drugs. Marijuana and cocaine are widely used and readily available, but recent offshore seizures of Colombia's top exports have raised prices in the last two or three years. Possession (though not selling) of one and a half ounces or less is no longer an arrestable offence.

The area code for Boston is 617.

Information: Greater Boston Convention and Tourist Bureau, Prudential Plaza West, Box 490, Boston 02199 (536-4100). There is a Visitor Center on the Fremont St side of Boston Common.
British Consulate-General: 4740 Prudential Tower, Boylston St (437-7160)
American Express: 10 Tremont St (723-8400)
Thomas Cook: 156 Federal St (267-5000)
Post Office: Post Office Square, opposite northern end of Federal St (223-2446).
American Automobile Association: 141 Tremont Street (482-8031)
Medical: Massachusetts General Hospital, Fruit St (726-2000).
24 hour drug store: Phillips Drug Co. Inc, 225 Charles St (523-1028)
Travelers' Aid: 711 Atlantic Avenue (542-7286). Also at the airport (569-6284), Greyhound Terminal (542-9875) and 312 Stuart St (542-7296).
Police: 145 Berkeley St (247-4200).

MASSACHUSETTS

Historic Sites. Cape Cod and the North Shore have their beaches and recreation areas, but most of the worthwhile day trips from Boston will involve cultural or historical sites. Lexington and Concord, now virtually suburbs of Boston, are the sites of the first fighting between British soldiers and the revolutionary "minutemen". You can get to Lexington on express bus 528 from Harvard Square in Cambridge. Concord is on the commuter rail line fron North Station. On Route 24 just outside of Concord lies Walden Pond where Henry David Thoreau lived. In Concord proper are several museums dedicated to the leaders of the Transcendentalist movement: the Antiquarian Museum — Ralph Waldo Emerson's old house — and the Alcott house, among others. The oldest continuously operating inn in America is in Sudbury, a few miles southwest of Concord. The Wayside Inn (443-8846) is the best place in the Bay state to have a traditional New England meal: try the Indian pudding, a sweet gooey delicacy made with cornmeal (ground maize) and molasses. The pilgrims loved it.

Further afield, you can see living history in two restored colonial villages, where centuries-old skills and crafts are demonstrated. One is Sturbridge Village, about 50 miles west of Boston, near Worcester just off the Massachusetts Turnpike. The other is Plimoth Plantation in Plymouth about 40 miles south of Boston. Plymouth is the site of the Pilgrim Fathers' landing in 1620. A replica of the Mayflower is on display there.

Cape Cod. Much of Cape Cod is now a state park featuring over 50 square miles of sandy beaches and dunes. It also has wildlife sanctuaries and is the site of Marconi's first transatlantic telegraph message. The offshore islands of Nantucket and Martha's vineyard (ferries from Boston, Wood's Hole, Falmouth and Hyannis) are old whaling communities and make for pleasant sea cruises on hot summer days. These islands attract artists, writers and Boston's high society, while Cape Cod itself is a much more proletarian holiday destination. You can rent a (fairly primitive) cottage in the Cape Cod National Seashore for $100-$175 per week from the Peaked Hill Trust, PO Box 1705, Provincetown MA 02657.

Western Massachusetts. The interesting areas begin about ten miles north of Springfield, in the Connecticut Valley. There are five colleges and universities in the triangle formed by Amherst (Amherst College, Hampshire College, University of Massachusetts), Northampton (Smith College) and South Hadley (Mount Holyoke). The so-called Five College Community is a miniature version of both Boston and Berkeley, with many fine restaurants, bookshops, cinemas, music, and an interesting and vocal feminist and leftist community. The colleges are linked by a free bus service.

Berkshires. Between the five college area and the New York state border is yet another distinct section of Massachusetts. If you have seen *Alice's Restaurant,* you'll be able to picture the scenery. In the autumn, the gently rolling Berkshire hills have magnificient foliage; in winter, skiing is popular. But the summer is the time the action takes place. The Boston Symphony Orchestra hold summer concerts at weekends at Tanglewood, located in Lenox. Tanglewood is also a music school and you can walk through the beautiful grounds and gardens and take in practice sessions, modern music concerts, etc. Lawn seats for the weekends are about $5. You can attend the rehearsals on Friday and Saturday morning for a nominal charge. There are also popular artists appearing in late August and early September at Tanglewood. Food — but not liquor — can be brought into the grounds. Check the local *Berkshire Eagle* newspaper or listings in the Boston newspapers or telephone (266-1492) for a performance schedule. During July and August there is a theatre festival in nearby Williamstown at the Adams Memorial Theatre at Williams College (597-3408); the summer Dance Festival at nearby Jacob's Pillow is also worth checking out. Some of the brightest lights of the American stage come to perform.

On route 20 heading into New York state is the Hancock Shaker Village, located in Pittsfield not Hancock. There are the original buildings and continious demonstrations of various crafts (carpentry, tinsmithing, bread baking, etc.) The beautiful surroundings are gradually being put back under the plough and made agriculturally viable again. If you are going to be in this area for a few days check the schedule in the Visitor's Center of the village. They often have intensive one-day courses open to the public on subjects such as herb cultivation, cane weaving for chairs, etc.

THE NEW ENGLAND COAST

Starting with New York City's dormitory towns in southern Connecticut, the coastline becomes more interesting as you travel northeast beyond New Haven, site of Yale University. I-95 hugs the coastline within a few miles of dozens of historic fishing and boatbuilding harbours overlooking Long Island Sound

Mystic, Connecticut, for example, has a maritime museum and aquarium (and a colonial-style shopping centre called Olde Mystick); Newport, Rhode Island is the home of the Regatta and of the Jazz Festival; New Bedford and Nantucket, Massachusetts have outstanding whaling museums. Fall River, Massachusetts has two excellent maritime museums: Battleship Cove and the Marine Museum.

North of Cape Cod, the coastline is a patchwork of active ports (Boston, Portsmouth and Bath); very garish seaside resorts (Revere, Salisbury, Hampton Beach, and Old Orchard Beach), and the more upmarket Oqunquit; and quaint old towns and fishing villages (Gloucester, Rockport and Newburyport in Massachusetts, the Strawberry Banke district of Portsmouth, and Kittery, Kennebunkport and Freeport in Maine). Portland Maine is a busy fishing and shipping city which has some wonderful examples of what happened to Victorian architecture when it reached the USA. The new Portland Museum of Art is surprisingly good, and has a Mona Lisa which some art experts theorize could be Michelangelo's original.

Northern New England is an outdoors experience with little in the way of historical or cultural entertainment. The states of Vermont. New Hampshire and Maine have turned their wildernesses into tourist areas offering hiking and camping, hunting and fishing, skiing, canoeing, whitewater rafting, mountaineering, rock climbing or just getting away from it all. The area is perhaps at its best in September and October when the bright maple foliage is spectacular. There are even "leaf-peeping" reports on radio stations giving the locations of the most dazzling colours. Summer is the time when mosquitoes and other biting insects abound. Spring is the season for tasting maple syrup, for which Vermont in particular is renowned.

Inland in Maine, the Baxter State Park is the start (or finish) of the Appalachian Trail, stretching as far as Georgia and is typical of the kind of wilderness area, you will find across the northern reaches of New England. Accommodation for hikers on the Trail is provided in mountain-top huts.

The Maine wilderness is on a scale that is unsurpassed in New England. From Greenville to Ashland, a predominantly dirt road winds 120 miles with barely a sign of habitation. If you park your car at a random point on that road and head northwest, you can walk another 120 miles without seeing any sign of human life. Since you can easily lose your way doing this, you should remain on established trails. Maps can be obtained by contacting the Baxter State Park Authority, 64 Balsam Drive, Millinocket 04462 (207-723-5140). Mount Washington in New Hampshire is a peak of extremes. The highest in the northeastern USA at 6,288 feet, scene of the strongest winds recorded anywhere in the world of 320 mph and subject to the worst winter weather outside the Poles. It was described by showman P.T. Barnum as the "second greatest show on Earth", but sadly the peak has been spoilt by drab tourist facilities, reachable by any vehicle which can handle 30% inclines. The cog railway is a less terrifying journey.

Hunting and Fishing. Hunters and fishermen should head north to Maine, New Hampshire or Vermont in the appropriate seasons. All hunting and fishing is closely regulated, however, and licences are required. Information on regulations and seasons is available in booklet form from any town or city hall in the state you are interested in visiting. Non-residents always pay more for licences than residents do.

Skiing. Skiing is also big business in the northern states, and Bostonians are willing to travel to Killington or Stowe, Vermont or Waterville, New Hampshire rather than settle for the lesser slopes of Massachusetts or Connecticut. With the aid of snowmaking machines, the season can stretch from mid October to early June. Northern ski resorts advertise seasonally in the travel pages of the *Boston Sunday Globe,* which also gives weekly reports on ski conditions in the main resorts. Tourist-conscious New Hampshire has its own information centre in Boston, the Ski New Hampshire store at 6 St James Avenue (423-7676). Most radio stations give daily ski conditions as well, or you can phone toll-free 1-800-258-3608. You might also like to browse in *Roxy's Ski Guide to New England* which describes and compares the downhill ski areas of New England.

Cross country enthusiasts might wish to ski in the orchard of the Nashoba Valley Winery at 100 Wattaquadoc Hill Road, Bolton (799-5520), 35 miles west of Boston.You must provide your own equipment (which can be hired in Boston), but the skiing, winery tour and tasting are free.

Calendar of Events

mid-March	New England Crafts Festival, Worcester Massachusetts
April	Maple Festival, St Albans Vermont
April (Monday nearest 19 April)	**Patriot's Day, Massachusetts**
April (last Monday)	**Fast Day, New Hampshire**
early July	Harborfest, Boston
July	Lobster Festival, Rockland Maine
mid-August	Jazz Festival, Newport Rhode Island
September	Oyster Festival, Norwalk Connecticut
mid-December	Re-enactment of the Boston Tea Party

Public Holidays are shown in **bold.**

Washington and the Mid-Atlantic States

The Capitol Building

Delaware   Maryland   New Jersey   Pennsylvania   Virginia   West Virginia

Like the Vatican, the District of Columbia is small in area but large in influence. It was designated capital of the United States in 1800 after a long political struggle with Philadelphia. The title "District" distinguishes the capital from the 50 ordinary states it governs. Where there is such power and wealth, culture is liable to flourish. So within the five square mile heart of Washington, there are numerous museums, theatres, parks, historical monuments and shopping areas, as well as government buildings. There is enough in this central location to keep the most curious and hardy visitor busy for weeks.

Washington is a fulcrum set between two geographical areas: to the north are the industrial and financial centres of America with their hectic pace of life; to the south begins a more tranquil and rural way of life. It is not surprising then that you find an unlikely synthesis of the two in Washington, such as frenetic businessmen with soft Southern drawls and genteel manners.

In 1882, Henry James attributed DC with "a charming climate and the most entertaining society in America". The former has never been true, and the latter claim would have been laughable until the 1970s. Until then Washington was somewhat provincial. Since then it has come a long way, and while it may not have the glamour of New York, it does have an enormous number of things to see and do. DC may be special because, or in spite, of its being the capital of the United States, but it nonetheless exerts a unique charm and fascination.

THE NATIVES

If you define natives as anyone who has lived in the District for more than five years, the natives of DC are comprised of blacks and bureaucrats. Those who come to Washington to find jobs, might live in the District with a roommate for a few years, but as soon as they start moving up the career ladder and can afford to move, they buy a house in the city suburbs in Virginia or Maryland. Housing in Washington itself is either very expensive (hence the need for roommates) or very decrepit, though there is an increasing trend for middle class whites to buy up and renovate old houses in the north-east part of town. In the poor sections of the city you will find blue collar workers who cannot afford to move to the wealthier suburbs and poor blacks. The more established and upwardly mobile ethnic communities such as Koreans and Cubans have joined the white commuters in the Maryland and Virginia suburbs.

Making Friends. A book claiming to teach how to "make friends and influence people" is a perennial bestseller in the USA. In Washington, however, it is easier to make friends if you already influence people. Washington is full of very bright, eager and ambitious men and women in their twenties and thirties. You may not find this stereotyped career-obsessed newcomer to Washington very congenial company. It is the norm for these lawyers, economists, management consultants and lobbyists to work 14 hour days, not to take holidays (only business trips) and to have few interests outside their niche of government.

Since Washington thrives on paper work, and therefore secretaries, there are about nine women for every man working in Washington. This means that if you are a young man you needn't be too wealthy, influential or handsome. The most popular nightspots for this crowd are in Georgetown, about two miles from the White House. The noisiest pubs and bars are on M St and on Wisconsin Avenue in Georgetown, but the lettered side streets (O and P, especially) off Wisconsin are just as nice and tend to be more discreet.

There are also a good number of universities in the District. Between the White House and Georgetown around 20th and Pennsylvania, is George Washington University. Georgetown University, American University and Howard University (predominantly black) have active social lives, if you can manage to lock into them.

The Mall is a strip of greenery where the natives come to play frisbee or softball, to attend free concerts, to jog, busk and picnic.

CLIMATE

If you think anything over 85°F/30°C is hot, absolutely avoid Washington during June, July and August. It is unbearable, since the unrelieved heat almost always brings with it a lot of humidity. Unless you are used to that kind of weather, be sure to get air-conditioned accommodation or, if you plan to rent a car, a vehicle with air-conditioning. Other than those three months, the weather is not too bad, though Americans certainly don't vacation in Washington for its climate. The autumn is chilly and often damp. During the winter you can expect freezing temperatures and a quantity of snow and slush. April and May are the beautiful spring months in DC when the cherry blossoms are at their best. The air is clear and dry, though it may become slightly cool in the evening. Dress very warmly for the winter, bring a sweater and light jacket in the spring, and wear as little

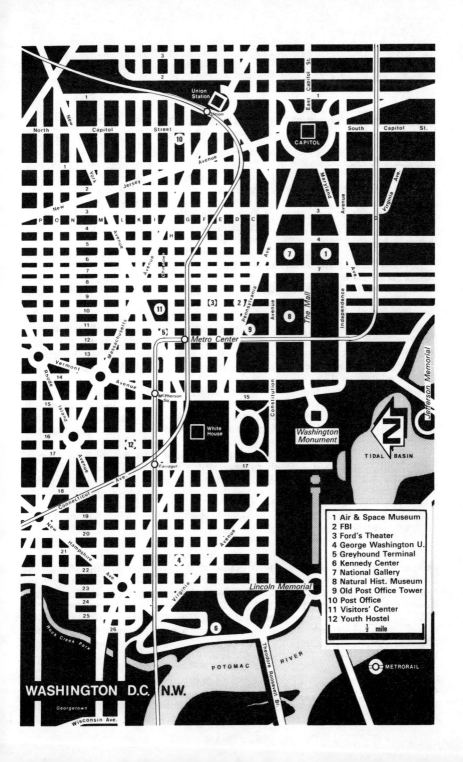

as possible during the summer. Be sure to bring a raincoat, regardless of the season.

For a short-term forecast for DC dial 936-1212, while for the five-day forecast call 899-3240.

ARRIVAL AND DEPARTURE

Air. There are three major airports serving Washington, though none is actually in the District of Columbia: Dulles (IAD) in Virginia, National (DCA — domestic only) also in Virginia and the Baltimore-Washington International Airport (BWI — between DC and Baltimore in Maryland). If you are flying in from Europe you will probably arrive at Dulles, 26 miles west of Washington. Call 661-8040 for information. Apparently the authorities are searching for an alternative name to avoid the number of visitors who get confused with Dallas. Going through customs can be slow or fast, depending on how many people the customs officials want to hassle that day. The rather impressive airport was designed by Saarinen, so if you have time, look at the building from the parking lots. The trip into town on the Airport Bus takes 45 minutes and costs $9.75. A taxi will cost at least $40.

National Airport is in Alexandria, Virginia but only three miles south of downtown Washington. It is a very busy airport, with hourly shuttle flights to New York, for which you need not book. The usual flight path into National follows the Potomac River so you get a good view of Washington if you are sitting on the left side of the aircraft. The Blue Line subway (part of the underground system) has a station at National Airport, which makes getting into DC very fast (18 minutes) and cheap (80c off-peak). Walk out the main doors of the airport, turn right, walk about 100 yards and you will see the station above some parking lots. Trains leave every ten minutes or so. From BWI (301-261-1000) there are Amtrak trains to Washington as well as bus links operated by Airport Connection II (301-859-3000).

Air fares to New York on the Trump Air and Pan Am Shuttles (from National Airport) are high, but rates to other US cities and abroad can be reasonable. Council Travel in Georgetown (1210 Potomac St NW; 337-6464) has cut-price charter, student and youth fares for overseas flights.

Bus. The Greyhound Terminal (565-2662) is at 110 New York Avenue, close to Union Station.

Train. Union Station (484-7540) is the only railway station in the District and is easily reached by metro (the stop is called Union). It is on Massachusetts Avenue north of the Capitol, just east of the Post Office on North Capitol Street. There are frequent Amtrak services to Boston via New York and Philadelphia. Washington to nearby Baltimore costs about $18, to Philadelphia $40 and to New York City $65. Metroliners, the high speed trains which take under three hours to travel between Washington and New York, levy a surcharge of about 25%. They operate hourly from 6.50am to 7pm, with all but the first departure on the hour.

Driving. If you are travelling by car and want to get into the heart of DC, take the 14th St Bridge coming from Virginia. You may get confused as you approach the bridge because I-95 and I-495 seem to merge and then split. Follow I-495. If you are arriving from Maryland, take the Beltway, I-495 and exit at either Wisconsin or Connecticut Avenue. From there it is another 15 to 30 minutes to get into the heart of Washington. Connecticut Avenue will eventually put you within two blocks of the White House; Wisconsin Avenue will take you into Georgetown.

There is little reason to have a car since the public transport network is good, as described below. It is not worth the exasperation of competing with the hordes of knowledgeable government drivers and the expense of paying $10 a day in parking charges (or much more in fines). If you do bring a vehicle in from out of state and plan to drive in DC for more than two weeks, you should apply for a visitor's permit from the Bureau of Motor Vehicles (727-6679). A better idea would be to stay at a motel and leave the vehicle parked (free of charge) for the duration of you Washington sojourn.

Unless otherwise marked, you are not supposed to exceed 45 mph on expressways or 25 mph in built-up areas. If a test shows you have over 0.5% alcohol in you blood, you are considered to be under the influence; twice that is considered intoxication.

Hitch-hiking. If you want to hitch-hike it is best to get into Maryland or Virginia first. All the good roads are high-speed (i.e. Turnpikes, Beltways, etc) so it is difficult to hitch within the city. For I-95 north to New York, take the Metro to New Carrollton, Maryland and hitch along I-295 to the junction with I-95 or the Baltimore-Washington Parkway. This may also be successful for those heading south. Do not accept a lift to Baltimore unless you actually want to visit the city.

The *Washington Post* classified advertisments list people or agencies wanting cars driven across country. During mid-December and late May try the universities for ride-sharing — in the university newspaper or bulletin board in the student union. All America Auto Transport have their headquarters in DC (347-4200) and should be able to fix you up with a driveaway vehicle without too much trouble.

CITY TRANSPORT

City Layout. The District of Columbia is divided into four parts: North-West (NW), North-East (NE), South-West (SW) and South-East (SE). It is important that you use these designations when addressing mail or giving instructions to a taxi driver, if the address is at all obscure. The areas are formed by the intersection of Constitution Avenue and North and South Capitol Streets, where the distinctive domed Capitol Building is located. Streets which are named by a letter, e.g. C Street, M Street, run east/west and streets which are named by a number, e.g. 3rd Street, 25th Street, run north/south. Thus if you found yourself at the intersection of 3rd and D, NW you would be three blocks across and four blocks up, i.e. seven blocks from the Capitol.

After the alphabet has run its course, the street names revert to the alphabet but become two syllable words, e.g. Adams, Bryant, Channing then three syllable words and so on. In addition to this grid of letters and numbers, there are streets radiating like spokes which are named after states, such as Connecticut, Massachusetts, Rhode Island. Having explained the complicated road system, you will probably spend most of your time fairly close to the Capitol in NW.

The two main types of transportation to get through this maze are buses and subways (officially called Metrorail and Metrobus). Phone 637 7000 for transit information. Whether you use these, taxis or cars, remember that between 7.30am and 9am and between 3.30pm and 6pm, you will be competing for space with tens of thousands of civil servants who flood to and from DC every day. In addition, traffic in the centre of Washington is often disrupted by demonstrations.

Bus. Buses run quite frequently between 7am and 6pm from Monday to Saturday. However, the service in the evening and on Sunday is patchy and you may have to wait up to an hour for a bus. Unless you have a transfer ticket, you will have to pay your fare with the exact change. Within DC fares are 75c off-peak, 80c peak. Ask for a free transfer if you wish to change to another bus.

Metrorail. The comparatively new subway/underground system is still surprisingly clean and quiet, and the air-conditioning works. Its good condition may be attributable to the fact that it runs mainly in the wealthier areas of the city, and is sometimes called the Yuppie Line. Like the buses, it runs into the immediate surroundings suburbs in Virginia and Maryland. Each Metro station entrance has a large cement post outside with the letter 'M' in brown and white. Inside the station are good Metro and local maps, and attendants are always on duty. The train driver will announce each stop, but usually unintelligibly, so look for the station signs. There are colour-coded route maps all around, much like the London Underground. This means of transportation is highly recommended in the summer, when you can get hot and exhausted trying to move around on foot.

The difficulty for the first time user is the ticket system. The best thing to do — and all the tourists do it — is to stand in front of the automatic farecard dispenser and watch someone more experienced use it. What most people fail to realize is that a) the ticket machine can give change back if you so desire and b) you can add more money if you have to later at yet another machine, inside the actual entrance and exit gates to the trains. The cheapest fare is 80c off-peak, $1.05 peak. (Peak hours are defined as 5.30am-9.30am and 3.30pm-6pm, Monday to Friday). If you buy a farecard for $30 or more, you get a free bonus of 5%. Note that fares have not increased since 1984, and are likely to go up soon. Help yourself to a transfer from one of the machines found in metro stations if you want to continue your journey on a bus. It is not possible to transfer free of charge from a bus to a metro.

The system is still being extended, so maps can be confusing: older one don't show lines which are actually running, while new maps show routes which have yet to open. Underground railway buffs might like to know that Bethesda has the longest escalator in the world (215 feet), but is shortly to be superseded by the moving stairway at Wheatley, which will be 228 feet.

Taxis. Taxis abound, especially in the central part of the District. Even so, you may encounter shortages at certain times of day. You can flag them anywhere, so pick a busy corner. You are charged by the number of zones you pass through and pay a lot to go into Maryland or Virginia. If you plan to use the taxis a lot, read the zone maps on the back seat of the cab; it will make things clearer and may save you some money. Charges begin at $2 for the first mile, then 50c per half mile. By law, not all taxis are allowed to leave the District, so make clear your destination before getting in. All the drivers expect big tips. There has recently been news about cabbies overcharging, so beware.

Cycling. Bike rentals are available in DC, Maryland and Virginia. Try the Thompson Boat Center, Rock Creek Parkway and Virginia Avenue NW,

(333-9711), or check the Yellow Pages for other listings. Always lock your bike; bicycle theft is rife in the capital, so don't rent anything bright and shiny. Rock Creek Park is a nice place to cycle and has cyclists' lanes. You can get a free booklet called *Bicycle Paths in the Washington Area* from the Metroplitan Council of Governments (1224 Connecticut Avenue NW) or a paperback called *Greater Washington Area Bicycle Atlas* for $3 which is useful for cycling throughout the mid-Atlantic states. The book is available from Washington Area Bicyclist Association, PO Box 27185, Central Station, DC 20005; 544-5349. Bicycles are allowed on Metrorail trains after 7pm on weekdays and all day at weekends. You need, however, a permit to show you have completed a safety course; call 962-1116 for details.

Accommodation

The fact that there are so many free things to see in DC is offset by the expensive accommodation. It is sometimes hard to find accommodation at any price, so book ahead if at all possible. Not only are there tourists but government conferences, conventions, rallies etc.

Motels. Motels in Maryland and Virginia tend to be a bit cheaper and still within 30 to 45 minutes from downtown Washington. The best thing to do is look in the Yellow Pages under hotels and motels and phone ahead for rates. Prices are generally higher in the summer though many places have special weekend or other special deals.

Hostels. The best place to stay is the International Youth Hostel at the corner of 11th and K Streets NW (737-2333), three blocks north of Metro Center. Prices are about $15 for a stay of one night and drop down to $10 for a stay of six nights. Breakfasts are served but cost about $5 extra. An alternative is Davis House, 1822 R St NW (232-3196), which is open only to foreign visitors and costs $20 per night. The International Guest House at 1441 Kennedy St NW (726-5808) is a bargain at under $20 per night including breakfast and afternoon tea.

There are two YMCAs in Washington which will accommodate visitors but no YWCA: the city headquarters at 1711 Rhode Island Avenue NW (862-9622) or the Alexandra Y in Virginia which accepts women guests as well as men at 420 E Monroe Avenue (549-0850).

Bed and Breakfast. Two agencies arrange accommodation in private homes: the Bed and Breakfast League, 3639 Van Ness St NW (363-7767); and Bed 'n' Breakfast of Washington, PO Box 12011 (328-3510). Rates are high.

Camping. Of the six sites in Maryland and Virginia close to DC, the Capitol KOA Campground (768 Cecil Avenue, Millersville MD; 301-923-2771) has the best transport links with Washington.

Eating and Drinking

The range and quality of restaurants in and around Washington is truly marvellous. Because of the great ethnic mix in the area, the embassies and a general interest in gourmet dining, you can easily find everything from French to African to Thai cuisine. The Yellow Pages list the restaurants not only alphabetically but by national cuisine as well. There is a Chinatown, around H and 7th NW, which has many Chinese restaurants but others scattered around DC and environs are just as good. There are excellent Vietnamese restaurants in Georgetown and in the Virginia suburbs. Washington's only authentic diner is at 5532 Connecticut Avenue, open 24 hours a day.

Of course there are also the fast food chains. But for good, cheap lunches go into some of the large office buildings, especially around K St between 15th and 21st Sts. They often have little carry-outs tucked in the rear of the ground floor. If you can do with just a quick hot-dog and soda, try "Best of the Wurst" at the corner of K St and Connecticut Ave (metro stop Farragut West). They have a choice of six or seven American and German hot dogs. Then go cross the street and eat in the little park. Given fair weather, you always see masses of people "brown-bagging" it — eating in the park, lunch being a home-made sandwich or two, piece of fruit and yoghurt and a drink. It is fairly easy to find a vegetarian lunch or supper. Even the expensive restaurants will gladly make up a salad, vegetable saute, etc.

Many of the museums, including those compromising the Smithsonian complex, have very good cafeterias open to the public. Try the one between the new East Wing of the National Gallery and the old National Gallery. The view from the basement of an indoor waterfall is quite extraordinary. There are street food vendors in good weather around all the museums and government buildings. If you want to see planes approaching National Airport down the Potomac, go up to the balconies of the Kennedy Center, for lunch or supper. All in all, it is easy to have a cheap, filling lunch anywhere in Washington.

The price of supper can be anywhere from $10 upwards. The prices on the menu do not include tax which is another 6%. Most places open for lunch at 11am and dinner at 5pm or 6pm. Some restaurants close on Mondays.

Bars in Washington tend to serve drinks only, though some around the Capitol do very good lunches as well. Almost every bar has a happy hour between 4pm and 6pm and many have certain days when women get some free drinks. Both bars and restaurants advertise heavily in the *Washington Post* and local magazines. There are always embassy parties going on, if you can get in. The longest beer list in DC is at the Brickskeller (1523 22nd St NW, 293-1885) which has nearly 600 from 46 countries.

Entertainment

About the only two types of entertainment you won't find in DC are beaches and gambling, and even these are just a few hours away in Delaware and New Jersey. The number of things you can do and see is extraordinary. The best way to approach the question is to decide whether you want to pay for it or not. Phone 737-8866 for "Dial-an-event".

Each Friday the *Washington Post* publishes a "weekend" supplement, an extensive list of daytime and evening events in the DC area. The paper also lists opening and closing times of the museums, telephone numbers, current exhibitions etc. which will be useful in organising your time.

The best — but not the highest — viewpoint in Washington is from the Old Post Office Tower, on Pennsylvania Avenue between 11th and 12th Streets. Queues are short and the view from the 315-foot clocktower is impressive. The 555-foot Washington Monument is well worth ascending, but the queues around the base are long. As a rough guide, allow 40 minutes for each complete circuit made by the queue.

Most sights in the nation's capital hark back to the days when Presidents were chosen for their statesmanship rather than TV appeal. The main landmark in Washington is the domed Capitol Building which houses the Senate and House of Representatives. Visitors are welcome to sit in on debates. Heading north west along Pennsylvania Avenue, you come to the headquarters of the FBI, and after a further four blocks, the White House. Free tours of all these famous buildings are available, although a visit to the White House requires a certain degree of planning. You should be queuing at the National Park Service office on the Ellipse by 8am, in order to get a ticket for a tour that day. The ticket is for a specific time between 10am and noon. Many doubt whether this laborious procedure is worthwhile; in contrast, the exhibits, films and laboratory activities at the FBI are very interesting. The tour guide at the FBI will point out the pictures of America's 12 most wanted criminals, and ask visitors if they recognize any as friends or acquaintances. Over the years several villains have been tracked down by this method. Bear in mind that the death penalty still applies in some states, so think twice before turning in a pal.

A tranquil walk along the Potomac River at the west end of the two-mile long Mall will take you between the Lincoln and Jefferson Memorials. Not far from the Jefferson Memorial is the Bureau of Engraving and Printing (C and 14th Streets, SW) where all paper money is designed and printed; free tours are available during the week, but the last one starts around 1pm. Across the Potomac from the Lincoln Memorial, the Arlington National Cemetery is a sombre memorial to thousands of American servicemen who died at war from the Revolution to Vietnam. It also houses remains of John F. Kennedy, and has Tombs of the Unknown Soldiers. Unfortunately the cemetery is touristy and tastelessly commercialised, with Tourmobile having a monopoly on tours; these range upwards from a $1.55 "express tour". A much simpler and more moving memorial is the wall near the Lincoln Memorial which bears the names of the Americans who died in Vietnam.

Museums and Galleries. Most of the impressive buildings and monuments which give Washington its imposing character are within a square two mile area extending from the White House to the Capitol. The main complex of museums in Washington is the Smithsonian Institution which encompasses many different museums situated between the Washington Monument and the Capitol in an area called the Mall. They include Air & Space (a spectacular building showing the history of aviation with aircraft and space vehicles suspended from the ceiling), the National Gallery (both wings housing American and European art), Freer (Asian art, including sculpture and pottery and a James McNeill Whistler Art Nouveau drawing room), Natural History (with some of the best special exhibitions); the US Botanic Garden and several others. Also part of the Smithsonian but a few blocks away at 8th and F St NW, are the National Portrait Gallery and the National Collection. All are free. They are generally open 10am-5.30pm daily, with later opening in spring and summer; call 357-2700 for precise times. During 1989 the Smithsonian Information Center will open in the Castle in the middle of the complex.

Other museums include the Renwick at Pennsylvania and 17th (American folk art, textiles and design), the Folger Shakespeare Librabry, 201 East Capitol Street (Shakespeare and his times), and the National

Archives, 8th St and Constitution Avenue (Declaration of Independence, Constitution and Bill of Rights and the Nixon tape recordings). The National Museum of Women in the Arts (13th St and New York Avenue, 783-5000) is worth visiting even if you have no interest in women or art. It is housed in a beautifully restored 19th century building and its cafe is about the best place to relax in the capital. The Museum is devoted to the contribution of women to art over the last four centuries, and is by turns fascinating, intense and startling.

A word of warning: you can get culturally burned out very quickly as you somersault through time, history and different cultures. Don't bite off more than you can view. Most of the museums have very good gift shops and cafeterias; set a leisurely pace and don't feel compelled to be a culture vulture.

Music. There is usually a choice of classical music, whether at the Kennedy Center (off Virginia Avenue at the Roosevelt Bridge, 254-3770), local colleges and churches or some of the art galleries. In summer there are free lunchtime concerts each Thursday from noon to 1pm on the north side of the reflecting pool near the Lincoln Memorial. Concert tickets (as well as theatre tickets) are often discounted on the day of performance; phone Ticketplace (842-5387) for details. This outlet also sells off tickets to outdoor events at the Wolf Trap Farm Park for the Performing Arts, a few miles from Dulles Airport, staging everything from the ballet to pop concerts. For popular music including jazz, check the *Washington Post* listings. Because of its large black population, DC has always been an important area for jazz. Most jazz at nightclubs is performed at the weekends.

Theatre. The Kennedy Center, next to the Watergate Hotel, offers a full schedule of concerts, plays, ballet, opera and film. For theatre there is also Ford's Theatre (where Lincoln was assassinated). Arena Stage and Folger Theater.

Film. The American Film Institute (785-4600), also in the Kennedy Center, is the icing on the cinematic cake. Movie theatres in the District show the full range of movies from the newest releases to old classics, from foreign festivals to retrospectives of American directors and stars.

The Circle and Inner Circle theatres at Pennsylvania and 21st show the classics, both old and quirky. The Outer Circle at 4849 Wisconsin Avenue has the better new releases. The Biograph and Cerebus Theatres in Georgetown show both old and new movies. And there are plenty of free showings at the National Archives 5th Floor Theatre (523-3000) and the Museum of National History. If you love movies, Washington is a great place to be.

Nightlife. Head west towards the Potomac River to find Georgetown, an area of gracious old houses and trendy boutiques. This is where the most interesting bars and clubs may be found, along Wisconsin Avenue, M St and their side streets. Jazz, blues, rock and soul are easy to find. For stand-up comics, go to the Comedy Cafe at 1520 K St (638-JOKE). If you have dinner with the show you pay $15.95, if not $7. Thursday is open-mike night for only $3.49.

SPORT

Major sports events, such as the Redskins football games, take place at the Robert F. Kennedy Stadium at the corner of E Capitol and 22nd Streets SE.

Phone the stadium box office (546-2222) for ticket availability, though be prepared for a disappointment. The Bullets play basketball (October to March) at the Capital Center in Landover, Maryland. The nearest major league baseball team are the Baltimore Orioles. Soccer is surprisingly popular, and DC supports two professional teams, one in each of the Northern and Southern Divisions. The former are the Stars, the latter the Diplomats. Seats for these events costs between $5 and $15, and there is a good bus service to all these venues. For horse racing head north to the Freestate Raceway at Laurel Maryland.

Participation. The young and energetic bureaucrats enjoy everything from archery (at Kenilworth Park, 926-0492) to windsurfing (on the Potomac, 548-9027). All the options are listed in the "Weekend" section of the *Washington Post*. For miles around the neighbouring areas contact the Sierra Club on 547-2326.

Parks and Zoos. The National Zoo has two of the few giant pandas in the West. During the past ten years, the zoo has been trying to make the settings more natural and though they still have further to go, it is a good zoo. It is located on Connecticut Avenue, metro stop Cleveland Station. The buildings are open 10am-4.30pm, and early birds catch the keepers feeding the animals. Admission is free, with limited parking.

Washington has many parks dotting its corners. The largest park, running through the District and into Maryland is Rock Creek Park. You can picnic and barbecue in certain parts of the park. It is a pleasant to walk around the Tidal Basin, an area around Jefferson Memorial, and around the reflecting pool in front of the Lincoln Memorial, especially when the cherry trees are blossoming in April. Or walk along the Potomac River from Georgetown to the Tidal Basin. Try Fletcher's Boat House in Georgetown for rides on an old barge up the Chesapeake and Ohio Canal, or simply walk or cycle along the canal-side path.

SHOPPING

The main shopping areas are around 10th St, along F and H Streets NW, just a few blocks from the Mall and Georgetown. The former has the large department stores, the latter the boutiques. Connecticut Avenue also has expensive shops of all kinds. Stores are generally open from 10am to 6pm though the ones in Georgetown tend to stay open later.

Across the street from the railway station North Capitol between G and H streets NW is the Government Printing Office. The bookstore inside has very interesting publications about not only DC but the rest of the United States as well. There are plenty of excellent bookshops in Georgetown.

For cut-price designer clothing, go to Potomac Mills ("the world's largest outlet mall") at exit 25 on I-95, 20 miles south of DC. Phoenix Tours (462-9100) run shuttle buses to the store.

THE MEDIA

Anyone who has seen *All the President's Men* will know that the *Washington Post* prides itself on its investigative journalism. The rival morning daily is the *Washington Times,* indirectly owned by the Unification Church. There is also a monthly magazine about the city and its environs called *The Washington.*

All the national public broadcasting corporations are based in Washington and, as you might expect in the seat of government, there is a higher proportion of news and current affairs stations than elsewhere. WAMU

(88.5 FM) is one of the few American stations to broadcast radio drama (for five hours per week), although this is complemented by current affairs, bluegrass and big band music. WETA (90.9 FM) has its own version of *Desert Island Discs* broadcast at 9am on Saturdays, and plays plenty of highbrow music. For news, try WTOP (1500 AM); for sport, WMAL (630 AM). WYCB (1340 AM) is a good example of an all-gospel station of the kind that proliferate south of Washington.

Crime and Safety

Despite the safe and antiseptic atmosphere of the white buildings and wide streets, Washington has a high crime rate. There is on average one murder per day in the American capital. Pickpockets are active in the White House and Capitol Hill area. Those busy areas can become empty and spooky at nights. Police patrol on foot and in cars and at night tour the parkland around the Mall instructing pedestrians to "clear the area immediately" for their own safety. The highest crime rate is in the poor black neighbourhoods in the southeast quadrant. Georgetown is relatively safe (since the streets are thronged at night), though if you're in the northwest quadrant, don't go lower than Washington's Broadway, i.e. 14th St.

Drugs. Possession of any amount of marijuana is punishable by up to one year's imprisonment and a fine of $100-$1,000. The corner of U and 14th Streets is notorious as a drug-dealing spot which you should avoid if you want to be sure not to be involved in one of the occasional shoot-outs here.

Help and Information

The area code for Washington is 202.

Information: Washington Convention and Visitors Association: 1455 Pennsylvania Avenue NW, Washington DC 20005 (789-7000). The volunteer-staffed International Visitors Information Service on the third floor of 733 15th St (783-6540) is friendlier and dispenses plenty of maps and information.

British Embassy: 3100 Massachusetts Avenue NW (462-1340).

American Express: 1150 Connecticut Avenue NW (457-1300).

Thomas Cook: 1624 I (Eye) St NW (872-8470).

Post Office: Corner of North Capitol and Massachusetts Streets (523-2323). Open until midnight.

Western Union Telegrams: 737-4260.

Medical: George Washington University Medical Center, 901-23rd St NW (676-3211).

All Night Drug Store: People's, 1121 Vermont Avenue NW (628-0720) and 7 Dupont Circle (785-1466). Both open 24 hours a day.

Travelers' Aid: Union Station (347-0101) and also National Airport.

Visa Information: Department of State, 515 22nd St NW (632-1972).

Further Afield 61

From the tawdry glamour of Atlantic City to the country roads of West Virginia, there is more to the mid-Atlantic states than domed government buildings. The climate of Virginia, West Virginia, Maryland, Delaware, New Jersey and Pennsylvania may be roughly similar to that of Washington, but the topography, people and culture vary considerably. So do the accents; don't expect to be understood unless you pronounce Maryland as "Mer'lnd" and New Jersey as "Noo Joisee". Expect crisp colourful autumns, cold bitter winters, bright warm springs and hot humid summers.

These states are well served by public transport as well as having an extensive road network. There are two main Amtrak routes through the region and an extensive network of bus routes. It is difficult to avoid I-95 the primary north-south route linking New York, Philadelphia, Baltimore, Washington, Richmond and on south to the Carolinas. if you do have time, however, take an alternative route such as US 13 through Delaware which eventually leads to US 1 along the coast, or US 209 and State Highway 611 along the Delaware River in Pennsylvania.

There is a ferry service from Cape May, New Jersey to Lewes, Delaware. The hour and half trip runs fairly frequently, with some twelve sailings per day in the summer. Taking the ferry gives you quick access to the Maryland Eastern Shore. Phone (609) 886-2718 for further information.

VIRGINIA

Virginia is America's gateway to the south. Many would argue that it has become urbanized and "northernized", which may be true of the civil servant suburbs around Washington and down the coast; however the remainder of the state still retains its southern charm and hospitality. As you go west into the Allegheny Mountains, life is as rural and slow as elsewhere in the south, amidst a great deal of quiet wealth.

If you are an (American) Civil War buff, Virginia is heaven, since many of the battle and skirmishes took place here. The main urban centres are Richmond and Norfolk on the coast, and Charlottesville (the intellectual centre) and Roanoke inland. Be a bit careful if people start discussing religion with you. There are a lot of fundamentalists and evangelical types who take their religion and prejudices very seriously.

Northern Virginia still relies heavily on Washington for its entertainment, intersting restaurants and nightlife. For sports there are lots of riding clubs and even fox hunting if you choose to cultivate the right connections. You can swim at Virginia's Atlantic beaches, which are not as crowded as those of Maryland Delaware, between May and September.

Williamsburg is a very large reconstructed (by Rockefeller wealth) colonial village, a bit too shiny for many people, but featuring craftsmen working on colonial machines. It is very crowded and you often feel pressured to see things too quickly. Five miles away is Jamestown, the first English settlement in America. It is now only a few ruins but nearby are replicas of the ships that carried these early settlers.

The capital of the state, Charlottesville, was also the home of Thomas Jefferson, third American president and author of the Declaration of Independence. At a distinguished gathering in the White House, John F. Kennedy once said, "This is the greatest gathering of intellectuals in this room since Thomas Jefferson dined here alone." Jefferson's home of

Monticello is not only scenically splendid but shows the many sides of Jefferson, as social critic, inventor, gardener, architect, etc. If you are travelling south from Washington, this should definitely be one of your stops.

Richmond is a fine introduction to the gentility of the south, and you begin to hear that famous southern drawl. Much historic renovation has taken place here and its rich traditions are still maintained.

MARYLAND

With the rejuvenation of Baltimore as its focus, Maryland has become a more interesting state for visitors. It retains much of its colonial flavour, particularly in Annapolis and on the eastern shore, and its scenery from Chesapeake Bay to the hills and mountains of western Maryland is equal to far better known areas of the USA. For something completely different, visit Barry Parzow's "Popcorn Circus" in Springfield, where you can choose from over 100 flavours of popcorn.

Once away from Baltimore and the suburbs surrounding Washington (Prince George and Montgomery Counties) the pace of life slows down, the sense of history is strong and you may find yourself spending more time in Maryland than you had planned. Of all the mid-Atlantic states this is the one where it is worth getting off the super highways and turnpikes to discover an older but not ossified America.

Maryland represents an interesting cross-section of American life. This is best exemplified in Baltimore, which has the usual middle class natives, but also strong blue collar sections, traditional Polish areas, poor whites and blacks, a famous university and an important Catholic heritage. In the rural areas in the extreme east and west of the state, you will find an authentic quiet rural hospitality, rather than the more flamboyant and famous Southern one.

The coast is not as attractive in Maryland as in the surrounding states. Only if you are interested in industrial archaeology and decaying urban landscapes should you take US 1 along the coast.

Baltimore. Baltimore has a number of colleges and universities, the most famous of which is John Hopkins, just on the outskirts of downtown. This is a good place to find bars and good conversation. The city is easier to get around now that the new subway system has been added to the Mass Transit Administration (539-5000) and some of the terrible traffic congestion has been relieved. Baltimore has a long and fine tradition of seafood and quaint bars. Crab-eating in the Chesapeake Bay area (in any non-posh restaurant) is a memorable experience. Explore the downtown restaurants, especially along Charles St and E Lombard. The huge indoor Lexington Market (Lexington and Eutaw) offers everything from seafood to pizza to German sausages. There are many small ethnic shops around the Market also. It is not difficult to find a good dinner for under $6 and a decent lunch for half that amount.

While Baltimore is still dependent on Washington for some of its cultural activity, it boasts many fine attractions itself. These include a good local symphony, the Baltimore Museum of Art (especially good for early 20th century French art), the Walters Art Gallery at Charles and Center Streets (American art, and excellent topical exhibitions), the National Aquarium at the Inner Harbor (largest in the US), Morris Mechanic and Lyric Theaters, and the Inner Harbor, perhaps the finest example of urban renewal in America. The very fine Peabody Institute of Music often has excellent music recitals which are free.

At one time Baltimore was infamous for its red light districts. The nightlife is more sedate nowadays, but you can easily find any type of entertainment you desire. The Baltimore Orioles were, until recently, perennial winners of the World Series in baseball, but have since lost a record number of games. They play at Memorial Stadium, as do the Baltimore Colts football team. John Hopkins University boasts one of the best lacrosse teams in the country. Pimlico Race Track, on the outskirts of thecity, is one of the major race courses in the USA. The highlight of the racing calendar is at the end of the city-wide Preakness Festival in mid-May.

PENNSYLVANIA

Pennsylvania is nearly as large as England. There are three main areas within this gigantic state: Philadelphia and environs with its financial and historical interests, the middle through which run the Allegheny Mountains dotted with vacation resorts, and the industrial coal-mining west around Pittsburgh. Until recently Pennsylvania was the largest steel producer in the world and served as the gateway to the industrialized Midwest (Ohio, Michigan and Indiana). While Pittsburgh has recently enjoyed something of an urban rebirth, unemployment is rampant in the steel regions of western Pennsylvania. If you do find yourself in the blue collar areas of Pittsburgh, there are very good cheap diners in the great American tradition. While the movie *Rocky* takes place in Philadelphia, the people portrayed are more indicative of the west of the state: blue collar workers, conservative and tough, and quick to fight. Some may think that the most interesting thing about Pittsburgh is that it is virtually the only "burgh" in the US to retain the "h", which it did by local legislation in 1894.

Philadelphia. Philadelphia was very important as a cultural and governmental centre in colonial times, and boasts as former residents two very famous Americans, William Penn the Quaker and Benjamin Franklin. It is as diverse a city as you will find in the States, although it still has a very wealthy population, most of whom live in exclusive suburbs near the city. While there is no dominant ethnic community, there are ethnic neighbourhoods throughout the city, including a substantial and upwardly mobile black population. The many university and art colleges add a slightly bohemian atmosphere to what has always been considered a strait-laced city. The University of Pennsylvania's campus is the focus for small boutiques and quaint restaurants.

The 12 mile journey from the airport is blissfully easy: trains run to 30th St Station (the Amtrak terminal) in 18 minutes, costing $2 off-peak, $3.50 peak. Philadelphia's subway system is mostly as grotty as New York's, but it will take you to most of the major sights downtown. The subways are integrated with a good bus system. Call SEPTA on 574-7800 for transport information. The flat fare is $1. The Convention and Visitors' Bureau (3 Penn Center Plaza, 568-6599) will kit you out with good maps and guide.

Low-cost accommodation is in short supply. The Youth Hostel is at Chamounix Mansion at West Fairmont Park (878-3676) and is very popular; try to book ahead between 4.30pm and 8pm. For bed and breakfast call 735-1137 or 688-1633.

You can find the entire range of restaurants in Philadelphia. Be sure to eat at some of the Jewish delicatessens; the delis here are just as good as the more famous ones in New York City. And don't leave without trying a hoagie, a sandwich filled with Italian salami, peppers, onions, provolone cheese and olive oil; Philadelphia is their home, and specifically Antoinette Ianelli's place. The cheap and trendy place at night is Jimmy's (corner of South and 6th Streets), for excellent steak sandwiches and beer.

Other attractions include the splendid Philadelphia Orchestra, the Philadelphia Museum of Art, the Rodin Museum, the Pennsylvania Academy of Fine Arts, the American Philosophical Society, the US Mint and the Liberty Bell. Top sports teams include the '76 basketball team with its star, Julius Erving, "The Doctor", who makes Nureyev look clumsy, the Flyers hockey team, the Eagles football team and the Phillies baseball team.

The Interior. Go to Lancaster, about 80 miles inland from Philadelphia, to see the Amish farmers. The Amish, like the Mennonites (mentioned in the chapter on Ontario), have clung to their strict traditional heritage ever since they fled religious persecution in Germany in the early nineteenth century. They are often referred to as the Pennsylvania Dutch, which is a corruption of "Deutsch". They dress all in black, drive horses and buggies (which they refuse to defile with the flourescent sticker required by law for slow-moving vehicles) and use traditional farming methods. In fact, they are a very wealthy people and their organic farming newspaper is considered to be among the best in the world. These early ecologists have kept this part of the country one of the most fertile and productive in the world. Try to sample their produce and Pennsylvania Dutch cooking generally. The food tends to be a bit heavy in the German style (e.g. dumplings and stews), but interesting and fairly inexpensive. Unfortunately the area fills with tourists in search of this anachronistic community, and so prices have been driven up.

DELAWARE

Some claim that Delaware is almost feudal, for it is completely dominated by the DuPont corporation, manufacturers of chemicals. The northern part of the state is heavily industrialized, especially around Wilmington. As you travel south and then east to the beaches, the state becomes increasingly typical of rural, small-town America, not particularly scenic or quaint but leisurely and quiet. Sometimes, when you drive through one of these small towns, you will think you are in a 1930's Hollywood movie set.

Delaware is famous for its locally raised chickens and for its crab dishes. But the main attraction is not the food but the beaches (not all of which have especially appealing names), including Slaughter Beach, Broadkill Beach, Dewey Beach and Rehoboth Beach. These are more "social" than scenic beaches, especially the latter two which get crowds coming up from Maryland and Washington.

The major museum, and a very good one it is, is six miles from Wilmington. The Henry Francis du Pont Winterthur Museum (known simply as Winterthur) in the town of the same name is a treasure of American folk decorative art from colonial times, including a splendid collection of Pennsylvania Dutch art. There is an admission fee and reservations are necessary.

NEW JERSEY

New Jersey has seen better days. Although its population density is the highest of any state (at over 1,000 per square mile), its quality of life leaves a great deal to be desired. Its eastern beaches used to boast genteel and elegant resorts, stretching from Asbury Park to Cape May. Its cities and towns were once safe and solid; now they are full of slums and political corruption. The opening of gambling casinos in Atlantic City was just another nail in the state's coffers. The northern part of the state, within a 75 mile radius of New York City, has adopted all the bad habits of the metropolis without displaying any of its redeeming culture and glamour. Driving through Elizabeth or Newark is like being heaved into the middle of a Bosch painting or a post World War III world, and the state's designation as the "Garden State" will seem a mockery. Newark is one of the most dangerous cities in the US; crime throughout the state is serious and increases as you get closer to New York City.

The only genuinely scenic part of New Jersey is the Delaware Water Gap in the northwest corner of the state. The closer you get to Manhattan the more congested and ugly New Jersey becomes. Every road and bridge seems to demand a toll, so carry plenty of quarters. If you must drive through this area, avoid rush hours at all costs. New Jersey has become just a state to pass through as speedily as possible.

Atlantic City. Atlantic City is the east coast version of Las Vegas, and, in fact, does more business than its rival gambling haven. Although not as glamorous as Las Vegas, the wheels are honest and there's a lot of action. The locals hate the gambling for the underworld crime it has brought, but they don't complain about the increased employment and revenue. Apart from gambling, it is also the major entertainment centre in the area, with big name stars and the Miss America Pageant each September. The boardwalks in Atlantic City as well as Asbury Park and Ocean City, have lots of games, rides and junk food for the kiddies. You can reach Atlantic City easily by bus from almost anywhere in New Jersey (and Maryland and Delaware and New York and Pennsylvania too).

WEST VIRGINIA

There haven't been many tourists in West Virginia since people came from far and wide to see John Brown hanged in 1859. More's the pity, because if a tourist really wants to see traditional America, West Virginia is the place to go. The people are conservative in the best sense of the word: valuing family tradition, love of the land, sense of community, yet still politically liberal. With its mountains and coal mines, there is a resemblance to Wales, although the number of illegal whisky stills might be more reminiscent of Ireland.

West Virginia is in the heart of the Appalachian region, which has always been associated with uneducated hicks,"white trash", pregnant teenagers, people who don't mind living in an economically depressed coal mining region. But it is also possible to see the state as containing the last vestiges of a quieter, down-to-earth America, unsullied by the hectic pace and questionable glamour of the industrial north. Whereas states like New Jersey have given up any sense of history and tradition in favour of money-making gambling and urban stagnation, West Virginia is only backward as a craftsman might seem when compared to the machine which replaces him.

The two major cities in West Virginia are Charleston (the capital) and Wheeling, though with populations of 71,000 and 48,000 respectively they can hardly rank with other American cities. The highway system is good, but try to spend as much time as possible on the back roads. Drive or hitch through the mountains (West Virginia's popular name is "The Mountain State") to meet the natives, though be sure to plan ahead so that you wind up in town which has accommodation at the end of the day. Amenities, including motels, food and drink, are comparatively inexpensive. You won't find any grand restaurants but the portions are generous in any diner or coffee shop and you will be relieved to discover that not everyone in the States is trying to rip you off. All in all the scenery is beautiful, the people austere but compassionate, and the state an undiscovered gem.

Densely populated and heavily industrialized as the Northeast is, there are plenty of wide open spaces and spectacular scenery in the Allegheny and Appalachian Mountains which sweep along parallel to the coast, rising to nearly 6,000 ft in south-west Virginia. Furthermore they are a good place to escape the city heat and humidity.

Just an hour's drive west of Washington DC is Front Royal, the entrance to Shenandoah National Park and the Blue Ridge Mountains. There are excellent views and good camping facilities throughout these mountain areas which extend along the West Virginia border and beyond to North Carolina and Tennessee.

The more easily accessible the hills and resorts from New York, the more expensive they will be. For example the scenic Pocono Mountains of eastern Pennsylvania, whose deciduous forests are especially attractive in the autumn, are almost prohibitively expensive to stay in unless you have camping equipment. Accommodation is most expensive along the coast, and in mountain resorts. Many state and national parks have various types of camping and cabin facilities.

Ocean fishing and swimming are popular throughout the coastal areas. Assateague Island in Maryland, south of Ocean City, is a dramatic and beautiful strip of land where there are wild ponies and ample opportunities for beach exploration and fishing. Primitive camping facilities only.

All national parks have information booths which will advise on camping, hiking, picnicking, swimming, etc. Just as a short drive will take you from Manchester or Newcastle into beautiful countryside, so it is worthwhile getting past the suburbs of Baltimore and Philadelphia to find rolling countryside, horse farms and gardens.

Calendar of Events

early April	National Cherry Blossom Festival, Washington
early May	Apple Blossom Festival, Winchester VA
mid May	Preakness Festival, Baltimore
early June	Potomac Riverfest, Washington
late June/early July	Amish Folk Festival, Kutztown PA
early July	Freedom Festival, Philadelphia
late September	Maryland Wine Festival
late October	Halloween Celebration, Georgetown DC
early December	Lighting of National Christmas Tree, Washington

Chicago
and the Midwest

**Illinois Indiana Iowa Kansas Michigan Minnesota Missouri Nebraska
North Dakota Ohio Oklahoma South Dakota Wisconsin**

According to the Illinois Department of Tourism, Chicago is the city
"where the dandified East meets the Wild West" and the clash of
sophistication and gutsiness produces an entertaining city. Despite its
beautiful setting on the shores of Lake Michigan, Chicago is not a soft
dreamy place. Bustling with mercantile activity, "the city that works" still
does. The oft-quoted description by the poet Carl Sandburg captures the
no-nonsense concrete practicality of the Great American city:

> Hog Butcher for the World,
> Tool Maker, Stacker of Wheat,
> Player with Railroads and
> the Nation's Freight Handler,
> Stormy, husky, brawling,
> City of the Big Shoulders.

The reference to grain, livestock and freight-handling confirms Chicago's
role as capital of the Midwest, where the vast region's output is processed
and distributed. Its strategic location has resulted in its becoming the
nation's largest railroad centre, and (until supplanted recently by Atlanta)
having the world's busiest airport. Yet despite its importance as a
crossroad for shipping, it is self-reliant to the point of isolationism and
often parochial in its attitudes and tastes.

Sandburg's poem also captures the confidence associated with America's
second largest city (population 3.5 million). The well known nickname
"Windy City" refers primarily to the fierce winds, which occasionally blow
off Lake Michigan, but also to the hot air and inaction of its politicians,

particularly during Prohibition. The city's politics are complex and often scandalous, but always interesting. The claim made by a local alderman that "Chicago ain't no sissy town" still holds true. His choice of idiom also recalls the famous gangster names associated with Chicago — "Scarface" Al Capone and "Baby Face" Nelson. Not that you'll find much evidence of those infamous exploits; no stone marks the site of the St Valentine's Day Massacre of 1929 (at 2122 North Clark St) and few know where John Dillinger, Public Enemy Number One, was finally gunned down. (The wall, outside the Biograph Theater, against which he and his gang were shot has been moved to a restaurant in Vancouver).

Chicagoans are understandably more proud of their achievements in fields other than crime. The invention of the skyscraper is claimed by the city on the basis of a steel-skeleton building ten storeys high built in 1885. Appropriately, a hundred years later, Chicago has added 100 floors to its original record to boast the highest building in the world, the 110-storeys Sears Tower, 1,454 feet in height. Another achievement was the reversal of the Chicago River's direction of flow in 1900. By using a series of locks, the river was made to drain eventually into the Gulf of Mexico to prevent the pollution of Lake Michigan. Chicago has always been good at finding innovative and daring solutions to difficult practical problems.

THE NATIVES

A typical Chicagoan is as tough and no-nonsense as the city he inhabits. He is also likely to be friendly, especially if you are positive about his city and country (which is just good manners).

The ethnic diversity is almost as extreme as it is in New York. Under half of the population is white. There are many charming, plenty of not-so-charming ethnic neighbourhoods. The German and Scandinavian communities are predictably full of immaculately kept houses and gardens. There are more Poles than anywhere outside Warsaw. There are Italians, Lithuanians, Arabs, Koreans, Indians, Vietnamese and Irish. If you are interested in a particular ethnic group, there may well be a museum devoted to them, such as the Balzekas Museum of Lithuanian culture, the Spertus Museum of Jewish artefacts, the Polish Museum of America and the Swedish American Museum.

In addition to these communities of European and Asian people, there are large parts of the city dominated by over a million blacks and a half a million Latin people. Many of these areas are ghettos, concentrated on the dangerous South Side of town. White Chicagoans have not been known for liberalism and racial tolerance, and Chicago has traditionally been a strongly segregated city. But in 1983, they elected their first black mayor Harold Washington (just four years after voting in their first woman mayor). He died of a heart attack at his desk in City Hall in 1987, and was succeeded by an interim mayor, black alderman Eugene Sawyer. In typical Chicago fashion, it is alleged that Sawyer gained power by making deals with whites on the City Council opposed to the leading candidate Timothy Evans. The election scheduled for 1989 promises to be a hot one.

Making Friends. Rush Street is lined with bars and anyone with an open manner and a full purse should be able to meet fun-loving people. The Division Street bars are for the college-aged crowd, the most famous being Butch McGuire's (20 W Division) home of the Harvey Wallbanger (vodka, orange juice and galliano) and supposedly the first singles bar in the nation. Unfortunately many of the 4,500 couples who allegedly first met there still seem to be hanging around in pairs. A more open and lively singles bar is the Snuggery (15 W Division).

The city is full of young people, partly due to the high concentration of universities and colleges (second only to Boston). The prestigious University of Chicago with 9,000 students is one of the smallest; Northwestern, DePaul, Loyola and the Chicago Circle campus of the University of Illinois all have more.

A good way to meet people and get fit in the process is to join in one of the omnipresent softball, volleyball or basketball games in any of the lakefront parks. Some groups of friends play regularly, but most games are impromptu and newcomers are welcome.

CLIMATE

The Chicago summer is just as hot and humid as the New York summer with an average temperature of 75°F/24°C and many days over 90°F/32°C. Cool breezes sometimes have a moderating effect, and it's always cooler by the lake. Shorts and T-shirts are standard wear, though are not normally worn downtown.

Violent rain storms can occur over the summer, suddenly interrupting a brilliantly sunny day, but bringing relief from the heat. Spring and autumn are lovely. Winters are bitter with an average January temperature of 26°F/—3°C. The record low occurred in 1982 when temperature dropped to —26°F/—32°C; the wind chill factor took this to —80°F/—63°C, cold enough to make your tear ducts freeze. Call 976-1212 for the city forecast.

Getting Around

ARRIVAL AND DEPARTURE

Air. Despite its tremendous volume of over 50 million passengers, with 2,000 take-offs each day, immigration procedures at O'Hare International Airport are fairly brisk, seldom longer than 45 minutes. Its airport code, ORD derives from its previous name of Orchard Field. For flight enquiries dial 686-2200. Located 17 miles northwest of downtown Chicago, O'Hare is linked by the Kennedy Expressway. The road journey time varies from half an hour to two hours according to traffic and weather conditions. More reliable is the rapid transit link betweeen the International Terminal and Washington St Station in downtown Chicago. The trains are clean, safe and cheap ($1), and take only 45 minutes to reach Washington St from where you can transfer free to any downtown station.

Continental Air Transport (454-7800) runs frequent buses to suburban and downtown hotels including one located in Water Tower Square. The fare is $6.75. You must first take the free airport shuttle bus to the round entrance building between Terminals 1 and 2. There are several competing airport transfer services, however they take longer and charge more.

Taxis are plentiful at the airport and charge a fare of $20. Some taxis participate in a super-saver programme which facilitates taxi-sharing; look for the programme's bright yellow identifying flag.

If you arrive on a clear day, you can get your first glimpse of the Chicago skyline from the top of the multi-storey car park at O'Hare. You can also visit one of the observation decks to watch the planes, though the decks are disappointingly spartan and poorly situated.

Only a few carriers, notably Midway Airlines and Northwest Airlines use Chicago's second airport: Midway (MDW, tel: 767-0500), located on the South Side. Until O'Hare opened in 1961, Midway was the world's busiest airport. You can reach downtown either via the Chicago Transit Authority bus to Jackson Park Station or the minibus service costing $7.50 direct. Chicago's third airport is Meigs Field (tel: 744-4787), protruding into Lake Michigan from Lake Shore Drive a few miles southeast of downtown.

Cheap flights are advertised in the *Reader* magazine. Council Travel has a downtown office at 29 E Delaware Place (497-1497) and a branch in the suburb of Evanston.

Bus. The Greyhound bus station (781-2900) is opposite the gleaming State of Illnois Center, downtown at Clark and Randolph Streets. There are also direct services from O'Hare airport to eight destinations including Madison and Milwaukee.

Train. Chicago is the Clapham Junction of America. Eight major railway lines converge, bringing passengers and freight from every corner of the country. Trains run from the highly imposing Union Station at 210 S Canal St on the corner of Adams St (558-1075). Chicago is an Amtrak "International Gateway" city, with bargain fares to Minneapolis ($55 for the eight hour one-way journey), St Louis ($39, six hours) and Detroit ($39, seven hours). Commuter services to the six surrounding counties are operated by the Regional Transport Authority (toll-free 1-800-972-7000) and depart from Illinois Central and Northwestern stations. (Northwestern Station, downtown at Madison and Canal Streets, is a most impressive modern glass structure). A map of services is shown near the front of the Yellow Pages.

Driving. Among the cheapest car hire firms are Econo-Car (70 W Lake St, 332-7785; 850 N State St, 951-6262; and at O'Hare Airport), Dollar Rent a Car (50 W Lake St, 782-8736), Alamo (1-800-327-9633) and Fender Benders (1608 N Wells, Pipers Alley Mall, 280-8554) which claim to have the lowest rates in town.

A number of highways leading out of Chicago are toll routes, including I-294, I-90, I-94 and Route 5. Automatic toll booths are quite frequent near the city. Picking the outside lane usually speeds progress. Most tolls are around $1 and enforcement is taken seriously.

Driveaways. Driveaway cars are readily available in Chicago. Check the Yellow Pages and phone the agencies to find out what destinations are on offer and what perks, if any, are available. Auto Driveaway (310 S Michigan Ave 939-3600) is a good bet. Wilson Driveaway at the Xerox Center, 55 W Monroe St (236-0445) sometimes needs drivers to deliver cars to comparatively nearby cities, such as Columbus Ohio 300 miles away.

Ride-Sharing. The Metro Ride Board (929-5139) tries to match up lifts to other cities and to the airport. Ride-sharing opportunities are also advertised in the *Reader* magazine.

Hitch-hiking. There have been several reports of hitchers receiving tickets in Illinois, but most of the time you will just receive a warning. If you're heading west or north take the Howard el-train to Morse or Jarvis and walk north or south respectively to Touhy, which runs east-west to I-94 west. To get on any of the eastbound interstates, take the Dan Ryan el-train to 69th St, though this is not a safe neighbourhood.

CITY TRANSPORT

City Layout. Chicago's street pattern is the conventional grid, with major streets a mile or half a mile apart. The street numbering system follows the compass: State St divides downtown into east and west, and Madison St forms the division between the North Side and the South Side. Once downtown, walking is the best way to enjoy the city. The business and entertainment districts are conveniently close and compact.

Bus. The Chicago Transit Authority (836-7000) runs a frequent and economical public transport system consisting of buses linking in with the

'El', an elevated train service. (The CTA is probably the world's only public transport network whose name has been adopted by a major rock group i.e. Chicago, who originally called themselves "Chicago Transit Authority"). The fare on the system is $1 for adults, with transfers to another bus or train costing 25c. The transfer can be used as a return ticket if it is presented within one hour of purchase. If you plan to stay more than a fortnight, it might be worth buying a monthly pass for $50, which is valid for whole calendar months only. An all-day pass is available for $1.50 on Sundays. This is also the fare charged on the summer Culture Bus which leaves from the Art Institute. Buses run on every major street and some side streets, stopping at most intersections which are indicated by a sign showing route number and details. Although the transit system operates 24 hours a day, late night services are infrequent and can be dangerous outside the downtown area.

The El. Chicago's Metropolitan railway is distinctive for being elevated above ground. The downtown business district is known as the Loop and officially consists of an area five blocks by seven, bounded by Van Buren, Wells and Lake Streets and Wabash Avenue, i.e. the loop surrounded by the elevated Ravenswood CTA line.

The El is completely integrated with the bus network and the same procedures for boarding apply. There is a 20c surcharge on certain lines. Like the buses the El operates throughout the night, though many natives consider it too risky to use alone late at night. Like the New York system, it is very noisy, but retains many pleasing characteristics.

Get a map of the transit system ($1) from the Water Tower Information Center, the Regional Transit Authority office (300 N State St), the Illinois Tourist Information Center at O'Hare Airport or by sending $1.25 and a self-addressed envelope to Chicago Transit Authority, PO Box 3555, Chicago, IL 60654. Study the map carefully since some lines branch off, just as on the London Underground. Many trains are designated A or B depending on the stops they make; so if it's a B stop you want, be sure to get on a B train.

Car. The naming and numbering of expressways in Chicago can be confusing. The most famous route is the Lake Shore Drive (US 41), said to be one of the most scenic urban drives in the world. This north/south route passes between harbour, tennis courts and beaches on the east and the striking city skyline on the west. The Eisenhower Expressway (I-290) approaches from due west, passing through shabby industrial neighbourhoods, until it hits downtown and becomes the Congress Expressway. I-94, known outside the city as the Edens Expressway, is the main north/south artery. It becomes the Kennedy Expressway at the city limits, until it crosses the Congress Expressway whereupon it becomes the Dan Ryan Expressway. I-90 heads off southeast to become the aptly named Chicago Skyway. For traffic information downtown tune to 1610 AM.

Car parks fill early in the downtown area and are generally expensive. One of the more convenient ones is the one on Michigan Avenue just past Monroe St; there is a cheaper one (about $8 per day) a few hundred yards further away on Monroe near the lakefront.

Taxis. There are 4,600 cabs in the city, and many run throughout the night They may be hailed in any busy street and are relatively cheap. Do not expect to find taxis cruising for custom in rough parts of town. Order a taxi to pick you up, well in advance through Checker Yellow (829-4222) or American United (248-7600).

Cycling. There is an excellent bicycle path (albeit incomplete, with certain stretches which have to be covered by road) along the lake front which stretches 11 miles as far north as Evanston, site of Northwestern University. The flat terrain in the northern suburbs makes cycling almost as pleasant. You can rent bicycles from the Bike Stop (4810 N Broadway, 334-3547), the Village Cycle Center (1337 N Wells St. 751-2488), Cycle Smithy (2418½ N Clark St, 281-0444) and Spokesmen Inc (5301 S Hyde Park, 684-3737). There is also a bike rental kiosk in Lincoln Park at the corner of Cannon and Fullerton, just north of the Conservatory. Prices start at about $5 an hour or $20 for 24 hours. Car rack rentals, when available, cost an extra $15. Look for *Chicago and Beyond: 26 Bike Tours* by Linda and Steve Nash in local bookshops.

Boats. Sightseeing tours are available from Mercury Sightseeing Boats (332-1353), Wendella Sightseeing Boats (337-1446) and Shoreline Marine Sightseeing Co (427-2900), all docked on the south side of the Chicago River at 102 Wacker Drive. Cruises along the lakefront or on the Chicago River last one or two hours and cost $5-$10. In summer, boats leave from Navy Pier (744-3315) for cruises which include dining and drinking; these cost from $25 to $40.

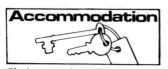
Accommodation

Hotels. Pick up the *Holiday Package* brochure from the Visitors Center for a complete list of hotels offering cheap two night weekends during the summer and Christmas shopping seasons. Usually the rates are between around $60 for a double room per night, not including the 9% tax on lodgings.

There is no particular area for cheap hotels, although some of the older ones downtown are reasonable. Similarly, there is no central booking service, though the Hotel and Motel Association (27 East Monroe St, Suite 700; 346-3135) will inform you of available vacancies.

Motels. All the approach roads into Chicago are lined with motels, although on I-55 they begin even further from the centre of town than usual. Chicago's Lincoln Avenue motel strip has a large number of motels in a reasonably safe neighbourhood, but the area is visually unattractive and is a 40 minute bus ride from downtown. Try the Spa at 5414 N Lincoln Avenue or the Summit at 5308; both charge around $45 for a room with two double beds.

One motel deserves particular recommendation — the Sheridan Chase Motel (7300 N Sheridan Road, 973-7440) located on the North Shore less than half block from the beach. It is close to the El and other transit routes. The cost is $40, $50 for a maximum of four to a room with savings by the week ($225 and $250). Shabby but convenient.

Hostels. The international youth hostel is on the North Side at 6318 North Winthrop (262-1011). A summer-only AYH hostel is run by the University of Chicago and located on the campus at 1414 E 59th (753-2270). It is open only between June 1 and September 9. It has the advantage of being just four blocks from Lake Michigan. The youth hostels office is 3712 N Clark St (327-8114).

YMCA. The Ys in Chicago are frequented by low-lifers and most are situated either in ghetto areas or in far distant suburbs. The most central is the Lawson YMCA at 30 W Chicago Avenue (944-6211). There are tolerable rooms at the Y at N Marshfield Avenue for about $20 a night. The YWCAs do not have accommodation.

Bed and Breakfast. Bed & Breakfast Chicago Inc (PO Box 14088, Chicago 60614, 951-0085) is a reservation service which handles a wide variety of accommodation in the Chicago area. The budget rate for two people is $40-$50 per night. A booking fee of $15 must be included with the reservation which is subtracted from the bill.

University Residences. Any student who will be staying throughout the period June to August should enquire about accommodation at Northwestern University's dormitories on Sheridan Road in Evanston, a lively and attractive lakefront suburb 30 minutes from downtown. Call the Office of Residence Halls on 649-8514.

Eating and Drinking

Fast food is a way of life in Chicago. The world's first McDonalds is in the northwestern suburb of Des Plaines. It no longer serves food, but has now been converted into a museum evoking the days when a burger cost 15c. You can reach it by RTA train to Des Plaines, then walking north for five minutes along Lee St/Mannheim Road. Tours operate Wednesday-Friday, but you should call ahead on 297-5022 to reserve a place. If you're hungry after the tour, a brand new McDonalds is across the road. The world's second-busiest McDonalds is in downtown Chicago at 600 N Clark St (at Ohio St). (It was the world's busiest until recently overtaken by the branch in the Hungarian capital, Budapest). Decorated in 1950s and 60s style, it has a couple of excellent juke boxes (one playing 78 rpm records) and some wonderful arcade machines which you can play for free. For good food and atmosphere, however, try Ed Debrevic's, a block away at Wells and Ontario Streets. Ed's is always crowded and, as the signs say, "If you think you have a reservation, you're in the wrong place!".

Street food seems equally popular and you can find decent little hot dog stands on corners all over the city. Also popular are Italian beef sandwiches (around $2) and *gyros,* a Greek sandwich comparable to doner kebabs. The word is pronounced guy-rose on the South-Side, he-ross on the North Side. True junk food addicts should betake themselves to Uncle Frank's (2651 N Halsted St).

Until recently Chicago tastes were conservative; plain steaks and chops were the favourite fare. But the polyglot nature of the city is becoming increasingly reflected in the range of restaurants. Restaurants which offer the most reasonably priced victuals are usually Thai, Mexican and Chinese.

The Rogers Park area along N Sheridan St abounds with inexpensive snack shops and restaurants: from Korean poolgogi sandwiches at the Poolgogi Steak House on Morse St to the White Hen Pantry which has takeaway lox and cream cheese on bagels for $1 and chocolate donuts for 50c. The Clark and Belmont vicinity has modestly priced Japanese fare and all manner of Oriental eateries. Other Oriental food can be found at restaurants and grocery stores on Argyll St. Dependable inexpensive Italian food can be found at Taylor St or 23rd and Oakley.

One statistician claims that it would be possible to eat out in Chicago every evening and never repeat oneself during a lifetime. The following will last you two weeks:

Chicago Pizza and Ovengrinder Co, 2121 N Clark (248-2570). Leading exponent of the famous Chicago deep dish pizza.

Pizzeria Uno, 29 E Ohio St (321-1000). Original Chicago-style pizza restaurant in a small Italian grotto with friendly relaxed service. If it's full, try the sister restaurant *Pizzeria Due* a block away at Wabash Avenue and Ontario St.

Dianna's Opaa, 212 S Halsted St (332-1225). Lively Greek restaurant in which owner Petros often starts up Greek dancing.

Chiam, 2323 S Wentworth Avenue (225-6336). Seating for 500. There are many other Chinese restaurants in Chinatown along Cermak Road and Wentworth Avenue.

Happy Sushi, 3346 N Clark St (528-1225). Reasonably priced flamboyant sushi bar.

Campeche, 7101 N Clark St. Family run Mexican restaurant charging $2-$6. Also located at 958 W Wrightwood in Sheffield.

Gaudalaharry's, 1043 N Rush St (337-0800). Food not great but a complimentary taco bar on Wednesdays and a long happy hour (4pm-8pm) most nights.

Nantucket Cove, 1000 N Lake Shore Drive (943-1600). Good fresh seafood.

Alexander's American Grill, 914 Ernst Court (944-0265). Crowded and open till 3am, 4am on Saturdays.

The Berghoff, 17 Adams St (427-3170). German food at reasonable prices with good atmosphere. It has its own beer, a delicious brew which is also sold elsewhere in the Chicago area, and its own bourbon.

Leona's, on Sheffield (near Belmont) and North Sheridan (near Morse). Ideal for an Italian binge.

Las Palmas, on Howard St. Great Mexican food, with musicians at weekends.

La Choza, on N Paulina St (near Howard St). Looks like a real dive, but has a lovely hidden outdoor garden and good, cheap food. Bring your own alcohol.

Heartland Cafe, on Lunt St in Rogers Park. Excellent vegetarian food.

If you want to dine in high style, many of Chicago's fine restaurants offer attractively priced menus at lunchtimes and at unfashionable dining times (5pm-6pm). For example, a small fixed-price dinner at the award-winning L'Escargot (Allerton Hotel, 701 N Michigan Avenue, 337-1717) can be had for $15.   You might also like to wander along Devon St, with numerous Indian restaurants which offer interesting buffets. The Billy Goat Tavern, *under* Michigan Avenue near Grand St, was made famous by the American TV show *Saturday Night Live*. It is patronized by rowdy sports fans and has a real live billy goat. For free food, loiter around the entrance floor of the Museum of Science and Industry and try to catch the eye of researchers from the adjacent Consumer Research Center, who seek out volunteers to taste new foods. Finally, you might like to take advantage of the substantial free hors d'oeuvres offered by bars such as Monday's (on Michigan Avenue near Grand St) and Dos Hermanos in the Sears Tower: both offer half-priced drinks during the Happy Hour.

DRINKING

Bars normally stay open until 3am Monday to Friday and 4am at weekends. Rush and Division Streets are full of trendy lively bars, many of which exact a cover charge. On a hot day go to El Jardin's (3335 N Clark St) for one of their 12 ounce killer drinks of tequila, triple sec and lemon juice. More serious drinkers still should head for Resi's Bierstube or Lashet's Inn

(2034 and 2119 W Irving Park Road). Locals speak highly of Quenchers (2401 N Western Avenue). One of Chicago's most famous bars — Frank's 113 Club Tavern (113 E 47th St) — is located in a risky ghetto area, but it is still crowded. The latest trendy area is River North, and you should try Ditka's Citylights at 223 W Ontario St (280-7660), owned by the coach of the Chicago Bears.

Many cheaper restaurants are unlicensed and permit you to bring your own booze. Try Sam's Wine Warehouse (756 W North Avenue) for the largest selection of American wines in the city.

Entertainment

You get superb views from both the Sears Tower and the John Hancock Center; admission is $3.25 and $3.50 respectively. At night it is particularly spectacular. For an interesting land-based view, take a horse and hansom cab tour from Water Tower Place ($30 for half an hour). A much cheaper option is the Chicago Transit Authority city tour, which runs on summer Sundays from the Art Institute of Chicago (Michigan Avenue and Adams St) every half-hour from 10.30am to 5pm. The fare is a bargain at $2.50.

The most comprehensive source of listings for performing arts, attractions and events is the *Reader,* which is published each Friday and is free from news stands, bookshops, restaurants, etc. *Chicago* Magazine (monthly $1.95) is also useful. The Chicago Convention and Tourism Bureau provides an Eventline for visitors (255-2323) with recorded information about theatre, sports, etc. Both the *Chicago Tribune* and the *Sun Times* include good entertainment guides, especially the Friday and Sunday editions of the *Tribune.* Hot Tix Booths sell half price tickets available on the day of performance for theatre, music and dance events; the downtown booth is at 24 S State St, with suburban branches at 1616 Sherman Ave, Evanston and Oak Park Mall.

There is an interesting presentation of the city and its history called "Here's Chicago" at the Water Tower on Michigan Avenue at Pearson St (467-7114). Also visit the ArchiCenter (330 S Dearborn St, 782-1776), an exhibition gallery which features points of interest in Chicago. Among these is the Broad of Trade (141 W Jackson Blvd at La Salle St, 435-3590) where you can watch the controlled chaos which contributes trading on the world's oldest and largest commodities futures market.

Buildings of Interest. Anybody with even a slight interest in architecture cannot fail to notice the innovative designs of the Chicago School, culminating in the work of Frank Lloyd Wright. The Chicago Architectural Foundation, dedicated to the preservation of this architectural heritage, gives 22 different guided tours on foot, by bus or even by bicycle from the ArchiCenter. (Hours and tour fees vary so call ahead). The Chicago Loop Tour is intended for people with a casual interest, whereas there are many more in-depth ones, including the Frank Lloyd Wright tour of Oak Park, Wright's home neighbourhood from 1889-1909. The Oak Park Visitor's center at 158 Forest Avenue (848-1500) should be the first stop for devotees of the architect. His own home (at Chicago and Forest Avenues) is open for guided tours daily, as is Unity Temple, his first public building. If you want to walk around Oak park without a guide to see the 25 buildings designed by Wright, not to mention the house where Ernest Hemingway once lived, take the Lake Street/Dan Ryan el to Harlem or Oak Park Avenue. There are no tours available for the Bach House (Sheridan and

Jarvis Streets), but it should not be missed by architecture buffs. You can take an architectural river cruise from North Pier abroad the *Fort Dearborn* for $10.

Some of Chicago's skyscrapers are stunning. Other buildings are simply strange. The former American Furniture Mart completed in 1926 has a ghastly blue-topped tower which glows ghoulishly at night and which was originally intended as a mooring for dirigibles (airships). Watch out also for the twin Marina Towers, a dozen storeys of parking lot topped by 20 levels of apartments. As an elegant contrast, head North on Sheridan Road to the Bahai House of Worship.

While wandering around the city, watch for sculptures and mobiles in public places (for information call FINE-ART). At 600 W Madison you will see a 100-foot sculpture of a baseball bat by Claes Oldenburg; outside the First National Bank Plaza is Chagall's "Four Seasons" mosaic; "Being Born" is at the corner of State and Washington Streets; and Picasso's "Mystery Sculpture" graces Daley Plaza. The lobby of Sears Tower is adorned by Alexander Calder's "Universe".

Museums and Galleries. The Chicago Council on Fine Arts located in the lobby of the Daley Center Plaza (Dearborn and Randolph, 346-3278) provides information on the city's art exhibitions, of which there are many. In addition to the collection of French Impressionists and Old Masters at the Art Institute of Chicago (Michigan Avenue at Adams St, 443-3600; free on Thursdays), there are many small and interesting galleries. These range from the collection of Eastern European prints at the Jacques Baruch Gallery (900 N Michigan Avenue, 944-3377) and the Photography Museum at 364 W Erie St to the Du Sable Museum of African American History (740 E 56th Place in Washington Park, 947-0600) which traces the history of blacks in America.

Most popular of all museums is the mammoth Museum of Science and Industry (Lake Shore Drive at 57th St, 684-1414), housed in a magnificent 1893 building. You can reach it from downtown Chicago on bus 1 (Indiana-Hyde Park) or 6 (Jeffrey Express). The museum opens 9.30am-5.30pm in summer and on winter weekends, 9.30am-4pm during the week in winter. Its 14 acres include replicas of the human heart and a collection of foetuses showing pre-natal development. Although admission is free (which is only proper since many of the exhibits are exercises in public relations for American industries) some of the major attractions such as a German U-boat and a full-sized model coal mine charge $2 admission. The Field Museum of Natural History is also enormous and contains dinosaurs' skeletons and much more. It is located on Lake Shore Drive at Roosevelt Road (922-9410), opens daily from 9am to 5pm and costs $2 ($1 for students).

Further along at 1300 Lake Shore Drive is the Adler Planetarium (322-0304) whose sky shows "combine cosmic theater and multi-sensory adventure." All this for just $2. It opens daily from 9.30am to 4.30pm, with late opening on Fridays to 9pm.

Music. For exhaustive listings of the Chicago music scene, consult Section Two of the *Reader*. The Chicago Symphony Orchestra under Sir Georg Solti performs in Orchestra Hall (220 S Michegan Avenue, 435-8111) from September to May. For concert information call 664-0858. Watch for their outdoor performances during the Ravinia Festival in Highland Park (782-9696) which lasts from June to September. The Lyric Opera Orchestra put on free performances at the Grant Park bandshell on certain days in the summer. Free lunchtime concerts can be heard at the First National Plaza at Dearborn and Monroe Streets.

Major rock artists perform at the Rosemont Horizon (6920 N Mannheim Road, Des Plaines, 635-6600) and outdoor concerts are given at Poplar Creek Music Theatre (W Higgins Road, 426-1222). For forthcoming attractions call 842-5387 and for ticket information 454-6777. *Chicago Music Magazine,* free from record stores and bars, is a good source of information about up-and-coming musicians.

Electric blues originated in Chicago and thrives there still. One of the original clubs on the South Side, the New Checkerboard Lounge (423 E 43rd St, 624-3240) is still going strong. Take a taxi. On the safe North Side, you can choose between two blues clubs across the road from one another on N Halsted St, B.L.U.E.S. (582-1012) and Kingston Mines (477-4646). The average cover charge is only $4 with cheap drinks, and they both have the crowded smoky atmosphere appropriate for blues dives. Blue Chicago (937 N State, 642-6261) is a little more upmarket.

The style of jazz called "Chicago" from the 1920s and 30s can still be heard alongside more modern jazz. Try Rick's American Cafe in the Lake Shore Drive Holiday Inn; it features good artists but charges steeply ($5-$10 cover plus very expensive drinks). Try also the clubs on N Lincoln Avenue or one of the following:

The Green Mill at Lawrence and Broadway features 1930s decor (it was one of Al Capone's hangouts) and super music.

Biddy Mulligan's on N Sheridan is a popular place for jazz/blues and sometimes reggae and rock. Low cover charge and dancing.

The Moosehead Bar & Grill on Wells St. (downtown) is more upmarket and features a wide variety of jazz artists.

The Blackstone Hotel on S Michigan (near the Hilton) is the home of Joe Segal's *Jazz Showcase,* where a long tradition of jazz is upheld.

Phone the Jazz Hotline (666-1881) for details of other events and venues. The Chicago Jazz Festival takes place in late August at Grant Park.

Chicago has one of the strongest folk scenes in the country. The pick of the folk clubs is Holstein's (2464 N Lincoln, 372-3331) since the venerable Earl of Old Town has been taken over by B.L.U.E.S. For those who maintain "if it ain't country, it ain't music", there is Nashville North (101 E Irving Park Road, 595-0170) and Sundowners at the R.R.Ranch (56 W Randolph St, 263-8207). Also good for folk music is the No Exit Cafe on Glenview in Rogers Park.

Theatre. Chicago has experienced a boom in theatre over the last few years. The International Theater Festival (held in May and June) is an excellent showcase. There are more than 50 professional theatre groups in the city. Many prominent actors, directors and playwrights have had their debut at the Goodman Theater, housed in the Art Institute Complex. Many shows which have either come from, or are bound for, Broadway are put on at the Shubert Theater (22 W Monroe St, 977-1710), at the Blackstone Theater (66 E Balbo Avenue, 977-1717) and at the Arie Crown Theater (2300 Lake Shore Drive, 791-6000). In addition there are many "off-Loop" theatres on the North Side which present original material. The League of Chicago Theaters provides recorded messages on ticket availability and brief interviews with critics and actors (977-1755). The Chicago Alliance for the Performing Arts (176 W Adams St, 372-5178) sells vouchers, often at a discount, to many community theatres.

Some theatres advertise in the "Wanted" section of the *Reader* for volunteer ushers, which is a handy way to see some plays for free.

Nightlife. Acid house fans will like the Exit (1653 N Wells St, 440-0535). Dancers with more conventional tastes in music should try Eddie Rocket's (9 W Division, 787-4881) for good value, or F/X (1100 N State, 280-2282) for chic.   One of America's most innovative comedy clubs is Second City (1616 N Wells St, 337-3992), where Alan Alda and John Belushi began their careers. It is housed in a converted Chinese laundry; space is limited, so advance bookings are essential. Some comedy fans maintain that Friday and Saturday nights at the Improv Institute (504 N Wells St, 782-6387) are better still: even if you don't catch all the local humour, you should learn a little about the Chicago psyche and have a good laugh.

Gambling is illegal in Illnois, but serious poker players should find it easy to join a game.

SPORT

Chicagoans take their professional sports very seriously. Indeed, the quickest way to popularity is to demonstrate some familiarity with their clubs. Generally ticket prices for professional games range from $3 to $12, though hockey is slightly more expensive. The better of the two baseball teams is the White Sox who play at Comiskey Park (35th St and Shields Avenue, 924-1000); however the Chicago Cubs are still Chicago's favourite, playing at Wrigley Field on the North Side (Clark and Addison Streets, 281-5050). The installation of floodlights at Wrigley Field in 1988, following the takeover of the Cubs by the *Chicago Tribune,* was a major national event.

Soccer is played quite successfully by the Chicago Sting at the grandiose Soldier's Field on S Lake Shore Drive at McFetridge St (558-5425) and, during the indoor season, at Chicago Stadium (1800 W Madison St). American football is played by the Chicago Bears (known as the Monsters of the Midway and featuring William "Refrigerator" Perry) also at Soldier's Field (663-5408). The Black Hawks play ice hockey and fight at the Chicago Stadium (733-5300). Horseracing and betting take place at the prestigious Arlington Park racecourse 20 miles northwest of downtown Chicago. After a disastrous fire, the course has been rebuilt and is now among the finest tracks in the world.

For participatory sports there are numerous tennis courts and golf courses. Despite Chicago's location at the edge of Lake Michigan, there is no point in taking your aqualung. But fishing, swimming, sailing, water-skiing and windsurfing are easily accessible. During a storm, however, Lake Michigan can become very rough and should be avoided.

Parks and Zoos. The Brookfield Zoo can be reached via the Congress El to Forest Park; take the Des Plaines Avenue exit, then transfer to the tiger-striped zoo express bus. The zoo includes species which are extinct in the wilds, some of them in a simulated tropical rainforest. It also has a few Koalas, for whom fresh eucalyptus leaves are flown in from a farm in Florida. The zoo is free on Thursdays. The zoo in Lincoln Park is far less impressive, but is free every day and is well-kept. There's also an indoor Conservatory just north of the park. The Chicago Botanical Gardens in the far north suburb of Winnetka (off Lake Cook Road) are impressive, but afficionados prefer the Morton Arboreatum out at Lisle. The world's largest aquarium is the Shedd Aquarium at 1200 S Lake Shore Drive (939-2426) which is best visited at feeding times: 11am and 2pm daily, with an extra feed at 3pm during busy periods. The aquarium opens at 9pm (March-October) or 10am (November-February) and closes daily at 5pm. Admission costs $12.

Chicago has the longest stretch of beachfront of any major city. Lincoln Park lies along the lake on the North Side, and the beaches and yacht harbours are always crowded. Try Rogers Park, beginning at Pratt Street, where the relatively undiscovered beaches stretch for blocks and are provided with municipal life guards, so swimming is permitted. If you are unwilling to leave downtown, just head east to Oak St beach.

SHOPPING

The shopping area is concentrated along a one mile stretch of State Street, a pedestrian precinct since 1978. All the major department stores are here, notably the magnificent Marshall Field's, built in 1892 with natural lighting by means of a skylit courtyard (now adapted to the age of electricity). One of the store's most famous employees, a Mr Selfridge, carried on the department store tradition in great style.

Explore the whole nine blocks of State Street from Wacker Drive to Congress Parkway. For information about special events and activities call 782-9160. North Michigan Avenue is known as the Magnificent Mile or "Boul Mich" and has all the fine speciality shops selling everything from antique Oriental carpets to Burberry raincoats. For less exclusive items, any of the city's 50 Woolworths or Walgreens drugstores should suffice. Men should visit any of the eight clothing Clearance Centers in Chicago: clothes costing les than half retail prices can be found. "You may go in a loft door and up in a creaky elevator but you get one hell of a buy" (*Newsweek*).

At the northern end of the Magnificent Mile is the much vaunted Water Tower Place (825 N Michigan Avenue, 440-3460) which includes a seven-level atrium shopping mall comprising over 100 speciality stores and glass enclosed elevators.

The best-stocked book store in town is Kroch and Brentano's on Wabash. For good bargain books, visit Crown Books and if you are feeling homesick, visit Stuart Brent's on N Michigan Avenue, which is modelled after Blackwell's in Oxford. There are plenty of secondhand bookshops in the Lincoln Park area on Clark St and Lincoln Avenue.

The sales tax in Chicago is 7% and is applied to all purchases except non-processed food not for immediate consumption.

THE MEDIA

The radio station for classical as well as other kinds of music is WFMT 98.7 FM; listen to the famous programme *Midnight Special* on Saturday nights at 10.15. Soft rock is played on WXRT (93 FM), adult rock on 101 FM and Country on WAMQ 670 AM. The leading black station is on 102.7 FM, while WCKG (105.9) promises "classic rock and less talk". For the nearest thing to BBC Radio One, try WLS 89 AM with a moderate teenage-orientated selection (listen to Animal Stories at 9.45am and 5.45pm, a humorous short news programme featuring anecdotes about animals). For serious news programmes tune to 780 AM for WBBM, 670 AM for WMAQ, 92 FM for the National Public Radio station WBEZ or try to find the Canadian Broadcasting Corporation. On television, PBS can be found on channel 11.

Newspapers. The *Chicago Tribune* was once in the same league as the *New York Times* and the *Washington Post*. Despite a decline in its reputation, it is still a fairly reliable newspaper. The *Sun Times,* formerly a liberal and gossipy newspaper, is now part of the Murdoch group. Both papers cost 35c, $1.25 on Sundays. Try also the *Chicago Defender* for local news that the two main papers don't print.

The fact that Chicago is a tough city should not be underestimated. On average, two violent crimes occur every minute. The sound of gunshot is considered commonplace in the rougher sections of town. It is not advisable for tourists to wander off exploring. This is particularly true on the South Side, but also in the unsavoury sections of the normally safe North Side. Certain places such as the Cabrini Green housing project just west of Rush Street are places you should simply not go unless you have a police escort. Late night revellers should not wander along Division St west of Clark St, for things change dramatically. Bus and train travellers should be careful in the vicinity of the terminals. If possible stay north of Roosevelt Road (1200 South) and east of Ashland (1600 West).

Do not walk at night in deserted areas and do not venture into the South Side unless your car is mechanically sound, all doors are locked and you have the route firmly fixed in your mind. Tactics popular among villains include deliberately colliding with other motorists, then attacking them when they get out to inspect the damage; other robbers simply smash the windows of stationary cars with baseball bats. (Some South Side locals ignore red traffic lights for fear of sudden attack). Taxis are the best solution. Visitors should ask a policeman, cab driver or even a reasonable looking stranger for advice about safe versus dangerous neighbourhoods.

Law enforcement of drug violations is erratic so do not assume that just because everyone else is doing it you won't be arrested. Dealing even in small amounts of marijuana is taken very seriously by the police. The police are very vigilant in their pursuit of drunk drivers, who face mandatory prison sentences.

The area code for Chicago is 312.

Information: Chicago Tourism Council, Water Tower, Michigan and Chicago Avenues (225-5000). Maps and brochures are also distributed from the Visitor Information Center at East Pearson St and Michigan Avenue.

British Consulate General: 33a N Dearborn St (346-1810).

American Express: 625 N Michigan Avenue (425-2570).

Thomas Cook: 435 N Michigan Avenue (828-9750).

Post Office: 433 W Van Buren and Canal Streets (886-2575).

Medical Emergencies: Northwest Memorial Hospital, Superior St (649-2000).

Dental Service: 726-4976.

Late night drugstore: Walgreen's Drugs, 1130 N State St (787-7035).

Crisis Center: 929-5140.

Travelers' Aid: 327 S LaSalle St (435-4500). Also at Union Station, the Greyhound Terminal and O'Hare Airport.

Away from the cities and industrial centres, the vast area of the Midwest stretching from North Dakota south to Oklahoma, and up along the Great Lakes is an area of small towns scattered thinly across flat farming country. There are of course some topographical surprises, but driving across these 13 states does not admit of much variety. If on the other hand you have grown weary of traffic, noise, hurry, expensive bars, beautiful people, and all the other features of urban America, it might be time to expose yourself to one of the sleepy Midwestern towns tenuously linked by miles of straight often deserted roads. People who choose to stop in one town for a while need not worry that they are missing anything new or different in the next town, the next county or even the next state.

In the Spring 1988 edition of *Granta,* Bill Bryson — a native of Des Moines, Iowa — placed his home state "in the middle of the biggest plain this side of Jupiter" and described the state capital thus:

> "A thousand miles from the sea in any direction, 600 miles from the nearest mountain, 400 miles from skyscrapers and muggers and things of interest, 300 miles from people who do not habitually stick a finger in their ear and swivel it around as a preliminary to answering any question addressed to them by a stranger. To reach anywhere of even passing interest from Des Moines by car requires a journey that in other countries would be considered epic."

The summer drought of 1988 had a devastating effect upon the people of Iowa and the rest of the Midwest. Crop yields fell by half, driving many farmers out of business and reviving memories of the Dust Bowl of the 1930s. Yet the resilience of rural Americans (characterised in the Nanci Griffith song *Trouble in the Fields)* means that you can expect a warm welcome even when the times are hard.

On the outskirts of a small town, the population sign separates the monotonous wheat and corn fields from the houses, gas station, post office and shop, whether it's Deadwood South Dakota (population 2,409) or Peculiar Missouri (population 705). Sometimes the town sign offers more information, such as "Home of the Ottertails", "Welcome to our Town" or even "Population 1,863... 1,862 nice, friendly folk and one old grouch". If you want further information, pull into the gas station where, unless the owner is the one old grouch, you will get reliable information about local weather, road conditions, events, the way to the old Methodist church or a shortcut to Pete and Jim's World Famous Bakery.

The spirit of the Midwest resides far more in these small, neat communities than in the handful of large cities in the region. Only St Louis, Kansas City, Minneapolis/St Paul, Milwaukee, Cincinnati, Cleveland, and Detroit have populations exceeding half a million. These cities are often the butt of jokes by people from the East and West Coasts: for example, Cleveland is claimed to be the one place in North America where you ask for a room *without* a view. Many state capitals are not the largest cities. Springfield Illinois, Topeka Kansas, Jefferson City Missouri and, smallest of all with 10,000 inhabitants, Pierre South Dakota, all are the thriving hubs of yesteryear.

Perhaps Detroit has the best claim as the Midwest's second city. It was also until recently the American city most worth avoiding. Its role as the world centre of motor car manufacturing gave it the appearance of a huge, sprawling Dagenham, then the decline of the industry in the face of foreign competition resulted in a far uglier face, where violence was rampant and the downtown area a slum. The epicentre of soul music (Motown=Motor Town=Detroit) was a crumbling shell, but has been energetically revitalised. While there are still vast areas of the city where it is unwise to venture, the downtown area has been enhanced by gradual gentrification and an efficient elevated People Mover railway. A day could be well spent at the University Cultural Center (which hosts six museums as well as

Wayne State Univerity), and Tamla Motown fans should brave the badlands and venture out to the Motown Museum, "Hitsville USA". You should call first (875-2264) for an appointment before heading out to the recording studio at 2648 W Grand Boulevard.

The Natives. The small town Midwesterner does not want to keep up with city slickers in fashion, taste or income. His spirit of competition is more likely to manifest itself in the energy with which he combats the frightful winters, or at sporting contests between rival small towns. His demands and aspirations are usually modest ones, and can make a refreshing change from the ambition and aggression so evident in most of urban America. You will find the people extraordinarily open, welcoming and delighted (though perhaps a little puzzled) at your choice of destination. In 1988, for example, South Dakota was the state with fewest foreign visitors; less than 500 British travellers ventured there.

They are moderate in most things from their accents (no twangs or drawls, except in the Southern parts of the region) to their politics and religion. Although the local church often plays a central role in small communities, the enthusiastic revival type of worship is uncommon. The Amish, Huttites and Mennonites have communities in Illnois, Ohio and Indiana, but do not impose their beliefs on others. There is much less ethnic variety in these states despite an early influx of Scandinavian settlers, some of whom came to set up utopian communes. On average 93% of the population is white, much higher than in the South or on the coasts. Oklahoma provides an interesting exception. Over 5% of the population is American Indian, the highest concentration in America. Also a higher proportion of Indians in Oklahoma are integrated into society rather than living on reservations. There are many historical sites and museums throughout Oklahoma which allow the visitor to learn about Indian culture. In southern Wisconsin you can visit reconstructions such as Little Norway and the Swiss Historical Village, to learn about early European immigrant life.

Climate. The extremes are cruel, and can seriously impair your travelling pleasure if you are unprepared. Even permanent residents caution each other prior to motoring journeys during the winter. And heatwaves can be very debilitating. It is virtually impossible to rent or buy a car without air-conditioning in St Louis.

In Minnesota the average January temperature is a full 15 Fahrenheit degrees below freezing and some people are experimenting with half-buried houses to escape the cold. July temperatures rarely fall below 70°F/ 21°C even at night. The southern stretches of the Mississippi River valley can become so hot and humid that you might think you were in the tropics. The northern states bordering Canada are much drier.

Natural disasters such as tornadoes, floods and dust storms are real possibilities. (In the *Wizard of Oz*, Dorothy's life in Kansas was turned upside down by a tornado). Even if there is no actual catastrophe, storms can have eerie effects on the atmosphere and on the quality of the light. Watch for the Northern Lights which are often visible from the Dakotas, especially in late summer.

The natives take all these inconveniences and dangers stoically. They emerge the morning after a blizzard wrapped up like Eskimos, greet their neighbours and set to work cooperatively with shovels to restore normality. Dozens of winter carnivals are celebrated with snowmobile races, sleigh rides, and baseball games in ice.

EATING AND DRINKING

Dining in the Midwest is often a basic down-home affair. The larger cities can satisfy the fanciest of tastes but the local greasy spoon is where you will find the residents eating their steaks, hamburgers and french fries in any small town. Summer barbecues are popular. One Midwestern establishment claims to serve the best barbecues in the world (*pace* Texas): Arthur Bryant's Barbecue, located in a rundown section of Kansas City Missouri. And if you're up in Wisconsin, be sure to try the cheese and ice cream produced in America's Dairyland.

The Central US is crammed full of McDonalds and a host of other food chains (Country Kitchens are among the best). The enormous Gateway Arch in St. Louis (at 631ft the tallest manmade monument in the US) should not be mistaken for the galactic headquarters of McDonalds, although close by is the world's first floating McDonalds.

Drinking. Often there is not much to do in a small town if you don't want to see the drive-in movie, except to go to the bar. Unlike sophisticated New York cafes or New Orleans blues bars, these small bars function more like British pubs, with a core of regulars who may look upon their local as a second home. Try to fit in with the customs of the local clientele and avoid initiating any hostility. Ask the bartender to recommend a beer; you may not get the best beer you've ever had but you will have showed your willingness to defer to local practice.

Milwaukee Wisconsin is the brewing capital of the US and is the headquarters for Miller, Pabst and Schlitz (which "made Milwaukee famous"). The breweries organize tours which include free samples. The world's biggest brewery, however, is Anheuser-Busch at 1127 Pestalozzi St; St. Louis; call 557 2626 for a free tour.

State liquor controls can be strict; for example in Iowa no beer containing over 3.2% alcohol can be sold, which means that Iowans close to state borders shop in neighbouring states before parties. Bars close punctually at 1am, unless the bartender is a special friend. The big cities —Chicago is a special case — have after-hours establishments which are often private clubs and of dubious character.

ENTERTAINMENT

From the state tourist literature you will be able to select the attractions both natural and manmade which interest you. An impressive combination of the two can be found at Mt Rushmore, southwest of Rapid City in south Dakota. Sculptor Gutzon Borglum carved the "Shrine of Democracy", bearing the likeness of Lincoln, Jefferson, Washington and Roosevelt. Or you might like to visit one of the world's largest amusement parks, "Marriott's Great America" in Gurnee Illinois (about 40 miles north of Chicago). Its main attraction is "Shock Wave", the world's tallest and fastest roller coaster (designed by an ex-NASA scientist). Some have described it as costly and crowded. More spectacular is the lunar landscape of the Badlands in South Dakota. More charming is the Mark Twain Museum and Home in Hannibal Missouri on the banks of the Mississippi, where there are numerous Huckleberry Finn and Tom Sawyer associations. More curious is the Cowboy Hall of Fame and Western Heritage Center in Oklahoma City, though a visit hardly seems necessary in the state where the man-in-the-street often looks and talks like an actor in a cowboy movie. (Try to see these cowboys bareback bronco riding, steer wrestling and calf roping at a rodeo). More restful is the rolling, wooded countryside and large wilderness preserves of Wisconsin and Minnesota. More bizarre is the radio station in Cincinnati Ohio, WCVG, which plays nothing but Elvis Presley records, linked by Presley trivia.

If you hope for something more sophisticated than bars featuring Elvis impersonators, seek out towns with sizeable universities. For example Madison Wisconsin has the University of Wisconsin's main campus. With 30,000 students, the university dominates the town, which is set between two large lakes. Clean, lively and friendly, there is plenty to do in Madison, and it provides a good base for exploring the natural beauty of Wisconsin's hills, lakes and forests.

Since so much of the Midwest is flat, outdoor recreations have adapted accordingly: jogging, cycling and cross country skiing are all popular. But the most widely enjoyed activities are boating (Minnesota has more boats per capita than any other place in the US), fishing and hunting for which you will need a licence. Every small bar in the appropriate areas has a display of enormous antlers or a stuffed walleye, and will be able to give you details about obtaining a licence and when the season begins and ends. Game includes deer, rabbit, pheasant and duck. For a guide to the wilderness areas of the Midwest, consult Bill Thomas's *Mid-America Trips and Trails*.

There are excellent opportunities for wilderness canoeing in the Boundary Waters Canoe Area, an area of three million acres of interconnecting rivers and lakes in northeastern Minnesota spilling over the Canadian border. Enquire in Crane Lake, Winton or Grand Marais for information about outfitters and canoe rentals which are available May to October. The Lake of the Ozarks region of Missouri, which begins an hour's drive southwest of St Louis, is a land of high limestone bluffs and caves, of blue heron and wild turkey, beaver and bass; it is perhaps best appreciated from a canoe. Hemingway venerated this part of the country as the true America, and returned throughout his life for the fishing and solitude.

Calendar of Events

January	Winter Carnival, St Paul Minnesota
February	Chicago Auto Fair
May	Indianapolis 500 motor race
May	Chicago International Art Exposition
June	Detroit Grand Prix
July	Lumberjack World Championship Hayward Wisconsin
August	Ohio State Fair (the nation's largest)
late August/ early September	Chicago Jazz Festival
October	Chicago Marathon
October	Pumpkin Show, Circleville Ohio

Miami and Florida

Everglades Wildlife

In the good old days of 1981 when your parents flew to Miami for £82 courtesy of Freddie Laker and a pound would buy them $2.50, the Sunshine State was generally thought of as an ideal summer destination. They could live there almost as cheaply as in Spain, with the bonus that the language was English, McDonald's hamburgers were more reassuring than *paella*, and Walt Disney World was only a short drive away.

What the package tourists failed to realize was that Florida is a winter playground. Nobody save Englishmen and the occasional mad dog goes to Florida in the summer because of the extreme heat and humidity. The other fact about Miami which the tour operators suppressed from their literature was that amid the glamorous world of big yachts, beachfront high society and posh nightclubs has grown an extremely depressed urban area, suffering from drug problems, high levels of racial tension and with one of the worst crime rates in the United States. Trafficking and processing drugs (especially Columbian cocaine) has become a major industry.

Miami has created many of its own problems; its string of high rise beachfront hotels, once such a symbol of the city's affluence and robustness, now seems tawdry and timeworn. The hotels are no longer full either, a fact which hasn't stopped their proprietors from continuing to charge phenomenally high prices. But the biggest blow to Miami's status as capital of the Southeastern Sunbelt has come from the competition of newer Florida resorts like Orlando, Tampa-St Petersburg and Sarasota, which have exploited the state's climate and ambience for touristic and commercial purposes, without having been victimized like Miami by the problems of urban growth.

Yet Miami still draws 13 million visitors each year, not all of them drug smugglers and illegal aliens. Its many museums and universities make it the centre of the state's cultural life. Most of the fine restaurants and bars which were opened in the city's heyday continue to operate. Though Miami is no longer the capital of American resort life, it remains its symbol, and most first-time visitors to the city with strong preconceptions are not unduly disappointed.

THE NATIVES

Florida continues to grow too swiftly to permit attempts to stereotype or categorize its population. Schools in the area teach children from 114 countries. However, a few general trends in the history of its settlement are worth noting. Miami's boom came with the influx of wealthy Northeastern industrialists, and its composition reflects that period to this day: a large number of its upper class are East Coast WASP's or Jews, who have retained their New York and New England lifestyles and accents.

The fact that Miami is America's chief air link to Latin America and the first stop for political refugees or "boat people" from Cuba, has made it one of the major Hispanic and Caribbean centres of the United States. Haitian refugees have arrived in even larger numbers without jobs or means of support, and relations between Miami's natives and immigrants — and between rival immigrant groups — remain strained. Unfortunately, amongst the highest stresses are those between blacks (making up 25% of the population and the hardest hit by "Reagonomics") and the prospering second-generation Cubans. Meanwhile, racist whites display bumper stickers reading "Will the last white man leaving Miami please take the American flag with him".

Making Friends. The first problem is to decide if there is actually anyone you would like to befriend. Blue-rinsed Yankee widows, Spanish-speaking drug dealers and underprivileged minorities might not be your cup of tea, and you would certainly not be theirs. But the pleasure and perils of meeting like-minded people in Miami are not much different from those in other cities. Beaches are anonymous enough for people to feel quite uninhibited about chatting with strangers. As in any American community where neighbourhoods are hacked up by freeways and people isolated by automobiles, singles bars are an important way of meeting people. These range from high-pressure meat-market establishments to cosy lunchtime spots with their regular and amiable clienteles. If such places give you the jitters, the bars around the University in Coral Gables have a more casual atmosphere, though they can be cliquish too. It's unfortunate — but important to remember — that recent problems with racialism and street violence have left Miami natives more chary than most Americans about meeting foreigners.

Anywhere in Florida, the time where you'll meet American youth in its largest numbers is from mid March to mid April, when most of the universities in the Northeast schedule their spring breaks, and undergraduates converge on the state in droves turning Fort Lauderdale, Daytona, St Petersburg and Jacksonville into month long beach parties. Most of the students are so wound up about impending final examinations that they're never more than half-sober, and those desiring intimacy with the opposite sex can expect to dispense with formalities.

CLIMATE

Miami enjoys warmer winters than any other city in the continental United States, with daily high temperatures even in January averaging 76°F/23°C, and lows seldom dropping below the 50°. The north of the state is less balmy and less predictable; snow is extremely rare but not unheard-of. Every few winters, storms moving up from the Gulf of Mexico meet cold fronts from the north, causing freezing rain. This decimates the state's vital orange crop and sends tourists home in their thousands.

Nonetheless, barring such flukes, shorts and T-shirts are the order of the day, plus one pair of trousers and perhaps a jumper for evenings. Average July temperatures peak at 89°F/32°C. June, September and October are the rainiest months, and July and August are often stormy as well. Winter and spring are the best times to visit, for those who can brave the crowds. Call 661-5065 for the Miami weather forcast.

ARRIVAL AND DEPARTURE

Air. A large percentage of the drugs that arrive in the USA and not a few exiled dictators and revolutionaries enter via Miami International Airport (MIA, 871-7515), seven miles northwest of downtown. As such, if you are stopped here you can expect the customs officer to be extremely diligent. Once you're through, its less than an hour's bus ride downtown. Metro Transit Authority buses 3 and 20 leave the upper level of the main terminal hourly from 6am to 10pm, and charge $1 (exact change needed, no bills). A 25c transfer, valid for two hours, will take you to all other points in Dade County. Bus 34 leaves every 45 minutes for Miami Beach. The Airport Limousine service (526-2300) is plusher and more frequent, and charges $6 to Miami.

Yellow Cab (885-1111) will take you into town for a flat fare or on a running meter. The meter rates of $2 for the first mile and 35c for each additional quarter mile make it about a $12 investment. If you can get a flat rate of less than $10 from what looks like a reputable cab, you're doing well. Shared taxis are possible — there's a path where people queue for them — and are often a better bargain than the limousine. Note that taxis within the airport area charge a flat rate of $5.

Miami is the USA's gateway to the Caribbean and Latin America. Bargain fares to Barbados or Bolivia are advertised in the *Herald.*

Bus. Greyhound-Trailways is located at 300 NW 32rd Avenue (638-6700). Coaches leave from downtown Miami seven times a day for Tampa on the Gulf of Mexico for $35. There is a thrice-daily Greyhound service southwest direct from Miami Airport to Key West ($30) leaving at 7.25am, 12.30pm and 6.20pm.

Train. After building the line right down the east coast of the USA, the railroad company must have run out of funds a few miles short of the intended terminus, since Miami station is five miles northwest of the centre at 8303 NW 37th Avenue (638-7321). Take bus L from Miami Beach. The *Silver Meteor* departs daily at 8.34am, arriving in New York 26½ hours later. The *Silver Star* to New York leaves at 5.19pm and takes an hour less. The inbound trains arrive at 6.43pm and 11.38am respectively. "International Gateway" fares for foreign visitors cost $45 for the round trip to Orlando or Tampa; but for the same price you can buy an unlimited travel pass valid for 45 days throughout Florida. These fares must be booked in advance from outside the USA.

Driving. America's two chief east coast highways I-95 and US 1 pass through the centre of Miami. I-95 is more modern and charges tolls along its whole

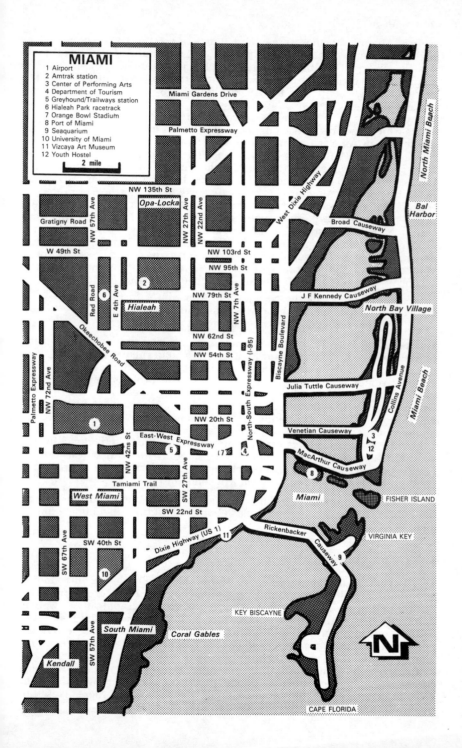

MIAMI

1 Airport
2 Amtrak station
3 Center of Performing Arts
4 Department of Tourism
5 Greyhound/Trailways station
6 Hialeah Park racetrack
7 Orange Bowl Stadium
8 Port of Miami
9 Seaquarium
10 University of Miami
11 Vizcaya Art Museum
12 Youth Hostel

2 mile

Miami Gardens Drive

Palmetto Expressway

NW 135th St

Opa-Locka

Gratigny Road

W 49th St

NW 57th Ave

NW 27th Ave

NW 22nd Ave

NW 103rd St

NW 95th St

Red Road

E 4th Ave

Hialeah

NW 79th Ave

NW 7th Ave

NW 62nd St

NW 54th St

Okeechobee Road

Palmetto Expressway

NW 72nd Ave

NW 20th St

North-South Expressway (I-95)

NW 42ns St

East-West Expressway

NW 27th Ave

SW 27th Ave

Tamiami Trail

West Miami

SW 22nd St

SW 67th Ave

SW 40th St

Dixie Highway (US 1)

SW 57th Ave

South Miami

Coral Gables

Kendall

West Dixie Highway

Broad Causeway

Bal Harbor

North Miami Beach

J F Kennedy Causeway

North Bay Village

Biscayne Boulevard

Julia Tuttle Causeway

Venetian Causeway

MacArthur Causeway

Collins Avenue

Miami Beach

Miami

FISHER ISLAND

Rickenbacker Causeway

VIRGINIA KEY

KEY BISCAYNE

CAPE FLORIDA

N

length. Miami's business areas and tourist attractions are connected by highways; you'll certainly find it easier to get around if you have a car. Traffic can be difficult on Miami Beach, but in general is no worse than in similar cities throughout the US. Potential trouble spots include the I-95 on-ramps at weekends and the Airport Expressway at rush hour (7.30 am-9 am and 4.30 pm-6 pm).

If you arrive by air, there is no point in looking beyond the car rental desks which line the arrivals hall. Competition is intense and the rates are the lowest in America. Downtown, ring around the listings in the Yellow Pages but don't be surprised if you find the best deals are at the airport. Most rental agreements restrict use of the car to Florida and Georgia, and impose high drop-off charges. To overcome both obstacles, ask about the possibility of returning hired cars, particularly to the Northeast of the US.

Note that the insurance requirements for hired cars in Florida are very lax so make your own arrangements for extra cover. Like most American states, Florida has stiffened its drunken driving laws in the wake of a growing number of highway deaths. Fines can reach hundreds of dollars and jail terms are not unusual for second offenders. For lesser offences, you can pay a fine on the spot or have it waived by attending "traffic school" (where offenders are lectured on good driving techniques).

Driveaways. Many wealthy Northerners who winter in Florida want their vehicles driven home at the end of the winter. As usual, check Yellow Pages for names of auto-delivery companies to phone.

Hitch-Hiking. Miami's drug and racial problems, and the fact that so many of its deprived areas are located near or underneath freeways make hitching anywhere near the city inadvisable, to say the least. Bus fares within Greater Miami are cheap enough so you probably won't feel the need to hitch locally. Although US 1 carries a good deal of traffic south to Key West, the Greyhound service is excellent. If you must hitch north, you'll probably feel safer taking the bus 25 miles north to Fort Lauderdale, and starting from there:

Florida presents other serious problems to the hitch-hiker. In the southern part of the state, many of the cars are too full of vacationing families to have the room or the inclination to stop. In the more provincial north, xenophobia and red-neckism will come into play.

Boat. SeaEscape operates a daily service between Miami and Freeport in the Bahamas. The 5½ hour trip costs about $100 return, including a buffet meal.

CITY TRANSPORT

City Layout. Dade County refers to Miami, Miami Beach, the surrounding suburban sprawl and part of Everglades National Park. It is crucial to realize that Miami and Miami Beach are distinct, geographically as well as culturally. To get from the city across to the long reef of Miami Beach and to the Keys of Virginia and Biscayne, you have to cross Biscayne Bay via one of seven causeways, two of which (the Rickenbacker and the Venetian) charge tolls.

Roads which run north-south are Avenues; those which run east-west are Streets. The key intersection is the junction of Flagler St and Miami Avenue, at the heart of the commercial district. Using these axes, the quadrants are prefixed NW, NE, SW and SE.

Bus. The Metro Transit Agency runs bus services in Dade County. Free maps can be picked up from their headquarters at 3300 NW 32nd Avenue, or during working hours from the kiosk at the corner of SE 1st Avenue and Flagler St, in front of the Chandler Shoe Store. Call 638-6700 for route information between 6 am and 11 pm. Most buses run from around 5 am to midnight.

The flat fare is $1 (exact fare, coins only) with transfers valid for two hours costing 25c. A special service links downtown Miami with the Omni Center, a huge shopping mall northeast of downtown: the Roun'Towner is a minibus shuttle with a 35c flat fare. It starts from Bricknell Avenue — just south of the Miami River — and meanders around the downtown area before heading north along Biscayne Boulevard. Services run every ten minutes between 8-30 am and 5.30 pm Monday to Friday.

Buses C,K,D and S link downtown Miami with Miami Beach. The latter two cover the most ground, travelling north along Collins Avenue as far as 194th St.

Metro. Miami has a brand new elevated train system known as Metrorail. It has also been billed as a "Downtowner People Mover" (DPM), which authorities claim "combines the fun of a theme park ride with the efficiency of above-street-level transport". The fare of $1 is fed into machines at each station. To transfer to a connecting bus, you pay an additional 25c.

Car. Parking is difficult and risky in downtown Miami. However, there is plenty of free on-street parking in Miami Beach, from where buses will take you to the centre.

Taxis. Taxis charge about $2 for the first mile and 35c for each additional quarter. There is no shortage on Miami Beach, in Coral Gables or the business district in Miami (west of Biscayne Park). You'll have a great deal of trouble finding one in less affluent areas, and cabbies can and will refuse to drive you into many ghettos such as Liberty City. Taxis run through the night.

Cycling. This is not ideal cycling territory. Too many of the roads are highways clogged with cars and cut off from the beach by massive hotels. However there are some cycle paths, and Key Biscayne and Coconut Grove are picturesque. Contact the Parks Department for further information (579—2672). Cycle hire charges start at about $3 an hour, $12 a day. You'll need $50 deposit or a credit card.

Accommodation

Hotels. Miami's beachfront highrises are astronomically priced. The hotels at the other end of the spectrum are normally in dangerous areas. But there are some places in between, most of which are listed in the Tourist Authority's excellent pamphlet *Hotels*. The Hotel/Motel Infomation number for Miami is 371-2030. If you'd like to stay in Miami Beach, there are a number of spots on Collins Avenue and on the lower part of Ocean Drive which will allow you to cram two or three into a bedroom for about $50. Downtown Miami is cheaper than Miami Beach: try the centrally located cheap-but-pleasant American Hotel (273 NE 2nd St, 373-0672) which charges about $35 a double. If it's booked, then try the nearby Leamington (307 NE 1 St, 373-7783) or Urmey (32 SE 2nd Avenue, 374-5147).

Motels. The hotel/motel distinction is blurred in Miami. Try the Golden Nugget Motel at 1855 Collins Avenue (932-1445) in a posh section of Miami Beach, with rooms at the comparatively low price of about $40. The incoming highways, Routes 41, 441, 835 and US 1 are lined with motels, though many cater to first-time visitors who overestimate the tightness of the accommodation market in Miami and are willing to pay through the nose during the tourist season. In fact all accommodation is much more expensive between Thanksgiving and Easter. Off-season you can get some real bargains, particularly for longer stays.

Bed and Breakfast. Contact the Bed and Breakfast Company, 105 Mariposa Avenue 233, Miami 33146 (661-3270).

Hostels. The AYH Youth Hostel is at 1438 Washington Ave (534-2988) in Miami Beach. It's a comfortable place, and although the neighbourhood is not terribly inviting, the staff is; the rates ($8 a night for members in 3-bedded rooms) are the cheapest you'll find in Miami.

University Residences. If you'll be in Miami between June and August, call the Housing Office at the University of Miami (248-2211) about the possibility of renting one of their dorm rooms in Coral Gables. This student section of town is lively, safe and pleasant. Availability at the dorms varies, but if you're set on staying in Coral Gables, the University Inn at 1390 S. Dixie Highway (667-2437) is a good bet, with single and double rooms at about $50 a night.

Camping. The two closest sites to downtown Miami are the Kobe Trailer Park (11190 NE 16th Avenue, 893-5121) and Miami North KOA (14075 Biscayne Boulevard, 940-4141). For information on sites elsewhere in the state, call the Florida Campground Association on 1-800-FLA-CAMP.

Eating and Drinking

Miami grew up around ostentatious displays of wealth; as a result the dominant cuisine in its restaurants remains the upmarket staples of the American middle class: steak, seafood, various ribs and chops in sauces, and similar fare. Some use is made of Caribbean and Gulf seafood, with crayfish, conch (pronounced konk) fritters and tuna well represented. Stone (or *morro*) crabs are available fresh only in Miami. They are in season from mid-October until mid-April. Try also a local speciality Key Lime Pie, a pastry filled with condensed milk, lime juice, eggs, sugar and topped with meringue, served cold. Don't miss Wolfie's, a traditional Miami Beach deli famous for corned beef sandwiches on rye and cheesecake at 21st and Collins Avenue (538-6626), open 24 hours. There are also several Kosher dairy cafeterias, specializing in vegetarian dishes like felafel and noodle pudding. Try Early Bird dinners at cut rate prices if you're hungry at 5/6 pm.

Miami's other endemic cuisine is the food of "Little Havana", the community of pre-and post-revolutionary Cuban expatriates, located between SW 12th Avenue and SW 25th Avenue, particularly around 8th St. (known as *Calle Ocho*). Best bets for budget dining; long thin doughnuts to accompany cafe cubano. The food is mainly lightly spiced meats, vegetables and soups, and Cuban pastries and desserts, most notably rich fried *churros.* For typical cheap but good Cuban food, try La Rumba in Miami Beach on Collins Avenue at 20th Street (538-8998). Many restaurants serve traditional Spanish dishes as well; of these, La Tasca at 2741 W Flagler St enjoys almost universal acclaim.

DRINKING

Miami suffers from a degree of schizophrenia as far as alcohol is concerned. While much of the city supports the great American lager industry, the areas dominated by tourism (hotels, beachfront singles bars, etc.) have a vested interest in keeping the city's Caribbean image intact, and push drinks like Pina Coladas, melon balls, frozen daiquiris, and the like. A rule that should be self-evident is that you can do the former sort of drinking more cheaply than the latter.

The drinking age of 21 is not enforced quite as rigorously as elsewhere in the US. Women will always find it easier to buy in liquor stores and bars if they are so inclined. According to spring break travellers, things ease up in March to allow proprietors to make a killing.

Take advantage of warm tropical nights to sit on the beach with a six-pack and watch the moon rise. For the more ambitious, a popular nightspot that used to be the Z Club is club 1235 at (you guessed it) 1235 Washington Avenue, Miami Beach (531-1235). There is a cover charge of $5 to $12.

Miami has few attractive areas in which to stroll, but the art deco apartments and hotels in old Miami Beach are well worth checking out. In particular, the Carlyle and Tides hotels on Ocean Drive and the Delano at Collins and 16th St are eyecatching. Try to join a Miami Design Preservation League walking tour, every Saturday at 10.30am for $6; call 642 - 2014 for more details.

The *Miami Herald* has daily reviews of concerts, exhibitions and shows; Friday's edition includes the most detailed listings of upcoming events. The *Miami* monthly magazine, available from newsstands, also lists events, but is intended more for the geriatric nightclub set. Tickets for many events can be bought through BASS (633 - 2277).

Museums. It should not be surprising that a city with as little history as Miami is short on museums, but the quality of the few museums the city does have comes as a pleasant surprise. The Bass Museum of Art (2100 Collins Avenue, Miami Beach, 673-7350) has an extensive collection of European art, especially a collection of Rubens and paintings from the 19th and 20th centuries. The Museum of Science, 3280 South Miami Avenue (854-4247) has impressive exhibits of the local wildlife Miami has largely supplanted, but lacks the sort of hands-on gadgetry typical of other American science museums. The Vizcaya Museum, 3251 South Miami Avenue (579-2813) is the one you can least afford to miss. It's a collection of Continental artefacts housed in the massive Spanish-style villa that was home to the American industrialist James Deering. Newspaper magnate William Randolph Hearst brought one of Spain's treasures to Miami, the 12th-century Segovian Monastery of Saint Bernard, now at 16711 West Dixie Highway (945 - 1461); daily guided tours are offered. Have a look into the Cuban Museum of Arts and Culture, 1300 SW 12th Avenue in Miami (858-8006) for a surprisingly beautiful display of colours and designs.

Theatre and Cinema. Miami's large population of expatriate New Yorkers may have brought the frenzy of the Northeast with them but they are largely responsible for the number of good theatres in the city (not to mention the exorbitant price of theatre tickets). The Theatre of the Performing Arts, at 1700 Washington Avenue, Miami Beach (673 - 8300) is perhaps the most renowned, and draws the best of local and national talent Miami has to offer, theatrical and otherwise. The Dade County Auditorium, 2901 W Flagler St (642-9061), is home to the Miami Opera Guild. During the off-season, many top-notch theatricals are mounted. For serious drama year-round, the Players Theater is quite respectable; they operate at the Coconut Grove Playhouse, 3500 Main Highway (442-4000). Avant-garde productions thrive at the Ring Theater on the University of Miami campus (284 -3355), and the prices are generally cheaper than those at other theatres. For cinemas, try the Roxy Theater or the Surf Theater, both in Miami Beach.

Nightlife. Dade County has some good venues for improvizational comedy, including A.C.T.O.R.S. at 2960 SW 28th Lane, Miami (448-1011); Coconuts Comedy Club at Howard Johnson's, 16500 NW 2nd Avenue, Miami Beach (948 -6887); and the Comedy Woom at 1590 S Dixie Highway, Coral Gables (667-2008). Admission costs $5 -$10, often with a minimum drinks order.

Music. For instant listings call the following recorded information hotlines: Jazz (382-3938), Blues (666-6656) and Folk (531-3655). Major rock acts appear at the James L. Knight Center in Miami itself, the Cameo Theater in Miami Beach and at the Hollywood Sportatorium.

SPORT

Miami retains its Southern-ness in nothing so much as its fanatical love of football. Though the local Dolphins are no longer the powerhouse they were in the seventies when they took three consecutive Super Bowl championships, they remain one of the best, and probably the most sophisticated, of National Football League teams, and their fans continue to raise the hackles of their rivals with the gloating way they wave their handkerchiefs after every touch down. The Dolphins play in the enormous new Joe Robbie Stadium; tickets may be obtained at the club's offices on 4770 Biscayne Blvd in Miami (576-1000). For a lot less money, though, you can watch professional baseball. Florida is where the major teams perform their spring training in March before the actual season starts. You'll find the New York Yankees in Fort Lauderdale, the St Louis Cardinals in St Petersburg, the Baltimore Orioles in Miami. All play exhibition games against one another. Florida has no professional sports teams of its own in baseball or hockey, but the university baseball teams at Tampa and Miami are always in the running for the national championships. For basketball, watch the Miami Heat at their downtown arena.

Although the Hialeah Race Track at Hialeah Park (105E 21st St, 885-8000) is open only six weeks of the year, it is considered to be one of the most important race tracks in the US. For something out-of-the-ordinary, you can watch *jai-alai,* a ball game something like a cross between squash and lacrosse which orginated in the Pyrenees; ring 633-9661 for schedules.

With beaches as famous as Miami's you will have to go swimming at least once, and possibly take up some watersports too. The beaches on Key Biscayne and Virginia Key are among the best. Surfing and scuba diving are also possible at many places. Miami and environs have many public marinas where you can rent any type of boat. Fishing, on-shore and off-shore, abounds.

Parks and Zoos. For a city whose cramped urban landscape can easily become depressing, Miami is short on parks. But those the city does possess have been imaginatively landscaped and well tended. Many people pass an idle hour under the palm trees watching the boats in Biscayne Bay in Bayfront Park. The North Shore Open Space Park occupies 54 acres of oceanfront Miami Beach along Collins Avenue, and is pleasant especially in the off-season. The Japanese Garden on Watson Island (MacArthur Causeway, 579-6944) was given to Florida by a Japanese businessman, and its delicate blossoms and variegated grasses now occupy a quiet niche in Biscayne Bay between Miami and Miami Beach. Hialeah Park is pleasant and lush, and occupies over 200 acres, but again its main points of interest tend to be overrun by tourists.

Not surprisingly Miami is full of zoos; the city has so ravenously gobbled up the lovely landscape surrounding it, that the only way to preserve local wildlife has been to hide it in pockets of 20 acres or so. The city's great animal attraction is the Metrozoo at Coral Reef Drive and SW 152nd Street (251-0400), 200 acres of animals from all over the world in a setting that has revolutionised zoo planning everywhere. Here, it is the animals who roam free, while the people move along caged walkways and inside vehicles, viewing the wildlife in its natural habitat.

The same philosophy has been adhered to at Monkey Jungle (14805 SW 216th Street, 235-1611), where you can walk through a simulated jungle and meet with chimpanzees, monkeys and apes of every description. The Parrot Jungle on the other hand (11000 SW 57th Avenue, 666-7834), is in a more domesticated environment: these birds have been taught to count, recite, and ride bicycles. Despite the heavy pandering to tourists, it provides the visitor with some unique fun. The big attraction however is the Miami Seaquarium on the Rickenbacker Causeway (361-5705) where thousands of tourists arrive each day to marvel at trained killer whales, dolphins, seals and walruses. The next biggest attraction, nowadays, is Planet Ocean. The only ocean showplace of its kind in the world, it enables visitors to 'visit' the birth of oceans, touch Florida's only iceberg, and climb into a genuine submarine.

SHOPPING

Where there is money, there will be places to spend it, and Miami's shopping facilities run the gamut. Perhaps the prettiest is Miami Beach's Lincoln Road Mall, a pedestrian street landscaped like a tropical garden, which stretches from Washington Avenue to Alton Grove. Prices are more reasonable than one would expect. North of Lincoln Road is the pricey Bal Harbour shopping area.

Shopping in Miami proper is also mall-orientated. The ultramodern Omni Shopping Complex is at the end of Biscayne Boulevard's prestigious market area, which runs from Flagler to 16th Streets. Flagler Street itself is full of shops and department stores. Coconut Grove is the quaintest of Miami's shopping meccas, full of little "ye olde" boutiques for tourists.

For bargains, the Tamiami Trail in Little Havana is full of discount shops, and the Tropicaine Drive-In Theatre (7751 Bird Road) hosts a large flea market on Saturdays and Sundays.

THE MEDIA

The major American broadcasting networks have television stations in Miami: Channel 4 (CBS), Channel 7 (NBC), and Channel 10 (ABC). Channel

2 (WPBT) is the public broadcasting station. For radio news, listen to WIOD (610 AM). The classical station is WTMI (93.1FM), while WHTE (100.7 FM) is the top rock station. The *Miami Herald* is the city's major daily. It is consistently ranked among the top ten papers in the States.

Crime and Safety

On average there is at least one murder each day in Dade County. Miami's crime problems stem generally from two factors, race and drugs, but this doesn't mean that a sensible attitude to both will guarantee you safe passage. Many of the city's Hispanics and blacks are living below the poverty line and feel themselves ignored by a wealthier white community and beleaguered by a hostile police force. This has left the police understandably nervous, leading to a Catch-22 situation in which the most dangerous areas are the most poorly policed and making it doubly important to avoid trouble spots. These are easy to recognise, and any native will steer you away from them if asked. From the airport bus, you can see teeming slums with some of the most threatening looking street corners in America. The car hire desks at the airport even issue a map of dangerous areas to incoming British travellers.

Be particularly careful around the bus terminals. If you're leaving on a night bus, try to get to the terminal in daylight; if this is inconvenient, take a cab. Try to avoid deserted areas at night, such as the normally-safe business district west of Biscayne Park. A good general rule is to stay near the seacoast resort areas: Miami Beach is generally safe, and the high-rise hotels of Miami are well-lit and extensively policed, often by private security agencies. Given that Miami is America's principal point of entry for illegal drugs, one might think that minor offences like smoking marijuana would be overlooked. It is true that many America's states have liberal laws on grass, but Florida is not one of them. Cocaine is treated even more seriously, but is used so widely that police estimate that every bank note in the city has 35 micrograms of cocaine adhering to it.

Help and Information

The area code for Miami is 407.

Information: Metro-Dade County Department of Tourism, 234 Flagler St (579-4694). Maps and brochures also available at the Greater Miami Visitors' Bureau, 4770 Biscayne Boulevard (573-4000).
Handicapped Travellers: Center for Survival and Independent Living, 1335 NW 14th St (547-5444).
Medical Emergencies: Randle-Eastern Ambulance Service, 35 SW 27th Avenue (642-6000); Mt Sinai Hospital, 4300 Alton Road (674-2200).
All night drugstore: Robert's Drugs, 590 W Flagler St (545-0533).
Crisis Center for Women: 667-1049.
American Express: 1759 NE 163rd St, N Miami Beach (945-0835).
Thomas Cook: 380 Miracle Mile, Coral Gables (448-0269).
Post Office: 500 NW 2nd Avenue (371-2911).
Telegrams: 358-0808.
Weather Forecast: 661-5065.

Crisis Lines: Suicide-Drug Abuse Hotline (358-4357); Rape Treatment Centre and Hotline (549-7273).
British Consulate: Brickell Bay Office Tower, 1001 S Bayshore Drive (374-1522).

Further Afield 61

The big west-Florida cities — Tampa, St Petersburg, and Fort Myers — were the first focus of America's retirement industry, and continue to bear the stigma of being towns for the "newly-wed and the nearly-dead", though this image is becoming less and less appropriate as an influx of young professionals continues to diversify the population. The Florida Keys, especially Key West, have long been a centre for Florida's cultural communities. Lifestyles of the Old South, predominant throughout Florida until about a half-century ago, today live only in the northern part of the state, particularly in the "Panhandle" region along the border with Georgia and Alabama.

THE KEYS

This archipelago, is strung together by 42 narrow bridges and causeways of US Route 1 (including Seven Mile Bridge) and has always had a romance about it. Hemingway lived here, as did Tennessee Williams, and Humphrey Bogart squared off against Edward G. Robinson on Key Largo in the film of the same name. The Keys continue to attract people from all quarters, most noticeably Cubans, gays, gangsters, artists and tourists. Many visitors to Key West arrive by the 5-hour Greyhound bus from Miami for $30 one way; it's quicker in summer when towns are less crowded and stops less frequent.

The AYH Youth Hostel on Key West is at 718 South Street (296-5719). The dormitories are a little cramped but the hostel is cheaper than elsewhere on the island, at $10 a night. They also rent bicycles and snorkel equipment at reasonable rates. The Key West Visitor's Bureau is at 402 Wall St (294-2587).

Most visitors come to "waste away in Margaritaville" as one songwriter once put it. Sloppy Joe's, on Duval St, was Hemingway's local, while The Fountains nearby has filling hors-d'oeuvres at its afternoon happy hour. The best Cuban restaurant in town is La Lechonera, at 900 Catherine St.

There's not a great deal to do in Key West besides visiting the homes of the famous people who lived here. You can visit Hemingway's house at 907 Whitehead St (294-1575), and that of naturalist John Audubon on Greene St (294-2116). Tennessee Williams's house has become a tourist attraction. In the evenings, especially in winter, there's usually folk music in the streets at Malloy Square Rock. Other watering spots include the Two Friends, a noted Dixieland jazz bar; The Green Parrot, favourite haunt of divers, boating community, hippies and international travellers; and La Bodega, a kind of grown-up student cafe boasting a noticeboard with events and accommodations. For those who still smoke, there's the Cigar Factory which sells cheap "Cuban" cigars made by exiled Cubans.

FORT LAUDERDALE

Fort Lauderdale (population 150,000) is hardly the "Venice of America", as the tourist office credits it, but its canals, lagoons, and inland waterways certainly provide a placid and more stately alternative to Miami, 25 miles south.

Rigorous zoning laws have kept Fort Lauderdale's six-mile stretch of sandy beach relatively unspoilt, and the fact that there is so little to distract one's attention here makes it more relaxing than its more industrial neighbour to the south. The mansions and life-styles of the nearby Palm Beach area are Florida's stateliest, and the locals would have you believe that the area's natural beauty is pre-eminent as well.

The AYH Sol Y Mar Youth Hostel on 2839 Vistamar Steet (566-1023) is the cheapest spot in town with rooms for members at $10.50 (non-members $13.60) and is nice, new, clean and with pool.

Surprisingly enough, Fort Lauderdale is one of the premier dining spots in the United States, with a glut of fine French restaurants. Some of them are beyond young travellers' means, like the gourmet Windows on the Green, overlooking the harbour and Marina. But Wolfie's, at 2501 East Oakland Park Boulevard, is one of the best-known Jewish delis in a state full of them, and eminently affordable. Durty Nellie's, named after the original beneath Bunratty Castle in Ireland, is also on Oakland Park Boulevard. It's a bit loud in the evening, but the hot dogs are free for drinkers. If you're still up at breakfast time, try R Donuts, and be the first in your neighbourhood to talk about doughnuts served by topless waitresses.

Entertainment. Fort Lauderdale is not exactly full of exciting things to do, except during spring break (around Easter) when college students descend on the place for a month of revelry. The Henry Morrison Flagler Museum on Whitehall Way in nearby Palm Beach (655-2833) is an imposing mansion full of china, jewellery, silverware, and other curios. An hour's drive west of Fort Lauderdale on Route 441 is Lake Okeechobee, the largest lake in the United States outside of the Great Lakes region. You can rent canoes for a paddle on the lake at Pakokee Marina (924-7505). Suggestions for other activities and daytrips are available from the Fort Lauderdale Chamber of Commerce, 4201 North Ocean Boulevard (776-1000).

ORLANDO

Very few Americans had even heard of Orlando twenty years ago. But since Walt Disney World, now the largest single tourist attraction in the United States, opened 20 miles to the south, many have come to appreciate the beauties of the city. Orlando is indeed a handsome city, full of parks, rivers and lakes. Although it has been overrun by hucksters and opportunists, and continues to fight against its image as a slightly ramshackle and prefab town, Orlando continues to draw and to impress tourists.

Numerous international flights arrive at the city's overcrowded airport; you can reach the downtown bus terminal for 75c on bus 11. Central Orlando has three hostels. The AYH Orlando Youth Hostel (423-1671) adjoins the Travelodge at 409 Magnolia Avenue. The other AYH Hostel is in the Young Women's Community Club at 107 East Hillcrest Street (425-2502), restricted to women aged 16-36 who are card-carrying hostel members staying less than three days. The American Christian Youth Hostel, slightly more austere, is at 426 East Jordan Street (420-9793) and charges $15 a night.

Walt Disney World. To dismiss Disney World as American tackiness and gadgetry is to miss the point (and the pleasure). It is gaudy, it is primarily child-orientated, but anyone who doesn't enjoy the dozens of dazzling rides and audio-visual presentations must be a real misery.

The older part of the complex, the Magic Kingdom , is a set of six parks modelled on the original Disneyland in Anaheim, California, but on a much larger scale: Tomorrowland, Libertyland, and so on. Main Street USA is where most of the tourist bureau photos of dancing Mickey Mouses are taken; trains leave from here for the different parks. Space Mountain is probably the biggest single attraction in this part of the park, an amazing roller-coaster ride that simulates a trip through outer space.

The much newer EPCOT Center was conceived by Walt Disney himself as a model community where new ideas could be tested by scientists, with public viewing and participation. The acronym stands for Experimental Prototype Community of Tomorrow. Sadly, perhaps, EPCOT has become something of a vehicle for corporate sponsorship: among the miracles unfurled in the Spaceship Earth exhibit (housed in the geodesic dome which dominates the Center) is the telephone, understandable enough as the sponsor is AT&T.

EPCOT is divided into Future World — with rides and exhibits such as World of Motion (sponsored by General Motors) — and the World Showcase, a series of stylized miniature villages representing different nations grouped around a large lake. For some reason most people visit Future World first and World Showcase in the afternoon, so you should do the reverse. Don't miss the newest addition, the Disney/MGM studio complex. Like Universal Studios in Hollywood, it offers tours which include seeing films and television recordings in progress. (Universal is now building its own studios 15 miles away, modelled on its Hollywood complex). After taking in a movie set, a dozen different countries and sensory overload at Future World, don't be suprised if you're exhausted: EPCOT, as they are pleased to remind you, also stands for Every Person Comes Out Tired.

The least busy days at the complex are Thursday, Friday and Sunday. Even for those without the seemingly mandatory Florida hire car, reaching Walt Disney World is easy: there are plenty of bus tours from both Orlando and Miami, costing around $10 and $25 return respectively. A one-day pass for either the Magic Kingdom or EPCOT (but not both) costs $28. The three-day ($78), four-day ($96) or five-day ($110) passes allow free access to any part of the park. If your time is limited, look out for people selling unexpired passes. Some visitors have seen enough after a couple of days, and sell off the remaining ticket for five or ten dollars. To make the most of your time, get to the complex early; 8.30 am is ideal: although the gates do not officially open until 9am, at busy times they have been known to open early. Head straight for Space Mountain in the Magic Kingdom to get your thrills before the crowds arrive. Since the Magic Kingdom is open until 10pm or midnight in peak season, you can see everything in a day if you don't mind feeling shattered at the end of it.

Sea World. This is what people came to see in Orlando before Disney World opened. The largest man-made marine environment in the world, Sea World is like Miami's Seaquarium several times over. The killer whales, penguins and dolphins are here, as are the trained seals, but the *coup de grace* is the 150,000 gallon main tank, with a transplanted barrier reef marine environment. Sea World (351-3600) is just west of Orlando on I-4; day admission costs about $15.

Spaceport USA. The launch pads and buildings of the Kennedy Space

Center spread across miles of swampland east of Orlando on the Atlantic coast. A host of side industries has sprung up to cater for the Center's visitors: in Cape Canaveral you can stay in the Gateway to the Stars Motel, and eat at the Galaxy Station restaurant in Cocoa Beach.

As many Americans have a deep emotional attachment to the US space programme, visitors numbers are steadily growing again after the Challenger disaster in 1986. Dial 1-800-432-2153 (toll-free, Florida only) for launch information.

More information on tourist attractions in and around Orlando is available from the city's Chamber of Commerce, 75 East Ivanhoe Boulevard (425-1234).

TAMPA/ST PETERSBURG

The Gulf of Mexico resorts were developed later than the Atlantic Ocean ones and are noticeably less vulgar and built-up. Flanking Tampa Bay, these two communities complement each other ideally as twin capitals of Florida's Gulf Coast. Tampa is a busy industrial centre, the seventh-largest port in the United States and home to one of the country's oldest Hispanic communities. St Petersburg ("St Pete") is a lush peninsula guarded by the lovely breakwater of the Holiday Isles from the Gulf of Mexico. Started as a retirement community and still one of the largest in the USA, St Petersburg has made a smooth transition into a resort centre. There is no need to worry about bad weather; every day that the sun doesn't shine the local newspaper is given away free, which in 60 years has happened only a handful of times. Taken together, these two communities offer the traveller all the amenities of a Florida vacation with enough history and non-tourist activity to save them from the crass commercialism one finds elsewhere in Florida.

Accommodation. St Petersburg is a more pleasant base than Tampa, and one of the best places to stay is the Detroit Hotel/St Petersburg International Hostel (215 Central Avenue, 813-822-4095). Foreign visitors can get dormitory beds for $10 per night, while double rooms cost $20 per night; there are discounts for long stays.

Eating and Drinking. In addition to the usual range of fast food establishments, there are Tampa's excellent and authentic Spanish restaurants. The most famous, the Colombia Restaurant at 2117 East Seventh Avenue (813-248-4961) will set you back at least $15 a head. A couple of doors down, JD's (2029 East Seventh Avenue, 813-247-9683) serves similar dishes at about $5 a plate. For drinks, most of the young people in town flock to the University area, especially to Bennigan's Tavern, 2206 East Fowler Avenue, which serves good lunches as well.

Entertainment. Downtown St Petersburg is not the most likely place to find an exceptional modern art gallery, yet it is the location for the Salvador Dali Museum with the largest collection of the surrealist's work in the world. The new Performing Arts Center in Tampa is also worth checking out. Otherwise, the Tampa/St Petersburg area is not a place for cultural offerings, but for its varied outdoor attractions, especially Busch Gardens, 3000 Busch Boulevard (813-971-8282). This is a man-made African jungle on a Disney World scale, complete with wandering elephants and lions, and space-age monorails and conveyance cars. Hillsborough River State Park is a beautifully landscaped grove on Tampa's waterfront, full of tropical flowers and tourists.

St Petersburg is even richer in outdoor attractions. Its Sunken Gardens, 1825 Fourth St (813-896-3186) are one of the best collections of tropical birds and flowers in the United States. Pass-a-Grille Beach is only one of the better of the city's waterfront areas, while Fort deSoto Park, at the peninsula's southernmost tip, is a leafy haven with plenty of campsites.

Shopping. Tampa, like much of Florida, relies heavily on the mall to please its shoppers; the largest is the Franklin Street Mall near the river, a fortunately tasteful project. Nearby is the Nostalgia Market, a restored cigar factory in the Hispanic Ybor city section. With a host of boutiques, ethnic cafes and folk exhibits, it is more typical of America's Northeast, and well worth a visit.

For more information, contact the Greater Tampa Chamber of Commerce (801 E Kentucky Boulevard, 813-228-7777) and the St Petersburg Chamber of Commerce (225 Fourth St, 813-821-4715).

JACKSONVILLE

Jacksonville is the major city of northern Florida and the second largest in the USA behind Los Angeles in total land area. It stretches from the scenic St Johns River to the Atlantic where Fort Clinch State Park and Little Talbot Island State Park preserve the least uncrowded and developed beaches between the Carolinas and Cuba. It is also the home of the University of Florida whose welcoming atmosphere and reasonably priced goods and services are not unlike those found on the campuses of Ann Arbor, Madison or LA for that matter. Students from the U of F make up much of the audience of the Jacksonville and All That Jazz Festival held in mid-October and for which no admission is charged.

The main disadvantage of Jacksonville, however, is the absence of cheap accommodation, especially in the tourist months. Lesser evils include its 9% sales tax added to everything and its dismal public transport which makes travel between lodging and the beaches a nightmare. Motels such as the Ambassador Inn (354-5611), Silver Sea Motel (249-1746) and Salt Air Motel (246-6465) will set you back about $20 a night.

You do better with food than lodgings. Ryan's Family Steak House chain will provide fish or steak for about $4 a plate. You can also enjoy all the shrimp you can eat at The Ritespot Restaurant for $7. And at the Center Street Station Restaurant, near Fort Clinch, a mere $3.75 will get you a meat and potatoes dinner.

EVERGLADES

The large swampy areas of southern Florida, known as the Everglades, are further south than Cairo and Delhi. Everglades National Park covers the whole southwest corner of the state and is traversed by Highway 27. Near the park entrance there is a boardwalk over the swampy grasslands where you can see alligators, brightly coloured birds and all manner of subtropical flora and fauna (including swarms of mosquitoes). For a more serious study of this unique area, you can charter a boat and guide who will take you to one of the many backcountry campsites. Camping is free provided you get the permission of the Park Ranger in Homestead, a small town easily accessible from Miami by Greyhound.

New Orleans and the South

Mississippi River Boat

**Alabama   Arkansas   Georgia   Kentucky   Louisiana   Mississippi
North Carolina   South Carolina   Tennessee**

Zsa Zsa Gabor, in one of her more perceptive comments, once said that New Orleans was "the most European of all American cities, not alone for its architecture but also because of the people's attitude towards life."

La Nouvelle Orleans was founded in 1718 as a French colony, then ruled by the Spanish from 1762 to 1803, when it went back to the French; Napoleon promptly sold it to the US as part of the famous Louisiana Purchase when the US government paid $15,000,000 for all the land between Canada and Mexico, and from the Mississippi to the Rockies. New Orleans is known as the Crescent City, because of the bend in the Mississippi River, also (enigmatically) as the "City That Care Forgot". While New Orleans is a large city (population 600,000) and the second largest port in the US, the much smaller city of Baton Rouge, 77 miles upriver, is the state capital of Lousiana.

Most of New Orleans is below sea level and the whole of it lies below the high water mark of the Mississippi River. It is easy to understand why the graves in New Orleans are caskets placed above ground.

New Orleans was, of course, the home of many jazz greats: Louis Armstrong, Jelly Roll Morton, Sidney Bechet, Bix Beiderbecke, Fats Domino. And jazz still flourishes in the bars and clubs of the French Quarter (Vieux Carre). The city also has a long and distinguished literary tradition, and Tennessee Williams wrote several of his books here.

New Orleans has a unique atmosphere and is full of oddities reflecting the city's history. The French Quarter consists mainly of 19th century buildings, some of which still show evidence of the Spanish influence, though most of the 18th century houses were destroyed in the great fires of 1788 and 1794. There are no high-rise blocks in the Quarter, and no traffic lights. At 1140 Royal St the ghosts of manacled slaves are said to appear on rainy nights.

Jackson Square, where the French Quarter meets the river, is dominated by St Louis, the oldest cathedral in the US. Though not old by European standards (built in 1794) the rest of the Square — with its old government buildings, palm trees, horse-drawn carriages and street artists — is reminiscent of Seville. Visit early in the morning when pigeons outnumber people and you might hear a lone Creole playing the trumpet to the sky. There is outdoor jazz here on Saturdays throughout the summer, when thousands of locals and visitors throng the shops, bars and restaurants around the Square.

Many of the more endearing curiosities of the city will be found by chance or, rather, by walking. You will discover streets with stranger and more enchanting names than perhaps anywhere in the world. The French and Spanish Catholic legacy is responsible for streets such as Annunciation, Assumption, Ascension, Piety, Ursulines; the Greek classical influence for Calliope, Terpsichore, Socrates, Melpomene. And who knows that fanciful thoughts inspired the street names Benefit, Desire, Pleasure, Mystery, Industry, Abundance, Genius, Harmony and Humanity?

New Orleans is indeed a most attractive city, but its attraction is beginning to present serious problems. Tourism has unquestionably had a deleterious effect in the last few years, and old hands say the city has demeaned itself in the unceasing quest for revenue. Travellers are now looking further afield for Southern towns and cities less riven by commercialism: Charlotte and Charleston are more charming, Memphis has more authentic music and Atlanta — self-styled capital of the "New South" — is more dynamic. But New Orleans' unique history and culture will always make it worth a visit.

THE NATIVES

The two most interesting ethnic groups in and around New Orleans are the Creoles and the Cajuns, which are sometimes mistaken for one another. The Creoles are the descendants of the original French settlers who first arrived in 1682. The term is a confusing one since elsewhere in the US, Creole refers to people of mixed race. The Cajuns (also known as Acadian people) were French deportees from British rule in Nova Scotia who arrived in the 18th century.

The present ethnic spectrum of New Orleans is wider than that of any other city in the States, embracing a complete range of colour from lily white to jet black, without much of the usual racial antagonism. Ernest Nathan "Dutch" Morial is described as New Orlean's first black mayor though his skin is quite pale. Almost half the population of New Orleans is said to be black. There are also large Irish, Italian, and German communities, Early English-speaking settlers chose to live further upriver from the French Quarter; this is now known as the Garden District, where most of the prosperous antebellum houses may be found.

The principal religious affiliation of the region is the Southern Baptist Church, but there are many extremist groups which preach their particular visions of salvation with varying degrees of fervour and intolerance. Fundamentalism (that is, a literal belief in the Bible) is very widespread. Tune in, if possible, to Rev. Ernest Angley (TV Channel 11, Sunday morning), for the full evangelical treatment complete with faith healing. Or listen to Jerry Falwell, leader of the Moral Majority, denounce sex education in schools and equal rights for women. An interesting alternative is the gospel flavour of many churches in black communities.

Making Friends. Travellers will find that the high reputation of Southern hospitality is deserved. Visitors from the UK are especially fortunate because many white Southerners are proud of their British roots, and most are intrigued by the sound of a British accent, which can be a valuable asset in environments ranging from singles bars to police stations. Offers of help and hospitality are frequent and genuine, especially if you strike them as a conservative and law abiding type.

Traditional Southern hospitality survives as well as could be expected in the big city, and people are generally easy to get on with. The French Quarter is unquestionably the best place to eat, drink, sleep and meet people. The atmosphere is friendly and the people so gregarious that there should be little difficulty in making contact. People in New Orleans have few inhibitions and enjoy noisy exchanges.

Bourbon Street abounds with bars, although many of the so-called "burlesque" bars are sleazy strip joints. Seek out those offering live music, whether Dixieland Jazz, swamp rock or Country and Western. Further down Bourbon Street at Dumaine Street, most of the bars are gay. Side parallel streets are more representative of the Quarter. Making friends requires not much more than the ability to penetrate the Southern drawl and to understand local idiom, so that you'll know what city they are referring to when they talk about N'Awlins.

The Mardi Gras festival takes place every year during the two weeks before Shrove Tuesday (late February/early March). It is impossible not to be caught up in the merry-making and this is a great opportunity to make friends.

CLIMATE

New Orleans is normally spared extreme temperatures with December in the 50s and July in the 80s. A temperature of 70°F/21°C is recorded every month of the year. Because of its sub-tropical delta location, the humidity can be very high at any time of the year and rainfall occasionally heavy. The best time to visit is between September and the spring, when the weather is cooler without the threat of hurricanes.

Though New Orleans has not been hit by a hurricane for many years, a "Tropical Storm Outlook" is issued every day of the summer, and the mayor's office has a "Hurricane Evacuation Plan". If a storm warning persuades you to leave the city in a hurry, do not do so by crossing the Lake Pontchartrain road causeway. One day in 1976 after a hurricane scare, so many thousands of people wanted to get out of New Orleans that it took four hours to drive the 24 mile distance. As the lake is only 15 feet deep, it is not hard to imagine the sort of tidal wave which could be caused by a hurricane.

Getting Around

ARRIVAL AND DEPARTURE

Air. New Orleans International Airport (MSY) is 12 miles northwest of the city centre along I-10. Ring 729-2591 for flight information. An Orleans Transit bus (737 9611) runs from the airport to

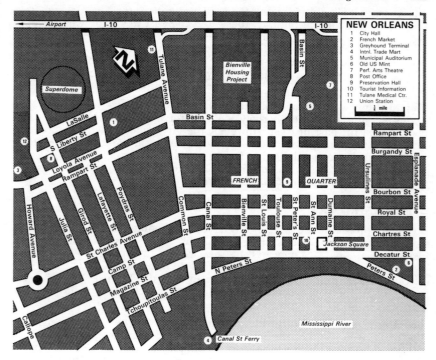

hotels in the business district and French Quarter. The journey takes about 30 minutes, and costs $6. A taxi will cost around $20.

Bus. Greyhound's Terminal (525-9371) is adjacent to Union Station in the western part of the city centre, behind the Bienville Monument and nestling beneath the freeway as it crosses Loyola Avenue. Most services also pick up and drop off passengers closer to downtown at the corner of Basin and Canal Streets. There are frequent long-distance services from Houston (eight hours), Miami (24 hours), New York (32 hours) and the California coast (48 hours).

Train. More interestingly, you can arrive in New Orleans by train. Amtrak operates from Union Station at 1001 Loyola Avenue near the Superdome. There are three main line services: *The Crescent* (from New York, Washington and Atlanta) arrives at 6.20pm daily after a 29-hour journey which ends by crossing Lake Pontchartrain, with the return journey 7.30am; the *City of New Orleans* (made fleetingly famous in the song of the same name by Arlo Guthrie) arrives every day at 12.50pm from Chicago and Memphis, returning at 3.50pm; the *Sunset Limited* arrives from Los Angeles via Phoenix, Tucson and El Paso at 7.45pm on Tuesdays, Fridays and Sundays, and departs west on Mondays, Wednesdays and Saturdays at 2.35pm. The journey to LA takes a few hours less than two days.

Driving. Although the 24 mile toll causeway which runs north from New Orleans across Lake Pontchartrain is undeniably the longest bridge in the world, it is more a long unimpressive flyover than a stunning piece of engineering. I-59 and I-55 flank the lake and both enter New Orleans from the north. Outside the the city, these join the east-west I-10 which sweeps right through downtown New Orleans. Drivers wishing to go straight through from Florida to California are advised to leave I-10 at Slidell and use I-12 to Baton Rouge, where I-10 rejoins. This is a shorter journey, and avoids the heart-stopping tension of trying to cruise through on a freeway which also fulfils the role of New Orleans' Main Street.

Hitch-Hiking. I-10 cuts right through the city centre and there are numerous junctions, notably the Canal St intersection, which provide a fair chance of a lift east or west. However, the city police strictly enforce the law against hitching from the roadway and make it clear that they don't like hitchers polluting their city. For a less hazardous start to your journey, take the Canal St bus to its terminus at I-10 heading west, and hitch around Lake Pontchartrain for destinations north and east.

CITY TRANSPORT

Although there are no longer any streetcars named Desire, there is a streetcar named St Charles and a diesel bus named Desire. Buses and the two streetcar lines are operated by the Orleans Public Service, known as *Transit*. Ring 569-2700 for route and schedule information, or call into the office at 317 Baronne St. The best way to tour the French Quarter is on foot, though there are horse-drawn carriages which leave from Jackson Square.

Bus. There is a 30c shuttle bus which operates in the Central Business District between the Convention Center and the Superdome, along Poydras and Canal Streets. This service operates Monday to Saturday 6.30am-6pm.

Other buses are identified by the points they serve in the suburbs, e.g. "Elysian Fields" and "Desire". Routes commence from Canal St and mostly run east-west, many until 3am. The flat rate fare is 60c for local buses and 75c for expresses. Exact change is required. Transfers (5c) are available from the driver. These are valid on the St Charles streetcar and on the Vieux Carre minibus which runs around the French Quarter from 5am to 7pm. Fares have not gone up for years, but are set for an increase soon.

Streetcars. The St Charles line is a National Historic Monument and claims to be the oldest continuously running street railway in the world. It runs along St Charles Avenue for seven miles between Canal St and Audubon Park (which has a zoo). On the way you pass through Lafayette Square which has three statues, none of them of Lafayette. The new streetcar line links the foot of Julia St with Esplanade Avenue. Fares and transfers are as for local buses.

Car. Except during Mardi Gras, the volume of traffic is no more oppressive than in other American cities. A good city map such as that given away at Tourist Information Offices, will help you come to terms with the unusual freeway numbering system (I-610 is actually a by-pass for I-10) and the unpredictable twists and turns of the Mississippi.

Don't try to drive in the French Quarter, let alone park. You can park all day (Monday to Friday) for a couple of dollars at the Superdome allowing easy access to the shuttle bus (see above). If the Superdome lot is full, use one of the off-street lots near the freeway, and walk the extra distance. Expect to pay $10 for 24 hours of parking. The alternative is to create your own Park'n'Ride system by parking in a quiet suburban street (e.g. near the western terminus of the St Charles streetcar line) and using public transport to the centre.

For low-cost car hire, try Cheapie Rent-a-Car (3215 Dublin St, 486-3986), Car-Temps Rent-a-Car (8814 Veterans Boulevard, 455-7278) or Snappy Car Rental (near the airport at 1710 Airline Highway, 464-6251).

Cycling. Bicycles may be hired from the St Charles Guest House (1748 Prytani St, 523-6556) or the Youth Hostel (523-3014). Both City Park near Lake Pontchartrain, and Audubon Park by the Mississippi, are fun to cycle around.

Ferry. For a brief and fascinating glimpse of the port, take *SS Natchez* (a sternwheeler paddle steamer) from Toulouse Street Wharf near Jackson Square. The *Natchez* takes 1,600 people on a two hour trip down the river to the site of the Battle of New Orleans, where General Jackson slaughtered the British in 1815, and up river past the site of the 1984 World Fair. Ring New Orleans Steamboat Company on 586-8777. The port of New Orleans handles 1,000 ships a month, and exports principally coal, grain, cotton and citrus fruit. Several of the grain tankers are Russian.

There are other boats — *Mark Twain, Cotton Blossom, Voyageur* — which cruise further, through the waterways of the bayou country, and also do evening trips. (Bayous are the marshy offshoots of lakes and rivers). There is a free ferry which travels between the bottom of Canal St and Algiers, the area on the opposite shore.

Hotels. Most tourists visit new Orleans primarily for the French Quarter, and accommodation rates reflect this. Cheaper hotels inside the square mile cost $35-$45 for a double, those outside at least ten dollars less. Yet the advantage of staying within or very close to the Vieux Carre is not just snob appeal: New Orleans is very much a night-time city, with after dark entertainment focussed sharply on the French Quarter. A long, daunting journey back to a distant hotel, with the added expense of a taxi ride, compares most unfavourably with a leisurely stroll home (lit by flickering gas lamps) from the bars and bustle of Bourbon St.

Within the Quarter, the friendly Hotel Villa Convento (616 Ursulines, 522-1793) is reasonably priced with a complimentary breakfast in the palm-shaded Victorian courtyard. Near the Quarter, try the St Charles Guest House (1748 Prytania, 523-6556) or the Old World Inn (1330 Prytania, 522-1793; both have easy access to the Vieux Carre by the St Charles streetcar. On St Charles Avenue itself, try the Hummingbird at number 804 (561-9229) which has doubles for about $30 and gives discounts for students. For longer stays, there are some rooms available in the Quarter starting at about $50 a week, sharing a bathroom.

Bed and Breakfast. Contact New Orleans Bed & Breakfast (PO Box 8163, New Orleans 70182, 822-5046) or just ask at the Visitor Center in Jackson Square.

Hostels. The AYH Youth Hostel (2253 Carondelet St, 523-3014) is very popular and so it is advisable to ring ahead. It is housed in a gracious pre-Civil War mansion just one block from the St Charles streetcar (get off at Jackson Avenue). The price is $8.50 for members in the summer, with one or two private doubles available for about $25. There is an unofficial hostel called l'Auberge in the heart of the French Quarter (717 Barracks St, 523-1130) which is deceivingly tatty from the outside. The room prices of $25/$40 for a single/double are fair in view of the amenities and restoration.

The characterless YMCA (936 St Charles Avenue, 568-9622) costs about $20 single, $30 double.

Camping. There are two KOA Campgrounds: one in the west (467-1792), on the Jefferson Highway which follows the north shore of the river, and the other in the east (643-3850) near Highway 433 on the northeast edge of Lake Pontchartrain. The fee is about $13.

Eating and Drinking

A southern menu might also require some interpretation: hushpuppies (cornmeal fritters), grits (ground corn boiled in milk) and chitlins (the small intestines of pigs, crisply fried, which taste better than they sound) are items which should be tried at least once, not forgetting such better known native crops as peaches, pecans and peanuts.

One of the principal reasons — perhaps the best reason — for visiting New Orleans is its food. Mark Twain wrote that dining here was "as delicious as the less criminal forms of sin". There are so many good eating places that it is difficult to go wrong. New Orleans is famous for its Creole cooking which specializes in gumbos (originally a Bantu word which refers to okra and meat or seafood stews) and jambalaya, the Creole version of pilaff, a rice and meat dish. Many dishes are served with spicy sauces. All the tabasco sauce in the world is made under licence from one factory in Avery Island, Louisiana, about 130 miles west of New Orleans, the place where the sauce was invented about a hundred years ago. Bottles of tabasco in New Orleans are the size of ketchup bottles. Go lightly until you are converted. For a 2½ hour introduction to Creole cookery visit the New Orleans School of Cooking in the Jackson Brewery (525-2665).

The seafood is superb. Oysters are better eaten cooked; uncooked they are not as tasty as English oysters, though they can be found for a little as $3.50 per dozen e.g. at the Desire Oyster Bar on Bourbon Street. Soft shell crab is delicious, but make sure it is in season and not frozen. A po-boy sandwich is cheap and filling and can be found almost anywhere: it is made with French bread and stuffed usually with roast beef with sauteed oysters, hot cream and tabasco, originally said to have been bought by errant New Orleans husbands on their way home when the bakers were baking to placate their wives.

Two of the best restarants in New Orleans, Galatoire's (209 Bourbon St) and K Paul's (416 Chartres St) refuse to take reservations so that you may have to queue outside. But the Creole and Cajun dishes which await you are inside are worth it. Brennan's (417 Royal Street) serves an outstanding "breakfast" until lunchtime, including a cocktail which it likes to describe as an "eye-opener". The famous Antoine's whose speciality is Oysters Rockefeller (poached oysters with anise flavoured spinach puree) is overpriced and overrated. You can get coffee and *beignets* (doughnuts) in the French Market at any time of the day or night. Try the chicory coffee at the Cafe du Monde (Decatur St and St Ann). Breakfast is served at The Clover Grill (corner of Dumaine and Bourbon) 24 hours a day by staff who are refreshingly sarcastic.

Of the cheaper places to eat, the Gumbo Shop (630 St Peter St in the French Quarter) is in a delightful 18th century courtyard surrounded by huge cheese plants, and Houlihan's (315 Bourbon St) has a jolly atmosphere. It is the sort of place — found only in America — where an omelette is served with hollandaise sause and fried oysters, and also garnished with a few fresh strawberries. Houlihan's also offers fried pieces of baked potato skin, which eaten with various hot tomato and horseradish sauces, are delicious. The local's favourite, however, is Johnny's Po-Boys, two blocks from Jackson Square at 511 St Louis. Avoid the tourists and join the queue of workers at lunchtime for the best fried catfish po-boy sandwich in town: "Even my failures are edible", boasts Johnny.

DRINKING

The great drink of the south is bourbon, corn-based whisky first produced in Bourbon County, Kentucky. The great soft drink of the South is Coca Cola, invented almost a century ago by an Atlanta pharmacist, but which no longer contains cocaine. It is certainly worth trying the traditional cocktails which are large and ingenious: mint julep (bourbon, soda, ice, sugar and mint leaves) Sazerac, Ramos gin fizz, Hurricane. The latter contains rum and passion fruit juice, and comes in a glass shaped like a hurricane lamp, which the waiter will try and persuade you to buy (he will propably give it to you if you don't buy it). When ordering you're unlikely to be asked for ID since, unlike most other states, Louisiana imposes no strict liability on the establishment which unintentionally serves someone under 21; only the drinker gets fined.

Among the more amusing bars are Pat O'Brien's (718 St Peter Street) which claims to have invented the Hurricane cocktail, the Old Absinthe House (Bourbon St, corner of Bienville), Napoleon House (500 Chartres Street) where classical music not jazz is played and the gay Cafe Lafitte in Exile (901 Bourbon Street). The Blue Crystal Dacatur (in the 1100 block) draws a young crowd and is a far cry from the tourist crassness of much of Bourbon St.

 **Entertainment**

You might wish to begin your stay in New Orleans by joining one of the guided walking tours of the French Quarter. The Friends of the Cabildo have tours starting from Louisiana State Museum in Jackson Square from Tuesday to Saturday at 9.30am, and 1.30pm, and on Sundays at 1.30pm. The cost is $7, but Thursday includes admission to two museum buildings call 523-3939 for details.

Music. It would be unthinkable to go to New Orleans without considering a visit to the Preservation Hall (726 St Peter St, 523-8939). If you're prepared to queue long enough, you can hear the original Dixieland jazz at its best, played by Louis Armstrong look-alikes most of whom are in their 70's. The bands change each evening, and for $2.50 a session (between 8.30pm and 1am) you may sit or stand in a room bare of furniture, decoration or a bar, and listen. You may be fortunate and hear Willie Humphrey (aged 88, clarinet) and his brother Percy (83, trumpet). Clearly, they cannot go on for very much longer; most of the younger musicians who are gradually replacing them are white.

To find other places for musical entertainment, the best advice is to walk down Bourbon St and listen, for example at the Famous Door (339) and the Paddock Lounge (309). Check the weekly entertainment papers called

Gambit or *Figaro*, or the *New Orleans Times Picayune* for details of performers and venues; the latter paper has a special "What's On" section (the "lagniappe") every Friday.

Also seek out the distinctive Cajun music, lively, foot-tapping tunes played on fiddles and accordions with vocals in the incomprehensible bastard French still widely spoken by natives. You may want to visit Cajun country known as Acadiana, west of New Orleans, which is particularly interesting in mid-September when the Festival Acadien is held in Lafayette. The black version of Cajun, know as *Zydeca,* is well worth hearing. The place to go is the Maple Leaf bar (8316 Oak St, 866-LEAF) five miles west of the French Quarter.

Special Events. Mardi Gras parades have been held in New Orleans to celebrate "Fat Tuesday" (the last day before Lent) since 1837. The carnival season officially begins on January 6, but parades start in earnest two weeks before Mardi Gras day. In 1989 this is February 7; in 1990, February 27; in 1991, February 12; and in 1992, March 3.

In addition to Mardi Gras, the Spring Fiesta takes place during the fortnight following the first Friday after Easter. Some of the gracious and picturesque 19th century aristocratic mansions open their doors to the public. These buildings may be found in the Garden District bounded by Jackson Avenue, Louisiana Avenue, St Charles Avenue and Magazine St. For information about the Spring Fiesta, contact 529 Ann St (581-1367).

Nightlife. The girls in the numerous strip clubs along Bourbon St are attractive principally for their lack of professionalism. Both straight and transvestite clubs are situated mainly between Bienville and St Peters Streets on Bourbon St, and can be inspected briefly without charge, since the doors are open. In spite of the variety of nightlife to be enjoyed, Bourbon St has a friendly almost innocent atmosphere; and the area is well policed. Basin St is now entirely respectable, no longer the "street of sin" of former times.

While renting a car the cheapest and most convenient way to visit the ante-bellum mansions and plantations around New Orleans, the great swampy swathes of Bayou country — with its unique Acadian culture — are best seen on a tour. The bayous consist of thousands of acres of oak and cypress forest, permanently flooded by the Mississippi. The area is a wilderness of backwaters, half submerged trees festooned with Spanish moss and isolated villages accessible only by boat. Bayou country is a haven for birdlife (including egrets and beautiful Louisiana herons), deer and even the occasional alligator. Try to see the film *Southern Comfort* for a vivid, if scary, view of the swamps.

The Acadian people (Cajuns) seek to preserve the simple lifestyle of fishing, hunting and trapping that has been followed since their ancestors arrived from Nova Scotia in 1755. Their distinct culture, cuisine and music has survived, and the latter has grown in recognition since Paul Simon adopted the style in some of the songs on his *Graceland* album. The most rewarding day tours (by bus and boat) are led by the Cajun guides of Acadian-Creole Tours, 828 Chartres,New Orleans (524-1700).

Festivals. Louisiana boasts festivals connected to some kind of activity or appetite more or less year-round; check with the Office of Tourism in Baton Rouge. For example there is a Boudin Festival every February in Broussard, just south of Lafayette the (capital of the Cajun region), to honour the Cajun sausage made from ground pork, rice, onions and peppers.

Other dates on the gourmet's calendar include the bi-annual Crawfish Festival at Breaux Bridge, self-proclaimed crawfish capital of the world (early May in even-numbered years), and the less appetizing sounding Louisiana Shrimp and Petroleum Festival at Morgan City at the beginning of September each year. Near Shreveport in the northwest of the state, you may attend the Poke Salad Festival held on the second weekend in May to celebrate a plant called poke (or sometimes "polk"), a vegetable akin to spinach which sustained many local people during the Depression.

SPORT

Baseball, football and boxing may be watched at the Superdome, the world's largest domed stadium (1500 Poydras St). Call 587-3800 for tickets, or 587-3810 if you want to take a tour of the Superdome. Horse racing takes place all the year round, including some Sundays, at Fair Grounds (November to April) and Jefferson Downs (April to November).

There is no shortage of golf courses, tennis courts, or of facilities for riding (ask at the Crescent Riding Academy) and sailing and water-skiing on Lake Pontchartrain, where you can swim without charge.

According to popular mythology, the driving skills acquired in transporting illicitly distilled "moonshine" whisky rapidly over country roads produced the early heroes of stock-car racing, today one of the South's most popular spectator sports in spring and summer.

Zoo. Audubon Zoological Garden is close to the western end of the St Charles streetcar, linked to the line by a free shuttle bus. The address is 6500 Magazine St (861-2537). Its biggest attraction is a collection of red wolves, originally native to the region but now extinct in the wild. Admission costs $5.50, and the zoo opens daily at 9.30am; closing times vary between 4.30pm and 6pm. As well as the streetcar, you can also reach the zoo on the Magazine bus, or by boat from Canal St aboard the *Cotton Blossom* (586 -8777).

SHOPPING

The colourful French Market is open daily along the 800, 900 and 1,000 blocks of Decatur St. Along with wonderful produce and seafood, you will find a shop called The Bombay Company which flies the Union Jack, a shop called Santa's Quarters which sells Christmas presents throughout the year, a shop at 536 Royal Street which sells a huge variety of colourful umbrellas and parasols, and a Religious Order of Witchcraft and Voodoo which holds classes and sells all sorts of incense, herbs, occult jewellery and 'witches closet collectables'. The usual selection of glamorous shops can be found at the converted Jackson Brewery on the river, and at the New Orleans Center near the Superdome. If you happen to want some turf laid in a garden, consult the *Yellow Pages* under the heading 'Sod and Sodding'. Legislation in Louisiana allows for overseas visitors to avoid sales tax; it is always worth asking if a store will do this.

THE MEDIA

New Orleans' only daily paper is the *Times Picayune*. *Gambit* is an informative and entertaining weekly newspaper. The University of New Orleans station (WWNO 89.9 FM) is part of the National Public Radio network. In addition, there are many religious stations and one (WRBH 88.3 FM) for the blind. For news try WWL (870 AM), for classic jazz WWOZ (90.7 FM), for soul Q-93 (WQUE 93.3 FM), for soft rock WLTS (105 FM) and for heavy metal WLMG (102 FM).

Crime and Safety

The New Orleans Visitor's Map does not mince its words. The Bienville Housing Project (north of Basin St between Canal St and St Louis St) is marked "CAUTION: KEEP OUT". In fact that is an unnecessarily hysterical reaction. The only place which should be avoided altogether is (ironically) Desire.

The Vieux Carre is well lit, frequently patrolled and generally safe at all times. You must, however, watch out for pickpockets and tricksters who are drawn to tourist areas everywhere. During Mardi Gras, criminals flock to New Orleans in almost greater numbers that tourists. Bagsnatching is particularly popular. Outside the French Quarter, stick to the main thoroughfares after dark.

New Orleans cops are not to be messed with (as throughout the south) and Louisiana justice makes it easy to put someone behind bars.

Help and Information *i*

The area code for New Orleans is 504.

Information: The New Orleans City State Tourist and Visitor Information Center, 527 St Ann, Jackson Square (568-5661).
American Express: 158 Baronne St, (568-8201).
Thomas Cook: 728 Canal St, (568-1964)
Post Office: 701 Loyola Avenue (589-2201). Near Union Station.
Western Union Telegrams: 568-1440.
Medical Emergencies: Tulane University Medical Center (588-5711); emergency entrance at 217 LaSalle.
24 hour drugstore: Eckerd Drugs, 3400 Canal St, (488-6661).
Travelers' Aid Society: 211 Camp St (525-8726).
Police: 822-4161.
Louisiana Department of Wildlife and Fisheries: 7612 West End Boulevard (1-800-442-2511).
British Honorary Consulate: 321 St Charles Avenue (524 -4180).

Further Afield 61

The South is as diverse and diverting as any region of the United States. Geographically, it stretches from the Atlantic to Texas, and from the bayous of Louisiana to the peaks of Appalachia. Culturally it clings to its heritage while moving fast into a high-tech future. The spirit of progress has had such tangible results as the civil rights legislation of the 1960s and the waning popularity of the Ku Klux Klan. Yet alongside the new, the Old South lives on, white-columned mansions and wretched sharecroppers' shacks, physical evidence of long enduring attitudes and values. The old Confederate flag is widely displayed, and visitors may well come across Resentment of "Yankees" and thinly veiled racial intolerance: MARTA, the acronym for Atlanta's public transport system, is interpreted by racists as "Moving Africans Rapidly Through Atlanta".

Dixie is the name for the name for the Southern states and should not be taken in vain. There are several explanations for its origin, the most common of which is that in the early 19th century, many of the $10 bills in circulation in the southern states were issued by a bank in New Orleans which printed *dix* on them (French for 'ten'). Dixie should not be confused with the Mason Dixon Line which separated the South from the North in the Civil War.

LOUISIANA

For an historical perspective on the society and economy of the South, hire a car to see some of the old sugar plantation houses which straddle the Mississippi between New Orleans and Baton Rouge. One of the most interesting is the Oak Alley Plantation, built in the 1830s. Visitors are shown around by the servants of the last occupying family. The exterior of the house and its quarter-mile avenue of evergreen oaks appear in advertisements for Southern Comfort.

For an early example of American excess, visit some of the other houses built before the Civil War in the style of Greek Revival. These include the 18th century Destrehan Plantation near New Orleans, San Francisco further along the north shore of the Mississippi and Ashlands which is close to Baton Rouge, though there are many others. It is even possible to stay overnight at some of the plantations. The free Lutcher car ferry which crosses the Mississippi a few miles from Oak Alley permits access to more colonial homes such as Madewood on State Highway 308, due west of New Orleans. An organized tour to a couple of these houses costs about $40 with Southern Tours, 7801 Edinburgh St (486-0604).

MISSISSIPPI

The Old South lingers on in Mississippi, in its cotton fields and in the ante-bellum mansions of Vicksburg, Natchez and Columbus. The Southern heritage is brought to life during the Spring Pilgrimage (March-April) in Natchez, when many historical buildings are open to the public. Reminders of the war between the States are constantly on view in the 1,700 acres of the Vicksburg National Military Park, where well preserved cannon trenches, memorials and markers attest the bitter siege of the town in 1863. Vicksburg's commanding position overlooking the Mississippi, which afforded great strategic importance in the war, is today one of the town's attractions for visitors. Another is the chance to go on a riverboat cruise: details of cruises on the *Delta Queen* and *Mississippi Queen* are available on 1-800-543-1949.

Tupelo, 200 miles northeast of the state capital Jackson, is best known as the childhood home of the king of rock 'n' roll. The Elvis Presley Birthplace and Memorial Chapel is a diminutive shack at 306 Elvis Presley Drive (842-9796).

The south coast of Mississippi is dotted with resorts. At Bay St Louis, the National Space Technology Centre (688-2321) is a free and intriguing introduction to the NASA Space Shuttle.

ALABAMA

Car number plates ("tags" in American parlance) in Alabama proclaim the state to be the "Heart of Dixie", which accurately describes its location.

And it is in many aspects a microcosm of the region — mountains in the north, Gulf Coast beaches in the south, a major space centre within view of cotton fields little changed since the last century, with a sizeable belt of heavy industry thrown in for good measure.

Huntsville, in the north, contains both present and past NASA activity: the Marshall Space Flight Center is the home of the space shuttle programme where the machinery is designed and engineers trained, and the Earth's largest Space Museum, which recreates earlier achievements. You can tour the former by bus whereas the latter invites more direct contact, offering (for example) simulated space travel complete with weightlessness.

There's also a space theme at the Gayle Planetarium in Montgomery, the state capital, a city more evidently rooted in the past. It was the first captial of the Confederacy in 1861, and a century later, the scene of early and angry civil rights demonstrations.

Way down south on the Gulf, the attractions of Mobile are well-preserved buildings and fresh seafood, not forgetting a ten-day Mardi Gras celebration around Shrove Tuesday (February or March). That is a good time to see Mobile, for it also marks the beginning of the city's Azalea Trail celebration, centred around the profusion of blooming flowers and is the best time to visit the beautiful Bellingrath Gardens and Home, outside the city.

ATLANTA AND GEORGIA

The most populous settlement in the southeast USA, with the world's busiest airport, Atlanta is prime candidate for the title of capital of the "New South". Downtown development has produced a towering skyline of concrete and reflective glass, and the sprawling Peachtree Convention Centre — with underground shopping malls and glass-enclosed overhead walkways — brings the American dream of a 100% air-conditioned enviroment to fruition. Atlanta has certainly rebound from Civil War days when General Sherman burnt nine-tenths of the city to the ground for the Union cause. Unfortunately for the budget traveller, Atlanta's modern boom has given it the appearance of a tough northern business centre miraculously transported to the humid heat of Georgia.

Arrival and Departure. *Air:* "When you die and go to heaven", complain jaded air travellers, "you have to change plans at Atlanta". Hartsfield International Airport (530-2081 for information) is the USA's number one air hub with over 2,000 arrivals and departures daily. Despite its size it is surprisingly easy to reach and use. MARTA runs a rapid rail link to downtown (journey time 15 minutes) for only 60c, daily from 5.30am to just after midnight. There are two private bus services: Atlanta Airport Shuttle (524-3400) charging $7 to downtown, $10 to suburban hotels; and Northside Airport Express (952-1601) with scheduled services to six Northside locations, fare $9.75. Competition from Atlanta to major US cities is fierce, so there are some bargain flights to be found. For international air tickets, try Council Travel (12 Park Place South, 577-1678).

Bus: The Greyhound bus terminal (522-6300) at 81 International Boulevard NW (one block from the Peachtree Center) is, like the airport, a major hub for transport in the south.

Train: Atlanta is not nearly so well served by long-distance trains. The Amtrak station is three miles north of downtown at 1688 Peachtree St N. It is linked by bus 23 to Arts Center station on the MARTA network. The *Southern Crescent* stops at Atlanta daily on its run between New Orleans ($100 one-way) and Washington DC ($120).

Driving: As may be expected in a city which derives a great deal of its income from convention visitors, there is plenty of choice in car rental. Atlanta Rent-a-Car (763-1160) at 3185 Camp Creek Parkway, three miles from the airport, is one of the best value companies. Motoring around Atlanta is made confusing by the 26 roads and streets named Peachtree (after Georgia's leading fruit crop). The main Peachtree St is a major north-south artery, along with Spring St and Piedmont Avenue. Ponce de Leon and North Avenues are the primary east-west throughfares. To add confusion, downtown Atlanta is a jumble of plazas and streets which meet at odd angles and are regulated by a convoluted one-way system. Given the cheap and efficient public transport, a car is an unnecessary encumbrance.

City Transport. The dazzlingly hi-tech Metropolitan Atlanta Rapid Transit Authority (MARTA) system is a combined rail and bus operation. Dial 848-4711 for information. The two rail lines intersect at Five Points station in downtown Atlanta. Each station has a name and code, e.g. Arts Center N5 is five stops north of the hub. Every bus route begins at one of the 27 rail stations, so having taken a train to the nearest station you can reach your final destination by bus. The MARTA system runs daily from 5.30am to 12.30am. The flat fare is 60c (with free transfer if you pick up a ticket when you pay your fare), or you can buy a weekly pass for $7. With efficient security and camera surveillance in every station, MARTA is one of the safest urban transport systems in the USA.

Accommodation. Atlanta caters unashamedly for visitors with expense accounts. If you don't have one, you could head out to cheap motels lining I-75. The YMCA at 22 Butler St (659-8085) is crowded and dirty, and there is no downtown Youth Hostel. For young people and students, however, a trial scheme offers rooms in cheap (but clean) downtown hotels for under $10 per person. People under 24 or ISIC cardholders should ask the Convention and Visitors Bureau (659-4270) for details.

Atlanta's cheap and efficient public transport makes camping a viable alternative to a dreary hotel or motel room. Try Arrowhead Campsites (948-7362), ten miles west of downtown, or Stone Mountain Family Campground (948-5710), 16 miles east. Both are served by MARTA and have excellent facilities for around $5 per person per night.

For those seeking a taste of the famed Southern Hospitality, two organizations will find you a room in a private guest house: Bed & Breakfast Atlanta (875-0525) who give a 10% discount to students, and Atlanta Hospitality (493-1930). Most rooms cost $25-35.

Eating and Drinking. If someone else is paying, grab a pint at Reggie's British Pub in the CNN Center, take a taxi to Nikolai's Roof restaurant for a Russian meal (rated the best restaurant in Georgia) before drinks at Le Parasol in the Peachtree Center, under a 13-ton metal parasol hanging 23 storeys up. Atlanta offers every conceivable cuisine at all-too-easily imaginable prices. For cheap eating, try the Cha Gio Vietnamese Restaurant, 996 Peachtree St NE near the Arts Center rail station. Or experience the ultimate in glorious American junk food at the Varsity, 61 North Avenue NW (close to North Avenue rail station). This is the world's largest drive-in where you can eat chilli-dogs and fries in giant television rooms (one for each channel).

For an evening drink, swallow hard and go up to one of the roof-top bars in the hotels around the Peachtree center. The night-time view of the city (almost) makes up for the prices of the drinks.

Entertainment. The most interesting sites are scattered around the city. An excellent introduction to the city is to take one of the four walking tours provided by the Atlanta Preservation Center (84 Peachtree St NW, 522-4345). The Monday and Sunday tours include the Fox Theater with its fantastical minarets, onion domes and Egyptian art-deco interior.

Until you leave the city centre, it is easy to forget that Atlanta is one of the USA's great black cities. The Martin Luther King Jr Historic Site is a mile east of the Peachtree Center, an interesting walk (safe in daylight) through gradual deteriorating surroundings as white neighbourhoods change to black: faded pictures of King are still displayed in store windows. The site is also served by bus 3 (marked Auburn Ave/MLK) from Five Points. It contains the first home and grave of one of the 20th century's greatest figures, plus a museum (524-1956) and the Ebenezer Baptist church where both King and his father preached, and where his mother was murdered.

In complete contrast, visit historic Buckhead (the city's most beautiful residential district containing the Greek Revival-style Governor's Mansion) and the houses of the Atlanta Historical Society (3101 Andrew Drive NW, 261-1837) to see how the other half lived.

For some, Atlanta is synonymous with the struggles of Rhett and Scarlett O'Hara. *Gone With The Wind* fans will wish to see the Margaret Mitchell exhibition in the Atlanta Public Library (Carnegie Way and Forsythe St). The remarkable writer is buried in the Oakland cemetery, worth a visit not least for its Civil War graves. For those requiring a refresher course, *Gone With The Wind* is shown daily at the CNN Center (577-6974).

Music and Theatre. Check the latest edition of the free magazine *Creative Loafing* or the weekend supplement to Friday's *Atlanta Journal* for full listings. In summer, look out for free concerts in the city's parks. The main indoor venues are the Woodruff Arts Center, 1280 Peachtree St NE (892-2414) and the Atlanta Civic Center, 395 Piedmont St (523-6275). The historic Fox Theater at 660 Peachtree St (881-1977) has recently been restored.

In early August in even-numbered years the National Black Arts Festival dominates the cultural life of Atlanta: call 681-7327 for details.

Nightlife. Atlanta after dark can be both varied and inexpensive. The most popular nightspots are the Limelight Disco (3330 Piedmont Road NE, in the Peachtree-Piedmont shopping centre in Buckland) and Club 668 (668 Spring St NW at 3rd St), which features frentic dancing to live bands nightly except for Wednesday's epilepsy-inducing rock video night. Push your way through the crowds into Blind Willie's (828 N Highland Avenue, 873-BLUE) and listen to black Chicago-style blues in a genuinely dark and run-down Chicago atmosphere. Live music starts at 10pm.

For a more relaxed evening, eat a pizza while you watch a movie at the downstairs Cinema-Pub at the Excelsior Mill, 695 North Avenue (577-6455) or listen to jazz and folk in the company of students at the cafe Erewhen, 60 N 5th St NW (892-6253). There is a standard cover charge of $3-$5 for all these venues, but drinks are half the price of city-centre locations. It is also interesting to watch the way in which emigres from the northern USA take on the more relaxed attitudes of the South as the evening progresses.

Sport. With maturing players replacing ageing veterans, the Atlanta Braves baseball team will be well worth watching in the next few seasons as they claw their way up from the foot of the National League. See them between April and September at the Atlanta/Fulton County Stadium. This arena is home during winter for the Atlanta Falcons football team. You can reach the stadium from downtown on MARTA, but start the journey at least two hours before the game begins. Tickets for both teams can be scarce: call 522-7630 for the Braves, 261-5400 for the Falcons. If you can't get tickets, watch the match at Jack and Jill's Indoor Sports Bar (112 10th St). It can be just as entertaining to watch the packed clientele of armchair enthusiasts in front of the 60-inch big screens.

Shopping. The malls and boutiques in and around the Peachtree Center make for amusing window shopping but, for most wallets, little else. More practically, the Flea Market Center (5300 Peachtree Industrial Boulevard, in the suburb of Chamblee) will be of interest if your interest in trimmings and trinkets has been fired by visiting ante-bellum mansions. It opens daily except Saturday from noon to 7pm.

The largest bargain bookstore in the South — with an enormous selection of used, remaindered and damaged books — is Oxford Too Books at 2395 Peachtree Road. The neighbouring Oxford Books store stays open until 2am on Saturday nights, dispensing bedtime reading.

Crime and Safety. Atlanta has one of the highest murder rates in the country. Most killings, however, take place in poorer neighbourhoods well away from places of interest to tourism and convention visitors. The well-lit and policed downtown area is safer than most city centres in the USA. Nevertheless, avoid the area east of I-85 after dark.

Help and Information. The area code for Atlanta is 404.
Information: Atlanta Convention and Visitor's Bureau, Harris Tower, Peachtree Center (659-4270). Open 9am-5pm, Monday to Friday.
Post Office: 39 Crown Road (at Hapville St); 221-5307.
British Consulate-General: 225 Peachtree St NE (524-5856).
Medical Emergencies: Crawford W. Long Memorial Hospital of Emory University, 550 Peachtree St NE (892-4411).
Traveler's Aid: Greyhound station, 81 International Boulevard (527-7400). Open 8am-8pm Monday to Friday, 10am-6pm on Saturdays. After hours, dial 522-7370.

Further Afield. Sixteen miles east of the city, on US 78, lies Stone Mountain Park (498-5600), a 3,200-acre recreational area of forests and lakes which includes an antebellum plantation and Civil War exhibition. The main attraction, however, is the world's largest bas-relief sculpture, carved into the side of the granite mountain. There is a stunning laser show against the mountainside each summer night at 9.30pm. Take MARTA bus 120 from Avondale rail station. On weekdays the last bus leaves the park at 7.50pm, although you can easily camp for the night at the park's campground.

You will see some of Georgia's more interesting features if you follow the general direction of Union General Sherman's well known passage of fire and sword southeastward from Atlanta to the Atlantic, commemorated in the song "Marching through Georgia" (not sweet music to Southern ears). From Atlanta, I-20 takes you to Augusta via (with short detours) Madison and Washington, all containing fine antebellum buildings spared by Sherman. Augusta is best avoided during the Masters' golf tournament every April: tickets are harder to obtain than for an English Cup Final, and accommodation costs soar.

Savannah. On the coast, the port city of Savannah has in a rather un-American way emphasized preservation over development. It has retained its 18th century layout of elegant squares, the wrought-iron clad buildings full of history but many still in use as homes and offices. An interesting sight in the city and throughout the so-called Low Country coastland running up to Charleston, S Carolina is the Spanish Moss which cloaks many trees in eerie grey festoons. Savannah is also the gateway to the Sea Island resorts of Georgia and South Carolina, with their miles of white sand beaches and healthy fun of the sailing/surfing/tennis/golf variety.

You can fly, drive or bus into Savannah from Atlanta; alternatively, it is on Amtrak's New York-Florida route, and just off I-95, the main East coast highway.

The Interior. Other places of interest in Georgia include Franklin Roosevelt's Little White House at Warm Springs, 60 miles south of Altlanta, where he "took the waters" for his paralysis, and another 60 miles south, the hometown of a more recent president, Jimmy Carter, though today Plains is a shadow of the boomtown it became during his term of office.

In the north of the state, you can pan for gold at Dahlonega, site of America's first gold rush in the 1820s, which led the government to drive out the last of the Cherokees. New Echota, on 1-75, midway between Atlanta and Chattanooga, was the Cherokee capital, today the site of a restored Indian settlement.

SOUTH CAROLINA

The far west of the state nudges into the spectacular scenery of the Blue Ridge Mountains, but the majority of South Carolina's tourist attractions lie along the coast. Chiefly, they comprise the picturesque and historical city of Charleston and numerous fun-in-the-sun beach resorts.

Charleston. Charleston has preserved its sleepy Old South charm, and you can tour its historic districts at a suitably leisurely pace in a horse-drawn carriage. The Old Slave Mart museum, now a black crafts centre, is an interesting reminder of the city's earlier principal activity, while Charles Towne Landing, where the first settlers arrived in 1670, is today a delightful park.

A few miles north of the city is Middleton Gardens which are landscaped in a Capability Brown fashion. You may even see huntsmen in pink (a rare sight in America) if you're there on a Sunday.

Charleston comes to life each year for two weeks around the end of May for the Spoleto Festival USA, a wide-ranging arts package of international calibre. You can obtain information on tickets, and accommodation from Spoleto Festival USA, PO Box 157, Charleston SC 29402, tel: 803-722-2764 (apply early). If you are not arts-minded, the Festival is a good time not to visit Charleston.

Beaches. Any time from March through October is fine to visit the beaches. Kiawah and Hilton Head Islands are distinctly up-market vacation spots, but all tastes and budgets are catered for at Myrtle Beach and the 55-mile Grand Strand running south from there. The Easter break from colleges brings droves of students from the chilly north in search of a good time.

Festivals. Inland, the biggest jamborees are at Darlington, site of the Rebel 500 (mile) stock-car race in April, and the even bigger Southern 500, over the Labor Day holiday weekend at the beginning of September.

NORTH CAROLINA

It's not that the Tar Heel state is too slow, it's just that the tourist — racing from the bustle of the northeast to the excitement of Florida — drives too fast. North Carolina boasts of no great cities: its beautiful island coastline and western mountain ranges are essentially places of quiet and solitude (unless you choose to visit the Great Smoky Mountains National Park on a holiday weekend). Postpone the thrills, spills and queues of Walt Disney World for a couple of days, try a hike through the oaks and pines of the Appalachian Trail or search for wild ponies on Ocracoke Island in the Outer Banks off the coast (see *The Great Outdoors*). Time is of the essence. To appreciate the state, take the slow side roads branching off the Blue Ridge Parkway and talk to the modest, almost indifferent inhabitants of the mountains selling home-made food and craftwork at their roadside stalls. Forget North Carolina if you're in a hurry: finding a place where patience and silence are appreciated in themselves will only frustrate someone looking for instant charm.

Whether or not you have time to get to know the people, stop off in the Burlington/Greenboro area and join the shoppers who come in by the busload from hundreds of miles away to shop for cheap, high quality merchandise, especially clothing and shoes, at the factory outlet stores. Or try a visit to the tobacco auctions and cigarette factories of Winston/Salem and Durham, notably the R J Reynolds Whitaker Park HQ off 1-40 in Winston/Salem. As befits a state whose economy is heavily supported by the tobacco industry, attitudes to smoking are more tolerant than elsewhere, and cigarettes much cheaper.

Charlotte. Direct flights from Gatwick by USAir make Charlotte a convenient launchpad for exploring the southeast. Walt Disney World is a day's drive south (through Atlanta or Charleston) while the Great Smoky Mountains, Nashville and Memphis lie to the west. The area code is 704.

Budget (359-5000) and Dollar (359-4700), among others, operate car rental services at the Charlotte/Douglas International Airport (359-4000); some of the cheapest unadvertised car deals in the South are reportedly at Alamo (1-800-327-9633), three blocks from the Airport. It takes 15 minutes to the city centre (cab fare $10, limousine service $4) where the downtown Greyhound Bus Terminal (601 West Trade St, 527-9393), offers several buses a day to Atlanta, Savannah and Washington DC (also served by Amtrak, 375-4416).

Unfortunately Charlotte itself doesn't have much to offer the tourist. The main throughfare, Tryon Street, with its skyscrapers and plazas is clear evidence of the claim that at $57 billion, Charlotte's banking resources almost outstrip Atlanta's and Miami's combined. This is a mixed blessing for the tourist. Money generated from businesses has allowed major operations of civic restoration such as Spirit Square and the Victorian Fourth Ward area. Unfortunately, places of interest are dwarfed and squeezed out of the city by downtown development: the old Federal-style US Mint (now at 2730 Randolph Road, 337-2000) was simply taken to pieces, moved three miles, and rebuilt in the northern suburbs to serve as an excellent art museum.

A self-guided tour of historic city sites is available from the Charlotte Convention and Visitors Bureau, 229 North Church St; call 1-800-231-4636 from outside North Carolina, 1-800-782-5544 from inside the state. Don't miss the beautifully renovated Fourth Ward, an area of fanciful wooden homes of the 19th century upper middle classes, two blocks west of North Tryon Street. It is the most pleasant place to stroll in the city, especially in the early evening.

Good, reasonably-priced restaurants are few in the downtown area. The Best Western Motel at 900 North Tryon St serves food 24 hours a day, or try lunch at the restaurants in Ivey's Department Store, 127 North Tryon Street. Its founder, a devout Methodist named J. B. Ivey, balanced his conscience and profession by pulling the blinds of the street level shop windows on Sundays. The young Billy Graham was more forthright. At age 17, he would exhort uptown shoppers from the steps of the nearby First Baptist Church, 318 North Tryon (now the Spirit Square Center for the Arts).

If you have a car, the cheapest beds can be found at the numerous motels on the city outskirts: just follow Tryon St north or south. In town, try the Oxford Inn, 601 N Tryon Street (372-2300) at a more reasonable price than the big name motel chains. Travellers shell-shocked by the flight from England, or just seeking genuine Southern hospitality, might contemplate skipping a sterile motel room and staying at The Homeplace, a Victorian wooden house, at 5901 Sardis Road (365-1936), just 15 minutes drive southeast of downtown Charlotte. A double room costs $55-$65 including full breakfast.

THE APPALACHIANS

The mountains of western North Carolina are divided into the "High Country" around Boone, 100 miles north of Charlotte, and the more touristy Great Smoky and Pisgah forested mountains around Asheville, 100 miles to the west. Both towns are just off the beautiful Blue Ridge Parkway (open only from April to November), which winds through the Appalachians to Pennyslvania. The Blue Ridge, Great Smoky, Black, Craggy, Pisgah and Balsam Mountains are a budget traveller's dream: cheap campsites abound, along with inexpensive (if elusive) Youth Hostels and ski lodges.

Boone. This mountain town, aptly named after the famous frontiersman Daniel Boone, seems to exist solely for rigorous outdoor exercise. For information on the surrounding High Country ask the Boone Area Chamber of Commerce, (264-2225), near the central bus stop, or the National Park Information Desk, Milepost 294 at the Parkway Craft Centre (295-3782).

You need a car to get to the best trail-heads. Hitching in the remoter areas is slow but viable (the normal risks apply). Sometimes the Youth Hostels at Blowing Rock Assembly Grounds (295-7813), or Trailridge Mountain Camp, Bakersville (688-3879), will pick you up from the nearest bus stop along the Blue Ridge Parkway. Inexperienced hikers should consider joining one of the guided expeditions run by Edge of the World, PO Box 1137, Banner Elk (898-9550). Two-day hikes cost around $60 including food and equipment.

Asheville. Asheville is the unofficial capital of the Carolina mountains which surround the city and give it its spectacular panorama. Asheville has several attractions apart from the landscape. The Biltmore Estate (704-225-

1700), a magnificent 250-room Renaissance Chateau transported to a New World setting in 1895 by George W. Vanderbilt, is the largest private home in America. More humble but equally interesting is the Thomas Wolfe Memorial, 48 Spruce St, (253-8304). The writer's "rambling, unplanned, gabular" childhood home is immortalised as "Dixieland" in Wolfe's first novel *Look Homeward, Angel*.

Asheville celebrates the rich Appalachian fold culture with festivals and craft fairs throughout the year, During the summer, don't miss the Mountain Dance and Folk Festival (1-800-257-1300) or the unique Mountain Sweet talk, a show combining banjo, clog dancing and story-telling. It is performed by the female duo "The Folktellers" at the Folk Arts Centre Theatre (258-1113) during July, August and the second half of October.

For more information about local events contact Visitors Information, 151 Haywood St (258-3858). The proximity of cheap camping has kept motel prices cheap ($25-35); start looking on Merrimon Avenue, north of the city. Most approach Asheville on the scenic I-40. If however you wish to by-pass the city and head straight for the mountains, travel along US 64-US 276 between Chimney Rock and Waynesville through the Pisgah National Forest (once part of the Biltmore Estate) and on into the Cherokee Indian reservation on US 19. This is probably the most scenic stretch of highway on the East Coast. The Cherokee Reservation's main attractions are rather tacky, its inhabitants self-conscious tourist attractions without the proud autonomy of the Navajo and Pueblo in the Southwest.

The half-million acres of the Great Smoky Mountains National Park cannot be fully appreciated except upon foot. There is a much greater variety of trees and wild flowers than in the parks of California and Wyoming, and the vistas are best seen as the light gradually changes and mists rise. Arm yourself with the invaluable *100 Favorite Trails* ($2), published jointly by the Carolina Mountain Club and Smoky Mountain Hiking Club, and widely available in Asheville and Gatlinburg. There are plenty of good guided tours and places in Boone and Asheville to buy or hire equipment, so there is no reason to be ill-prepared. Summer nights can be bitterly cold and even if you don't meet one of the 600 resident black bears, you're sure to meet the resident mosquitoes.

TENNESSEE

If your taste in music is country, blues, or bluegrass, you're in the right place. Tennessee stretches over 400 miles east to west and contains three distinct cultural regions; in the east it's hillbilly country, fiercely independent villages scattered throughout the mountains and forests of the Great Smoky Mountains National Park; in central Tennessee the landscape levels out into rolling countryside where local farmers' music combined with the wilder eastern hill music to turn a quiet cotton-farming centre called Nashville into "Music City, USA". Finally the land flattens out entirely as it meets the banks of the great Mississippi and the city of Memphis —where the natives were influenced by the great river route between New Orleans and Chicago which brought southern gentility to the Memphis upper classes and blues music to the lower classes. It's easy to find things to do in each area and to have a good time; the less interesting the scenery gets, the more friendly the people become.

The area code for Nashville was made briefly famous by the local band Area Code 615; prefix Memphis numbers with 901.

Nashville. If Johnny Cash leaves you cold, and you can't see anything special in Patsy Cline's last cigarette lighter, then in Nashville you'll probably experience that occasional panic that *you're* the one who's insane. The city has little else of interest to offer other than Country and Western music. To see the few sights (including a full-sized replica of the Parthenon) quickly, take one of the Nashville Trolleys (25c) that cruise around the vaguely historic downtown before depositing you in Music Row: a street of souvenir shops and "personal museums" (effectively souvenir shops owned by the stars themselves). Most amusing is the Country Music Hall of Fame, 4 Music Square East. Included in the admission price of $5 is a tour of RCA's studio B where Elvis crooned his Christmas albums (each August).

For live music the biggest venues have been purpose-built (with the emphasis on glitter) on the city outskirts. The Nashville palace (2400 Music Valley Drive, 885-1540) dishes it out seven nights a week, and the famous Grand Old Opry (next to Opryland USA, a C&W/Disneyland combo) has big names every Friday and Saturday night. It is easiest to find tickets ($10-$15) for the matinee performances held between March and September; call 889-3060 for details. The shows are slick, wholesome and footstomping, but probably not ideal if you prefer "real" Country. There is a trend away from the Nashville sound of digital recordings and orchestral backgrounds, and a return to native bluegrass and more excitingly raw hillbilly sounds.

Cheap accommodation is hard to find in Nashville; try the motels on I-65 or the Tudor Inn (244-8970) on James Robertson Parkway. Whatever else you do, make sure you have one meal at the Elliston Place Soda Shop, 211 Elliston Place. It is hard to say which is its better attribute: the low prices or the perfectly preserved 1950s decor.

In Hendersonville, some way northeast of Nashville, you can take in the Johnny Cash Museum (824-5110), Conway Twitty's "Twitty City" (822-3210) and the Marty Robbins Memorial Museum. Instead you could head southeast to Lynchburg for a tour of the Jack Daniels Distillery (759-7394).

MEMPHIS

It is evident even to the casual visitor that Memphis' fortunes are on the upswing. Originally the city's position on the Mississippi made it the hub for the Southern cotton crop, and a boom lasted through the first half of this century. It was to Memphis that Vernon Presley drove with his wife and young son Elvis Aaron when he couldn't make ends meet in Tupelo Mississippi in the 1940s. With the decline of the cotton market, two decades of economic and inner city decline set in from which the city is only now recovering. Its improved fortunes are due largely to the influx of white-collar work as major corporations move to Memphis, attracted by low prices and its central position in the South.

Memphis has learned from the errors of other cities and is handling its revival by renovating rather than replacing the interesting 1920s buildings with skyscrapers. Despite its large size (the 15th most populous city in the USA), the atmosphere is relaxed and almost provincial. There is a great deal to do and see; Memphis seems likely to become one of the main tourist attractions in the USA in the next decade.

Getting Around. Memphis International Airport is 15 miles south of downtown. There is no airport bus service, and a taxi might easily cost $15. The cheapest way downtown is to take a hotel courtesy bus away from the airport area (when you arrive at the hotel say you'd like to stay but can't afford to), then take a local bus.

Greyhound services operate from the terminal at 203 Union Ave at 4th St (523-7676), two blocks north of Beale St.

The perimeter of the city is orbited by I-240, from which Poplar Ave and Union Ave run east-west through the heart of the city. Madison Avenue divides the north and south addresses: basically the large black community and the poorest areas are to the south. The Mississippi runs north-south, providing the western boundary to the city and the focal point for much of the new development.

Visitors to Memphis are fortunate in that almost all tourist sites are easily accessible by foot within the downtown area. Even so, the Memphis Area Transit Authority (MATA: 274-6282 for information) runs "show-boats" (ill-disguised buses) on a fixed route between all the major attractions — stops are marked by red and blue flags. An all-day pass costs $2 for adults, $1.25 for children. Buses run every few minutes, seven days a week. The only sight not covered by the "showboats" is the greatest, Elvis' Graceland; take bus 13 (marked "Lauderdale/Elvis Presley") from 3rd and Union Streets (85c each way).

Accommodation. As with many cities experiencing regeneration, the downtown area has seen the growth of many expensive hotels while more reasonable accommodation requires a car or bus journey. The only cheap downtown location is the TravelLodge at 265 Union Avenue (527-4306 or 1-800 255-3050) where singles cost $35, doubles $38. Check the rates also at the Days Inn Downtown, 164 Union Avenue (527-4100 or 1-800-272-6232). Both are across from the Greyhound Bus station: when occupancy is low these hotels indulge in price-cutting battles which can sometimes mean doubles for less than $30.

The Lowenstein — Long House/Castle Hostelry (AYH) 217 N Waldran (527-7174) offers both expensive bed and breakfast in a Victorian Mansion as well as rooms in the small adjacent youth hostel ($10). The YMCA, 3548 Walker Avenue (458-3580) is nine miles east of downtown; since it is often full, you should call ahead. Bed and Breakfast in Memphis (726-5920) can suggest various local homes for around $40 double or more.

Visitors with a car can try the numerous cheap motels further out along Union Avenue or near Graceland on Elvis Presley Boulevard south of the city. Be warned that rooms are scarce from August 11-17 during the week commemorating Presley's death in 1977.

Eating and Drinking. Memphis deserves its reputation for good "soul food" and the best Southern barbecue. For the finest ribs go to the Rendezvous at 52 S 2nd St, in the alley between Union Avenue and Monroe St across from the Peabody Hotel. A measure of its success is that it now sells barbecue ribs by mail order. Other good restaurants include the Marmalade at 153 Calhoun Avenue (522-8800) which has live music, and Leonard's Barbecue Pit, reputedly an old Presley haunt, at 1140 Bellevue Boulevard (948-1581).

Entertainment. However much the city develops, Memphis' greatest tourist attraction will always be a surprisingly small house set in a quiet residential district ten miles south of the centre: Elvis Presley's Graceland, 3794 Elvis Presley Boulevard (332-3322; 1-800-238-2000 toll-free from out-of-state). Visitors buy tickets and souvenirs across the road before being bussed up to the house for a guided tour. This has allowed the mansion — itself a Mecca of glitz and tastelessness — to escape the worst ravages of tourism. You can sense the isolation and loneliness behind the mirrored ceilings and stacked televisions. Disbelievers in Elvis' mortality may wish to enquire why the upper floor is out-of-bounds. Graceland opens daily from 8am to 6pm, admission $7.

Presley's two greatest influences were the blues and gospel. Explore the restored Beale St, which is to Southern blues what New Orleans is to jazz. To experience the inspiration and fervour of black gospel music, try to attend a service at the Reverend Al Green's church, the Full Gospel Tabernacle, 787 Hale Road (396-9192). Three blocks south of Beale St, in a now derelict area, is the place where Martin Luther King Jr died. On April 4 1968, while staying in Memphis to support a strike by sanitation workers, the great civil rights leader was assassinated at the Lorraine Motel, 406 Mulberry St. There are plans to renovate the site and build a National Civil Rights Center, but many locals claim the money should be spent instead on badly needed housing.

Examples of successful restoration well worth a visit include the mansions of the Victorian Village; the luxurious Peabody Hotel at 149 Union St where ducks swim in the central indoor fountain and are ceremoniously escorted to and from the elevator daily at 11am and 5pm; and the historic South Main district (details of a self-guided walking tour from the Visitor Information Center at 207 Beale St, 526-4880).

The most interesting museum in Memphis is the Mississippi River Museum on Mud Island (576-7241); the island itself is an amusement complex on a former mud bank, connected to the shoreline by a monorail. The museum traces the history of the river from its earliest Indian settlements and on through the Civil War using a combination of standard artefact displays and ingenious full-scale audio-visual replicas. Mud Island also had an open-air scale model of the Mississippi, 800 yards long, flowing into a one acre Gulf of Mexico. Cool off on a hot day by walking in the river, covering several miles with each stride. Admission to all Mud Island attractions plus the monorail ride costs $4.

Other places of interest in the city include the Brooks Museum of Art (722-3500), Libertyland amusement park (274-1776) and the Memphis Zoo (726-4775). Shopping for presents ceases to be much fun after the hundredth souvenir shop selling Elvis Presley baseball caps. Instead, try A. Schwab's store on Beale St which has the catchy motto "if you can't find it at Schwabs, you're better off without it."

Nightlife. The city has the best blues scene outside Chicago. Check the "Playbook" section in Friday's *Memphis Commercial Appeal* or the monthly *Memphis Star* to find out what's on. Rock and jazz concerts are held in summer at the amphitheatre on Mud Island and at the Overton Park Shell. For blues, stroll along Beale St and choose the bar where the music sounds best. Most bars have a disarmingly informal clientele, and are good places to meet people. Except in trendy Overton Square, prices are lower than in most American cities. Try the Rum Boogie Cafe at 182 Beale St, with live entertainment and dancing. When there is no guest band, the house band steps in, often to be joined for a jamming session by a megastar unwinding after a performance on Mud Island.

Crime and Safety. Immediately outside the central downtown area (north of Madison Avenue and south of Linden Avenue) lives a population which has yet to feel the benefits of Memphis' current boom. Crimes committed there against travellers have little to do with drugs but much to do with poverty.

KENTUCKY

The Kentucky Derby is the state's most notable attraction. It lasts for a few minutes each year on the first Saturday in May. Kentucky's other great creation is bourbon whisky, which can be enjoyed every day of the year.

The Derby is the pinnacle of a multi-million dollar horse breeding and racing industry centred on Lexington, which is active year-round. You can visit many of the neat, white-fenced horse farms (free), see horses change hands for huge sums at auction (especially Keeneland, in July), watch them perform at shows, polo games and races, and even race them yourself. For information contact the State Racing Commission, 535 W 2nd St., Lexington (502-564-5859). Lexington is the centre of Kentucky's bluegrass region, and hosts a festival featuring the music of the same name every June.

Louisville is the home of the Derby, which you might want to attend for the same reason as you would say, the FA Cup Final: both are experiences as much as sports events, and you don't have to care about the result to enjoy the occasion (though a bet does sharpen your interest). General admission to the field costs $10; phone (502) 636-3541 for further information. The city was also the birthplace of Mohammad Ali, "The Louisville Lip", who has a boulevard named after him. You can visit the Colonel Sanders Museum if you are interested in the history of Kentucky Fried Chicken, or distilleries in Louisville, though you have a wider choice in Bardstown, an hour's drive south. Free samples are not permitted.

Mammouth Cave in the centre of the state, is the world's longest known cave system, 235 miles in length. Indians, lived there 3,000 years ago; today you can take tours of varying lengths and depth, and eat lunch in a cafeteria nearly 300 feet below ground. Remember to take a sweater.

Other places of interest in Kentucky include Hodgeville, birthplace of Abraham Lincoln, and Berea, a town and college community preserving the traditional way of life of the Appalachian mountain people. There is a museum and an annual festival (spring) of music and crafts. Another group whose past has been preserved are the Shakers, a sect who seceded from the Quakers and found settlements in Kentucky and eleswhere, where they practised temperence and celibacy. Unsuprisingly, they have virtually died out, though there is a small Shaker community in Maine. If you are passing Shakertown near Harrodsburg, take a look at their restored homes and austere and beautifully-made furnishings.

ARKANSAS

The gentle, forest-clad Ozark Mountains in the north of the state are the home of some of America's true backwoods people. The Ozark Folk Center at Mountain View is a comphrehensive collection of all aspects of this rustic culture — weaving, woodwork, pottery and, above all, music. Ozark music is real downhome hootenanny stuff full of banjos and fiddles and mandolins. Hootenannies are foot-stomping celebrations or jamborees. The highpoint of all this is the Arkansas Folk Festival at the Center, which runs over two week-ends in April. The religious side of the mountain people is shown especially in the Passion Play performed five nights in a week in summer at the spa town of Eureka Springs, in the far northwest of the state.

Thermal springs are one of Arkansas's varied aquatic attractions. As well as a Eureka, you can get yourself into hot water at the city of Hot Springs in mid-state, which embraces a National Park full of bubbling mineral springs with supposedly healthful properties. The Mississippi forms the eastern border of Arkansas as it heads south through cotton country towards the Delta.

The Great Outdoors

Although Southerners are not as geared to energetic outdoor activity as the hyperactive Northerners or the moutain-obsessed natives of the West Coast, there are plenty of opportunities for enjoying the great outdoors while travelling in the Southern states.

An almost-complete long distance path, the Natchez Trace, follows an ancient Indian track from Nashville via Jackson to Natchez. It runs nearly 500 miles through rolling countryside and swampland. For a map, write to the Tupelo Visitor Center, Rural Route 1, Tupelo MS 38801.

Fishing is popular year round, either salt water fishing in the Gulf of Mexico and Atlantic or fresh water fishing in the numerous inland lakes and rivers. There is also duck, wild turkey, snipe, quail, raccoon, possum and deer shooting, as well as fox hunting.

In Louisiana you can explore Acadiana west of New Orleans, a region rich in scenic and cultural interest. For information on tours of the swamps look under the *Further Afield* section. It's also possible to rent canoes in many of the small towns, where fishing is always the favourite past-time. No self-respecting general store is without its gruesome tub of live bait.

Arkansas offers a remarkable scope for water sports: water-skiing, sailing, canoeing and fishing. In the north, Mountain Home and Beaver Lake are the major centres; if you are crossing the middle of the State on 1-40, Lake Dardanelle near Russellville is convenient and excellent. Experts give high marks to the canoeing on the Buffalo River south of Mountain Home.

The mammoth Tennessee Valley Authority provides facilities for swimming, sailing and fishing. In winter you can ski, skate and toboggan near Gatlinburg, chief town of the Tennessee region of the Great Smokies and full of tourists year round. The Smokies continue into North Carolina which offers two recreational contrasts: hiking, rafting and skiing in its western mountain ranges, or swimming, snorkelling and fishing on the Outer Banks, a strip of long, narrow islands stretching for 100 miles in a lazy arc as they follow the Atlantic coastline. The islands are linked by route 12, connected to the mainland in the north by US 64 and in the south by a ferry from Ocracoke Island. While hitching is possible, the islands' minimal public transport makes a car or bicycle worthwhile.

Head for two unspoilt southern islands, Ocracoke and Hatteras, both part of the protected Cape Hatteras National Seashore. (A flying visit on the way to the Wright Brothers National Memorial at Kitty Hawk on the commercialized Bodie Island is quite sufficient). As well as the pleasures of sun and surf, favourite activities include birdspotting on Pea Island National Wildlife Refuge at the northern tip of Hatteras Island, and stalking wild ponies on Ocracoke Island. There are official camp sites on both islands (reserve in advance at the Whalebone Junction Information Centre, Bodie Island). While it may not be possible for the authorities to enforce the rule against sleeping on the beaches, the night time beach-buggy races across the dunes may make you think twice.

Both the Gulf and the ocean coasts are dotted with resorts. The Mississippi coast has been much developed taking advantage of miles of sandy beaches, and offers a full range of resort facilities to suit all budgets. Between May and September you can take a boat from Biloxi or Gulfport to Ship Island, 12 miles offshore, first landfall of French explorers at the beginning of the 18th century.

There are also many state parks in South Carolina as well, including Edisto Beach Park and Hunting Island State Park. The flora and fauna of South Carolina are particularly interesting and exotic, including scarlet cardinals, egrets and flowering magnolia trees.

Calendar of Events

January 8	**Battle of New Orleans Day (Louisiana only)**
January 19	**Robert E. Lee's Birthday**
late February/early March	Mardi Gras Festival, New Orleans
March	Pilgrimage, Natchez Mississippi
late March/April	Spring Fiesta, New Orleans
April	Arkansas Folk Festival, Mountain View
May (first Saturday)	Kentucky Derby
June (first Monday)	**Confederate Memorial Day**
July	Blessing of the Shrimp Fleet, Bayou la Batre, Alabama
early August (even-numbered years)	National Black Arts Festival, Atlanta
mid-August	Elvis Presley International Tribute Week, Memphis
September	Delta Blues Festival, Greenville, Mississippi
October	Pilgrimage, Natchez Mississippi
October	National Peanut Festival, Dothan, Alabama

Public holidays are shown in **bold**

Texas

Cattle and Oil

You can't deny that Texas is big. Until the admission of Alaska to the Union, it was by far the USA's largest state. Texas is bigger than France, Belgium, Holland and Switzerland combined. Not only is its area immense but the buildings and companies and wealth it contains are enormous also. Despite the economic downturn caused by the fall in oil prices, the continually expanding number of gleaming skyscrapers in Dallas and Houston testifies to the State's unbridled optimism and prosperity.

It is worth stressing the size of Texas because it explains a lot about the state. It is what gives Texas its enormous variety of landscape, weather, flora and fauna, cuisine, sport, art and outdoor activities. More importantly, the immense area gives Texans a different sense of distance and space which in turn shapes their personalities. It explains a Texan's restlessness, pride, adventurousness, melancholy and hospitality. It would not be at all unusual for Texans to set off on the spur of the moment to visit a place 150 miles away, and then, if it happened to be in a dry county, drive a further 100 miles to slake their thirsts. They would drive the distance between London and Edinburgh on a whim.

Texas wasn't always a place where the inhabitants could take comfort and security for granted. Five flags have flown over Texas. The first was that of Spain, carried there by the Conquistadores. The second was that of Mexico, from whom Texas won its independence in 1836 at the decisive Battle of San Jacinto, a battle that followed three weeks on the heel of the Amercans' defeat at the Alamo.

Texas remained an independent republic until 1845 when it became the 28th state in the Union and the Stars and Stripes was raised. Fifteen years later, Texas and other southern states sided with Confederacy in the Civil

244

War, and the Confederate Flag flew throughout the state. When the Union triumphed, the Stars and Stripes was again hoisted.

After a brief bitter period of reconstruction, Texas began to prosper by raising herds of Longhorn cattle to provide beef for the growing nation's westward expansion. By the turn of the century, oil production was underway and it soon became apparent that Texas sat on top of immense reservoirs of oil. Texas now provides over one third of the USA's oil needs and is home for much of the country's technologically-based industry. In addition to its extensive mineral wealth it is the second largest agricultural producer after California.

CLIMATE

Unless you can cope with really hot weather — 85°-100°F (29°-38°C) — avoid Texas during July and August. It is not unusual for one out of every three days to be over 100°F/38°C. The high humidity especially in Houston is enervating and produces what the natives call "Gulf weather". They escape it by resorting to a network of carpeted underground tunnels downtown. The city's annual air-conditioning bill is $700,000.000.

Winters are usually mild — 45°-65°F (7°-18°C) — but there can be sudden drops in temperature to below freezing, and ice storms in December and January are not unknown, though, mercifully, of short duration. The best times to visit are March to May and mid-September to mid-November. Because the extremes of Texas' weather are compensated for by chilling air-conditioning during heat spells or excessive heating during cold snaps, light to medium weight clothing should see you through without pneumonia or heat prostration. For weather information, dial 654-0116 in Dallas, 228-8703 in Houston.

In a state so big, there is obviously a lack of uniformity in the climatic conditions. Partly due to the wide range of elevation from sea level to 8,000 ft, the rainfall varies from 10 to 55 inches per year, and the vegetation varies accordingly from desert shrub to thick forest.

THE NATIVES

Texas has a population of 15 million. Nearly every ethnic group found in the USA exists in Texas: Anglos (i.e. whites) make up 66%, Hispanics 21%; blacks 12%. The population growth was once the fastest in the nation. This was once due largely to a massive migration from the northern United States to the "Sun Belt", which is now showing signs of diminishing as the economic boom levels off. But during the heyday major companies such as Caltex and American Airlines relocated from New York to Dallas, in search of what they perceived to be a better business climate which discouraged trade union membership and consequent high wages.

Texans are predictably friendly to tourists, if only because it gives them a new audience for boasting about their state and a chance to do some leg-pulling, at which they excel. Beware when they start to tell you the recipe for chilli armadillo on the half shell or that the one-legged crane is the state bird (they mean the building crane). Knowledge of Europe is often comically limited, but they love talking about themselves. You might learn more than you want to about embryo implants in Santa Gertrudis cows, but after enough ice cold beers even talk of a cherished collection of 100 varieties of barbed wire can become interesting.

Although tourists are welcomed, not all outsiders are gathered to the

Texan bosom. for example the influx of unemployed Northerners willing to work for less than the going wage were (and are) resented, and the "sight of a Yankee in a one-way U-Haul" (a small do-it-yourself moving van) has become a Texan's pet hate. In fact many of those migrating families soon became disillusioned and there is now a stream of U-Hauls going in the reverse direction.

Texans can be even more hostile to each other than to outsiders. Houston has the title of Nation's Number Two Murder Capital (after Miami). Most homicides take place in the ghettos and arise out of domestic quarrels. It has been said that Texans, used to lots of breathing space, get very touchy when crowded together. A further sign of not-so-neighbourly behaviour is the sight of countless pick-up trucks with hunting rifles and shotguns in full view on gun racks mounted behind the driver. Hand guns can be bought for a $49 down payment and $5 a week for a month, or purchased mail order from a catalogue. Texans are the chief exponents of the citizen's right to bear arms. So avoid the rough neighbourhooods in big cities whenever possible, and avoid quarrels with strangers and motorists.

Religion. Texas is a very conservative place. Although many of the newly arrived Northerners spend their weekends worshipping nature or Mamon, Texans are still church-goers. Profanity in front of (or by) females is frowned upon, not to mention kinkiness and pornography. Baptists have the larest religious following, with two million members, followed by Roman Catholics, Methodists and numerous others. The world's largest Methodist, Baptist and Presbyterian churches are all in Dallas.

Texans are very work oriented. It's common for a person to work part-time or nights, in addition to holding down a regular job: truckers will also drive school buses; law enforcement officers do hotel security work. For many public sector workers, retirement means collecting a pension and starting a new career. You continually meet Texans who have a small business venture on the side: a stall at a flea market; a "piece of the action" in a bar or restaurant; a mail order deal; or a few video machines sited at a local country club. College students work during their three-month summer vacantion at amusement parks or children's camps and also part-time during term. Texas has a competitive, non-union work market and unemployment is now less than 5% and falling.

Making friends. Despite all this, it is not difficult to make friends with the locals. There are plenty of singles bars, discos, dance halls, night clubs and student lounges, especially near the various campuses of the University of Texas. Colleges with a religious affiliation like Southern Methodist University (SMU), Baylor, Rice of Texan Christian University tend to be very staid. But outside therse places most Texans have an earthy, if not particularly sophisticated, interest in heterosexual sex.

The biggest gay community is in Houston, where it numbers around 250,000, but a frightening number of Texans are fiercely anti-gay. The spread of AIDS has increased their influence, and verbal or physical abuse of homosexuals is becoming more common. Discretion is advised.

ARRIVAL AND DEPARTURE

Air. Flying, particularly between Dallas, Houston and San Antonio, can be the cheapest method of transport between cities more than 200 miles apart. Keep an eye on newspaper advertisements for truly silly deals when hostilities break out between competing airline companies. The current fare has crept up but is still only around 12c a mile for the 214-mile trip.

Bus Greyhound-Trailways has eight buses a day from Dallas to Houston and vice versa; the fastest takes 4¼ hours and the one way fare is around $24.

Train. There are only two lines in Texas: from San Antonio north to Dallas and beyond, and the southern transcontinental route from Houston to El Paso through San Antonio. The *Eagle* train from Chicago to Los Angeles passes through Dallas, Austin and San Antonio on Monday, Wednesday and Saturday; in the reverse direction Tuesday, Friday and Sunday. The route across the south of the state collects passengers at Houston on Monday, Wednesday and Saturday evenings and deposits them in El Paso the following afternoon. The train in the opposite direction arrives in El Paso from Los Angeles on Monday, Thursday and Saturday afternoons, and arrives in Houston 18 hours later. San Antonio-Dallas costs around $40 one way; San Antonio-Houston about $30.

Driving. Despite the long distances between cities, Texan drivers usually observe the national speed limit of 55 mph. A few miles (up to five) over the limit is usually all right, but Texas police do enforce the laws. It is worth keeping an eye out for the speed trap cops concealed behind low ridges. Seat belts are compulsory for drivers and front seat passengers; the penalty for non-compliance is a fine of $50.

Freeways link the major cities, while rural areas are served by "farm-to-Market" (FM) and "Ranch-to-market"(RM) roads; sometimes these are little more than dirt tracks.

Hitch-Hiking. Most Texans don't understand it; "If you can't afford a car, why aren't you home working so you can buy one instead of sweating by the side of the road like a hobo?" In a state where the car is a traditional high school graduation present and the murder rate is among the highest in the nation, a lack of sympathy for hitch-hikers is understandable. Hanging around the market, meat-packing areas or truckers' gas stations of larger Texas cities like Dallas, Houston, San Antonio or El Paso could turn up a lift with a truck driver who owns his own vehicle and wants some company.

Cycling. In the same two words, forget it. Just contemplate those vast distances on inhospitable roads under a fierce sun. Cycle rentals are available in cities for recreational cycling. It could, though, be dangerous as Texans are just not used to sharing roads with cyclists. The determined cyclist might like to get hold of the free *Texas 'Lone Star Bicycle Route'* from the Texas Cycling Committee, c/o John Gaynor, 711 West 32nd, Room 133, Austin TX 78705.

Eating and Drinking

Food is cheaper in Texas than in most states. Lower restaurant prices reflect both cheaper labour and cheaper agricultural produce. The most economical way to eat is to buy your food at a supermarket. There will be at least one open 24 hours a day, seven days a week, in every major Texas city. Because of the increase in the number of single people and childless couples, it is possible to buy single items of fruit, chops, etc.

There are two kinds of cuisine at which Texas excels — Tex-Mex and barbecue. Tex-Mex food is described in detail in the introductory chapter on *Eating*. Highly recommended is the take-away food to be found each Sunday at the "Tortilla Factory" in every Texan town with a large Hispanic population. Low-priced delicacies include maize and flour *tortillas* (sold in multiples of 10); *menudo*, a tasty tripe stew; *barbecao*, the Mexican barbecue which is closer to a pot-roast than meat broiled over-coals or logs; home-made *tostados* (vastly superior to the packaged brands found in shops and supermarkets) and *salsa verde*.

The second cuisine of Texas is the barbecue. Nowhere in the USA is there tastier barbecue. Every Texan has his favourite establishment, and taste does vary from place to place according to the type of logs over which the barbecue is cooked, cuts of meat, and most importantly, the quality of the barbecue sauce. Try a combination plate of beef, pork and rings of sausage which go by the name of "hot links" on the menu. You may wish to avoid the sexist barbecue restaurant in the town of Cut 'n Shoot in eastern Texas, where a sign reads "Men — no shirt, no service. Women—no shirt, no charge"; the proprietor gives away beef sandwiches to topless customers.

DRINKING

The sale of alcohol is against the law in 76 of Texas' 254 counties, and only beer and wine can be bought in 14 others. Take-away liquor can be obtained only in state-licensed "package stores" from 10am to 9pm, except on Sunday. Beer and wine can be bought in package stores, supermarkets and food shops, between 7am and midnight, except on Sundays, when the sale of beer and wine begins at noon.

Licensed restaurants, bars, taverns and nightclubs in wet counties serve alcohol beverages seven days a week until losing time. However, all sale of alcohol must cease by 2am throughout the state.

It's not illegal to have an opened bottle of liquor, beer or wine in your car while driving. As a matter of fact, it's not illegal to drink while driving. Only being drunk while driving is an offence.

Crime and Safety

Perhaps the hot climate is to blame for the high crime rate across the southern states (especially Texas) but the fact remains that travelling in the southern US is more dangerous than it is in southern England or southern Canada. Be especially mindful of the advice given in the introductory chapters about exercising caution with fellow motorists and policemen. The person you find yourself confronting in anger may be one of the trigger-happy minority. Although you won't be shot for speeding, you should be aware that any traffic violations are likely to be noticed by the police.

Drugs. Drugs are not difficult to obtain in the big cities. Marijuana, smuggled by private planes and ships from Latin America, is the most frequently used drug with cocaine popoular among the young affluent set. Heroin is almost completely restricted to ghetto areas. Although a fine is the most usual punishment for marijuana, jail sentences for anything stronger are by no means rare.

Sleeping Rough. Don't sleep rough. Besides waking up even poorer than you were when you went to sleep with clothes and shoes you could be courting trouble in a state that enforces its stringent vagrancy laws.

DALLAS

THE NATIVES

The most striking feature of Dallas and Dallasites is their concern for wealth. It sometimes seems that the city exists solely for business, and caters only for success. The average age in "Big D" is 28. The city proper has a population of 950,000, the metropolitan area 3,000,000. A highly visible element of the population is the "singles" set: extroverted, obsessed with the body-beautiful, rather amoral with a widespread acceptance of computer-dating and one-night stands. Many of these thrusting young Dallas residents live in the pristine desirable suburbs, which line the airport road, shop in the smart shopping malls and work in gleaming towers.

Check the Classified Section of the free *Dallas Observer* to get an idea of what relationships can be formed. There is a prominent gay community to be found mainly in the Oak Lawn area (its gay bars are nearby on Cedar Street). The gay community is active in "neighbourhood watchdog committees", though the AIDS era has severely tarnished their image. Many restaurants and hotels discriminate against them in matters of employment.

Making Friends. It might be worth visiting the campus of the University of Dallas (3113 University Avenue) or the Southern Methodist University (University Park) to meet the outgoing students and check the notice boards for rides and items for sale.

ARRIVAL AND DEPARTURE

Air. Dallas/Fort Worth International Airport (DFW; 574-6720) lies 17 miles west of Dallas, midway between the two cities. The size of Manhattan, it's the largest airport in the world. By bus, take the Surtran airport bus (for schedule information, telephone 574-2142), operating a service every half hour between 6 am and 11 pm to dowtown Dallas and luxury hotels on the way on a journey taking 35 minutes and costing $10. The taxi ride will be expensive, at least $30 to downtown Dallas, but ride-sharing could halve this (telephone Yellow Cab 426-6262).

Love Field Airport (DAL; 670 6073), seven miles from downtown Dallas, is for domestic flights. (Don't get the two airports mixed up as the character in a Hank Wangford song did, "I waited for you at DFW but you must have been in Love"). The frequent flights to other Texan cities are competitively priced, e.g. the forty minute flight to Houston 250 miles away costs about $35 one way. By bus, take Transit Bus 38, 70c to downtown Dallas, running every half hour from 5.30 am to 10.30 pm. Surtran also runs a service for $5. If you want to rent a car, check with Jartan Truck Rental near the airport on 3704 Maple Avenue (526-8496) who rent used cars, free mileage up to 50 miles per day, $18 per day (for a minimum of three days) or $89 per week.

As well as cheap flights to US destinations, Dallas has bargains to Latin America and Europe. Try Council Travel at Suite 101, 3300 W Mockingbird (350-6166).

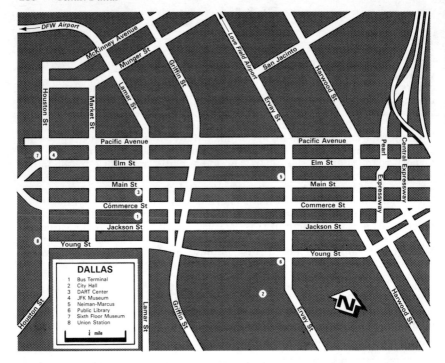

DALLAS

1 Bus Terminal
2 City Hall
3 DART Center
4 JFK Museum
5 Neiman-Marcus
6 Public Library
7 Sixth Floor Museum
8 Union Station

¼ mile

Bus. Greyhound services operate from 205 S Lamar St (741-1481).

Train. Union Station is a well restored terminal, full of shops and restaurants, on Houston St at Young St (653-1101).

CITY TRANSPORT

The downtown area is suprisingly small, and is negotiable by foot, On the Dallas Area Rapid Transit (DART) System (979 1111) bus rides cost 70c to $1.50 (exact change required) depending on the length of ride. Buses are air-conditioned. The Customer Assistance Center, 1501 Main Street, Dallas is open weekdays from 7am to 6pm. Citywide service is available from 5.30am to 11pm. The staff are helpful in person and on the phone. Discount passes are available, as are easy-to-read bus route maps.

Texas Bus Lines services between Dallas and Fort Worth cost about $4 and take about an hour.

Accommodation

There is virtually no reasonably priced accommodation in the city centre, no youth hostels or Y. There are Y's however in Fort Worth, 34 miles east (YMCA: 512 Lamar Street, 332-3281 and the

YWCA: 512 4th St). An outfit called Bed and Breakfast Texas Style (298-5433) can arrange rooms in a private house for about $20 a night. Motels ring the city but are inaccessible without a car. Every other year when football teams of the University of Texas and the University of Oklahoma meet at Texas Stadium in Dallas, hotel rooms in the city are as rare as free drinks at a Temperance lecture. If you are a militant non-smoker you might enjoy staying at the Non-Smoker's Inn near the Texas Stadium, where residents who smoke in their rooms are fined $100.

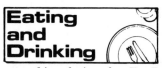

Eating and Drinking

Because Dallas is on the whole full of wealthy residents and visiting businessmen, restaurant food tends to be expensive. Try to stick with Tex-Mex served in ethnic cafes. Try Pepe's (3011 Routh at Cedar Springs) or Rosita's (4906 Maple Avenue) which serves a hearty Tex-Mex breakfast. If you want to sample inland seafood at a reasonable price try S & D Oyster House (2710 McKinney) where you can have seafood gumbo (gumbo is a soup or stew), fried shrimp and raw oysters. To purchase your own natural food groceries try H & M Natural Food Store (2106 Lower Greenville).

Although beer is the most popular drink throughout Texas, there are outdoor wine tastings for $2 at the Winery (2404 Cedar Springs) on Sunday evenings during the summer. The drinking laws in Dallas are convoluted, since some parts of the metropolitan area are designated "dry" (which means drinking is only possible in private clubs). Even in "wet" areas, no strong liquor is sold on Sundays. Licensing hours are liberal, however, and run from 7am (noon on Sundays) to midnight or 2am.

Entertainment

Consult the *Times Herald* and *Morning News* for city entertainment listings. Note that Friday is the weekend edition. Both papers, but especially the *Times Herald*, give extensive coverage to local and area attractions, forthcoming and past. See also *D*, a monthly magazine on Dallas. Phone Artsline, operating 24 hours a day, for theatre, music, museum events and free public performances (522 2659).

The John F. Kennedy Museum (501 Elm Street, 742-8582) is near the "grassy knoll" where JFK was killed on November 22, 1963. The building nearby was formerly the Texas School Book Depository where Lee Harvey Oswald hid before the assassination. It is now the Dallas County Administration Building, and 25 years after the President's murder, a small museum was opened on the sixth floor from where the fatal shot was fired.

Go on, go out to Southfork Ranch, home of the Ewings in TV's Dallas. The ranch ceased to be a private residence in September 1984 and has been turned into a hotel and entertainment complex (442-6536). If you can't afford to stay there, take a snapshot of yourself and companion standing by the gate. (Everybody should behave like a tourist once). Souvenirs include a tiny barrel of real Southfork crude oil and plots of land on the ranch itself (one square inch for $10). Take US 75 north out of Dallas, until exit 30, then follow the Parker Road five miles east to FM 2551. While in the city, be sure to notice the First National Bank skyscraper which serves as the head office of Ewing Oil on the TV *Dallas*.

Museums and Galleries. The new Museum of Art (1717 North Harwood, 922-0220) is the first building in a planned huge arts complex in downtown Dallas that will eventually include a Symphony Hall, promenade, outdoor restaurants, cafes and art galleries. The museum boasts a fine modern collection and excellent pre-Columbian art.

City Hall (749-4321) on the east corner of Young Street and Ervay Street is a striking building designed by I. M. Pei; the plaza has an enormous Henry Moore sculpture. Free tours take place daily at 2pm.

Music. Classical music concerts are given at the Southern Methodist University (SMU) Caruth Auditorium (692-3680). The Festival in the Park, held from April to June, includes symphony concerts, opera and ballet, free performances on summer weekends and holidays in the city's park.

Theatre. Drop into the W. A. Criswell First Baptist Church (on Ervay and San Jacinto) run by the Reverend A. Criswell, who broadcasts every Sunday morning at 10.30. It's a revelation. For theatre of a more traditional kind, visit the Dallas Theater Center, 3636 Turtle Creek Boulevard (526-8857). Daily tours of the theatre, designed by Frank Lloyd Wright, are available, There are also interesting experimental productions a 15-minute stroll away Theater Three in the Quadrangle 871-3300 July and August sees free Shakespeare in the park (954 0199).

Nightlife. For night-life, try the jazz bar Strictly Tabu (4111 Lomo Alton) which serves excellent pizza, the Tango Disco (1827 Lower Greenville) and for country and western music, which is so popular in Texas, the Longhorn Ballroom (216 Corinth). Greenville Avenue is the current rage of the "singles set". Lower Greenville caters for younger, more budget-minded people while Upper Greenville is for those people with expense accounts.

SPORT

Dallas boasts top collegiate and professional sport: football by the Dallas Cowboys (556-2500) who play at Texas Stadium in Irving (between Dallas and Fort Worth) baseball by the Texas Rangers, (273-5100), soccer by the Dallas Sidekicks (760-7330), basketball by the Dallas Mavericks (658-7068) etc. There's also pro hockey, world class tennis and top track and field. Consult your local paper for events. For thoses who want something different, head for the Rodeo Kowbell in Mansfield halfway between Dallas and Fort Worth. Rodeo is performed every Saturday night year round (477-3092).

Parks and Zoos. A water recreation park called White Water (264-6211) offers a giant "wave pool" and a terrifying water slide, for which you will need a swimming costume. the admission is expensive (about $12, reduced after 6pm), but it is easy to find on I-30 at Belt Line between Forth Worth and Dallas.

SHOPPING

Going shopping is unlikely to be a problem in a city which has no fewer than 630 shopping centres. The most famous department store is Neiman-Marcus (Main and Ervay) which carries such items as an exercise bicycle with a video screen showing scenes of the Grand Canyon or New York's Central Park. Every year their catalogue includes something for the couple who has everthing, from evening capes made from Russian lynx bellies to a live ostrich.

Bargain shops for second-hand clothes include the Salvation Army Store, on Inwood Avenue. It is open 9am to 5pm and sells off its daily intake of unsold stock from major downtown stores. Also try Linda's Surplus (4323 Maple Avenue) which has inexpensive trendy casual wear for men and women.

There is a Farmers Market (1010 South Pearl, 748-8582) selling fruits and vegetables in season brought in pick-up trucks by "old boy" Texans from East Texas farms. It starts at 6am daily. About $4 should feed two people for a day.

THE MEDIA

There are no fewer than 16 AM and 21 FM radio stations plus numerous TV channels in Dallas, so spin the dial until you find something congenial. Note however that a dozen of the radio stations are Christian. There is a Broadcast Museum for the state on 1701 N market St with displays of early radio studios, famous old programmes etc.

The two principal newspapers are the *Morning News* and the *Times Herald* which has afternoon and evening editions. If you want to get a free Sunday newspaper (normally $1) buy a large cup of coffee to take away for 99c from any of the shops in the 7-11 chain.

The Reading Room in the public Library (west corner of Young Street and Ervay Street, opposite City Hall) carries newspapers from abroad including the *Times*.

Help and Information *i*

The area code for Dallas is 214.

Information: Dallas Convention & Visitors Bureau, 1201 Elm St, Suite 2000 (746-6702). There are Visitors Centers at Union Station and Love Field airport.
British Consulate: 813 Stemmons Tower West, 2730 Stemmons Freeway (637-3600).
American Express: Renaissance Tower, 1201 Elm St (748-8606).
Thomas Cook: 1801 Commerce St (747-1563).
Medical Emergencies: Baylor University Medical Center, 3500 Gaston Avenue (820-2501).
Pharmacy: Rexall Drugs, 4101 Bryan St (824-4539); Eckhard Drugs, 2320 West Illnois Avenue (331-5466). Both open 24 hours.
Handicapped Visitors: Access Dallas, 4300 Beltway (934-9104).
Suicide Prevention: 828-1000.
Post Office: 400 N Ervay St (760-7200).
Telegrams (Western Union): 747-8821.

HOUSTON

THE NATIVES

You won't be in town for long before someone informs you that the first word spoken on the Moon was "Houston". The natives are proud of the city's associations with NASA, high technology and the Texas Medical Center, although few boast about the appalling crime statistics. Houston is the fourth largest city in the USA with a population of over 3,000,000 whose average age is 29. An industrial-business complex, it's the most cosmopolitan city in the Sun-Belt with 57 foreign consulates. Huge peacock-coloured mirror-glass buildings give Houston a "Space City" look and provide a vivid contrast to its rougher districts with their massage parlours and sleazy clubs featuring "coach-dancing" (of which, as Louis Armstrong said, "If ya gotta ask what that is, you nevah gets to know, because no one gonna explain it to you.").

There's a lot of *nouveaux riches* in Houston with a pretention to artistic interests, and the city buys up art for its museums, orchestras and conductors for its symphony, etc. with breath-taking abandon.

As one might expect in a high-technology town, there are plenty of northerners educated at top engineering, business and law schools who have flocked to Houston. Aggressively on the make for power, wealth and status, they lack the provincialism found in cities like Dallas and San Antionio. They also strike visitors as more interested and more ionformed about what's going on in the world outside.

If you want to get to know a Houston family, contact Americans-at-Home (223-5454), a voluntary organization which arranges visits with friendly locals.

Getting Around

ARRIVAL AND DEPARTURE

Air. Coming directly from abroad, you will arrive at Houston Intercontinental Airport (230-3000), 20 miles north of downtown. The Airport Express bus (523-8888) goes into the city centre every half hour from 6am to 10.30pm (cost $7.50). For a cheaper and slower ride into town, follow the signs for "Economy City Busses" *(sic)*. The same ride by taxi will set you back $40 plus tip. Beware of the "Solicitation" desk at the airport: charities take turns to use the desk to ask for money for various causes, and the staff seem to be on a percentage of takings judging by their persistence in hounding hapless travellers.

A more "user-friendly" domestic airport is Hobby (635-6597) only nine miles south-east of downtown. You should confirm which airport you will be using as some airlines use both and it is routine on a foggy winter's day for domestic flights to be diverted from one airport to the other. The limo service into town costs $5 (644-8359) and serves the Downtown Terminal at the Hyatt Regency on Polk St. A taxi costs around $15.

Bus. The Greyhound-Trailways terminal is at 1410 Texas Avenue (222-1161).

Train. Amtrak offices are located at 902 Washington (224-1577). Union Station is on Jackson St at Prairie. Houston is on the line between New Orleans and Los Angeles.

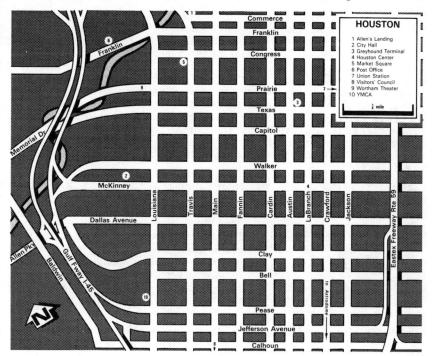

Driving. More rental cars will be available at the airports than downtown, though many of these will be pre-booked. An economical choice is Thrifty Rent-a-Car (449-0126 at Intercontinental and 644-3351 at Hobby). Another is Rent-a-Heap Cheap at 5722 Southwest Freeway (977-7771). It provides used cars from $11.50-19.95 with 50 miles free, then 12c per mile.

Houston is notoriously difficult for motorists, who find that along with the heavy traffic on the freeway loop system, the exit numbers and even the names on signs do not correspond with their maps. For instance, I-45 at the approach to Houston is called the "Dallas" or "North" Freeway; south of Houston I-45 changes to the "Gulf Freeway". I-10 east of the city centre is called "East Freeway"; west it becomes "Katy Freeway". I-610 is the "Loop" which encircles the city about six miles out; the direction of the road in relation to the city centre is added to the direction you are driving in, thus "North Loop East". The Beltways (Texas Route 8) provide another orbital route, about twelve miles out from downtown. For road conditions dial 681-6187.

Ride-sharing possibilities are good at the end of term times (Christmas, Easter, late June) if you want to leave Houston. Check the notice boards at the central campus of the University of Houston (4800 Calhoun St) or Rice University (6100 Main St).

CITY TRANSPORT

People who naively think it might be nice to "walk downtown" from the suburbs are likely to get picked up for "suspicious behaviour" — or for their own protection. Within the downtown area, much of your walking is likely to be underground on the four-mile network of subterranean sidewalks connecting shops, offices and hotels. For an interesting above-ground walk, try the Walking Tour organised by the Greater Houston Preservation Alliance (861-6263) on the third Wednesday of every month.

Houston Transit System, known as "Metro Buses", is based at 403 Louisiana (635-4000). There is a "Shopper's Bus" system which allows you to get around the downtown area for only 20c. Other services, alas, are infrequent and the routes in the sprawling metropolis inadequate. Fares are 60c assuming you can locate a bus: exact change required. If you don't have a car, you may have to resort to taxis. These are among the most expensive in America, costing $2.45 for the first mile then $1.05 for each subsequent mile. To call a cab, dial Liberty on 695-6700 or United on 699-0000.

Cycling. You can get a pamphlet from the Parks and Recreation Department (PO Box 1562, Houston, TX 77001) called *Houston Hike & Bikeways.*

Hotels and Motels. As in Dallas, most of the downtown area is brand new, leaving no room for older budget hotels. Try Fannin Street which is about four blocks west of the Greyhound terminal. The cheaper motels are on the western fringes of town. Alternatively, head out of town towards Galveston Bay for cheaper accommodation.

Hostels. The Houston Downtown Y, 1600 Louisiana St (659-8501) charges about $25 a night (plus 7% tax), but is for men only. There is no YWCA. There is a clean and friendly youth hostel at 5302 Crawford St (523-1009). Reservations are recommended. The University of Houston College Center, 101 Main (225-1781) charges $40 a night and is near Allens Landing, an up-and-coming area.

Bed and Breakfast. The B & B Society of Texas, based at Sarah's Bed and Breakfast Inn at 941 Heights Boulevard (868-1130) has rooms at 24 Houston homes costing from $35 double; Sarah's Inn itself costs $50 double.

Eating and Drinking

The Luling City Market (4726 Richmond) near the Galleria Shopping Center has a reputation for the best barbeque in the city, but isn't cheap. A better bargain is the Cortez Delicatessen (2404 West Alabama near River Oaks) which has cheap Mex-Tex Food, large portions, lunch counter style; try the *menudo.* Glatzmaler's Seafood (809 Congress Avenue) downtown on Market Square serves a Texas equivalent of fresh fish and chips in a cafeteria style. It's good value, and always crowded. Then there's Otto Barbeque at 5502 Memorial Drive. A plate of beef is about $4.25. Houston's small Chinatown is around the junction of McKinney and St Emanuel, and is worth a visit for the experience of Chinese cuisine meeting Tex-Mex head on. Quan Tam Luncheonette (1117 Bell) is one of the several cheap Vietnamese eateries that have sprung up and cater mainly for lunchtime office workers. If you're worried about your diet, you can Dial-a-Dietician (827-2458).

Anheuser-Busch runs free tours of its brewery at 775 Gellhorn; call 670-1695 for bookings.

Entertainment

For current offerings by the Houston Symphony Orchestra, ballet, opera and theatre, phone 227-ARTS or get a free *Performing Arts Calendar* available from the Greater Houston Convention and Visitors Center; or write to Arts for Everyone Inc, 1950 West Gray, Houston, TX 77019 (522-3744 for ticket information). The Wortham Theatre Center (near the river at Smith and Prairie Streets) is worth a visit even if you don't see a show there, since the scale and elegance are impressive. The Center is home to the Houston Ballet (523-6300) and Grand Opera (546-0200), whose seasons run from late September to early June.

The International Festival in March attracts a good range of drama, music and dance companies; call 654-8808. You can see some new movies during the International Film Festival in April (965-9955), while the venue for the Jazz Festival in August is the Miller Outdoor Theatre in Hermann Park (528-6740).

Take the Harbor Cruise Excursion of the nation's third largest port aboard the *Sam Houston* at Gate 8 of the port, Clifton Drive (225-0671). It's free, but advance reservations are sometimes necessary, so write to the Port of Houston, PO Box 2562, Houston, TX 77001.

To many the US space programme is synonymous with Houston. The Lyndon B. Johnson Space Center (NASA), 25 miles south by the I-45 (483-0123), is open daily and the Visitor Orientation Center features splendid displays of spacecraft, lunar rocks and space-shuttle training. In addition, free guided tours are available by advance arrangement to Mission Control Center and the Space Simulation Lab (483-4321). If you can't get advance reservations for the day you want, arrive there before noon and queue up at the Tour Reservations Desk where cancellations (usually considerable) are given out on a first-come-first-served basis.

You can also visit parts of the huge Texas Medical Center, southwest of downtown: go to the Assistance Center at the corner of Bertner and Holcome Streets (790-9505) for a tour, which normally starts at 10am on weekdays.

Museums and Galleries. The Contemporary Arts Museum on the corner of Montrose and Bissonnet (526-3129) is open Tuesday-Saturday from 10am to 5pm, Sundays noon-6pm, and contains a fascinating collection of post-World War II American art. The museum shop has inexpensive and imaginative gifts and small toys. The Museum of Fine Art (526-1361), also on Bissonnet at number 1001 has works by Western artist Frederic Remmington, plus collections of Impressionists and European Old Masters that only money can buy. The museum lies in an attractive shady sculpture garden, and admission is free. A new museum, the Menil Collection at 515 Sul Ross (529 9400), displays Classical and modern art. It opens Wednesday-Sunday from 11am to 7pm.

Nightlife. World famous is Gilley's, on Houston's southeast perimeter in Pasadena (4500 Spencer Highway, 941 7193). The place is outsized, honky-tonk and tops for Western singers and bands. Listen to songs with titles such as "If You Want To Keep Your Beer Cold, Put it Next to My Ex-Wife's Heart." NRG at 901 North Shepherd Drive (863-0010) is bigger still, and has a 15,000-watt sound system. Rockefeller's (3620 Washington Avenue; 861-9365) is the best jazz club for name bands, but cover charges range from $10-$15. Cardi's (5901 Westheimer) specializes in folk/rock and is both cheap and friendly.

The Montrose area of town is a multi-racial, tolerant neighbourhood and has a large male gay community. Disco bars and wine bars come and go or change names, but Numbers (300 Westheimer) is a large, long established disco with a friendly atmosphere. Finally there is Escape (8670 South Gessner), a late night mixed crowd disco, open till 4am on weekends.

SPORT

Don't miss the Astrodome, home of the Houston Astros baseball team (799-9555) and the Oilers football team (797-1000). It is situated on the I-610 and Kirby Drive. With a capacity of 66,000 is it the world's largest enclosed stadium. There are daily guided tours that feature a dazzling display on their giant scoreboard; admission $5. It might well be worth putting the money towards a cheap ticket for a baseball or football game instead. For sports events, see *Day and Night* distributed by the Convention and Visitors Center (telephone 526-7220 for ticket information).

SHOPPING

The Galleria is a unique shopping experience. Located in the Magic Circle Area, Post Oak and Westheimer, it has luxury stores, restaurants, an Olympic-sized skating rink and even a medical clinic where for a mere $500 you can have a thorough health examination and receive your results the same day.

Downtown Houston has an underground weather-controlled shopping and dining area. Enter the Hyatt-Regency Hotel or at the large banks on the 800 to 1400 blocks of Main Street.

The best buys are to be found at Loehmanns Outlet Store, 7455 Southwest Freeway (777-0164). Also recommended is browsing through *The Underground Shopper-Houston* in any bookstore for specific details on bargain stores of every variety.

For unbeatable flea-market items, try the sidewalks of Montrose. To keep cool in this relaxed, slightly bohemian area, try a peach ice cream at Udder Delight (1521 Westheimer).

Crime and Safety

Houston ranks near the top in almost every category of crime on the FBI table, from car theft to murder. So be even more careful here than in other American city centres, especially after the workers go home to the suburbs and the streets are largely deserted. Strolling is not a safe activity. Many local women drive around with cowboy-hatted dummies strapped to the passenger seat, and the rich employ security guards.

Drugs. Illegal narcotics are not in short supply, but neither are members of the drug squad. Caution is suggested. Affluent Houston citizens may be able to afford a $500 fine plus legal expenses better than you.

Help and Information

The area code for Houston is 713.

Information: The Greater Houston Convention and Visitors Council, 3300S

Main (523-5959; toll-free 1-800-392-7722 within Texas, 1-800-231-799 from outside the State). The staff seem to be genuinely interested in helping visitors. They give out free maps, walking tours, a detailed calendar of events, etc.

British Consulate: Suite 2250, 601 Jefferson Avenue (659-6270).

Travellers' Aid: 2630 Westridge (668-0911) and 1410 Texas (223-8946); a desk in C terminal of the Intercontinental Airport is manned during office hours.

American Express: First West Building, 1307 Travis St (658-1114)

Post Office: 70 San Jacinto (227-1474)

Telegrams (Western Union): 224-1705.

Medical Emergencies: General Hospital, Ben Taub Loop (791-7300)

Pharmacy: Cunningham Pharmacy, 6033 Airline Drive (697-3261). Open 24 hours.

Gay Switchboard of Houston: 529-3211.

EL PASO — Population 500,000

El Paso's main business is the building and testing of nuclear missiles, including Cruise and Pershing. Obsolete models decorate many buildings including high schools and churches, as well as fulfil practical uses such as bases for goal posts, animal troughs and pot plants. Once a year there is a nuclear holocaust exercise, so try to schedule your visit accordingly. Fort Bliss, close to the airport, trains servicemen from the USA and allied nations to fire the weapons. Its museums (568-2121) show the contribution it makes to "peace and freedom".

An interesting aspect of El Paso is the preservation of North American Indian culture. Visit the Ysleta de Sur Pueblo Museum (869-7718), which traces the history of the Pueblo Indians, or the Tiquas Indian Reservation where you can see handicraft being made and eat Indian bread with Tiquas chillis.

Nearly two-thirds of El Paso's population is Hispanic, and there is a great deal of traffic across the Mexican border into the large town of Juarez. It costs 5c walk across the bridge over the Rio Grande and 10c to walk back. There is no need to bother with the Grayline Tour which is just for little old ladies.

El Paso and environs are on Mountain Time, one hour behind the rest of Texas.

AUSTIN — Population 345,000

The capital city, Austin, provides a liberal oasis in the midst of conservative Texas. It has a tradition of tolerance which has attracted artists, writers and artisans. You would not automatically be thought a lunatic here if you happen to be a hitch-hiker. Folk singers may be found in many of the bars, especially on Guadalupe Street. Visit the student-oriented area called 'The Drag' where you will find cinemas, book stalls and trendy clothing shops. The friendly relaxed atmosphere of Austin is enhanced by its extensive park system which provides relief from traffic, heat and noise. You might even be invited to join in an informal game of baseball.

Assuming you won't be in hot pursuit of memorabilia concerning Austin's 'favourite son', ex-President Lyndon Baines Johnson, you might be interested in the McDonald Observatory, located at Painter Hill and 24th Street. It is freely open to the public every Friday night after dusk. You can even do some homework by phoning 'Skywatcher Reporter' on 471-4478 for a two-minute recorded talk on what stars, planets and satellites are visible.

Austin is surrounded by hills, lakes and reservoirs which offer superb recreational and camping facilities.

SAN ANTONIO — Population 780,000

The further south you go, the stronger the Mexican influence becomes. If you are in the laid-back city of San Antonio you can watch Mexican folk dancing on summer evenings or attend the Mexican version of rodeo called *charreadas* at a local ranch. You must also pay a visit to the state shrine of Texas, the Alamo, where Davy Crockett and other heroes died trying vainly to fend off the much larger Mexican army in 1836. It opens daily from 9am to 5.30pm.

San Antonio is one of the few southern cities where it is not only feasible but safe to walk around. The distances between attractions are easily walkable though there is the El Centro bus around downtown (exact fare 40c). Join the relaxed parade of people on the River Walk and enjoy the sidewalk cafes and outdoor entertainment. There is also a colourful Mexican market, and the new Sea World of Texas just northwest of (tel: 512-225-4903) the city. The star is Shamu, a three-ton killer whale, who performs daily in a 4,500-seat stadium. To find out about the people who make Texas what it is, visit the Institute of Texan Cultures in the Hemisfair Plaza (home of the 1968 World's Fair). It opens daily except Mondays, 9am to 5 pm, and is free.

MEXICO

You may want to cross the Mexican border to shop in the markets, eat the food, see a bullfight or just to say you have been to Mexico.

Crossing the Border. If you are planning to cross the border, you will need a green tourist card for visits of 72 hours or more and a passport. If you intend to return to the US, make sure you have a multiple entry visa. Tourist cards are available at no charge from any Mexican consulate or in any major Texan border town such as Brownsville or Laredo (as well as El Paso). If you want to take your car over the border you will need Mexican insurance which is available from numerous travel agencies on the Texas side of the border. When returning to the USA you may bring back duty free $400 worth of purchases, a litre of alcohol and 200 cigarettes. A little known Texan law prohibits the import of alcohol in containers smaller than a half pint, thereby disqualifying miniatures.

The Great Outdoors

The National Parks and Wildlife Refuges are primarily meant to preserve nature, and are accordingly undeveloped. They are ideal for backpacking and primitive camping. Only three are dealt with here. A comprehensive guide to all the state parks of Texas, including points of interest, phone numbers for booking and camping regulations can be obtained free by writing to Texas Parks and Wildlife Department, 4200 Smith School Road, Austin, TX 78744 (512-479-4800 or from out of state, toll-free 1-800-792-1112).

In Big Bend National Park, you will find 700,000 acres of desert, remote canyons and mountains on the US/Mexican border. There are excellent hiking trails and free permits for overnight camping. Highly recommended is the South Rim Trail overlooking the Rio Grande (at dawn, you can hear the cocks crowing and donkeys braying across the river in Mexico). Riding and commercial raft trips are available as well as hiking. If you prefer, you can drive around the park on almost 200 miles of adequate roads, but check with Park Rangers first for information on possible rock slides. For details and literature, write to the Superintendent, Big Bend National Park, TX 79834 (915-477-2251). Well worth a detour from the park is a trip to nearby Terlingua which hosts the world famous "Chilli Cook-Off" in the late autumn.

The second major recreational area is the Padre Island National Seashore. Here visitors will find one of the nation's last unspoilt natural seashores with 80 miles of white sand, excellent surf casting, beachcombing, and numerous shore birds and animals to view. Highly recommended is the Grasslands Trail over the dunes. For details, and literature write: Superintendent, Padre Island National Seashore, 10235 South Padre Island Drive, Corpus Christi, TX 78418 (512-937-2621). Officials here have been known to waive the $2 camping fee.

The third national park worth visiting is the Guadalupe Mountains National Park. On the New Mexico/Texas border, this 78,000-acre park includes within its boundries Texas' four highest peaks, deep canyons and an extensive fossil reef. Some of its trails, though, are for experienced climbers only. Highly recommended is McKittrick Canyon with its spectacularly colourful foliage in late October. Camping is permitted only in some areas. For details and literature, either visit Frijole Information Station, Pine Springs, TX, or write Carlsbad Caverns National Park, 3225 National Parks Highways, Carlsbad, NM 88220 (915-828-3385). From the latter, you can also obtain information on nearby Carlsbad Caverns, famous for the unique flight of bats at sunset.

Camping. Texas also maintains over 90 state parks which preserve much of Texas' historical heritage as well as places of unique rugged beauty and natural phenomena. An annual entrance permit for unlimited visits to any park is $20 and 24-hour tickets can be purchased for $3 each. Camping is encouraged at most parks; RV (Recreation Vehicle, pronounced by the natives Vee-hickel) hook-ups are provided at $5 per day, and at some sites rustic cabins sleeping 4 to 8 people can be rented for as little as $20 a night; this is one of the best bargains Texas has to offer. However, you must book in advance and, in most instances, put up a deposit.

Camping is also allowed in Texas' four National Forests, plus some municipal parks offer RV hook-ups. For a free complete list of all campgrounds in the state, write to Texas Public Campgrounds, Travel and Information Division, State Department of Highways and Public Transportation, PO Box 5064, Austin TX 78763. And for a free map of privately-owned campgrounds, write to the Texas Association of Campground Operators, 1301 North Watson Road, Arlington, TX 76011.

Lovers of the great outdoors should also take advantage of Texas' small, well-landscaped roadside parks with tables, benches, shade trees and cooking grills. All you need is a bag of charcoal, "hamburger" meat (ground beef), hot dogs or steaks (about $2 a pound), halved tomatoes, *jalepenos,* corn on the cob (you grill it with husk on which acts as an oven and keeps in the juices!) and a bag of "Fritos" (corn crisps). Be warned that many of the roadside parks do not allow the consumption of alcoholic beverages. Many have drinking water, spotlessly clean rest rooms and "Infoboards" giving details about various attractions within easy reach.

Armed with a map, be adventurous and try an occasional detour. For instance, half way between Austin and San Antonio, take FM-306 towards Sattler some ten miles away. Here you can go "tubing" on the Guadelupe River. You will find places that will rent you inflated lorry inner tubes and then pick you up downstream when your ride is finished. Wear old tennis shoes to protect your feet and do not forget sunglasses and hat, and also a styrofoam cooler with beer which you tie to your tube.

Wildlife. In the south-west part of the state, there are herds of pronghorn antelope and mule deer, as well as coyotes, jack-rabbits and gophers. Some of the rarer animals, mountain lions and grey fox, can be found in the woodlands of the Big Bend region. Many of the more nocturnal animals, opossums, raccoons, and armadillos, are seen only as road casualties.

If you're a birdwatcher, bring a pair of binoculars. Three-quarters of all known American birds are represented in Texas at any time of the year, and the number increases during times of migration. Ivory-billed woodpeckers (once thought to be extinct) and bald eagles can be seen in East Texas, wild turkey in the Central Texas Hill Country and in the south-west, kites and fleet-footed roadrunners (immortalized in a famous American television cartoon). The world's few remaining whooping cranes winter on the coastline at the Arkansas National Wildlife Refuge.

Texas is the only state in which every variety of poisonous snake in North America can be found. Some places even have rattlesnake baiting contests, culminating in a rattlesnake roast.

Traces of long-extinct wildlife also remain in Texas as fossilized skeletons and footprints. Pre-historic Texas was covered by salt-water and lagoons, and so, for the same reason that Texas is rich in petroleum products, it has numerous superb fossil sites. Collectors have every chance of finding speciments of sought after minerals, topaz, petrified wood and fossils. Ask for a free copy of *Texas Rocks and Fossils* at any tourist bureau or the State Department of Highways and Public Transportation (address above). They will also provide free copies of *Flowers of Texas*. The Department of Highways and Public Transportation is a jewel in the crown of the state government; not long ago they had the brilliant idea of sowing wild flower seeds on highway "shoulders" which resulted in riots of colour in springtime.

Calendar of Events

January 19	Confederate Heroes' Day*
March 2	**Texas Independence Day**
March	Houston International Festival
April	Houston International Film Festival
May	Hot Air Balloon Festival, El Paso
July/August	Shakespeare Festival, Dallas
August	Blessing of the Shrimp Fleet, Galveston Bay
August	Houston Jazz Festival
August 27	Lyndon Baines Johnson's birthday*
September	Fiesta de las Flores, El Paso
late September/late October	Texas State Fair, Dallas

As well as the statewide holiday on March 2, some businesses close on the days marked above with an asterisk

Denver and the Rockies

Colorado Mountains

Colorado   Idaho   Montana   New Mexico   Utah   Wyoming

In the space of a few miles, you switch from the laser-straight roads of the Midwest to tortuous tracks winding between snowy peaks. Against the backdrop of the red foothills, caught between the prairie and the peaks, is Denver (city population 500,000), self-appointed capital of the Rocky Mountains. The Mile High City is so-called because it is 5,280 feet above sea level; to be more precise, the 13th step of Denver's Capitol Building is at that elevation. Your first impression of Denver will depend on whether you arrive from the east or west. From the endless plains of the Midwest, the city appears as a stirring introduction to the Rockies, but if you've travelled over the mountains, the relatively flat streets of Denver can be a welcome relief.

Some vestiges of the gold mining days remain: tackily restored Larimer Square, the house of Molly Brown (heroic Titanic survivor) and the grave of Buffalo Bill on nearby Lookout Mountain. But the log cabins and tents have been superceded by shiny skyscrapers and sprawling suburbs. Denver is now second only to Washington in terms of federal employees, and headquarters for many energy corporations. Even with this influx of men and money, sophistication is not a feature of Denver life. To compensate, the university town of Boulder, half an hour northwest among the foothills of the Front Range, acts as a civilised antidote to the rawness of Denver.

THE NATIVES

The population of Colorado in general and Denver in particular is very mixed: while bureaucrats, some descendants of the 19th century pioneers who tamed the country; a few Indians who survived the taming; Hispanics (about 20% of Denver's population), blacks (about 12%), and more recently Asian refugees. In 1983 Denver's first Chicano mayor, Frederico Pena, was elected.

In the last decade, there has been a huge influx of middle class immigrants from the northern states who viewed Colorado as a growth state. The state government has found it necessary to discourage new immigration; a Bouder city ordinance goes even further by restricting growth to 2% per year. The population of the metropolitan area (which included Boulder) is 1,650,000.

Making Friends. The leisure sections of local newspapers and magazines are full of listings of the clubs and singles bars frequented by the young and well-off. Most of the action occurs on Leetsdale Drive in Glendale. The Boulder, where over 25,000 students (out of a total population of 76,000) are waiting to be befriended.

The large gay population meets in the area to the south of Denver's Capitol Hill and frequents Cheeseman Park.

CLIMATE

Along with many aspects of day-to-day living, the weather is affected by the altitude. Although the altitude of Denver is lower than most of Colorado, the thinness of the atmosphere has some unexpected effects. For example, water boils at lower temperatures (i.e. about 95°C/200°F) which means that cooking takes longer; there is even a book called *The New High Altitude Cookbook* which tells you how to cope.

The effects on the body take some getting used to. Very young or old people are particularly prone to shortness of breath and faintness. Do not over-exert in the first few days. Smokers and drinkers should moderate their habits: smoking may leave you gasping for breath, and the effects of alcohol are exacerbated by the thin air.

As for the weather itself, there is little to fear. Denver makes the somewhat unilluminating claim that it is the "climate capital of the world". By this they mean it has more hours of sunshine than Florida and Texas, as any of the several hundred solar power companies based in Denver will hasten to tell you. Unfortunately it also has a pallid yellow smog which clings unpleasantly to the city due to temperature inversions caused by the proximity of the mountains. The internal combustion engine does not function as efficiently at high altitude and the by-products of petrol are enough to produce smog which rivals that of Los Angeles. Every weather forecast includes a smog report with ratings of "mild" to "dangerous". There is very little rain to wash the smog away.

The temperature varies from —25°C/—12°F to 38°C/100°F, but the dryness makes even the extremes bearable. From May to September it is usually warm, sunny and comfortable during the day, cooling noticeably towards evening.

However, clear summer skies sometimes give way to sudden and violent thunderstorms with dazzling displays of lightning and occasional flash floods. Autumn weather is unpredictable. Snow sometimes falls as early as September 1st, but during the autumn there are more warm days than there are crisp and cold ones. December to March is as extreme as winter in any other part of the USA. Heavy clothing, boots, gloves and a warm hat are essential. High up in the mountains, the weather is unpredicatable whatever season. Be prepared for any eventuality, and heed official

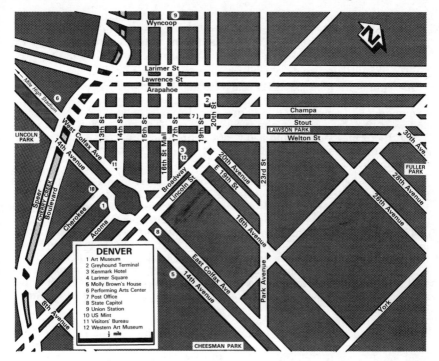

warnings. Denverites take snow conditions very seriously and after a snowfall of more than three inches, you can expect TV specials all evening about the heroic efforts of snow-clearing crews. For recorded weather information call 639-1212 (Denver only) or 639-1515 (state of Colorado).

ARRIVAL AND DEPARTURE

Air. Stapleton International Airport (DEN), is the eighth busiest airport in the world. Dial 1-800 - AIR 2 DEN for information. It lies within the city limits seven miles east-north-east of the city centre with a direct road link to I-70, making access easy. Buses 28, 32 and 38 cover the journey downtown in half an hour for $1.25. Bus AB runs direct to Boulder in about 70 minutes and costs aound $3. Taking a taxi to downtown Denver will set you back only $15 or so, a bargain compared with most airport journeys. The limousine service to the bus station and the major hotels costs $5. Go to lower level door 5 to catch a bus, taxi or limousine.

The international concourse is little used, so Denver is a very good place to clear customs and immigration (assuming your papers are in order). Despite the obscure law that prohibits the importation of alcohol from outside the state, luggage is not normally searched on internal flights. There are many cheap domestic flights available from Denver, as an important airline hub. Services to nearby resorts such as Aspen are very expensive; take the bus.

Bus. Greyhound (623-6111) operates from the bus terminal at 1055 19th St, at the junction with Arapahoe St. Rural bus services in the mountains can best be described as sparse and sporadic; in addition, their inability to negotiate the more interesting mountain roads may persuade you to try an alternative form of transport such as a four-wheel drive vehicle.

Train. Union Station (893-3911) is at 17th and Wynkoop Streets on the edge of the financial district. The northbound service to Cheyenne was recently suspended, and now there is only one line through Denver: east to Chicago, and west to Salt Lake City and the West Coast. The run to Salt Lake City, along the former Denver and Rio Grande Railroad line, is spectacular. One Amtrak through-train (the *Californian Zephyr*) runs each way daily: eastbound at 9.20 pm, westbound at 8.55 am.

Driving. Most of the rental agencies are on Colfax Avenue east and west of the city centre. Rent-a-Wreck is at the junction of Colorado Boulevard and West Colfac Avenue; Cheap Heaps is 16th Avenue at Colorado Boulevard (393-0028); and Compacts Only has a desk in the airport arrivals hall (388-0948). Some agencies hire out four-wheel-drive off-road vehicles for the mountains. I-25 and I-70 intersect just north of the city centre and provide fast, easily accessible routes for long distance traffic. Many other roads — including US 36 to Boulder — are fast dual carriageways. One road hazard best avoided is the stampede of young, rich inhabitants of Denver who clog the roads towards the mountains on Friday evenings, and return *en masse* late on Sundays.

Most mountain passes over 8,000 ft close completely during the winter, and driving is generally dangerous. Some, like Squaw Pass on Highway 103, are not far from Denver.The Colorado State Patrol provides information on road conditions and closures: call 639-1234 for Denver routes west, 639-1111 for I-25 and routes east. Always heed storm and blizzard warnings. During the summer forest fire season in the mountains, any vehicle using an unnumbered road must be equipped with a shovel, bucket and axe.

Ridesharing. Boulder has a well-used ride board in the University Memorial Center (UMC) on Euclid Avenue. Alternatively, call the Denver-based National Ride Center (837-9738) for lifts anywhere.

Hitch-Hiking. Hitch-hiking in the Rockies is a risky business, particularly for women. It is not unusual for hitchers to be robbed, raped or killed and many of the nicer sort of drivers do not stop for hitch-hikers for fear they may be armed. Even so, many hitchers enjoy problem-free journeys through the mountains, with a large proportion of lifts in the back of pick-up trucks. To get a ride out of Denver, try any downtown Interstate intersection and use a sign.

CITY TRANSPORT

City Layout. Most of the city is spread out in the familar grid pattern, except in downtown Denver where rivers and I-25 conspire to upset the pattern. The Interstate snakes around the centre in an arc to the west, roughly following the course of the South Platte River. North of Colfax Avenue (the main east-west thoroughfare) the grid pattern becomes tilted to form a diagonal grid on the map. The central business district is contained in this area which has numbered streets. (Although Colfax Avenue is the main east-west route, the numbering system is based on Ellsworth Avenue). The 16th St Mall is a pedestrian precinct. Numbered avenues are confined to east-west roads north of Alameda Avenue. All other roads are named, until you get to the suburbs when numbering resumes. If you become grossly disoriented, then just find a local telephone directory, which contains a map and street index at the end.

Bus. The Regional Transportation District (RTD) runs all buses in metropolitan Denver and the surroundings, including Boulder. The bus service is known as "The Ride", a slogan liberally plastered over every vehicle, bus shelter and ticket. The system is efficient and well-used although crosstown journeys sometimes involve two or three changes. Most buses run from 6 am to midnight every day. For information call 628-9000 or visit the Downtown Information Center at 626 16th Street.

A free shuttle service runs along 16th St. Other journeys within the city cost 35c off-peak, with one free transfer within 40 minutes. Peak hour services (6 am-9 am and 4 pm-6 pm) cost 70c, or $1.05 on the express buses to the suburbs which run mainly during rush hours. Exact change is required. Outside the city, fares increase to $1.75. The Denver to Boulder run operates at approximately hourly intervals but more frequently during rush hours.

Car. As long as you avoid the 16th St pedestrian precinct and successfully negotiate the straightforward one-way system, there should be few problems. To get through the traffic lights in downtown Denver without having to stop at a single red, it is recommended that you travel at a steady 10 mph.

Parking is not easy to find and expensive. Multi-storey downtown car parks cost around $3 per hour, and meter regulations are strictly enforced by tow trucks. If you arrive before 8 am you can take advantage of "Early Bird" cheap rates in downtown lots for around $7 all day. It is much cheaper to find a suitable suburb with a good bus service to central Denver and park for free.

Try to avoid driving in the downtown area after a snowfall. Anyone parking in a designated "snow route" may be towed away.

Taxi. Do not count on being able to hail a cab, though there is a rank at the airport and some major hotels. Call Ritz (294-9199), Yellow (292-1212), Zone (861-2323), or Metro (333-3333) in Denver or Yellow (442-2277) in Boulder. Fares start at $2 for the first mile, $1 per mile thereafter. There is a flat charge of 40c for each additional passenger. In serious snowstorms taxi drivers charge by the minute.

Cycling. Denver is mainly flat and so theoretically fine for cycling. However, the numerous potholes on downtown streets can prove dangerous, as can the appalling traffic fumes. The city authorities are actively promoting cycling in an effort to reduce smog levels, by providing special bikeways and smoothing out the streets. Bicycles can be hired from I Like Bikes, 4730 E Colfax Avenue (393-7391) or J & E Sports, 4365 S Santa Fe Drive (781-4415). For information, contact the Denver Planning Office, 1445 Cleveland Place (575-2736) or the Denver Bicycle Touring Club Hotline (794-9443). If you prefer to watch, the Coors International Bicycle Classic is based in Boulder in early July.

The visitors bureaux at the airport and at 225 W Colfax Avenue (892-1112) can book you into moderately expensive hotels. Bed and Breakfast Colorado (PO Box 6061, Boulder 80306), lists somewhat cheaper accommodation (442-6664). Fortunately there are a number of cheap hotels in central Denver. Try the Kenmark at 17th Welton Streets (623-6113), La Quinta, 3500 Fox Street (458-1222) or the Harris, 1544 Cleveland Place (825-6341). For cheap motels, head south on Broadway from Colfax Avenue.

Denver's youth hostel at 1452 Detroit St (333-7672) is reached by bus 15 to East High School on E Colfax Avenue then walking two blocks south. The YMCA is more central at 25 E 16th Avenue (861-8300). Similarly the YWCA is on Tremont St between 15th and 16th Streets. KOA operate two "Kampgrounds" on the outskirts of Denver.

Cheap accommodation in Boulder is very hard to find. The Youth Hostel, 1107 12th St at College Avenue, 442-9304 (which boasts a water fountain fed by a glacier) is often fully booked. During the vacations there may be student residences available, but in term-time your best bet is to try to find a cheap motel or go to the KOA Campground, 5856 Valmont (449-1812)

Eating and Drinking

The local specialities are mountain trout and steak, but Denver is a good place to try ethnic fare in a variety of settings ranging from "nouvelle southwestern" to prime examples of American junk culture. If you happen to see "Rocky Mountain oysters" on a menu you might spare a tear for the young bull so cruelly cut off in his prime to provide the local delicacy.

Mexican food is to Denver what Indian food is to London: spicy, filling, and cheap. Downtown, La Loma (2527 W 26th Avenue; 433-8307) features authentic south-of-the-border cooking. Try the fajitas (grilled strips of marinated chicken or beef rolled up in a tortilla with peppers, onion, and refried beans) and, for dessert, fried ice-cream. Cafe Santa Fe (2955 E 1st Avenue; 355-2955) has live music on weekend nights as well as commendable Mexican food.

Denver has some excellent pizza joints: Beau Jo's is a local chain with two in town (2024 E Colfax Avenue; 388-7600, and 2700 S Colorado Boulevard; 758-1519) and one in Boulder (1165 13th Street; 449-3090). You buy pizza by the pound, selecting from a myriad toppings. The Old Spaghetti Factory is a popular and inexpensive place for pasta in a converted cable car shed at 1215 18th Avenue (534-0537); it is noisy and crowded.

Don't leave Denver without going out for a thick charcoal-broiled steak (unless, of course, you are a vegetarian). The Buckhorn Exchange (1100 Osage; 543-9505) is the steakhouse of steakhouses — a local historical landmark — and they are celebrated for their trout and buffalo as well as for their delicious navy bean soup. Lutz's (2651 S Broadway; 744-6141) is less expensive and it boasts one of the best beer lists in town.

As a rule, restaurants touting "southwestern cuisine" are as pretentious as they are expensive. The Rattlesnake Club (901 Larimer; 573-8900) is no exception but the locals simply rave about it and you may find yourself tempted to eat there. Look for dishes using native southwestern ingredients, like blue corn.

DRINKING

None of your fancy Californian wines nor southern spirits for the Denver drinkers: they drink beer. Every autumn, Larimer Square is swamped by the Oktoberfest where the participants get as merry as they do in Munich. The local brew is called Coors and is brewed in the surburban town of Golden west of Denver. Although Coors is gaining popularity in out-of-state places like Florida, most Coloradans deride it and prefer Michelob or imported beers. Tours of the brewery at 13th and Ford Streets in Golden run from 9am to 4pm except Sundays, but should be booked in advance; call 277-BEER. After the mandatory look-round, you can sample the brews. Many discerning beer drinkers prefer Boulder Bitter brewed at an exclusive little brewery in Boulder. You can tour the brewery at 2880 Wilderness Place by calling 444-8448 in advance.

Cocktails, particularly tequila-based margaritas and rum daiquiris are nearly up with beer in popularity. Hours vary, but few bars stay open past 1am. Alcoholic purchases to take away must be concealed in brown paper packages; and open bottles or six-packs cannot be carried in a car, Only "3.2" beer can be bought on Sundays from package stores and after eight o'clock on Sunday nights, restaurants may not serve alcohol and they remove unfinished drinks. There are "3.2 clubs" for people under 21, where at least the dance floors tend to be bigger than at the over 21 clubs. Amazingly, a barman who serves someone who later gets into an accident while under the influence can be sued, so bar-owners take out special insurance.

A little of the Colorado gold not housed in the Mint has been used to cover the dome of the State Capitol at E Colfax Avenue and Sherman St. The finest view of Denver can be had from the gallery at the top. Admission is free every day from 9 am to 3 pm. A good way to get your bearings is to follow the walking tour featured in a brochure issued by the Convention and Visitors Bureau.

If you are looking for high culture, you will soon exhaust Denver's resources. But if your tastes are sufficiently eclectic, you should find something to enjoy: the nightclubs and rock venues of Denver, sophisticated student events at Boulder, and even the odd topless doughnut bar.

Museums. An interesting state statute requires that 1% of capital spending must be used to buy art to "create a more humane environment." You can best see the results of this law around the Civic Center, at the junction of Colfax Avenue and Broadway. Judge for yourself.

The Art Museum at 14th Avenue and Acoma St (575-2793) is a fortress-like building which houses a fascinating collection of native art and craftwork. As well as travelling exhibitions, it features a good collection of European art from early Roman to Monet and Picasso. Opening hours are 9 am-5 pm, Tuesday to Saturday and noon-5 pm on Sunday; admission $2.50 (Students $1.50).

Three blocks northwest at W Colfax Avenue and Cherokee St is the US Mint (as distinct from the Bureau of Engraving in Washington). Five billion of the nation's coins are produced here each year and the vaults contain the largest amount of gold bullion outside Fort Knox. There are free 20-minute guided tours every working day except in late June (no reservations needed). Call 837-3582 for opening times.

Many of the other museums are a little shabby and commercial, or of interest only to connoisseurs of transport, wax and cowboys. Buffalo Bill's Museum (526-0747) is at the place on Lookout Mountain in Golden (about 15 miles west of the city centre) where William F. "Buffalo Bill" is buried. Adults may be more impressed with the panoramic mountain view than the memorabilia. Denver's only other celebrated resident — "unsinkable" Molly Brown, a survivor of the Titanic, who is credited for saving the lives of dozens of children in that Atlantic disaster, is honoured at 1340 Pennsylvania (832-4092), her former home now restored in her memory. Opening hours are 10 am-3 pm from Tuesday to Saturday and noon-3 pm on Sundays. The Pearce-McAllister Cottage at 1880 S Gaylord (322-3704) provides a glimpse of home life in turn-of-the-century Denver.

For train buffs the Colorado Railroad Museum in Golden (17155 W 44th Avenue, 279-4591) presents a fascinating collection of railroad memorabilia. The Heritage Center at 1300 Broadway (8682-3682) has Indian artifacts and exhibits on the history of Denver, which is, after all, one chapter in the settling of the American West. And in the large City Park at Montview and Colorado Boulevards is the Denver Museum of Natural History (370-6300) which houses outstanding specimens of Rocky Mountain fauna (stuffed, though) as well as dinosaur fossils and Indian artifacts. It boasts one of the world's largest movie screens in the IMAX Theater, and watching a feature there is well worthwhile.

Music. There are free open-air concerts in City Park nightly from July 4th to August 18th except Mondays, some of which feature the renowned Denver Symphony Orchestra. During the winter season, the Orchestra is based on Boetcher Hall, part of the Center for the Performing Arts, a mammoth complex on 14th St between Champa and Arapahoe Streets (592-7777). Although the Hall seats 2,700, no one is more than 85ft from the stage. Free tours of the Center take place each weekday at noon; call 893-4200.

Opera buffs should head for Central City, 30 miles west of Denver. In the 1870s residents of the "richest square mile on Earth" devoted some of its mineral wealth to an Opera House (16th and Tremont Street, 571-4435). The season runs from April until November.

For information on rock bands check the local press. The bigger bands play the Rainbow Music Hall at 6260 E Evans Street (753-1800), one of several Boulder venues or the spectacular Red Rocks amphitheatre (575-2637). This natural auditorium lies in Red Rock Park about 16 miles west of Denver and even if the music is disappointing, the scenery makes it worthwhile. Local rock groups can be found in the bars around Larimer Square and in Boulder dives. The Arvada Center for the Arts and Humanities at 6901 Wadsworth Boulevard (422-8050) sponsors everything from jazz to classical.

Theatre. In an attempt to rid the city of its image as a cultural backwater, the new Center for the Performing Arts 1050 13th Street (893-4000) has three regular theatres plus an amphitheatre and the Auditorium Theatre. The Denver Center Theater Company can be seen here, along with numerous touring shows and more avant-garde productions.

There are many smaller experimental theatres in the city and in Boulder. These include the Arvada Center which hires its actors literally off the streets (422-8050), Germinal Stage Denver 1820 Market Street (296-1192), and the Changing Scene, 1527 Champa Street (893-5775). The Colorado Shakespeare Festival is held in July and August at the Mary Rippon

Outdoor Theater (492-8181) on the Boulder campus (advance information from Campus Box 261, Boulder, CO 80309).

The Elitch Theatre at 38th Avenue and Tennyson Street (455-8801) is the oldest summer-stock theatre company in the nation. It brings in big-name performers so tickets are usually sold out early.

Nightlife. Downtown Denver has been largely drained of nightlife,but there are still a few bars, some with live music, particularly around Larimer Square. Nightlife now centres on E Hampden Avenue between I-25 and Havana Street. Here you will find nightclubs from the cheap, informal "No Fuss Grill" (jeans, hamburgers and beer) to the more sophisticated Bobby McGees at 10175 E Hampden (attractive decor, waitresses dressed as cartoon characters and a disc jockey). There is even a 60s style club complete with Stones, Beatles and other early pop music...and cheerleaders. El Chapultepec at 19th Street and Market (295-9126) is the place to go for jazz.

Clubs with no cover charge may seem like a good idea but if you're out to drink rather than dance, beware. Prices can start as high as $3 for a Coke, so ask before ordering. Some clubs have special deals such as "Ladies Nights" when "ladies" can have unlimited drink from as little as $2. Leetsdale Drive in Glendale has most of the rock and disco action. Turn east off Colorado Boulvard. Neo (321-1118) is the most popular dance club currently.

The nightlife in Boulder is cheaper and less brash. There are bars featuring stand up comics, jazz bands playing for free, and street cafes which afford a good view of the numerous local posers. Try the Mall on Pearl St or the university area. Pleasant, relaxed evening entertainment can be enjoyed in the dozens of smaller establishments that feature folk or country music performers. Check the newspapers.

SPORT

In football, the Denver Broncos (nickname: Orange Crush) have a near-fanatical following. They play from September to January at the Mile High Stadium, 17th Avenue and Federal Boulevard (433-7466) which usually has a good crowd atmosphere, great weather and magnificent mountain views. Although the stadium seats 74,000, tickets are hard to come by since most seats are held by season ticket holders. There is even a waiting list of 20,000 for season tickets. The Bears, a minor league baseball team, share the Mile High Stadium (433-8645) in summer. It is a source of much civic frustration that Denver has been unable to acquire a top-flight baseball team.

The 18,000-seat McNichols Arena is the venue for the Nuggets basketball team (575-5833) from October through May, and the Colorado Rockies ice hockey team (534-PUCK). The US National field hockey team is based at Colorado Springs. The low oxygen level due to altitude and equable climate of Colorado make the state a favoured training ground for international athletes.

Horse racing takes place at the Centennial Race Track (794-2661) in the southern suburb of Littleton from May onwards. The dogs race at the Mile High Kennel Club, 6200 Dahlia St from January to March. Off-course gambling, if any, is covert but on track betting is legal. Rodeos are held at the Coliseum: call 892-1000 for details of forthcoming events. The National Western Stock Show and Rodeo is held in Denver each January.

There are plenty of venues if you feel like a little exercise yourself.

Sports complexes contain some combination of a swimming pool, water slide, bowling alley and, for the more sedentary, a wall of video games. Try the swimming pool in Congress Park. There are hundreds of municipal tennis courts for hire in virtually every park, and half a dozen golf courses. Anglers should contact the Colorado Division of Wildlife, 6060 Broadway (825-1192) for details of seasons and permits.

Parks and Zoos. The City Park (between York St and S Colorado Boulevard off E Colfax Avenue) contains the excellent Denver Natural History Museum. There is also a planetarium which features a laser display and a zoo where animals are kept in something approximating their natural habitat. Other attractions include a miniature railway, boating and outdoor skating in winter.

Denver has a hundred other parks, including the Botanic Gardens (1005 York St, 575-2547) which lie within Cheesman Park (admission $2). For those more interested in fun than flora, there are two good amusement parks: Elitch Gardens (4620 W 38th Avenue at Tennyson St, 455-8801) with a huge roller coaster and Lakeside (4601 Sheridan Boulevard at W 44th Avenue, 477-1621). They open at weekends only in May, then daily from June to Labor Day.

SHOPPING

The main shopping area in Denver is on and around the 16th St Mall running from Court Place to Arapahoe St, although as usual prices are lower in the numerous suburban shopping plazas. Expensive boutiques are grouped around Larimer Square. In Boulder, the Pearl St Mall and the university area are the best bets.

As you might expect, Denver excels in outdoor gear and equipment, though it is more expensive than in Europe. If possible, buy during the end of season sales: January for skis and skates, July for boots, tents and backpacks. There are also numerous Indian art and jewellery shops where you can find beautiful silver and turquoise pieces.

THE MEDIA

There are two competing dailies, the *Denver Post* (broadsheet) and the *Rocky Mountain News* (tabloid), each costing 25c. Both have extensive entertainment and classified sections. The "Center Section — Friday" of the *Rocky Mountain News* or the "Sunday Round-Up" of the *Denver Post* are the best sources of listings. The Boulder newspaper is the *Daily Camera* and free University of Colorado paper called the *Colorado Daily* can be picked up in many shops, bars and restaurants.

Some of the more informative and offbeat weekly magazines include *Denver Downtowner, Up The Creek* and *Westworld,* all of which are free from shops, restaurants and hotels. *Denver Magazine* is available from news stands if you prefer to pay for more complete information.

Among the 35 radio stations serving Denver is KOA (850 AM) which gained fame with a deliberately offensive phone-in host named Allan Berg (who was eventually murdered by an outraged listener). Also of interest is KCFR (90.1 FM), the university station which is affiliated with the National Public Radio network, and KDEN (1340 AM) offering NBC news 24 hours a day. There are three other stations offering undiluted country and western, and five religious stations. The small town of Oak Creek in northwestern Colorado offers what is claimed to be the world's only wind-powered commercial radio station, as well as good rock-oriented programming.

Denver is unusual in having two publicly-sponsored TV stations. In addition to the regular PBS (channel 6), KBDI (channel 12) provides independent local programming.

You should be cautious rather than paranoid about street crime. Daylight attacks are rare. If you avoid the Five Points area downtown and the gangland area around N Federal Boulevard after dark there should be no problem. Lone women should steer clear of the rougher parts of E Colfax (especially around the Crazy Horse Bar) at night, since this is the red light district. Denver has one of the highest incidence of rape in the country. Wise women never venture out alone at night nor in the early morning hours.

Drugs. Boulder has a justified reputation as the cocaine capital of the Rockies. Along with high pay goes high living, including a large and casual drug consumption. Many of the jaded but wealthy younger generation do not find it strange to spend $500 a week on white powder: legislators have made penalties for possession more severe and drug users have made themselves less conspicuous.

The area code for Denver and Boulder is 303.

Information: The Convention and visitors' Bureau of Denver and Colorado, 225 West Colfax Avenue (892-1112) has maps and information for both city and state. The bureau also has a branch at the airport. For tourist information in Boulder, visit the Chamber of Commerce, 1001 Canyon St (442-1044) for free maps and event listings.

American Express: Anaconda Tower, 555 17th St (298-7100).

Thomas Cook: 8775 E Orchard Road, Englewood (694-6860).

Post Office: 1823 St (837-3536).

Police: 575-2011.

Medical Emergencies: St Joseph Hospital, 1835 Franklin St (837-7111). Denver General Hospital, W 8th Avenue at Cherokee St (893-6000).

Dental Emergency: Metropolitan Denver Dental Society (789-0573) or the United Denver Network (363-8605).

Travelers' Aid: 1245 E Colfax Avenue (832-8194). Also at Stapleton International Airport (398-3873). Similar services are offered by the International Hospitality Center, 980 Grant St (832-1234).

THE ROCKY MOUNTAINS

The states of New Mexico, Utah, Colorado, Wyoming, Montana and Idaho are dominated by the most famous range of mountains in North America, The Rockies. These mountains, so deservedly beloved by environmentalists and outdoorsmen cover an enormous area; in the state of Colorado alone they occupy an area six times that of the Swiss Alps. A feature common to each state (except Utah) is that the Continental Divide runs through them. Ever since pioneering days, the Divide has been of profound significance to Americans. All rivers to the west of the Divide flow eventually into the Pacific: all those to the east, into the Gulf of Mexico or Atlantic.

Unlike other great mountain ranges in the world, the "roof of America" is very accessible. The mountains are traversed by a well maintained cycling, walking, skiing or canoeing through any part of the Rocky Mountains becomes a great pleasure in the fresh air, hospitable summer climate and stunning terrain. It is one of the most beautiful places in the world, and one of the most dramatic.

Cities of the Rockies. People don't generally travel to the Rocky Mountains for the cities: they go for the rugged mountains and dramatic scenery. Denver is the undisputed capital of the region, and the only other city of significant population is Salt Lake City. But there are other smaller cities worth mentioning that are a better choice for the traveller who wants to maximize his or her time communing with the great outdoors. AYH hostels are to be found in little towns across the Rockies; call the regional office on 301-576-8880. The smaller, more obscure towns tend to have lower prices for accommodation and have been more successful at withstanding the homogenizing influence of the rapidly expanding tourist industry. You will probably come across some interesting characters in the local bars and restaurants.

COLORADO

The USA's most mountainous state, Colorado is smitten with lust for tourism dollars and its towns tend to be well-groomed, cosmopolitan and disappointingly lacking in authentic western charm. It is worth travelling to for the hiking trails leading from the outskirts of Boulder into some beautiful sandstone formations called the Flatirons.

Seventy-five miles south of Denver on I-25 is Colorado Springs, in the Pike National Forest. While the city is losing what little character it had retained from Wild West days to rapid high-technology industry growth, it is a good place to visit if you want a whirlwind nature tour. Pikes Peak (14,645 feet), the awesomely quintessential rocky mountain, looms ominously in the background and the Pikes Peak Incline Railway runs trains from town to the summit from where you will be able to see as far as the eye can see. An hour southwest of Colorado Springs is Royal Gorge, a 1,250 foot deep canyon carved by the Arkansas River. West of Colorado Springs on Route 24 is the Garden of the Gods — a 940-acre park full of strange red sandstone formations from the Paleozoic era — and to the south on Cheyenne Mountain is Seven Falls, where a roaring river cascades down a steep, 1,000 foot deep chasm in seven distinct stages. During summer the falls are illuminated at night and can be viewed from a cable car. Bed and breakfast places are abundant in Colorado Springs. Call the statewide listing service (301-630-3433) and reserve a place before you go.

Estes Park is a town in the heart of Rocky Mountain National Park and, while surrounded by stunning mountain pine forests and beautiful scenery, one of the biggest tourist towns in the Rockies. Avoid it in summer, when over two million people visit the park. Aspen, Vail, and Breckenridge are famous ski resorts and expensive all year round.

Greyhound/Trailways Buses (292-2291) run from Denver's Stapleton Airport to most of the towns and cities in Colorado. For help deciding where to go and finding accommodations, call or visit the Colorado Tourism Board in Denver (1625 Broadway, Suite 1700; 592-5410, or outside Colorado 1-800-433-2656).

NEW MEXICO

Albuquerque is the state capital and a wonderful place to live (residents claim), but simply not interesting or attractive enough to entice travellers. If you're passing through, call in at the Museum of Natural History and try the excellent fish at the Cafe Oceana. If you visit during the first half of October, the International Balloon Fiesta is a fine sight with mass ascents and hot-air balloon races; call the Albuquerque Visitors' Bureau on 1-800-321-6979 for details. Albuquerque also has one of the best and cheapest Mexican restaurants in the southwest: the M & J Sanitary Tortilla Factory, 403 2nd St SW. The *carne adovada* burrito merits at least an hour's detour.

On August 4 the most exciting remaining Indian dance takes place on the saint's day of Santa Domingo Pueblo, 30 miles north of Albuquerque. Festivities last all day, and include 1,000 dancers in the intricate corn dance. The event is for the benefit of the local *pueblos*, but non-locals are welcome; no photos or sketches. Gallup, a small town 150 miles to the west, makes much ado about the Inter-Tribal Ceremonial that takes place there every August. Avoid it like the plague: it is a tourist trap at best and Gallup is really nothing more than a grubby strip of highway.

Travelling between Albuquerque and Gallup, make sure to stop off at Acoma Pueblo, one of the oldest continously inhabited settlements in America (well over 1,000 years), perched dramatically on top of a tall *mesa* (flat-topped mountain). Intricate silver and turquoise Navajo Jewelry is sold in all the reservations, however the cheapest place to buy good-quality is the pawn shops on Gallup's Main St. Make sure you buy silver that has been initialled by the Indian silversmiths, e.g. GHB — Great Hunting Bear.

Santa Fe, nestled among the splendid peaks of the Sangre de Cristo mountain range, is one New Mexico city worth stopping in. Founded in the 1540s by Spanish roman Catholic missionaries, Santa Fe retains its Latin heritage in its architecture and lifestyle. Yet at the same time it has evolved into the epicenter of southwestern culture. A colony of artists has established itself there, cohabiting the town with the heavily Indian and Hispanic citizenry, so galleries and studios abound. Outside of town, the mountain scenery is arguably the most spectacular of the Rockies. For information about hiking trails, camping, or picnic grounds, call the Santa Fe National Forest Service (505-988-6643). In town, there is always a wealth of cultural events, high and low, taking place. Call the local Tourism Office (505-827-0291) for a calendar of events and help in finding accommodation.

UTAH

The semi desert state of Utah is a curious blend of religious doctrine, salt flats and ancient canyons. What permeates every aspect of life in Utah is the Church of Jesus Christ and Latter Day Saints (often abbreviated to LDS) whose followers are universally known as Mormons. After having a vision of the angel Moroni, Joseph Smith recruited some disciples and set off from the East Coast in search of a settlement where they could practise their religion in peace. Their first choice was Illinois, where Joseph Smith was murdered. His heir-apparent Brigham Young continued the Mormon trail westward, and finally settled in the shadow of the mountains on the banks of Great Salt Lake. The salinity of this lake (second only to the Dead Sea) is due to the dissolved minerals brought by streams from the surrounding mountains. Since there is no outlet from the lake, the minerals are trapped, and evaporation increases the concentration of salinity.

Mormons comprise nearly half the state's population and there is no escaping their influence. From the complexity of the liquor laws to the towering temples of Salt Lake City, the followers of Joseph Smith have made their mark. Utah in general, and Salt Lake City in particular, are extremely rich. This does not stem only from industrial, agricultural or mineral wealth, but from the requirement that Mormons must pay 15% of their earnings to the church. The wealth is reflected in the no-expense-spared architecture in Salt Lake City. Brigham Young, the first city planner, designated Temple Square as the centre of the city and of the street grid system. It is dominated by the six-spired Temple which looks suspiciously like something out of Disneyland. The public may attend rehearsals of the Mormon Tabernacle Choir here (8 pm on Thursday) and broadcasts (9.30am on Sunday). Guided tours of the Temple are offered every half hour.

The Visitor Information Station is at 180 S West Temple St (521-2822). Call 533-TIPS for recorded event information, and 532-BIRD for recorded wildlife information. The *Walking and Driving Tours* brochure (free) details all the main attractions. Of particular interest to non-believers are the converted tramsheds of Trolley Square, the Marmalade Historic District around Quince St (where the efforts of British and Scandinavian architects to adapt their building methods to the blistering heat are fascinating) and the grave of Hiram BeBee in the City Cemetery, reputed to be the Sundance Kid. Two hours out of town, at Sundance Mountains, lives Robert Redford who played the film role of the Sundance Kid against Paul Newman's Butch Cassidy.

Liquor Laws. Alcohol, like tea, coffee and Coke, is forbidden to Mormons. Although you'll have little problem in finding coffee or beer, anything stronger requires a certain amount of planning. If you are staying in one place for a while, take out guest membership at a private drinking club. However, these are not particularly pleasant places, and, furthermore, they do not serve food. If you wish to enjoy your drink with a meal, there are two options. You can either buy alcohol in advance from one of the many state liquor stores (which accept cash only and have erratic opening hours) and order a mixer or "set-up" at the restaurant, or wait until 4pm (noon on Sundays) whereupon most restaurants will serve miniature bottles of wine or spirits, which you must actually fetch yourself from the cashier since waiters and waitresses are prohibited from serving spirits. If you are a serious drinker there are many better places to be than Utah.

WYOMING

Set up on a high, barren prairie, the state capital Cheyenne is basically a cattle market surrounded by rundown bars, with a rather Latin air of lethargy. It is only worth visiting during Frontier Days in July when the city hosts the most prestigious rodeo in the world. Contact the Wyoming Travel Board (1-800-225-5996) for information. At the entrance to the majestic Grand Teton Mountain range, just east of the state line, the town of Jackson is given over to promoting its "nouveau-western" image: rather cosmopolitan yet imbued with the spirit of the old west. From Jackson you can travel by bus (Jackson/Rock Springs Stages 301-733-3133) into the Tetons or further north to Yellowstone National Park. In winter Jackson is one of the most chic ski resorts in the Rockies, and in other seasons you can ride the ski lift 2,100 feet up Snow King Mountain for a panoramic view of the immense wilderness. Each summer Jackson hosts a fine arts festival, summerstock theatre, and symphony, and the dozens of galleries in town buzz with activity. In spite of the town's trendiness, it is possible to find inexpensive accommodations there. AYH runs a hostel in Jackson. Scenic hiking trails, lakes, and rivers surround the town.

IDAHO

This boot-shaped state is the most obscure of the Rocky Mountain states, primarily because it lacks the accessibility afforded by the bus lines, excellent roads and tourist industries of the other states. Only if you have a car and want to go to a less-frequented, under-developed side of the Rockies does it merit a visit. Ketchum-Sun Valley is the best place to stay. It is within a short drive of the wildlife-rich Sawtooth Mountain Range and Craters of the Moon National Monument: a vast, ancient lava flow that covers over 100 square miles, and Mount Borah, Idaho's tallest peak 13,000 ft. Ernest Hemingway liked Ketchum so much he died there and is buried in the local graveyard.

MONTANA

Montana's Rockies are full of rustic mountain towns whose inhabitants remain untouched by the vitiating impulses of modern life: the rest of America refer to them as "good people." Helena, originally known as Last Chance Gulch, is the only city in the Montana Rockies. The richest city in the country during the gold rush of the 1860s, it is now a quiet little capital, convenient to beautiful canyons, mountains, and a sulphurous hot springs. Unlike the rest of the Rocky Mountain states, sightseeing by train is eminently rewarding in Montana. You can board in Helena and journey through some spectacular scenery to Glacier National Park and then east across the north of the state. There are AYH hostels in Missoula (406-728-9799) and Polebridge (406-862-0184).

The Great Outdoors

This of region scenic splendour does not rely solely on the mountains for its beauty and interest. Canyons, caverns, craters, geysers and glaciers dot the maps of these six states, mostly inside the bounderies of the 11 National Parks. In addition National Monuments, Forests, Recreation Areas and Grasslands preserve vast tracts for the lover of the great outdoors. The Rockies are the best place to stop for a while if you're crossing the country. Opportunities for outdoor activities are endless: hiking and backpacking, rafting and inner-tubing, windsurfing and sailing, wilderness trekking with horses and even llamas, panning for gold (it is still possible to make a little money) and, of course, skiing and snowmobiling. For information about any of the National Parks write to the National Park Service, Rocky Mountain Regional Office, Denver Federal Center, West 6th Avenue, Denver, CO 80225.

The environs of Denver contain many places of breathtaking scenic and natural beauty. Only 60 miles southwest of Denver is the highest paved automobile road in North America which takes you to the summit of Mount Evans (14,262 ft) where there is a view of mountains and prairies. Mostly above the tree line, rare alpine flowers and 2,000-year-old bristlecone pines grow. And, as the map below shows, there are numerous National Parks within relatively easy reach of Denver and the other cities of the Rockies.

PARKS

Rocky Mountain National Park, Colorado. If you visit only one national park in your lifetime, you will not be disappointed if you make it this one. Because of its proximity to Denver and Boulder (less than 50 miles), it suffers from some commercialism, but it covers such a vast area that the interior remains untouched. Here you can see some of the most exhilarating scenery in the Rockies, on either side of the Continental Divide which bisects the park.

There are 107 peaks over 11,000 feet high within the park's 405 square miles; even the valleys are a mile and half above sea level. The traces of glacial action are so clear that an untrained eye can recognise them. Much of the area is above the tree line with bleak alpine terrain. The weather at this altitude is highly changeable: wrap up well, and never stray from the beaten track in inclement weather. The beaten track in this case is the 50 mile-long Trail Ridge Road — the highest continuous highway in the USA — which follows the course of an ancient Indian track. You can actually look down on 10,000-foot mountains. The drive ($3 toll within the park) takes around three hours, but the hardy can hire a bike from Cosmic Wheels Cyclery, 340 W Riverside Drive (586-2975) in Estes Park. You can procure hiking trial maps at the Visitors Center in Estes Park and Deer Ridge Junction.

Wildlife is abundant, with elk, deer and Rocky Mountain bighorn sheep. Although coyote, black bear mountain lions, bobcat and smaller carnivorous animals all live here they are seldom seen by park visitors. You are very unlikely to see the "jackalope" — a cross between a jack-rabbit and an antelope, beloved by Coloradan practical jokers —except on postcards.

The 240-miles drive from Denver via Boulder, Estes Park (including the hotel where the filming of *The Shining* was done), Grand Lake (the world's highest yacht club with opportunities for boating, swimming and trout fishing), and Idaho Springs is along one of the most impressive circular routes in the country.

Mesa Verde National Park, Colorado. Whereas Rocky Mountain National Park is pre-eminent for mountain scenery, Mesa Verde allows the visitor to have a rare glimpse of America's distant history. Mesa is a Spanish word meaning a table shaped landform; the "Green Table" in the extreme southwest of the state contains excavated cliff dwellings. Anasazi Indian tribes lived in these caves until the end of the 13th century, when they mysteriously fled leaving behind all their possessions for the delight and bewilderment of archaeologists.

The cliff palace is a capacious dwelling 15 storeys above the canyon floor and containing 200 rooms. The park lies about nine miles east of Cortez on Route 160, and there is a bus service from town.

San Juan National Park, Colorado. One of the most pleasant and unusual ways to see some of the dramatic San Juan Mountain range is by train on the old Durango-Silverton narrow gauge railway, left over from mining days. The round trip takes a day, winding through some of the most photogenic scenery of the Rockies. You need to reserve a seat in advance: the address is 479 Main Avenue Durango, CO 81301 (303-247-2733). North of the Park is the immense Black Canyon of the Gunnison — a craggy, black gorgy nearly 3,000 feet deep — which you stumble upon the midst of a bleak plateau. At the bottom of the canyon lies the powerful Gunnison river and some excellent opportunities for fishing.

Dinosaur National Monument, NW Colorado (on Utah border). One of the world's largest concentrations of fossilized dinosaur bones is found in this 325 square mile park. Nearly 2,000 such bones are on view as a permanent exhibit on a cliff face and visitors can watch technicians still working to uncover the skeletons of brontosauruses (which are unique to Colorado and Wyoming) and other prehistoric creatures.

The scenery itself is remarkable: there are many narrow gorges with sheer, strangely-carved, red-tinted sandstone cliffs. From Harper's Corner there are spectacular views of the confluence of the Green and Yampa Rivers at Steamboat Rock, over 2,500 feet below. River trips lasting between one and five days are available.

White River National Forest, Central Colorado. The forest was once the hunting ground of the Ute Indians. Within its boundaries lie the Mount of Holy Cross, Glenwood Canyon and the Snowmass wilderness. But most visitors are attracted by the ski resorts of Vail and Aspen. If you are not there during the ski-season, try to attend the music festival in July and August, where the Aspen Music School, Ballet West and the American Theatre Company all perform. Summer visitors may also try white water rafting. River Runners in nearby Salida run reasonably priced trips on the Arkansas River and have a toll free number to check prices and availability (1-800-332-9100). About 50 miles downriver near Canon City is a remarkable canyon called Royal Gorge which narrows to 30 feet and is spanned by the world's highest suspension bridge (1,053 ft).

Carlsbad Caverns, New Mexico. The only National Park in New Mexico features the largest caverns in the world, many of which have not been fully explored. There is a choice of walking tour depending on your adventurousness. For the two hour torch lit tour of the "New Cave" you should reserve in advance (505-785-2233).

Near Albuquerque New Mexico, the Basque del Apache National Wildlife

Refuge harbours over 300 species of birds, including the gravely endangered whooping crane.

Yellowstone National Park, Wyoming. A whole generation of *Yogi Bear* viewers grew up firmly believing that the correct name for this park is Jellystone. In fact the name comes not from the sandstone which millenia of geographical disturbance have shuffled into a rugged, bubbling wilderness, but rather from the yellow cleft of the Grand Canyon of the Yellowstone River. This is the biggest expanse of wilderness in the continental USA, covering an area greater than Wales. Yellowstone was the first National Park and although a large proportion of its forest was destroyed by fire in 1988 it is still a delightful place.

Most visitors head straight for the huge geyser known as Old Faithful. Park rangers can predict its steaming sulphurous eruptions by the intensity and duration of the previous one, and on average they take place every hour to the delight of the gathered hordes of tourists. There are other less predictable geysers in the Mammoth Hot Springs area to the north. Once the novelty of geysers wears off, the Yellowstone River has canyons and waterfalls of a less intermittent nature.

Yellowstone is becoming more accessible during winter — as long as you are prepared to pay. Snowmobiles and snow coaches (half-track vehicles carrying up to a dozen passengers) transport visitors to view Old Faithful and other sights without the crowds which plague the area in summer. Intrepid cross-country skiers can make the same journey independently. The wildlife is so accustomed to the masses that it is not uncommon to see a bear on the road accepting handouts from passers by.

Grand Teton, Wyoming. Not far from Yellowstone, this park is indeed in the grandest part of the Teton Mountains. The glaciated features of the mountains — cirques, valleys and reflecting lakes — contribute to the grandeur. It is the winter feeding ground of America's largest elk herd. The Tetons are rugged and less-frequented than other parts of the Rockies. They harbour tremendous hiking trails which will lead you to places like Death Canyon — a steep-walled chasm full of wildlife — and the static Peak Divide, the highest point in the park.

Zion National Park, Utah. Zion is an excellent antidote to the commercial excesses of some of the more heavily visited parks, especially Grand Canyon which is only 100 miles away (see page 297). It is on a smaller scale, more easily accessible (a few miles from I-15) and virtually deserted. If you base yourself in the centre of the park (a pleasant grassy area that meanders alongside the river), there is a selection of trails around the peaks and waterfalls. The gentlest stroll would not overexert even a Los Angeleno deprived of his car; the hardest, an ascent of the Angel's Landing, required the skill and courage of an experienced mountaineer.

Bryce Canyon National Park, Utah. Although Bryce is only 50 miles from Zion, it is almost a different world. Instead of sub-tropical flora clinging to the rock faces, Bryce has nothing but sandstone. The desert winds have carved this stone into designs which look completely out of place on Earth. The feeling is like walking around caves or catacombs with the roof taken off. There are trails of varying severity, and unobtrusive food and accommodation services.

There are three other national parks in Utah: Arches, which contains giant red sandstone arches and other evidence or erosion; Canyonlands, with extensive evidence of prehistoric Indians; and Capitol Reef, a 70-mile uplift of cliffs dissected by steeply-walled gorges.

Glacier National Park, Montana. The park comprises the larger part of the Waterton-Glacier International Peace Park, which straddles the Canadian border. If you wish to cross between Montana and Canada, note that the border post at Chief Mountain with the park is not open 24 hours: check locally for crossing times. Glacier is much more difficult to reach than most other parks in the Rockies and consequently far less crowded during the height of the summer, when it is at its best. Like the Trail Ridge Road of Colorado, the "Going-to-the-Sun" route permits the motorist or cyclist to cross the Continental Divide. It is even more rewarding to leave your vehicle behind and take advantage of some of the 800 miles of hiking trail, in order to see mountain goats, moose, possibly a grizzly bear and a wealth of wild flowers. The park is best from mid-June to mid-September, and even then it is still substantially covered by snow. Hiking in this park is serious business: watch out for bears and never stray from the trail. Contact Glacier National Park HQ, West Glacier, MT 59936 (406-888-5441) for maps and information.

SKIING

The Rocky Mountain states offer the most reliable skiing in North America, whether in Wyoming's Grand Teton National Park at Jackson Hole, with the best Black Runs in the USA; Idaho's Sun Valley; or in the numerous Rocky Mountain resorts in Colorado, New Mexico and Utah.

Aspen, the ski capital of USA, is becoming so chic and expensive that it is losing ground to skiing "theme parks" like the twin resorts of Winter Park and Mary Jane also in Colorado. These operate on a non-profit basis and, among other things, encourage the disabled and very young children to take up skiing. One of the cheapest and least crowded resorts is Loveland Pass about 50 miles west of Denver; head out I-70 toward the Eisenhower Tunnel. Another good one is Telluride, a working silver mining town until 1972 and still not over-commercialized. Hydro-electricity was invented here. During the summer all manner of informal arts festivals take place. Utah offers excellent skiing at the resorts of Park City and Snowbird for instance, but lousy apres-ski due to the state's repressive liquor laws.

On the whole, ski resorts in the Rockies have a relaxed and democratic atmosphere. Ski packages are rare and most resorts offer a wide range of accommodation, equipment hire facilities and instruction which anyone can take advantage of without much prior planning. The season usually starts in late November and runs until late April. Equipment for cross-country skiing is available in all the resort towns.

Calendar of Events

mid March	Winternational World Cup, Aspen, Colorado
late July	Frontier Days rodeo, Cheyenne, Wyoming
August	Colorado State Fair, Pueblo
early September	New Mexico State Fair, Albuquerque
late September	Oktoberfest, Worland, Wyoming
early October	International Balloon Fiesta, Albuquerque, New Mexico

Los Angeles and the Southwest

Disneyland

Arizona　　**Nevada**　　**Southern California**

Southern California is a free-wheeling land of sun, sea and surf. Although the beach parties attended by Annette Funicello and Frankie Avalon in the movies of the 1960s are more likely to be private these days, the pleasure-seeking lifestyle persists. Suntanned surfers of both sexes haunt the beaches in search of the perfect wave and perfect partner. One of the questions most frequently asked by visitors is "When do people here do any work?"

The atmosphere may be one of indolence, but there are a great many people who have made a great deal of money. And this is not a place for disguising your wealth. Rolls Royces (6,300 in Beverly Hills alone) and swimming pools (one fifth of the nation's total) abound. And yet there is great natural beauty in Southern California: forests, mountains, deserts and sea cliffs. At the centre of all the beauty is the Great Wen, Los Angeles with a population of nearly thirteen million, the supremely artificial nerve centre of the southwestern USA.

Sprawling and undisciplined, it covers more than 460 square miles. It has been described many times as "50 suburbs in search of a city" and Quentin Crisp calls it "New York lying down". But suburbs with such evocative names as Hollywood, Beverly Hills and Malibu Beach help to console the visitor who is disappointed by the lack of a city centre.

It is almost essential to have a car in this straggling city: 97% of all daily trips in Los Angeles are made by car (and 97% of those vehicles carrying only one person). To participate in the spirit of Southern California it is necessary to spend time lane-hopping on the freeways — negotiating the intersection where five cars pass every second — and join in the general madness.

For lunacy is the norm; nothing is taboo. The more outrageous the style, the more probable that it will set a trend. Although some of the glamour has faded from the Movie Capital of the World, the inhabitants — even the 375,000 expatriate British — still perpetuate the myth among themselves that Los Angeles is the most "with it" place in the world (even if that expression no longer is). This busy, bright and ever moving city is an altogether bizarre place, unlike any other in America.

THE NATIVES

Los Angelenos are as uninhibited as their city's growth pattern. Go to the beachside area of Venice just south of the popular beaches at Santa Monica where you will see amazing street life — drag queens, women pumping iron, even a roller-skating Sikh in full regalia. In fact the beach itself is quite lovely and yet it is the artifice which attracts both performers and spectators. Or go to one of the places where movie moguls hang out, like the Polo Lounge of the Beverly Hills Hotel or the Colony and Trancas Supermarkets in Malibu where the stars do their grocery shopping.

If you are unlucky enough not to see a famous personality, you can safely assume they are seeing their divorce lawyers, plastic surgeons or analysts. In Los Angeles you don't have to be a movie star to be into the study of "interpersonal exploration". The old joke — Q. Why does it take 12 Californians to change a light bulb? A. One to change the bulb; 11 to share the experience — is well aimed.

Making Friends. So if you want to meet the natives, you can start by inviting them to change a light bulb with you. Or go to one of the beaches, rent a surf board and find someone to teach you. Or arrange for a friend to page you at the Polo Lounge, and the unemployed actors waiting for their own big break will sit up and take notice. Or visit the informal Original Pantry (9th and Figueroa Streets) at any hour of the day or night where waiters park you wherever there is a free seat, often at other people's tables. You will find it easier to strike up acquaintances if you're not too prim and proper. At some southern Californian communes you may even encounter the "hug patrol", always on the lookout for unhappy mortals in need of comfort.

Westwood, home of the University of California at Los Angeles (UCLA), is the suburb neighbouring on Beverly Hills. This area teems with interesting bars and restaurants frequented by students.

If you make a particularly good friend of the opposite sex, you can take advantage of California's instant wedding industry. Chapels advertise "no blood tests, no waiting, open Sundays" or offer free champagne to the happy couple. At a pinch you can marry in 20 minutes for less than $200.

CLIMATE

The casual, outdoor-oriented lifestyle of Southern California would not be possible in a colder climate. The sun shines most of the year (except for a few weeks in February or March). Santa Monica Beach (a few miles from Hollywood) boasts a year round average temperature of 68°F/20°C. In downtown LA, there is no measurable precipitation in May, June, July or August. Take advantage of the warm ocean currents because a couple of

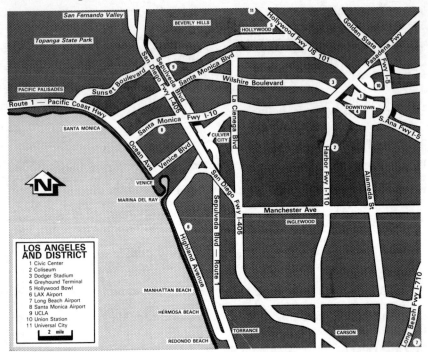

hundred miles up the coast they are replaced by cold ones. Dial 554-1212 for the Los Angeles weather forecast.

The one (literal) blot on the horizon is the smog for which the city is notorious. The reason is not that Los Angeles has more heavy industry than most; it is a combination of car exhaust fumes and the lie of the land which traps the air. It is said that God occasionally rolls back the smog to check that LA is still there, then puts it back so He doesn't have to look at the city. The smog is at its eye-stinging worst during the summer, when smog warnings are issued on radio and TV. You can report vehicles with smoky exhausts by calling 1-800-CAR-SMOG. Alternatively, escape to the sea or to the interior.

ARRIVAL AND DEPARTURE

Air. Los Angeles International Airport (LAX) underwent a $100 million facelift for the 1984 Olympics, but clearing immigration and customs at the Tom Bradley International Terminal is by no means a streamlined operation. At busy times (early morning and late afternoon) you can often face a wait of an hour or two.

The San Diego Freeway (I-405) passes LAX but the airport is normally surrounded by traffic jams. If you are not in a hurry you might still be tempted to rent a car from any of the dozens of airport rental outfits. Tune into 530 AM, the airport radio station, for up-to-the-minute traffic reports.

Buses run from all eight airport terminals to downtown 24 hours a day

(723-4636). The cost is $7 and the 17-mile journey takes anything from 40 minutes to two hours depending on traffic, terminating at the Greyhound Station at 6th and Los Angeles Streets. There is a link by public transport to downtown: catch a combination of the freeway Express 607 and Local 872. Cabs are prolific but not cheap, at least $25. Limousines and vans run to the suburbs of Anaheim (for Disneyland, $15), Pasadena ($19) and Burbank ($33). For door-to-door service without spending a fortune, call SuperShuttle (777-8000) for a shared van trip.

There are four other airports in the Los Angeles/Orange County region which are used by various domestic carriers, and — depending on your final destination — you may find it easier to fly into Orange County's John Wayne Airport (for Disneyland) or Long Beach.

Fares on major routes from LA are competitive, e.g. $49 to San Francisco and $149 to east coast cities. For cheap international flights, check the travel section of the *Los Angeles Times.* Student Travel Network, Suite 507, 2500 Wilshire Boulevard (380-2184) has good fares for normal people as well as students.

Bus. The Greyhound terminal is downtown at 208 E6th St (corner of Los Angeles St, 620-1200). Conveniently, this is also the terminal for the local Rapid Transit District buses. Inconveniently, this is a seedy and dangerous neighbourhood. There are many daily services north to San Francisco (8 to 12 hour journey for $46) and south to San Diego. A cheaper option to San Francisco is the Green Tortoise service every Friday and Sunday night for $30; you should book in advance on 392-1990.

Train. Union Station would have been even more impressive in the days when it was in full use. Admire the combination of Spanish and Art Deco architecture from 1930s. There are eight daily services to San Diego ($18 for the three hour journey) and one to Oakland/San Francisco ($60 for the ten hour trip). If you're planning to take the train to Chicago, note that the *Southwest Chief* is nearly 24 hours faster than the *Eagle* which has a circuitous route via Dallas.

Driving. Some people claim you should rent a car even if you are going to stay for no more than a few hours. In addition to the full range of standard rental companies both at the airport and elsewhere, there are many low-priced outfits: as well as Rent-a-Wreck and Ugly Duckling, you might try Rite Rate (670-7633) where rentals start at $15. Free mileage arrangements are preferable in a city as spread out as Los Angeles.

If you are driving your own car and have trouble with your exhaust system, you may want to visit Tijuana just over the Mexican border 150 miles south of LA, where there is an inexplicable preponderance of establishments specializing in cheap "muffler" repairs.

Driveaways. Having your car delivered for you is a very common practice among the locals, and driveaway companies proliferate. Most cars need to be delivered to the east, but it is worth enquiring about any destinations up the Pacific coast.

Hitch-hiking. It is difficult to get a lift out of Los Angeles since so much of the freeway traffic is local. But in view of the high proportion of students and alternative types, it is worth having a go. Just choose any freeway entrance heading in roughly the right direction and be sure to use a sign.

CITY TRANSPORT

City Layout. Downtown Los Angeles is just one of many separate areas, and not necessarily one in which you will want to spend much time. The distance between Beverly Hills and Anaheim (where Disneyland is located) is over 40 miles and one of LA's main streets, Wilshire Boulevard, is 27 miles long. It is possible to base yourself between Beverly Hills and Hollywood so that you can walk to both; however, walking any distance is not a rewarding experience. The Los Angeles Police Department zealously enforce the laws on jaywalking, and ignoring a "Don't Walk" sign can earn you a $25 ticket; recent victims include the US Attorney General and the head of the CIA.

Bus. You wouldn't want to have the job "Park and Ride" co-ordinator in a city as car-crazy as LA, but amazingly there is such a person. In fact there is a surprisingly extensive network of city buses in Greater Los Angeles operated by the Rapid Transit District or RTD (626-4455). The system is complicated and buses run infrequently in many cases, but it is cheap — $1.10 a ride (exact change only) or 10 tickets for $9. There are surcharges on express buses and transfers cost an extra 25c. If you simply want to go in a long, straight line, the service is fine; otherwise a trip can take half a day.

There is a downtown minibus service, DASH (1-800-874-8885), which operates very frequently during the day Monday to Saturday just in the downtown area. Having a foreign passport makes you eligible for the tourist pass which permits unlimited travel on the whole system for $2 a day. A monthly pass, valid from the first day of the month, can be bought a week on either side of the day for $30. If you're in LA for a short time and simply want to visit one or two of the major attractions (Disneyland, Universal Studios, etc.) it is probably easiest to join a sightseeing tour.

Car. Over half a million cars pour into downtown daily. Two-thirds of the surface area of the business district is swallowed up by streets and parking lots. Even so, parking can be tricky and rush hours are a nightmare. Try to find a residential area behind the major commercial thoroughfares where it is usually possible to park on the street for free.

If you are going to be in LA for a few days, get hold of a full street directory (about the size of a phone book). It is almost impossible to navigate the hundreds of miles of freeway with tourist or gas station handouts.

Taxis. Taxis are difficult to find except at major hotels. They do not cruise to streets for fares. The initial charge is $2 plus $1.50 a mile, making them amongst the most expensive in North America. If you want to order a taxi from the Yellow Pages, make sure the company you choose is located in your section of town.

Cycling. You can hire bicycles at Santa Monica and Venice, the original beach resorts of the area. You can them set off along the beachside bicycle path as far as Palos Verdes 28 miles away. The UCLA campus and Griffith Park just north of the Hollywood Bowl are also pleasant venues for cyclists. The City Department of Recreation and Parks (485-5555) publishes a pamphlet with maps called "Seven Bikeways in Los Angeles" and the *Los Angeles Times* features cycle touring maps.

Accommodation

Assuming you do not have the income of Harrison Ford, you will probably not be able to afford the faded splendour of the Chateau Marmont Hotel in Hollywood, hangout of pop stars. Nor is the Beverly Hill Hotel, where Victor Mature entertained starlets, a possibility. You must first decide which area of Los Angeles you wish to make your base. Your choice will probably be made from five areas: downtown, Hollywood, Beverly Hills/Westwood, the beaches and the San Fernando Valley. The disadvantage of downtown is that it is not a safe place to walk around after the offices and shops empty at 6pm. There are plenty of cheap and sleazy hotels from $10 a night in the neighbourhood of the Greyhound terminal but these are not recommended for the faint at heart. Reasonable accommodation may be found at bargain prices at the following:

L.A. Huntington Hotel (752 S Main St, 672-3186) doubles for $30.
Orchid Hotel (819 S Flower St, Downtown, 624-5855) doubles from $37.
Crescent Hotel (403 N Crescent Drive, Beverly Hills, 274-7595) doubles $35-$45.

The cheapest accommodation in the Southwest is located over the Mexican border. Hollywood is probably the liveliest area in which to stay. The San Fernando Valley, known simply as the Valley, is a sprawling suburban area full of young upwardly mobile families. There are plenty of inexpensive motels along Ventura Boulevard, the Valley's main artery. A car would be essential.

Santa Monica and the southern beaches of Manhattan, Hermosa and Huntington have many attractions for the visitor. On Santa Monica's Ocean Avenue, however, very ordinary motel rooms go for $60 a night and up. Smaller motels some 20 blocks back from the beach offer rooms for about a third of that price and buses run past the door every few minutes for the beach.

Hostels. There are two AYH hostels in LA, plus one which shares the YMCA premises. The largest one is in Building 613 in Angels Gate Park at 3601 South Gaffey St, San Pedro (831-8109). The second hostel is in Westchester, two miles from the International Airport, but opens only from June 1 to September 15. The address is 8015 S Sepulveda Boulevard (776-0922) Advance bookings are usually unnecessary, except perhaps at the height of the summer tourist season. If these locations are too farflung to suit you, try the YMCA Youth Hostel in Hollywood (1553 N Hudson Avenue, 467-4161) between Sunset and Hollywood Boulevards and four blocks west of Vine St, where a single will be $27. The LA Guest Hostel (1518 Rockwood St, 250-7921) is quite convenient for both LA and Hollywood and has dormitory accommodation for $10 per night; advance reservation is recommended since there are only 16 beds. In Venice, try the International Network Hotel at 2221 Lincoln Boulevard (305-0250) which has dormitory beds for $10. Or, for longer stays, the Share-Tel International Hostel (20 Brooks Avenue, 392-0325) has shared apartments from $105 per week.

Bed and Breakfast. Contact Bed & Breakfast International (151 Ardmore Rd. Kensington 94707, 415-525-4569) the oldest B & B agency in the state, with over 300 listings. There are several other smaller agencies, some of which also impose a two-day minimum stay: California Houseguests International (6051 Lindley Avenue #6, Tarzana 91356; 818-344-7878), or

Bed & Breakfast of Los Angeles (32127 Harborview Lane, Westlake Village 91361; 818-889-8870). Rates start at about $40 for two.

House Exchanges. If you plan to spend several weeks in Southern California, you may want to consider swapping houses with a resident, a practice which is well established in this part of the US. See the introductory section *Accommodation* for details and useful addresses.

Camping. Many American families, who pour into California in the summer, camp near Disneyland in Orange County. It is usually necessary to book in advance; this can be done through Ticketron outlets (670-2311). Get a list of campground addresses from the LA tourist office. All campsites are a long way from downtown. The cost per site is about $15.

Eating and Drinking

Because of the large Hispanic population (well over a quarter of the total) there are many very good Mexican restaurants and cafes. The cheaper and more unpretentious the decor, the better the quality of the food is likely to be. The greatest concentration of Mexican restaurants and stalls is along Olvera Street, near Union Station, site of the original Spanish settlement.

There is a small Chinatown in Hill Street a few blocks west of Union Station but it is not in San Francisco's league. Try also Koreatown and the Little Japan area. To shop for your own produce visit the municipal market betwen Hill and Broadway, in preference to the more swish Farmer's Market near Century City.

If you have begun to tire of ethnic cuisine, visit Johnies Steak House on Hollywood Boulevard, reputed to be the cheapest place in town. Or try Larry Parker's Beverly Hills Diner (206 Beverly Drive) where you can get any kind of omelette at any time of the day or night. If you are willing to spend a little more for the possibility of seeing a famous actor or actress, eat breakfast at Duke's Coffee Shop on Sunset Boulevard. (The working breakfast is said to have been invented in LA). Most of the pricier restaurants cater for the steak and seafood clientele and some locals regard eating out as a spectator sport. Sheridan Morley overhead a diner berating her companion with "never mind what's on the menu, honey, just show me what's on the chairs." Note that smoking is prohibited in all Hollywood restaurants.

One of Hollywood's classic eating houses is the Musso and Frank Grill at 6667 Hollywood Blvd, which has remained (self-consciously) unchanged for two generations. It is a cheap oasis, which goes some way to evoking the old style Hollywood. The Sunset Grill on Sunset Boulevard was made famous by Don Henley in the song of the same name; at live perfomances he dedicates the songs to the owner, Joe Frolisch. The best burger in town is reputed to be at Pete's Grandburger 1033 W 6th St and the best hot fudge sundaes at C C Brown's (7007 Hollywood Blvd.

The Original Pantry has already been mentioned as a good place to meet people. Go to this restaurant whose motto is"we never close" on the corner of 9th and Figueroa Streets. To prove the point, there are no locks on the door. Once run by ex-cons it is a place with lots of local colour. Eat steaks while you marvel at the statistics quoted on fact sheets which circulate, including such fascinating information as the number of celery sticks which have been served since the establishment opened in 1924. You may have to queue.

Londoners might recognize familiar names like the Hard Rock Cafe (8600 Beverly Blvd) and Joe Allen's (8706 W Third St) both in West Hollywood. If you are feeling really homesick, you might like to try some British-owned pubs: the Cat & Fiddle in Hollywood or those in the Santa Monica area such as the Old King's Head, corner of 2nd St and Santa Monica Boulevard, which serves shepherds pie, steak and kidney pie and faggots and peas.

DRINKING

Along with your faggots and peas at the Old King's Head, you can drink Guinness, Sam Smith's and Fullers. There are numerous offbeat bars, including one — the Beverly Hills Juice Club, 8382 Beverly Boulevard — which sells grass nectar (of the lawn variety) and another which serves nothing but mineral water. If you want exotic cocktails, visit the bars in the Marina-del-Rey area. The drink of Southern California is Margarita, based on tequila.

If you want to rise above the evils of freeways and parking hassles, visit the bar at Yamashiro not far from the Hollywood Bowl and on top of a hill. The view at sunset is superb.The opening scenes of the Faye Dunaway film *The Firefly* took place at the Firefly bar, two blocks down from Hollywood Boulevard. Until local fire chiefs objected, the counter was set alight nightly.

Some bars open as early as 6 am, but all close by 2 am (and that means you must be outside by 2 am). Los Angeles is not a late night city.

Entertainment

The best view of the spectacular suburban sprawl is from Griffith Park Observatory, where James Dean filmed the car scene in *Rebel Without a Cause*.

Los Angeles (or at least Hollywood) promotes itself as Entertainment City USA. Without attending a single concert, film or fantasyland you may feel adequately entertained by traversing the 30 miles of Sunset Boulevard from downtown to the beach or driving round Beverly Hills, spotting celebrities' houses. (Don't linger too long in front of the security signs which read "Armed Response" for fear of arousing suspicion.)

East coasters do not think much of west coast's cultural achievements. If it is string quartets and Byzantine icons you are into, this may not be your favourite American city, and visitors do not as a rule come here for highbrow entertainment. If they come on Monday they won't have any choice since all LA museums are shut on that day. There are several excellent collections at the LA Museum of Art, the Norton Simon Museum in Pasadena and the J Paul Getty Museum in Malibu, said to be so rich that its funding equals the Grass National Product of Australia. But rather than attend conventional art exhibitions, people come to LA to see how David Hockney has painted the exterior of his house off Mulholland Drive or to attend the Museum of Neon Art (704 Traction Avenue) which includes a neon Mona Lisa and elaborate movie house marquees from days gone by.

Some visitors come to see the stars, which is partly why the Universal Studios tour is so popular (see Cinema, below). If you want to see films being made on location, the Hollywood on Location Company (8644 Wilshire Boulevard, Beverly Hills; 659-9165) sells maps showing "where the stars are filming today" for $29. More grisly is the Grave Line tour, aboard a hearse which takes you to the grave of Marilyn Monroe, the house where Sharon Tate was murdered and the place where Janis Joplin took her terminal overdose (7047 Franklin Avenue, Room 105).

The Calendar section of the Sunday *Los Angeles Times* provides a fairly thorough run down of what's on in the city. The *Los Angeles Weekly* and the *Los Angeles Reader* — both free from most liquor stores and other outlets —are informative and essential if you want full entertainment listings of alternative things to do.

Music. The 17,630 capacity Hollywood Bowl features a varied programme of classical music from July to mid-September. There is so little rain that in 40 years there have been just three postponements. It is worth going just to sit under the stars and watch the people. The bandshell was designed by Frank Lloyd Wright's son. At the other end of the spectrum are the pop video emporiums especially popular among teenagers.

In between these cultural extremes, there is an astonishing choice of excellent rock acts; everybody in search of a record contract ends up performing in LA. A staggering one third of the world's pop and rock music is recorded in the city. The Museum of Rock Art at 6427 Sunset Boulevard in Hollywood is devoted to rock music memorabilia such as album covers and vintage TV shows. It opens Wednesday - Saturday from noon to 4.30pm, and the $4 admission includes access to the video theatre. Some of the top venues include Whisky A Go Go and the Roxy, both on Sunset Boulevard, Club Lingeries and the Palace (both in Hollywood) and At My Place in Santa Monica which specializes in lesser known but equally good blues/ rock performers. For information about traditional blues gigs, look for the black population's paper published on Thursdays called the *Los Angeles Sentinel.* The mecca for country fans and star names like Jerry Lee Lewis and Rick Nelson is the Palomino at 6907 Lankershim Blvd, N Hollywood (818-764-4010) where it is hard to move for cowboy hats.

Many of the bars and restaurants along Ventura Boulevard in the San Fernando Valley feature excellent bands and groups on a regular basis, with no cover charge. For good jazz, try the Blue Note Cafe at number 11941 (tel: 818-760-3348).

Throughout the summer the open air Greek Theater (2700 N Vermont Avenue near Griffith Park) and the Universal Amphitheater (Hollywood Freeway at Lankershim Blvd) star big show business names such as Frank Sinatra and Bette Midler. Tickets can be bought at Ticketron offices throughout the city.

Theatre. LA is an important centre for live theatre. Many productions star famous film and television actors, tired of the celluloid art. Try the Center Theater Group who perform in the round at the Mark Taper Forum (972-7211), or the Westwood Playhouse near the UCLA campus (208-5454). Major Broadway productions are staged at the Shubert Theatre (2020 Avenue of the Stars, Century City) and the Music Center in downtown LA.

Cinema. Rather than just see a newly released film, you may want to see where films are made, though you will have to be prepared to queue for up to several hours. Contrary to popular belief, the major film studios are not in Hollywood, but are spread around the suburbs. Universal Studios in Universal City (818-508-9600) specialize in showing visitors around in "glam trams". You will be attacked by the shark from *Jaws,* be besieged by enemy aliens from the Battlestar Galactica and barely survive all manner of disasters including rock slides, collapsing bridges, fire, flood and an earthquake measuring 8.3 on the Richter Scale. *The Star Trek Adventure* is a must for Spock fans. The tour takes several hours and costs $16.95.

If you are interested in movie memorabilia, visit Mann's Chinese Theater at 6925 Hollywood Boulevard, where you can see foot, hand, elbow, etc. prints of movie stars in the cement outside.

Nightlife. Sunset Strip (a short section of the Boulevard) is still the centre for LA's nightlife. In addition to bars and nightclubs of every persuasion, try out the Comedy Store which features some very talented comedians. Only the young and fit should sample some of LA's wilder clubs such as the Scream (Embassy Hotel, Grand St, Fridays and Saturdays at 11pm). The Troubadour (9081 Santa Monica Boulevard, 276-1159) is a more established club and hosts good bands.

Theme Parks. Anaheim, about 40 miles from downtown LA, is the site of the original Disneyland created in 1955 and should not be confused with the much newer Walt Disney World in Florida. No trip to Southern California would be complete without a visit to this fantasy world. It takes more than a day to see everything, including the magnificent electric parade and evening fireworks display. The Space Mountain ride in which you experience a flight through outer space is worth the hour-long queues, as is the new Splash Mountain waterslide and the Captain E/O show starring Michael Jackson. You can see storybook characters, join pirates and cruise the jungle. A passport to all this costs $21.50. And since it is an alcohol-free zone, you won't spend much more than that. The monorail from Disneyland drops passengers off at the licensed Disney Hotel just outside the park.

There are other fantastic entertainments in the region. Six Flags Magic Mountain (I-5 north at Valencia) has the Colossus, the world's largest dual track wooden rollercoaster, as well as the Revolution in which thrill-seekers turn a terrifying upside-down circle in a vast loop. Knotts Berry Farm at Buena Park (close to Disneyland) is not a pick-your-own-farm as its name suggests, but another amusement park with a variety of daredevil rides. At Long Beach you can view the largest aircraft ever to fly and visit the biggest ocean liner afloat. The *Queen Mary* is moored at Pier J, alongside Howard Hughes' flying folly, the eight-engined *Spruce Goose* built mainly of birch and weighing over 200 tons. The complex (which predictably has restaurants, shops and a tacky "Londontowne" area) opens 10am-6pm in winter, 9am-9pm in summer.

SPORT

Spectator Sports. Los Angeles can probably boast more major league teams than any other US city inlcuding New York. There are two professional football teams, the LA Rams and the LA Raiders. The LA Dodgers (National League) delight baseball fans at Dodger Stadium in Chavez Ravine, while the California Angels (American League) play in Anaheim. Even if baseball is a closed book to you, you will find that you thoroughly enjoy sitting in the sun, drinking beer, eating hot dogs and soaking up the atmosphere of the Dodger fans all around.

The Los Angeles Kings (ice hockey) and the Los Angeles Lakers (basketball) both play in the Forum near the airport. Since the demise of the Aztecs, there is no longer a professional soccer team in the area, although there are dozens of soccer leagues.

Horse racing is at the Hollywood Park and Santa Anita tracks and, further south, at the beautiful Del Mar racecourse, just north of San Diego. Throughout the summer there are volleyball competitions all the way down the costal strip and the Championship Surfer Meet in Huntington Beach in September packs the town of Huntington with spectators.

Participation. A great deal of the social life of Southern California revolves around activities. After an ideal morning sunbathing, perhaps you will feel inclined to get some exercise on the ski slopes. There are 15 major ski areas inland from Los Angeles, offering all types of slope. The season usually runs from November until April.

Ocean sportsfishing services are available at Long Beach, Marina del Rey, Malibu, Redondo Beach, San Pedro, Santa Monica, Seal Branch, Dana Point and Newport Beach. Marina del Rey is the world's largest man-made pleasure boat harbour and is home to over 6,000 recreational boats.

Roller skating is another popular form of exercise and transport along the boardwalks bordering the beach. Skates can be rented for about $2 an hour; additional protection and wrist guards are usually a dollar or so extra, but are a good investment for the amateur.

There are thousands of tennis courts in the area, including private, pay-for-play and free public facilities. Most of them are floodlit for night play as well. When they're not skiing, fishing, skating or volleying, most Los Angelenos are out jogging. For details of organized runs, consult the "On the Run" column in Saturday's *Los Angeles Times.*

SHOPPING

Shopping runs the gamut from high-priced quality department stores and trendy boutiques to inexpensive national chain stores. The West Coast's influential garment industry is centered on downtown LA, the city that claims to have invented both the bikini and blue jeans. The stores are shabby rather than glittering in the garment district and specialize in selling casual and sports clothes at bargain prices.

Beverly Hills — and Rodeo Drive in particular — is a mecca for sophisticated shoppers. Visit on a Saturday when the posers are out in full force. Some of the world's most expensive shops like Gucci's, Giorgio's and Hermes are all congregated in a two block area around Rodeo Drive. Don't try to browse in the ultra-exclusive Bijan; you have to make an appointment. The Beverly Center Mall is less exclusive.

For the trendiest clothing, Melrose Avenue has developed into what King's Road, Chelsea used to be in the sixties. It is worth a stroll along the street just to see the weirdly dressed promenaders. If you are fed up with LA, visit Thomas Bros Maps & Travel Bookstore (603 W 7th St) or Maps to Anywhere (1514 North Hillhurst Avenue, Hollywood) to plan your escape.

THE MEDIA

Television. Tours of the NBC Television Studios (3000 W Alameda Avenue, Burbank, 840-3537) are available for $7. You might get a chance to see a programme being taped. Other TV studios also throw open their doors to the public. Enquire about tickets at the Visitors Information Center, or contact CBS Studios (7800 Beverly Boulevard, LA 90036).

Radio. KFWB (980 AM, 98 FM) gives local and national news 24 hours a day; KMPC (710 AM) is best for sport, KRLA (1110 AM) specializes in old rock music; KROQ (106.7 FM) is the station for the latest hits. KKGO (105

FM) plays virtually nothing but jazz; KFAC (92.3 FM) is the 24-hour classical music station. For those interested in information about cheap flights to and from Britain, KFAC (1330 AM) presents a two-hour programme for British expatriates every Sunday morning at 10am, and also plays old Tony Hancock radio favourites. If you've seen the movie *American Graffiti,* you may wonder if Wolfman Jack is a real disc jockey. He is, and can be heard performing in his over-the-top fashion on Pasadena's KRLA.

Newspapers. The *Los Angeles Times* is the main daily newspaper. British papers are on sale at the University City Library (630 W 5th St). A magazine for the British community in and around LA is called *British Weekly.*

Los Angeles is one of the most dangerous cities in the world. Random killings are almost commonplace. Even so, the statistical chances of being involved are minute. Most crimes involving visitors tend to be thefts from hotel rooms and the occasional purse-snatching in the street. There are no strict rules, but it is a good idea to avoid the area of Santa Monica Pier and the Venice beaches after dark, and also MacArthur Park. The downtown area attracts all sort of wierd and seedy characters at night, and Hollywood and Vine can be similarly creepy. Boys and girls sell themselves in broad daylight along the more sordid sections of Sunset Boulevard. East LA, outside the downtown area, is notorious for armed battles between rival street gangs. These gangs, which derive their income from drug dealing, are now spilling over previously civilized suburbs.

Marijuana has been decriminalized in the state of California for quantities under one ounce. Many Southern Californians drive down to Tijuana where drugs which require a prescription in the US are freely available.

As well as the threat from malevolent humans, LA is in constant danger of a severe earthquake. The last serious tremor killed six people when is struck in 1987, and seismologists estimate that there is a 50% chance of a massive quake striking the area in the next 30 years.

Help and Information

The area code for Los Angeles is 213; for the San Fernando Valley dial 818. Orange County is 714.

Information: The Greater Los Angeles Visitors and Convention Bureau is on Level B of the ARCO Plaza at 505 S Flower St. (624-7300). There are several regional information offices e.g. at Anaheim (714-999-8999) and at Santa Monica (393-9825). These offices provide maps, calendars of events and tickets for TV shows. Also ring the Info Line (686-0950) for a 24 hour information and referral service.
British Consulate-General: 3701 Wilshire Blvd (385-7381).
American Express: Beverly Center, 131 N La Cienega Blvd #706 (659-1682).
Post Office: 900 N Alameda (617-4491).
Western Union: 687-9750.
Medical Emergencies: USC Medical Center, 1200 N State St (226-2622).
Dental Service: 481-2133
24 hour drugstore: Thrifty Drugs, 3rd St and Vermont Avenue (381-5257).

Traveler's Aid: Greyhound Bus Terminal (625-2501) and International Airport (646-2271).
Hollywood Lifeline: 963-5433.
Sex Info Hotline: 653-1123.

Further Afield 61

SAN DIEGO

In terms of population, San Diego rather than San Francisco is California's second city. Just 15 miles north of the Mexican border town of Tijuana, San Diego is blessed with clean air, miles of beaches and weather once voted the most perfect in the USA. Once a haven for senior citizens, the median age has dropped and the city is undergoing a facelift. A $140 million convention centre with a sail-like rooftop structure has already become an architectural landmark on the city's skyline. San Diego has ample attractions including the USA's best zoo, the fascinating museums of Balboa Park and Old Town and an environment infinitely more pleasant than that of LA.

Arrival and Departure. San Diego International Airport (Lindbergh Field) is at the northwest edge of town, across from Harbor Island, and has services from most major North American cities plus London. Fog sometimes delays take-offs and landings. Take San Diego Transit bus 2 downtown for $1 or a cab for about $7. You can take a bus to San Diego both by Greyhound whose terminal is at 120 W. Broadway at 1st Ave (239-9171) and Green Tortoise (1-800-227-4766). Amtrak rail services terminate at Santa Fe Depot, 1050 Kettner Blvd (239-9021), which is also the terminus for the Trolley to the Mexican border. If you plan to cross into Mexico, see page 260 for details of formalities. The main freeway approaches to San Diego are 1-5 which runs down a lovely coast road from Los Angeles, and 1-8 which comes in from the desert to the east. Hitch-hiking along either is difficult.

City Transport. Downtown is easy to find your way round because of its grid design of streets: consecutive numbers running north-south, letters A-L running east-west. San Diego is safer than most American cities.

It is easy to reach most areas in the city on the regional transit system. A new Bayside trolley line, which will serve the convention centre and downtown, is expected to be completed in 1989. Fares vary: 60c for North County transit routes, $1 for local routes, $1.25 for express bus routes, and $2.25 for commuter rides; some transfers are free, others are free. Exact change is required. Some buses have bike racks! The Transit Store at 449 Broadway sells a one-day unlimited travel pass for $3, two-day for $5, three-day for $7.

You can rent a car at standard California rates. Best bargain: Rent-a-Car Cheap at 1747 Pacific Hwy (232-2041) where there are bangers going for $8 a day unlimited mileage plus insurance for another $8 a day. San Diego is cyclist's paradise. Caltrans, 4080 Taylor St (231-24530) provide maps and pamphlets of bike hire shops and paths. Most shops will also rent you skates, boogie boards, and even surfboards.

Accommodation. As tourism is booming, making reservations makes sense. Inexpensive digs can be found in hostels, Y's, and even no-frills motels for anywhere between $13-18 a night for a single. There are AYH hostels at 3790 Udall St (223-4778) and 170 Palm Avenue, Imperial Beach (423-8039).

The Armed Services YMCA Hostel at 500 W Broadway (232-1133) has dormitory beds for only $5 a night.

Eating and Drinking. San Diego boasts Afghan, barbecue, Brazilian, Cajun, Greek, Middle Eastern, Mexican, Oriental, seafood and vegetarian restaurants. For Mexican, try La Veva's Mexican Cafe on 939 E St (234-7795) where two enchiladas with rice goes for $2.85; for vegetarians, there's the House of Nutrition on 1125 6th Ave (239-9453) where herbed soy loaf with mushroom gravy costs 89c; for Chinese, try Hong Kong Restaurant at 3781 4th Ave (291-944) where Cantonese, Mandarin or Szechuan main dish, soup, rice and eggroll can be had for about $4; for good value, San Diego Chicken Pie Shop at 3801 5th Ave (295-0156) where pie, whipped potatoes, vegetables, roll and dessert sets you back a staggeringly slight $3.10. Go to the Farmer's Bazaar for cheap fresh fruit and vegetables. The best barbecue in California is Gellerosa Ranch at 120 Ash St (232-2838), featuring wood burning pit, Oklahoma secret sauce, beef, ribs, chicken, hot links and crab salad. You might overdose on protein.

San Diego has plenty of good bars, and some reasonable wineries to visit and sample in the Temecula Valley an hour away.

Entertainment. Like LA, San Diego has a lot going for it with the additional advantage of having it contained within a reasonable area. Don't leave town without seeing the zoo in Balboa Park (234-3153); and visit Sea World at Mission Bay unless you've visited its counterparts in Florida, Ohio or Texas. To find out what's going on, consult the *Reader,* a free weekly paper that lists dates, places and prices, or call Arts & Entertainment Hotline (234-ARTS). The Arts Tix Ticket Center on 121 Broadway & 1st Ave features half-price day of performance tickets to theatre, music and dance events. In summer, Shakespeare is performed in the outdoor Old Globe theatre in Balboa Park.

Plenty of music and dance is provided by the San Diego Foundation for the Performing Arts (701 B St, 234-5855), the San Diego Opera, San Diego Performances and San Diego Symphony (1245 7th Ave 699-4205). The best clubs for blues or rock include the Mandolin Wind at 308 University Ave (297-3017), the singles bar Confetti's at 5373 Mission Center Rd (291-8635) whose Happy Hours between 5-8pm include two-for-the-price-of-one drinks and free chow, Diego's Club and Cantina, a surfers' hangout on 860 Garnet Ave (272-1241).

Like most Americans, denizens of SD think they have a comic genius. If you're interested in seeing budding comics, try either The Comedy Store on 916 Pearl St in nearby La Jolla (454-9176) or The Improv at 832 Garnet Ave (232-3121).

San Diego had some impressive museums, particularly the Museum of Photographic Arts, San Diego Museum of Art and the Timken Art Gallery in Balboa Park, a park larger in area than downtown SD and ideal for picnics. A "Passport to Balboa Park" gives you entrance tickets to four museums for $8 (Information Center in the House of Hospitality, 1549 El Prado, Balboa Park, 232-2053).

Sport. A major feature of the local lifestyle, especially watersports. On any weekend at Mission Bay Park, a 4,600-acre aquatic park, countless swimmers, sail surfers, water-skiers and rowers are afloat on the Pacific. There's also horseracing nearby and both greyhound racing and jai alai 15 miles south in Tijuana. For those interested in spectator sports, there's the San Diego Chargers for pro football and the San Diego Padres for baseball.

Basketball fans might appreciate one of the best American college teams called the San Diego State University Aztecs. The oddest (and perhaps most enjoyable) SD sport, though, has to be whale watching. There's a free whale-watching station at Cabrillo National Monument on Point Loma, as well as cruises provided by the National History Museum. However, it's only during winter months that the California Grey Whale and others migrate close enough to shore.

Shopping. Try the Price Bazaar at 1140 Broadway, Chula Vista, where 60 shops include a constantly changing bazaar with handmade items; Clothing Clearance Centers (three locations) with designer men's clothes at discount prices; and the Southpaw Shoppe at 803 W. Harbor Dr, featuring items for left-handed people. Bargains on liquor and Mexican goods may be obtained in Tijuana.

Help and Information. The area code for San Diego is 619.

Information: Visitor Information Center, 11 Horton Plaza (236-1212) and San Diego Convention & Visitors Bureau, 1200 3rd Ave, Suite 824, San Diego, CA 92101 (232-3101). The last named will send you free the best package of maps, brochures, calendars and fact sheets of any American city.

Post Office: 2535 Midway Dr (221-3310).

American Express: 1640 Camino del Rio N. (297-8101).

Travelers Aid: Airport, 231-7376.

Women's Crisis Hotline: 232-3088.

Lesbian and Gay Men's Center: 692-GAYS.

Apart from the road south to San Diego, there are two principal escape routes from the glitter and glamour of LA. Many people set off on the eight or nine hour drive to San Francisco, preferring to take the very scenic Highway 1 which hugs the cliff-lined coast. There are many worthwhile stop-overs such as the quintessentially Southern Californian lotus-eating town of Santa Barbara where everyone sips cocktails by the pool all day, and Big Sur, once an important hippie landmark. It is possible to sleep rough on the beaches along this coast, though campsites are readily available in the national forests and parks.

The other direction which might tempt you is inland, to visit forests, deserts, and Mount Whitney, which is the highest mountain in the continental USA. Place names like Yucca Valley, Cactus Gardens and Palm Desert immediately convey the climate and geography of much of the area. The states of Arizona, Nevada and southern California are very dry and attract hayfever and rheumatism sufferers from all over the country. Palm Springs is the millionaire oasis resort about 120 miles southeast of LA. Not only is every home and pulic building air-conditioned, but the city planners are working on ways to air condition outdoor areas such as restaurant patios and complete streets. This is not surprising, considering that the average daily maximum between June and September is over 100°F.

Death Valley's temperatures are even more horrifying. This enormous area on the border with Nevada is almost intolerably hot in summer (average July high is 115°F), and therefore heavily visited in winter. But the coloured landscape and odd rock formations make a visit worthwhile. Be sure to take enough water in the summer (see the section on *Summer Driving* in the Introduction).

For spectacular natural scenery in more temperate conditions, the adjoining national parks of Sequoia and Kings Canyon, due north of LA, are worthwhile. the hardwood trees called Sequoia Gigantea (after a Cherokee chief) grow to mammoth proportions: the largest is 275 feet tall and 102 feet in circumference.

And for the be-all and end-all in natural wonders, you will want to make the pilgrimage to the Grand Canyon in northern Arizona. Its immensity and beauty are sufficient to compensate for the crowds and commercialism which are never absent from this unmissable tourist destination. All manner of accommodation is available, but must be booked well in advance. Ring the central Hotels Switchboard for reservations (638-2401) or for campsite information try the Backcountry Reservations Office, South Rim Visitors Center (Grand Canyon National Park, Arizona 86023, 602-638-2474).

It is possible to hike to the base of the canyon (which is a mile deep) to the Colorado River, but this should not be undertaken lightly. It is normally a two day trip and accommodation at the base must be secured in advance. It is however a sure way of leaving behind the folks who are continuously disgorged from tour buses.

Strange and striking landforms, abound in these states and it is most worthwhile to take a leisurely drive which takes in the Petrified Forest and Painted desert in eastern Arizona full of colourful geological formations, canyons, caves,sand dunes, meteor craters, mesas (table-shaped hills) and buttes (isolated flat-topped hills). There is also an abundance of interesting flora and fauna. Six hundred species of plants live in the isolation of Death Valley, many of which are unique to the area.

LAS VEGAS

Few visitors to the Southwest can resist the temptation of a few days in Las Vegas. Between Death Valley and the Grand Canyon, this neon-lit monstrosity rises improbably out of the desert. The artificiality and lavishness of "Glitter Gulch" as downtown Las Vegas is known, is more extreme than anything Los Angeles can offer and is best appreciated after a drive across the tranquil, elemental desert rather than after a flight.

Las Vegas's undisguised vulgarity and hectic commercialism can easily be made into a symbol for modern American life — or at least one important aspect of it — and this alone is a reason to visit. There is very little of historic interest ("Old Vegas", out of town, is a pure tourist trap) although you may care to glance up at the top floor of the Desert Inn where Howard Hughes spent the last ten years of his life. Especially after you have bankrupted your own coffers, it may strike you as a morally bankrupt place where the drunken and boisterous rabble come only to visit gambling houses, quickie divorce lawyers or brothels. Nevada is the only state in which prostitution is legal, though it has recently been banned in several counties, including Las Vegas County. For detailed information about the 38 brothels in the state, consult a book available in most Nevada bookshops called *The Layman's Guidebook to the Brothels of Nevada*. The going rate for straight sex is about $100 per hour.

Most people come to Las Vegas prepared to squander a little (or a lot) along the famous four-mile Strip or in downtown Las Vegas which is some distance away and offers less fashionable and less expensive casinos and hotels. Professional gamblers congregate at Binion's Horseshoe Casino on Fremont St, where the poker World Series is held each Spring. The entrance to Binion's features a horseshoe enclosing one million dollars in

$10,000 bills. Among high rollers a "nickel" is $500, a "dime"is $1,000 and a "big dime" is $10,000. Everyone, whether feeding quarters into machines or staking "big dimes" at the poker table, is hoping for the gold at the end of the rainbow. Three billion dollars are fed annually into the slot machines alone. Normal self-restraint evaporates in the midst of an atmosphere which intoxicates. Night and day blend together in one long orgy of gambling and pleasure-seeking, for the bars and casinos never close and there are no public clocks.

Whereas gambling is expensive, everything else is cheap. Food, drink, entertainment (including the latest Broadway extravaganzas) and accommodation (cheap motels from $20 a double) are often subsidized by the casinos. Many hotels offer buffet breakfasts, lunches or dinners for ridiculously low prices, say $1.99, served at anytime of the day or night. There is no admission charge to any casino and you may be offered a free drink as soon as you stroll in. If you stand at a slot machine with a stack of quarters, judiciously inserting one whenever a waitress passes, you may be set up for an evening of free drinks. Everything is geared to bribe the reluctant gambler to part with some money. Competition among the casinos is fierce and books of coupons, which are given away at hotels or on the street, might entitle you to a free deck of cards or miniature of bourbon, sometimes even bags of coins for the slot machines (which you should change into notes to avoid temptation).

Even travelling to Las Vegas is subsidized: advertisements placed in LA and San Diego newpapers offer 24-hour trips to Las Vegas for a nominal $5. The condition is that you must spend six hours in the casino that sponsored the bus (and your attendance will be checked), although there is no compulsion to gamble.

If you are tempted to participate in any of the more serious games like blackjack, roulette, baccarat or craps, spend as much time as possible watching the game being played and have the rules mastered before putting down any money. *The Biggest Game in Town* by poet Al Alvarez (Flamingo Books) provides a good introduction. For big-time losers, destitute cardholders can order up a few hundred more dollars at cash machines in every casino.

There is also plenty of gambling at Reno (a slightly less brash version of Vegas), the south shore of Lake Tahoe and Carson City which all offer well-run and big name casinos. In between, virtually every truck stop and hole-in-the wall bar in Nevada has gambling facilities of one kind or another. The one exception is Boulder City, which was built to house the workers on the nearby Hoover Dam.

Calendar of Events

January 1	Tournament of Roses Parade, Pasadena
April	Tucson Festival, Arizona
early July—early August	Flagstaff Festival of the Arts, Arizona
July	Hollywood Bowl Summer Festival
September	Mexican Indepedence Day
late November	Hollywood Christmas Parade
December	Waiters/Waitresses 5km race, Beverly Hills

San Francisco and the Northwest

The Golden Gate Bridge

Northern California   Oregon   Washington

The authorities use Alistair Cooke's sobriquet to describe San Francisco as "everyone's favourite city". They do not dwell on the San Andreas fault, upon which the city was rebuilt following the 1906 earthquake. The city now has two parapet inspectors. Their sole function is to enforce the Parapet Law which requires that potentially dangerous overhangs be removed from buildings.

When people speak of San Francisco, they often mean the whole Bay Area: the city itself, plus the counties of San Mateo, Contra Costa, Marin and Alameda (which includes the cities of Oakland and Berkeley). Together they have a population of well over three million. Marin County has recently become full of very rich San Franciscans who moved north across the Golden Gate Bridge hoping to enjoy the company of the artists and writers living around Sausalito. Unfortunately, this creative community has largely been dislodged because of high property prices, and many have moved on to Oregon and Washington (where it is popular to subsidize creative talents with a little illicit agriculture).

Oakland has long been regarded as the poor relation of San Francisco, although this reputation is becoming less deserved as the city gentrifies. Neighbouring Berkeley is dominated by the radical-yet-respectable campus of the University of California, once teeming with radical students and drugs, now for more sedate and less opposed to the tenets of yuppie materialism.

San Francisco was originally settled because the Bay provided a natural harbour. This was of critical importance prior to the transcontinental railway, since the sea route was the easiest way to the West. The village of

Yerba Buena (now submerged beneath Chinatown) was the obvious ocean base for the 1848 / 49 Gold Rush.

Nowadays, with its winding streets and cultivated inhabitants, San Francisco is perhaps the most European of American cities. But it also reflects many of the most appealing features of the USA. The architecture varies from cosy hill terraces to stunningly dramatic skyscrapers, including the not inconspicuous TransAmerica pyramid and the 52-storey Bank of America, the largest (but not the tallest) building in the USA. There are also many oases of calm and charm. One such is Nob Hill, which might be reminiscent of Montmartre or Hampstead were it not for the proliferation of luxury hotels. The food is superlative in range and quality. The arts are well-patronized and arguably superior to the offerings of New York, despite San Francisco's much smaller population.

It is a city of great class and many contrasts, yet compact enough to walk around. And if the hills become too much for your feet, you can take advantage of the most varied urban transport system in North America.

THE NATIVES

The people of San Francisco take great pride in their city. They never refer to it as "Frisco", which they consider a vulgar appelation. They are among the nation's richest citizens, with an average income of nearly $20,000. The population is comprised of 60% white, 15% Asian, 13% Black and 12% Hispanic. The Asian contingent consists mainly of 65,000 Chinese crammed into a few acres of Chinatown, although there is also a substantial Japanese population plus increasing numbers of Koreans and Vietnamese. The city fosters ethnic diversity and the various groups which make up the city's population are remarkably tolerant of one another.

There are no accurate figures for the number of gay people in San Francisco. although it is certainly a large, visible and vocal minority of probably more than 100,000. It is the only city in the States where the gay community has real political power; gay activists are involved in the whole spectrum of political life, from voter registration to holding office. Even though AIDS has cast a pall over life in San Francisco, gays continue to exert a powerful political force, and the Bay Area is arguably the most politically radical area of the USA. Mayors tend to be Democrats with liberal persuasions, and an extraordinary range of social welfare laws are in force. Smoking, for example, is forbidden virtually everywhere that the public congregate. Whether you consider this legislation to be evidence of advanced civilization or creeping authoritarianism may indicate whether or not you will feel at home in San Francisco.

Making Friends. Try the bars, bookshops and trendy restaurants in and around Sproul Plaza in Berkeley (once famous for its sit-ins). Bancroft and Telegraph Avenues are particularly promising. The Berkeley campus attracts foreign students in large numbers, so if you're yearning for a chat with a compatriot then you should be in luck. Even if you don't make a friend instantly, you can't fail to enjoy an espresso and pastry at one of the many street cafes.

In San Francisco, the singles bars lining the south-eastern half of Columbus Avenue and nearby streets cater for a slightly older and predominantly heterosexual clientele, who will waste no time in striking up conversation with unfamiliar faces. Be prepared for detailed psychoanalytical case histories.

San Francisco's gays meet in clubs and bars throughout the city, with the highest concentrations around Castro and Polk Streets. Check the listings

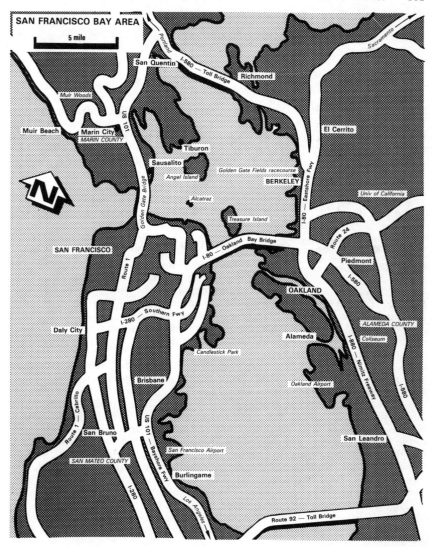

in the *Advocate* for the currently fashionable venues. Most establishments are single sex, usually male.

California is still a stronghold for the Unification Church, better known as the Moonies, though the power of the church has waned. Pairs of religious fanatics prowl the streets, airports and bus stations in search of innocent tourists. However genuine their offer of coffee and a meal may seem, you are advised to be very wary.

There are few hippies left over from the flower power era; if you want to meet the survivors, note that they have abandoned their former haunts around the junction of Haight and Ashbury Streets and can now be found in Berkeley. To meet more conservative San Franciscans, call 986-1388 for details of the "Meet Americans at Home" Scheme; at least 48 hours notice is required.

CLIMATE

Mark Twain is quoted as saying "the worst winter I ever spent was summer in San Francisco". The city has a reputation for being permanently enshrouded in the mists that roll in under the Golden Gate from the Pacific. But in fact there are 162 clear days each year, compared with 93 in New York and 57 in Seattle. Between June and August there is virtually no precipitation, but you have to contend with the hordes of tourists. Spring and autumn are much less crowded, and it is quite possible to chance upon a spell of fine, sunny weather. There is usually an Indian summer from mid-September to mid-October which is a delightful time to visit. Between November and April take a raincoat. You won't need much cold-weather gear since temperatures almost never fall below freezing. This is fortunate in view of the chaos which would ensure if the slopes of San Francisco iced up. Dial 936-1212 for the latest weather forecast.

ARRIVAL AND DEPARTURE

Air. San Francisco International Airport (SFO) lies 15 miles south of the city. International travellers arrive at the Central Terminal and connections to onward flights are easy. If your outbound flight is delayed, you could try the sauna (mezzanine floor, South Terminal) or the beauty shop. With any luck, you won't be delayed long enough to need the services of the airport morgue.

The recommended taxi fare is posted outside the terminal: $24 to downtown, $28 to Fisherman's Wharf. The Airporter bus (495 - 8404) links the airport with various hotels in central San Francisco. Departures are approximately every 20 minutes from 6am to midnight then hourly through the night. The journey takes 30 minutes normally, an hour in rush hours and costs $4 one way, $7 return. If there are crowds of passengers waiting for the bus, just walk up one floor to pick up the bus as it deposits departing passengers before descending to the arrivals level. Other buses run directly to all points in the Bay Area for slightly higher fares. Slower buses will take you into San Francisco (express 7F or local bus 7B), or the metro (called BART) terminus at Daly City (bus 3B) for about a dollar. They are operated by SamTrans (761-7000) which allows large amounts of luggage only on specially designated buses. If you're loaded down or just plain exhausted, use the SuperShuttle van service to anywhere in downtown San Francisco for $8; call 558-8500 to arrange a pick-up upon departure.

Hitch-hiking south from the airport is feasible: walk straight out of the terminal area to the sliproad leading to US 101 (Bayshore Freeway).

Oakland International Airport (OAK) is across the bay in south Oakland, about 18 miles southeast of San Francisco. It is much more convenient for Berkeley and all points east. Many frequent travellers also prefer it for its compactness (maximum walk: five minutes) and relative quietness. *Airporter* buses run every half-hour to San Francisco (40 minutes eastbound, 50 minutes westbound) for $5 each way, with another service to 320 20th St in Oakland. The Oakland Air BART bus (AC57) links the airport with Coliseum/Oakland Airport BART station, it takes ten minutes and costs $1.

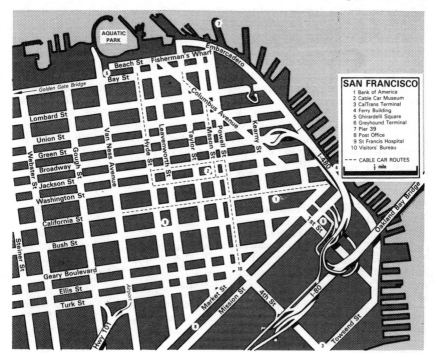

Travellers looking for a cheap flight to the Far East should check the travel agencies in Chinatown; their low fares to Asia are also advertised in the classified columns of the *San Francisco Chronicle* and the *Examiner*.

Bus. The counties bordering on San Francisco are served by buses from the Transbay Transit Terminal at 1st and Mission Streets. AC Transit (635-3535) serves Berkeley, Oakland and the rest of Alameda County; SamTrans (761-7000) runs south through the peninsula to San Mateo County; Golden Gate Transit (332-6600) operates buses across the Golden Gate bridge to Marin County, plus ferries across the Bay (see below).

Greyhound (433-1500) operates from the depot at 1st and Mission Streets, beneath the freeway sprawl and close to Market St and the Civic Center. Green Tortoise (821-0803) and Grey Rabbit (621-1550) run sleeperbuses to the East Coast and up and down the West Coast; the Friday and Sunday night services to Los Angeles on Green Tortoise cost $30 one way.

Train. The CalTrain depot at 4th and Townsend Streets (557-8661) operates commuter services only, although connections with the Amtrak line to Los Angeles are possible by taking a train to the terminus at San Jose. Otherwise, prospective train travellers must take the free Amtrak shuttle bus from the Transbay Terminal to 16th St Station in Oakland (982-8512). There is one train daily (the *Coast Starlight*) to both Los Angeles and Seattle; another runs south through central California but only as far as Bakersfield; and the *Californian Zephyr* departs daily to Chicago via Denver. Sample one-way fares are Los Angeles $65, Seattle $110 and Chicago $350.

Driving. San Francisco has no Los Angeles-style network of freeways. The road system in this hilly, compact area consists mainly of two- or four-lane streets with traffic lights at every intersection. Out of town, the main highways of interest to travellers are State Highway 1, the most spectacular coast road in America, though beware of fog; US 101, a freeway for most of its length as it winds along the coast a little inland (and the road that cross the Golden Gate Bridge); I-80, straight to New York; and I-5, an eastern by-pass for the city used only by philistines in too much of a hurry to get from LA to Seattle to stop.

Urban freeways reserve the extreme left-hand lane for buses and pool cars. The remaining lanes are crowded and frantic during rush hours, so try to plan your approach and departure at other times.

Tolls on the two strategic bridges — the Golden Gate and the Oakland Bay — are charged only inbound to San Francisco.

Driveaways. Because the Bay Area is such a popular destination for settlers, there are more inbound than outbound driveaways. In addition, there is a large student community and many like-minded visitors all in search of driveaways. Don't bother trying to find one around the end of the university terms. At other times, try all the companies listed in the Yellow Pages and resign yourself to a long wait. The most likely destinations are Texas and the East Coast; there is little driveaway traffic up or down the West Coast, because the distances are too small.

Ride Sharing. Ride sharing is a major industry; check the noticeboards around the campus at Berkeley, or ring the radio station KALX (642-1111). Los Angeles is by far the most popular destination, followed by Seattle, Vancouver and the East Coast.

Hitch-hiking. Hitchers may wish to visit 29 Russell St in San Francisco, where Jack Kerouac wrote *On the Road*. Hitch-hiking in the Bay Area is probably better than when he wrote about it: there is a large student population, thousands of motor-borne tourists who take pity on their pedestrian kin and a widespread acceptance of the practice. For US 101 south to Los Angeles, start from San Francisco Airport. Heading north on US 101, try the approach roads to, or the exit from, the Golden Gate Bridge. A faster route north is I-5 which you can pick up by taking BART to Berkeley, then the free bus (Monday-Friday only) to University Avenue. Although often choked with hitchers, no one seems to wait around for long. Berkeley is also a good bet for I-80 east. An alternative is to take BART to Concord, then hitch on I-680 which leads on to I-80.

CITY TRANSPORT

Walking is an excellent way to get around the compact city centre, but can be exhausting because of the hills. "If you get tired of San Francisco", said columnist Herb Caen, "you can always lean against it". Or you can take advantage of the efficient MUNI public transport system, which includes buses, streetcars (trams) and the famous cable cars. For information ring 673-MUNI and tell them which intersection you are near and where you want to go. You can pick up a map showing all MUNI services from their office at 949 Presidio Avenue.

Buses and Streetcars. Whenever you board a vehicle, pay the driver the flat fare of 75c (25c for under 18s). Always ask for a transfer. This is a timed ticket valid for two hours on any MUNI service, although return or circular journeys are prohibited. Visitors staying for several weeks are advised to get a Fast Pass which allows unlimited travel on the MUNI system for 30 days for $25.

Note that some streetcars — lines J to N inclusive — run through tunnels in the city centre equipped with proper stations.

Cable Cars. This anachronistic mode of transport is both a National Historic Monument and an integral part of the MUNI system. Looking like a cross between an old railway carriage and a Disneyland ride, each is operated by a crew of two. The driver uses a level-operated pincer to latch on to the cable which runs along a channel beneath the tracks. This pulls the cars up the one-in-six slopes and retards them on the downhill run. He also has a selection of brakes at his disposal, the most effective of which gouges chunks out of the road, tracks and cable to stop the car in an extreme emergency. The conductor collects fares ($1.50) and issues transfers. The system of fare registration and signalling is a Heath Robinson network of levers, rods and bells.

The cable is driven at a constant 9 mph from the Powerhouse at Mason and Washington Streets, also the site of a free museum describing the building and running of the system. The recent refurbishment has not affected the construction nor quaintness of the system. Its main purpose seems to have been to satisfy the clause in the City Charter that the cable cars shall run forever.

If there is a queue at the terminus where you wish to join, walk a block or two to the next stop; the conductor ensures that the cars leave with enough room to pick up passengers en route. As benefits a National Historic Monument, there are special rules for riding. When you board, you are supposed to move inside to the spartan cabin. Many visitors ignore the rules (until admonished by the conductor), and cling to the hand rails as the car lurches around corners. There are three lines: Powell-Mason, Powell-Hyde and California St, which intersect close to the summit of Nob Hill.

The Bay Area Rapid Transit - BART. The BART system is San Francisco's above and below ground railway and extends deep into the border counties. It provides a cheap and fast means of transport once you've mastered the method of payment. This involves finding a computer-like ticket machine at the station, pushing the button for your destination, then feeding in coins or notes to the amount shown. At some machines, change is given automatically. The minimum fare is 80c; highest fare (for a 25-mile journey) is $3, with most fares between $1 and $2. For information call 788-BART. There is an excellent pamphlet called *All about BART* which explains the whole system clearly. There is also one entitled *Fun Goes Further on BART* which lists all the attractions in the Bay Area and how to reach them by public transport. Services start at 6 am (9 am on Sundays) and run through to midnight. There is a handy free bus between the Berkeley BART station and the University campus called the Humphrey Go-BART bus, which operates Monday to Friday.

Car. Rights of way will be asserted by cable cars and streetcars. If you'd like to test your brakes, steering and nerve, then try Lombard Street between Hyde and Leavenworth Streets; ten hairpin bends in a single block, down a one-in-six slope. It is ungrammatically described as the "Crookedest Street in the World".

Parking is a constant nightmare for residents, and visitors hardly stand a chance. The whole city is zoned: red means don't even consider parking: an enthusiastic posse of towing trucks roams the streets ready to pounce on offenders (minimum recovery $75); yellow zones permit parking after 6 pm and before 8 am; green means you can park for ten whole minutes during the day, or any time from 6 pm-8 pm. Even if you do find a street space, you have to ensure your car won't roll away. A city ordinance requires that all cars be left in gear (the "parking" setting on automatics) with the wheels turned towards the kerb. The best plan is to use a free Park'n'Ride lot (signposted on all approach routes) or to pay the $12 per day demanded by downtown parking lots.

The "49-mile Drive" is a well-signposted circuit of the city and its sights, but not worth undertaking during business hours because of the severe downtown congestion.

Car hire is among the cheapest in the USA, and you should find a good deal by ploughing through the 15 Yellow Pages on the subject in the local directory. Rent-a-Heap-Cheap (776-5450) 777 Van Ness Avenue, is a local alternative to Rent-a-Wreck (776-8700) at 555 Ellis St.

Mopeds. In the last few years numerous moped rental firms have sprung up in the city. McCall's Moped Rentals (112 Gough St, 552-6561) hire out 80cc Honda Elites for $60 per day; this sounds expensive, but the bikes carry two people, fuel is cheap and parking problems are alleviated. A 50cc Honda goes for $40. A full driving licence is required.

Taxis. Downtown San Francisco is choked with yellow, blue, red, orange and mauve cabs. They congregate outside the major hotels and at the foot of hills, to tempt foot-weary pedestrians. Away from the city centre, taxis are hard to find; ring Allied (826-9494) Luxor or DeSoto (673-0333) for strategic bridges inbound to San Francisco.

Cycling. San Francisco is not the easiest (because of the hills) nor the safest (because of the cable car and streetcar tracks) city in which to cycle, although many residents are not perturbed. To hire a bike, try the Bike Shop, 4621 Lincoln Way (665-3092) or any of the bike shops on Stanyan St adjacent to Golden Gate Park. Cycling maps of the Bay Area are available from Caltrans at 150 Oak St (557-1611) and show the two dedicated scenic cycle routes. One goes through the Park and on to Lake Merced, while the other goes from the south of the city over into Marin Country. Riding a bicycle across the Golden Gate Bridge is a splendid experience (it is also possible to walk). There is no special bicycle path across the Oakland Bay Bridge. To obtain a BART bike permit, call 465-4100 extension 569.

Those visitors to the city in May or September each year may wish to join a three-day cycling tour of the backcountry roads of Marin and Sonoma. For details of the Golden Gate Bike Trek, call 543-2880.

Ferries. The Marin County towns of Sausalito and Tiberon are served by commuter launches from the Ferry Building at the foot of Market St in San Francisco. Golden Gate Ferries (332-6600) run to Sausalito for about $4. The Red and White Fleet (546-2896) also serves Sausalito as well as Tiberon from Pier 43½ at Fisherman's Wharf. Even if you don't have an overwhelming desire to visit Marin County, ferries offer a cheap alternative to sightseeing trips around the Bay.

Accommodation

San Francisco is a very popular place to be, and this is reflected in the high cost of rooms. Rock-bottom hotels (in terms of both price and standards) are available, but may involve sharing a dormitory or a mattress on the floor. Try one of the following which (in 1988) offered double rooms for $30 per night or less: *All Seasons,* 417 Stockton (986-8737); *Pensione Internationale,* 875 Post St (775-3344); *Golden City Inn,* 1554 Howard St (431-9376). Across in Oakland, the Hotel Touraine (559 16th St, 832-2100) has the advantage of toll-free numbers for advance reservations: call 1-800-421-7548 from outside California, 1-800-238-4916 from within the state. The Convention and Visitors Bureau in Hallidie Plaza (974-6000) will happily place you in more respectable hotels; if what they have to offer is too expensive, then there is also a hotel information desk in the airport (arrivals hall of the North Terminal). Motels (mostly chains) line the Bayshore Freeway (US 101) from the city south to the airport.

On top of the usual sales tax, a "transient tax" is added to your accommodation bill adding 11% to the total. The extra tax is used to finance culture in the city.

Hostels. The YMCA has hostels at 220 Golden Gate Avenue (885-0460) and 166 The Embarcadero (392-2191); a double costs $35. The Youth Hostel Centrale, 116 Turk St (3HO-STEL), is not a member of the AYH, but does have cheap rooms: $10 per night sharing a double, with reductions for weekly rentals. The city's AYH hostel is at Building 240 (a former Army dispensary and a registered historic building) inside Fort Mason Park. It lies at the corner of Bay and Franklin Streets just west of Fisherman's Wharf (771-7277) and costs $10 per night. There is another hostel across the Golden Gate in Marin Country, but it is so inaccessible that even the AYH handbook recommends hiring a cab from Sausalito to reach it. For the hardy, its address is 1941 Fort Barry (331-2777). Several more worth investigating include the European Guest House, 761 Minna (861-6634) for $9 a per night and the International Network Cotel, 10 Hallam Place (431-0540) for $10 per night.

Student Residences. If you are staying for a month or more in summer, then the student residences at Berkeley present an economic alternative. Most are privately owned. Consult the *Berkeley Barb* or simply look around the streets for a suitable vacation let. San Francisco State University's Housing Office (338-1067) is worth contacting during summer if your an overseas student. Reckon on $20 per night there.

Bed and Breakfast. The cost of bed and breakfast in San Francisco is in line with hotel prices. Do not be misled by the numerous Bed and Breakfast Inns: these are small, smart, expensive hotels rather than private homes. One of the most pleasant of these is the Golden Gate Hotel at 775 Bush St (392-3702) near the Powell St cable car route. Tasteful doubles cost $45 which includes an excellent breakfast of croissants and coffee. For the real thing, call Bed and Breakfast International (151 Ardmore Rd, Kensington 94707, 525-4569). It might also be worth contacting the California Office of Tourism at 1121 L Street, Suite 103, Sacramento, California 95814, for their free directory of bed and breakfast inns throughout the state.

The city ordinance which prohibits camping or sleeping out is strictly enforced in the parks and beaches. For official sites, go north to Marin County or south to the environs of Palo Alto. Reservations may be necessary in the summer.

Eating and Drinking

The choice of restaurants in the Bay Area is awesome. While the Manhattan Yellow Pages carries 33 pages of restaurants, the San Francisco edition runs to 46. The average San Franciscan spends $800 each year on eating out, and there is one restaurant for every 200 inhabitants. In Berkeley alone there are 18 French restaurants (most of them lining Shattuck Avenue) serving a population of only 100,000.

If you're in town for only a short time and are keen to save money, try Kublai Khan's Mongolian BBQ, 1160 Polk St (885-1378), Marcello's Pizza at the corner of Haight St and Filimore St (621-6700) and Cafe Orient, 438 Castro St between 18th and 19th St (863-6868), where truly delicious and filling meals can be had for about $4. Family-style Italian cooking is available at Capp's Corner, 1600 Powell St (989-2589); a 3-course set menu costs $10. And don't overlook San Francisco's salad bars. At Sizzler (Eddy and Leavenworth Streets), for example, you can eat avocado, various fruits and diverse salads and vegetables and cheese until you're gorged for $4.79. And San Francisco is an excellent place for do-it-yourself eating. There is plenty of fresh, cheap food, and the famous sour dough bread makes for delicious open sandwiches.

Many of the restaurants in Chinatown (enclosed by Powell, Bush and Kearny streets and Broadway) seem to cater purely for tourists who won't ever come back, and standards are accordingly low. Some natives claim that Chinatown is not the best area for Chinese food. For lunchtime Dim Sum, try Yank Sing, 427 Battery St (362-1640). Your bill is calculated by the number of empty dishes (around $15 for a filling meal). If you choose to dine in Chinatown, select a place where Chinese people are eating, and no menu in English is displayed.

Lesser-known Japantown (know as Nihonmachi — around Geary Boulevard and Webster Street) is less of a tourist trap and makes fuller use of the abundant seafood. Mexican restaurants are dotted around the city rather than concentrated in a particular area. Little Italy is centred on Washington Square and offers authentic Italian cuisine as well as Americanized Italian fare. Naturally, fish figures prominently in the San Francisco diet. The Fisherman's Wharf area (on the Bay between Hyde and Powell Streets) is crammed with American fish restaurants, but the same Pacific salmon and Dungeness crabs are far cheaper a few blocks inland. There is a lot of frozen fish around, so beware. One place to find the fresh article is the Tadich Grill at 240 California St. You can tell from the queues outside that this is among the best fish restaurants in town. Decadent cakes and chocolates may be found in the cafes and confectioners of Ghiradelli Square (pronounced Gear-ar-delly), the site of an old chocolate factory just west of Fisherman's Wharf. For example, the Ghiradelli Soda Fountain and Candy Shop sells a stupendous "Golden Gate Banana Split". Berkeley is renowned for its ice cream parlours: try McCallum's on Solano Avenue, or Vivoli's which is run by feminists.

As with other American cities, cafeterias are the bargain basement of eating well; there's no tipping, service is fast, you see what you eat beforehand, and you can get up and go if you don't like what you see. Try Brother Juniper's Breadbox at 1065 Sutter St, Lipp's at 201 9th St, Manning's Cafeteria at 1275 Market St and Papa Joe's at 1412 Polk St for American food. For Mexican food served cafeteria-style, there's La Cumbra at 515 Valencia, Taqueria Pancho Villa on 16th and Valencia and La Olla at 2417 Mission St which combines Mexican with Nicaraguan and Argentinian dishes. There is a surprising number of bars in San Francisco where for a $2-2.50 drink, you can stuff yourself on free hot and cold hors d'oeuvres. Favourites include Templebar on 1 Tillman Place, White Elephant at 480

Sutter St, Front Page at 20 Annie St, MacArthur Park at 607 Front St and Jay'n Bee's Club at 1223 Polk St.

If you are down to your last few dollars, you should try the employee's cafeteria of the fancy Fairmont Hotel on Nob Hill. Go through the hotel loading dock and eat for $3.

DRINKING

Apart from Californian wine and standard North American fizzy beer, the city claims an affinity with Irish coffee for obscure historical reasons. Some bars serve little else and have elevated the drink to an art form. The Buena Vista at 2765 Hyde St (near Fisherman's Wharf) claims to have invented the drink. For a better view while you warm yourself, try Phineas T Barnacle at the Cliff House (1090 Point Lobos Avenue) which overlooks the Seal Rocks and the Pacific.

For a truly spectacular view while you drink, try Henri's on the 46th floor of the Hilton or the Carnelian Room on the 52nd floor of the Bank of America. Be prepared for sky high prices. For the ultimate straight singles bar, try Perry's, 1944 Union St (922-9022 for details of current happy hours and brunch specials). There is not much difference between Perry's establishment and the East Side bars in New York: advertising executives ogle graphic designers, unemployed actresses chat up accountants, etc.

If you want to spend an evening drinking seriously, away from the singles bars and perhaps with some jazz thrown in, try the North Beach area, around Columbus Avenue and Green Street. Or, if you consider anaesthesia a good plan, share some murderous Mai Tai with the residents of Chinatown.

Anchor Steam Beer is one of America's original naturally matured beers. You can tour the 19th century brewery and sample the end product; if you call in just prior to Christmas, taste the powerful Old Foghorn brew. Ring 863-8350 for an appointment at 1705 Malpas St. If you're feeling homesick you might want to visit the Pelican Inn in Marin County. It is a genuine British pub, imported bit by bit, and serves Guinness plus a range of British beers.

Wine Tastings. A day trip to the Napa Valley is highly recommended (see *Further Afield)*. In San Francisco itself, Sonoma Vineyards have a walk-in tasting and sales shop at 2191 Union St, as does the Napa Valley Winery Exchange at 415 Taylor St. The Wine Museum at 633 Beach St does not offer samples, but houses a collection of wine-making equipment dating from Roman times. It opens daily except Mondays.

For at least a few days you may find strolling around San Francisco is sufficient entertainment in itself. Yet it would be a shame to overlook the cultural offerings of the Bay Area, which have breadth and depth matched only by New York. Tickets for more formal events are sold through BASS (dial TELE-TIX for information) which began life as Bay Area Seating Services and has since spread nationwide. For cut-price tickets on the day, visit the STBS kiosks from noon (Tuesday-Saturday) located on the Stockton St side of Union Square. For a recorded summary of the day's events, dial 391-2000.

Museums. The island of Alcatraz, standing starkly in the middle of the Bay, was a prison from which reputedly no one ever escaped alive. It is now a museum of penal servitude. The only way to reach the island is to join a boat trip from Pier 41 or 43 ½. Call Red and White Fleet on 546-2805 for further details. The fairly energetic tour includes being locked into a cramped cell — but for half a minute rather than half a lifetime. Other options include trail walks, and cassette tours of the prison narrated by ex-cons and guards. There is a superb view of the Bay from the island.

The most prestigious museum is the M.H. de Young Memorial Museum at 8th Avenue and JFK Drive in Golden Gate Park (558-2887). It contains a range of classical art and historical treasures and houses various travelling exhibitions. In the same building is the Asian Art Museum, $3. It's free on the first Wednesday of every month.

The Museum of Modern Art in the Civic Center (863-8800) will not disappoint fans of Dali, Matisee or Picasso. Opening hours are 11am-5pm from Friday to Sunday; 10am-5pm on Tuesday and Wenesday; 5pm-9pm Thursday; closed Monday. Entrance costs $3, free on Tuesday.

The galleries and gardens of the Oakland Museum, 10th and Oak Streets (273-3401) feature the history, art and ecology of California. It opens from 10am-5pm, Wednesday-Saturday, noon-7pm Sunday.

Music. Rock'n'roll and jazz roar out from every other bar along Columbus Avenue and neighbouring side streets. The more popular live bands play at the Opera House or the Civic Auditorium; rock groups consisting largely of ageing hippies play Golden Gate Park on summer Sundays. The Fisherman's Wharf area is the venue for scores of comedians, magicians, mime artists and buskers — including a human juke box.

To find more jazz, discos and cafes, you have only to stroll around North Beach, the Haight-Ashbury area and Castro Street. Country and Western fans should try High Chaparral, 2124 Market (861-7484), where there's no cover charge, but there are dance lessons and all the beer or soft drinks you can consume for $4.

The transient tax ensures a good supply of entertainment for classical music fans. The San Francisco Symphony Orchestra (one of America's best) plays "pops" concerts (i.e. light classical music) in the Civic Auditorium in summer. For the rest of the year, a more serious repertoire is performed at the Louise M Davies Hall in the Civic Center (431-5400) at Van Ness and Grove Avenues. The Beethoven Festival takes place each June, while the Midsummer Music Festival (outdoors at Sigmund Stern Grove) has free Sunday afternoon concerts from late June to August.

Opera. The three-month San Francisco Opera season commences in early September with a performance in Golden Gate Park. The remainder of the season continues at the War Memorial Opera House in the Civic Center at Van Ness and Grove Avenues (431-1210). Each June, the International Summer Festival includes grand opera in repetory. Seats are hard to come by and extremely expensive, although cheap tickets can sometimes be had by queing on the morning of the performance. Chances are better at the Pocket Opera, which specializes in comic opera and performs at the Theater on the Square in the Kensington Park Hotel at 450 Post St and the Herb St Theater; 398-2220 for details.

Dance. The San Francisco Ballet (621-3838) shares the War Memorial Opera House. The season begins each year with Tchaikovski's Nutcracker Suite in December and lasts through until May. For avant-garde dance, try the Oberlin Dance Collective, 3153 17 St (863-6606).

Theatre. The Geary Theater at Geary and Taylor Streets (673-6440) — also known as the American Conservatory Theater — has a repertory season from October to June. The Orpheum Theater, 1192 Market St (474-3800) is host to local and travelling companies, plus (for Gilbert and Sullivan fans) the Civic Light Opera from May to July. For something a little different, try to catch a performance at the theatre of the Chinese Cultural Center (on the third floor of the Holiday Inn at 750 Kearny St). Call 886-1822 for forthcoming events. In both San Francisco and Berkeley there are plenty of Equity-waiver theatres staging largely experimental works. Check the *Chronicle* or *Berkeley Barb*. Of particular note is the One Act Theater Company, 430 Mason St (421-5355). The young actors present three one-act dramas nightly.

Nightlife. You could begin a Friday evening at the Hyatt Regency Hotel, enjoying a tea dance complete with English tea, then move on to the Embarcadero Center for some dancing. It might be wise to avoid the quaintly-named "Dance Your Ass Off" disco. Most nightclubs are concentrated near the junction of Broadway and Columbus Avenue. The waterfront north of Market St used to be known as the Barbary Coast because of the dubious nature of its night spots; the topless bars and strip joints seem to have moved elsewhere (see *Crime and Safety*) and the area has been taken over by the shops and cafes.

SPORT

The 49ers are the local football team and play at Candlestick Park (eight mile south of downtown on US 101; 468-2249), which they share with the baseball-playing Giants (467-8000). The East Bay teams are generally superior to their San Franciscan rivals, particularly in the specialist art of referee-baiting. The Oakland A's (baseball) use the Oakland Coliseum, easily reached by BART from San Francisco. The Oakland Raiders football team turned into the LA Raiders a few years ago.

For soccer, you have no choice but to cross the Bay to see the Oakland Stompers in action. The San Francisco Warriors represent the city at basketball. Horse racing takes place at the Golden Gate Fields (across the Bay at Albany; 526-3020) during the spring, and at Bay Meadows (at San Mateo southeast of the city) at other times of the year. The Grand National is not a race but a rodeo held each October at the Cow Palace (469-6055). bets may be placed on this event and other race meetings on-course; for other forms of gambling you must cross the border into Nevada.

If you feel up to seeing most of San Francisco's sights in a little over two hours, join the city's Marathon in late July. Competition for places is fierce, so apply in advance to PO Box 27385, San Francisco 94127.

Parks. The vast Golden Gate Park becomes the focus of the entire city on summer Sundays. Among the many attractions are the Japanese Tea Garden, the Strybing Arboretum and the Conservatory of Flowers. Turn a corner and you stumble upon a field of buffalo. If you tire of walking (or jogging), rent a pair of rollerskates from the stalls on JFK Drive or, even better, hire a horse from the Golden Gate Park Stables (668-7360) for a guided tour. There a plenty of other parks for picnicking or simply watching the natives. At Aquatic Park, you can fish for free from the muncipal pier; no closed season, no licence required.

Zoo. San Francisco's excellent zoo is at 45th Avenue and Sloat boulevard; dial 661-4844 for recorded information, 661-2023 for specific enquiries. The zoo is particularly hot on primates, containing Gorilla World, Monkey Island and the Primate Discovery Center. It opens daily from 10 am to 5 pm.

It is quite common to see sea lions alongside Fisherman's Wharf. The Bay also has sharks, but only three-foot long ones which eat rubbish at bottom of the water; they present no threat to bathers.

Beaches. Don't try swimming at North Beach since it's mile inland. Bathing near the Golden Gate is hazardous due to the strong currents flowing between the Bay and Pacific; that's why they chose Alcatraz Island on which to build a prison and most popular with residents. But the water is very, very cold. This part of the West Coast gets the Alaskan current.

SHOPPING

The arcades of Fisherman's Wharf, Ghirardelli Square, the Anchorage and the Embarcadero Center are great for window or gift shopping. More ordinary purchases may be made at the department stores on Market St, or the suburbs for cheaper shopping. If your interests are specialized, head for the Ghirardelli complex (which used to be a chocolate factory), where you will find shops such as Hammock Way which could provide one answer to an accommodation crises, and Come Fly a Kite, whose proprietor Diresh Bahadur claims a world *indoor* kite-flying record of over two hours. The Cannery (formerly the world's largest fruit-canning factory) and Pier 39 are also worth strolling through. The famous gift shop Gumps is at 250 Post St.

Among the many specialist book and record shops supported by the local community of artists and intellectuals in the avant-garde City Lights books, 261 Columbus Avenue, run by poet Lawrence Ferlingetti. Others can be found over six pages of the Yellow Pages!

If you're in the market for used clothing, your best bet is Purple Heart (veterans' charity) Thrift Store on 1855 Mission St (621-2581). There's a good selection of outdoor clothing, suitable camping gear including sleeping bags ($35), tents and mess kits. Another highly rated shop is the Salvation Army Thrift Store at 1509 Valencia (695-8040) where you pick up designer labelled mens shirts for $2, trousers ($3), jeans, sports clothing, shoes, boots, women's separates, suits, sweaters, T-shirts ($1), shoes, records (99c), books and home furnishings. At St Vincent de Paul Society on 1519 Haight (863-3615), helpful staff will help you find what you're looking for, and while stock varies, it's very cheap. When you've purchased clothes which are not cleaned and pressed, they can be washed and dried for $1.50 at nearby launderettes.

THE MEDIA

Radio. KALX (90.7 FM) broadcasts from the University of California at Berkeley. The station specializes in rock music punctuated by community news and information exchange, such as ride-sharing announcements. The 34 other stations serving the Bay Area include outfits which cater strictly for gays, and others broadcasting to the Chinese, Filipino, Spanish and Irish minorities. The nearest equivalent to BBC Radio 3 or 4 is KQED (88.5 FM) which is the public broadcasting station. If homesickness strikes, you can hear BBC programmes on KAWL (91.7FM). For Country, tune to KSAN (94.9 FM); for black music, KSOL (107.7 FM); and for news, KGO (810 AM).

Newspapers. The *San Francisco Chronicle* for 25c ($1 for Sunday edition) is the "quality" daily paper (though it's no *New York Times*), and its listings are fairly comprehensive. *The Oakland Tribune,* while not so good for listings, has excellent news coverage. For complete details of the less formal brands of entertainment, try the *Berkeley Barb* or the free weekly *San Francisco Bay Guardian.* The *Advocate* lists gay events.

The British tourist killed in San Francisco when two gangs tried to mug him simultaneously was extremely unlucky. Tourist haunts in the Bay Area are relatively safe, at least during daylight, and the main thoroughfares are well-lit and heavily patrolled at night. After dark, stay on the Van Ness side of the Civic Center. Women may be harrassed by kerbcrawlers. At night the panhandle of Golden Gate Park including lower Haight St attracts malevolent loiterers, only some of whom are plain-clothed police, so stay away after sunset. Other places to avoid include the skid row area south of Market St at 5th and 6th Avenues, and Candlestick Park at night. The Western Addition (west of the Opera House beyond the flyover, bounded by Gough, Hayes, Steiner and Geary Streets) is the sort of place that gives inner cities a bad name: avoid it at all times. Across the Bay, Oakland is not a good place to be during the hours of darkness, nor are the off-campus areas of Berkeley.

Drugs. Marijuana is widely grown in the Northwest USA and has now become California's leading cash crop, worth over three billion dollars a year. Consequently marijuana is readily available. The possession of small amounts in the state of California (i.e. under one ounce) will not get you a criminal record but might get you a fine of $100. Street dealers are often untrustworthy; those on campus in Berkeley are the least unreliable. The possession and use of cocaine and opium derivatives is still a felony, and buying from street dealers is a highly risky business. LSD is no longer popular among the young, upwardly-mobile set who comprise the major part of the drug-taking community in San Francisco.

The area code for San Francisco and the Bay Area is 415.

Information: San Francisco Convention and Visitors Bureau, on the lower level of Hallidie Plaza at Powell and Market Streets (974-6000). You might also try the voluntary International Visitors Center on the 4th floor of 312 Sutter St (986-1388). For fast computer information, find one of the many *Chronicle Videofax* terminals within the city and at the airport.

British Consulate: 120 Montgomery St (981-3030).

American Express 237 Post St (981-5533); 295 California St (788-4367); 400 21st St, Oakland (834-2833).

Thomas Cook: 175 Post St (392-2378); 1730 Franklin St, Oakland (893-3846).

Travelers' Aid: 38 Mason St (781-6738); also at the Transbay Terminal, 1st and Mission Streets, and on the departure level of San Francisco International Airport.

Medical Emergencies: St Francis Memorial Hospital, 900 Hyde St (775-4321). There is also a 24 hour-clinic at 2339 Durant St in Berkeley (548-2570).
Late night pharmacy: Hub Pharmacy, 1700 Market St (431-0068). Open 7.30am to 11.30pm.
Helplines: Dial-a-Story 626-6516; Lesbian/Gay switchboard 841-6224; Women's Switchboard 431-1414; STD Hotline 327-6465; Dial-a-Quake 642-2160; San Francisco Drug Line 752-3400; Rape Crisis Line 647-7273.
Post Office: 1076 Mission St (556-2381).
Legal Aid Society: 864-8848.

The geography of Northern California, Oregon and Washington approximates to a series of north-south strips. Along the coast, a range of mile-high mountains towers precariously above the Pacific. Inland lies a valley containing some of the richest agricultural land in the world. The Cascade Mountains (so called because of the many waterfalls which pour down from the ice- and snow-capped peaks) form the eastern barrier to the huge Central Valley. The rain shadow of the Cascades means that the extreme east of the region is a rocky desert considered fit only for military installations and Indian Reservations. Travel further east, and you reach the foothills of the Rockies.

The whole of the coastal area is alive with seismic activity, from the San Andreas fault in the south to the northern volcanoes of unreliable dormancy, of which the most notorious is Washington's Mount St Helens. The eruption on May 1980 has had an effect on the climate of the whole world.

Climate. Rainfall near the coast is heavy throughout the year: Corvallis, Oregon — one of the wettest places in America — is jokingly described as having an English climate. However, the temperature of the sea actually rises as you move north because of the warming influence of the Japanese current, thereby encouraging many coastal holiday towns to flourish. Try one of the oldest: Seaside in northern Oregon.

NORTHERN CALIFORNIA

Northern California is normally defined as everything north of Fresno, a rather dull market city which does not conform to the Californian image. Economic life in Northern California is a tale of three valleys: the great Central Valley which stretches almost the length of the state and whose fruit supplies much of the western world; the Napa Valley, northeast of San Francisco and California's answer to the Loire in both scenery and produce; and the so-called Silicon Valley, a swathe of land in Santa Clara County south of the Bay, where earth tremors have not deterred the creation of the world centre for microelectronics.

Of these valleys, the Napa is likely to be of greatest interest to the traveller. Centred upon the small, lively town of St Helena, it produces the best wines in the USA. Most wineries along Highway 29 offer guided tours and free tastings. Christian Brothers Winery (off Redwood Road) is picturesque and generous with tastings. Robert Mondavi in Oakville offers an excellent tour and produces first class wines. The Sterling Winery in Calistoga is reached by a $5 cable car and provides a splendid view of the Valley. Take a picnic lunch and visit several wineries. (This is one occasion when hitch-hiking is probably safer than driving). The new Napa Valley Train operates six round trips daily between St Helena and Napa, costing $25, in 1915 Pullman carriages. Try to avoid the tourist buses which operate to Napa from San Francisco, unless your idea of fun is sipping a thimbleful of wine prior to being herded into the buying room. A tour is especially lively around harvest-time in October; just as in Europe there is a festive atmosphere surrounding the *vendange*. For more information, contact the Napa Valley Vintners' Association, 900 Meadowood Lane, St Helena 94574 (tel: 707-963-0148).

South from San Francisco. The Monterey Peninsula, 80 miles south of San Francisco, is also a wine-producing area, but the local economy relies more upon the rich and famous who live there and the hordes of tourists who flock to see them. Unlike Beverly Hills, the Peninsula deserves a visit for the charms of its scenery rather than of its inhabitants. The former fishing village of Monterey acts as the northern gateway to the Peninsula. Dating back to the 1770s, the town provides excellent (if overpriced) wining and dining. Its Fisherman's Wharf resembles a miniature version of San Francisco's. Visitors to the Wharf can feed the entertaining (and overfed) sea lions, then dine in one of the smart seafood restaurants such as Rappa's: the clam chowder is excellent, but prices are high, so go for the "Early Bird Dinner". The newest attraction in Monterey is the multi-million dollar Bay Aquarium. A few miles west lies Cannery Row, where John Steinbeck wrote the novel of the same name.

The 15 mile drive south from Monterey to Carmel takes you past some of the most splendid homes in Southern California. The town's most famous resident (and former mayor) is Clint Eastwood. He owns the Hog's Back restaurant in San Carlos St where you can sample such delights as a Dirty Harry burger. It is often very busy with diners hoping that Clint might be filling in as a waiter for the evening. To enjoy the area properly, you need to get out of your hire car and walk or cycle around the Peninsula. For cycle hire try Freewheeling Cycles, 188 Webster St, Monterey (373-3855).

The "Seventeen Mile Drive" winds along the coast to Point Lobos, where you can see otters and sea lions. A $5 toll is charged. Most of the Peninsula's 16 golf courses are open to the public, though they are expensive.

A few miles further south is Big Sur, an area replete with redwoods, majestic cliffs and beautiful beaches, the most spectacular being Pfeiffer Beach. Big Sur has a small but lively artistic community. There are many camping facilities and other inexpensive rustic accommodation. You will find there the quintessential Californian restaurant called Nepenthe, originally built by Orson Welles, which affords a superb view of the ocean.

Just off Highway 1 at San Simeon is the strange and wonderful former vacation home of the late newspaper publisher William Randolph Hearst. Hearst Castle is open for tours every day of the year except Thanksgiving, Christmas and New Year. Its construction began in 1919 and took 27 years to complete. As well as being a newsman, Hearst was also a great movie mogul and would often invite stars to come and stay: Charlie Chaplin and the Marx Brothers were frequent visitors. You can take four different walking tours of the castle, the three guest houses and the gardens. Tour 1 is recommended for your first visit but it is advisable to book: in California call MISTIX on 1-800-446-PARK (from outside the state the number is 619-452-1950). After office hours tickets can be booked at the Holiday Inn in San Simeon.

Continuing south from San Simeon, the friendly town of San Luis Obispo is also worth visiting especially if you can make the Farmers' Market held each Thursday evening. It is much more than just a market...barbecued food of ever description is available, there are bargain fruit stalls (four pounds of oranges for one dollar) and entertainment from local bands, jugglers, clowns and the local radio stations. If your visit does not coincide with a Thursday evening, most of the central coast towns also have Farmers' Markets.

The outstanding views from Highway One continue with interruptions from towns like Pismo Beach where many activities are available including horse riding on the beach, fishing off the pier and surf fishing.

Muir Woods. For those without the time or resources to make the long journey to the spectacular Yosemite National Park, Muir Woods to the north of San Francisco offers a scaled-down but rewarding version of Yosemite. Only 12 miles north of the Golden Gate Bridge, this beautiful and fascinating forest covers an area of 560 acres. The tallest redwood is 252 feet high and 14 feet across and most of the mature trees are between 500 and 800 years old. The park is open all year round, from 8am to sunset. It is cool, shaded and moist all year so jackets are advisable. The forest has six miles of walking trails, details of which are available from the Visitor Center on arrival. Picnicking and camping are not allowed but facilities are provided nearby.

Californian Redwoods. Giant redwoods abound along the Californian coast north of San Francisco. The coastal scenery and charming fishing villages (actually yacht marinas) through which Highway 1 passes are well worth visiting. You may think there is little to distinguish the attractive villages of Inverness, Bodega Bay and Mendocino from villages along the New England coast, except that the sun sets rather than rises in the Ocean.

But as you move further north, the crowds and commercialism fade and the coast becomes more rugged. The highway is lined with state parks providing camping facilities and ample opportunities to admire the famous trees, culminating in the world's tallest tree (just short of 400 feet high) in Redwood National Park near the Oregon border.

The terrain is ideal for hikers and backpackers, but you'll need strong legs as little public transport exists. Campsites abound, but range from the primitive ($1) with outhouses to the well-equipped ($10) with flush toilets and hot showers. There's a new Redwood Youth Hostel at 14480 Highway 101 (482-8265) with rooms going for $6.50 a night. By far the best way of seeing the Napa Valley and Redwoods is the Green Tortoise bus. A "hostel on wheels" when you're not camped out, you can do a six-day looping trip of Northern California for $149, plus around $35 for food and drink for the entire period, and all you need is a sleeping bag.

Sacramento. The state capital of California (population 275,000) looks remarkably similar to many other state capitals except larger since it administers the most populous state in the Union. There is little of interest in the city itself apart from the restored section near the river, but it is a good base from which to explore the '49er territory southeast of Sacramento. Ghost towns like Rough and Ready are all that remain of the 1849 gold rush which led to the opening of Northern California. All the gold has been exhausted, but that does not stop the descendants of fortune hunters from hiring out gold pans.

Take the appropriately-numbered State Highway 49 from Loyalton south to Oakhurst. This road runs the entire length of the principal gold seam; hence the name Mother Lode Highway.

OREGON

Oregon's only large city is Portland (population 400,000) which faces Washington State across the Columbia River, one hundred river miles from the Pacific. Portland originally developed as a staging post for the lumber cut upstream, but is now a thriving modern city, divided into east and west by the Willamette River. Despite the mushrooming of shiny office blocks, it remains informal and peaceful. Portland claims to be the "City of Roses": if you visit between May and late September, you will understand why. The 17-day Rose Festival is held every June. On clear days, Portland is overlooked by Mount Hood, 40 miles distant but over two miles high. Do not be misled, like some travellers, by the apparent proximity of Canada. The signs pointing across the river to Vancouver refer to a small town in Washington state, not to the city in British Columbia.

Getting Around. Portland has arguably the best public transport of any American city. Buses are free within the downtown "Fareless Square" area, Four 80-year-old Portuguese trams trundle around the city centre and an efficient light railway known as MAX serves outlying areas. All services are run by Tri-Met; call 233-3511 for information.

Accommodation. Portland is probably the easiest town on the West Coast to find cheap digs. There are two hostels, a YMCA and lots of cheap (albeit dingy) hotels downtown for about $8 a night. Those that like camping in relative comfort will find hot showers at the sites in Ainsworth State Park, Milo McIver State Park and Battle Ground Lake Washington State Park; the rate is about $6 per person per night. An organisation called the Northwest Bed and Breakfast, 610 SW Broadway, Portland 9705 (243-7616) has a list of places starting at $14 a night, but you have to pay an initial £15 to join. The Convention and Visitors' Association (SW Front and Salmon Streets, 222-2223) can help with other suggestions.

Eating and Drinking. The local speciality is fresh seafood, particularly oysters and Portland salmon. Mother's Deli, a student hangout, at 1802 SW 10th St and Fuller's at 136 NW 9th are best value selections. Portland Saturday Market at 108 W Burnside St is where you go to eat the best and cheapest fruit and vegetables. Oregon produces excellent wines, and there are 35 wineries just west of Portland.

Entertainment. Take your pick along the Riverside Marina on the river between Marquam and Hawthorne bridges for the best music and atmosphere. If you're longing for English beer and pub grub, look in at the Horse Brass Pub on 4534 SE Belmont (232-2202), which has darts, Trivial Pursuit and 14 imported British beers.

Further Afield. The only other towns of any size in Oregon are linked to Portland by I-5, part of the Pan-American Highway. Eugene has a population of only 76,000, but the concentration of 16,000 students attending the University of Oregon in such a small city adds a respectable amount of life. Similarly, the state capital Salem has the usual collection of public buildings and bureaucrats but good nightlife thanks to Willamette University.

The small town of Ashland (population 12,000) in the south of the state is notable for having a Shakespearean theatre modelled on the Globe.

Performances are given year round, outdoors in summer when the weather is always perfect. Despite the occasional but unmistakable disparity between the quality of the star actors imported from afar (usually Britain) and the local cast, the productions are usually excellent.

WASHINGTON

Seattle. The largest city (population 500,000) in Washington likes to forget that Olympia is state capital and that Juneau is capital of Alaska, and has assumed de facto responsibility for both states. Puget Sound, upon which it lies, is the southern terminus of the Alaska Marine Highway (although this will switch to Bellingham in 1990), and the Alaska operations of many corporations are based in Seattle. The sheltered harbours have turned the city into an important international seaport. The Space Needle provides a 605-foot panorama of the city. Puget Sound and Mount Rainier in the Cascade Mountains. It is a solidly middle-class city thriving on the lumber and aircraft industry, neither of which is much evidence in the city centre. Seattle also regularly tops polls of USA holiday destinations.

Henry M Jackson International Airport (known as Sea-Tac, short for Seattle-Tacoma) is one of the least fraught American gateways for international air travellers, even if there is a large sign up in the Customs hall warning travellers not to make jokes with the officers. After passing through customs, you are whisked under the runway to the main terminal building.

Once downtown, buses are free within the "Magic Carpet" zone, bounded by the freeway and the waterfront. Outside this area, fares are cheap, $2.50 buying you an all-day pass. One peculiarity: on buses heading out of the city centre, you pay on leaving the bus; on inbound buses, pay on entry as normal. For information, ring Metropolitan Transit (Metro) on 624-7277 or call in at the information bureaux at the airport and 7th and Stewart Streets. A monorail links Westlake Mall (in the centre of the city) with Seattle Center, site of the 1962 World's Fair. Departures are every 15 minutes from 10 am until midnight and the fare is 50c. The journey takes one and half minutes. Note that Seattle Center, an arts complex, is not actually in the centre of Seattle.

Cheap accommodation is not hard to find in Seattle: try a couple of blocks inland from the port. There is a good AYH hostel at 84 Union St (622-5443) and several Ys. Eating cheaply in Seattle is not difficult either. The Market Cafe at 1523 1st Avenue (624-2598) gives you a $3.50 breakfast that keeps you going all day; the Manila cafe at 624 S Weller 682 (223-9763) has delicious but cheap Filipino food; the Fran-Glor's Creole Cafe at 511 South Jackson has an immense gumbo from $4.50, with free Dixieland jazz thrown in; and the feminist The Cause Celebre at 254 E 15th Ave (323-1888) has sensational ice cream and baked goods.

Calendar of Events

late January/early February	Chinese New Year celebrations, San Francisco
late March	Festival of Jazz, University Portland
April	Cherry Blossom Festival, Japantown, San Francisco
May	Northwest Folklife Festival, Seattle
early June	Rose Festival, Portland
August	Washington State International Air Fair, Everett
late August	Oregon State Fair, Salem
October	Festa Italiana, San Francisco

Hawaii

The fiftieth state to join the Union is a string of tropical islands jutting out of the Pacific Ocean 2,500 miles from the Californian coast. The largest island is Hawaii ("the Big Island") which gives its name to the whole state. The most populous (and popular) is Oahu. The island is dominated by Honolulu, the state capital, population 770,000, and the adjoining excesses of Waikiki Beach. Next most important in terms of tourism is Maui, midway between Oahu and Hawaii. The only other islands of significance are Molokai, Lanai, Kauai and Nihau.

Although the economy partly revolves around fishing and farming, most of the population depends to some extent on the burgeoning tourist industry. For millions of Americans and Canadians, the islands of Hawaii provide the same mixture of sun, sea and sin that has Europeans flooding to the Mediterranean. And just as on the Meditteranean, travellers can either succumb to the pleasures of mass tourism or stray away from the beaten track to find more unspoilt attractions.

Be warned, however, that Hawaii can be extremely expensive for those not visiting as part of a package tour. As in the Soviet Union, tourism in Hawaii is geared towards visitors on organized holidays. For around $400 you can get a return flight from the West Coast, a few nights in a beach motel and a hire car. To make the same trip independently will cost much more: the air fare alone is about $400, motel rooms booked by private individuals cost upwards of $50 per night, and regular car rental rates are high. If you plan to go it alone, take advantage of the good bus services and cheap hostels on Oahu, and consider buying a packaged side-trip to another island: these are as little as $100. Maui is lively and commercialized, the

Big Island best for the great outdoors (although very wet). The smaller islands offer a degree of peace and tranquility.

The Natives. Hawaii's population consists of indigenous Polynesian inhabitants, Asian immigrants (mainly Japanese and Filipino, including ex-President Marcos), American settlers and many combinations of these. Most of the million residents are pleasant and approachable, as you'd expect from a state which depends for its prosperity on pleasing visitors. You can hardly turn around without having someone greet you with "Aloha" and put a lei (wreath) around your neck — commercial but fun. British visitors seem particularly popular, and Hawaii likes to emphasise its links with the United Kingdom: the state flag bears the Union Jack in one corner.

The Hawaiian language has the shortest alphabet in the world, which explains why place names appear to be indistinguishable combinations of the letters a, e, h, i, k, l, m, n, o, p, u, and w. Hawaiian scrabble must be a very dull game. Fortunately everyone speaks an approximation of American English, though embellished with some native and Asian vocabulary. Since the Hawaiian language is largely phonetic, you shouldn't have too much trouble getting your tongue around place names: practise with Likelike (lee-kay-lee-kay) and Lahaina (la-hyena).

Making friends. You are most likely to make friends with fellow travellers. Should holiday romance blossom, you can take advantage of Hawaii's liberal and imaginative marital laws. Family court judges will perform a marriage for $25 (phone 548-2075). Weddings can be arranged almost immediately, and some state religious authorities specialize in unusual ceremonies. Recent marriages have taken place 50 feet underwater and while jogging along a cliff path. Divorce is not so easily arranged.

Climate. Hawaii is the only state in the Union which is in the tropics. The climate is predominantly hot and damp, though the heat is moderated by ocean breezes and the wet can be minimised by choosing your location and timing carefully. For example you will want to avoid Mount Waialeale on the island of Kauai, which is one of the wettest spots on the earth (rainfall record 486 inches in a year). But the average rainfall is more likely to be 20-50 inches, and the consistently balmy temperatures (70's in winter, 80's in the summer) make up for the occasional downpour.

There is nothing to stand between this chain of volcanic islands and thousands of miles of unpredictable Pacific Ocean weather.

For a hair-raising account of a wild Hawaiian storm, read *The Curse of Lono* by Hunter S. Thompson. A mile or two up in the mountains, the skies are unpredictable and ofter heavy with cloud. The only time you are likely to need warm clothes is for high altitude journeys. The summits of Mauna Kea and Mauna Loa on the Big Island have snow in January and February.

Arrival and Departure. Unless you arrive by cruise liner or wangle your way onto a freighter from the West Coast, you'll get to the state in an aircraft bursting at the seams with tourists, businessmen and a few more serious travellers en route to the Far East and Australasia. Almost all flights arrive at Honolulu (HNL), the state capital on the island of Oahu. Most of your fellow passengers will be herded on to charter buses or will head for the car hire desks. Local buses 19 and 20 run to downtown Honolulu and Waikiki Beach every 20 minutes for just 60c.

Transport. Oahu, Maui and the Big Island have the most substantial road networks. Note that car rental companies are most particular about where

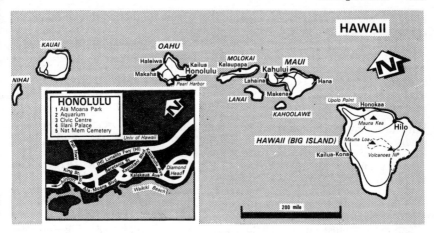

their vehicles may be taken, so don't stray too far from the beaten track. Hitch-hiking is usually easy, not least because of the large numers of holiday couples in rental cars. Taxis are expensive. Oahu has an extremely cheap bus service (60c maximum, anywhere on the island); call *The Bus* on 531-1611 for a schedule information.

Inter-island flights are very frequent, with a staggering 200 flights a day between Honolulu and Kahalui (on Maui). If you approach the airlines direct you'll find fares are high (e.g. $80 between Honolulu and Hilo on the Big Island), but most travel agents sell discounted tickets.

Accommodation. Resorts devoted to package tourists tend to be expensive for independent travellers, and Hawaii is no exception. (In the summer low season, however, you might be able to strike a good deal). Sleeping rough can be wet and risky. A better option is to camp (see *The Great Outdoors*). The authorities in Honolulu operate a number of beach parks where you can camp free for up to a week. Contact the Department of Parks and recreation (650 S King St, 523-4525) well in advance, since reservations are invariably required.

There are two AYH hostels in Honolulu: one near the University at 2323A Sea View Avenue (946-0591), and the more central Hale Aloha Hostel at 2417 Prince Edward St (926-8313). The International Network Cotel near Waikiki Beach (2051 Kalakaua Avenue, 955-5457) has dormitory beds for $12. You could also try the YMCA at 250 S Hotel St, Honolulu (524-5600) where a double costs about $40.

Bed and Breakfast Hawaii (PO Box 449, Kapaa, HI 96746; 822-1582) has about 75 host homes charging $40-$100 for a double room and breakfast.

Eating and Drinking. Tropical fruits of all kinds, especially pineapples, and macadamia nuts are cheap, plentiful and delicious. But a lot of other foodstuffs are imported at great expense from the mainland. Because of this and because of the inflation caused by wealthy tourists, eating out can carve massive holes in your budget. The way to eat most cheaply is to stick to coffee shops and fast food restaurants, though for a splurge you might go to a Polynesian or Japanese restaurant. Avoid the restaurants in Waikiki, though the much-touted tourist trap Wagonwheel International Market

Place — serving food from around the world to the accompaniment of country and western music — can be a laugh.

Contrary to popular opinion, not everyone in Hawaii drinks only pinacoladas (rum, pineapple juice and coconut milk). Most of the locals stick to beer and American or Japanese whisky. Prices are higher than in comparable bars and restaurants on the mainland, but virtually every bar in Hawaii has a happy hour (usually 5pm - 7pm) whith half price drinks and free snacks.

Entertainment. Although there is a Honolulu Symphony (537-6171), Hawaii Opera Theater (521-6537) and a Honolulu Academy of Arts with a good collection of Pacific art, the state is not renowned for its high culture. The best museum is the Contemporary (2411 Makiki Heights Drive). The Honolulu Zoo and Waikiki Aquarium are both worth a visit for their tropical fauna. The only royal palace in the USA is the Iolani in downtown Honolulu, the 19th century residence of King David Kalakaua. It is open to visitors at King and Richards Streets.

The closest most vistors get to a museum is the voyeuristic trip to Pearl Harbor, site of the 1941 Japanese attack which dragged the USA into World War II. The harbour, located a few miles northwest of Honolulu, is still an important naval base. It also has a Visitor Center and a tour around some of the scenes of destruction. A free shuttle boat runs daily except Mondays between land and the Arizona National Memorial, which is on the hulk of the sunken ship of the same name. Sadly you cannot escape regimentation even at this sombre monument, and after 12 minutes studying the submerged wreckage and reading the names of those who died, visitors are herded back onto the boat.

Live entertainment revolves around nightclub cabarets often with a hackneyed Hawaiian slant: steel guitar renditions of old pop songs accompanied by garlanded dancing girls whose origins are just as likely to be in South Dakota as the South Pacific. There is also a very wide range of special events from Buddha Day in April to a Ukulele Festival held each July in Waikiki.

Sport and Recreation. Sport in Hawaii usually means participation, and the most popular of all is surfing. Try to buy, borrow or rent a surf board. You should pay about $10 an hour for a surfboard and $20 for a surfing lesson. Oahu is one of the world's surfing headquarters, and many beginners like the gentle waves of Waikiki. More advanced surfers prefer Makahana Beach on the northwest coast, where 20-foot waves are not uncommon. Wherever you surf, always take note of weather and tide warnings; the ocean that produces titanic waves can easily drag anything or anyone out of reach. Beaches and bays on the neighbouring islands offer a wide range of surf to suit both the novice and the thrill-seeking expert, and are not as commercial and crowded as Waikiki.

Other water sports like deep-sea fishing, windsurfing and snorkelling are almost as popular and are very easy for the beginner to dabble in. Equipment and lessons are available on popular beaches, or at an Ocean Activities Center of which there are several. Golfers and tennis players flock to the islands for their annual vacations because of the year-round balmy weather and excellent facilities. A round of golf at a mid-range course might cost about $50 per person including hire of clubs and a buggy; most golfers in Hawaii are too lazy to search hard for lost balls, so you can find plenty.

Shopping. Reasonably priced shops can be found in downtown Honolulu, away from the waterfront, and at the 155-shop Ala Moana shopping mall on Atkinson Drive between downtown and Waikiki Beach. If you are a souvenir collector, go for shell and coral jewellery, sun hats woven from palm leaves or brightly printed fabrics sewn into muumuus (loose-fitting dresses for women) or aloha shirts for men. For kitsch collectors, Hawaii is a paradise.

Help and Information. The area code for the state of Hawaii is 808.
Tourist Information: 2270 Kalakau Avenue, Honolulu (923-1811).

The Great Outdoors. If you head inland on any of the islands, away from the strands of tourist development along ocean shores, you can easily find true wilderness. Mountain hikes should not be undertaken casually, since the weather and terrain are unpredictable, and many of the trails are tough going. But at least there are no snakes in Hawaii. A useful companion is Hilary Bradt's *Backpacking in Hawaii.* Contact the State Forestry Division (1151 Punchbowl St, Honolulu; 548-2861) for maps which show the trails on all the islands. Organised group hikes are advertised in the newspapers.

Most visitors make for one or both of the National Parks. Haleakala on the island of Maui is the smallest National Park in the USA. It consists of the oblong crater of the dormant volcano Haleakala ("House of the Sun"). The terrain is mainly bare volcanic lava, but is fascinating to geologists and interesting to laymen because of the colourful streaks which successive eruptions have produced. There is a Visitor Center at the southwestern entrance to the park where you can find out about the ecology and geology of the volcano, and make reservations for one of the three crater cabins. In addition there are four free primitive campsites dotted around the park. A favourite day trip is to join a cycling group to freewheel down from the crater rim to sea level. It costs around $80 including meals and hire of a mountain bike.

The Hawaii Volcanoes National Park, about 30 miles south of Hilo, is much larger and grander than Haleakala, and consists of tropical jungle clinging to the sides of two volcanoes. The higher is Mauna Loa, over two and a half miles above sea level, and requires an arduous three day climb.

Camping is so popular in Hawaii that state and federal campsites are very often full whatever the time of year. Sometimes places are allocated by lottery held two months prior to the requested dates, so unless you are very organised, you might not get your first choice or none at all. It is more difficult to obtain a cabin than it is to find a place to pitch your own tent, especially in view of the fact that cabins are free or nearly free.

There is no central reservation service covering the entire state. So you must contact the Parks Division of the island you wish to visit.

Calendar of Events

January/early February	Narcissus Festival (Chinese New Year)
March 17	St Patrick's Day Parade, Honolulu
March 26	**Prince Kuhio Day**
late March/April	Cherry Blossom Festival
May 1	Lei Day
June 11	**Kamehameha Day**
August (3rd Friday)	**Admission Day**
September	Aloha Week Festivals
October 12	**Discoverers' Day**

Public holidays are show in **bold**

Alaska

Barrow Eskimo Settlement

Alaska is radically different from the "Lower 48", as the residents refer to the other states of the Union. Its unique weather, wildlife and ethos make a visit highly rewarding, despite the expense. Alaska is full of bush pilots, trappers and prospectors, taciturn but colourful characters who belong to a distinctively North American pioneer tradition which breeds legends and heroes. The frontier spirit flourishes in a terrain and climate as hostile as Alaska's. The supreme test of frontier endurance takes place every March in the form of the 1,049 mile Iditarod Trail Race of husky drawn sledges between Anchorage and Nome. Even the six mile Seward Mountain Marathon, held each Fourth of July, is demanding. It is claimed to be the second oldest race in America (the oldest being the Boston Marathon), and involves running up and down a 3,000-foot mountain.

THE NATIVES

Just as fortune hunters once came in search of gold, many "state-siders" (migrants from the Lower 48) have poured into Alaska ever since oil was discovered at Prudhoe Bay on the Arctic Ocean at 3.18pm on February 18, 1968. The completed pipeline runs between the extraordinarily inhospitable north and Valdez (pronounced Val-deez) near Anchorage, and has created jobs and prosperity for residents and newcomers alike. Many "johnny-come-latelys" — most of them people of vigour and enterprise — are zealous converts to the northland and will sing its praises to a responsive visitor. With an average age of 27, the state is very welcoming to young travellers.

The true natives are the Eskimos and Indians. Their numbers have been much diminished in the past few centuries and they now constitute only

324

15% of the state's population. There are Inuit, Aleuts (ruthlessly persecuted during the period of Russuan rule and now very few in number), Athapascans, Haidas, Tlingit and Tsimpshian. Their folk tales can be riveting: listen for the one about the Eskimo girl whose lover is killed, only to return to her as a mosquito. Or the modern legend of the Eskimo youth whose headless body was discovered on the snow next to his snowmobile, supposedly having been decapitated by the dropping curtain effect of the northern lights.

Making Friends. Eskimos are a very friendly people. Although there is some latent ill-feeling towards Americans (as a result of US government deals which deprived them of their land) they show great curiosity about Europeans, and the British accent fascinates them. Almost all Eskimos speak English, though they are fiercely proud of their heritage and retain their native languages. Getting along with the Eskimos is easy providing you behave as a guest in their country.

If you intend to look round or camp in an Eskimo village, seek out the head man and ask for his permission, which he will not hesitate to give. Your arrival will arouse the curiosity of the local community who will turn to their head man for an explanation. It will cause embarrassment and loss of face if he can't satisfy their curiosity.

The pace of life is generally laid back in the villages except during the salmon runs in July and September. Don't get in the way during a salmon run, but offer to help if you feel you can make a contribution, and you could make a friend for life.

CLIMATE

Alaska is not a frozen waste year-round; Anchorage, the largest city with a population of around 200,000, is hot and dry during the summer with temperatures sometimes reaching the 80s and 90s. The southeastern panhandle towns of Ketchikan, Sitka and the capital Juneau are warmed by the Japanese Current and have a relatively mild and rainy climate akin to that of the Western Isles of Scotland (although Ketchikan has 236 days with precipitation compared to the Hebrides' 102).

Winters can be spectacularly cold. From late October to early May the rivers are frozen over, and most of Alaska is buried under snow. Temperatures of —40° are commonplace. Without properly insulated footwear, headgear and clothing, you will not survive — let alone enjoy — a winter visit. The lowest temperatures in the world have been recorded deep in the interior near the Yukon border. Where the oil wells are, between the Brooks Range of mountains and the Arctic Ocean, blizzards bring the worst windchill factors in the world apart from the South Pole. Winter visitors who fly to Nome, which is not very far from Siberia, are lent the necessary parkas by the airline.

If possible, visit in the summer not just because of the balmy temperatures, but because of the midnight sun. The Arctic Circle, which is defined as the line north of which the sun never sets on midsummer's day, passes north of Fairbanks. Even many miles south of the Circle, night consists of a brief twilight during the early hours of the morning.

Getting Around

ARRIVAL AND DEPARTURE

Air. For decades Anchorage has been an aerial crossroads, a refuelling stop linking Europe with the Far East. It is

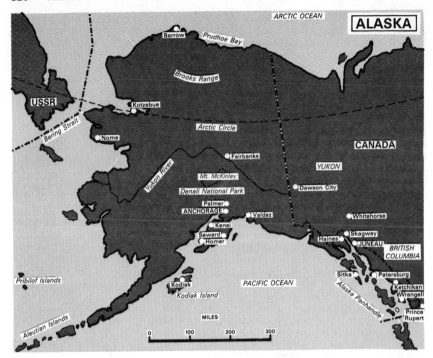

therefore easy to reach Alaska's largest city: at the time of going to press, British Airways flew several times a week from London Heathrow to Anchorage en route to Tokyo and Seoul. Clearing immigration and customs at Anchorage International Airport is probably easier than anywhere else in the USA: so few passengers disembark that you would be unlucky to wait in line for more than a few minutes.

The main air link between Alaska and the 'lower 48' is the 1,445 mile hop between Anchorage and Seattle, with numerous daily flights each way; there are also non-stop services to Chicago and Minneapolis/St Paul. Fares, however, are sky-high. Although you could get to Anchorage from London for just £199 in 1988, the cheapest flight one-way to New York was over $600; it can be cheaper to fly from Anchorage to New York via London. There are no cheap flights between the continental USA and Alaska, and the best you can hope for is a 25% reduction for taking a night flight: this brings the Anchorage-Seattle round trip down to around $600.

Anchorage International Airport is six miles southwest of the city centre. If you are not too laden down with luggage, ignore the taxi drivers ($15 to downtown) and the ACE minibus ($5). Instead, look for the People Mover bus 6 which costs 75c and allows free transfers to other destinations.

Bus. The Coachways System (part of Greyhound) runs as far north as Whitehorse on the Alaska Highway in Canada's Yukon Territory. From Whitehorse there is an intermittent service to Fairbanks Alaska on Norline Coaches based in Whitehorse (3211-A 3rd Avenue). Norline does not honour Greyhound's Ameripass, and the one way fare for the 600 mile journey is about $100. This service is available only between June 21 and September 4.

Train. There are no railway routes into Alaska from Canada. The narrow gauge route originally built for the Gold Rush in 1899 between Skagway on the Panhandle and Whitehorse in Canada's Yukon has been suspended due to high operating costs.

Driving. The motor trip along the fairly primitive Alaska Highway, which officially starts in Dawson Creek, British Columbia, can make an interesting change from driving on the predictably well maintained highways of the Lower 48. Much of the Highway is unpaved, and sections are regularly washed out in the late spring run-off, so be prepared for delays, sometimes lasting more than a week. The total length of the Alaska Highway from Dawson Creek in Canada to Fairbanks, Alaska's second largest city, is over 1,500 miles.

Ferries. The Alaska Marine Highway ferry system is the primary mode of transport for many Alaskan towns. As of 1990 the southern terminal will move from Seattle to Bellingham, quite a coup for this pleasant Washington university town (population 45,000) near the Canadian border. Ferries travel up through the Inland Passage, making calls at Prince Rupert on the coast of British Columbia, and Ketchikan, Wrangell, Petersburg, Sitka and Juneau, all in the Alaska Panhandle. The service continues up the fjord (always ice-free) to Haines — which is linked by road to the Alaska Highway — and Skagway. The whole trip takes 60 hours and costs about $200 deck class. If you are coming from Canada, you can travel by land as far as Prince Rupert (or take a British Columbia ferry from Vancouver or Vancouver Island to Prince Rupert) and catch the Alaska ferry there. The 24 hour trip from Prince Rupert to Juneau costs about $100.

TRAVEL WITHIN ALASKA

Alaska covers an intimidatingly large area (over twice that of Texas) and it will not be possible to see the whole of it. There are several regions from which to choose, for their intrinsic interest and their ease of access.

The Alaska Panhandle extends for over 500 miles down the coast which should logically belong to British Columbia. Some of the state's most picturesque towns such as Sitka, Ketchikan and Juneau are in this (relatively) mild region. Juneau is connected by neither road nor rail to the rest of the state and so the ferry service is vital.

Anchorage is a useful — if not very agreeable — base from which to explore other regions of Alaska. The most heavily travelled route from Anchorage (much favoured by back-packers and Japanese tour groups) is north to spectacular Denali Park and Mount McKinley. The Kenai Peninsula which stretches south and west of Anchorage is the preferred playground of Alaskans (and therefore crowded). For more deserted wilderness, take the ferry from Homer or Seward on the Peninsula to Kodiak Island. The adventurous may want to visit more distant islands in the Aleutian archipelago, to watch birds, go fishing, etc. These islands are accessible only by chartered or scheduled flights.

Air. Flying is often the only practical way of travelling around the great expanses of land. Residents of remote communities do not think twice about flying into the nearest centre on a shopping expedition. For example the airport in Sitka, an interesting town on the Panhandle which retains Russian architectural features, is only a ten minute walk from downtown. There are more private aircraft per capita in Alaska than anywhere in the world, Small aircraft which are equipped with floats in summer and skis in winter can be easily chartered. Many of these operate as shared taxis, and you may have to wait until there are enough people going in your direction.

Bus. There are several locally based companies which offer scheduled services. Alaska-Yukon Motorcoaches (326 F St, Anchorage, 276-1305) covers several routes including the Anchorage to Fairbanks route via Denali. Some services are integrated with the ferries. Bus services are curtailed between November and March.

Several minibuses run between Anchorage and Denali, including Denali Express (1-800-327-7651) which costs $108 for a day trip, and Eagle Custom Tours (258-2901) charging $38.50 for one-way, $70 return.

Train. The Alaska Railroad (265-2494) operates from Anchorage to Fairbanks, 11 hours into the interior. It is extremely important as an all-year communication. There is a departure daily at 9am from both Anchorage and Fairbanks, and all trains call at Denali. The one-way fare is $88, which allows a stopover at Denali. Even if you don't get off at Denali, you will be able to admire the twin peaks of Mount McKinley (highest mountain in North America) from Milepost 279. *Aurora,* the crack express which is equipped with vista domes and diners, runs year round. Among the worst headaches for engine drivers are the moose which prefer to move along the tracks than across the exhausting muskeg. The only other railway route in the state connects Anchorage with nearby Whittier (a port of call for the ferries) for $18.

Driving. The network of roads in Alaska is neither dense nor well maintained. However motor home touring is very popular and there is a choice of rental outlets in the cities. Discount car hire firms like Rent-a-Wreck, Rent-a-Dent and Cheepie Auto Rental have all penetrated to the last frontier. In Anchorage, call Rent-a-Dent on 243-2277 or Rent-a-Wreck on 561-2218 for an airport pick-up; Rent-a-Wreck also have an office in downtown Anchorage at 1120 E 5th Avenue (279-9611). Rentals are more expensive than elsewhere because of harder wear and tear on vehicles. And despite the abundance of oil which flows through the pipeline to Valdez, petrol is expensive because all the oil leaves Alaska to be refined in the south.

Hitch-hiking. Many travellers have found Alaska to be one of the most rewarding places in which to hitch. Perhaps because of the slow pace of life and frontier hospitality, residents and visitors seem more prone to pick up hitchers. Long distance lorry drivers tend to be "characters". For ride-sharing advertisements, check the classified section of the *Anchorage Times.*

Sleds. Motor-powered sleds are a popular means of transport during the winter, though for limited journeys only. The one-man version is called a skidoo. These may be available for hire, so enquire locally.

Ferries. There are two main ferry systems: the Southeast System joins up towns on the Panhandle, and the South Central System operates between towns near Anchorage (though not including Anchorage) like Whittier, Homer and Valdez. Surprisingly there is no ferry link between the two systems, although they are both run by the same company. Frequency is much greater in the summer.

City Transport. The People Mover bus network in Anchorage is fairly cheap and efficient. The flat fare is 75c, and free transfers are allowed.

Most buses arrive and depart from the Downtown Transit Center at 6th Avenue between G and H Streets. For bus information ask at the Transit Center or call the Rideline on 343-6543. Note that only a skeleton service operates on Sundays, and that no buses at all run on public holidays. In winter the schedules are sometimes put out by heavy snow: dial 786-8205 for a recorded report of delays and cancellations. In addition to the People Mover system, there is an independently operated double-decker bus which links downtown Anchorage with Lake Spenard and the University. For a flat fare of $2 you can stop off anywhere en route and continue your journey on a later service.

Accommodation

Motels, hotels and inns throughout Alaska are more expensive than in the rest of America. Standards are high, however, especially when compared to those in neighbouring Yukon. A few older hotels have affordable accommodation, such as the Palace Hotel in Anchorage (4th and Barrow Streets), the Hotel Palmer in the town of the same name north of Anchorage (745-4111) and the six-cabin Aurora Motel in Fairbanks (456-7361).

There are bed and breakfast associations in most towns. Rates start at about $30 single. Contact the Juneau Bed & Breakfast Association (526 Seward St; 586-2959), Stay with a Friend (3605 Arctic Boulevard #173, Anchorage 344-4006) or Alaska Private Lodgings, 1236 W 10th Avenue, Anchorage (258-1717). One of the most interesting lodgings in Anchorage is Bed & Bike (243-7878) which provides a double room and two bicycles for $60 per night.

The AYH Anchorage International Hostel is downtown at 700 H St (junction with 5th Avenue, 276-3635); the nightly rate is $10. There is another 45 minutes' drive away at Alyeska ski resort (277-7388). Both these Youth Hostels are open all year, as are those at Mentasta Mountain, Snow River (near Seward), Sitka and Juneau. Other hostels — at Delta, Tok, Sheep Mountain (near Palmer), Haines and Ketchikan — open only in summer. (Many facilities in Alaska operate only in summer, a season whose starting date is indeterminate.) Some hostels in remote locations do not hire out bedding, so you should take your own.

Accommodation is non-existent or fearsomely expensive in most small towns, so a tent is essential if you plan to travel in remote areas. Summers are warm enough to permit comfortable camping, though you should be mindful of potentially dangerous wildlife. The standard fee for a private campsite is $10. The state government operates a number of free campsites in parks and along highways. Write to the Alaska State Division of Parks for details (Suite 210, 619 Warehouse Avenue, Anchorage, AK 99501, 274-4676). In addition the US Forest Service operates a number of primitive cabins, usually equipped with wood-burning stoves and outside toilets. These cost a mere $15 per party, but are often booked up six months in advance. Write to the District Ranger, PO Box 10-489 Anchorage, AK 99511, 345-2519.

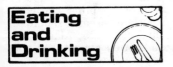

Eating and Drinking

The cost of living is high throughout Alaska and this is particularly noticeable when buying food. Expect to pay nearly twice as much for meals in Alaska as in

California. Even the best agricultural areas of the state have growing seasons for only 120 days and therefore most produce must be imported at great expense. Fortunately state taxes are minimal due to oil wealth. Salmon, both smoked and fresh, is very cheap indeed. Many towns have salmon bakes at which you can typically eat as much salmon barbecued over an open fire as you want, plus sourdough bread and salads for about $15. The best salmon in the Anchorage region is served at Max's, south of the city near the Alyeska ski resort. McDonalds has found its ways to Alaska and fast food restaurants abound. Relatively cheap diners often stay open 24 hours a day.

Meat and fish are the staple diet of the village natives. Moose is popular and tasty, similar to beef in taste and appearance. Traditionally, a great deal of fish and meat were eaten raw, but nowadays that diet survives only among the elders living in remote areas. Sun-dried is often a staple on hunting expeditions.

The most authentic native food in Anchorage is served at the Tundra Club, part of the Alaska Native Medical Center at 250 Gambell St (278-4716); you can reach in by bus 45 from downtown. As well as a $5 set lunch, you can sample *agutak* (Eskimo ice cream), Indian fry-bread and reindeer sausage. It opens 7am-3pm from Monday to Friday.

Drinking. Drinking in an Alaskan bar is not much more expensive than elsewhere in the US; a bottle of beer costs about $2.50 in a typical Anchorage bar. Most sizeable bars supply a free floor show of topless or naked dancers (many of whom are not averse to supplementing their income in other ways). One of the more restrained Anchorage bars is Chilkoot Charlie's (Fireweed Lane and Spenard Road, 272-1010), whose motto is "We cheat the other guy and pass the savings on to you".

Although alcohol is widely available in the big towns, its sale is controlled in Eskimo villages. Like the native Indians of North America, Eskimos have difficultly coping with alcohol, although they have borne up well in most other respects under the relatively sudden "American invasion". Most Eskimos will drink whatever is offered and regularly pass out after over-indulging. Although it is fine to offer the village head man a drink, do not let it be known that you have large amounts of alcohol. Otherwise you can expect a continual stream of visitors until your supply has been consumed. Too much alcohol often transforms the normally placid temperament of Eskimos, and violence and unpleasantness can ensure.

Entertainment

Only Anchorage can claim to have much cultural life, based at its new Performing Arts Center (5th Avenue and F St) and at several theatres in the city. Unfortunately Alaska is so out-of-the-way that few major performers appear. Even so, bars in the biggest towns often feature some very talented rock bands; Chilkoot Charlie's (see above) is especially recommended. Folk, blues and country and western are all given a good airing. Many Eskimos are remarkably adept at blues guitar.

If they are not picking guitars during those long nights on the tundra, they are playing cards. Eskimos have an affection for gambling, and both men and women are shrewd card players. In the outlying areas it shouldn't be too difficult to get in on a game. Pool is popular all over Alaska but mainly in large towns where big-money games are often played, and you must beware of hustlers.

In the more touristy areas traditional native music and dance is often on display. Special entertainments commemorate the history of Alaska: for example performances of Russuan folk dance in Sitka and the Ragtime Revue in Juneau which recreates the atmosphere of a Gold Rush saloon. Skagway, now a National Historic Site, has been preserved intact from the Gold Rush days which made it an important port for the Klondike. The steep and rugged Chilkoot Trail is popular with hikers who want to follow in the footsteps of the original gold prospectors.

Shopping. Because the cost of shipping to Alaska is so high, items in the shops are very expensive. Village stores often get away with charging what they like. For example, a set of fishing tackle might cost five times as much as it would in Britain. One of the few bargains is salmon, and most shops will pack it with ice for an extra dollar or so, which will keep it in good condition for several days.

Native crafts are on sale throughout the state. There are many cultural centres at which native artists carry on old traditions of wood carving, silverwork, beadwork and spinning from musk ox wool. Eskimo arts flourish best in the Far North in communities like Kotzebue and Barrow.

The Media. Anchorage has thorough and regular news programmes as well as music for everyone. Folk, blues and rock are all found somewhere on Anchorage radio, as well as coverage of the British music scene. In the more remote area, the choice of listening is limited and the radio is somewhat monopolized by religious programming between the news and music. Nome radio disc jockeys are renowned for trying to convert their listening audience between records.

There is a surprisingly large range of television stations in and around the big cities. As with radio, the choice of programmes is more limited in remote regions, though most Eskimo homes have a television if there is good reception. British movies, old and new, are watched with avid interest out on the tundra.

Crime and Safety

Alaskan cities have their fair share of street crime, but you can usually identify dodgy areas by the preponderance of seedy bars.

Drugs. The smoking and possesion of under four ounces of marijuana is legal. Many native Eskimos, especially in areas where alcohol is scarce, use marijuana as socially as Europeans use alcohol. As in the rest of the USA, harder drugs are strictly illegal.

Natural Disasters. Earthquakes are a risk in many parts of the state. Anchorage was seriously damaged by one in 1964 (an Earthquake Park has been established on the Knik Arm out of town to show the extent of damage). The old town of Valdez was wiped out by an earthquake and tidal wave a few years before the coming of the pipeline, when a small new city was erected close to the old site.

Health. In the outlying places, medical facilities can be sparse. Serious accidents or illness victims are flown out to big centres, so make sure your insurance covers such as an expensive contingency.

CB radio is slowly being superseded by the cellular phone, but is still a way of life in Alaska, where most trucks, cars and village homes are equipped with one. A portable CB should be borrowed if possible for unguided walks in any desolate area. A special channel is kept clear for emergency calls only; enquire locally and make sure you remember it.

Wildlife. It is not advisable to wander about in the wilderness without a knowledgeable guide. Information about guides and outfitters is available from the Alaska Wilderness Guides Association (360 K St, Suite 246, Anchorage; 276-6634). For tips on how to avoid contact with wolves, porcupines, etc. see the Canadian introductory section on *The Great Outdoors* on page 351.

Mosquitoes are the most annoying natural hazard and you are guaranteed to meet them in the summer. Every portion of exposed flesh must be covered with repellant; locals recommend a product called "Cutter". Although they are not a serious problem in built-up areas, they can make a visit to the tundra, where they swarm in their millions, a downright ordeal.

The area code for all of Alaska is 907.

Information: Anchorage Convention and Visitors Bureau, 546 W 4th Avenue (274-3531). Recorded visitor information: 276-3200.
   The Southeast Alaskan Tourism Council, PO Box 7055, Ketchikan (225-167) provides information only on the Panhandle.
Parks and Forests Information Center: 540 W 5th Avenue, Anchorage.
American Express: 333 W 4th St, Anchorage (263-6250).
Alaska State Auto Club: 525 W 3rd Avenue (276-3236).

Wilderness backpackers and canoeists flock to some of the more accesible natural wonders of the state. The abundance of flora and fauna which appears when the snows are gone makes Alaska a naturalist's paradise.

Even if your time is short, and you are restricted to the environs of Anchorage, there are good opportunities for exploring. The Sierra Club (276-4048) runs numerous free hikes, bicycle tours and canoe trips. The Portage Glacier and Chugach National Forest are little more than an hour away from Anchorage; get to the glacier sooner rather than later, since it is expected to have receded from its valley by the year 2020. Back Trail Tours (276-5528), who have a stand across the road from the Visitor Information Center in Anchorage, run a convivial "Sunset Tour" to the glacier for $35. They also offer daily hikes in the hills around Anchorage.

Skiing takes place at the Alyeska resort, 45 minutes south of Anchorage, from the end of November until the end of April. Equipment can be hired locally, and a daily lift pass costs $20-$30. Although the resort failed in its bid to host the 1994 Winter Olympics, facilities are improving all the time.

Mount McKinley (20,320 feet) is the highest mountain in North America; its summit rises nearly four miles above the 900-foot elevation of the Tokositna Glacier below it. The Eskimo name for the mountain is Denali ("The Great One"). Buses and trains travelling between Anchorage and Fairbanks stop at Denali National Park, admitting access to the mountain. A trip to the top of McKinley will take a month, but there are shorter trails within the park. In summer a free bus operates the 84-mile journey between the park entrance and Wonder Lake. Ring 683-2294 for details of campsites, trails etc.

Short cruises from Juneau or Valdez take you past floating glaciers, which occasionally crack and split in front of you. The vibrations set off by loud noises (such as a ship's horn) often induce ice avalanches. Whales and porpoises sport alongside the boats in summer. Whale-watching is possible at Glacier Bay from May to September. For details, write to Glacier Bay National Monument, PO Box 1089, Juneau.

Kodiak Island, a huge island southwest of Anchorage, is the home of the world's largest carnivores, the giant Kodiak bears. It is also where the huge 20 or 30 pound King Crabs are caught, a delicacy favoured above salmon.

The fishing is tremendous throughout Alaska. King salmon can run to 70 pounds or more. Trout and pike are plentiful, as well as a local species called "shee-fish" which can be found throughout the year in the Yukon River. Tackle can be hired in the tourist centres but Eskimos in remote places will view someone fishing with anything but a net as slightly mad. Permits may be needed so enqure at the local fisheries office. Hunting is very popular, and plenty of trips are organised. Unfortunately a broad interpretation of fair game is used, which means that even the innocent Dall mountain sheep are hunted.

Swimming, windsurfing or boating can be fun in the quiet backwaters, but unless you are of Olympic standard, stay out of the Yukon River (the third longest river in North America). Its powerful currents and 70 foot depths can be dangerous. The water level of Alaskan rivers tends to fall gradually as the summer wears on, and a safe course between the sandbanks and rocks one day may not be safe the next.

For the ultra-adventurous, the Brooks Range sweeps across northern Alaska and contains some of the largest unexplored regions remaining on earth. Almost as remote are the Pribilof Islands which are the summer breeding ground for one and a half million fur seals.

Calendar of Events

January	Winter Festival, Ketchikan
early February	Iditaski cross-country ski race
February	Festival of Native Arts, Fairbanks
early March	Iditarod Trail Sled Dog Race
mid April	International Music Festival, Anchorage
May	Crab Festival, Kodiak
mid June	Midnight Sun Marathon, Anchorage
June (third week)	Spirit Days
early August	Alaska Scottish Highland Games
late August/early September	Alaska State Fair, Anchorage
late September	Equinox Marathon, Fairbanks
December	Christmas Boat Parade, Sitka

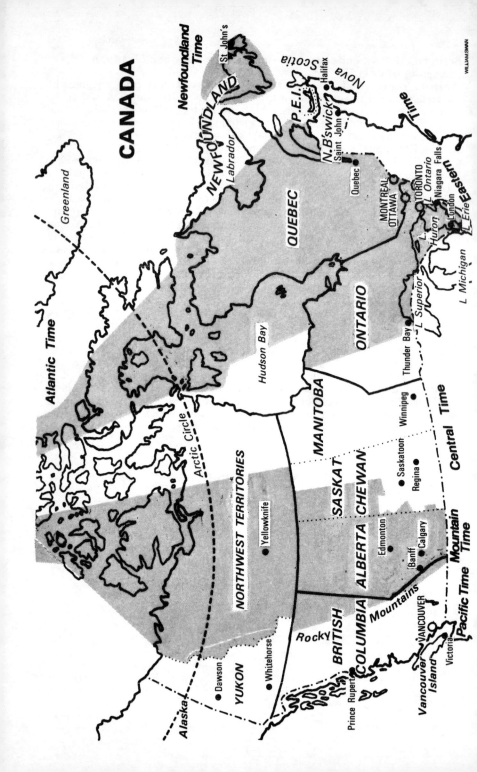

CANADA

THE PEOPLE

The fastest way to antagonize a Canadian is to mistake him or her for an American, and then to say "well there is not much difference anyway". It is difficult to avoid confusing the American and Canadian accents unless you have an ear attuned to the sound "ou" which Canadians say in a short clipped way, almost like "abote" for "about". Or listen for the characteristic "eh?" at the end of sentences. (Apparently, there is a computer installed in Ottawa which invites commands with "eh?") But once it is revealed that you are addressing a Canadian, you must instantly acknowledge that you have committed a gross error.

Canada is heavily dependent on the USA both culturally and economically. This is not too surprising considering that 80% of the Canadian population lives within 200 kilometres of the US border. And yet your average Canadian will fiercely defend Canada's uniqueness. There is considerable anti-American sentiment in schools and in the media which became particularly evident during the 1988 federal election, in which the controversial Free Trade Agreement was the central issue. Although in some ways the differences between the two countries are ones of degree rather than kind, in other ways they are fundamental. For example televised political debates in Canada are genuine debates and therefore quite unlike their American counterparts.

The reputation of Canadians as being cautious, conformist, humourless and dull inspired the writer Saki to say "Canada is all right, really, though not for the whole weekend." The strong influence of Scottish puritanism during the early days of the colony persists, and the work ethic and a wholesome boyscoutishness continue to hold sway. The fact that Canada is the most heavily insured nation per capital in the world does suggest that the natives lack a certain flair.

On the positive side, they are less brash than their American neighbours, not as noisily self-confident. Because they do not take themselves quite as seriously as Americans they are more prepared to laugh at themselves, so you can risk a few good-natured insults. Your overwhelming impression will be that people both in public office and private business are efficient and polite.

Canada's claim to uniqueness is best justified by the French influence. The highest concentration of French-speaking people is in the province of

335

Quebec (over 82% French) though there are large numbers of French-speaking people in the Maritime provinces, Ontario and Manitoba.

Bilingualism has been an important political issue for many years and an uneasy truce now seems to have been reached. All packaging, government documents, street signs, etc. must by law be in both languages across Canada. Government employees, from switchboard operators to politicians, are supposed to be bilingual, though in many cases they have no more than a smattering even after attending compulsory immersion courses. Railway conductors have been known to announce first in English "The train is arriving in Montreal" and then in their French version, "the train is arriving in Mon-ray-al".

The fact remains that 6,300,000 Canadians or a quarter of the population claim French as their mother tongue (compared to 17,000,000 English speakers) and this fact creates welcome contrasts in culture and outlook among various regions and the total population of 25.3 million.

Canada is as ethnically diverse as the US, but without a large black population. With Italians and Germans numbering half a million each, Ukrainians and Chinese over a quarter of a million each, plus large populations of Greeks, Portuguese and Koreans, no one can complain that Canadians are all alike. One in five Canadians was born outside the country. Canada prides itself on being not so much a "melting pot" as a "salad bowl", though second generation immigrants seem to assimilate thoroughly. Since immigration is declining steeply (because of stricter government measures in the face of dire unemployment), the ethnic mosaic may not be as colourful in future generations.

NATIVE PEOPLE

There are only 300,000 Dene (Indians) and 23,000 Inuit (Eskimos) left in Canada, comprising less than 2% of the national population. The majority live on reservations in Ontario and the four western provinces (especially Saskatchewan) where poverty and unemployment are rampant and the levels of alcoholism and crime are alarmingly high. Although Canada has a better record than the US — for example the Indian wars in Canada ended in treaties rather than military defeat — the disadvantaged position in modern Canada of the native peoples reflects their early mistreatment.

The situation has been improving over the past 20 years. Many Indian groups have negotiated settlements for mineral development on their lands held by treaty, substantially improving their standard of living. The federal government has encouraged and funded native rights lobbies to present their cases, though most groups continue dissatisfied.

Few Natives have integrated into modern Canadian society. Although the rare individual becomes a lawyer or an accountant, the ones who move away from the reservations can often be seen standing on city street corners, usually outside the liquor stores passing a bottle. Unemployment is very high, and most Natives have little choice but to live on federal subsidies. At the same time as they are unable or unwilling to integrate, they have also lost many of their traditions. Very few dress in their traditional costume unless for the benefit of tourists who seem happy to pay a dollar or two to photograph them. Only a handful speak their own languages.

Because Indians no longer rely on their traditional means of livelihood —hunting moose, caribou and buffalo, fishing for salmon, etc. — many of their practical skills are disappearing. Furthermore many of their ceremonies were banned by law, notably the potlatch during which hereditary privileges are passed on. As a result many of the traditional arts and crafts were jeopardized. But with government support, there has been a revival in Indian arts in the past couple of decades, arts such as mask-carving on the west coast, the folk songs of Shingoose, and the ancient vocal music of the Inuit called Katadjait, throat songs which reflect things in the environment from babies to boiling water. Belatedly money is being poured into Native arts centres where the old arts of carving totem poles and ritual painting can be passed on to younger artists.

In a further effort to prevent the cultural erosion, there are summer wilderness camps where Indian children (who, like most Canadian children, are avid television-watchers and junk food eaters), are taught the ways of their elders. It is even possible for foreign visitors to work as volunteers on such camps and to participate in local events such as moose, bear and porcupine roasts. There are also opportunities for volunteers to help on building projects lasting two months in remote northern Native communities over the summer. (Contact Frontiers Foundation, 2615 Danforth Avenue, Suite 203, Toronto, Ontario M4C 1L6). Inuit communities have not altered as much, since their contact with white society is often limited. (See the chapter on the *Great White North*).

Hunting and fishing lodges are often on Indian land and it is possible to hire a Native guide to take you fishing or hunting. Unfortunately the remote locations of these wilderness retreats make them prohibitively expensive for many people.

To experience the life of Canada's original inhabitants at second hand, the books of Farley Mowatt are highly recommended. His descriptions of the traditions and customs of the people of the far North, as in *People of the Deer* and *The Snow Walker,* are especially evocative.

CLIMATE

Although Canada's climate has its flaws, it is often wrongfully maligned. It is not unknown for an American tourist to drive over the border in July with a pair of skis strapped to his car roof, only to find the temperatures in Calgary higher than those in San Francisco and warmer in Ottawa than in Massachusetts. If you travel around Canada in July and August you will be almost as hot as you would be in the States, with the exception of the West Coast where summer temperatures remain a little cooler, though still very balmy. The majority of shops and public buildings are air-conditioned. High summer is ideal for enjoying the Great Outdoors (give or take the odd swarm of biting insects), though it can cool down considerably in the evenings. Although there can be heat waves in June and September, they are the most comfortable months in which to travel. As for the proverbial Canadian winter when temperatures hover around 0°F/-18°C, you really will have to acquire a warm and waterproof pair of boots, woollen hat, scarf and mitts and a down or woollen coat. But even in Canada, you are not guaranteed a white Christmas.

WEIGHTS AND MEASURES

One difference between the US and Canada which will immediately strike the visitor is that Canada has "gone metric". Road distances and speed limits are all in kilometres (pronouced *kill*-o-meet-ers), petrol is sold in litres, temperatures are quoted in centigrade and butter is sold in grams. The programme is well advanced now and most Canadians have made the adjustment. There were a few dodgy moments in the early stages, for instance when the tank of an Air Canada jumbo jet was filled with litres instead of gallons of fuel, and the pilot had to make an emergency landing in the middle of nowhere. (He was promptly fired).

Occasionally, groceries are labelled in both Imperial and metric, but in most cases you will have to do a lot of mental arithmetic if you are interested in comparing Canadian prices with those in the States or at home. The chart below provides some useful approximations. Failing this, you can apply the conversion technique used by Canada's two backwoods humorists Bob and Doug Mackenzie who multiply the metric measure by 2 and add 30 to arrive at the Fahrenheit temperature. Unfortunately this also had them going 90 mph in a 30 km/h zone and getting 42 metric bottles of beer for the price of a six-pack.

Length

1 centimetre = 0.4 inches   1 inch = 2.5 cm
1 metre = 3.3 feet   1 foot = 30 cm
1 kilometre = 0.6 miles   1 mile = 1.6 km

Weight

1 gram = .035 ounces   1 oz = 28 g
1 kilogram = 2.2 pounds   1 lb = 45 kg

Temperatures

$(C D° \times 9/5) + 32 = F D°$ $(F D° - 32) \times 5/9 = C D°$

Volume

1 litre = 2.1 pints (Imperial)   1 pint = .47 litres
1 litres = .22 gallons   1 gallon = 4.5 litres

Red Tape

Immigration. British and Commonwealth citizens do not require visas to enter Canada as tourists. (If you are from Greenland you don't even need a passport). A passport with six months validity remaining is sufficient. To work or study legally in Canada, you must obtain the appropriate visa before you leave your home country.

If you are arriving as a tourist, you will probably be granted a stay of 90 days. If you intend to stay longer than three months, you may argue your case (in advance) to the Canadian High Commission in London (Immigration Division, MacDonald House, 38 Grosvenor Street, London W1X OAA; 01-629-9492). Failing this, you should declare your intention at the port of entry, giving reasons and, providing you can show a return flight and sufficient funds, you may be granted up to six months.

Those who arrive for more than a couple of weeks holiday may be asked to show a return ticket and enough money to support themselves without working. A couple of credit cards and the address of a Canadian relative or family friend should clinch your case. As long as you look like a regular tourist you should have no problem. Canadians on the whole are suspicious of eccentrically dressed and coiffed people. People under 18 travelling without an adult may be asked to show a letter of permission from their parent or guardian, to check up on runaways.

Many European travellers enter Canada via the US. If you plan to return to the States you should make sure you have a multiple entry visa. A single entry visa will mean that you are turned back at the airport or border when you try to go back into the States. Although it is possible to apply for a second visa at any of the eight American consulates in Canada, you will find it easier to persuade the US Embassy in Britain to issue a multiple entry visa in the first place.

CUSTOMS

Purportedly because of Canada's anxiety about animal and plant diseases, there is no red and green channel system in airports. All incoming travellers must fill out a form declaring the potentially dubious contents of their luggage, e.g. plants, firearms, alcohol, tobacco and gifts. The customs inspector looks at the form before you reclaim your baggage, so if he trusts your form (and your face) you are all right and will escape having your luggage searched. You may bring in as many gifts as you like duty free provided none had a value of more than $40.

The duty free alcohol allowance is 1.1 litres (40 ounces) of liquor or wine, or 8½ litres of beer. You cannot import liquor unless you have reached the legal drinking age of the province of entry. The minimum age is 18 in Prince Edward Island, Quebec, Manitoba and Alberta and 19 in the rest. If you want to bring in more than your allowance (as you might find it worthwhile to import fine wines or Scotches unavailable in Canada) you are allowed to bring in up to 9 litres more provided you pay the duty and obtain a permit at the port of entry.

People 16 or over may bring in 50 cigars, 200 cigarettes and 1 kg (2.2 lbs) of tobacco duty free.

There are restrictions on the import of some food products in certain provinces. You may bring in as many tropical fruits as you like, since these are not grown in Canada and therefore don't present an agricultural threat. Fruits and vegetables which are grown commercially in Canada may be prohibited depending on where they come from. For example, peaches, plums and apricots must be sprayed before they are allowed into British Columbia, and apples are prohibited. Vegetables from certain parts of the US (mainly southern and mid-western states) are not allowed in. Better to eat your apples and carrots before arriving at the border. While you're at it, you might as well smoke your dope too. If you are caught with a small amount of illegal substances, you will not be allowed in; with larger amounts of hard drugs, you will be prosecuted.

HEALTH AND INSURANCE

Canada's reputation as a safe and clean country may tempt you not to worry too much about potential health hazards. But a simple fall on the ice in winter, or from a jetty in the summer might necessitate hospital treatment. And at $750 a day, you will rue the day you decided to skimp on insurance.

Foreign visitors can buy last minute insurance by the day called "emergency cover" from Blue Cross, represented in most cities across Canada (e.g. 429-2661 in Toronto). You pay about $4 ($7.50 for a family) for every day you want to be covered and can pick up the forms from Canadian drug stores such as Boots and at information centres. You can then pay for as many days as you need at any bank. You are not eligible to apply if you have been in the country for more than ten days. The maximum period of cover is six months. A cheaper alternative is the Hospital Medical Care plan offered by John Ingle Insurance, 710 Bay Street, Toronto (597-0666). For extensive medical cover they charge around $35 for 15 days increasing to $150 for three months.

Visas. In 1987 the Canadian government eased its restrictions on foreign students working temporarily in Canada, partly in response to a sudden increase in the number of unfilled summer vacancies now that the products of the baby boom are too old to take on summer jobs. For a general outline of the possibilities request the leaflet *Student Temporary Employment In Canada* from the Canadian High Commission (Immigration Division, Macdonald House, 38 Grosvenor St, London W1X 0AA). All participants in the official work exchanges must be British citizens aged 18-30 years and must have proof that they will be returning to a tertiary level course on their return to Britain.

Students who have a job offer from a Canadian employer can apply directly to the High Commission in London for an employment authorization which will be valid for a maximum of 20 weeks and which is not transferable to any other job. The other and more flexible possibility is to apply to BUNAC (232 Vauxhall Bridge Road, London SW1V 1AU; 01-630-0344). Their new Work Canada programme offers about 600 students the chance to go to Canada for up to six months and take whatever jobs they can find. The only requirements are that applicants have $1000 (or $500 and a letter of sponsorship from a Canadian relative), a return ticket and proof of an approved medical examination (which costs £50-£70).

Certain other categories of work may be eligible for authorization, such as for the tobacco harvest in Southern Ontario and qualified nannies who are in great demand but must stay for a minimum of one year. In Britain contact European Nannies (5 Wimblehurst Road, Horsham, W Sussex RH12 2EA) or Childminders Canada (61 Woodland Gardens, London N10 3UE) for further information on nannying in Canada.

Australians should write to the Canadian Consulate in Canberra, Sydney, Melbourne or Perth and request an application form for a working holiday visa which is an open employment authorization valid for a year from the date of issue, available to young people aged 18-30.

Seasonal Jobs. Travellers who are not eligible for a work visa do manage to pick up casual jobs, though this can be risky. In the most prolific areas, immigration officials are vigilant and carry out frequent raids (see *Crime & Safety* below). The key to getting a job is to have a nine-digit social insurance number; employers seldom ask to inspect the actual document.

Wages are fairly good in Canada with statutory minimum wages (e.g. $4.55 per hour in Ontario). In June last year, it was reported that there were 26,000 unfilled job vacancies in Toronto and employment was much easier to find than affordable accommodation. Count on having to spend at least $60-$75 a week on food and rent in the cities. The employment situation is tighter in Vancouver than Toronto, which is not surprising in view of the high rate of unemployment in British Columbia (i.e. 14%).

Many jobs exist in summer resorts especially in and around Banff in the Canadian Rockies, and in the Muskoka District north of Toronto. Jobs here usually come with accommodation. As in the US, waiting and bartending staff must depend heavily on tips. Banff attracts many casual workers and is a good place to make enquiries. Try the notice board at the youth hostel. The going rate for hotel/catering staff is $4.50-$6 an hour.

Harvesting and other outdoor jobs proliferate in the spring and summer, especially tree-planting. The interior of British Columbia and around Prince Rupert BC are among the most promising areas. The season normally lasts from the end of March to the end of July. The work is just as hard as any farming or construction work but is also very well paid. Novice planters should be able to earn over $100 a day and by the end of the season $200+, with camp living expenses amounting only to $15 a day.

The Okanagan Valley of BC is a destination famous among travellers looking for fruit-picking work, though wages tend to be low ($30-$40 a day) and the risk of discovery high. The best crop is apples which are picked after the soft fruits, i.e. in September and October. There is also an important apple harvest around Annapolis Royal in Nova Scotia.

Still in the Maritimes, tobacco farmers in eastern Prince Edward Island are major employers of planters in May/June. Opportunities for tobacco pickers in Southern Ontario (around Aylmer and Strathroy) have diminished in recent years with the drastic fall in the demand for tobacco worldwide.

For brief spells of employment investigate special events. Expo 86 in Vancouver and the Calgary Winter Olympics in 1988 absorbed a number of foreign workers with few questions asked.

Money

For a couple of years now the pound has been equal to C$2 give or take five or ten cents. Gone are the days when Canadians could proudly claim that their dollar was stronger than their neighbours' dollar. At the time of going to press, the Canadian dollar was worth about 80 US cents, which represents a slight inprovement over the situation a year or two ago. So your European travellers cheques will go further in Canada than they will in the States.

Both Thomas Cook and American Express issue travellers cheques in Canadian dollars which you will have no problem cashing and which can usually be used in hotels, restaurants and major stores. American and British currency or travellers cheques can be negotiated at any large bank though a hefty commission is often charged. US currency may be accepted in some establishments heavily visited by American tourists, but you are unlikely to receive as favourable an exchange rate as at the bank.

Banking hours are normally 10 am-3 pm Monday to Thursday, and 10 am-5 pm on Fridays. Trust companies (loosely analagous to building societies) offer most of the services that banks do and are open longer hours including Saturdays. If you arrive in Canada with a large sum of money, you might consider opening a bank account in Canadian dollars. You can open an account on the spot providing you have two pieces of identification, preferably showing a local address. An account holder at Canada Trust, one of the leading trust companies (which stays open 9 am-9pm six days a week), can withdraw money from any branch across Canada without delay or service charge. If this system appeals to you, get a list of the branch addresses beforehand, to make sure you will have access to your money in the places you want to visit.

The bright colours of Canadian notes (bills) and the smiling face of HM the Queen may come as both a shock and a relief after American greenbacks. The $1 bill is green, $2 pink, $5 blue, $10 purple, $20 pale green and $50 orange. The terminology used for coins is the same as in the US: penny, nickel, dime and quarter. Although there are 50c coins, you will not often see them in circulation. A new eleven-sided $1 coin is to be introduced in 1989. Quarters are the handiest coins for telephone booths, newspaper and other vending machines, parking meters, etc.

Telephones. The Canadian telephone system, run by private enterprise, certainly outflanks the deregulated American one for efficiency and economy. There are many aspects which are similar such as the dial tone, toll-free numbers and dial-a-joke service. Local calls from a private phone are invariably free, so it is quite permissible to ask in a restaurant or store if you can make a quick local phone call. If you are staying in a private home, you need feel no compunction (from the financial point of view) in chatting for hours on the phone. Local calls from call boxes cost 25c. A three minute long distance call (e.g. Toronto to Vancouver) costs about $6.50.

Post. Canada Post, a crown corporation, is notoriously slow and inefficient. Canadians you meet will be amazed to hear about the British system, and green with envy of next-day delivery including Saturdays. Post offices are not as numerous as they are in Britain (which admittedly has the highest ratio in the world) and will be further reduced in number once the government replaces many rural post offices with private outlets. In cities there is often a postal counter in the foyer of shopping malls where you can buy stamps and send parcels. An ordinary letter or post card within Canada costs 38c and to Europe 74c for the first 20 grams. Poste restante mail should be sent c/o General Delivery and be collected within a fortnight of its arrival.

Telegrams. Telegrams can be dictated over the phone to CN/CP Telecommunications and the cost will be charged to a telephone bill. If you don't know anyone whose number you can use for this purpose, you will have to send your message in person from any CN/CP office (address in phone book) which is distinct from the post office.

AIR

Unlike the US, internal air fares in Canada have not been deregulated, and are accordingly high. For example, the one way fare Toronto to Vancouver is about $550 and to Halifax $254. These fares can be reduced by a third by buying VUSA tickets before arrival in North America (see page 48). Students with ISIC cards can obtain cheap one-way fares (e.g. $250 from Toronto to Vancouver) at offices of the Canadian student travel organization travel CUTS. Excursion return fares are cheaper than one way fares (e.g. $427 return Toronto-Vancouver). In general, prices vary according to the season. The three major carriers — the government owned Air Canada, Wardair and Canadian Airlines International (formerly CP Air) — offer identical rates and discounts, including some standby fares for the under 21's. Before leaving Britain, you can get information and make bookings through travel agents or by ringing Air Canada (01-759 2636),

Wardair (0800-234444) or Canadian Airlines International (01-930 5664).

One way air tickets are sometimes sold privately through the "travel" Classified ads of major newspapers like the *Toronto Globe & Mail* or the *Vancouver Sun.* Watch for last minute adverts such as "One way Vancouver-Montreal. Female. $190 obo (or best offer)". The reason gender is specified is that technically airline tickets are non-transferable. Although the airlines don't bother to check your identity, they might feel obliged to make a fuss if they see that your sex does not match the one stated on your ticket. As long as you are flexible enough to travel on the date specified, this is probably the best bargain.

All airports in Canada are coded to begin with Y and bear no relation to the place name. Following the lead of a number of US airlines, Air Canada and Canadian now issue air passes for tourists. The price and conditions are similar and both offer a cheaper version for travellers willing to fly standby. You can purchase passes which allow four, six or eight stopovers for C$537, $605, or $672, which must be used within 60 days. The standby passes are sold at a 20% discount. Canadian offer more stopovers (but not at the standby rates): ten stopovers cost $740 and 12 costs $807. All these air passes are valid throughout North America and must be purchased outside the continent. Canadian and VIA Rail now offer a Skyrail pass which allows three sectors of air or train travel. The pass costs £225 (£45 less for travellers flying to Canada on Canadian), with extra sectors priced at only £22.50 each.

BUS

Greyhound Lines of Canada offer the greatest number of services, especially in Western Canada, though there are dozens of smaller operators with names like Moose Mountain Lines and Voyageur Colonial. For a copy of the *Official Bus Guide* which provides schedules for services throughout Canada as well as the USA, contact Russell's Guides Inc, PO Box 278, Cedar Rapids, Iowa 52406 (319-364-6138). Greyhound's Canadian headquarters are at 877 Greyhound Way SW, Calgary, Alberta (403-265-9111). Greyhound's transCanada *Scenicruiser Service* takes the better part of four days to go from Toronto to Vancouver.

In the past, a number of companies have cooperated to offer discounted one-way or return excursion fares but it was not certain that these would be repeated. The maximum single fare between a point in Ontario and anywhere in the four western provinces is around $150 one way. The Canada-wide maximum is about $199. So the 4,250 mile trip between Halifax and Whitehorse could work out at a mere 5c per mile, and allow unlimited stopovers within a 30-day period.

The Greyhound Ameripass (described in *Getting Around USA:* Bus) is valid only for brief forays into Canada including around Ontario and Quebec on Voyageur and Voyageur Colonial Lines. It is no longer valid for trans-Canada travel unless at the time of purchase you pay an extra US$50. If you intend to add extra days to your Ameripass ($15 a day), be sure to do this before your ticket expires in Canada.

A Canada-only version of the Ameripass costs $189 for seven days, $249 for 15 days and $349 for 30 days.

TRAIN

The building of the railway across the country plays a large role in the popular imagination and the national identity. The Canadian poet EJ Pratt wrote an epic poem called the *Last Spike* and Gordon Lightfoot's opus magnum is *The Canadian Railroad Trilogy*. The trans-Canada rail trip on the Canadian is one of the classic railway journeys of the world. The epic three-and-a-half day journey Toronto to Vancouver is an attractive alternative to the expensive flight. The basic one-way rail fare between these two cities is $261 for a reclining seat, with various supplements for more luxurious sleeping accommodation. For example there is a supplement of $200 for two people in a curtained-off double bed called a "Section". The fare permits stop-overs. It is sometimes possible to negotiate a discounted berth once you're on the train if these are available; ask any of the porters. Apex return fares which must be purchased at least two weeks in advance often represent considerable savings. There are also worthwhile savings to be made if travelling during the low season (January to early June and mid-September to mid-December.

The terrrain through the Prairies and the wilderness of Northern Ontario can become monotonous (as can the food in the dining car). But the section through the Rockies is spectacular. Occasional glimpses from the domed observation car of a herd of elk or moose stampeding away from the tracks or of a lonely little Ukrainian Orthodox church, generate enough interest to keep most travellers happy.

The most dense network of rail services is in the Ontario-Quebec Corridor which connects Montreal with Windsor. VIA Rail (pronounced *Vee-ah)*, which runs most of the passenger services in Canada is heavily subsidized by the government and is under constant pressure to axe services. (One of their economies was to close their London office near Trafalgar Square). VIA has introduced some futuristic new trains called LRCs (Light, Rapid, Comfortable) and is doing its best to compete with airlines. This has some advantages for travellers (computerized bookings, deluxe service) but some disadvantages (e.g. the necessity of reserving a seat in advance instead of simply buying your ticket and boarding your train). The express services in the Corridor are called "Rapido" and are equivalent to the Intercity 125 service of British Rail. The 325-mile (523 km) journey between Montreal and Toronto takes less than five hours on a Rapido, and the cost is $51 single, $82 for a seven-day return. If you are travelling on or near a holiday period, be sure to book a seat.

You can purchase a rail pass called a Canrailpass from any VIA station. Prices vary according to the age of traveller and region of the rail network. The fare for the whole country is $299 for 15 days, with extra days (maximum 15) costing $9 each. Shorter passes are available for the Maritime region, the Eastern and Western regions, and cost $99, $189 and $199 respectively for eight days. Youth discounts of 35% are available to those under 24.

DRIVING

Dependence on the automobile is just as rampant in Canada as it is in the USA. A Canadian without a car is an eccentric Canadian. If you plan to travel around any sparsely populated regions such as the Maritimes or the Northland, a car is virtually essential.

Car Hire. Rent-a-Wreck is just as strongly represented in Canada as in the States. Their toll-free number is 1-800-663-6727. Rates begin at $17 a day plus a 9c kilometre charge. The weekly price is $99 plus 9c per kilometre (charged on half the kilometres you do) plus $7 a day collision waiver and

$2 a day insurance. If you want to go for one of the large companies like Tilden, Budget or Avis, you can get a sub-compact for $75 a weekend which includes 600 free kilometres, or $200-$400 a week depending on the mileage arrangement. Camper vans may be hired for about $600 a week, unlimited mileage. Remember that provincial sales tax (up to 12%) will be added to the bill. The minimum rental age is 21 in most cases.

Petrol. Petrol is sold by the litre across Canada and the variation in price is extreme, from about 40c to 75c per litre. The average should be not much over £1 per Imperial gallon.

Rules of the Road. Driving laws are made at the provincial level, so rules and practices vary from province to province. For example you can drive with your UK licence for only 30 days in the Yukon but for six months in British Columbia. You can turn right on a red light (after stopping) in every province except Quebec. The speed limit in built-up areas across Canada is 50 km/h (30 mph) except in Prince Edward Island where it is 60 km/h (37 mph). On the open highway, the limit varies from 80 km/h (50 mph) in rural areas to 100 km/h (62 mph) on major arteries. All limits are clearly and repeatedly signposted in kilometres only.

The minimum driving age across Canada is 16 except in Newfoundland where it is 17. Seat belts are compulsory in BC, Ontario, Quebec, New Brunswick and Saskatchewan.

There are some rules which apply in all provinces. For instance, you must stop for school buses no matter in which direction you are travelling; and driving with over 0.08% alcohol in the blood is a serious offence. After a first offence, your licence will automatically be suspended for at least three months and you will normally get a $150-$300 fine. Speed traps are frequently set up by the police. Approaching motorists will often warn you by flashing their headlamps.

Insurance. Visiting drivers must have full liability insurance. The minimum cover varies from $50,000 to $200,000 according to province. Information is available from either the Insurance Bureau of Canada (181 University Avenue, Toronto; 416-362-2031) or from the Canadian Automobile Association (1775 Courtwood Crescent, Ottawa; 613-226-7631). The CAA is fully affiliated with the AA and RAC and will provide maps, itineraries, an emergency service, etc. to members of both organizations. The highway map issued by the tourist office is as detailed as most people require for long journeys.

Winter Driving. If you're visiting Canada during the winter, you'll have to have nerves of steel to drive. White-outs and black ice are common, even on the main highways. Police will normally block a road if it is considered too dangerous to navigate. Listen for warnings on the radio. If you are driving in rural areas, you are advised to carry a shovel, sand, flashlight, flares, extra clothes, a blanket, ice scraper and a candle placed inside a tin can. (A candle gives off enough heat in an enclosed space to sustain life for a considerable length of time). If you do get stranded stay in your vehicle and wait for help. Cautious drivers wait out storms in private houses or hostelries on their route. There is even a Canadian word for this: people talk about being "storm-stayed" for several days.

Driveaways. Under the heading Automobile Delivery in the Yellow Pages you will find a selection of driveaway agencies, just as you do in the USA. From the west coast, cars need to be delivered to California or Ontario; from Toronto, most of the traffic is destined for Florida or western Canada.

You should have no difficulty finding a driveaway car during the winter, but there may be delays in the summer.

HITCH-HIKING

There are fewer crazy drivers in Canada than there are in the USA, and hitching is less dangerous in Canada than it is south of the border. There is a large measure of hostility to hitchers among the more conservative elements of society, but on the other hand there is a strong pro-British feeling which should work in your favour if you sport a Union Jack on your luggage. Just as in the USA it is difficult to hitch out of big sprawling cities. But hitching is an accepted practice in country areas, especially in summer. In winter, only the brave or foolhardy would want to try.

As in the USA, most budget travellers choose from youth hostels, cheap downtown hotels (often attached to a bar) or motels. Hotel addresses given out by tourist offices or hotels associations tend to be expensive, at least $45 for a double. Try asking for guest houses or tourist rooms which will be cheaper. Similarly, bed and breakfasts are often interesting places to stay but rarely cheap. Consult *John Thompson's Country Bed & Breakfast Places of Canada* if you're interested. Double rooms in motels start at $35, though you must take into account the additional cost of commuting into a city centre. Also look for signs on residential homes "Approved Accommodation" which indicates a private guesthouse.

Canada is not very well endowed with youth hostels; it has a total of 60 with a concentration in the Rockies and in Nova Scotia. Charges vary from $4 to $13.50 depending on the degree of luxury. Some of the ones in the Rockies for instance are very primitive, little more than a log shelter. A list of hostels is available from any hostel shop or from the National Office in Ottawa (333 River Road, Tower A, 3rd Floor, Vanier, Ontario K1L 8H9; 613-748-5638).

University residences are usually open to visitors out of term, i.e. mid-May to late August. There may be restrictions such as a minimum stay of one week or priority for visiting students. Enquiries should be addressed to the University Housing Officer of the university of your choice as far in advance of your visit as possible. Charges are about $20 a day single, with reductions for longer stays. The Travel Canada Card allows the holder to stay in a number of university residences. It can be purchased for $20 from the Conference Office, St. Mary's University, Halifax B3H 3C3.

There are over 50 KOA campsites in Canada, mostly in eastern Canada, as well as a large number of government and other privately-run sites nationwide. The Canadian headquarters of KOA is at 6-A Tilbury Court, Brampton, Ontario L6T 3T4 (416-453-7080). ·

You have to go out of your way to find uniquely Canadian dishes. Any you do find are regional specialities, from the famous French Canadian meat pie called *tourtiere* to fried cod's tongues in Newfoundland. Occasionally a restaurant will serve pemmican (originally a Cree word describing meat which has been dried and pounded with berries), bear and groundhog, but this is very rare. Freshwater fish are delicious and best enjoyed over a lakeside fire a few hours after having been caught. British Columbian salmon is famous and cheaper than Scottish salmon. Many west coast households own their own salmon smoking devices with a choice of wood flavouring. The most famous Canadian food product is maple syrup, preferably enjoyed with a plate of fluffy pancakes. A small tin of maple syrup is one of the tastiest souvenirs of Canada you can take home.

Apart from a few regional specialities and the excellent French cooking available in many Montreal and Quebec City restaurants, eating out in Canada is almost indistinguishable from eating out in the US: fast food frachises, coffee shops, delis, steak and seafood restaurants and a huge range of ethnic restaurants in the big cities. And if you want to eat in rather than out, you can have food such as pizza or Chinese food delivered to your door. Check the Yellow Pages for the restaurants that deliver.

Tipping. As in the US, a 10-15% tip is usual in restaurants. Canadian waiters and waitresses may not display their wrath quite as openly as their American counterparts if you undertip, but they will certainly feel it.

DRINKING

Canadians consume more alcohol than the British and the Americans, most of it in the form of lager-style beer. As in the US, more beer drinking takes place in front of the TV than in public. But beer drinking, like all alcohol consumption, has been declining. As an expensive marketing ploy to revive the habit, some brewers have replaced the characteristic stubby bottle with a taller American-style bottle.

Canadian beer has long been held in high regard not only by nationalistic Canadians but by Americans too, for being slightly stronger and considerably tastier than American beer. It is therefore surprising that American beers have penetrated the market as effectively as they have over the past few years, especially Miller and Budweiser. The Canadian company Molsons brews a version of Lowenbrau to compete with the American imports, though it tastes more like ordinary Canadian beer than the stuff brewed in Munich. However, the three principal Canadian breweries continue to dominate: Carling, Labatt and Molsons, all of whom brew a range of beers. Most beer drinkers buy a 24-pack or "two-four". A deposit of about 10c is charged in bottles and cans. Domestic bottled beer costs about $2.50 for a 20oz bottle, $3.50 for an import. The most unusual brews are Carling's Buckeye, Labatt's IPA and Molson's Brador. If possible sample some of the beers brewed regionally. Some, like Moosehead which is brewed in the Atlantic provinces, have become well known, but there are other small breweries known only to a local clientele.

Many people are surprised to learn that a country associated with snow blizzards produces wine. The industries of both British Columbia and Ontario are expanding and producing more mature wines. Some examples are given in the relevant chapters.

Canadian whiskey is drier than American bourbon but quite different from Scotch. Browse in a liquor store for some unusual indigenous liqueurs, for instance Yukon Jack or a liqueur made from maple syrup.

The minimum drinking age is 18 in Alberta, Manitoba, Quebec and Prince Edward Island, and 19 everywhere else. ID must often be produced when purchasing alcohol just as in the US. Hours of opening vary from province to province and are dealt with in the regional chapters. Due to the puritanical influence of the early settlers, the sale of alcohol is strictly controlled by the provincial governments. Government-run off sales usually keep normal shop hours (9am-5.30pm) and so a certain amount of advance planning is necessary. It is also illegal to drink alcohol in public and you may well witness the spectacle of police officers emptying can after can of the demon drink at the entrance to beaches, stadiums, etc.

Most bars fall into one of two categories: rough hang-outs or expensive neon antiseptic haunts where you are constantly hassled to buy another drink, since the staff are trying to supplement their meagre wages with tips. There are also increasing numbers of replica British pubs which never quite come off.

THE ARTS

Canada is less paranoid about its culture than it once was. For years, talented Canadians in every field have drifted over the border for recognition in the US, people like Oscar Peterson, Joni Mitchell, Neil Young, Donald Sutherland and William Shatner. In an effort to stem the tide and to promote Canadian Culture, the government has legislated a minimum level of Canadian content in radio and television broadcasting. There is also a strict Hire-Canadians-Only policy. Xenophobic immigration and employment laws have made it difficult for theatre companies and orchestras to hire British and American stars as directors, conductors and players. The hiring of less well known Canadians in favour of foreign celebrities often results in bitter controversy.

The generous government subsidies of Canadian talent have complemented private patronage to boost the arts. Toronto, Montreal and Vancouver have a great deal to offer the theatre-goer, opera lover, music buff and balletomane, both mainstream extravaganzas (some shows are imported from the US it must be admitted) and experimental works. The Royal Winnipeg Ballet and the Canadian Opera Company regularly tour the country and every city has its own symphony orchestra. The Canadian Film Board is known internationally for the quality of its shorts, documentaries, animations and, more recently, for a controversial anti-nuclear film *If You Love This Planet* which was banned in public cinemas in America. On the whole, though, the Canadian film industry has lagged behind the Australian one; it has produced only two or three films which have achieved some international recognition such as the film *The Decline of the American Empire* and the brilliant *I've Heard the Mermaids Singing*. Entrance to cinemas costs about $6 while tickets for mainstream theatre and concerts start at about $12. Watch for "rush-seats", unsold seats which are sold at a discount on the day of performance.

The splashy new National Gallery in Ottawa, the Art Gallery of Ontario in Toronto and Vancouver Art Gallery have international art collections and have visiting exhibitions from Europe and the US. In every town there is a regional gallery which displays art and artefacts from both early and contemporary Canada, which can be fascinating to visitors from the Old World.

Popular Music. Although famous musicians like Joni Mitchell and Ian Tyson are Canadian in origin, they have gone to the US for recognition. Artists who remain in Canada normally depend on a regional following. Toronto based bands are often unknown on the west coast and vice versa. Groups like Rush and the Band have earned themselves large international audiences. For the newest and best, you'll have to ask the locals or guess from listings in the alternative press.

Folk music thrives across Canada and any of the annual folk festivals are very worthwhile attending, especially Mariposa in Ontario and the Vancouver Folk Festival (see regional chapters for details). Quebec has a strong and unique tradition of French folk and popular music which is continued by home-grown *chansonniers*.

Television and Radio. The strict laws which prescribe a minimum of Canadian content in the media mean that programming in Canada is quite different from that of the States. Almost all Canadian households have cable TV which allows them to pick up programmes on all three American networks plus Public Broadcasting. The Canadian Broadcasting Corporation shows some American drivel, but also some worthwhile drama series and documentaries (some bought from the BBC).

The CBC schedules of radio programmes are listed in the monthly magazine *Radio Guide.* Many Americans close to the border tune in to the CBC news, since it is reputed to be more impartial and international than American radio news. The Corporation operates two national English-language services. Many stations across the country devote all or part of their schedules to ethnic programming. Some northern broadcasts are in Indian and Inuit languages. For more details about programming, contact CBC Audience Services, Box 500, Station A, Toronto.

Newspapers. As in the US, Canadian newspapers are bulging with advertisements. When you see the size of an average city daily, you will understand why the forests of Canada, vast as they are, are being depleted faster than they can be replaced. Overall circulation of newspapers is exactly half of Britain's (219 per 1,000 people as opposed to 441). The only newspaper which can justifiably claim to be a national paper is the *Toronto Globe & Mail* which is published in a western edition as well. Even so, the circulation is only 312,000, so its influence is limited. The price of the newspaper varies between locations. In Toronto the Monday-Friday editions cost 25c while the Saturday edition cost $1; elsewhere in Ontario the price is 50c every day.

SPORT

Canadians are even more avid sports fans than their American neighbours. Extensive media coverage, especially of ice hockey (always called hockey), guarantees that most Canadians are familiar with stars' names and team standings. As in the US, the baseball season takes place in summer, football in the autumn and hockey throughout the winter.

Hockey. It is the rare Canadian who does not learn to skate at a very early age. By about the age of nine, most children — predominantly boys — play hockey either informally or in a local league. In former days, boys would gather on any frozen river or lake with their portable nets, hockey sticks and puck and play for hours until their extremities were numb with cold. These days, most hockey is played in indoor arenas, and when those aren't available, the neighbourhood kids dispense with skates, get together on the road, strap old telephone directories to their shins to act as protection, and take shots at each other's goal. Hockey is ingrained in the national consciousness. There is even a Canadian novel about the game called *The Last Season* by Roy MacGregor.

In the good old days (pre-1967) the National Hockey League consisted of six teams, the Toronto Maple Leafs, Montreal Canadiens, Chicago Black Hawks, Detroit Red Wings, New York Rangers and Boston Bruins, all battling for the top prize, the Stanley Cup. Despite the American location, any Canadian would have told you with pride that the vast majority of the players were Canadian. To the great satisfaction of Canadian fans, the Stanley Cup passed back and forth between Montreal and Toronto during the 1960's. But then the league expanded, eventually to embrace 16 more teams including such unknowns as the New Jersey Devils and Buffalo Sabres. Although many fans lamented the dilution of the league, they don't seem to have become any less fanatical.

The game itself is fast, exciting and easy to follow. If you're in Canada during the season (October to April) and can't see a live game, try to see one on television. One aspect of it that may take you by surprise is the fisticuffs which regularly develop. It is a strange sight to see a heavily padded sportsman trying to pull the opponent's jersey over his head while balancing on skates. Regrettably, the fans love it.

Lacrosse. This indigenous game was adapted from a Native Indian ball game called bagataway. Early explorers reported that games involved as many as 1,000 players, and that broken bones and even death regularly ensued. Although the modern version is not played on so massive nor so violent a scale, it is a fast and rough game, well worth the effort of tracking down.

GAMBLING

Gambling in casinos is illegal in all provinces, with one exception. In the former gold rush town of Dawson City in the Yukon Territory, you can gamble at a reconstruction of Diamond Tooth Gertie's casino. There is a maximum bet of $25 on black jack, roulete and poker. There is no off-track betting.

Perhaps because Canadians have always been deprived of the pleasures of gambling, lotteries are amazingly successful. If you like to spend time dreaming about what you would do with a prize of $20 million then by all means buy a ticket. Most stationery and newspaper shops sell them.

In a country whole capital means "buying and selling" in an Indian language, it is not surprising to find an obsession with commerce. The inventor of the shopping mall is reputed to have been a Canadian (who went south to make his fortune). The rate at which suburban shopping complexes continue to spring up makes the casual observer wonder how there can possibly be enough consumers to go round.

The principal department stores are Eaton's, Simpson's, Woodwards (in the West) and the Bay, descendant of the original Hudson's Bay Company. With a few exceptions, these department stores are found downtown. The major discount department stores like Zellers, K-Mart, Woolworths and Canadian Tire are found in suburban plazas. The Bay carries high quality merchandise including the distinctive Hudson's Bay blankets.

Sales tax varies from zero in Alberta, the Yukon and the Northwest Territories to 12% in Newfoundland. As in the USA, the tax is not included in the published price. If you plan to make any expensive purchases, enquire about having the sales tax deducted or how to reclaim tax paid. Normally the shop will deduct the tax only if they ship the item directly out of the province. If this is not convenient, contact the local government offices to find out the procedure for reclaiming.

A number of shops allow youth hostel members a discount, so hostellers should obtain the list of participating merchants.

Most shops open from about 9.30 am to 5.30/6 pm with late night shopping on Thursdays and Fridays. The laws prohibiting Sunday shopping are being strenuously challenged, but for the most part you will have to rely on convenience stores (such as Mac's Milk and Beckers) on Sundays.

Clothing and shoe sizes are identical to those in the USA (see page 104).

The Great Outdoors

For many people, the reason for a trip to Canada is to explore the wilderness. Pleasant and interesting as Canada's cities are, the forests, mountains and lakes are what give the nation its special appeal. Although the distances between city and undeveloped countryside can be large, every visitor should make the effort to leave the cities. In a country where raccoons and skunks are periodically spotted in southern Ontario backyards, and where the Northern Lights *(aurora borealis)* can occasionally be seen from city parking lots, the call of the wild is not far away.

The trouble with all that virgin wilderness is that it can be inaccessible, and inhospitable once you get there. Dense forests criss-crossed by rivers and dotted with lakes make difficulties for the uninitiated backpacker. The dream of a coast-to-coast National Trail is still a long way from realization. Most hikers head for maintained trails, usually in national and provincial parks. Ironically, these can become crowded. In order to control the numbers, park authorities are now insisting that you book ahead for some of the most popular trails. The reservation is not for a specific campsite but simply for the right to hike. Make enquiries to the park ranger well ahead if you are interested in doing a specific route (addresses of individual parks available from provincial tourist offices or the regional office of Parks Canada). There is no such restriction on day hikes. Topographic maps costing from $7-$10 (including postage) are available from the Canada Map Office Department of Energy, Mines and Resources, 615 Booth St, Ottawa K1A OE9. A free index of maps will be sent on request.

Parks. In addition to a host of provincial parks, there are 29 national parks in Canada from the Pacific Rim in the far west to Terra Nova Newfoundland accounting for 50,000 square miles (about the size of England). Each park has a distinctive feature such as a glacier, a herd of roaming bison, geological formations or rare flowers and plants. They all offer access to Canada's backcountry as well as tamer opportunities to join organized hikes, rent canoes or attend a naturalist's slide show. Vehicles pay $3 for a single day's admission to a national park, $6 for four days and $20 for the whole season (usually May-September). Camping fees range from $5 for a primitive site to $13.50 for a deluxe site with electricity, showers, etc. Firewood is normally supplied at a cost of $1. Campsites cannot be booked in advance, so you have to take your chances when you arrive. You can't stay longer than two weeks at any one campground, and many are open only in the summer. Consider carefully what provisions you take into a primitive campsite, since you'll have to carry all your rubbish out again. In many parks, tins and bottles are completely banned. Occasionally parks are closed when there is an exceptionally high risk of forest fire. For a guide to the national parks write to Parks Canada, Ottawa, Ontario K1A 1G2 (819-

997-2800). The five regional addresses have been listed in the regional chapters.

Wildlife. Seeing a spouting whale off the Pacific coastal trail or a bewhiskered Rocky Mountain goat high on a crag or hearing the haunting morning call of the loon (a diving bird) could be the highlight of your whole trip. On the other hand confronting swarms of mosquitoes or a bear might be the low point. If you do plan to go into the bush, make sure you take all the anti-bear precautions you can. Most bears attack because they are suddenly frightened or because their cubs appear to be threatened. So it is advisable to make a lot of noise as you hike; some people even wear a special bell called a bear-scarer around their necks. Bears tend to wander along the same route every day, creating shallow trenches which a native guide will probably be able to recognize. At night always hang your food from a tall tree branch; never keep it inside your tent. If you woud rather watch a bear from the safety of a car, visit a rubbish dump in northern areas just after sunset. Sometimes the local council even erects a sign at tips warning bear-watchers to stay inside their cars.

Wolves are much less dangerous, since they will rarely confront a human, though an injured person left alone could be in danger. It is a good idea to carry a whistle to blow in an emergency, both to notify potential rescuers and to frighten away animals. Porcupines are commonplace but present no threat unless you try to handle one in which case you will find a mass of sharp needles embedded in your hand. Skunks (from the Algonquin word "segonku") are a nuisance. When frightened they spray a very offensive odour which lingers not only on the victim but in the air for days. The remedy for an afflicted human (including clothing) or pet is a bath in tomato juice.

Insects. One of the worst trials to the outdoors-person is the succession of biting insects. The mosquito season is said to begin in earnest in June; however it is possible to be driven wild by them in May. The blackfly season also lasts for the months of June and July. Blackflies are tiny insects with a vicious bite. You must apply a strong evil-smelling repellant at regular intervals. Look for a brand which is composed of 100% active ingredients viz. diethyl toluamide, colloquially known as DEET. Experienced hikers also recommend eating lots of garlic which apparently offends insects as much as humans. Make sure there are no holes in your tent. Another way of avoiding the pests is to plan to take a trip after the first frost which usually occurs in late September. For instance if you choose the Thanksgiving weekend in mid-October, you may find yourself camping either in hot sun or in snow, but at least there won't be any bugs.

Equipment. Canada is as good a place as any to purchase good quality camping equipment, though prices are no lower than in Britain. It may also be possible to hire rucksacks or tents in places like Banff, or from university co-op shops. Some addresses are included in the regional chapters. Certainly skis and canoes can easily be rented from private outfitters or at resorts.

It is ironical than in a country as heavily forested as Canada, there are often restrictions on the use of wood by backpackers to build fires. Forest fires are a very serious problem and although many of them are caused by lightning, a few are caused by careless campers. When firebuilding is permitted, the rule is that you can burn only dead wood and fallen branches. Along heavily travelled trails, you may have to penetrate deep into the bush to find enough wood. So unless you are carrying your own stove (as most campers do) be sure to start setting up camp well before dark.

A waterproof container for matches is often essential, since downpours can be very heavy. One solution is to use a film canister and glue the striking surface of the match box inside the lid.

Hunting and Fishing. All non-residents must purchase provincial hunting and fishing licences. Fees range from about $10 to $25 for a licence lasting a few days. To shoot migratory game birds you need a special federal licence available from post offices. Hunting rifles or shotguns may be imported into Canada without a permit. Whereas hunting is not allowed in Canada's national parks, fishing permits are available for a small sum from any national park office and valid in all parks. For information about licences, equipment and species, contact either the provincial tourist office (addresses listed below in *Help and Information*) or the provincial government division of Fish and Wildlife.

Canoeing. The placid lakes found throughout Canada are ideal for the beginner. There is also plenty of whitewater for the more adventurous. The cost of an organized trip will be at least $60 a day including log cabin or tended accommodation.

Crime and Safety

Although the population of Canada is one-tenth that of the USA, it has about one-thirtieth of the murders, rapes and so on. It is not only the statistics which are reassuring, but also the atmosphere. Walking alone at night is not nearly as terrifying in Ottawa as in Washington nor as dangerous in Montreal as in Memphis. Even in the biggest cities, there are virtually no areas which you need to avoid. You should of course exercise caution just as you would at home but, on the whole, there is little cause for anxiety. people who have hitch-hiked around North America report that their heart rate drops as soon as they cross into Canada. One explanation for the lower level of violence is that there is far less racial tension, and no history of segregation in Canada. Although the Native Indians' resentment against the white man occasionally flares up in barroom brawls, you are unlikely to be involved.

As in the USA, laws vary from province to province. Some provinces have a dial-a-law telephone number which will provide the basic legal facts about such topics as drugs and immigration. There are also several levels of policing, from the federal Royal Canadian Mounted Police (who are more associated with synchronized riding than with tracking the Mafia) down to municipal policemen who sometimes seem like glorified traffic wardens.

If you decide to work without proper authorization, you should be aware that you are breaking the law. If you are working in a high-profile job, you may well be raided by immigration control (rather than the police whose jurisdiction does not include immigration offences). If you have insufficient funds you may be deported. Otherwise you will be given a "departure notice" which allows you to travel to the US. If caught you should contact the nearest legal aid lawyer whose services are free.

Drugs. The drug laws in Canada are federal rather than piecemeal by province. Possession of marijuana is a criminal offence under the Narcotic Control Act, despite the fact that one national organization estimates that over four million Canadians indulge. The penalty for a first offence is a fine of up to $1,000 and/or six months in prison. It is to be presumed that a traveller would not be so foolish as to put himself in the position of committing a second offence, whereupon the penalty is a $2,000 fine and a year in jail. Importing and exporting is punishable by up to life imprisonment, but not less that seven years. Incredibly the penalties for marijuana are identical to those for heroin and other opiates. Despite this, the cultivation and use of marijuana by average people of all social backgrounds is just as widespread in Canada as in the US.

The provincial tourist offices publish many informative and useful leaflets, so it is worth writing to them. (Half of them have only a box office address). Their addresses are listed below, alphabetically according to province. Toll-free numbers are valid within North America only.

Travel Alberta: 10025 Jasper Avenue, 15th Floor, Edmonton T5J 3Z3. Tel. 1-800-661-8888.

Tourism British Columba: Parliament Buildings, Victoria V8V 1X4. Tel: (604) 683-2000.

Travel Manitoba: Department 7020, 155 Carlton St, 7th Floor, Winnipeg R3C 3H8. Tel: 1-800-665-0040.

Tourism New Brunswick: PO Box 12345, Fredericton E3B 5C3. Tel: (506) 453-2377. Toll free: 1-800-561-0123.

Newfoundland Tourism: PO Box 2016, St John's A1C 5R8. Tel: (709) 576-2830. Toll-free: 1-800-563-6353.

Nova Scotia Tourism: PO Box 130, Halifax B3J 2M7. Tel: (902) 424-5000.

Ontario Ministry of Tourism: 77, Bloor St W, 9th Floor, Toronto M7A 2K9. Tel: (416) 965-4008. Toll free: 1-800-268-3735.

Prince Edward Island Tourism: PO Box 940, Charlottetown C1A 7M5. Tel: (902) 892-2457.

Tourism Quebec: C. P. 20,000, Quebec G1K 7X2. Tel: (514) 873-2015.

Tourism Saskatchewan: 2103, 11th Avenue, Regina S4P 3V7. Tel: (306) 787-2300. Toll free: 1-800-667-7191.

Northwest Territories: (TravelArctic): Yellowknife X1A 2L9. Tel: (403) 873-7200.

Tourism Yukon: PO Box 2703, Whitehorse Y1A 2C6. Tel: (403) 667-5340.

Travelers' Aid. The few offices which Travelers' Aid maintains in Canada are in financial difficulty. You may discover that their offices, usually located in downtown railway stations, are closed due to shortage of staff.

Consulates. The British High Commission is at 80 Elgin St, Ottawa K1P 5K7 (613-237-1530). There are also consulates in Montreal, Toronto, Vancouver, Edmonton and Halifax (addresses in following chapters).

PUBLIC HOLIDAYS

There are ten statutory holidays celebrated across Canada plus a few holidays unique to some provinces:

January 1	New Year's Day
March/April	Good Friday
	Easter Monday
May (Monday preceding May 25)	Victoria Day
July 1	Canada Day (formerly Dominion Day)
September (1st Monday)	Labour Day
October (2nd Monday)	Thanksgiving
November 11	Remembrance Day
December 25	Christmas Day
December 26	Boxing Day

In addition, most individual provinces observe additional public holidays as shown below; Quebec's festival on June 24th is also known (significantly) as Fete Nationale, while Newfoundland has no less than five provincial celebrations.

March (second Monday)	St Patrick's Day (Newfoundland only)
April (fourth Monday)	St George's Day (Newfoundland only)
June (third Monday)	Discovery Day (Newfoundland only)
June 24th	St John Baptiste Day (Quebec only)
June (last Monday)	Memorial Day (Newfoundland only)
July (second Monday)	Orangemen's Day (Newfoundland only)
August (first Monday)	Civic Holiday/Heritage Day (*not* Quebec, Atlantic Provinces or Yukon)
August (middle Monday)	Discovery Day (Yukon only)

Toronto and Ontario

CN Tower

Ontario is the richest and most heavily industrialized of Canada's ten provinces. For this reason and because Southern Ontario is geographically buried in the central USA, it is sometimes thought to be more "American" than many other parts of Canada. In many ways it is envied and resented by the other provinces for being the most powerful and sophisticated. Certainly there are giant Ford assembly plants and huge American-style agri-businesses in Southern Ontario, not to mention sprawling suburban shopping plazas and neon-lit motel strips. But there are also charming country towns like St Mary's and Fenelon Falls, gracious farming communities, thriving Mennonite markets and thousands of square miles of forest, parkland and even some Arctic tundra, all of which are as yet uncontaminated by minigolf courses and fast food joints. Ontario is an interesting place to start your holiday.

Toronto is likely to be the first taste of Canada which many travellers will have. With a population of 3.2 million, it has recently overtaken Montreal as the leading city in Canada, and is making a bid for the 1996 Olympics. Toronto is renowned throughout North America for its cleanliness and low crime rate, and for having avoided the development of a wasteland between downtown and suburbs so characteristic of North American cities. Much of its architecture and atmosphere are glossy and new, and yet it has retained many of its old neighbourhoods which lend the downtown area some character. You will probably confine yourself to the pleasingly dense downtown, most of it negotiable by foot, before setting off to explore the rest of the province.

The rest of Ontario has much to offer by way of outdoor recreation. Just a short distance from Toronto there are ski hills (admittedly not very spectacular) and a further hour will bring you to the lakes and forests which you may have come to Canada expressly to find. With its 1.75 million acres, Algonquin Provincial Park is the most well-known destination for canoeists and campers, but there are many others, 130 other provincial parks to be exact. And if you are not as keen on wilderness solitude as on picturesque landscapes, you might like to cycle through Prince Edward county west of Kingston to the shore of Lake Ontario, or take the ferry across to the very rural Manitoulin Island, where fishing and blueberry picking seem to be the main activities, or visit Point Pelee National Park, the most southerly point in Canada, to see the exotic birds and flowers. Any Ontarian will be very happy to recommend his or her favourite little out-of-the-way discovery, and you cannot do better than to take that advice.

THE NATIVES

Ontario is the only province of Canada whose urban population is over 80% of the total, and the natives seem more sophisticated and fast-living than in the other provinces. Ethnic communities thrive in Toronto and the Italian, Chinese, Portuguese and German populations are numerous and culturally strong. There is an Austrian club where old men play chess on the weekends. You can attend United Church services (the largest Protestant denomination in Canada) in Korean, Hungarian and many other languages. You can watch soccer being played by Greek and Portuguese teams, and buy Armenian and Korean newspapers.

Outside Toronto, there is a small but influential group of people called Mennonites. Originally they were German settlers, and they continue to dress only in black and drive horses and buggies for religious reasons. Their celebrated produce and cuisine is available at markets and specialist restaurants in the Waterloo area.

Making Friends. Judging from the number of singles bars and lonely hearts advertisements, Toronto seems to be full of people in search of a partner. They seem to favour the bars and singles clubs (like Earl's Tin Palace) near the corner of Yonge and Eglinton (sometimes dubbed young and eligible). The popular singles night is Thursday. Bars at the University of Toronto are few and dismal, but there are plenty of lively off-campus places which students can recommend.

CLIMATE

Although Toronto is on the same latitude as Nice, do not expect a balmy winter. Toronto has a typically Canadian climate which specializes in extremes. The average temperature in July is 70°F/22°C and it can feel particularly hot and muggy during the summer. Most public buildings are air-conditioned and many private houses have at least one air-conditioned room. In January the average is 24°F/-4°C. There is an annual snowfall of 141 centimetres (55 inches), however snow is promptly removed from sidewalks and roads so a pair of snow shoes would look distinctly out of place. You may, however, need a pair of waterproof boots to wade through the slush caused by melting snow.

Bicycles are not normally ridden between approximately December and April, since the ice and slush make cycling not only unpleasant but dangerous. All buildings are heavily insulated and centrally heated, often to about 70°F/21°C which can seem uncomfortably hot to visitors from Britain, where the legal maximum in public buildings is 68°F/19°C. There is some form of precipitation on 134 days of the year making a total of nearly 80 centimetres (31 inches). Although July and August are the wettest months, the heavy rains fall infrequently, and are unlikely to be a serious nuisance. The best months are probably May and September. It can become very windy, especially among the downtown skyscrapers where people have been knocked flat by the whirling winds. In Toronto, recorded weather information is available on 676-3066.

In Northern Ontario, the summers are not as hot as in the south of the province, the winters are colder and longer and the snowfall considerably more.

ARRIVAL AND DEPARTURE

Air. The Lester B. Pearson International Airport is named after the Nobel Peace Prize-winning Prime Minister of Canada who led the country during the 1960s. The airport is located 30km/18 miles north-west of the city centre. There are express airport buses operated by Gray Coach (979-3511) between the airport and the ends of the public transport system or between the airport and downtown. Buses leave from the arrivals level of both terminals every 40 minutes between 6.45am and midnight to take passengers to the Islington subway stop near the western end of the Bloor subway line or the Yorkdale station on the Yonge line (pronounced Young); one way fare is $4.25 and $4.75 respectively. The third destination is York Mills subway station which costs $5.25, though there is no advantage unless you are staying with people who live in the York Mills area. For $8 you can be taken right downtown. The Airport Express Downtown Service runs every 20 minutes between 6.50am and 12.10am. Travel time to the Royal York Hotel (opposite the main railway station) is about 30 minutes unless it's rush hour. The cost of the taxi ride is about $30.

Commuter flights to Ottawa and Montreal operate from the STOL-port (short take off and landing) on Toronto Island.

For low-cost onward flights, contact Travel CUTS at 187 College St (1-800-268-9044).

Bus. The Bus Terminal is located on Bay Street north of Dundas Street, just around the corner from Toronto's Chinatown. It is Canada's busiest bus terminal, and is currently being renovated; when completed, arrivals and departure areas will be separated. Information is obtainable on 979-3511 between 7am and 11.30pm. Gray Coach (as distinct from Greyhound) operate most of the routes within Ontario although the Ottawa-based Voyageur Colonial operates the services between Toronto and Kingston/Ottawa/Montreal. Buses leave for Montreal and for London and Windsor/Detroit about a dozen times a day. There are five buses daily to Huntsville, a small town in the heart of the scenic Muskoka region; the journey takes about four hours. The cost of bus travel works out a very approximate 8c per kilometre (13c per mile).

Train. There are two rail routes from the USA to Ontario. Amtrak run a daily service from New York's Grand Central Station departing at 8.45am and arriving in Toronto at 8.10pm. The one way fare is $77 (in Canadian funds). Customs formalities take place at Niagara Falls. You may decide to break your journey if you want to spend some time admiring the famous waterfall.

Union Station, at the southern extremity of the subway line, is a Beaux Arts architectural delight, which was saved from the wreckers' crane in the 1970's. You may even recognize it from the final scene of the *Silver Streak* when an incoming train fails to stop and ploughs into the station wall. Union is very close to the O'Keefe Arts Centre and the St Lawrence Market, and is only about a 15 or 20 minute walk from the Bus Depot.

The daily trans-Canada service, called (inevitably) *The Canadian,* arrives in Toronto Union at 7pm, three days and eight hours after leaving Vancouver. The train heading west leaves at 12.35pm. Information about all rail schedules and prices is available on 366-8411. Some sample single fares from Toronto are $45 to Ottawa, $31 to Sarnia, $21 to Huntsville, $4 to Niagara Falls. As a very rough guide, the price of a single is 10c per kilometre (16c per mile) and less for a seven day return. This calculation ceases to be valid for longer journeys. If you want to go to Moosonee in the far north via the Polar Bear Express (a classic train ride), you will have to spend $170 on a return ticket and be prepared to spend 16 hours on the train each way.

Rapid commuter services called "GO Trains" (Government of Ontario) feed into Union Street from other towns in the Toronto conurbation. They go as far east along the shore of Lake Ontario as Whitby and as far west as Hamilton. Ring 630-3933 for information.

Driving. Entry into Toronto by road is well sign-posted and comparatively swift. Car drivers coming from Detroit/Windsor in the west or Montreal and Kingston in the east will approach via Highway 401, now cumbersomely renamed the Macdonald-Cartier Freeway. This is a typical North American highway: straight, wide and not very scenic, with a speed limit of 100 km/hr (62 mph). The highway from the south (Niagara Falls) is the Queen Elizabeth Way (QEW to the locals) which cuts off the western tip of Lake Ontario and no longer charges a toll. From the east you'll approach downtown on the Don Valley Parkway, whose traffic jams are so bad sometimes that locals call it the Don Valley Parking Lot. The standard speed limit on Ontario highways in the 400 series (400, 401, 402 ...) is 100 km/hr.

To reach many of the scenic highlights and lakeside parks in Ontario, you will have to rely on a car whether as a hitch-hiker or as a driver. The road heading north out of Toronto is highway 400. Avoid this at the beginning and end of summer weekends, because it soon becomes clogged with city-dwellers escaping to their summer cottages north of Toronto.

There are many rental offices for Budget and Tilden in Toronto, both charging about $35 a day including 200 free kilometres per day. Tilden's weekend rate is $70 with 600 free kilometres. You can drop the car off in another centre but this is very expensive. For example one-way rentals are available from Budget at the airport for $50 a day plus 104 per kilometre. Rent-a-Wreck is represented in Toronto, at 374 Dupont St (961-7500), close to downtown.

Petrol in downtown Toronto costs about 55c a litre ($2.50 a gallon), though price wars can bring this down. Prices are usually highest on the highways. In cities, Canadian Tire gas stations usually charge a low price. Also try Discount on 961-8006.

Driveaways. Although there are driveaway companies in Toronto, they almost never need drivers for destinations within the province. Most of the traffic is to Florida or to the Canadian West in early winter or back in the spring. You are permitted four days to get to Florida and eight days to get to Vancouver. In winter they are so desperate for drivers that some companies even pay for the gas. Try the Auto Delivery Company, 5803 Yonge St (225-7754).

Hitch-hiking. Hitchers heading west should take a GO-Train from Union Station to Mississauga, an outer suburb, and stand on the ramp approach to the 401. Waits can be long here. People heading east usually have better luck; they should stand on the Ajax ramp after taking the GO-Train to Ajax. It is technically illegal to hitch on the highways themselves.

CITY TRANSPORT

City Layout. Like American cities, Toronto is based on the grid pattern, though the streets are named not numbered. The main north-south street is Yonge Street which according to the *Guinness Book of Records* is the longest thoroughfare in the world at 1,700 km. Bloor Street is the main east-west thoroughfare.

When trying to locate a specific address, bear in mind that all east-west numbering begins at Yonge Street, which is the boundary between east and west. So Dundas Street is called Dundas East or Dundas West according to which side of Yonge you are referring to. The further away from Yonge, the greater the street number. An added trick is that on east-west streets, the even numbers are always on the north side, and on north-south streets, even numbers are on the west side. Street signs are yellow for east-west streets and blue for north-south; they are clearly visible at night due to helpful lighting.

Toronto Transit Commission. The TTC is credited with being the safest, cleanest and most efficient public transport system in North America. It runs an integrated service which includes subways, buses and street cars. It successfully transports 1.3 million passengers a day, from all backgrounds and income brackets. Information about all routes and times is available by ringing 393-4636. Pick up a free copy of the TTC *Ride Guide* available from most subway stations, and at the TTC Transit Information Centre in the Yonge and Bloor subway station.

The flat fare of $1.05 (and rising) allows you to travel on any one or a combination of these vehicles in order to get to your destination, as long as it's a one way journey without stopovers. It is more economical to buy your tickets or tokens (small aluminium discs) in bulk: eight cost $7. A Metropass is valid for unlimited travel for a month and costs $46 plus a $2 photo charge. A Sunday or public holiday pass costs $3.75 and can be used by up to two adults and three children.

If you start your journey above ground, you must have the exact fare, either $1.05 in cash or a prepurchased ticket or token. If you intend to switch on to another vehicle, ask the driver for a transfer which will indicate the time of purchase. You then present this to the driver of the connecting bus or streetcar, or to the ticket taker at the subway stop. If you have to use a third vehicle, show the transfer to the second driver but hold on to it. If you start your journey on a subway, pay the ticket taker (who can give change) or use a token in one of the automatic gates. Just past the barrier, you will find an automatic transfer dispenser. If you need to continue your journey above ground, push the large red button. Transfers

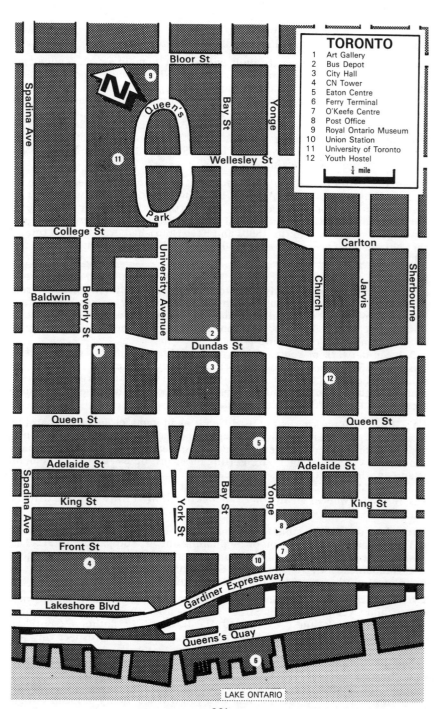

TORONTO

1 Art Gallery
2 Bus Depot
3 City Hall
4 CN Tower
5 Eaton Centre
6 Ferry Terminal
7 O'Keefe Centre
8 Post Office
9 Royal Ontario Museum
10 Union Station
11 University of Toronto
12 Youth Hostel

¼ mile

Bloor St
Spadina Ave
Bay St
Yonge
Queen's
Park
Wellesley St
College St
University Avenue
Carlton
Beverly St
Baldwin
Church
Jarvis
Sherbourne
Dundas St
Queen St
Queen St
Adelaide St
Adelaide St
Spadina Ave
King St
King St
York St
Bay St
Yonge
Front St
Gardiner Expressway
Lakeshore Blvd
Queens's Quay
LAKE ONTARIO

are not needed if you simply want to change on to the other subway line at Yonge and Bloor. If in any doubt at all, take a transfer.

Subway. The subway lines are built under the two main streets Yonge and Bloor and constitute a simple cross shape. The Yonge line has been augmented and loops around Union Station and up along University Avenue to bisect Bloor again at the Royal Ontario Museum and north to form the Spadina line. The system is very easy to master. The stops are almost all named after the cross street, unlike the London underground or Paris metro. The subways start running at about 6 am and continue until after 1 am. The last subways leave Union Station at 1.40 am. Exact times are given in the TTC *Ride Guide.*

Street Car. Street cars run east and west along College Street, Dundas, Queen, King and St Clair Avenue, all of which correspond with subway stations on the Yonge Street line. The north/south streetcar runs along Bathurst, four subway stops west of Yonge. Electric streetcars were first introduced to Toronto in the 1890s and have flourished ever since. A few of the old model cars from the 1940s are still in use, though they are scheduled to be phased out.

Bus. Buses ply most of the other main roads and provide a more frequent service to the suburbs. Many downtown buses are trolley buses, powered by an overhead electric cable which makes them very economical. A few longhaul suburban trips fall outside the TTC's jurisdiction. Name your destination to the TTC operator on 393-4636 and they will give you a further number for connecting services.

A basic network of routes operates all night, including a Yonge Street bus every 15 minutes, a Bloor/Danforth bus every 30 minutes, and the King, Queen, College and St Clair streetcars. Each TTC bus and streetcar stop is marked with its own individual telephone number which carries a recorded message of the schedule 24 hours a day.

Car. Downtown parking is not as difficult as in many cities of comparable size. Avoid parking in a "tow-away zone" (normally 4-6 pm) since these are rigidly enforced. If driving on a road with streetcars, you must not pass on the inside while passengers are getting on or off, unless there is a cement island on which waiting passengers can stand.

A stiff Metro Toronto programme called RIDE (Reduced Impaired Driving Everywhere) means that random breathalyzer tests to find drivers over the .08 limit are common.

Taxis. It is usually possible to hail a taxi in the downtown area, but easier to find them at Union Station or by phoning ahead. You pay about $1.30 as soon as you enter the taxi, plus about 65c per kilometre. One of the biggest taxi companies is Metro Cab on 363-5611 which has 800 cabs, though there are plenty of others listed in the Yellow Pages.

Cycling. Bicycles may be rented for $12 a day or $30 a week from Brown's Sports and Cycle, 2447 Bloor Street West (nearest subway station is Jane) or from North Bathurst Cycle and Hardware, 3549 Bathurst (south of Wilson) for somewhat more. Ring 763-4176 and 781-6333 respectively for current prices.

See the section *Climate* for the effect the Canadian winter has on cycling. If cycling on a street with streetcar tracks, beware of letting your wheel slip into the groove.

Cycling has become very popular and you will see plenty of locals out on their racing bikes or trail bikes. There are miles of cycle paths many of which stick to some of Toronto's 354 parks, following ravines which are invisible from the road. The Martin Goodman Trail is a paved route which runs along the waterfront from the area known as the Beaches in east Toronto to Ontario Place in the west.

Ferry. Although Toronto has a fairly important commercial harbour, there is not much picturesque shipping to observe. Scenic boat trips are offered from Queen's Quay but these are not much better than the ordinary ferry ride to the Toronto Islands. Between June and September ferries leave frequently from the bottom of Bay Street to one of the three islands just ten minutes away. Foot passengers pay $2 return; bicycles travel free though there are some restrictions to Centre Island at very busy periods. The islands are a favourite Torontonian retreat from the heat, since there are beaches, ice cream vendors and lake breezes. Ring 392-8186 for details. Centre Island is the most popular though it is best suited to young children who enjoy the funfair atmosphere and the McDonalds cuisine. In preference try Ward's Island which is partially residential but which has a secluded beach on the lake rather than the city side and small canteens which serve an interesting range of snack foods.

Accommodation

Hotels. A modest hotel room will cost at least $35 single, $45 double. Many of the cheap hotels are also bars and clubs and may be very noisy. Cheap downtown hotels include St Leonard, Selby, Isabella and Catnaps Guest House all on Sherbourne Street, several streets east of Yonge. The Victoria (corner of Yonge and King) and the Strathcona (York and Wellington) are more expensive with doubles from $70. One of the cheapest is the Rex Hotel at 194 Queen St West which charges $22 single, $26 double. For further details of the facilities available in other budget hotels, contact Accommodation Toronto (34 Ross Street; 596-7117), a free service operated by the Hotel Association of Metro Toronto. The provincial government imposes a sales tax (5%) on transient accommodation though out-of-province visitors may be exempted, so enquire when checking in. If you are visiting Toronto between December and February, ring 979-3143 for information on hotel discounts.

Tourist homes and guest houses tend to be cheaper (from $35 double) and less central then hotels. A good area to head for is King St W where you will find the Candy Haven at number 1233 (532-0651), AT King-Jameson Tourist Home at 1409 (532-4822) and Grayona Tourist Home at 1546 (535-5443). A more central bargain is the Karabanow Guest House, 9 Spadina Avenue near Bloor (923-4004).

Motels. Motel accommodation is not usually any cheaper, and of course is not centrally located. The two strips of motels stretch along the Lakeshore Boulevard heading west to Hamilton (Inn-on-the-Lake, Lakeshore, North America, Westpoint, etc.) and the Kingston Road on the road to Kingston. The Greater Toronto Motel Association is located at 2733 Kingston Road, Scarborough.

Hostels. The Toronto International Youth Hostel is located at 223 Church Street (3 blocks east of Yonge just below Dundas) and costs $9.50 for members, $13.50 for non members. This address is adjacent to the regional hostelling office, so if you are not already a member, you can join here.

YMCAs. The YMCA run an emergency shelter for men aged 16-29 who may stay up to seven nights for a pittance. The YWCA (80 Woodlawn E near the Summerhill Subway, 923-8454) charges about $35 for a single, and $50 for a double (women only).

Bed and Breakfast. Bed and breakfasts are catching on in Toronto and there are several B & B organizations. The Metropolitan Bed & Breakfast Registry located at 72 Lowther Avenue (928-2833) publishes a list for $3 which provides a great deal of detail about a small number of places and makes them sound charming. Unfortunately, they average $50-$55 a double. Also try Bed & Breakfast Homes of Toronto on 363-6362 which has 13 member establishments, All Seasons Bed & Breakfast, 383 Mississauga Valley Boulevard (276-4572) whose houses are somewhat cheaper and less central, and finally the non-smoking Downtown Toronto Group of Bed & Breakfast Guest House, PO Box 190, Station B, Toronto (977-6841).

University Residences. University residences are good value if you are looking for accommodation out of term i.e. mid-May until late August. The University of Toronto Housing Service (214 College St; 978-8045) can provide a list of residences along with their rates. Bookings should be made directly to the residence of your choice as far in advance as possible. University of Toronto (known as U of T) residences are very centrally located, and will cost $22 a day, $145 a week; and with full board $35 and $200. The other university in Toronto is York University, which keeps residences open in the summer for visiting students only. Ring 667-2100 for details. Singles will be about $25 and twins $18 each.

There is a popular "college-hotel" called Neill-Wycik at 96 Gerrard Street, also open only in the summer. Singles with breakfast cost $30 - $32 and doubles $35 - $37 (977-2320).

Camping. Campsites are generally open May to September. A directory of campsites is available free of charge from the Ontario Travel Information Service (Macdonald Block, Bay and Wellesley; 965-4008). It will indicate which campsites take reservations. There are two campsites in Scarborough which fall within the city limits: Woodland Park (282-1270) and Glen Rouge Park (367-8092). There are seven other campgrounds within reach of downtown including two KOA sites; check the Yellow Pages. Ring 364-4722 in July and August for campground vacancy reports, covering 53 Southern Ontario parks. Private campsites will charge between $10 and $18 per site depending on the facilities available. The camping fee in provincial parks is $8 or $10 depending on whether there is electricity.

Eating and Drinking

Eating out in Toronto is a delight. If you have become bored with the ubiquitous hamburger, you may wish to avoid the many burger and fast food outlets in Toronto. Because of the large ethnic mixture of people in Toronto's population, the range of interesting restaurants is superb. For example, there are over a quarter of a million Italian speakers in Toronto, the largest Italian-speaking community outside Italy and a correspondingly large number of Italian eating establishments, as the 14 Yellow Pages under "pizza" will attest. (Most listed will deliver a pizza to your door for a small extra charge.) Try the wood-oven pizzas for $7 at Pat and Mario's (Church and Front Sts) which also has a dance floor. For informal Italian eating, try John's Italian Caffe at 27 Baldwin Street near the Art Gallery.

Chinatown flourishes along Dundas Street west of Bay and north along Spadina. The Chinese population in Toronto is now reputed to be greater than in any other North American city. You get a range of regional Chinese cooking, so that a Szechuan place will be next door to a Mandarin, and Cantonese next to Hunan, not to mention Vietnamese and Korean variations. Try the Lee Gardens (358 Spadina) where long queues attest to its quality. If the decor is mostly formica and the menu is written only in Chinese characters, you can be assured of some authentic oriental cooking. Spadina Avenue south of College, offers an excellent choice of Asian restaurants. Explore the nearby Kensington Market (west of Spadina and south of College) for Portuguese, Brazilian, Jewish and Jamaican restaurants. Hungarian, Japanese, Indian and Middle Eastern restaurants are scattered liberally throughout the city. Greek restaurants are concentrated "out the Danforth" as Torontonians refer to the eastern extension of Bloor Street while the Indian quarter is on Gerrard St E (take a College streetcar heading east). For a cheap and friendly meal, try Dooley's Irish Dining Parlour at 23 Bloor St E which serves good clam chowder. For upbeat cafes, try the Queen Mother at 206 Queen West or the Kensington Kitchen on Harbord St, west of the University, though there are many others. There is also a plethora of good restaurants in the moderate and expensive categories, such as the Bangkok Garden on Elm St just west of Yonge (977-6748) and La Bodega (30 Baldwin St) which for many years has been serving creative French cooking (though it's run by a Brit). Consult the monthly magazine *Toronto Life* (available at newsstands for $2) for further inspiration.

DRINKING

Drinking may be less congenial than what you are used to at home, despite the licensing hours of 11am to 1am. Sundays are dry unless you're dining. Downtown bars tend to be ritzy, expensive and not very lively, or just seedy dives. The trendy place to drink in the summer when tables line the sidewalk is Yorkville, north of Bloor between Avenue Road and Yonge. It's more expensive than most but the beer is still affordable. Ontario Place, open May to October, has several beer gardens. There is a new influx of imitation British pubs such as the Elephant and Castle in the Eaton Centre which are meant more for fashionable Torontonians than for homesick Brits who may baulk at paying $4.50 for a pint of Double Diamond. Some places now have special pub licences which mean you can buy a drink at the bar and thereby avoid being served by a tip-hungry waitress. However, this is still the exception; in shabbier places you are served at a table and pay for each round as it arrives, in others you run up a bill. If you are eager to continue drinking after the bars close at 1am, cultivate the friendship of a waitress or bartender who knows where to find a speakeasy, usually located in disused warehouses.

If you want to combine a cocktail with a view of the dramatic night-time skyline in Toronto, go to the bar at the top of the Manulife Building (Bay and Bloor) or the Park Plaza Hotel (Bloor and Avenue Road) but the price of the high rise view will be included in your drink. For the most expensive drink of all, make the pilgrimage to the CN Tower, the tallest free standing structure in the world. The elevator costs $6 (return) and a bottle of beer at 1150 feet will cost $3.50. Still, if you want to say you have been up the tallest building in the world.

The sale of alcohol is controlled by the provincial government and so neither beer nor wine is ever available from grocery stores. Beer must be bought from the Brewers Retail outlets, and wine and spirits from the LCBO (Liquor Control Board of Ontario). Most LCBOs now display their wares on open shelves, but you may still encounter some where you must choose from a catalogue and fill out a slip which you hand in at a counter. The catalogue rates the sweetness of wine from 0 (very dry) to 23 (Sacramental Jewish wine). Brewers Retails are usually open Monday to Thursday 10am -10pm and Friday/Saturday 10am-11pm. Some LCBOs are also open till 10 but most close at 6pm.

The drinking laws are barbarous in many respects. Strictly speaking, it is illegal to transport liquor anywhere except between the place where it was bought and your home, though this law is hardly ever enforced. However, you may not consume liquor in any public place, which means that wine at picnics is sometimes consumed from tea cups and poured out of a thermos flask. You cannot carry alcohol except in the boot of your car and it must be unopened.

Ontario wines are grown around Niagara and are improving in quality. Avoid the pop-like Baby Bear and Cold Duck, and try Inniskillin Brae Rouge ($6). Unfortunately, Canada does not encourage its own wine industry as Australia does and there is almost as large a mark-up on domestic wines as on imported wines. For a larger choice of imported bottles than is available at your run-of-the-mill LCBO, try the Rare Wines and Spirits store at 2 Cooper St, off Queen's Quay.

Beer enthusiasts will want to try Connor's beers brewed in Toronto, including a bitter, an ale in the Scottish style and a hoppy Pale Ale, available at many Brewers Retail stores. Though more typically Canadian in character, Upper Canada ale is also worth trying.

Entertainment

There is no shortage of music, theatre or film in Toronto. The key to Toronto's entertainment scene is the free entertainment guide called *NOW* published on Thursdays and available from many downtown shops and restaurants. In addition to entertainment listings, it carries lots of adverts for interesting eating places and shops. Also check the Saturday edition of the *Star,* an excellent guide to what's on, or the Thursday and Saturday editions of the *Globe and Mail* for reviews and listings. You might want to get hold of the University of Toronto handbook which contains good advice about bars, clubs and entertainment. Visit the Varsity office at 91 St George and ask for a free copy of the *Varsity Student Handook* which they will give you if they have any left. Also look for the free TTC brochure (*Exciting Toronto by TTC*).

The established theatre, ballet and opera venue is O'Keefe Centre on Front Street (393-7469). Tickets to mainstream cultural events will not normally be less than $12 unless you get student standby tickets. Ring the box office for details. There are last minute ticket booths, comparable to the one in Leicester Square, called Five Star and in the main rotunda of the Royal Ontario Museum, located outside the Eaton Centre (596-8211). They sell discounted tickets on the day of performance, but unfortunately the choice is not usually very great. Tickets for the big shows can be purchased through Bass (698-2277) or Ticketron (598-0437).

Harbourfront is a relatively new entertainment complex which offers theatre, music, antique markets and food. Although open year round, it is especially pleasant in the summer when most of the entertainment takes place in the open air. Take Spadina bus 77B from the Spadina subway station or from Union Station, or the new Harbourfront Light Rapid Transit line due to open soon.

Museums and Galleries. The Art Gallery of Ontario (corner of Dundas and Beverley; 977-0414) has a small international collection, including the world's largest collection of Henry Moore sculptures, and several rooms of Canadian art, as well as some excellent special exhibitions. There is an admission charge of $3.50 (free on Thursday evenings) and an excellent book and card shop. A better representation of Canadian art including native work may be found at the McMichael Collection at Kleinberg (893-1121) which is outside the city limits but accessible by a combination of TTC and Vaughan Transit: take the subway to Islington, transfer to Islington bus 37 north to Steeles and then take Vaughan Route 1 to the collection. Ring 832-2281 for bus times and fares. Admission is $3.

The Royal Ontario Museum (or ROM) has an outstanding general collection including some exhibits on Native cultures. The imposing building stands on the corner of Bloor St W and Avenue Road. Next door there is a planetarium which puts on interesting shows of the constellations.

Music. The Toronto Symphony plays at the dazzling new Roy Thomson Hall (593-4828) near King and University. The acoustics are remarkable though parking was such a problem that the whole structure was lifted while an underground car park was built. Concert tickets start at about $13.

For rock and blues, try the El Mocambo on Spadina, the Hotel Isabella on Sherbourne, the Brunswick (Bloor past Spadina), or the Rivoli (334 Queen St W). Jazz may be heard at the Bluenote on Pears Avenue, Bourbon Street (180 Queen West), George's Spaghetti House (290 Dundas St E) or at the after hours jazz club at Meyer's Deli (185 King St W). Folk is performed at the Free Times Cafe (320 College), and at the Spadina Hotel at 460 King St W. A country and western venue with a difference (it's feminist) is the Pine Tree on Queen St W near Bathurst.

The Mariposa Folk Festival, at one time the best known folk festival on the continent, is held in the middle of July at Molson Park near Barrie, an hour's drive north of the city. Phone 769-3655 for details of ticket prices, camping arrangements, etc.

Theatre. The Royal Alexandra on Adelaide St is the theatre which mounts Broadway productions at Broadway prices. It is owned by Ed Mirvish, the Toronto businessman who has bought up the Old Vic in London. There are plenty of smaller, more experimental theatres in Toronto, consult *NOW* for times and locations. The well-established Tarragon Theatre (30 Bridgman Avenue; 531-1827) puts on Sunday afternoon productions on a PWYC basis, i.e. Pay What You Can.

The Shakespeare Festival in Stratford, Ontario (about a two hour drive from Toronto) is internationally acclaimed. The lavish productions are well worth the effort of getting to this quiet, scenic little Southern Ontario town. Phone 364-8355 in Toronto for details. Similarly there is a Shaw Festival each summer in Niagara-on-the-Lake, not far from the famous falls. Ring 361-1544 for information.

Cinema. Along with New York and Los Angeles, Toronto is the third city in North America where films are likely to premiere, especially during the

Toronto Film Festival held in September. The price of a ticket at a downtown "movie theatre" will usually be $6. Toronto has a space-age style cinesphere with a screen six storeys high. There are several repertory cinemas such as the Bloor Cinema (506 Bloor St W) and the Fox Beaches (2236 Queen St E) which show a good selection of films at a low price (about $3). You might prefer to become a member ($5) whereupon you can see films for 99c. The once famous 99c Roxy Cinema (Danforth and Greenwood) has now become an alcohol-free nightclub open until 3 or 4 am on weekends. Free films are shown at Harbourfront; ring 973-3000 for details.

Special Events. The most longstanding summer event is the Canadian National Exhibition (called CNE or the Ex; 393-6000) which takes place during the last two weeks of August and the first of September. It is located on the lakefront by the stadium, and consists of lots of rides, junk food, good food, international exhibits, circuses and big name entertainers.

Caravan takes place in late June and features a number of ethnic pavilions scattered around the city where the various communities within Toronto offer their native food and entertainment. Canada Day (July 1st) is celebrated by a picnic at Queen's Park (the provincial legislature) with 5c hot dogs.

SPORT

The performance of Toronto's one-time champion hockey team, the Maple Leafs, has become so abysmal in recent years that "fans" have taken to pelting the players with rubbish and abuse. Games are played at Maple Leaf Gardens (Carlton east of Yonge; 977-1641). Tickets tend to sell out in advance, so it is wise to enquire as soon as you arrive in Toronto if you are interested in seeing a game. The cheapest seats and standing room are $8 and the best seats are $25. Scalpers (i.e. ticket touts) are always present outside the Gardens to sell you a ticket for an inflated price. Failing this, you can watch a hockey game on TV three or four nights of the week between October and May.

The Toronto Argonauts, winners of the 1983 Grey Cup, play their games of football (not soccer) at the Exhibition Stadium (595-1131), as do the Toronto Blue Jays, comparatively recent but formidable members of the American Baseball League (595-0077 for ticket information and schedules). In fact Torontonians have become passionate about baseball and to make friends with a local, ask about the Jays. A controversial and expensive new domed stadium is being built next to the CN Tower.

The thoroughbred racing season opens in mid-March at Greenwood, culminating in the Queen's Plate in mid-July (698-3131). The Canadian national sport of lacrosse is more popular in small Ontario towns such as Owen Sound and Peterborough than in the big cities.

If you want to have a crack at ice skating, you will have to buy or borrow a pair of skates, since rinks don't hire them. If you simply want to watch, you should go to the outdoor rink at the foot of the architecturally striking Toronto City Hall, corner of Bay and Queen. If you visit the national capital, Ottawa, in the winter, you will find many citizens skating on the solidly frozen Rideau Canal which goes through the centre of town. It is a common sight to see civil servants skating to work, wearing toques (double thickness woollen caps) and carrying brief cases.

Parks and Zoos. The Metro Zoo covers over 700 acres and is well worth a day trip. Take the subway east to Kennedy and transfer to Scarborough bus 86A. Admission to the Zoo seems steep at $5 but it is worth it. Cross-country skis are available in winter.

SHOPPING

Shopping hours in Ontario are generally 9 am-6 pm Monday to Saturday, and till 9 pm on Thursdays and Fridays. The Liberal provincial government recently made Sunday shopping legal but leave it to each municipality to decide. The ubiquitous Beckers, 7-11 and Mac's Milk corner stores are open 24 hours in many cases, or 7 am to midnight in others.

The provincial sales tax of 7% is added onto all goods except children's clothes, shoes under $30, books, magazines and groceries. If you are taking goods out of the province, you can avoid paying tax by arranging for the shop to ship your goods out of the province. In order to reclaim tax, you should pick up a leaflet from the tourist office called "Sales Tax Refunds for Visitors to Ontario" and send it along with proof of export (e.g. a foreign customs declaration) to the Ministry of Revenue, Retail Sales Tax Refund Unit, PO Box 628, 33 King St W, Oshawa, Ontario L1H 8J6.

The multi-level Eaton Centre in downtown Toronto is one of the best examples of a lavishly appointed North American shopping complex, a veritable cathedral to consumption. It has been claimed that it is the most popular tourist attraction in the country. You can buy choice quality Florida fruit just next to Algonquin Indian carvings. This is not a place to find bargains. The shops in the Centre are open 9am-9pm Monday to Friday and until 6pm on Saturday only. The stunning architecture can best be appreciated on a Sunday when the shops and most of the restaurants are closed and the Centre nearly deserted. There is an alarming number of posh indoor shopping malls in the downtown area, many of which contain chain stores. For an opposite atmosphere, visit Honest Ed's Warehouse (Bloor and Bathurst) where a wealth of everyday objects are available at bargain prices. For more quirky shopping, try Queen Street West between University and Spadina. For chic stores, visit Yorkville, just north of Bloor west of Yonge. You will even find a shop called Lovecraft (63 Yorkville Avenue) which sells edible underwear.

The large vigorous ethnic communities are often responsible for the quality and abundance of food available in the markets. The best markets are the Kensington Market (near Spadina and College) with its wonderful range of fish, tropical fruit and wholefoods, and the St Lawrence Market (Front Street East) where a lively Farmers' Market is held on Saturdays. The quality of the produce is high, as are the prices.

THE MEDIA

There are three main newspapers: the *Toronto Globe and Mail*, the *Toronto Star* and the *Sun*. The *Globe* is the closest thing to a national paper that Canada has, and its international coverage is the best available though still not extensive. You will be surprised by the weight of the dailies; don't get excited, it's mainly ads. Homesick Brits may want to get hold of a monthly tabloid called *Britannia* published for UK expatriates (690-4307). At least it will tell you the football scores. Toronto also supports its own French language weekly *(L' Express). The Times, Telegraph, Daily Express* and the Sunday papers are sold in W. H. Smith in Toronto Dominion Centre (King and Bay) for a hefty $3. *Guardian* readers will just have to suffer in silence.

You may consult the *Times* and the *Guardian Weekly* at the Metropolitan Library (Yonge north of Bloor) or visit the British Consulate (777 Bay St) although there is no reading room.

There are many radio stations both AM and FM. Most are more or less similar to Radio 2: popular light music and bright chit-chat from DJs. Students tend to favour one of the FM stations, such as CHUM-FM (104.5) or CFNY (102.1) which plays more interesting rock music. The non-profit CJRT FM (91.1) carries the World Service news at 8 am. The Canadian Broadcasting Corporation (CBC) runs an FM station which offers a more diverse programme (classified music, jazz, current affairs, etc.) on 94.1. CBC AM can be found at 740 on the dial.

Many hotels equip the rooms with a TV. You may choose one of the Canadian networks: CBC (channel 5), CTV (channel 9), TV Ontario (channel 19) or any of the American networks available on cable.

Crime and Safety

There is remarkably little violent crime in Toronto for a city of 3 million; in fact the crime rate is declining, one of the few in North America. The majority of crimes which are committed are hold-ups of corner stores and gas stations in the suburbs rather than muggings on downtown streets. Some lone women have expressed anxiety at walking along the streets running east from Yonge Street south of Bloor especially in the area known as "The Track" bounded by Isabella, Wellesley and Church Streets. Gerrard and Jarvis is another district with red light overtones, however there are some luxury hotels in the neighbourhood as well and most tourists do not feel nervous. Stay on the main arteries rather than the side streets and alleys if you are feeling anxious. Even in tough areas there have been few incidents of violence reported, and for the most part anxiety is unwarranted. The number to dial in any emergency is 911.

Although not as popular as it was ten years ago, cannabis is still favoured by students and young professionals. The maximum penalty in the province of Ontario for a first offence of possession is six months in jail and/or a fine of $1,000. So be careful. Growing-your-own is a widespread practice. If you do get in trouble with the law contact 24-hour criminal law firm, Neuman & Grant for advice (961-7400).

The police are very quick to spot drivers who have been drinking and generally show no mercy. Especially in the weeks preceding Christmas, they administer thousands of breathalyser tests. Their campaign has been fairly successful and as a result the taxi business is booming while tavern owners complain of a slump. If visiting one of Southern Ontario's provincial parks between May 1st and June 17th, make sure that it is all right to drink alcohol. Because of rowdiness and violence, alcohol was completely banned from 13 parks for this period, but may be reintroduced if campers behave themselves.

Help and Information

The area code for Toronto is 416.

Tourist Information: Eaton Centre (368-9990). Additional pavilions are set up during the summer on Yonge outside the Eaton Centre and at several frequently visited locations around the city.

Ontario Travel: Eaton Centre (965-4008).

Parks Canada: Ontario Region, 132 Second St E, Cornwall K6H 5V4 (613-938-5866).

Travellers Aid Society: Union Station (366-7788).

Post Office: 21 Front St W (973-5757).

American Express: 50 Bloor Street W (967-3411).

Thomas Cook: 777 Bay St (922-0804).

British Consulate: 600 Sherbourne St, Suite 303 (593 1267).

Metropolitan Police: 967-2222. All emergencies - 911.

Canadian Automobile Association: 2 Carlton St (964-3111). Emergency road service — 966-3000.

Community Information Centre of Metro Toronto - 863-0505 (24 hours).

"Teleguide" terminals have been installed in many public buildings, and shopping centres. You type in the information you require, for example "Restaurants - Japanese" or "Shopping - Sporting Goods" and the machine provides a list of names and addresses. The information is far from comprehensive, since only paying advertisers are included, but the machines are fun to play with.

Further Afield

THE GREAT LAKES

Whereas western Canada is famous for its Rocky Mountains, eastern Canada has the Great Lakes. The five Great Lakes are by far the largest bodies of fresh water in the world. The largest and furthest inland lake is Superior. Next is Lake Michigan which is entirely in the US, then Lake Huron, Lake Erie and finally Lake Ontario which flows into the St Lawrence Seaway. A series of locks and canals between the lakes allows ships to avoid Niagara Falls and other natural impediments and to penetrate all the way to the Lakehead at the furthest end of Lake Superior. Thunder Bay, the city at the Lakehead, is the third largest sea port of Canada, and yet it is roughly half way between the east and west coasts. Although these bodies of water are lakes, their large size means that stormy weather can create large waves, and there have been many shipwrecks on the Lakes. You can visit some islands including Manitoulin Island in Lake Huron, the largest fresh water island in the world. It is accessible by a long land route via Sudbury or a charming ferry ride from Tobermory.

The shores of Lake Ontario and Lake Erie are more densely populated on both the American and Canadian sides than Huron and Superior. Consequently, those lakes are more polluted. The sight of dead fish along a holiday beach is a shocking reminder of the environmental crimes committed in North America during the 1950s and 1960s. You will notice that a favourite Canadian ploy is to blame the Americans for this (and many other) evils. In view of the fact that the effluent and petrochemicals in the Cuyahoga River — which flows into Lake Erie at Cleveland Ohio — once caught fire and burned for three days and three nights, there is some justification for the complaint. Measures are now being taken to clean up the lakes and now Toronto's beaches remain open except during long hot spells when the algae builds up.

Lake Superior is the least developed lake, and its north shore is virtually unmolested wilderness. Not surprisingly, it is also the least accessible. Since it is nearly a 500 mile (800 km) drive from Toronto to Lake Superior Provincial Park just north of Sault (pronounced Sue) Ste Marie, it will be feasible to visit this part of Ontario only if you are heading west. The largest of the Great Lakes is several degrees colder on average than Erie or Ontario. The Lakes are too large to freeze solidly, though skating along the shores is a favourite winter recreation. Sometimes the ice is thick enough to take the weight of cars, and it can be quite an eerie sight to see headlights far out "at sea" between, for example, Kingston and Wolfe Island a mile or two offshore.

Niagara Falls. The sight which few tourists will have the courage to miss is Niagara Falls. The mighty falls are located on the Niagara River which connects Lake Ontario and Lake Erie 85 miles/140km from Toronto. Without a car, you might find it convenient to join a tour out of Toronto for example the day trip offered by Toronto Tours (869-1372) for about $50. Any self-respecting Canadian will assure you that the view of the 176 foot drop is much more spectacular on the Canadian side than the American. A trip on the *Maid of the Mist* boat or a walk down through tunnels cut from the rock behind the falls both allow you to experience the pounding noise and spray of the Falls at close range. There are lots of tacky tourist sights around the town. If you are a devotee of junk culture, you will have a field-day in the Honeymoon Capital of North America. If you are eligible, you can get a Honeymoon Certificate from the mayor of Niagara Falls. Try to visit nearby Niagara-on-the-Lake, a charmingly reconstructed 19th century town, home of the Shaw Theatre.

The Great Outdoors

In addition to the Great Lakes with their much-visited provincial parks, sandy beaches and holiday havens, there are thousands of smaller lakes in the Ontario hinterland. Travelling north from Toronto you should head for the Haliburton Highlands or the Muskoka District centred around the towns of Huntsville and Bracebridge. Both these areas admit of easy access to the 3,000 square mile (7,500 square kilometre) Algonquin Park. Canoeing, hiking and camping are the favourite ways of enjoying the park in the summer.

Despite the great amount of publicity which the pollution by acid rain of these lakes has received they will seem to you crystal clear and will be safe to swim in for at least another 15 years. The worst form of pollution is caused by the noisy motors favoured by boat-owning cottagers. If you do not want to be bothered getting hold of camping equipment, you should consider hiring a cottage for a week or more. Study the brochure distributed by Tourism Ontario (965-4008) called *Accommodations in Ontario,* which lists housekeeping cottages and fishing lodges as well as hotels and motels. Prices start as low as $100 per week for a small cottage, but most cost $150-$200.

The May 24th long weekend is traditionally the time when people "open up" their cottages after the long winter, and take their first (brief) dip in the lake. The cottage season ends either on the Labour Day weekend (early September) or more unusually at the Thanksgiving weekend (mid-October).

If you are attracted by the far north, you can travel on the Polar Bear

Express, a rail service between North Bay and Moosonee, an old Hudson's Bay Company fur trading post. Contact Ontario Northland (805 Bay St, Toronto; 965-4268) for details. From Moosonee, there is a short boat ride to Moose Factory Island, the original trading post, or a trip by freighter canoe led by Indian guides to Fossil Island where it is possible to collect many interesting geological specimens.

Skiing. Although there are no real mountains in Ontario, skiing is extremely popular. The resorts within easy striking distance of Toronto are Chicopee to the west, Dagmar to the east and resorts around Barrie to the north. The resorts popular with more serious skiers are Collingwood in the Blue Mountains or the Huntsville region several hours north of Toronto. Phone 963-2911 for recorded cross country ski information and 963 2992 for downhill conditions. A lift ticket will cost $15-$30 a day and equipment rental $10-$15. There are excellent facilities for cross-country skiing scattered throughout the city and province. Horseshoe Valley near Barrie and Camp Fortune near Ottawa are both superb. It is possible to hire equipment at both. Travel CUTS (187 College St, Toronto M5T 1P1) organize cross-country ski trips combined with dog-sledding in Algonquin Park. For information about accommodation in ski resorts, ask for the free brochure *Good Times Guide* available from Resorts Ontario, 10 Peter St N, Orillia (363-1100). Gray Coach (979-3511) run buses to the slopes departing Toronto about 7am and returning in the late afternoon; the return fare of $35 includes a lift-pass.

Montreal and Quebec

For North Americans, a trip to Quebec is a convenient (and inexpensive) substitute for a trip to Europe. Montreal is the Paris of North America and the second largest French-speaking city in the world. Visitors are attracted not only by the sound of spoken French, by the old world architecture, the fine restaurants and sophisticated fashions, but by a distinctly European atmosphere which has little truck with northern prudery. Whereas Toronto was once known as the City of Churches, Montreal was Sin City, where liquor was available during Prohibition (and is still served later than in any other part of Canada) and where art and nightlife were not censored.

Its political life is certainly more lively than that of the other provinces, and politics are discussed into the wee hours of the morning in restaurants and bars. In 1980 the provincial government held a referendum to discover whether the voters wanted Quebec to separate from the rest of Canada and become independent. Many ardent separatists were hopeful that at last the opportunity had come to cast off the galling yoke of English domination. English speakers had dominated the province's business and banking in spite of the fact that a large majority of the inhabitants are French-speaking. But the "Non" votes outnumbered the "Ouis" by about 59% to 41% and so the separatists have had to be satisfied with laws which protect and promote French language and culture, e.g. hiring and schooling practices which positively discriminate in favour of French. The tension which this created has begun to subside (partly because many English companies panicked and moved their head offices to Toronto) but Quebec is still politically a very stimulating place to visit.

One of Quebec's most dynamic politicians was Jean Drapeau, mayor of Montreal from 1954 (with a brief interruption) until 1986 who was responsible for bringing first Expo 67, the world fair, to Montreal to celebrate Canada's centennial year and then the 1976 Olympics. These events live on in the "Man and his World" exhibit on the site of Expo, and in Olympic Park, both of which are worth a visit. They also live on in the memory of the city's taxpayers, who are still footing the bills.

So alongside the quaint and charming side of Quebec is the aggressively and lavishly futuristic. The city fathers are very proud of their underground city, in which cars, public transport and pedestrians are channelled along separate tunnels among shops, banks, sporting complexes, cinemas and art centres. In fact it is not much more advanced than the underground developments in Toronto, but you will not be tempted to quibble if you happen to be in Montreal in the winter and can take advantage of the climate-controlled atmosphere of the underground city.

THE NATIVES

The Quebecois are not just like the French of Paris or Marseille or Toulouse. They are avid hockey fans, for example; they drink bottles of Molsons beer (brewed by a prominent Montreal family) and speak a kind of French which is sometimes incomprehensible to a Parisian. According to one theory, the French spoken in rural Quebec is much closer to the French spoken by the 17th century peasants, who were among the first arrivals in the New World, and it has survived relatively unchanged. By now, the Quebecois language has adapted many English expressions such as "hambourgeois" just as the Quebecois people have absorbed many Anglo-North American influences into their culture. Try to speak French if possible though Montrealers are no more tolerant than Parisians of hearing their language mangled. Altogether it is fascinating to visit a place where cultural and ethnic traditions have been so vigorously maintained over such a long period (the British defeated the French in 1763) in order to fend off assimilation by English-speaking culture. For example St-Jean-Baptiste Day (June 24) is energetically celebrated with fireworks and parades (especially in Mount Royal Park), rather than Victoria Day (late May) which is celebrated in the other provinces. Quebec is a very lively place with something of a Latin character, though, like the rest of Canada, its people are caught up with the making and spending of money.

CLIMATE

After certain point, you may think that all versions of the Canadian winter become indistinguishable, but the cold is noticeably more extreme in Montreal than in Toronto and still colder as you move east to the provincial capital of Quebec City, and further towards the Gaspe Peninsula. With the possible exception of Moscow, Montreal gets more snow than any other major city (i.e. about 100 inches a year), so dress accordingly if you're visiting between December and April.

The summers are a different matter, hot and still, ideal for sitting at outdoor cafes long into the evening.

ARRIVAL AND DEPARTURE

Air. There are two international airports serving Montreal: the original Dorval (about 12 miles/20 km west of downtown) and the new showpiece Mirabel, over twice as far away. Mirabel has one of the largest areas of any airport in the world and the fewest passengers, or so it seems. Somehow it has never caught on, and most passengers travelling from points within North America still land at Dorval. Except for its inconvenient location, Mirabel has wonderfully modern facilities.

Aerocar operates a bus between the principal downtown hotels and both airports; dial 397-9999 for details. The one way fare from Mirabel is $9, between Mirabel and Dorval is $9, and from Dorval is $7. The suburb of Dorval is on the train line, but the area between the station and airport terminal is a jungle of overpasses, cloverleafs and fast highways. You can try to persuade a taxi driver to take you the short distance to the train station, but they usually want to wait until they can get a more lucrative fare to downtown i.e. $35.

A frequent air shuttle between Toronto and Montreal, run by City Express, is much quicker and not much more expensive for non-students than the rail journey. The downtown office of Travel CUTS is at 1613 St Denis (843-8511).

Bus. Greyhound can carry only international passengers in the province of Quebec. Greyhound buses depart from the Port Authority Bus Depot in New York seven times daily, taking eight hours to reach Montreal. There is also a seven hour service from Boston operated by Vermont Transit.

The domestic carrier is Voyageur whose depot and head office is at 505 Boulevard de Maisonneuve at the Berri-de-Montigny metro stop. Phone 842-2281 for information. There are frequent services into the Laurentian Hills north of Montreal and the Eastern Townships south of the city. Voyageur operates a bus service between Montreal and Ottawa, with buses leaving almost every hour on the hour from 6 am until midnight. Journey time is 2 hours 20 minutes. The one-way fare is $16; a same day return costs $19.90. If you don't leave on a Friday and stay less than 10 days, the return fare is $25. Otherwise it is $32. Similarly there are buses to Quebec City (journey time three hours), every hour on the hour from 6 am to 9 pm, and two evening buses at 11 pm and 1 am. The fare is $24.95 one way, day return $30.95, less than ten days, departure other than Friday, $34.95. Over ten days; $49.90. Smoking is prohibited on all services.

There are six express buses arriving daily from Toronto. One way, either to or from Toronto, is $39.95. a less-than-10 days return is $55.90, more than ten days return is $71.90. Travel time is usually between six and seven hours.

If you plan to do a lot of travelling within the provinces of Quebec and Ontario investigate the "Tourpass". The pass entitles you to 10 days of unlimited bus travel between June 15 and October 15 and costs $99. The pass may be extended at a cost of $9.90 per extra day, but the extension must be specified at the time of purchase of the Tourpass.

Train. The railway link between New York and Montreal slightly predates the one between Toronto and Montreal. There is only one train a day operated by Amtrak (1-800-426-8725) from New York now that the *Montrealer* has been suspended. The *Adirondack* trip lasts about 9 hours and departs at 10.45 am. There are six trains a day between Toronto and Montreal. A one-way ticket costs $51, a return for five or less days $82.

There are two stations in Montreal: Central Station at 935 Lagauchetiere St W, 871-1331 (metro Bonaventure) under the Queen Elizabeth Hotel, and the old and dignified Windsor Station nearby at the corner of Peel and Lagauchetiere. Windsor handles more local traffic including commuter services. There are six trains a day to Quebec City; the fastest *(Rapidos)* take three hours from Central Station. The one way fare is $28, a return for under five days $45. Similarly there are seven trains a day to Ottawa. This journey takes about two hours and costs $20 single, $32 for a return of five days or less. There is one train per day to Gaspe, over 620 miles/1,000 km east of Montreal. This trip lasts 18 hours and costs $75 single, $113 return.

Driving. The road network in and out of Montreal can be fairly daunting to the uninitiated, so study your map carefully before entering the fray. On autoroutes (freeways) the speed limit is 100 km/h (62 mph) maximum and 60 km/h (37 mph) minimum. On other provincial roads the limit is 90 km/h (56 mph). In cities and towns, the limit is 50km/h (30 mph). Both the provincial and the local police use radar to check drivers' speeds. Front seat belts are compulsory in the province. Quebec is the only province in which it is illegal to turn right at a red light and to pass in a right hand lane. If leaving Montreal on a Friday, be prepared for heavy traffic.

Highway 401, the major highway through southern Ontario, continues east from Toronto along the north shore of Lake Ontario and the St Lawrence River to the Quebec border. Here it changes to Autoroute 20 and joins Autoroute 40 from Ottawa before turning into the Blvd Metropolitain north of Montreal. To enter Montreal, take exits Decarie, St Denis or St Hubert. To bypass Montreal, and continue to Quebec City, stay on Autoroute 40 which travels along the north shore of the St Lawrence.

If approaching from south of the river, you will either be on Highway 15 leading due north from the American border or on the Trans-Canada (Highway 20) from Quebec City. Coming from this direction you will be more aware that Montreal is built on an island since you will cross one of the following bridges: Jacques-Cartier, Victoria, or Champlain. The latter is a toll bridge charging 25c.

Discount car rental firms were slow to come to Montreal but now there are many outlets of Rent-a-Wreck in Montreal where the company is called Via Route Auto Location. Phone 355-1335 or 521-5221. Tilden, Budget, etc. all charge at least $35 a day. Ask about renting a van at the Complexe Desjardins. Because of the high provincial tax on gasoline (40%), driving can be an expensive proposition.

CITY TRANSPORT

Finding your way around Montreal is not made easy by the gradual changing of English street names to French ones. In particular, the main east-west Boulevard formerly known as Dorchester has just become Rene-Levesque, but few maps of the city so far show the change.

Metro. Montrealers are justifiably proud of their metro. The metro stations all have unique murals and decorations and the trains themselves run almost silently on pneumatic tyres (unlike the clattering subways of NYC). the north-south and east-west lines bisect at the station Berri de Montigny near the corner of Blvd Montigny and St Denis. The metro stops which permit access to old Montreal, a part of town ideally suited to strolling, are Champ-de-Mars, Place d'Armes and Victoria. The metro has been extended across the river to the Isle Sainte-Helene for Man and his World and on to Longueuil on the south shore.

As in Toronto the metro system is completely integrated with the bus network. Once you have purchased your ticket for $1 (a *carnet* of six tickets costs $5.50) you are entitled to complete your journey by presenting the transfer pass comparable to the one offered by Toronto's TTC. For all information concerning public transport, ring AUTOBUS (or 288-6287)

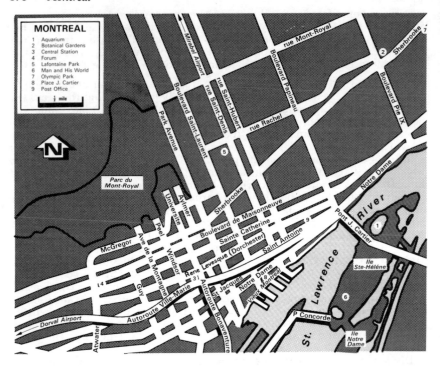

between 5 am and 12.30 pm weekdays or visit the office at 159 St Antoine W. The metro starts operating about 5.30 am and stops at 12.30 am.

Car. Taking after their Parisian counterparts, Montreal drivers have been variously described as fiendish, maniacal and suicidal. So be prepared to drive aggressively or not at all. (Pedestrians should also be alert and not put any blind faith in crosswalks). The streets of Montreal, originally laid out by Sulpician monks in 1672, are fairly straightforward to navigate though several of the main thoroughfares are one-way. As you might expect, parking can be tricky, even if there are 9,657 parking places in the underground city. Parking is particularly difficult in Old Montreal and the picturesque Place Jacques-Cartier and nearby streets are closed to cars during the summer months. It is best to leave your car at the park by the Champs-de-Mar metro station, and walk from there.

Taxis. Cabs are easily hailed on any downtown street at anytime.

Cycling. Bicycles can be rented for about $14 a day, $60 a week from the following stores, which also rent cycling accessories: Cycles Peel, 6665 St Jacques West (486-1148), La Cordee, 2159 St. Catherine St East (524-1515), Yeti-Plein-Air, 5127 St. Laurent (271-0773).

Carriages. You may wish to splurge and have a ride in a caleche or horse-drawn carriage (sleighs in winter) in Montreal or Quebec City. Needless to say, these exist solely for tourists and usually come with a guided tour by the driver. Although it may be possible to bargain a little, you have to be prepared to spend at least $30 an hour, though if you are in a group of four or five, this may not seem too steep. You will find them parked in the Place Jacques-Cartier.

Accommodation

Hotels. The budget range of hotels in Montreal are called *maisons de tourisme* or tourist lodges, and tend to be less expensive than their counterparts in the other major cities of Canada. It is always worth asking for an off-season discount between November and April. Doubles can be found for $25-$35 around the metro St Laurent. Other streets to check are rue St Hubert, accessible from the next metro stop along (Berri-de-Montigny) and very near the bus terminal at St Denis. Turning left out of the terminal will bring you to the Hotel le Breton (1609 St Hubert), and on the same street to the Hotel Kent (number 1216) and the Hotel Viger Centre-Ville (number 1001). Continuing north to the next metro stop (Sherbrooke) try the north side of Sherbrooke west of St Denis for the Hotel Manoir Sherbrooke and the Armor Tourist Lodge, where doubles will all be similarly priced in the $30-$45 range. St Denis St has a number of relatively cheap hotels: Hotel de la Couronne (number 1029), Hotel des Touristes l'Americain (number 1042) and the Hotel St Denis (number 1254). Also cheap and conveniently central are the Vines Tourist Rooms (1208 Drummond) and Maison Andre (3511 University). Somewhat more upmarket is the renovated Royal Roussillion Hotel at 1610 rue St Hubert.

There is a bed and breakfast registry called Montrealers at Home (932-9690) whose B & Bs are cheaper than those in Toronto.

Motels. If you have a car and want to stay in a motel, look along Taschereau (Highway 124) on the south shore, especially around the bridges, or along Saint Jacques West. Few doubles will be less than $40. The cheapest is on neither of these roads; the Metro Motel at 9925 Lajeunesse (382-9780) charges $28 for a double.

Hostels. The province of Quebec is generally well provided with youth hostels, and the one in Montreal is particularly popular. If it is full, you may be referred to other temporary summer hostels. It is at 3541 rue Aylmer at Milton (843-3317) near the McGill metro stop. If you supply your own bedding, the cost is $10 per night. This hostel is open year round from 8 am-2 am, and you will probably be limited to a five-night stay.

YMCAs. The YMCA is at 1450 Stanley (849-8393) and offers singles from $28, doubles from $44.50. The YWCA is a few blocks away at 1355 R-Levesque West at the corner of Crescent (866-9941). Although it is very large, it accepts women only. Charges begin at $26 single $42 double. Enquire about dorm prices.

University Residences. There are several universities and colleges in Montreal, which rent out residence rooms between May and August. The University of McGill on Sherbrooke West offers the best location and so rooms should be booked in advance (398-4455). Singles go for $27 a night, $150 a week, with substantial reductions for students. Much cheaper is the residence of the French-speaking University of Montreal north of Mount Royal at 2500 Edouard-Monpetit (343-6531) which has over 1,000 rooms to rent for $16 if you have a student card. The Concordia University Student

Residence at 1455 de Maisonneuve W (848-3830) charges $19 single, $28 double.

Bed and Breakfast. In Montreal itself contact Montreal Bed & Breakfast on 738 9410. Even if you do not have camping equipment you can stay in the country either at a country bed and breakfast or at a farm. Contact Vacances Families (870 Blvd de Maisonneuve E, 282-9580) or Le Gite du Passant (4545 Avenue Pierre de Coubertin, 252-3000) for lists of addresses. The standard rate is $25 for an adult, $7 for a child occupying the same room, and they are usually open May to September. The nearest country B & B to Montreal is Coteau-du-Lac 25 miles/40 km away. The same organization can help you arrange a farm holiday, either staying in the farmhouse itself or in a cottage on the property similar to *gites* in France. These will cost around $220 per week, including two meals daily . Often these rural French families take pride in their dining rooms and serve regional specialities. For example if you are staying at a farm at St Urbain de Chateauguay south of Montreal, you should try their cheese and yoghurt made from goat's milk.

Camping. People with cars might want to consider staying even further away from the city than in motels. There are a couple of campsites less than 30 miles/50 km away. One is the Pointe des Cascades west of Montreal on route 338, just before you cross over to Montreal Island coming from the west. Charges begin at $15 here which includes use of the swimming pool. On the south shore there is camping at Cote-Ste-Catherine, 23 miles/37 km from downtown on route 132. For $9 you can pitch your tent or park your trailer and take advantage of facilities for swimming, fishing and picnicking between early June and September.

Eating and Drinking

Whereas the most rewarding places to dine out in Vancouver or Toronto are the ethnic restaurants, in Montreal, predictably, French is the cuisine to go for. Creperies, bistros and cafes abound in the inexpensive range and haute cuisine French restaurants at the other end of the spectrum. There is a provincial tax of 10% on meals over $3.25. It is customary to calculate the 12%-15% tip before adding the tax. Out of 250 restaurants listed by the Montreal tourist office, over a third serve French cooking. Visit les Filles du Roy (415 Bonsecours, 849-3535) to find Quebecois specialities, such as maple products, rabbit pie, *gibolette* fish stew, blueberries, Quebec cheese, maple-cured ham and so on.

There are literally thousands of restaurants in Montreal and dining out is part of the Montrealer's way of life. Don't be overwhelmed by the choice; it is difficult to go wrong. You need stray no further than rue St Denis to keep you eating well for months. This is the so-called Latin Quarter of Montreal and attracts students, artists and the beautiful people as well as tourists. Sitting outdoors at one of the many cafes, it is possible to amuse yourself for hours watching the passers-by. Or try the creperies which are normally licensed, such as Triskells at 3470. At all these places it is possible to lunch or dine for under $12 and many stay open long into the night. Le Fripon (436 Place Jacques-Cartier) serves $10 weekend buffets. Between these casual eating places there are plenty of more formal French restaurants, not to mention cheap Swiss, Moroccan and Asian places.

If you follow St Denis as far south as it will go you will come to *le Vieux*

Montreal. The dedicated sight-seer will follow the complete walking tour of the historic buildings, but most visitors are distracted by the abundant choice of restaurants, and begin to fantasize about the next meal. Most tourists end up in the Place Jacques-Cartier at some point, which in the summer is filled with outdoor tables and chairs, none of them available it may seem. Naturally food and drink are more expensive in this popular area than elsewhere and more expensive outdoors than in. Still it is also more entertaining than other areas, as it attracts all manner of buskers, hawkers and dawdlers. Old Montreal also houses some of the city's finest French restaurants in elegantly restored old houses near the waterfront. As on most of the restaurant-filled streets of Montreal, there is a startling variety of establishments, including the fairly expensive ($20-$25) but worthwhile seafood establishment called Chez Delmo at 211 rue Notre Dame (849-4061).

Vegetarians and health food enthusiasts on a budget will enjoy Le Commensal, 680 Sainte-Catherine West (871-1480) and 2115 Saint-Denis (845-0248), where innovative food is sold by weight. Biddles Jazz & Ribs, 2060 Aylmer (corner of President Kennedy, 842-8656) allows the tired traveller to feast on a barbecued chicken and ribs, while listening to a live jazz band. Each table at the Kyoto, 2055 Mansfield (866-8061) features a hot plate upon which a Japanese chef prepares patrons' orders, serving delicious Japanese specialities with a flourish and turning the whole affair into a virtuoso performance. For travellers with money to spare or something big to celebrate, the following are pricey, but reliably good. For excellent cuisine, try le Mas des Oliviers, 1216 Bishop (861-6733). Terrific Greek seafood can be sampled at Milos, 5357 du Parc (272-3522).

Try the Blvd St Laurent for many inexpensive restaurants, Polish, Italian, Jewish, Greek and German as well as French. Several good Chinese restaurants are clustered in Chinatown (St Laurent and de la Gauchetiere). Two interesting delicatessens which sell a wonderful range of smoked meats are Main and Schwartz's, both of which have more atmosphere than the more famous Ben's on the corner of Maisonneuve and Metcalfe, or Dunn's at 892 Ste Catherine West. Also try to fit in a late-night pilgrimage to the classic St Viateur Bagel Factory which serves the best bagels with lox and cream cheese in the world (160 St Viateur E). Or try the trendy Prince Arthur Street at the base of Mount Royal for Greek, Italian and seafood, where it is customary for restaurants to have a "bring-your-own" licence. For fast foods, watch for *casse-croutes* which specialize in hot dogs *(chien chauds)* with French fries and cabbage. A pleasing alternative to this standard North American fare is the relatively recent but now firmly established Montreal favourite: a delicious cross between the French croissant and the North American sandwich, served in *croissanteries* throughout the city. Also watch for roadside booths, advertising excellent *patates frites* when you are travelling out of town.

DRINKING

Drinking in Montreal can be just as lively as eating, since many bars (as opposed to "taverns" which stop serving at midnight) are licensed until 3 am (Monday to Saturday). Many of these bars will feature live entertainment. So for instance when the bars close at 1 am in Ottawa, it is not unusual for people to cross the provincial border and carry on drinking in Hull, Quebec. Although there is a liquor control board in Quebec, it does not have the same monopoly as its counterpart in other provinces. Wine and beer may be purchased from grocery stores (*depanneurs*) though not supermarket chains, usually for a few cents more than in liquor stores. Quebeckers are traditionally heavy beer drinkers though wine is becoming more fashionable, as it is in many western countries. Try Quebecois cider which, unlike cider sold in other provinces, is alcoholic, about the same strength as beer. For a really lethal brew try Caribou, a Quebecois mixture of red wine and spirit which at its best tastes like cherry brandy and at its worst like hangover-inducing cough medicine. This is the refreshment which is consumed in such quantity at the Winter Carnival in Quebec City (see below). Quebec imports large quantities of French wine, bottles it in the province and sells it for about $6 a bottle.

Whereas taverns are still male-dominated, brasseries welcome women and often serve cheap pub food. For a rooftop drink, go to the 36th floor bar of the Chateau Champlain in the Place du Canada or the Royal Bank skyscraper at Place Ville Marie which has a disco on the 44th floor. This place is favoured by students as well as jet setters. If the evening is warm, drink on an outdoor terrace at one of the cafes in Old Montreal, St Denis and Crescent St.

The drinking age is 18.

Entertainment

Look for the free fortnightly tabloids *Montreal Mirror* (in English) and *Voir* (in French) in bookshops, museums and restaurants. Each gives extensive listings. Also check the Saturday *Montreal Gazette* newspaper for a full entertainment section in English.

The Place des Arts (metro stop of the same name) is the central arts complex hosting symphonies, ballets and operas. Just as the South Bank in London includes several different theatres and concert halls, so does the Place des Arts, which includes the Theatres Maisonneuve, Port-Royal and the Salle Wilfrid-Pelletier. Ring the box office (842-2112) for details of upcoming events.

Cruises on the St. Lawrence depart several times daily from Victoria Pier and Jacques-Cartier Pier in the old harbour of Old Montreal, from mid-June until September. They are operated by Gray Line (280-5327) and Montreal Harbour Cruises (842-3871). Jet boat rides through the Lachine Rapids are organized by Lachine Rapids Tours (284-9607 or 843-4745); departures from Victoria Pier in Old Montreal.

Museums. Museums in Montreal are normally closed on Mondays. In addition to the main Musee des Beaux Arts (1379 Sherbrooke W), visit the McCord Museum, a few blocks east on Sherbrooke. This museum displays objects of Canadian historical interest including Inuit works of art and Quebecois handicrafts.

The Chateau de Ramezay, 280 Notre Dame East (861-3708) in Old Montreal, houses a small collection of original native artifacts. The Musee d'Art Contemporain, located on Cite-du-Havre (873-2878) is Montreal's museum of Modern Art. The Chateau Dufresne, the city's Decorative Arts Museum, is at the corner of Pie-IX and Sherbrooke (259-2575); it closes on Mondays and Tuesdays. The Palais de la Civilisation, located on Notre-Dame Island in the former French pavilion of Expo '67, usually hosts several international exhibitions simultaneously. Take the metro to Ile-Ste-

Helene. A shuttle ferries visitors from the station to the museum (872-4560).

Music. If you are visiting outside the symphony season (September to April), the prestigious Montreal Symphony Orchestra under the direction of Charles Dutoit will not be at the Place des Arts, but may be performing summer concerts at Notre-Dame Church in the centre of old Montreal.

The famous Yellow Door Coffee House at 3625 Aylmer near the youth hostel no longer has folk music, but you might like to check the useful student notice board. For traditional Quebecois folk music clubs, look for *boites-a-chanson* in Old Montreal, especially along rue Saint Paul, for instance Au Pierrots at number 104 (861-1270). These often turn into friendly sing-alongs, which provide a good opportunity to practise your French accent. For folk dancing in the summer go to the man-made lake in Mont-Royal Park on Monday or Thursday evenings when the ethnic community put on free performances of their national dances.

The choice of jazz is especially good during the Montreal Jazz Festival held in Saint-Denis each July for 10 days. But there is plenty of jazz to be heard any time of the year at the bars along St Denis such as Le Central (metro Mont Royale) and elsewhere (for example Biddles with Oliver Jones at 2060 Aylmer). For rock music, try the Moustache (1445 Closse Street near the Atwater metro stop). Big name rock bands play at the Montreal Forum (also near the Atwater stop) or at the Theatre St Denis. Trendy nightclubs abound. In Old Montreal, try Brandy's, 25 Saint-Paul East (871-9093) Don't forget to admire their twenty-odd giant Tiffany lampshades, each of them unique. Crescent and Bishop, located in the western, Anglo half of downtown, are focal points of nocturnal activity. Deja-Vu (1224 Bishop, 866-0512) has live rock bands most evenings. Winnie's (1445 Crescent, 288-0623) comes highly recommended by resident yuppies, and the Beaujolais (1458 de la Montagne, 842-8825) boasts both posh interiors and a quiet rooftop terrace, allowing a bird's eye view of the teeming streets below.

Theatre and Cinema. If you are not interested in French films or French theatre, your choice of entertainment will be reduced. (Films are not always subtitled). Plays in English are put on at the Centaur Theatre in Old Montreal. There is an English language rerun cinema at 2155 Ste Catherine St (932-1139). The Montreal Film Festival is held annually in late August.

SPORT

To join in Quebec's favourite spectator sport, try to see a hockey game at the Forum (932-2582). The champion Montreal Canadiens have won the Stanley Cup two dozen times. The Montreal Expos baseball team plays at Olympic Stadium (metro Pie-IX) between April and September. Call 253-3434 for ticket information.

If you have any interest in sport or architecture, you will want to schedule a visit to Olympic Park 4141 Pierre-de-Coubertin, site of the 1976 Olympics. Built at huge and controversial expense, the scope and originality of the structures are very impressive. While you're there, don't forget to take the funicular railway up to the top of the stadium's inclined tower, where you get a good view of the city skyline. Take a metro to Viau. Hourly tours costing $4 ($3 for students) begin at the Centre d'Accueil Touristique. It is also possible to rent a bicycle for $2 to explore the site. The pools are open to the public; phone 252-4737 for details. While out in that direction you might also like to visit the spacious botanical gardens across Sherbrooke from the park (4101 Sherbrooke East, 872-1400, metro to Pie-IX). They are open 9am-6pm and admission is $3 (872-1400). As well as 25,000 floral species and the biggest collection of Bonsai trees outside Asia, the gardens have a new and fascinating Insectarium.

There is a 7-mile/12-kilometre bicycle path beside the Lachine Canal which can be enjoyed independently or as part of a group tour. There is another along the St Lawrence River which begins at the south side of the Victoria Bridge. There are also canoe launching places and cross-country ski trails along the Lachine Canal. Canoes may be rented at Rosario Faucher (4282 Brebeuf) for $10-$15 daily or from Cles Plein-Air (6533 Clark).

Just as Vancouver has its Stanley Park and Toronto its Centre Island as an easy escape from the downtown bustle, Montreal has its mountain. Mont Royal Park is the place where the locals can go walking along miles of trails, skiing, skating, snowshoeing in winter, and cycling, jogging and sunbathing in summer. Autumn is a particularly memorable time to explore the park when the maple trees turn brilliant red and orange. Excellent views of the city may be obtained from the sign-posted observation points.

It is very pleasant to spend a summer's day on one of the largely man-made islands in the St Lawrence River. Ile Notre-Dame is the site of an enormous floral park. The island has a man-made system of canals and lakes, and a Nautical Pavilion which offers an excellent rental service featuring boats, catamarans, canoes, sailboards, pedal-boats, etc. Wetsuits and lessons are also available (872-3374). On Ile Ste Helene is La Ronde, a fun fair offering some terrifying rides, open only during the summer. In June it hosts an International Fireworks Competition. Admission is $3 on weekdays. Other attractions on the island include the Montreal Aquarium (872-4656) and the David M. Stewart Museum of Discoveries, focusing on Canadian history (861-6701). These attractions can easily be reached from the metro station on the island.

SHOPPING

Normal shopping hours are 9.30 am-6 pm Monday to Wednesday with late night shopping till 9 pm on Thursdays and Fridays, and Saturday closing at 5 pm. The main shopping thoroughfare is St Catherine (near McGill metro) where the four major department stores may be found: Eaton's Simpson's the Bay and Ogilvy's; only the latter is unique to Montreal. For a high density of fashionable boutiques try Les Terrasses, Place Ville Marie or Place Bonaventure shopping complexes. The *haute couture* salons and elegant antique stores are found along Sherbrooke Street. The provincial sales tax of 9% is among the steepest in the country.

There are a number of excellent outdoor farmers' markets in Montreal, all of them closed on Sundays. Perhaps the best is the Marche Atwater at the southern end of Atwater (metro Lionel-Groulx). Six days a week from about 7 am -6 pm, farmers sell their produce at very reasonable prices. In the neighbourhood there are some interesting secondhand shops. A chaotic and colourful fish market is held on Saturday mornings on Roi St E. Particularly hardy travellers might be interested in the Marche Central Metropolitain at Cremazie and de l'Acadie in far north of the city, which is reputed to peak at 5 am. Also interesting is the market in the Italian district near the Jean-Talon metro stop.

The Canadian Guild of Crafts may be found at 2025 Peel St near the metro stop which stocks interesting quilts, textiles, mocassins and carvings. For less expensive traditional arts and crafts try le Rouet with several locations including Place Ville Marie and 700 Ste Catherine W.

Quebec produces two-thirds of the world's maple syrup. If you are interested in its production try to visit a maple bush in the early spring when the sap is collected and boiled down. Place Jacques-Cartier is full of boutiques which rely on tourists to buy presentation packs of maple syrup as well as the handicrafts and delicacies which they display.

MEDIA

The majority of radio and television stations and newspapers are in French. Tours are available of the headquarters of the CBC French network called La Maison de Radio-Canada (1400 R-Levesque East, 285-2690). CBC-AM in Montreal can be picked up on 940 AM and CBC-FM on 93.5 FM. Students favour CKGM on 980AM, CHOM on 97.7FM, and CJFM on 95.9FM, all of which play different shades of rock and pop music. The DJ chatter on the latter two will tend to fluctuate between English and French. CKOI on 97FM also plays rock music, but commentaries are exclusively in Quebecois. English-speaking television channels available without cable in Montreal are CBC channel 6 and CTV channel 12. The American television networks are all available on cable.

Five of the six Montreal dailies are in French from the serious *Le Devoir* to the sensationalist *Journal de Montreal.* The English language Montreal daily is the *Gazette.* British newspapers may be consulted at the Municipal Library on Sherbrooke near la Fontaine Park (nearest metro stop Sherbrooke).

Montreal has the reputation for having more than its fair share of organized crime, bank hold-ups being a regular feature, and a large proportion of the murders seem to have underworld connections. Innocent tourists can go about their business day or night without anxiety, and no area of Montreal is a no-go zone. Although there are slums in Montreal they do not seem to nurture violent crime and need not be avoided. The area around St Urbain was made famous in novels by Mordecai Richler such as *The Apprenticeship of Duddy Kravitz*, about a boy's struggle to escape a Jewish ghetto.

Possession of cannabis is an offence like everywhere else in Canada and just as prevalent.

The area code for Montreal is 514.

Tourist Information: 174 rue Notre-Dame East (871-1595). The Recreation and Sports Federation (*Regroupment Loisirs Quebec*), is an excellent source of information, not only on recreation and sports, but also on accommodation throughout the province, special events, and general tourist information. Youth Hostel members and International Student

Card holders should make a point of contacting Regroupement Tourisme Jeunesse at the same address in order to obtain a list of hotels, restaurants and shops across Canada which give discounts to members.

Maison du Tourisme: 2 Place Ville Marie (873-2015).

Parks Canada: Quebec Region, 1141 Route de l'Eglise, Ste-Foy Quebec G1V 4H5 (418-694-4177).

British Consulate: 635 Rene-Levesque W (866-5863).

American Express: 2000 Peel Building, 1141 de Maisonneuve W (284-3300).

Thomas Cook: 2020 University St (842-2541).

Emergency Health Aid (Greater Montreal Referral Center): 931-2292.

Post Office: St Antoine and de la Cathedrale, Place Bonaventure.

Telegrams: 861-7311.

Weather Information: 636-3284.

Road conditions: 873-4121.

QUEBEC CITY

By North American standards the provincial capital of Quebec, also called Quebec (population 575,000) is very ancient, having hosted the famous battle between Wolfe and Montcalm in 1759 well on in its history. The church of Notre Dame des Victoires built in 1688 rivals some of the 17th century Spanish missions in the American Southwest as the oldest European settlement in North America. Quebec City is the only walled city north of Mexico (it was declared a World Heritage Treasure by UNESCO in December 1985), and Laval University is among the oldest universities on the continent.

The city is divided into the Upper and Lower Towns, connected by steep and winding staircases, as well as a funicular railway. The narrow and random streets are best explored on foot. The atmosphere in Quebec City is more quaint and even more French than in Montreal, which is not surprising considering that 95% of its residents are French-speaking. The restaurants are renowned throughout North America for their French cuisine.

Unexpectedly the most popular time to visit Quebec is early February, when there is a ten-day Winter Carnival. Be prepared for the coldest temperatures you have ever encountered. (Significantly, the advertisement on the inside front cover of the Carnival brochure — "proud to be associated with such a splended event" — is for a remedy for chapped lips). Most people who attend the carnival drink large quantities of the local brew (Caribou) to keep warm, in between ice skating on the outdoor rink, going down the giant ice slide on Dufferin Terrace and admiring the snow sculptures at the Place du Palais. Participants from as far afield as China and Morocco, not to mention Inuit from the Canadian Arctic, come to compete in this unique and transitory artistic medium.

If you do plan to attend, try to book accommodation ahead of time (call 418-524-8441) for the latest updates). Similarly in July and August, the youth hostel and inexpensive guest houses fill up. Quebec has a brand new youth hostel: the Centre International de Sejour, 19 Ste Ursule (418-694-0755) which charges $9 a night. Double rooms are available at $25 a night. A bunk in the dorm is $6.50. Services are excellent, and include a fully equipped kitchen, laundry facilities, a baggage check, and a bicycle shed.

For detailed information on walking tours, historical background, hotels, restaurants and special events, contact The Quebec Urban Community

Tourist Information Center, 60 rue d'Auteuil, Quebec GlR 4M8 (418-692-2471); or the Maison du Tourisme de Quebec, 12 Sainte Anne (418-651-2882).

The Great Outdoors The Laurentian Mountains north of Montreal, the Eastern Townships south of the city, the Gaspe Peninsula 400 miles east along the St Lawrence River and the vast thinly populated north of the province all provide varied opportunities for outdoor activity. There are two national parks. La Mauricie 130 miles northeast of Montreal and Forillon at the tip of the very rural and French Gaspe Peninsula. Here there are wildlife observation facilities for seeing moose and deer on land, and whales and seals at sea. The Laurentians are particularly beautiful in the fall. Guided bus tours are available in September and October. Contact Grayline, 440 Rene-Levesque West (280-5327).

The provincial government publishes lists of many types of accommodation. The Ministry of Recreation even sponsors government inns and campsites, and runs a reservation service at its offices in Quebec City (418-643-5349). Contact the Ministry if you are interested in renting a self-catering cottage for a week or two, some of which are located inside provincial parks. Their detailed list of campsites is most useful; ranging in price from $5 a night for primitive sites to at most $15 for luxury.

Skiing. Skiing is the most universally popular sport. The ski resorts of the Laurentian Hills are within an hour's drive north of Montreal and are located in such places as Piedmont, Sainte-Adele, Sainte-Agathe, Val-Morin and Val-David. Murray Hill ski buses run between downtown and the Laurentians (Mt. Tremblant, St. Sauveur) or Vermont (Jay Peak, Smugglers Notch) (937-5311). Daytrips to Mt. Tremblant, Jay Peak and Smugglers Notch are $34. A day trip to St. Sauveur is $26, while night skiing from 6-12 midnight is $22. The price covers bus fare and lift ticket. Equipment can be rented at all resorts but prices are steep. If you are a foreigner and are boarding a "ski express" bus to Vermont, don't forget your passport and visa; otherwise, you're likely to spend the day at the border crossing, with the bus picking you up on the way back! The highest peak in the Laurentians is Mont Tremblant (nearly 3,000 feet/1,000 metres) 90 miles/150 km north of the city. This is part of a huge wilderness park which is also a worthwhile destination for people interested in rustic camping during the summer. Camping equipment may be rented in Montreal from Passe-Montagne, 5209 St. Denis (276-1643). The shop also rents cross-country ski equipment in the winter. Skis, boots and poles may be rented for $12 a day, $24 a week-end. One week ski packages cost about $250 including room, meals, lessons and lift tickets.

There are also major ski centres within a short distance of Quebec City including the relatively new Mont Sainte Anne development. For details of snow conditions phone 861-6670 in Montreal and 827-4579 in Quebec City. Skiing equipment can be rented at any of the resorts.

Canoeing, fishing and hunting are all extremely popular, and there are outfitters and rental facilities in many parks and small towns. If you want to hunt, you must purchase a licence ($10 or $25 depending on the game). To get this, you will have to have written authorization that you are competent with firearms. Non-residents are not allowed to hunt moose but most other game is available to them.

The Atlantic Provinces

Peggy's Cove, Nova Scotia

New Brunswick   Nova Scotia   Prince Edward Island   Newfoundland

The "hospitality industry" outstrips all other sources of revenue except fishing in New Brunswick, Nova Scotia, Prince Edward Island and Newfoundland. Some over-zealous planners have suggested that the Atlantic provinces should be depopulated and turned into a gigantic playground. Fortunately, this futurist dream will never be realized, and Maritimers will continue to pass on their rural lore and their hospitable traditions.

Strictly speaking, the Maritime provinces do not include Newfoundland, since the term was coined well before 1949 when Newfoundland ceased to be an independent British colony and joined the Canadian Confederation. A reminder of Newfoundland's isolation is the fact it has its own time zone, half an hour ahead in the winter and 1½ hours ahead in the summer of the other Atlantic provinces.

It often seems that the less prosperous a place is, the more slowly it changes. With an average income per capita of about two-thirds that of central and western Canada, the Atlantic region is definitely the least prosperous part of Canada. Change comes reluctantly to this region, and fishing and farming techniques remain relatively backward. Although the natives may grumble about the policies of the federal government, they are a peace-loving and traditional people who happily persist with the old ways of doing things.

Whether gentle rolling farmland, dramatic sea cliffs or forested mountains, the changing landscape is always pleasing. Furthermore, the man-made landscape is more picturesque in eastern Canada than elsewhere.

White frame farmhouses inland and fishing villages nestling around coves, old-fashioned one room school houses and wooden churches seem to have kept modern ugliness at bay. The scale of distances is more manageable than in the other provinces, so a motoring holiday is not quite the marathon exercise it can become in other provinces.

Halifax, with a metropolitan population of just 277,000, is the largest city of the region and the commercial and cultural hub. Yet the city retains much of its attractive quaintness, because of its situation along seaside bays. The other main cities are Moncton and Saint John in New Brunswick, Charlottetown Prince Edward Island (invariably abbreviated to PEI, which often comes out Pea-Eye) and St John's Newfoundland (pronounced Newf'nd-*land*). These small cities have more charm than sophistication and are worth exploring on foot.

THE NATIVES

There is a joke about an old-timer Newfoundland fisherman who boasts about how well travelled he is. "So what did you think of the mainland?" he is asked. "Oh, I ain't ever been to the mainland, but I'se been everywhere else". Although not every Maritimer is as home-loving as this, they tend to be neither very sophisticated not cosmopolitan. But they are renowned for their easy going nature and gentleness and you can go for weeks without hearing a voice raised in anger.

The accents of Maritimers are the most distinctive in Canada. Whereas it is impossible to distinguish between a Vancouverite and a Torontonian, a Newfoundland accent can be detected immediately. And because of the lack of mobility, communities within the same province have preserved different kinds of speech. In southern Newfoundland, there is a definite Irish lilt, whereas the north is more English west country. Plus the locals have a vivid homespun vocabulary (such as "yaffle" meaning a pile of dried fish) and more than their fair share of raconteurs. Try to make the acquaintance of one of these old salts in a local beer parlour, or lounge around the docks when the fishing boats are putting in.

The cultural influence of the British Isles remains surprisingly strong. On Cape Breton Island in Nova Scotia, for example, there are still Gaelic-speaking descendants of Scottish settlers, a Gaelic college and Highland festivals featuring Scottish dancing and bagpipe playing. In fact songs and dances are still performed more spontaneously in this part of Canada than in any other.

There is also a large French population, especially in New Brunswick, where over a third of the population is French. Instead of being concentrated in one part of the province, French communities are scattered among English-speaking ones. So you must exercise a little tact when addressing a townsperson for the first time. These French people are descendants of the early traders and settlers called Acadians. When the land of Acadia (now the Maritimes) was won by England at the beginning of the 18th century, over half the 10,000 French-speaking Acadians were expelled; some went to Quebec, others to New Orleans but many soon returned to the Maritimes. If you are in the area during August, try to attend the Acadian Festival in Caraquet when, among other traditions, there is the Blessing of the Fleet, just as in New Orleans.

CLIMATE

The sea is never far away and provides cool breezes in summer and a moderating effect in winter from the warm currents. PEI has the mildest temperatures. Whereas summer highs are in the range 60°F to 75°F/16°C to 24°C, winter temperatures hover around 32°F/0°C. The snow has usually disappeared by April and medium weight clothing is appropriate thereafter. The Maritimes are comparatively rainy, with some rainfall on nearly half the days of the year and also windier and foggier (especially Newfoundland) than other parts of the country.

Air. Air Canada, Canadian Airlines and Air Nova operate frequent flights from Toronto and Montreal to Halifax, the principal gateway. There are also international flights from London, Glasgow and Boston. The airport is 26 miles/ 42 km northeast of the city, a distance which can be covered in about 80 minutes on the airport limousine service (873-3525) for $8.

Bus. Because of the low density of population in the Maritimes, the coach services are fairly sparse. Greyhound does not operate in the provinces at all, although the Ameripass is valid in Nova Scotia and New Brunswick but not on ferries or on the two island provinces of Newfoundland and PEI. The services in Nova Scotia are mostly operated by Acadian Lines in Halifax (454-9321) with the service south from Halifax operated by MacKenzie Bus Lines in the nearby town of Bridgewater (543-2491). New Brunswick's only coach line is SMT (Eastern) in Saint John (506-658-6500). For the only public transport on PEI, contact the Island Transit Co-op in Charlottetown (892-6167) which operates only during the summer. Finally in Newfoundland, you will have to use Terratransport Roadcruiser Service (709-737-5900) which operates between St. John's and Port aux Basques where the ferry from Nova Scotia docks (see below). The 560-mile/900 km journey through such places as Come-by-Chance takes 14 hours.

Train. VIA Rail's *Atlantic* leaves Halifax daily at about mid-day for Montreal where it arrives the following morning (cost $90 single). There are daily services between Halifax, Saint John and Fredericton. There are no railway lines on PEI nor on Newfoundland where the only services are on coaches.

Driving. The Trans-Canada Highway links Riviere-du-Loup in Quebec with Fredericton (the capital of New Brunswick), Saint John, Moncton, Truro and North Sydney on Cape Breton Island. It even continues on PEI and Newfoundland. Although this is the fastest route, it is just two lanes wide for most of its distance. The minor roads are the ones which take you into the picturesque backwaters, though some become difficult to negotiate in muddy conditions. Coastal roads are invariably scenic, in particular the Cabot Trail which runs through Cape Breton Highlands National Park NS. This route is also popular with cyclists. Cars may be hired in any of the cities, though the big firms may be booked up in July and August.

Speed limits are similar to those in the rest of Canada: 100 km/h (62 mph) or 90 km/hr (55mph) on the Trans-Canada, 80 km/h (50 mph) on other highways and 50 km/hr (30 mph) in towns. There is less temptation to speed on these roads than on their much straighter and more boring counterparts in the Prairies. The RCMP patrol the highway and impose minimum fines of $50 for speeding. On the back roads, many of which are gravel, you will have to proceed slowly.

Ferries. In addition to the CN ferry between the mainland and PEI or Newfoundland, there are car ferries from Bar Harbor and Portland Maine to Yarmouth Nova Scotia. The 45 minute crossing between Cape Tormentine NB and Borden PEI costs about $2.50 for foot passengers and $6.25 for cars. Crossings are made frequently during the height of summer, so there is no need to book. This is not true of the daily crossing on the *MV Caribou* between North Sydney NS and Port-aux-Basques Newfoundland which is 600 miles/1000km from the capital St John's in the east. The trip takes five to six hours and costs about $65 for a car with two passengers. You can make reservations by calling toll free 1-800-565-9470 within the Maritimes, but you must collect your tickets two hours before the sailing. In the summer months only there is a thrice-weekly overnight service between North Sydney and Argentia, a town just 78 miles (130 km) from the capital St. John's, cutting out the long drive across the whole province; this trip costs $35 one way. For schedules and prices write to Marine Atlantic, 100 Cameron St, Moncton, New Brunswick E1C 5Y6. There are also other ferry routes in the Atlantic provinces, which are marked on the standard road map of Canada. There are rumours that cruises around the Minas Basin at the head of the Bay of Fundy are going to be introduced in the 1990s.

Bed and breakfast at a reasonable price has flourished in the Maritimes and there is a large choice of charming, inexpensive private homes. You can find double rooms in quiet rural areas for as little as $22. Self-catering cottages sleeping up to four are priced at about $200 per week. The one drawback of staying in country inns or as guests on farms is that it would be hard to manage without a car, since the rest of civilization is usually miles away.

Since tourism is such an important business, there is an abundance of facilities with the notable exception of Newfoundland, where prices tend to be higher. Even with a ratio of four visitors to every inhabitant (as there is on PEI), there seems to be enough hotels, bed and breakfasts, campsites, self-catering cottages and inns to go round. Campsites for $9 per tent represent especially good value, and are often near beaches and other recreation facilities. The provincial tourist offices publish detailed lists of campsites.

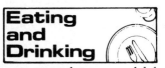

Fishing is the primary industry in the region and eating seafood is a primary occupation of both locals and visitors. You will notice piles of lobster traps in most coastal towns and lobster appears on most menus. There are also oysters (watch for oyster-shucking contests), scallops, mussels, quahaugs (an Indian word for a kind of round clam), Atlantic salmon and many others. There are plenty of seafood shops from which you can buy shellfish very cheaply to barbecue or cook yourself. An even more enjoyable way to eat the local produce is to attend a "lobster supper". These are organized periodically by local communities and held in church halls. Members of the local parish provide all the trimmings. Also watch for strawberry socials in the summer, and also maple syrup festivals in March and April during the sugaring-off season, when the maple trees are tapped for their sap. Many of these local culinary events cost a pittance. Although potatoes are the most important crop on PEI, there are no potato festivals. Delicious blueberries abound near the New Brunswick/Nova Scotia border.

In the more expensive restaurants you can find some very unusual dishes. For example Newman's Restaurant in Annapolis Royal NS has been known to feature bear stew on the menu.

The provincial sales taxes are fairly high, as high as 12% in Newfoundland. Inexpensive restaurant meals (e.g. under $4 in Nova Scotia) are exempt.

Drinking. The staunch Protestant background of these provinces has resulted in licensing laws which are no more liberal than in other parts of Canada. Off-licences tend to close at 10pm on Fridays, 6pm on other nights. Taverns usually close at midnight, though in some tourist areas their licences may be extended. Cocktail lounges and clubs in cities normally stay open until 2am. The drinking age is 19 throughout the region except in PEI where it is 18. Watch for Moosehead beer brewed in New Brunswick and Nova Scotia, as well as some newer and smaller breweries which brew German-style lagers free of preservatives and additives. In Newfoundland watch out for "screech", a Jamaica rum made specially for the Newfoundland Liquor Corporation.

Ask the tourist office for a list of events and look for Gaelic festivities, fiddle contests, country fairs, water regattas, etc. Two of the most famous events are the International Gathering of the Clans due in the summer of 1991, and the annual Antigonish Highland Games in early July. Canada's most popular musical ever, called *Anne of Green Gables,* is performed in Charlottetown every summer. There are also regional theatres such as the Ship's Company Theatre in Parrsboro NS.

With its early colonization and subsequent changes of ownership, the Atlantic region has a long and interesting history. Archaeologists have found Viking remains at the extreme northern tip of Newfoundland and dinosaur remains in western NS where a dinosaur museum may soon open. Among other highlights are the Citadel in Halifax, the Fort at Louisberg and the Alexander Graham Bell Museum at Baddeck. You can visit any of the 21 National Historic Parks, ranging from reconstructed fortresses to ruined lighthouses. Contact the Atlantic regional office of Parks Canada for details: Historic Properties, Upper Water St, Halifax B3J 1S9; (902) 426-3436.

The area code for Nova Scotia and Prince Edward Island is 902, for New Brunswick 506, and for Newfoundland 709.

Provincial tourist office addresses are listed in the introduction.

Fredericton Visitors' Information Centre: corner of Queen and York Streets (506-455-9426).

St John's (Nfl'd) Tourist Bureau: City Hall, New Gower St (709-722-7080).

Halifax Information Centre: Historic Properties, Lower Water St (902-421-8736).
Tourist Information Centre Charlottetown: 902-368-4444.
British Consulate: 1645 Granville St, Halifax B3J 1X3 (902-429-4230).
American Express: Island Travel, Confederation Court Mall, Charlottetown (566-1024); 300 Union St, Saint John (506-642-1055); 199 Water St, Saint John's (709-726-2543).
Parks Canada: Atlantic Region, Historic Properties, Upper Water St, Halifax B3J 1S9 (902-426-3436).

The Great Outdoors

The wilderness in the Atlantic provinces is more manageable in scale than elsewhere, though there are still vast tracts too remote to be accessible. Except in Labrador, the little-visited mainland part of the province of Newfoundland, there are no mountains over 3,000 ft (900m). The first efforts at conservation in Canada were made in Nova Scotia in 1794 to protect grouse and black ducks.

All outdoor activities associated with the seaside are easy to join in. Whether you take scuba diving lessons, go clam-digging ashore or "cod-jigging" at sea, swim on any of the supervised beaches or play frisbee, the miles of clean beaches and bracing ocean water should not be missed. Fishing outfitters are very easy to find. If you happen to be in Newfoundland in early July you can catch fish without any equipment during the "caplin scull", when millions of smelt-like fish called caplin come ashore to spawn and can easily be caught with the bare hands. Cycling is especially recommended because of the relatively high number of back roads and the absence of mountains. There are hire facilities in most towns.

You may see beaver, moose, raccoon, porcupine, deer, hare and even bobcats. There are many migrating birds and waterfowl, including the great blue heron, bald eagle and many others. One of the most exciting activities is whale-watching whether from land or sea. For example from the narrow isthmus which connects the Avalon Peninsula to the rest of Newfoundland, it is possible to see pothead and humpback whales in large numbers during the summer.

Vancouver and British Columbia

Confusingly, the city of Vancouver (population 1,300,000) is not on Vancouver Island, but on the mainland. (The much smaller city of Victoria is the main city on Vancouver Island and the capital of British Columbia). The popular image of the west coast is that it is more "laid-back" than the rest of Canada, that the inhabitants are more willing to experiment with alternative lifestyles. Vancouver is to Canada what San Francisco is to the States. This may not be immediately apparent if you find yourself caught in a rush hour traffic jam on one of the bridges leading to the eastern bedroom communities, surrounded by impatient motorists in business suits. However, a stroll along one of the city's beaches on a sunny day will give you a different impression. It is rewarding to mosey around the streets of Vancouver, sampling the food, music and local atmosphere, to see for yourself whether Vancouverites are as unhurried, tolerant and wholesome as they like to think.

It is more likely to be the scenery than the sociology which attracts you to Vancouver and to British Columbia generally. The forests and mountains for which Canada is so justly famous are easily accessible from the cities of BC. Just a 20 minutes drive from downtown Vancouver takes you to the bottom of Grouse Mountain (though there are no longer any grouse), from whence you take a cable car to the top for excellent skiing. Not surprisingly, there is a strong emphasis on outdoor recreation among British Columbians. Wilderness camping, skiing and watersports are all the rage, and you should try to arrange at least one expedition outside the city to experience the rugged terrain. Millions of acres of the province are protected as provincial or national parkland, with trails and campsites.

For the serious adventurer, BC offers intriguing possibilities. The inaccessible and thinly populated north of the province near the Yukon border is a land of unexplored mountains, a place where it is possible for modestly equipped amateur mountaineers to be dropped by a bush pilot in a remote area of the northern Rockies, to go hiking, then successfully submit suggestions for new place names to the Geographical Place Names Committee in Ottawa. Another epic trip which is possible now that the road along the east coast of Vancouver Island has been completed is to cycle its complete length, about 300 miles/500km.

THE NATIVES

The citizens of Vancouver are not as ethnically mixed as in Toronto or Montreal. The most prominent racial minority are the Chinese who are concentrated in North America's second largest Chinatown along W Pender St between Abbott and Gore Streets. A few blocks north, there is a smaller but thriving Japanese community. There is also a relatively large (for North America) number of Indians, mostly Sikhs.

The alternative lifestyle exerts a great deal of influence in Vancouver and environs, and a large number of unconventional young people were attracted here during the 1970s because of its freer atmosphere. Watch out for some of their more amusing excesses; some expensive alder firewood was advertised as being "hand hewn by people in the Gulf Islands wearing only natural fibre clothing". Look for the free newspaper *Common Ground,* which is an amusing source of information on such activities.

Making Friends. With two major universities (the University of British Columbia known as UBC and Simon Fraser), there are plenty of students around. If you want to meet people (and eat cheaply while you are at it) visit the UBC cafeterias open to visitors out of term (May to August). Try the Pit in the Student Union Building, which is the student pub. Another area to find pubs and cafes frequented by students is Kitsilano, where the youth hostel is located.

CLIMATE

By Canadian standards, the west coast has a relatively tame climate. Victoria — just across the water from Vancouver — is the only provincial capital in Canada to have a January mean temperature above freezing, with almost no snow fall. Houses in Vancouver are not as ruggedly built as they are in the rest of Canada; they do not come automatically equipped with double glazing and thick insulation. Although over 20in/51cm of snow are measured in an average winter, it rarely stays on the ground, and the usual winter business of shovelling and putting on snow tyres is not necessary. But there are usually one or two sudden cold spells and every winter a few car owners, who have rashly neglected to use anti-freeze, find their engine blocks have cracked.

Summer temperatures are very pleasant along the coast. The blistering heat experienced in the interior of the country is moderated by the sea to create a potentially ideal climate. That is the good news. The bad news is that it rains a lot, precipitation falling on nearly half the days of the year. Most of the rain falls in the winter, but it is quite possible to have a solid week of rain during the summer. That may be your cue to flee to the dry interior of the province where temperatures regularly soar into the 90°s (30°C). Once you get past the first mountain range (the Coastal Range) most of the precipitation has been off-loaded, and if you continue into the next valley, you can even find a patch of genuine desert. But on a sparkling sunny day in Vancouver, fleeing will be the last thing on your mind.

ARRIVAL AND DEPARTURE

Air. The approach into Vancouver is very dramatic. After flying over unrelievedly mountainous terrain, you suddenly swoop down over the sea and land on an island. Vancouver International Airport is located on Sea Island, about 8km (5 miles) south of the city on Granville St. The airport is modern and efficient. Luggage trolleys are freely available.

The Hustle Bus, operated by the Airport Bus Service (273-0071), travels between the airport and downtown every 15 minutes between 5.45am and 9.15pm. The cost of the service is $6.50. The best place to get off for the city centre is the Hotel Vancouver at 900 West Georgia. Other airport services are operated by Perimeter Transport (261-2299) and to the North Shore by Pacific Transport (273-7207) for $10. The cheapest way into downtown is to take a city bus from the US departure level to 60th and Granville and then transfer to a bus going downtown; the transfer ticket costs $1.25.

Canadian Airlines, Wardair and Air Canada operate services between Vancouver and most cities in Canada and around the province. The VUSA fare to Calgary, for example, is $61. The one way fare between Vancouver and Kelowna in the Okanagan Valley is $120 and between Vancouver and Prince Rupert $175. Ask any travel agent for details. There are also smaller seaplanes operated by Air BC which service smaller centres up the coast (273-2464). Also check the classified ads in the *Vancouver Sun* for people selling off unwanted tickets cheaply, either within the province, across Canada or overseas. Travel CUTS has an office at 1516 Duranleau St (1-800-972-4004).

Bus. The Greyhound Terminal is at 150 Dunsmuir St, at the corner of Cambie. Phone 662-3222 between 7am and 11.30pm for information about times and prices. There are many daily departures for Victoria operated by Pacific Coach Lines (737 Humboldt St, Victoria; 662-7575) via the Tsawwassen Ferry Terminal. The trip from Vancouver to Victoria costs $15.75 including the ferry and takes about 3½ hours altogether. Maverick Coachlines (662-3222) operate a through service from Vancouver to Nanaimo on Vancouver Island.

There are four Greyhound buses a day to Banff, and from thence across Canada. The ride to Banff is a wonderfully scenic trip lasting 16 hours and costing $55 one way, $90 return. If you want to visit towns in the Okanagan Valley, you will have to rely on Greyhound since there is no train line. There are six Greyhound services a day in each direction between Seattle and Vancouver; the express journey takes just 3½ hours. An alternative service is operated by Quick Coachlines (604-591-3571).

Greyhound has introduced a FlexPass which allows 10 days of bus travel (within a month) in Alberta or BC.

Train. There are two stations in Vancouver. The VIA Station is at 1150 Station Street at Terminal Avenue. The BC Railways Station from which you catch trains to northern BC terminating at Prince George is at 13 West First Street in North Vancouver (984-5246). The Canadian Pacific trans-Canada railway was completed to Vancouver in 1889. You really get the feeling in the VIA Station of being at the edge of a continent, since there is just one departure and one arrival a day. The Supercontinental service via

Jasper leaves at 4.30pm and arrives at 12.35pm daily. The *Canadian* departs at 3.55pm and arrives (from Montreal/Toronto) at 10am. A popular place to break the easternbound journey is Banff in Alberta, 21 hours from Vancouver; the trip costs $65. VIA Rail has a toll-free number in Vancouver: 1-800-665-8630. One of the interesting day trips which can be made from Vancouver starts at the North Vancouver Station. There is a six-hour return excursion by steam train (The *Royal Hudson*) to the logging town of Squamish, which costs about $12 (phone 689-9222 for details).

Driving. If you are approaching from the US border, just 24 miles/40km from downtown Vancouver, you will be on Highway 99 which turns into Oak Street running parallel to Granville Street, which in turn will take you right across town to North Vancouver, with a few signposted deviations. If you are approaching from the east you will be on the Trans-Canada (Highway 1) which turns into Hastings Street. Since the traffic in the downtown area can get very congested at rush hour, try to avoid those times of the day.

Some discount car rental addresses in Vancouver: Oldies but Goodies, 667 W 3rd Street (980-1515); Rent-a-Wreck, 350 Robson St (688-0001) plus 12 other locations; McKee's U-Drive Campers, 113000 Bridgeport Road (270-8565). Battered cars from Rent-a-Wreck cost from $18, and a camper van will cost four times as much. Gas costs are in the region of 50c per litre ($2.27 a gallon). There are no toll bridges or roads in BC though highway ferries in the interior of the province have begun to charge fees. All drivers must wear seatbelts.

In view of the expense of motoring you may prefer to share a ride. Hitch-hiking is common throughout the province and is usually very successful, even to remote places. Check in the *Yellow Pages* for drive-away companies. One is Auto Delivery, 19337 48th Ave, Surrey (576-1443). The most common destinations are Calgary, Toronto and Los Angeles.

Recorded reports on highway conditions in BC may be heard on 660-9775.

Ferry. You may want to make the journey between the US and British Columbia by ferry. The ferry service from Seattle to Victoria runs daily in summer ($25 one way, $37 return); the trip takes 3½-4½ hours. Year round services to Victoria on the *Black Ball* run from Port Angeles in northern Washington state. There are three or four ferries a day during the summer. A car with driver pays US$22 while a passenger with bicycle will be US$8.

Ferry information may be obtained from BC Ferries on 669-1211 or for recorded schedules 685-1021. There are 15 ferries a day to Vancouver Island during the summer, either between Tsawwassen and Swartz Bay 18 miles/30km outside Victoria or from Horseshoe Bay in West Vancouver to Nanaimo. During high summer both routes are very busy and if you have a car, you may have to queue for several hours. The cost is $21 for car and a driver, and $4.50 for foot passengers only. Both routes are very scenic looking back towards the Sunshine Coast or threading among the Gulf Islands. Sunrise is a particularly fine time to make the trip, and also the ferries are less crowded early in the morning. There is a ferry from Port Hardy at the northern end of Vancouver Island to Prince Rupert in northern BC ($50 single plus $95 for a car.) If you want to continue to Alaska, you must switch onto the Alaska State Ferry System at Prince Rupert (see *Alaska*).

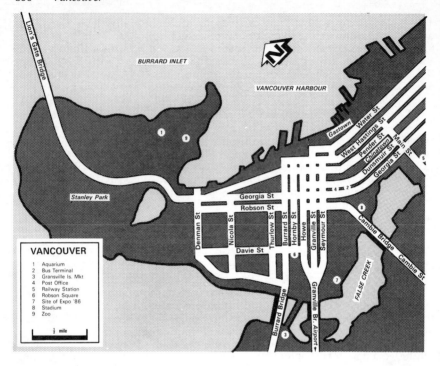

CITY TRANSPORT

Car. Because all of Vancouver's traffic must be funnelled across a handful of bridges, the congestion can be terrible. The Advanced Light Rapid Transit (ALRT) rail system, part elevated, part surface, part underground for EXPO 86 has improved the situation though its expense discourages many commuters. So at present the only way to avoid a snarl-up in rush hours is not to drive nor take a bus. If you are driving your own vehicle, watch the illuminated signs on the Lion's Gate Bridge, since they indicate changes in the direction of the middle lane to accommodate the flow of traffic. Also listen to Radio CHQM which gives rush hour traffic reports. There is an elaborate one-way system on roads which makes navigation difficult. Together with the great pressure on parking spaces, you are well-advised to use the public transport system.

Public Transport. There is a reasonable integrated network of bus routes in Vancouver. The transfer ticket fare of $1.25 allows travel on all buses, ALRT and the seabus to the north shore within 90 minutes in one direction (i.e. no backtracking). Information on all transit on the lower mainland is available on 261-5100 or you can buy a *Transit Guide* for $1.25 from newsagents. The fare must be paid in exact change when you board and preferably with coins not bills. The trip by seabus across the Burrard Inlet between North Vancouver and downtown takes just 12 minutes, but does permit you a new view of the city and is worth doing even if you have no real reason to go over to the North Shore. You catch the seabus, which departs every 15 or 30 minutes depending on the time of day, from the bottom of Granville Street. It is also picturesque at night, and you can pretend (for 12 minutes) that you are on a moonlit harbour cruise.

To get to the University of British Columbia (UBC) campus, take bus number 10 from Granville Street. To get to Kitsilano, take bus number 4 from Granville to Jericho Park. A few buses run along the main arteries (Granville, Georgia, Hastings) through the night. Ordinary buses stop about 1am.

Cycling. City cycling is popular in Vancouver, though it can be both very hilly and fumy. An obvious cycling destination is Stanley Park, the largest downtown "wilderness" park in North America. Just opposite the bus loop on Chilco Street inside the park is a bicycle rental shop (681-5581) which charges between $10 and $15 a day. You will have to leave an additional deposit of $10. Bike rentals are also available from Dunbar Cycles, 4219 Dunbar Street (224-2116) and Bayshore Bicycles, 1876 W Georgia (689-5071).

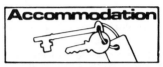

Accommodation

You can't do better than to use the provincial tourist office's *Accommodations* brochure. It contains details, including prices, of every sort of lodging from houseboats to hotels. There is a provincial guest tax of 8%.

Hotels. The cheapest hotels can be found in Chinatown around Main and Hastings, though there are fewer than there were before the council tarted up this once-rough neighbourhood for the 1986 World Fair. In Chinatown, prices can sink as low as $30 for a double but you will be getting no more than you pay for. A few blocks away from Chinatown, try the St Regis Hotel (corner of Dunsmuir and Seymour; 681-1135) or the Dufferin Hotel (900 Seymour; 683-4251). There is also the Niagara (435 W Pender; 681-5548), the Kingston (757 Richards; 684-9024) and the Buchan (1906 Haro Street; 685-5354) just a few steps from Stanley Park. Vincent's Guest House (1741 Grant St, 254-7462) has dorm beds for $10, singles for $20 and doubles $35.

Some of the sleazier establishments rent only by the week ($70 and up). If you do intend to stay in the city for more than a week, it is always worth asking about a discount. Your chances at successful bargaining will be diminished in high summer when there is a shortage of hotel accommodation. Try to book ahead. The Greater Vancouver Convention Bureau (Royal Centre, 1600-1055 West Georgia, 682-2226) run an Accommodation Reservation Service.

Motels. Motels will cost between $35 and $60 a double. Drive along Hastings East around Exhibition Park, along the Kingsway to Burnaby (the best bet) or along Marine Drive in North Vancouver.

Bed & Breakfast. For more upmarket places to stay, try the establishments listed in *Town and Country Bed & Breakfast* in BC which you can browse through in any Vancouver bookshop (cost $7.95). First Choice Bed & Breakfast International (875-8888) have private homes which charge $25-$30 single, $40-$55 double. Alternatively try Elsa Schamis in Kitsilano (224-1695) or Lillian Feist (873-0842).

Hostels. The youth hostel operates year round and is in the students and bohemian area known as Kitsilano, located on English Bay between downtown and the UBC campus. It costs members $8 and non-members $10. The bus number 4 from Granville to Jericho Park stops at Discovery

Street, then a ten minute walk. The hostel phone number is 224-3208. For a non-IYHF hostel, contact the International Network Hostel at 1263 Hornby (685-5176) where a bed costs $12.

YMCA. The YMCA at 955 Burrard (681-0221) accepts both men and women and charges $23 single. The YWCA further north on Burrard at number 580 (683-2531) has singles for $31 plus tax and no more dorm beds.

University Residences. Both Universities offer summer accommodation to visitors. UBC, about 7km from downtown, opens its enormous Walter Gage Residence from early May to late August (228-5377). There are considerable discounts for students, e.g. $20 for a single rather than $28. Even better is the nearby Vancouver School of Technology (228-9031) where the spartan rooms are yet cheaper. The Simon Fraser University campus is not as convenient, but it is also strikingly situated. SFU is 12 miles/20 km east of downtown Vancouver on Burnaby Mountain. Beds may be available for as little as $12 between June and August. Ring 291-4201 for details.

Camping. If you do have your own vehicle you may prefer to stay in a campground rather than in a motel. There are two campsites within range of Vancouver. Capilano Travel Trailer Park, 295 Tomahawk Avenue in West Vancouver (987-4722) and Timberland Motel and Campground, 3418 King George VI Highway in Surrey (531-1033). The cost of a site wwill be between $8 and $15 with access to whatever facilities are available, usually showers and launderette.

Longer Term. There are three main areas for longer term accommodation: the West End bordering Stanley Park (which is said to be the most densely populated three square miles in North America), the large East End east of downtown, and Kitsilano near the beach of the same name. You can visit the high rise apartment blocks in the West End to find vacancy notices posted in the entrance halls. The best place to head in the East End is on Commercial Drive around 1st Avenue (the site of Little Italy). Among the alternative establishments are Octopus Books at 1146 Commercial and Sweet Cherubim Health Foods across the road, where shared and cheap accommodation notices cover the front windows especially in the last week of the month. (Meat-eaters and smokers may find that their choice is limited). Kitsilano is one of those areas which has gone upmarket rapidly and so it is not as easy as it used to be to find cheap student-type accommodation here.

If all else fails check the Thursday edition of the *Vancouver Sun* for housing adverts. "Hydro inclusive" means that gas and electricity are included in the rent.

Eating and Drinking

Vancouver is reputed to have some of the most sophisticated restaurants on the continent. Certain areas of town are full of interesting and affordable establishments although, as is the case throughout North America, some are stronger on gimmicky decor and menus than on original cooking. In any case, it is easy to eat well and healthily since Vancouver is as health-conscious as any city in the world.

Gastown is an area which offers lots of choice. Down by the harbour, it was the site of the first settlement of Vancouver. It is not named for any petroleum product but after a colourful and loquacious Yorkshireman who started a pub here in the 1860s and who came to be known as "Gassy Jack". In the 1970s extensive renovations transformed the area from a slum into a picturesque area full of pubs and restaurants (and tourists). A stroll along Hastings and Water Streets will allow you to compare a wide variety of menus. You will pass the Old Spaghetti Factory restaurant (which has branches in other North American cities) and the Only Fish and Oyster Cafe, both of which are institutions. You will eventually come to the Harbour Mall where you can indulge in anything from an oatmeal cookie to Lobster Newburg.

Seafood naturally plays a large part in Vancouver menus and the inhabitants consume tons of shrimps and prawns annually. (Pacific shrimp are tiny whereas the prawns are bigger). For a good basic fish and chip restaurant try the Dover Seafood restaurant at 945 Denman, or the simple and inexpensive The Only Seafood cafe at 20 East Hastings downtown. You can sample them straight from the fishmonger if you like. The Granville Island Market fishmongers display their shellfish and other wares most temptingly. This is a gourmet's paradise and so a good place for buying the fixings for a picnic which you can take with you to one of the 150 parks in the city, and also good for general shopping and people-watching.

Another local tradition is to go out for Sunday brunch. Watch for the "All You Can Eat for $10" type of advertisement. You may prefer the Chinese version of brunch known as *dim sum* which is very good at Ming's (147 Pender SE). For health foods try Lifestream Foods (4th and Burrard) and the Naam (4th and MacDonald). With many ethnic communities, Vancouver's restaurants rival those of San Francisco and Toronto. The primarily Cantonese restaurants may be found along Keefer, East Pender, Gore and Carrall Streets. Try the Ho Ho Inn, the Green Door opposite which is clean, cheap, friendly and bring-your-own, the On On Tea Garden at 214 Keefer, which has become an institution, or Yang's (4186 Main). The best value Chinese restaurant is arguably the On Lok on Hastings past Commercial Drive, which serves large dishes for $3.50-$4. A recommended Vietnamese restaurant is the Saigon on 4th Avenue. Commercial Street has a concentration of Italian restaurants; try Joe's Cafe for wonderful cappuccinos.

One of the most memorable dining experiences you can have in Vancouver is at Quilicum (1724 Davie St, 681-7044) which serves native Indian cuisine such as fernshoots, wind-dried salmon and barbecued caribou. If you like Indian food try the Indian Nirvana Restaurant at 2313 Main St. Excellent Thai food is available at the Thai House on Robson St. For a fast food lunch of ethnic cuisines visit the main building of the Granville Island Market or try the Food Fair at Robson Square (just near the tourist office). There you can choose a Mexican taco, a Ukranian pyrogy (potato pastry) or a Chinese spring roll for between $3 and $6. You may have to queue at lunchtimes. Delicatessens throughout the city offer cheap and delicious sandwiches for lunch or snacks. Barbeque chicken dinners are cheap and popular with locals.

DRINKING

If you want to combine drinking with The Tourist Experience, then go to the top of the Blue Horizon Hotel (1225 Robson St) to the revolving Sears Tower on Hastings or the bar at the top of the Ramada Inn. It is always better to seek out aerial views just before dusk, so that you can see the city both by day and by night. An opposite drinking experience can also be had on Hastings St (corner of Carrall) where the Funky Winker Beans serves the cheapest beer in town at $1 a glass including a "meat ticket" for the hourly raffle.

In the 1980's the provincial government finally relented and granted a brewing licence to someone other than the major Canadian brewers (Carling, Molson and Labatts). The best known brewery is the Granville Island Brewing Company which brews an ale and a lager. The Troller pub in picturesque Horseshoe Bay in the west part of Vancouver serves Okanagan lager and stout and good food, though it no longer brews it own beer. There are a number of imitation British pubs in Vancouver including the Elephant and Castle (Pacific Centre off Dunsmuir), the Rose and Thorne Neighbourhood Pub (part of the Kingston Hotel at 757 Richards) and the Dover Arms (961 Denman near the fish and chip restaurant).

There has been a recent and encouraging increase in neighbourhood pubs in Vancouver (as well as in Victoria) which serve imported beers and offer no entertainment apart from dartboards and pool tables. Ask locals for their recommended watering-hole. A new yuppie craze for privately-owned beer stores which are upmarket off-licences has recently hit BC.

BC white wines are improving all the time, leaving the red wines far behind. Try Osoyoos Select white. Most wines cost about $6 a bottle, and like spirits and beer are available only in government liquor stores. There is a greater selection of Californian wines in BC than in eastern Canada.

The legal drinking age is 19. As in the rest of Canada, there has been a very significant crackdown on drinking and driving.

Entertainment

Try to find a copy of the free *Georgia Straight* which is published on Fridays, though it has degenerated slightly since Bob Geldof was involved with it. It contains fairly reliable listings of the music, film and theatre going on during the following week. The monthly *Discorder* is published by UBC students and is geared to more alternative and underground music, theatre and film. There are also several free entertainment guides such as *Key to Vancouver* and *Vancouver Guideline* which has more conventional reviews. Check the entertainment page of the evening *Sun*, especially on Saturdays. Mainstream entertainments can be booked by phone with Vancouver Ticket Centre on 280-4444. The Vancouver Arts Hotline is 437-ARTS.

Buildings of Interest. There are many noteworthy buildings in Vancouver. Even the domestic architecture offers more variety and interest than in other Canadian cities. The Law Courts on Hornby St are a stunning example of modern architecture. Even a seemingly ordinary office building like the Marine Building at the bottom of Burrard Street has many attractive 1920s decorative motifs inside and out consistent with its function as a maritime insurer.

Museums and Galleries. You should visit the Vancouver Art Gallery (682-5621) housed in the impressive old Law Courts at Georigia and Hornby. Its collection of Canadian art, especially the paintings of Emily Carr, is particularly strong. If you have a special interest in art, check in the foyer the schedule of lecture tours offered by knowledgeable volunteers. The tours are free but the admission to the gallery is $3, free on Tuesdays. It is open Tuesday to Sunday.

If you missed the "Living Arctic" exhibition on Indian and Inuit life at the Museum of Mankind in London in 1988, you should try to visit the

Museum of Anthropology on the UBC campus. Its collection of totem poles, masks, etc. carved by various groups of west coast Indians is very impressive. Admission $2, $1 for students, free on Tuesdays and closed on Mondays. Centennial Museum at Kitsilano Point has more artefacts from the culture of the Pacific Indians.

Music. The music scene in Vancouver is excellent. Unfortunately the proliferation and quality of bands is not matched by available venues and record labels, so very few gain a reputation outside the province. For jazz try the Hot Jazz Society (2120 Main) or the Landmark Jazz Bar (1400 Robson). Rock venues and discos are not in short supply while country and western music has a strong following (prairie cowboys who have migrated west?). The Commodore has a dance floor suspended on springs, while the ultra-modern and trendy Luv Affair in the heart of downtown appeals to some. For folk, try the Soft Rock Cafe (1925 W 4th St) or the Classical Joint Coffee House (231 Carrall St) in Gastown. Folk music thrives in Vancouver, especially during the annual Vancouver Folk Music Festival, a three-day event in mid-July. Most who have attended rave about the setting on Jericho Beach, the quality of the music and the general atmosphere. For information and tickets phone 879-2931. There is also now an annual jazz festival in late June.

Theatre and Cinema. The main downtown cinemas are concentrated in the Granville Mall. The Ridge Theatre (corner of 16th and Arbutus) offers cheap double bills throughout the week while the Vancouver East Cinema on Commercial and Broadway (253-5455) is also recommended. Films normally cost $5. There is a strong theatre following in Vancouver. Check the Arts Club and the Waterfront Theatre, both on Granville Island, or the Vancouver Playhouse on Hamilton St. During the summer musicals are performed under the stars in Stanley Park (ring 687-0174 for current programmes).

SPORT AND RECREATION

Most visitors catch the outdoor bug one way or another after falling under the influence of the locals. They have built a jogging track in one of the most beautiful settings in the world. And then there is Stanley Park, with its huge trees and fascinating Aquarium with breeding killer whales, lots of locally caught seals and some sea otters. But soon you may find yourself hankering after the real thing; forests out of the earshot of traffic, and whales spouting in the ocean. It is not necessary to participate in strenuous activity; you can get to the top of Grouse Mountain near Vancouver in a cable car ($10), but you may still feel guiltily sedentary when the skiers glide past.

Swimming, skating, skiing and hiking are within easy reach of the city. There is a skating rink at Robson Square and a number of city beaches. You need not be a dedicated sporty type to enjoy lounging on Kitsilano Beach or Spanish Banks. As is true throughout the world, beaches are good places to meet people. Wreck Beach is the nude beach, though you do not have to disrobe. There are superb hiking trails open year round, for example a six-mile sea wall around Stanley Park and numerous trails around the University Endowment Lands.

Spectator sports are also popular. The Vancouver Canucks (a slang word for Canadians) ice hockey team play at the Pacific Coliseum and the BC

Lions play the Canadian version of American football at the BC Place Stadium, the first covered dome in Canada.

The Canadian Lacrosse Hall of Fame is at 65 E 6th Ave in New Westminster (526-2751). Sports facilities at Victoria on Vancouver Island are being improved rapidly in preparation for the 1994 Commonwealth Games.

A less traditional spectator activity is to watch the harbour. Vancouver's harbour is the busiest on the west coast of the Americas and enormous freighters and container ships are constantly coming and going. You can discover the country of origin and the cargo of the ships in harbour and expected to arrive by phoning 926-7464, which provides a recorded message. You can also visit the Vancouver Container Terminal (Vanterm) to see a port in action. Phone 666-0101 for opening times and tours.

SHOPPING

Vancouver is bursting with boutiques and handicraft shops. Browse in Hill's Indian Crafts at 165 Water St, the Inuit Gallery of Vancouver at number 345 on the same street and the Indian Arts and Crafts Society of BC at 540 Burrard. The standard department stores, Eatons and the Bay, are connected by the underground Pacific Centre Mall while the western department store Woodward's is at 101 W Hastings. The market on Granville Island has an interesting selection of shops which sell books, crafts, toys and souvenirs as well as food. An interesting gift for any gastronomes you may know is wild rice, which may be purchased from one of the gourmet stalls. Upmarket fashions may be found on Robson St while Gastown is good for kitsch and authentic crafts.

Shopping hours vary from shopping centre to shopping centre but are basically 9.30am or 10am to 6pm, sometimes staying open until 9pm on Thursdays and Fridays. There is a provincial sales tax of 7% which can be avoided by shipping your purchases straight out of the province.

THE MEDIA

The daily *Vancouver Sun* has better coverage of international news than it once did and is very good for entertainment, local news, cheap flights and accommodation, not to mention coloured comics. *The Toronto Globe & Mail* is available in a national edition. The morning tabloid is called *The Province.*

You may consult the *Times* and the *Guardian Weekly* at the Vancouver Public Library at 750 Burrard Street, or at the British Consulate General (800-1111 Melville, 683-4421).

CBC-AM can be located on 690 and CBC-FM on 105.7. There are many local stations carrying all shades of popular journalism. CJAZ has a good evening jazz programme, CBC is best for current affairs and CITR, the student alternative station out of UBC, is worth a regular listen.

Crime and Safety

Hastings Street downtown is considered to be Vancouver's skid row, especially between Main St and Cambie. Also some of the side streets in Chinatown seem quite rough and some locals recommend avoiding these after dark. But on the whole, Vancouver is a safe city.

Marijuana continues to be popular and easily available, especially at music festivals. As in the other provinces you run the risk of being deported if caught, since possession is strictly illegal. "Campaign O" has resulted in the confiscation of vehicles of anyone crossing the border with any quantity of drugs, including seeds and even paraphernalia such as cigarette papers.

Legal aid information is available on 687-1831, while the Royal Canadian Mounted Police operate a Tourists Alert numbers (264-3111).

Help and Information *i*

The area code for Vancouver and all of British Columbia is 604.

Vancouver Travel Info centre: 562 Burrard St (683-2000).
Parks Canada: Western Region, Room 520, 220 Fourth Avenue SE, Calgary, Alberta T2P 3H8 (403-231-4745).
BC Tourism & Recreation: White Rock, 356 King George Vl Highway, Surrey (531-4442).
Post Office: 349 W Georgia, near Homer (662-5724).
Police or Ambulance emergency: 911.
Automobile Association: 999 W Broadway (733-6660).
Recorded weather information: 276-6109.
St Paul's Hospital Emergency Room: 1081 Burrard (682-2344).
British Consulate: 800-1111 Melville (683-4421).
American Express: 701 West Georgia (669-2813).
Thomas Cook: 220-701 W Georgia (688-0231).

Further Afield (61)

Victoria. The city of Victoria is renowned for being more British than the British. It is the one place in Canada where you might see a cricket game being played or daunting old dowagers in fur stoles (even in summer) munching on cucumber sandwiches at tea in the lobby of the grand old railway hotel, the Empress (provided they don't take their custom elsewhere because of the ambitious renovations taking place at the time of writing). Not many other cities in North America would support a newspaper called *The Colonist*. Because of Victoria's moderate climate, it is very popular as a retirement haven. Characteristically, the most popular tourist attraction on the island is a magnificent garden called Butchart Gardens, set in a former quarry, featuring many ornamental flower displays as well as shrubs and trees. They are located between the ferry port at Swartz Bay and Victoria (admission $6).

Victoria is not altogether geriatric, and will become livelier in the run up to the 1994 Commonwealth Games. Even now it has many big city amenities, such as good restaurants, without the blight of industrialization. Try for example the late-night Herald St Cafe, Pagliaccis, the Metropolitan Diner or Six Mile House, which are all popular with locals and cost $10-$20 for dinner. There are also some good pubs, such as the Stonehouse in Swartz Bay where the ferry docks, where the beer called Spinnaker's is brewed on site. Altogether Victoria is a charming city. Its Visitor Information Centre is at 812 Wharf St (382-2127).

The rest of Vancouver Island is well worth exploring especially if you enjoy backpacking. The train ride up the eastern coast to Courtenay costs $15 (see *The Great Outdoors*).

The Sunshine Coast. The Sunshine Coast refers to the 95 miles/150 km north of Vancouver. It looks particularly enticing at sunrise from the ferry to Nanaimo. It encompasses all that is great about Canadian scenery — mountains, ocean inlets, sandy beaches and fishing villages. There is no through road, so if you want to see the northern part of the Sunshine Coast, you will have to take one ferry from Horseshoe Bay to Langdale, another to Earl's Cove about 745 km along and then a third one across the inlet to Powell River.

The Okanagan Valley. If you are looking for a good place to relax on your way across the province, the Okanagan Valley is as good as any place. It is world famous for its fruit production, especially its apples, and the millions of acres of blossom in the spring are a wonderful sight. During the summer, roadside fruit stalls are impossible to pass by. The Valley also supports a thriving wine industry. Most of the wineries welcome visitors on tours and tastings. Try Calona Wines in Kelowna (762-9144), Okanagan Vineyards near Oliver (498-4041), Claremont Wines in Peachland, Casabello Wines in Penticton and Sumac Ridge Winery in Summerland. A further way you might benefit from the Okanagan fruit is that you might be able to earn a little extra money picking it. Ask at the Agricultural Employment Centre offices in Kelowna or Penticton. The whole area fills up with young people and professional transient fruit pickers (especially from Quebec), and it is possible to meet lots of interesting people.

If it is relaxation rather than work you want, the towns along Okanagan Lake are ideal. This is no wilderness, and so camping is a more social activity. Many campsites fill up in the summer. Two people in a tent can expect to pay about $13. Windsurfers can be rented in Penticton for about $12 an hour.

There is an infinite number of possibilities for other places to see and things to do, for instance the Queen Charlotte Islands off the coast of northern BC, home of the proud artistically gifted Haida Indians, or the province's theme towns such as Spanish Osoyoos and Bavarian Kimberley.

The Great Outdoors

There are several mountain parks within easy reach of Vancouver for hiking, skiing or wildlife (watch for bald eagles, deer and bears). For hiking try the relatively tame but scenic Lighthouse Park, or Cypress Bowl for skiing, both about 8km from downtown (take bus 250 from West Vancouver). Slightly further afield is Mount Seymour Provincial Park. Serious skiers will be interested in the world class resorts of Mt Whistler (64 km north of Vancouver), Panorama and Big White/Apex Alpine in the interior. There is a youth hostel at Whistler (932-5492) which is open year round. Winter rates at $10.50 for IYHF members are slightly higher than summer ones. Yet another huge wilderness area also 40 miles/64 km away is called Garibaldi Park. Getting from the car park to the campsite involves a full day of fairly serious hiking or cross-country skiing. Admission to provincial parks is free but camping costs about $4. Watch for bear tracks in the mud or the snow. Danger is slight except possibly at the first thaw, when the bears emerge hungry from their winter's hibernation.

The Outdoor Recreation Council of BC publishes a series of recreational maps showing trails, bridle paths, historic landmarks, etc. A catalogue is available from Suite 100, 1200 Hornby St, Vancouver V6Z 2E2. There are a great many camping and sporting goods shops in Vancouver, so you should not have any trouble getting yourself equipped. You can rent most equipment at Rudy's (3279 W Broadway) and skis are available for hire at the UBC Sport Store in the Student Union Building. The best outfitters are Taiga and Mountain Equipment Co-op which both have notice boards for buying and selling used equipment.

Watersports are also popular; windsurfing takes place off most of Vancouver's beaches. Powell River, 88 miles/142 km north of the city, has excellent diving including wreck diving. Contact the Beach Gardens Dive Resort in the town of Powell River for particulars. You can raft down the turbulent Fraser River for about $70 inclusive. Contact Whitewater Adventures in Vancouver (669-1100). You may prefer to experience the Fraser Canyon, which is a 2½ hour drive from Vancouver, from the safety of a cable car. Oyster collecting is possible along many of the bays and inlets of the Sunshine Coast, particularly in the spring and autumn.

There are many outfitters in the interior of the province who arrange trail riding in the mountains. Trips generally last one or two weeks. A one week trip will cost from $350. Consult Tourism British Columbia for suggestions.

Vancouver Island. What attracts so many people to the island (after the mild climate) is the wilderness. Vancouver Island is nearly 300 miles/500 km long (the largest island off the Pacific coast of North and South America) and is very thinly populated except in the southeast. Perhaps the most appealing destination is the Pacific Rim National Park, where there is a rugged and beautiful 7-day coastal trail, which was originally used as a way out for shipwrecked sailors. Many hikers are accompanied along their route by spouting whales and sea-lions, herons and humming-birds. One of the most beautiful sections is along Long Beach from Tofino. You can also visit Hot Springs north of Tofino by boat or plane only. Or try the Cowichan Valley, starting at Duncan, which offers canoeing and fishing as well as hiking and camping.

Perhaps the most isolated destination is Cape Scott at the northern tip of the island. Access is not as difficult as it used to be, for it is now possible to drive (or hitch-hike) all the way to the park, though the last stretch is a dirt logging road. Roads used by hitch-hikers are often privately owned by logging companies. Check with the tourist office before setting out because sometimes the logging companies permit access only at weekends. Interesting as the wilderness environment is in these coastal areas, make sure you have tested your camping equipment in Scotland or a tropical monsoon. Cape Scott gets hundreds of centimetres of rain every year, which sometimes turns the ground into a foot of mud. Still, in good weather, nothing can beat it.

It is also very pleasant to spend a day or two in the Gulf Islands (Salt Spring, Galliano, San Juan, etc.), easily accessible by ferry from Vancouver or Victoria, or by Washington State Ferries between Anacortes in Washington State and Sidney 16km north of Victoria. They are covered with wild flowers in the spring and summer and make for excellent walks and bicycle rides. It is easy to visit most of them on a day-trip.

The Prairies

Manitoba Saskatchewan Alberta

Most visitors vacationing in Canada — indeed many Canadians — think of the Prairies as "the land between the interesting places", i.e. the sights of eastern Canada and the Rockies. The bulk of Manitoba, Saskatchewan and Alberta, like Belgium or the Nullarbor Desert of Australia, is something to be crossed as quickly as possible. But the scenery and the people of the Prairies are such an essential part of Canada, that it would be a shame to fly over and miss it completely, though walking or cycling would probably be taking things too far. The Prairies are best appreciated by train or car. The miles of wheatfields broken occasionally by a grain elevator or a domed Ukrainian church provide a pleasant contrast with the forests in the east and the mountains in the west. Because of the flatness of the terrain, you will begin to notice and appreciate the magnificent skies.

The main cities of Winnipeg, Regina, Saskatoon, Calgary and Edmonton are, frankly, not very interesting. While the *Business Traveller* magazine voted Winnipeg the most boring city in the world, eastern Canadians were inventing the joke, Q: 'What is the difference between Calgary and yoghurt?' A: 'Yoghurt has live culture'. Regina bore the name "Pile o'Bones" until it was chosen as capital of Saskatchewan late in the 19th century, and renamed in a more dignified vein after Queen Victoria. As a rule Prairie cities are sprawling, crass and lacking in character. Calgary (sometimes called Cowtown) is the least aesthetically pleasing and seems to be designed primarily with the car park in mind, as though there is no such thing as a pedestrian. There could hardly be a euphemism more extreme than calling the inescapable expressways of Calgary "trails", but you will find a Banff Trail, a Bow Trail and so on. Even the frenzy of improvements which preceded the 1988 Winter Olympics could not alter the city's (non)-character. It is now hoped that tourism will replace oil as the next great boom in the economy, though this seems over-optimistic.

Edmonton and Saskatoon are more picturesque since they both straddle the fast-flowing North Saskatchewan River. Nevertheless, a tour of the main cities is likely to be fairly boring, unless you happen to be interested in provincial legislative buildings or in the history of the Royal Canadian Mounted Police, whose pioneer activities are extolled in several museums. You would be better off leaving the Trans-Canada Highway and visiting some smaller towns. Get a list of events from the provincial tourist offices and seek out some of the rural centres where genuine prairie hospitality prevails. You can choose from the Canadian Open Wellington Boot Throwing Championship in Dugald Manitoba, the World Championship Gopher Derby in Eston Saskatchewan or the Cowpoop Patty Throwing Contest (dried dung tosses) at the Kindersley Goose Festival. Culture, in its traditional sense, is not much in evidence on the Prairies, but since this is cowboy country, there is no shortage of rodeos, whether it be the Canadian Firefighters Rodeo in Virden Manitoba, or the famous Calgary Stampede, reputed to feature some of the biggest, toughest rodeo events in the world. Among the highlights are the Chuckwagon Races, when four-horse buggies pound around a track. During the ten days of the Stampede, which takes place every July, Calgary becomes very crowded attracting 100,000 people a day, and expensive, so if you hope to see this event, try to book accommodation and tickets ahead, or else arrive as far in advance as possible; write to PO Box 1060, Station M, Calgary T2P 2K8 for information (403-261-0101). Admission tickets go on sale months ahead and may vary from $10 - $40.

THE NATIVES

Even by North American standards, the settlement of the Prairies took place very recently, within the last hundred years. Until then the land was shared (not always amicably) between the fur traders and the Indians. Many of the original furtrappers were French, who intermarried with Indians. Their descendants are called Metis and still form a substantial part of the population. There is a much higher proportion of native peoples living in the Prairies than in other parts of Canada. For example there are nearly 150 Indian reservations in Saskatchewan alone.

The land was primarily settled by the British and French, mainly Scottish crofters and French noblemen escaping republicanism and heavy taxation. They were joined by many other nationalities. There are many people of Ukrainian descent and numerous towns have a Ukrainian museum or cultural centre and celebrate Ukrainian festivals with food, entertainment and dancing. The largest Icelandic settlement outside Iceland is in Gimli, Manitoba. Icelanders arrived in the 1870s and still celebrate their heritage every August with food, theatre, poetry contests and music.

One of the most interesting groups are the Dukhobors, who arrived from Russia at the turn of the century. Because of their mystical beliefs and anarchist politics, they were expelled from Russia and with the help of Leo Tolstoy and English Quakers, moved to Saskatchewan, where their practices continue to cause conflicts with the Canadian government.

Several Prairie cities have ethnic festivals comparable to Caravan in Toronto, when national pavilions are set up around the city, and a "passport" admits you to all the pavilions. There is Winnipeg's Folklorama in August, Saskatoon's Folkfest in early September and Regina's Mosaic in May. To give an idea of the range of cultural backgrounds of prairie folk, there is a radio station in Winnipeg (CKJS-810AM) which broadcasts in 18 languages from Filipino to Hebrew, Hungarian to Hindi.

CLIMATE

One wonders how the early fur traders and settlers, not to mention the Indians, survived the prairie winters. The provincial tourist offices are right to emphasize the blue skies and sunshine which accompany their winters, but the fact remains that they can be unimaginably cold. Weather reports sometimes provide a measurement in seconds or minutes which lets you know how long it will take before exposed flesh freezes. Waiting five minutes for a bus in Regina or Calgary when it is 40 degrees below becomes an ordeal. The locals dress in down, fur and wool and seem to manage quite happily, moving between their heated homes, cars, offices and stores. Provided you have enough warm gear, you should be able to avoid frostbite.

There is one climatic aberration called the chinook, a warm wind which blows down from the mountains and can raise Calgary's temperature by 30 degrees in a few hours, melting the snow and giving people headaches. (According to the manufacturers of negative ion machines, the chinooks upset the ion balance dreadfully and are responsible for an increase in accidents, suicides and ill health; the solution is to acquire your own negative ion generator.) This wind blew uncharacteristically often during the Winter Olympics so that there was much less snow than usual.

A better way of avoiding frostbite than waiting for a chinook is to visit in the summer. But then you will have to beware of sunstroke. The highest temperature in Canada was recorded one year at Regina, 110°F/43°C. During the summer months (especially July) it is quite usual for the Prairies to get over 300 hours of sunshine in a month, i.e. over 10 hours a day on average. Most motels are air-conditioned, as are the trains. If you are driving, roll down the windows and keep going; air-conditioning in hire cars adds $6 a day to the rental charges. You will not need to worry about sweltering in a traffic jam. Neither do you need to worry about rain, since the Prairies on the whole are very dry. The occasional thunder storm brings some relief from the heat and makes for exciting skies. Summers are so hot and dry that forest fires are a real danger, so be very careful with campfires and heed fire warnings on the radio.

Air. In addition to Air Canada, there are many regional airlines with such picturesque names as Calm Air International and Frontier Airlines which provide frequent services to communities, some of them quite remote, throughout the provinces. There are numerous fly-in lodges in the northern prairies mainly for keen hunters and fishermen. Services are good among the principal Prairie cities. There are, for example, five Air Canada flights a day from Winnipeg to Calgary. The economy fare is $210; Winnipeg to Regina is $135.

Bus. There are plenty of Greyhound services connecting the Prairie cities as well as more local bus lines serving smaller communities. The city terminals are as follows:

Winnipeg: 487 Portage Avenue (204-775-8301).
Regina: 2041 Hamilton St (306-664-5711).
Saskatoon: 50-23rd St E (306-664-5711).
Calgary: 850-16 St SW (403-265-9111).
Edmonton: 10324-103rd St (403-421-4211).

There are roughly three trans-Canada Greyhounds a day in either direction connecting Winnipeg, Regina and Calgary. The Calgary-Regina trip takes 12 hours, and then it is a further 8 hours to Winnipeg. To get to the northerly cities of Saskatoon and Edmonton which are on the Yellowhead Highway rather than the Trans-Canada, you will have to change. Some sample single fares are Winnipeg to Calgary $80. Winnipeg to Regina $40, Regina to Saskatoon $18, Calgary to Banff $9.

Train. The northern trans-Canada route via Jasper, Edmonton and Saskatoon has been reintroduced, so if for some reason you want to visit those northern cities, you will not necessarily have to break your train journey in Regina or Calgary. The *Canadian* from Vancouver arrives in Calgary at 2.25 pm, Regina at 1.35 am and Winnipeg at 9.25 am. The single fare Winnipeg to Calgary is $109, Winnipeg to Regina $54 and Regina to Saskatoon $18.

Driving. Because of the unendingly flat terrain, the Trans-Canada Highway goes in a seemingly straight line for hundreds of miles. The more northerly Yellowhead Highway is less travelled and just as uninteresting. The construction of some of the highways in the north of the provinces presented very difficult engineering problems; there is a 10 mile/16 kilometre stretch on Provincial Trunk Highway 10 in Manitoba which had to be built over floating muskeg, a Cree Indian word for swamp.

The rules of the road do not differ very much from province to province. The maximum speed limit in Alberta is 100 km/hr (62 mph) by day and 80 km/hr (50 mph) by night; in Saskatchewan it is 80 km/hr and in Manitoba 90 km/hr (56 mph). Littering in Saskatchewan is subject to a $200 fine.

Renting a vehicle is cheaper than in Toronto or Vancouver. Many people fly or take the train as far as Calgary and then rent a car or camper to explore Banff and the mountains.

Accommodation

Except in Banff and Calgary, accommodation in the Prairies is much cheaper than it is in Vancouver or Toronto. Double rooms in downtown hotels in Winnipeg or Saskatoon start as low as $20 a double. And the price of some motels is similarly low. Even in Banff you may be able to find accommodation in private homes for $30 a double (for example 521 Buffalo St). If you are on the back roads, you will find some great bargains like the Rama Hotel in Rama Saskatchewan (population 170) where the five so-called 'non-modern' rooms cost between $9 and $12. All the tourist offices publish complete lists.

Alberta is well supplied with 17 youth hostels as opposed to two in Manitoba and four in Saskatchewan. Prices range from $4 - $12 per night. Many of the Alberta hostels in the mountains are humble buildings with wood-burning stoves and few amenities. Even in summer the temperatures can drop at night and so down-filled sleeping bags are a necessity, as is food since there will be no shops or restaurants nearby.

Because of the hot dry summers and the many camping facilities available, camping is very popular. If you are crossing the country on a tight budget, your best option is to make use of the many free campsites. These are free of charge either because they are roadside stop-over places with few amenities, or because they are operated by a generous municipality. There is a fee if you want to camp in a provincial park, ranging from $4-$9, after you have paid the $2 or $3 park admission fee. You can also rent cottages in provincial parks from $18 a night for two people.

Since so much of the economy of the Prairies is based on agriculture, farm and ranch holidays are widely available. Although you are not obliged to help with the chores, there is not much else to do. Prices are from $30-$45 per person per day including all meals. Contact addresses are: Alberta Country Vacation Association, CMH Travel, 217 Bear St, Banff (762-4531); Saskatchewan Farm Vacation Association, Box 24, Bateman (648-3530); and Manitoba Farm Vacations, 525 Kylemore, Winnipeg (475-6624).

Eating and Drinking

Dining on the Prairies is not for the sophisticated. Stick to steaks and you will not be disappointed. Pancake breakfasts are often available and barbecues are popular. Try to sample a berry pie made from indigenous Saskatoon berries.

The licensing hours in the Prairie provinces are normally 9am-1am with some exceptions, such as beer parlours in Manitoba closing at midnight and cocktail lounges in Alberta staying open until 2am. Like the American Midwest, the Canadian Prairies are conservative. Beer and wine advertising was legalized in Saskatchewan less than a decade ago.

The minimum drinking age is 18 in Alberta and Manitoba, and 19 in Saskatchewan. The only beers served are standard Canadian beers. You will not be subsidizing the provincial government when you eat or drink in Alberta, since there is no sales tax in the province — a legacy of their oil boom.

Entertainment

If you are a confirmed urbanite who loves theatre, opera and fine dining, the Prairies would not be an obvious destination for you. Most of the popular music is country and western, though there is a large and excellent Folk Festival held in Winnipeg every July. The cinema listings for a large city like Calgary are very limited, though the University does have an arts cinema series. Your average Prairie native's idea of a good time is certainly not the ballet; it is more likely to be golf, curling (a tremendously popular sport) or watching *Hockey Night In Canada* on TV. You can obtain a free calendar of rodeo events from the Canadian Professional Rodeo Association, 223-2166 27 Ave NE, Calgary, Alberta T2E 7A6.

The Great Outdoors

Skiing is being heavily promoted by tourist officials following the Winter Olympics. A sample package costing £250 might include a week's car hire, accommodation and lift pass to several areas such as Lake Louise, Sunshine and Norquay. Hiking remains as popular as ever. Calgarians who find themseles apologizing for their city invariably finish by saying "But it's so close to the mountains". Although people in Saskatchewan or Manitoba are not very close to mountains, they have taken up cross-country skiing with a vengeance. There are thousands of parks in all three provinces providing the whole range of recreational opportunities from windsurfing to guided nature walks. For example try to visit Oak Hammock Marsh Wildlife Park in Manitoba where thousands of migrating snow geese may be seen in spring and fall.

Banff is by far the most popular resort in Canada, though it is remarkably small and unpretentious (though overpriced). Banff National Park was the first in Canada opened 1887. Jasper, 177 miles/287km north of Banff is slightly less crowded in the high summer and winter seaons, and in an even more beautiful setting. Banff and Jasper are located inside adjacent national parks, offering hundreds of kilometres of hiking trails and camping facilities both primitive and luxurious. Obviously, such popular tourist destinations get filled up so book ahead or be prepared to spend some time looking for accommodation. There is a privately operated room reservation service operated by Summit Vacations Ltd of Banff (762-5561) and by Take-a-Break Tours Ltd in Jasper (852-5665). Hostelling is probably a better bet.

Skiers will certainly want to visit in the winter. The mountains offer something for everybody from the most timid cross-country beginner to the most expert skier who wants to be put down by a helicopter at the top of a mountain. The avalanche season begins in February. For ski conditions at Banff and Jasper phone (toll-free): 1-800-661-6543. You might also get hold of a free 32 page publication called *Ski West Magazine* from travel agents, about resorts, prices, etc.

The area code for Alberta is 403, for Saskatchewan 306 and for Manitoba 204.

Parks Canada: Prairie Region, 391 York Avenue, Winnipeg R3C 4B7 (204-983-2290).
British Consulate: 1404-10025 Jasper Avenue, Edmonton (403-428-0375).
American Express: 501 5 St SW, Calgary (403-261-5982); 10305 Jasper Avenue, Edmonton (403-421-0608); Bay Department Store, Portage Avenue, Winnipeg (204-786-5671).

The Great White North

Yukon Territory   Northwest Territories

In addition to Canada's ten provinces, there are two thinly populated northern territories which are administered by the federal government. The climate of the Yukon Territory and the Northwest Territories (NWT) is even harsher than that of Alaska, with the average daily high staying below freezing between October and May in many parts. All homes have a wood-burning stove as a back up system in case of a power failure. It must be stoked every two hours to prevent freezing to death. But as in Alaska, summer temperatures are balmy, rainfall is slight, and summer festivities thrive in the near round-the-clock sunshine.

To get to Canada's two arctic territories, you will have to decide whether to invest time or money. There are daily flights — but few discounts —from the main cities of southern Canada to the Northland, e.g. the excursion fare Vancouver to Whitehorse costs well over $350. If you have several weeks, then you can consider going by land, bearing in mind that the 60th parallel is a very long way from the 49th; the distance between Toronto and the NWT/Alberta border is nearly 3,000 miles/4,800 km. There are several highways in the territories, the most recent of which was opened in 1983 (the Liard Highway linking Fort Nelson in northern BC with the Mackenzie Highway to Great Slave Lake). The Dempster Highway goes right through to the Arctic Ocean.

Just a glance at the map of these two northern territories will demonstrate their uniqueness. In an area as vast as the Northwest Territories (1¼ million square miles), there are just 60 communities with a population of over 20. Some of the place names convey the hostility of the land and the determination of the early fur traders and gold miners to stick it out: Repulse Bay, Fort Resolution and worst of all 'Wager Bay (Abandoned)'. Expanses of land hundreds of miles square, including some islands in the Arctic Ocean, are set aside as bird sanctuaries and reindeer grazing reserves. There is a dotted line indicating the "Northern Limit of Trees". But even below the treeline, this is forbidding country, and its barren beauty does not appeal to everyone.

Motoring holidays take on a whole new complexion in such terrain. The roads are gravelled not paved, since the frozen tundra would soon destroy a conventional road. Gas stops are few and far between, not to mention regular services in the event of a breakdown. Several of the highways cross major rivers by ferry in summer, by ice bridges in winter, but not at all in the month or so when the rivers are freezing over and then again when they are melting. Traffic on the Dempster Highway is sometimes limited because of the movement of the caribou herds. Some stretches become impassable during heavy rains.

Despite the hazards and difficulties of travel in the Arctic (or perhaps because of them), the government authorities are enthusiastically encouraging tourism. In fact both Tourism Yukon and Travel Arctic (the tourism bureau of the Northwest Territories) provide excellent detailed manuals listing all accommodation (which is sparse), methods of getting around the vast area and events, as well as providing background information on native history and culture.

If simple motoring is such a challenge, the two favourite outdoor activities of hiking and canoeing are more so. All travellers intending to venture into the wilderness are requested to register with the local Mounties in case an emergency arises. Less experienced lovers of the outdoors can hire the services of a local guide or outfitter. For local outings in the Whitehorse area, contact the Yukon Conservation Society (Box 4163, Whitehorse). Canoeing on the intricate network of lakes and rivers can be a superb way of seeing the arctic landscape and wildlife. It is possible to hire a canoe from any of the outfitters listed in the tourist literature. In the NWT you can arrange to pick up a canoe at any post of the Hudson's Bay Company and drop it at another. Book in advance through the National Stores Department, 77 Main St, Winnipeg, Manitoba R3C 2R1.

Amenities are, on the whole, scarce: for example there is only one hotel on the 420 mile/657 km Dempster Highway and it costs $90 a double. Camping facilities, open mid-May to mid-September, seem a better idea since many of them are free of charge. Most of the food served in cafes and restaurants will be expensive, conventional and frozen or tinned. As in Alaska fresh foods are at a premium because of the cost of shipping. You will have to get off the beaten track and become accepted by an Indian or Eskimo family before you will find traditional dishes such as acorn soup, baked skunk or boiled muskrat tails (said to be very sticky to eat). For some very unusual reading about the food prepared in the far north, look at Eleanor Ellis's *Northern Cookbook* which includes one of the strangest recipes of all times for chocolate sauce: the ingredients are simply two pounds of chocolate and a quarter block of paraffin.

One of the highlights of a trip to the Great White North must include glimpsing the life of the Inuit, many of whom continue to live at least partly by their old methods. One way of seeing some of the native traditions is to attend a carnival, jamboree or festival held in most communities, where there may be competitions in tea boiling (i.e. fire building), muskrat skinning, igloo building and harpoon throwing. Other festivals concentrate on the artistic traditions, for example the Folk Festival held in Yellowknife each June. (For further information write to the Society for Encouragement of Northern Talent, Box 326, Yellowknife, NWT). To see the handicrafts of the native people, visit any of the museums in the region, especially the MacBride Museum in Whitehorse and the Prince of Wales Northern Heritage Centre in Yellowknife.

Other books in this series:

Travellers Survival Kit: Europe..£5.95
"Enlarged to include even more useful tips"   *The Guardian*
Travellers Survival Kit: Australia and New Zealand.................£6.95
"An invaluable comprehensive guide"   *Sunday Express*
Travellers Survival Kit to the East..£4.95
"Packed with essential cool-preserving, life-extending information"
                                                                          SHE Magazine
Travellers Survival Kit: Soviet Union and Eastern Europe......£8.95
(to be published April, 1989)

Vacation Work also publish:

The Directory of Summer Jobs in Britain £5.95
The Directory of Summer Jobs Abroad £5.95
Adventure Holidays £3.95
Work Your Way Around The World.....................................£7.95
The Au Pair & Nanny's Guide to Working Abroad...............£5.95
Working in Ski Resorts — Europe......................................£5.95
Kibbutz Volunteer..£4.95
The Directory of Jobs and Careers Abroad £7.95
The International Directory of Voluntary Work £6.95
The Directory of Work and Study in Developing Countries................£6.95
Hitch-hikers Manual Britain..£3.95
Europe — a Manual for Hitch-hikers £3.95
The Traveller's Picture Phrase-Book £1.95

Distributors of:

Summer Employment Director of the United States............£7.95
Internships (On-the-Job Training Opportunities in the USA) £12.95
Emplois d'Ete en France..£6.95
Jobs in Japan £9.95
Teaching Tactics for Japan's English Classrooms................£5.95

Vacation Works Publications, 9 Park End Street, Oxford